The International Handbook of Consultation in Educational Settings

The rapid changes in the composition of school-age youth around the world have cata-lyzed a growing concern about how to address children's mental health and education. Grounded in this increasingly global perspective, *The International Handbook of Consultation in Educational Settings* is designed to provide a multicultural/transnational approach to consultation theory, research, training, and practice in educational settings. With chapters written by geographically diverse and prominent scholars across the field of school psychology, this handbook captures the range of ways in which consultation services are trained, implemented, and researched internationally. Written for practitioners, researchers, faculty members, and graduate students in the fields of school psychology, school counseling, special education, and educational psychology, this volume is the first of its kind to provide a comprehensive look at consultation in learning environments across the world.

The International Handbook of Consultation in Educational Settings offers various perspectives on models, implementation, training, and research on school consultation. After an introduction by the editors, contributors to Part II examine school-based consultation around the world to explore how consultation services are implemented in different countries. Part III addresses cross-cultural issues in consultation, particularly at a systems level. Part IV presents themes related to processes and issues in the implementation of consultation by focusing on approaches in various countries. The chapters in Part V focus on consultation training, offering insights into the development of students and professionals into effective consultants in cross-cultural and systemic contexts. Part VI describes how practitioners can contribute to the body of research on consultation through careful planning and implementation of their work. Finally, the editors summarize key concepts and findings in a concluding chapter.

Chryse Hatzichristou is professor of school psychology, director of the Center for Research and Practice of School Psychology, and chair of the Department of Psychology at the National and Kapodistrian University of Athens, Greece.

Sylvia Rosenfield is professor emerita and former co-director of the Lab for IC Teams at the University of Maryland, College Park, USA.

The International Handbook of Consultation in Educational Settings

Edited by

Chryse Hatzichristou

and

Sylvia Rosenfield

Routledge
Taylor & Francis Group

NEW YORK AND LONDON

First published 2017
by Routledge
711 Third Avenue, New York, NY 10017

and by Routledge
2 Park Square, Milton Park, Abingdon, Oxon, OX14 4RN

Routledge is an imprint of the Taylor & Francis Group, an informa business

© 2017 Taylor & Francis

The right of Chryse Hatzichristou and Sylvia Rosenfield to be identified as the authors of the editorial material, and of the authors for their individual chapters, has been asserted in accordance with sections 77 and 78 of the Copyright, Designs and Patents Act 1988.

Library of Congress Cataloging-in-Publication Data
A catalog record for this book has been requested

ISBN: 978-1-138-01347-6 (hbk)
ISBN: 978-1-138-01348-3 (pbk)
ISBN: 978-1-315-79518-8 (ebk)

Typeset in Minion
by Apex CoVantage, LLC

Dedicated to Nadine Lambert, a pioneer in international school consultation and an esteemed colleague who believed strongly in consultation training, practice, and research for school psychologists.
Sylvia Rosenfield and Sissy Hatzichristou

A special dedication from Sissy Hatzichristou:

Dedicated to Nadine Lambert, a mentor who led my way of thinking and practicing school psychology while studying at the University of California, Berkeley, Graduate School Psychology Program and then while developing a model of science and practice of school psychology in the Greek educational system. A dear friend whose consultative support throughout the years changed the trajectory of my life for the better.

CONTENTS

FOREWORD

International Handbook of Consultation in Educational Settings

In the *Theory and Practice of Mental Health Consultation*, Caplan (1970) defined consultation and based its practice within a community framework. He argued that consultation was a powerful process to support communities and prevent mental health problems. It is within this framework that consultation evolved and was eventually implemented in school settings. Today, consultation plays a pivotal role as school consultants support teachers, other school professionals, and parents while indirectly influencing students' educational and mental health functioning.

My own professional introduction to consultation was in the context of an instructional consultation course that I took with Sylvia Rosenfield (1987) in the mid-1980s as part of the first cohort of graduate students who completed the bilingual school psychology program at Fordham University. It was within the context of that course that I was introduced to the history and models of consultation. It was also within that context that I began to appreciate the nature of consultation as a comprehensive process that links problem identification, assessment, intervention planning and delivery, and evaluation to understand educational problems and work collaboratively with consultees to solve them. As a graduate student completing a practicum in consultation and eventually practicing my skills during my internship in New York City, consultation became a powerful tool to explore the challenges teachers encountered when working with students from diverse cultural backgrounds in schools. As I continued to evolve and eventually taught, practiced, and investigated consultation, I became increasingly aware of the importance of understanding the communities in which we provide consultation to be better able to use the process in ways that benefit those communities.

My reflections about community also extend to the consultation community itself as trainers, practitioners, and researchers seek to understand consultation and further its theoretical foundations and practical implications. Demographic data clearly indicate that the U.S. population continues to diversify, and thus consultants must develop the multicultural skills needed to collaborate effectively with consultees from diverse backgrounds who are directly responsible for clients who are culturally diverse. However, our own consultation community must be open to understanding consultation from a wider perspective as diversity becomes the norm and global opportunities via technology, travel, international educational exchanges, and migration provide us with ample opportunities to exchange knowledge and resources (Hatzichristou, 2002).

The *International Handbook of Consultation in Educational Settings* makes a unique contribution to the international consultation literature as Drs. Sylvia Rosenfield and Chryse Hatzichristou, experts in this field, have gathered an impressive cadre of authors that address a wide range of topics. Among the national and international cultural themes explored are systems consultation in Sri Lanka, Ghana, and Greece. The preparation of educational consultants takes a global approach through discussions of professional development in the U.S., the United Kingdom, and Vietnam. Differences between countries are highlighted in chapters that describe consultation models implemented in Hong Kong, Sweden, Canada, and Australia. The global application of consultation comes into sharp focus in chapters that describe working with families and English language learners, using an understanding of systems to enter international school settings, addressing school crises, and conducting research. The editors end the volume with projections of a global future for consultation.

This volume is noteworthy because it provides the forum for an exchange of information that transcends regional and national boundaries. Our worldview of consultation is enriched as the chapters within the handbook invite readers to think about how consultation is practiced, taught, and studied within different sociocultural and cross-cultural contexts. The handbook also provides us with opportunities to reflect upon consultation findings and practices that may be universal and others that may be more culture specific. Most important, this volume leads readers to question what we think are universal findings about consultation that may need to be reexamined using cross-cultural and international perspectives. The editors and contributing authors are commended for disseminating a powerful collection of chapters that enhance our worldview and advance the international exchange of knowledge across the global consultation community.

Emilia C. Lopez

REFERENCES

Caplan, G. (1970). *The theory and practice of mental health consultation*. New York: Basic Books.

Hatzichristou, C. (2002). A conceptual framework of the evolution of school psychology: Transnational considerations of common phases and future perspectives. *School Psychology International, 23*, 266–282.

Rosenfield, S. A. (1987). *Instructional consultation*. Hillsdale, NJ: Lawrence Erlbaum.

PREFACE

The multinational origin of this book has a long history. We, the two editors, one from Greece and one from the U.S., met for the first time in Sweden in 1995 as a result of the pioneering efforts of Nadine Lambert, to whom we have dedicated this handbook. She supported consultation in the Graduate Program of School Psychology, University of California, Berkeley, and was a mentor for one of us (CH). Not only did she put a lot of emphasis on consultation as a core concept for school psychologists in training, but she also encouraged consultation practice in schools in California and across the U.S. (Lambert, 1961, 1963, 1965). More relevant here, she began the first efforts to bring together school psychologists interested in consultation practice and training models from different countries. Nadine Lambert, Ingrid Hylander, and Jonathan Sandoval established an International Seminar on Consultee-Centered Consultation, with the initial meeting held in Stockholm, Sweden, in 1995; additional meetings were held in Stockholm in 1999 and in San Francisco, California, in 2001(Lambert, 2004). These meetings were followed by a book, edited by Lambert, Hylander, and Sandoval, titled *Consultee-centered Consultation* (2004), which included chapters by authors from multiple countries, many of whom had participated in the meetings. An additional International Seminar on Consultee-Centered Consultation took place in Boston in 2008.

Since that time, in various ways and in various venues, psychologists around the world interested in consultation theory, training, practice, and research in educational settings have sought contact with each other. The annual meetings of the International School Psychology Association (ISPA) have often been the sites of workshops and seminars about consultation, bringing together trainers, researchers, and practitioners from around the globe. Further, in 2012, the American Psychological Association Division of School Psychology supported the formation of the Globalization of School Psychology Working Group (WG) with the goal to further develop transnational/multicultural domains in school psychology science and practice. The WG has developed a database with transnational/multicultural readings and material on basic areas of school psychology science and practice, including a section on consultation.

This volume is designed to introduce some of those interested in consultation to each other and to a larger international audience, as well as to expand the knowledge base that has been growing with relatively little interaction across nations. As we worked to include a variety of authors from multiple countries and continents, we recognized our own limited ability to span the world. But in bringing together the current authors, we see an incredible potential for future interactions that can grow in scope. Our vision is the development of a transnational approach in consultation training, research, and practice and the promotion of partnerships and professional collaboration among faculty, graduate students, and practitioners in this field. We hope this handbook will inspire others to join the process.

Sylvia Rosenfield
Chryse Hatzichristou

REFERENCES

Lambert, N. (2004). Consultee-centered consultation: An international perspective on goals, process and theory. In N. M. Lambert, I. Hylander, & J. Sandoval (Eds.), *Consultee-centered consultation: Improving the quality of professional services in schools and community organizations* (pp. 3–19). Mahwah, NJ: Lawrence Erlbaum.

Lambert, N., Hylander, I., & Sandoval, J. (Eds.). (2004). *Consultee-centered consultation: Improving the quality of professional services in schools and community organizations*. Mahwah, NJ: Lawrence Erlbaum.

Lambert, N. M. (1961). How to introduce mental health consultation in a school. In *Programming consultation services to schools by mental health specialists* (pp. 23–27). Sacramento, CA: California State Department of Mental Hygiene.

Lambert, N. M. (1963, March). *School psychology: A search for identity*. Presidential address in conference proceedings, California Association of School Psychologists and Psychometrists, Lakeport, CA.

Lambert, N. M. (1965). *The protection and promotion of mental health in schools*. USPHS Mental Health Monograph, No. 5. Washington, DC: U.S. Government Printing Office.

Part I

INTRODUCTION

1

CONSULTATION SERVICES IN EDUCATIONAL SETTINGS
A Global Perspective

Chryse Hatzichristou and Sylvia Rosenfield

Education policy, practice, and training around the world are undergoing change at every level. Increasing demands on schools have emerged to stress staff and students alike. The composition of school-age youth around the world has become increasingly diverse in terms of culture, race, ethnicity, and language. These rapid changes have caused a growing concern about how to address children's mental health and education in developed and developing countries alike.

Given this context, consultants in educational settings make unique contributions to systems and to supporting educators and caregivers. Combined with a scarcity of direct service providers across the globe, there is a special role for educational and psychological consultants in the promotion of children's well-being in all aspects of their development. With strong training and a solid empirical base, their contributions are even more powerful.

CONSULTATION DEFINED

Consultation is a functional competency required for all psychologists (Fouad et al., 2009) and a major one for psychologists working in education. According to Fouad et al. (2009), the key competencies in this domain include: (a) identifying the appropriate consultant role in context, (b) selecting assessment tools and interventions to address the identified problem, (c) providing recommendations and feedback relevant to the situation, and (d) basing practice on research. Multicultural competence is viewed as a foundational competence for all practice, and it has a particularly strong role in consultation.

In addition to multicultural competence, the Society of Consulting Psychology (APA Division 13), which developed a set of consultation guidelines (APA, 2007), specified that one of the broad competencies for all consulting psychologists is competence in the international area. Much of the work on diversity in consultation thus far has been limited to an emphasis on multicultural dimensions of consultation training and practice models in the United States. However, over the past decade, consultation has enlarged the focus from concerns about multicultural issues to recognition of the importance of a more international/global perspective, which requires a more nuanced understanding of culture (Christopher, Wendt, Marecek, & Goodman, 2014).

SCHOOL CONSULTATION SERVICES: AN INTERNATIONAL BACKGROUND

Although consultation practice in educational settings has a long-standing history in some countries, including the U.S., the United Kingdom (UK), Israel and Sweden, as well as more recently Greece, a lack of training and practice models and relevant research has been consistently emphasized in the literature (see, e.g., Erchul & Sheridan, 2014). Early efforts to examine consultation practice and training models in different countries were initiated by Nadine Lambert, who had a pioneering role in initiatives supporting consultee-centered consultation in schools in California and across the U.S. (Lambert, 1961, 1963, 1965); she also was a pioneer in implementing consultation as a core domain of training in the UC Berkeley School Psychology Program (Lambert, 1974, 1986). In the mid-1990s, Lambert, Hylander, and Sandoval organized International Seminars on Consultee-Centered Consultation. The initial meetings were held in Stockholm, Sweden, in 1995; seminars were later conducted seminars in Stockholm in 1999 and in San Francisco, California, in 2001(Lambert, 2004). These meetings were followed by a book titled *Consultee-Centered Consultation: Improving the Quality of Professional Services in Schools and Community Organizations* (Lambert, Hylander, & Sandoval, 2004), which included chapters by a variety of authors from multiple countries, many of whom had participated in the earlier seminars.

Since then, relatively few papers on school consultation in various countries have been published in professional journals. More specialized journals, such as the *Journal of Educational and Psychological Consultation (JEPC)*, have rarely included a focus on the international dimension of school consultation research, training, and practice, although a special issue of *JEPC* included papers about consultation work of American colleagues in international settings (Worrell, 2014). This volume is the first since the book edited by Lambert et al. (2004) to focus on consultation in educational settings from an international perspective.

MULTICULTURAL/TRANSCULTURAL COMPETENCE: CENTRAL TO SCHOOL PSYCHOLOGY PRACTICE

Increasing diversity of student populations across the world has brought to the foreground the need to emphasize and promote multicultural competence in the training, theory, and practice of school psychologists. Current research has noted the lack of knowledge regarding the interventions that are most effective with ethnic minorities, migrants, and refugees in the U.S. (e.g., Abe-Kim et al., 2007; Fazel, Doll, & Stein, 2009; Kia-Keating & Ellis, 2007; Leong & Lau, 2001; Weisz, Doss, & Hawley, 2005) as well as in other countries (e.g., Carta, Bernal, Hardoy, & Haro-Abad, 2005). For example, the number of immigrant and refugee families and children, as well as the population of people of ethnic minority backgrounds, living in the U.S. continues to rise (Martinez-Fernandez, Kubo, Noya, & Weyman, 2012). Similar findings and themes are identified across different countries, as immigration has been an integral part of many countries' histories (Banks, 2008; Hollifield, 2013; Levitt & Jaworsky, 2007).

Culturally competent practices are required for school psychologists to effectively respond to the needs of students and families from various culturally and linguistically diverse backgrounds. Incorporating such a training philosophy requires, to a great extent, multicultural training and integration of content into courses (Newell et al., 2010).

However, limited consideration has been given to multicultural issues in current school psychology graduate programs worldwide. In the U.S., even though more graduate school psychology programs have incorporated multicultural training, either as a separate course or in the form of references and/or readings, programs continue to lag in integrating multicultural content into core training areas (Newell et al., 2010). Further, there is little evidence that multicultural training has been integrated with consultation skills (e.g., Sirmans, 2004).

An additional barrier includes a limited evidence base on the prerequisite professional competencies for working with culturally and linguistically diverse populations (Braden & Shah, 2005; Jones, 2009). There is a need for a meta-cultural or culturally synthetic approach to school psychology that focuses on similarities of cultures and individuals (common needs and adversities) and builds on positive potential, competencies, and strengths as a means of enhancing resilience. This view/philosophy implies mutual valuing of perspectives and cognitive exchange across cultures (Hatzichristou, Lampro-poulou, & Lykitsakou, 2006).

Others have focused on transcultural competence, which is "the ability to successfully deal with and develop solutions to issues and problems created by cultural differences within any cultural setting" (Glover & Friedman, 2015, p. 8). Such competence, especially valuable in the emerging global community, is thought to consist of four elements: recognizing cultural differences, respecting the differences, reconciling the differences through creative problem-solving skills, and implementing the reconciliation into practice (Trompenaars, 2015). Learning how to do that is a necessary competence for consultants in education.

BEYOND MULTICULTURAL/TRANSCULTURAL COMPETENCE: A GLOBAL CONTEXT

Globalization is the process of change structured by postnational forms of production and distribution of goods and services, information, communication and media technologies, worldwide migration, and the resultant cultural transformation and exchanges that challenge traditional values and norms (Arnett, 2002; Suárez-Orozco & Qin-Hilliard, 2004). Professionals around the globe are engaged in enhancing the education and mental health of children and families, as well as working with their school personnel. In this environment, psychologists need to be well prepared to respond to and consider the current major *global challenges* (i.e., telecommunications and media, poverty, migration and refugees, urbanization, global warming, war, health and disease, well-being and mental health, human rights violations) as well as the *global resources* (e.g., equal access to knowledge, advances in sciences and humanities, advances in medical knowledge, improvements in human rights, citizen activism, spirituality, growth of psychology); these challenges and resources are shaping and influencing children, families, and systems around the world (Marsella, 2007).

Given these challenges of today's world, a "new" psychology—a global psychology that recognizes and acknowledges the major global forces and events that are shaping the context of our daily lives and prizes the cultural variations in psychologies across the world—is required (Diaz & Zirkel, 2012; Marsella, 2007, 2012). Various alternative psychologies emerging around the world reflect the paradigmatic adjustments in psychology and a need for a new global or international perspective in psychology (Moghaddam,

Erneling, Montero, & Lee, 2007). New directions in school-based multicultural competence focus on transnational and transcultural differences as professional psychologists attempt to provide services in a global community (Ehrhardt-Padgett, Hatzichristou, Kitson, & Meyers, 2004; Hatzichristou, 2002, 2004; Jimerson, Oakland, & Farrell, 2007; Nastasi & Varjas, 2011). The globalization of psychology theory, training, practice, and research is well underway, and this has significant implications for the field of educational and psychological consultation.

THE GLOBALIZATION OF SCHOOL CONSULTING

The American Psychological Association (APA) Division of School Psychology, responding to the current multicultural and global challenges in school psychology, formed the Globalization of School Psychology Working Group (WG) three years ago; the goal was to further develop transnational/multicultural domains in school psychology science and practice (Hatzichristou, 2012; Hatzichristou, Nastasi, Jimerson, & Woods, 2012; Nastasi, Hatzichristou, & Hart, 2012; Nastasi, Hatzichristou et al., 2012). The initial objective of the WG was to develop a database with transnational/multicultural readings and material on basic areas of school psychology science and practice with the help of faculty members and their graduate students both internationally and within the U.S. The major thematic subgroups in the WG are (a) assessment, (b) prevention and school-based prevention programs, (c) transnational/multicultural school psychology, (d) consultation, (e)crisis intervention, and (f) evidence-based intervention.

The annotated bibliography of the *Globalization of School Psychology Working Group* (2012) examines important issues in theory, research, service delivery, education, and training for school psychology at national/multicultural and international/ global levels with the optimal goal of promoting future partnerships and professional collaboration among faculty, graduate students, and practitioners in this field. The consultation subgroup within the Globalization of School Psychology project (Lopez, Rubinson, & Hatzichristou, 2012) focused on (a) identifying subthemes representing major areas of practice and science under consultation, (b) summarizing readings addressing consultation practice and research, and (c) highlighting multicultural and transnational themes in the summaries for each of the readings. Implications for multicultural practices and research are addressed, and transnational perspectives are discussed in the context of several international readings (i.e., Greece, Spain, Sweden, and Estonia).

PURPOSE OF THIS HANDBOOK

Given the increasingly global perspective of psychology, this handbook is designed to provide a multicultural/transnational approach to consultation theory, research, training, and practice in educational settings. While other international handbook authors (e.g., Jimerson et al., 2007) have "provided a description of the specialty of psychology devoted to the provision of services to children and youth, their teachers, and parents" (p. 1), the goal of this book is to capture the range of ways in which consultation services are trained, implemented, and researched across the globe. While there have been international handbooks on other topics, none has provided an in-depth look at consultation in educational settings across the world. Although an earlier book explored the area of consultee-centered consultation (Lambert et al., 2004) with an international group of editors and authors, this is the first comprehensive international handbook on educational consultation.

STRUCTURE OF THE HANDBOOK

An array of international practitioners and researchers on school consultation contributed to this book; they represent a sampling of major conceptual and applied expertise in educational/school consultation. This book includes the following sections, which provide various perspectives on models, implementation, training, and research on school consultation.

After this introductory chapter, Part II, School Consultation Services across the Globe, examines school-based consultation in different countries to provide some perspective on how consultation services are implemented in a variety of international contexts. In Establishing Psychological Consultation Services to Promote Student Well-being in Schools and Preschools (Chapter 2), Ingrid Hylander describes the task of introducing teacher consultation as a student psychosocial health–promoting service to school management, principals, and teachers. Examples are drawn from 30 years of experience with psychological and psychosocial consultation to Swedish preschools and schools and from Swedish research on school consultation and student health teams. In the next chapter, Revisiting Canadian Consultation Models in School Psychology: Just the Same, Only Different (Chapter 3), Ester Cole and Judith Wiener describe how children's mental health is the focus of school-based consultation in Canada. Consultation is seen as part of a continuum of direct and indirect services, with the multidisciplinary team having a central role. Online resources are discussed as an important adjunct to the services. In the following chapter, Consulting in School Settings in Australia: Challenges, Positive Development, and Future Opportunities (Chapter 4), Terence Bowles overviews the complexities of providing consultation in the Australian context, examining how training and educational structures there challenge the provision of consultation services and the new opportunities that might address these barriers to consultation practice. In the final chapter in this section, A Multilevel Approach to System-Level Consultation: Critical Components and Transnational Considerations (Chapter 5), Chryse Hatzichristou, Aikaterini Lampropoulou, Georgios Georgouleas, and Spryridoula Mihou present a multilevel model for combining theory, training, and practice of consultation in the Greek educational and cultural context, emphasizing the need for development of a transnational model of consultation training and service delivery.

Part III, Crossing Cultures, specifically addresses issues in consultation across cultures, particularly at a systems level. In Chapter 6, A Transcultural Approach to Systems-Level Consultation, Bonnie Kaul Nastasi opens the conversation with a transcultural approach to systems-level consultation. She provides a model for conducting systems-level consultation using a participatory approach that involves stakeholders in the cultural construction of interventions focused on well-being of children and youth; case examples from Sri-Lanka and India exemplify the model. She takes an international/global perspective and addresses issues related to working across cultural boundaries. In the following chapter, Navigating the Cultural Complexities of School Consultation with Contemporary Families in a Globalized World (Chapter 7), Candice A. Hughes provides an analytic framework of consultation competencies that incorporates an understanding of the cultural realities and intercultural needs of families who represent diverse compositions and identities, alternate pathways related to international mobility, and different worldviews that shape their expectations about schooling for their children. She includes a toolkit of practices to facilitate this work with families. The chapter by Samuel O. Ortiz and Kristan E. Melo, Foundations for Consultation in Educational Settings with Second Language Learners (Chapter 8), outlines the various interrelated factors that provide a foundation in both the knowledge and skills necessary for effective consultation service delivery with bilingual or English language learning (ELL) populations. Abigail Harris and Mio Ueda, in The Entry Process in International Systemic School Consultation (Chapter 9), focus on the entry process in order to effectively use system consultation to support educational reform in developing countries. They share their extensive experience on best practice in entering another culture as external consultants. In International Collaboration to Develop a School Psychology Training Program in Vietnam (Chapter 10), Kimberly S. Kassay and Mark D. Terjesen describe the collaborative work they did as consultants to establish the first school psychology training program in Vietnam. The process of engaging in this work follows the project from its early stages through the planned outcome. Stephen E. Brock and Shane R. Jimerson, in School Crisis Consultation: An International Framework (Chapter 11), present a conceptual model for engaging in school crisis consultation at the international level. An international version of the PREPaRE Model, including prevention, preparedness, response, and recovery activities, is described.

Part IV, Implementing Consultation Services in the Schools, centers on themes relating to issues, processes, and difficulties in the implementation of consultation. Although discussed in other chapters (e.g., Chapter 4), it is the main focus of four chapters. In Consultation and the Role of the School Psychologist: Barriers and Opportunities (Chapter 12), Peter Farrell and Kevin Woods explore some of the barriers that have prevented school psychologists from abandoning traditional ways of working in favor of consultation approaches. They discuss ways to overcome some of the barriers to consultation practice in England. Facing a similar context, in Thinking *In* the Box: A Tool for Promoting Innovative Problem-Solving in Israeli School Psychology Services (Chapter 13), Sharone L. Maital describes a model for helping school psychologists adopt and implement a more systemic consultation approach to school services. Her case study of this tool provides the context for this chapter. In the next chapter in this section, Dealing with Difficulties: The Strategies of Instructional Consultants in Hong Kong (Chapter 14), Shui-fong Lam describes the difficulties in providing consultation to teachers in Hong Kong as the educational system undergoes change. Strategies that the consultants developed are highlighted. In the final chapter in this section, Ecological Consultation as a Means to Promote Child Rights (Chapter 15), Cynthia Hazel describes how a school-based ecological consultation model could serve as a means of realizing the Convention on the Rights of the Child's assertion that all children deserve protection and have the same rights. Implementation processes for two case studies of consultation in an urban United States school district are described.

Part V, Educating Effective Consultants, on consultation training includes three chapters. The chapter by Colette Ingraham, Training and Education of Consultants: A Global Perspective (Chapter 16), presents models and practices for the development of professionals to become effective consultants in cross-cultural and systemic contexts. She introduces the Consultation Learning and Development Model and discusses how it articulates global competencies and instructional approaches. The next chapter by Emma Kennedy, Sandra Dunsmuir, and R.J. Cameron, Professional Training and Development in Consultation: From Knowledge to Competence and Capability in Educational and Child Psychology Practice in the UK (Chapter 17), describes initial and in-service training in consultation, especially the development and maintenance of key skills, based on the English model. Their focus on supervision and feedback provides models of a critical feature of effective training. The third chapter in this section, Complicating the Thinking of Trainee Consultants in Consultee-Centered Consultation (Chapter 18), by Frank C. Worrell, Jessica Ernandes Naecker, Christine E. Gerchow, Chloe Green, Claire E. Kunesh, and Anna Casey, celebrates student voices. Students-in-training report how their training experiences impacted their growing skills in consultation and how they documented those changes using a unique method.

Part VI, Researching Consultation, includes a chapter on enhancing the research base of consultation. In their chapter, Conducting School-based Consultation as Publishable Research (Chapter 19), Stephen D. Truscott, Moriah A. Kearney, Yanique T. Matthews, and Kirnel Daniel describe how practitioners can contribute to the body of research on consultation through careful planning and implementation of their work. They present the prevailing models of consultation research, identifying the underlying assumptions of that work and explicating the challenges and opportunities available to international researchers. Given the dearth of research on consultation, their approach provides encouragement to practitioners across the globe to help develop an empirical base for consultants.

The last chapter, by the co-editors Sylvia Rosenfield and Chryse Hatzichristou, Mapping the Global Future of School-based Consultation (Chapter 20), summarizes key concepts and findings that emerged from the previous chapters and considers the future of consultation theory, research, and practice from a global perspective.

CONCLUSION

It is our intention that the work of the authors will provide an international snapshot of the current state of consultation in educational settings. The emerging picture will highlight the many similarities and some differences that exist. We also look forward to an international conversation about next steps: how to educate consultants for school settings, how practice can be implemented widely and successfully, and how research can provide a more solid empirical foundation for the field. Working across cultures and national boundaries can help us achieve these ends.

REFERENCES

Abe-Kim, J., Takeuchi, D. T., Hong, S., Zane, N., Sue, S., Spencer, M. S., . . . Alegría, M. (2007). Use of mental health-related services among immigrant and US-born Asian Americans: Results from the National Latino and Asian American Study. *American Journal of Public Health, 97*(1), 91–98.

American Psychological Association. (2007). Guidelines for education and training at the doctoral and postdoctoral levels in consulting psychology/organizational consulting psychology. *American Psychologist, 62*, 980–992.

Arnett, J. J. (2002). The psychology of globalization. *American Psychologist, 57*, 774–783.

Banks, J. A. (2008). Diversity, group identity, and citizenship education in a global age. *Educational Researcher, 37*, 129–139.

Braden, J. P., & Shah, K. G. (2005). A critique of multicultural training in school psychology: Rationale, strategies, and tactics. In C. L. Frisby & C. R. Reynolds (Eds.), *Comprehensive handbook of multicultural school psychology* (pp. 1023–1047). New York: Wiley.

Carta, M. G., Bernal, M., Hardoy, M. C., & Haro-Abad, J. M. (2005). Migration and mental health in Europe (the state of the mental health in Europe working group: Appendix 1). *Clinical Practice and Epidemiology in Mental Health, 1*(1), 13. doi: 10.1186/1745-0179-1-13

Christopher, J. C., Wendt, D. C., Marecek, J., & Goodman, D. M. (2014). Critical cultural awareness: Contributions to a globalizing psychology. *American Psychologist, 69,* 645–655. http://dx.doi.org/10.1037/a0036851

Diaz, J., & Zirkel, S. (2012). Globalization, psychology, and social issues research: An introduction and conceptual framework. *Journal of Social Issues, 68,* 439–453.

Ehrhardt-Padgett, G., Hatzichristou, C., Kitson, J., & Meyers, J. (2004). Awakening to a new dawn: Perspectives of the future of school psychology. *School Psychology Quarterly, 18,* 483–496.

Erchul, W. P., & Sheridan, S. M. (Eds.). (2014). *Handbook of research in school consultation: Empirical foundations for the field* (2nd ed.). New York: Routledge.

Fazel, M., Doll, H., & Stein, A. (2009). A school-based mental health intervention for refugee children: An exploratory study. *Clinical Child Psychology and Psychiatry, 14,* 297–309.

Fouad, N. A., Grus, C. L., Hatcher, R. L., Kaslow, N. J., Hutchings, P. S., Madson, M. B., & Crossman, R. E. (2009). Competency benchmarks: A model for understanding and measuring competence in professional psychology across training levels. *Training and Education in Professional Psychology, 3*(4, Suppl.), S5–S26. doi: 10.1037/a0015832

Globalization of School Psychology Working Group, APA Division 16 (2012). (C. Hatzichristou, chair and ed.) annotated bibliography document.

Glover, J., & Friedman, H. L. (2015). *Transcultural competence: Navigating cultural differences in the global community.* Washington, DC: American Psychological Association.

Hatzichristou, C. (2002). A conceptual framework of the evolution of school psychology: Transnational considerations of common phases and future perspectives. *School Psychology International, 23,* 266–282. doi: 10.1177/0143034302023003322

Hatzichristou, C. (2004). Alternative school psychological services: Development of a model linking theory, research, and service delivery. In N. M. Lambert, I. Hylander, & J. Sandoval (Eds.), *Consultee-centered consultation: Improving the quality of professional services in schools and community organizations* (pp. 115–132). Mahwah, NJ: Lawrence Erlbaum.

Hatzichristou, C. (2012, February). *School psychology and the global world.* Invited presentation at the Trainers of School Psychologist Annual Meeting, Philadelphia, PA.

Hatzichristou, C., Lampropoulou, A., & Lykitsakou, K. (2006). Addressing cultural factors in development of system/community interventions. *Journal of Applied School Psychology, Multicultural Issues and School Psychology Practice, 22*(2), 103–126.

Hatzichristou, C., Nastasi, B. K., Jimerson, S., & Woods, K. (2012, July). *Future directions in multicultural/transnational school psychology science and practice.* Symposium at the 34th International School Psychology Association Conference: Helping the world's children realize their dreams, McGill University, Montreal, CA.

Hollifield, J. F. (2013). The politics of international migration. In C. B. Brettell & J. F. Hollifield (Eds.), *Migration theory: Talking across disciplines* (pp. 137–185). New York: Routledge.

Jimerson, S., Oakland, T., & Farrell, P. (Eds.). (2007). *Handbook of international school psychology.* Thousand Oaks, CA: Sage Publications.

Jones, J. M. (2009). Counseling with multicultural intentionality: The process of counseling and integrating client cultural variables. In J. M. Jones (Ed.), *The psychology of multiculturalism in the schools: A primer for practice, training, and research* (pp. 191–213). Bethesda, MD: National Association of School Psychologists.

Kia-Keating, M., & Ellis, B. H. (2007). Belonging and connection to school in resettlement: Young refugees, school belonging, and psychosocial adjustment. *Clinical Child Psychology and Psychiatry, 12*(1), 29–43.

Lambert, N. M. (1961). How to introduce mental health consultation in a school. In *Programming consultation services to schools by mental health specialists* (pp. 23–27). Sacramento, CA: California State Department of Mental Hygiene.

Lambert, N. M. (1963, March). *School psychology: A search for identity.* Presidential address in conference proceedings, California Association of School Psychologists and Psychometrists, Lakeport, CA.

Lambert, N. M. (1965). *The protection and promotion of mental health in schools.* USPHS Mental Health Monograph, No.5. Washington, DC: U.S. Government Printing Office.

Lambert, N. M. (1974). A school-based consultation model. *Professional Psychology, 5,* 267–275.

Lambert, N. M. (1986). Conceptual foundations for school psychology: Perspectives from the development of the school psychology program at Berkeley. *Professional School Psychology, 4,* 215–224.

Lambert, N. M. (2004). Consultee-centered consultation: An international perspective on goals, process and theory. In N. M. Lambert, I. Hylander, & J. Sandoval (Eds.), *Consultee-centered consultation: Improving the quality of professional services in schools and community organizations* (pp. 3–19). Mahwah, NJ: Lawrence Erlbaum.

Lambert, N. M., Hylander, I., & Sandoval, J. (Eds.). (2004). *Consultee-centered consultation: Improving the quality of professional services in schools and community organizations*. Mahwah, NJ: Lawrence Erlbaum.

Leong, F. T., & Lau, A. S. (2001). Barriers to providing effective mental health services to Asian Americans. *Mental Health Services Research, 3*(4), 201–214.

Levitt, P., & Jaworsky, N. B. (2007). Transnational migration studies: Past developments and future trends. *Annual Review of Sociology, 33*(7), 129–156.

Marsella, A. J. (2007). Education and training for a global psychology. In M. J. Stevens, & U. P. Gielen (Eds.), *Toward a global psychology: Theory, research, intervention, and pedagogy* (pp. 267–298). Mahwah, NJ: Lawrence Erlbaum Associates.

Marsella, A. J. (2012). Psychology and globalization: Understanding a complex relationship. *Journal of Social Issues, 68*, 454–472.

Martinez-Fernandez, C., Kubo, N., Noya, A., & Weyman, T. (2012). *Demographic change and local development: Shrinkage, regeneration and social dynamics*. Paris: OECD/LEED.

Moghaddam, F., Erneling, C., Montero, M., & Lee, N. (2007). Toward a conceptual foundation for a global psychology. In M. Stevens & U. Gielen (Eds.), *Toward a global psychology: Theory, research, intervention, and pedagogy* (pp. 179–206). Mahwah, NJ: Lawrence Erlbaum.

Nastasi, B. K., Hatzichristou, C., & Hart, S. N. (2012, February). *Translating science to practice and policy: School psychology leadership initiatives*. Presentation at the National Association of School Psychologists Annual Convention, Philadelphia, PA.

Nastasi, B. K., Hatzichristou, C., Jimerson, S., Stoiber, K. C., Forman, S. G., & Shriberg, D. (2012, August). *Division 16 Initiatives—Social justice and child rights, Translating science to practice, and Globalization*. Symposium at the Convention of the American Psychological Association, Orlando, FL.

Nastasi, B. K., & Varjas, K. (2011). International development of school psychology. In M. A. Bray & T. J. Kehle (Eds.), *Oxford Handbook of School Psychology* (pp. 810–828). New York: Oxford University Press.

Newell, M. L., Nastasi, B. K., Hatzichristou, C., Jones, J. M., Schanding, G. T., Jr., & Yetter, G. P. (2010). Evidence on multicultural training in school psychology: Recommendations for future directions. *School Psychology Quarterly, 25*, 249–278.

Sirmans, M. (2004). *Culturally relevant consultation among school psychology practitioners: A nation-wide study of training and practice* (Doctoral dissertation). Retrieved from http://drum.lib.umd.edu/handle/1903/1499

Suárez-Orozco, M. M., & Qin-Hilliard, D. (2004). *Globalization: Culture and education in the new millennium*. Berkeley, CA: University of California Press.

Trompenaars, F. (2015). Foreword. In J. Glover & H. L. Friedman (Eds.), *Transcultural competence: Navigating cultural differences in the global community*. Washington, DC: American Psychological Association.

Weisz, J. R., Doss, A. J., & Hawley, K. M. (2005). Youth psychotherapy outcome research: A review and critique of the evidence base. *Annual Review of Psychology, 56*, 337–363.

Worrell, F. C. (2014). Developing international partnerships: American school psychologists consulting in other countries. *Journal of Educational and Psychological Consultation, 24*, 261–264. doi: 10.1080/10474412.2014.929967

Part II

SCHOOL CONSULTATION SERVICES
ACROSS THE GLOBE

2

ESTABLISHING PSYCHOLOGICAL CONSULTATION SERVICES TO PROMOTE STUDENT WELL-BEING IN SCHOOLS AND PRESCHOOLS

Ingrid Hylander

Educators have proposed a shift from a narrow diagnostic view to a holistic, ecological (Bronfenbrenner, 1986) and salutogenic (Antonovsky, 1987) perspective on students' school-related difficulties (Guvå & Hylander, 2012; Sheridan & Gutkin, 2000). A salutogenic approach focuses on factors promoting health and well-being in contrast to factors causing problems and ill-health—ease instead of disease (Antonovsky, 1996). Albeit a proposed shift, school psychologists and other school-based professionals around the world state that they are so busy assessing individual children that no time is left for preventive work or promotion of general well-being for students (Guvå & Hylander, 2012; Hjörne & Säljö, 2004; Hughes, Loyd, & Buss, 2008).

Several reasons for the lack of change, despite being talked about for decades, have been proposed. One reason for the slow shift may be a lack of understanding of what promotion of well-being in schools actually means. Another reason may be a lack of professional models and working methods, as well as training, to meet the new demands. A third reason is teacher and administrator expectations of individual student assessments from school psychologists and other school-based student health professionals (Hylander, 2011). In this chapter, the concept of well-being will be extensively discussed in relation to the introduction of school psychological consultation services. Examples are drawn from 30 years of experience of practice and research on psychological and psychosocial consultation to Swedish preschools and schools.

THE EVIDENCE BASE FOR PROMOTION OF WELL-BEING

Facts based on evidence sometimes need to be repeated, such as the fact that learning and well-being go hand in hand. Without student well-being, there is no or little learning, and without successful learning, student well-being is seriously affected (Dodge, Greenberg, & Malone, 2008; Gustafsson et al., 2010; Halonen, Aunola, Ahonen, & Nurmi, 2006; Masten et al., 1999; Morgan, Farkas, Tufis, & Sperling, 2008).

A Systematic Overview

In 2010, the Swedish Royal Academy of Science conducted a systematic overview of research on student achievement and mental health and well-being (10,717 refereed international articles) in order to communicate a common evidence base for school administrators, teachers and other school-based personnel (Gustafsson et al., 2010). Based on the sample of those articles considered to have experimental designs (randomized controlled trial [RCT] studies), high quality, and high relevance for the research questions—the effect of academic achievement on mental health and the effect of mental health on academic achievement (n = 51)—a few general conclusions could be drawn. The conclusions were as follows:

- School competence and achievement are related to mental health and well-being.
- High achievement has a positive effect on students' self-esteem.
- Factors related to self-esteem, such as motivation and sense of control, influence learning and achievements.
- Good relations with friends and teachers can prevent mental health problems.
- Low achievement and mental health problems tend to form a vicious circle that accelerates through the school years.
- High quality preschool may enhance reading and math competencies, but more research on this is needed.

These conclusions may seem self-evident to anyone with experience of teaching and bringing up children. What is new is that the scientific evidence is so strong for the link between psychological well-being and achievement. Perhaps the time has come to let this evidence become the basis for school curriculum and management for all children and specifically for children with special needs.

THEORETICAL FRAMEWORK FOR PROMOTION OF WELL-BEING

A Swedish study showed that interdisciplinary school support teams wanted their work to be preventive and to promote well-being, but in practice it turned out that they spent time diagnosing individual children (Hylander, 2011). Members of the team used the concepts of prevention and promotion of well-being interchangeably and did not seem to see any difference between them. The conclusion was that they had no common theory of health promotion and hence few professional methods and work models for the promotion of well-being (Guvå & Hylander, 2012; Hylander, 2011).

Salutogenic Approach

The traditional way of delineating preventive work comes from medicine (Caplan & Caplan, 1993). Primary prevention is aimed at reducing the risk of disease for a whole population. Secondary prevention is aimed at discovering risks and signs at an early state before any harm can be detected. Tertiary prevention is aimed at those already struck by disease to minimize the consequences of the illness. This medical model has been applied to psychosocial prevention (SBU, 2010) in schools in the following ways: (a) universal prevention (primary prevention) is aimed at the whole school population; (b) selected prevention (secondary prevention) is aimed at risk groups; and (c) indicated prevention (tertiary prevention) is aimed at those showing symptoms to reduce effects and prevent more problems. In many texts, preventive and health promoting interventions are used interchangeably, and some authors argue that universal prevention is the same as health promotion.

Antonovsky (1987, 1996), however, made a clear distinction between prevention and health promotion. He also provided a theory for health promotion: *salutogenesis.* Antonovsky (1987, 1996) developed his theory about salutogenesis, explaining how people manage stress and stay well. The term salutogenesis describes an approach focusing on the origin of health and well-being rather than on factors that cause disease. For him, disease and health are not mutually exclusive but rather on a continuum. There is always more or less disease, but people cope with difficulties in their own ways. Thus, the well-being of a person is as much a question of how stressors such as disease are handled as well as the disease itself.

In salutogenic theory, there are forces called *generalized resource deficits* (GRD) that move toward the disease end of the continuum and *generalized resistance resources* (GRR) that move toward the well-being end of the continuum. GRRs help individuals cope, avoid or combat stressors and strengthen their sense of coherence. *Sense of coherence* means that things are comprehensible and predictable, manageable through enough resources and meaningful by being worthwhile. GRDs will cause coping mechanisms to fail if a sense of coherence is not robust enough. It is thus a balance between GRDs and GRRs that determines whether a specific factor will be salutogenic and contribute to health or pathogenic and cause disease for an individual. Antonovsky (1996) also believed that preventive efforts were pathogenic in the sense of focusing on risk factors at the disease end of the disease–well-being continuum instead of the well-being end. Thus, according to his theory, interdisciplinary school support teams with the aim of promotion of learning, health, and well-being should focus on the GRRs strengthening coping mechanisms and sense of coherence.

The following example clarifies this theory. A number of children play on the beaches of a river, where water is rapidly flowing downstream; there are a few adults there to care for them. Some adults position themselves downstream in order to be able to save children who have fallen into the river from drowning. Other adults position themselves upstream to be able to make an early discovery and pick a child who just fell into the water. This is the difference between an early and a late discovery. Acting preventively would be to buy life jackets for all children and supervise their use of them. In contrast, an approach of health promotion would be to teach all the children how to swim.

A Model for Prevention of Ill Health and Promotion of Well-being in Schools

Classroom instruction and classroom climate are natural points of departure to raise achievements and enhance well-being among students. Although efforts made to enhance students' well-being could also enhance school achievement, the core processes of schools are instruction and learning. As much as well-being affects student motivation and learning, high achievement affects students' well-being (Dodge et al., 2008; Gustafsson et al., 2010; Halonen et al., 2006).

A similar argument can be made about school-related difficulties as Antonovsky (1996) made about disease and well-being. There is not a dichotomy between nonlearning students and learning students. All students have some difficulties in learning, and all students learn in some situations. Students are at different places on a learning versus nonlearning continuum. However, school difficulties are typically discussed in terms of nonlearning situations, not learning situations. In a Swedish study of individual intervention programs (IP) for children with school-related difficulties, it was concluded that even if teachers attended to positive sides of the student in writing the background of the IPs, these positive comments were never the basis for the intervention (Hylander, 2011).

In a Swedish study of student health and well-being (SHW) in primary school (grades one to nine), six different school-based professions (school psychologists, school nurses, school doctors, special educational teachers, principals and teachers; n = 87) were interviewed about their understanding of SHW and what type of services they wanted to contribute (Guvå & Hylander, 2012). They all emphasized that the approach of the services should be general prevention and promotion of student well-being. But they also agreed on the fact that this was not the case at the moment. Instead, time was spent on assessing and investigating individual problems in a traditional way. They all agreed on a gap between rhetoric and practice in school-based interdisciplinary services.

Interventions were considered from two perspectives, salutogenic and pathogenic, and on two levels, individual and general, which formed a matrix with four different meanings given to SHW interprofessional services (see Table 2.1).

- Screenings or preventive interventions for all students are examples of services from a pathogenic perspective on a general level (Table 2.1 section A), that is, services with the aim of avoiding or minimizing risk factors, such as antidrug or antibullying programs.
- Assessments and interventions aimed at targeted students with specific difficulties are examples of services from a pathogenic perspective on an individual level (section C). This is the position where most interprofessional school-based interventions are conducted today.
- Interventions aimed at promoting good school climate, constructive teacher leadership in the classroom, collaboration among teachers, good and wholesome food in the cafeteria and physical activities for all are examples of a salutogenic perspective on a general level (section B). System consultation is a way for members of interprofessional teams to contribute with their specific competence to promote well-being on a general level.
- Individual promotion from a salutogenic perspective refers to all interventions to an individual child that are provided in order to promote learning and well-being (section D). This is what teachers work with every day and where psychologists could support teachers with consultee-centered case consultation.

Table 2.1 Pathogenic and Salutogenic Perspectives on Professional Interventions to Schools (adapted from Guvå & Hylander, 2012)

	Pathogenic perspective	Salutogenic perspective
General level	A General preventions and interventions • Screening • Antidrug programs • Antibullying programs	B Promotion of general health, well-being and learning • System work • Teamwork
Individual level	C Individual prevention and interventions • Assessments • Individual interventions	D Promotion of individual health, well-being and learning • Support to teachers to develop interventions and understanding of individual students

Guvå and Hylander (2012) illustrated the salutogenic and pathogenic perspectives as dichotomies, but it is closer to reality to see them as a continuum. In providing interdisciplinary support services to schools, no one of the four positions in the chart should be neglected. However, the chart could be seen as a reminder of on which side the main tasks are performed and where they are supposed to be performed according to overarching objectives. Referring to the example of the river, no one can watch a child drowning without doing something. But if all resources are placed downstream, there is no one there to see the child fall into the water. If all resources are spent buying life preservers and supervising the use of them, there is no money left for swimming classes.

This table may serve as a reminder of the goal to move from the pathogenic end of the continuum to the salutogenic end. Consultee-centered consultation to teachers, as described later, is a means in this movement because it focuses on the ordinary classroom work either for one specific child or for a group of children. Consultation on a systemic level, to principals or teachers, may also move interventions from a perspective of avoiding risks to a perspective of creating good psychosocial and educational climates in the school.

The two levels of intervention can also be considered as a continuum. According to an ecological (Bronfenbrenner, 1986) or systemic view of interventions, if a change occurs with a single student in the classroom, it will also affect the classroom. Changing the classroom climate will change the climate for the individual student. A principal with a new approach to student health and well-being may change the situation for a large part of the student body, but a traditional teacher may also obstruct implementation of the principal's visions.

INTERPROFESSIONAL TEAMS IN SWEDISH SCHOOLS

In Sweden, a shift from a pathogenic to a salutogenic perspective is proposed through a new organization of school health and psychosocial services (SHW) with the distinct aim of psychosocial and physical health promotion in schools. According to the Swedish Educational Act (SEA) (Skollagen, 2010, p. 800), schools must now have access to resources such as a psychologist, social worker, doctor, and nurse and professionals with competency in special education. SEA also emphasizes that the approach of these interprofessional teams, which are supposed to provide educational, psychological and medical services to schools, primarily should have a preventive approach and promote general well-being among students.

Interprofessional teams have a long history in Swedish schools, but the teams now proposed to integrate two existing parallel services (school health care and psychosocial care) with special education into one system, student health and well-being (SHW). It is the responsibility of the principal to involve the SHW teams when an individual student is not attaining academic objectives. However, individual assessments from the SHW team should be limited to what is essential for the individual student's learning and for teacher instruction. This means that diagnosing medical and neuropsychiatric disturbances is not the responsibility of school-based professionals but should be attended to by other services such as child psychiatric clinics. Thus, a legitimate base for consultation services to schools is now attained.

Collaboration among School-Based Professionals
The proposals of the Educational Act (Prop. 201/02:14) emphasized that promotion of student health, well-being and learning requires collaboration among all school-based

professionals. Students' achievement and development are the objectives for all school-based professionals. The classroom is a context where not only children's competencies are developed but also peer-relations, social competency and self-esteem. To change destructive day-to-day experiences lasting year after year has much more influence on students' achievement and well-being than single individual interventions (Hughes et al., 2008). No more can students' psychological well-being be the professional responsibility only for the school psychologist, or students' health a professional responsibility only for the school nurse, or students' learning the professional responsibility only for the teacher. Teachers encounter the whole student in the classroom not only his or her cognitive competence. Different professions are there to contribute their specific competencies for the best of the students. No one profits from all professions taking on the same tasks, blurring the professional borders. The challenge is to use competencies and knowledge from all professions in such a way that students' learning and well-being profit (Hylander, 2011).

No teacher should be in a situation where they feel that it is their responsibility to care for the well-being, health and learning of all students in their classroom without support and complementary competence from other professionals. However, studies show that teachers feel alone with regard to difficult student problems because other school-based professionals, although they have a mission to promote general health, well-being and learning in schools, are stuck in traditional positions assessing individual children (Hylander, 2011).

Consultation as a Means for Transferring Knowledge and Understanding

Interprofessional teams in Swedish schools, which consist of psychologists, school social workers, nurses, doctors and special education teachers, have diverse professional competencies that could be used in developing school and classroom climates and promoting students' well-being and learning. But there is little use of this competence until it is translated to teachers so it can be used to create new understandings and promote developmental changes in classrooms and student environments.

Consultation is a way of transferring specific knowledge and understanding from the consultant to the consultee in a way that it is applicable in a certain context, such as the classroom. *Consultation* here is understood as a professional relationship between a teacher and a consultant focusing on a student, a group of students or an organizational issue where the teacher keeps the responsibility for implementations and is in charge of the start and the end of consultation (Lambert, Hylander, & Sandoval, 2004). Psychological consultation, such as consultee-centered consultation (CCC), is a method designed to enhance well-being among students by supporting teachers to handle students and issues with students in their own classrooms (Caplan & Caplan, 1993; Guvå & Hylander, 2013; Lambert et al., 2004). Instead of diagnosing and treating a child, the psychologist supports the system professionals to handle a problem within their own context, emphasizing individual growth and the shaping of a healthy environment. Furthermore, it aims at fostering teacher competency in handling similar cases in the future.

EVIDENCE FOR SCHOOL-BASED CONSULTATION

Scientific evidence for most preventive and general interventions to schools with the aim of promoting students' well-being is not overwhelming. It is seldom that consultation efforts in organizational development (OD) projects are delineated in such a way that conclusions can be drawn about specific consultant interventions (Illback & Pennington, 2008). With a few exceptions (Erchul & Sheridan, 2014; Rosenfield, Gravois, & Silva, 2014), this research has not been conducted. Most research on consultation is limited to single-case behavioral problems and short-term effects or to teacher satisfaction (Knotek & Hylander, 2014), which show good effects in meta-analysis (Erchul & Sheridan, 2014). In addition, a majority of studies are performed by university researchers who have undergraduate or graduate students acting as consultants (Hughes et al., 2008).

Swedish surveys have shown that teachers think that problems have been wholly or partly solved through consultation, and they think that what they learned about handling one child could be transferred to interacting with other children (Alzén, 2000; Brodin & Hylander, 1995; Knotek & Hylander, 2014). This indicates that a conceptual change, resulting in a change in interaction with the target child and other children, has taken place (Hylander, 2000, 2012). Hence, the promotion of well-being was successful. However, much more research is needed in order to better understand how sustainable the effects of consultation are with the aim of promoting well-being.

Experienced consultants working with an established school consultation practice are needed before studies with a more ecological and long-term approach can be conducted. Without practical experience with a well-identified and well-structured consultation model, would-be consultants will have difficulties negotiating consultation contracts with schools and teachers. Thus, developmental work and research have to go hand in hand in order to establish a scientific evidence base for consultation as a service that is both preventive and health promoting.

Meanwhile, empirical evidence as the basis for consultation as a preventive and health promoting service must be sought in other areas of research, such as research about teacher–student relationships (Hamre & Pianta, 2001; Hattie, 2008; Hughes, Zhang et al., 2005; Jerome, Hamre, & Pianta, 2009; Pianta, 1999; Pianta, Paro, Payne, Cox, & Bradley, 2002; Pianta & Stuhlman, 2004), general research on the relation between school success and well-being (Gustafsson et al., 2010) and research on successful schools (Grosin, 2002; Rutter, 1983). This research shows a consensus on the importance of good teacher–student relationships, open classroom climates, well-structured instruction and collaboration among teachers with common vision and objectives for school success. When and if psychological consultation can contribute to these objectives, consultation will be deemed effective.

CONSULTATION MODELS

There are several different models of school-based consultation (Erchul & Sheridan, 2014). Many school psychologists refer to consultation as a work method without referring to a specific model. This is typical in practice work. However, in order to promote consultation and explain to reluctant teachers and principals what effects it may have, nothing is as practical as a good theory and nothing so convincing as an abundance of experience from one model. The following section describes one model of school consultation.

Mental Health Consultation

Gerald Caplan developed and described mental health consultation almost half a century ago (Caplan, 1970). Caplan proposed two types of consultation focusing on individual cases, client-centered case consultation and consultee-centered case consultation, and two types of consultation focusing on administrative (or system-level) issues, program-centered administrative consultation and consultee-centered administrative consultation. Incorporating a salutogenic and a pathogenic approach can be done to give a new perspective to Caplan's four different types of consultation.

In *client-centered consultation* the focus is on the client. The consultant makes an assessment of the student on the basis of tests or other objective or reported data that are considered objective. Then, the consultant communicates his or her report and recommendations for interventions to the teachers. In this type of consultation, a pathogenic approach is most natural, as the difficulties the student encounters must be scrutinized and reported back to the teacher. As an example, a school psychologist is consulted by a teacher about a child who has difficulties in attaining academic objectives. The psychologist conducts a series of tests; after finding that the student is dyslexic, he or she talks with the teacher and makes recommendations for specific training and for other measures that will enable the student to participate in classes without being hampered by his or her difficulties. The psychologist sees the teacher a couple of times to follow up on how recommendations are implemented and how the student is doing.

In *consultee-centered case consultation,* the focus is on the interaction between the teacher and the student, specifically on the teacher's understanding of the case. The teacher makes the assessments and collects data. The challenge for the consultant is to contribute with understanding and competence in such a way that the teacher gains new perspectives and more understanding of the student so difficulties can be handled and new ways of interacting and instructing lead to more learning and well-being for the student. For example, a teacher consults with a psychologist about a student whom the teacher describes as not attaining academic objectives because of attention deficits and who disturbs other students by running around the classroom and talking out in class. The teacher is frustrated and has long ago passed the limits for what she considers a normal work situation in class. Through support and structured questions, the consultant and the teacher find areas where they need more information in order to help the student. The teacher carries out investigations and tries new ways to interact with the student on the basis of the new understanding attained during consultation. Hopefully, this new understanding will also help the teacher to change his or her approach in other situations to promote learning and well-being in the whole class.

Program-centered consultation means that the consultant investigates problems in the system and suggests that specific programs or recommendations be implemented. Typically the consultants are experts on the type of program they recommend. For example, a school psychologist is consulted because of problems with bullying in a secondary school. The psychologist investigates the problem by surveying all students about their experiences of bullying. In those classes where students have experienced bullying, the psychologist proposes a specific antibullying program and meets with the teachers to help them implement the program. Thus, this is a pathogenic approach in the sense that it focuses on a specific problem and a specific intervention to prevent that problem.

Consultee-centered administrative (system) consultation means that the consultant meets with members of a system who want to explore a specific issue. The consultant helps the consultees find ways to investigate the issue and, in collaboration with the members of the system, suggests different ways to develop the specific issue. For example, a principal wants to improve collaboration and teamwork among teachers in his school,

Table 2.2 School Consultation on Different Levels According to Pathogenic and Salutogenic Perspectives

	Pathogenic perspective	Salutogenic perspective
General level	A *Program-centered system consultation*	B *Consultee-centered system consultation*
Individual level	C *Client-centered case consultation*	D *Consultee-centered case consultation*

so he consults with a school psychologist from the central office. They talk things over, and the consultant has some suggestions on how the principal can involve the teachers in the planning of a project. The principal continues to see the consultant and discuss the development of the project over the year. At the end of the project, they discuss how the project can be evaluated and what the benefits for teachers and students were. This is a salutogenic approach focusing on promotion of collaboration among teachers as a way of promoting of student learning, health and well-being. Table 2.2 illustrates different meanings of SHW interprofessional services in relation to salutogenic or pathogenic perspectives and individual or general levels.

Psychological Case Consultation: A Consultee-Centered Model Developed in Sweden

The consultee-centered case consultation model that was developed in Sweden beginning in the 1980s, first as a consultation model to preschools and later to compulsory schools, is based on Caplan's Mental Health Consultation Model, and it can be briefly described as follows. When teachers are concerned about a child, they can contact the consultant directly. Consultants, primarily psychologists employed by the municipality school board, make an appointment shortly after the first contact. Typically teachers meet with the consultant for 1 to 1.5 hours every 3 or 4 weeks until they feel confident in handling the problem on their own (Hylander & Guvå, 2004). Surveys show that consultation usually occurs over three to five sessions (Alzén, 2000; Brodin & Hylander, 1995).

The consultation visit takes place in school/preschool, typically with a team of teachers in a room with no children present. The consultant focuses on understanding teachers' concerns and learning more about the interactions between the child and the teachers and between the targeted child and other children using a consultation guide designed to promote reflection and understanding of the case (Guvå, 2004). During this first session, teachers typically express their worries and frustrations. The aim of the first session is to negotiate a collaboration contract that the teachers will find hopeful and helpful. When it is possible for the consultant and the consultee to identify a common framing of the issue, an important part of the consultation process has already been accomplished. Between sessions the teachers make observations, conduct interviews or collect other data, the results of which are discussed with the consultant during the next session. Later, teachers implement strategies from a new understanding of the case that emerged from the discussion with the consultant (Guvå & Hylander, 2013; Hylander & Guvå, 2004).

This type of consultation is here regarded as promotion of learning, health and well-being on an individual level. The teacher may regard it as an intervention targeting an individual problem. From the perspective of the psychologist, however, it is health promoting in the sense of being solved in the context of the classroom within the learning relationship between the teacher and the student. The psychologist has done no diagnosing and has not categorized the child but instead has focused on the possibilities of growth and development for the child as well as for the teacher. The teacher has hopefully gained understanding and knowledge that other children will profit from.

INTRODUCING CONSULTATION IN PRESCHOOLS AND SCHOOLS

For psychologists who want to establish consultation as preferred service to schools and teachers, they need to be aware of the scientific evidence for the close relationship between school achievement and mental health, understand the salutogenic and ecological and systemic approach and know where, when and how consultation may be a successful service to schools. This section will provide a background for the difficult task of introducing teacher consultation as a student psychosocial health-promoting service to school management, principals and teachers. Particularly, facilitating factors for consultation are described; then, barriers to be overcome and steps to be taken in the task of introducing and establishing consultation will be considered.

It is a challenge for a novice school psychologist to explain to schoolteachers and principals how consultation can function in a constructive way and how psychological consultation may serve an important role in the promotion of students' well-being. Novice school consultants with basic training in consultation often claim that they know how to do consultation but that they don't get any practice because teachers don't ask for it. Too often, we see novice school psychologists working in school areas where no consultative services have been given before and where there is no or little understanding of the benefit of a whole school approach, promotion of well-being and preventive efforts. Then, these novice school psychologists with little or no training in consultation are supposed to be the ambassadors for consultation work. No wonder so many withdraw to the testing room!

Mandated prevention and promotion of well-being as a preferred school service is a prerequisite for consultation. But such a system-level change, particularly on a national level, requires advocacy not only from single school psychologists but also from national professional organizations. When promotion of learning, health and well-being, in contrast to a medical approach, is mandated by legislative acts and rules, would-be consultants can discuss and debate system-level barriers with principals and school administrators. However, even when promotion of well-being is proposed in educational acts, traditions and teacher expectations may hinder a development of consultative services. Furthermore, there are barriers related to the consultants. Such barriers include a lack of consultation network opportunities with other consultants, supervision on consultation and other types of support necessary for school psychologists not to feel lonely in their professional roles as consultants in an education environment. These prerequisites and barriers will be discussed later.

Introducing Consultation in Swedish Pre-Schools[1]

Psychological consultation services were successfully introduced to preschools during the 1980s in Sweden long before they were introduced in primary and secondary schools. Even though school psychologists have offered services to schools since the early 1970s, consultation became a regular service to primary schools later than to preschools. The legal prerequisites for consultation services to schools are now in many ways more similar to what was the case for preschools when psychological consultation services first were introduced in Sweden 35 years ago (Hylander & Guvå, 2004). With SEA, consultation is now a legitimate response to the quest for prevention and promotion of well-being among all students. Understanding the background to the development of the early childhood education and preschool movement in Sweden and consultation services to preschools is relevant also for consultation in compulsory schools. There are lessons to be learned from the introduction of consultation services to preschools that are applicable to the introduction of consultation to primary and secondary schools today.

A governmental proposal from 1972 set the basis for the Swedish preschools, which were established throughout the country during the late 1970s and 1980s. Since 1995, Swedish municipalities are obliged to provide high-quality, day-long preschools for all children whose parents work or study outside the home. Today more than 90% of all 2- to 5-year-old children attend preschools with a common national curriculum for at least 6 hours a day. Parents pay a low tuition because costs are governmentally subsidized. About 50% of the staff is preschool teachers with BAs in early childhood education, and 50% are assistant teachers with fewer years of educational training. A normal classroom, depending on age of students, has two to four teachers and 15 to 20 children, with a mean ratio of five children per teacher (Skolverket, 2012).

The special pedagogy in preschools was labeled *edu-care*, which means that in early childhood education, care and education are intertwined. Children's developmental competence, psychological wellness and safety are core responsibilities for teachers (Davies et al., 2009). Learning first takes place on the changing mat through smiles, talk and physical interaction between the baby and the adult. The holistic perspective of children's development and learning is emphasized in the national curriculum for early childhood education (LPFÖ 98, 2011). This perspective includes cognitive, emotional and physical development and all types of learning: learning in action, relational learning, and individual and group learning.

Thus, the rational for early childhood education in preschools in the 1980s was to promote well-being, individual development and learning. When behavioral and developmental problems occurred, it was within a teacher's range of responsibility to promote development and attend to them (Guvå, 2001). This is a basic prerequisite for consultation as it means that the teachers have the ownership of the problem.

However, it also means that the problem must be framed in a way that the teacher can handle it within the framework of the classroom. A request for an assessment of ADHD is not possible to solve within the classroom framework, in contrast to a request for how to understand and relate to a child with acting-out behavior and attention difficulties, which is within this framework. Naturally, many requests still came framed as requests for assessments or more bluntly stated that "Something is wrong with him/her!" The challenge for the consultant was to change that type of request to an issue of "what is the main concern for the teachers in interaction with the child and his or her parents?"

To help in this work, an interview guide for consultants was developed (Guvå, 2004). Through systematic questions to the teachers, the main concern could be agreed on and elaborated. The interview guide also served the purpose of making teachers curious about the child and want to inspect and inform themselves on issues they had ignored. The outcome of consultation, usually after three to five sessions, was a change of perspective—a conceptual change. Teachers reported that they saw things differently, they were not so upset or the child had changed and did not act out in the same way (Hylander, 2000).

Facilitating Factors of Consultation Services in Preschools

Besides the emphasis on the strong link between learning, development and health, there are several other aspects that facilitated the establishment of preschool psychological consultation services. These aspects will be discussed in relation to their relevance as possible prerequisites for school consultation.

Multilevel Advocacy as Facilitator for Consultation

At the time when introducing psychological consultation services to preschools in Sweden took place, all-day preschools for children aged 1.5 to 6 years old were spreading around the country. Psychologists were involved in the development of child daycare and preschool programs on governmental, municipality and local levels. They were also involved in teacher training and courses and workshops for teachers. Psychologists were thus well-known and visible on all levels of the preschool board administrations, nationally and on the municipality level, where they could explain and debate the advantages of preventive work and consultation services.

However, psychologists also met challenges and barriers when introducing consultation as psychological support to preschools. These challenges, and ways to address them, included principals questioning consultants as well as psychologists' role conflicts between being consultants and teachers and between being consultants and advocates.

First, principals could be afraid that consultations would challenge their authority by introducing new ideas to the teachers or, even worse, that organizational problems or problems in relation to the principal as a leader would be topics of concern during consultation. This challenge was met in several ways. Psychologists could invite the principal to join consultation sessions. This was sometimes deemed successful but could also cause new problems, such as teachers not daring to ventilate their deep concerns or the principal taking over and acting as a leader of the session. Another way was to invite the principal for the last session and, before that, discuss with teachers what they wanted to communicate to their leader. Psychologists also took great care in communicating with the principals; they participated with principals in meetings and conferences and offered workshops on child development and behavior.

Second, psychologists offered workshops and lectures to teachers. For consultants to offer lectures to presumptive consultees can be and was debated. As an introduction for teachers to get to know the consultant, workshops and lectures can serve as door openers, which Caplan pointed out (Caplan & Caplan, 1993). There is, however, a risk that consultees regard the lecturer as an authority, which may aggravate the coordinate relationship between the consultant and the consultee. This can be dealt with in consultation through the consultant's emphasizing the expertise of the consultee but, in the long run, having different professional roles in relation to consultees may hamper the consultation process.

Third, in the introduction phase of consultation services, multilevel work is typically a key, and psychologists need to advocate for the use of consultation as a practice to convince principals, school administrators and teachers about the benefits of consultation. However, there is a time in the consultation introduction phase when the consultant must choose to give up advocating strategies in favor of consultation strategies due to the crucial difference between the consultation process and the process of advocating (Hylander, 2014). In advocating, the consultant knows what he or she wants to implement and uses means of information, different strategies of influence and even power strategies. All these strategies are contraindicated in a consultation process, where the basis is voluntarism and coordinate relations. It may, however, be true that for the sustainability of consultation services, continued multilevel advocacy for consultation is necessary. Then it is preferable if there are several psychologists that can play different roles in the organization. If there is a coordinator of school psychology services, he or she may be the advocate. If there is more than one school psychologist and there is a request for system consultation, psychologists may work on different levels in the school organization. One psychologist consults with teachers and the other consults with principals in order to avoid the difficult task of acting as consultant on several levels in one organization (Guvå & Hylander, 2013).

Inclusion as Facilitating Factor for Consultation

In the 1980s, Swedish preschools were (and still are) inclusive, and teachers adhered to that policy. This meant that teachers seldom pushed for a child to be placed somewhere else. When the situation became too difficult for them to handle, they asked for support, irrespective of whether the child was assessed. The issue of teacher ownership of the problem was seldom at stake. There was no drive to have children placed in special educational groups. Preschool psychologists were specially employed to serve child daycares and preschools. They could offer consultation without having a press to also assess individual children. Assessments were not the responsibility of the preschool psychologists. Instead, psychologists at child health care centers serving all children and parents provided individual child assessments when necessary.

When teachers suspected severe disturbances before parents had come to that insight, teachers would ask for consultation. Sessions were then focused on how teachers could talk with parents, parents' expected crisis reactions and information on where parents could turn for help. In that way, teachers could be prepared to communicate with parents in professional and helpful ways and not upset them more than necessary.

Understanding Teachers' Work Situations as Facilitating Factors for Consultation

In order to contribute to the promotion of positive processes and the elimination of barriers to students' learning and achievement, a genuine understanding of teachers' work situations is key. When consultation was introduced to preschools, psychologists in general had a genuine and positive interest in the development of the curriculum for early childhood education.

External Position for the Consultant as Facilitating Factor for Consultation

When consultation was introduced to preschools, psychologists were centrally employed at the municipality level. This was necessary because preschools were generally small and no preschools could hire their own psychologists. This meant that even if psychologists worked in the same municipality, they came from the outside when visiting the preschools. Thus, they were not involved in the day-to-day activities with teachers and children, and they did not have the preschool principal as their immediate manager. In that sense, coming from the outside was seen as one important facilitator for consultation.

INTRODUCING CONSULTATION IN SWEDISH COMPULSORY SCHOOLS

Even if Swedish compulsory schools in many ways today have more legitimate and mandated support for consultation services than before, the process of introduction is still more complex than in preschools.

Inclusion as Facilitating Factor for Consultation

In Swedish compulsory schools (grades one to nine), the issues of inclusion and assessment are much more complicated than in preschools. Even when schools are considered inclusive, which Swedish schools are, there is always a possibility of creating a temporary "small group" with a special educational teacher or employing a special resource person to assist in the classroom. For such interventions no special diagnosis should be required, but diagnoses are still requested by principals as a way of prioritizing limited economic resources. Furthermore, it has not been made clear which assessments are the responsibility of school psychologists and which are the responsibility of the health sector. For psychologists in compulsory schools, the question of individual assessments has been complicated, and a good share of their time is spent assessing individual children. However, negotiations between local school boards and city council clinics are now taking place in order to clarify the type of assessments that are school psychologists' responsibilities. In that process, it should be made clear that the only assessments conducted in schools are those that are necessary for teaching and learning.

Still, a barrier to consultation in both compulsory schools and preschools is teachers not wanting to do anything until they know the result of an assessment. To turn a request for an assessment into a request for consultation is still one of the greatest challenges for school-based psychologists, just as it was 40 years ago (Lambert, 1974). Guvå (2004) discussed that issue and framed it as "how to help a teacher who asks for help but not for consultation." The only way to proceed is to start where the teacher is. That means listening to his or her representation of the problem and trying to negotiate a contract on what to do right now to collect more information about what can be changed in the classroom, irrespective of whether the child will be referred for an assessment.

Understanding Teachers' Work Situations as Facilitating Factors for Consultation

School psychologists, in contrast to preschool psychologists, work in a complicated system that has been long established and has rules, routines and approaches to children that they do not always agree with. However, without understanding teachers' dilemmas and their framing of problems, there is no way that consultation can be successful.

Teachers in all stages of the educational system experience children who upset classroom rules, disturb other students and are extremely difficult to handle, particularly in front of 30 other students. When teachers ask for help, typically they have tried to handle a problem for a long while and can see no other way out than having the child placed somewhere else, or the child will have a diagnosis and that medication will help. Not until teachers feel that they can communicate their dilemmas and hardships and have a sense of being understood are they open to collecting new information and looking for alternative ways based on new understandings. Few persons, teachers or others would, in a difficult situation where everything has been tried, ask for a new way of thinking. But in looking back, after consultation, this is typically what they report. In Swedish surveys of consultation outcomes, teachers reported as helpful consultants coming with new and different perspectives on the issue or just "somebody coming from the outside" (Hylander, 2000, p. 129).

For a consultant's understanding of the problem to be authentic, it is as much a challenge for the consultant to learn from the teacher as for the teacher to learn from the psychologist. Without learning about teachers' work in the classroom, a consultant cannot translate psychological knowledge of groups, leadership, child development and behavior in such a way that it will become useful to the teacher. This is perhaps the greatest challenge for many novice consultants who easily take the part of the student when there is a conflict and thereby close the door for further understanding of the teacher's dilemma. For new school psychologists, spending time in classrooms to learn more about teachers' work situations is highly recommended.

The consultation process has been described as a pendulum between approaching the teacher's representation of the problem and challenging it (Hylander, 2000). However, if challenges come too early in consultation, in a phase where the teacher seeks confirmation and feedback for his or her way of framing an issue, there is an immediate risk of consultation failure. Challenge cannot come until the consultee feels confirmed and is open to the collection of new data. Then, new information may surprise the consultees and also challenge their views. When such a conceptual change has occurred, suggestions of new ways of interacting from the consultant will be readily accepted. If such a change then leads to a new and favorable response from the child, the teacher will feel satisfied with the consultation work. And there is no better introduction of consultation to schools than one teacher being satisfied with the help he or she has received through consultation.

Coming from the Outside as Facilitating Factor for Consultation

Most school psychologists in Sweden are hired at a central level in the municipalities and do not have school principals as their immediate managers. In that sense, they come from the outside even if they are hired by the same central school board as the teachers. However, coming from the outside can also become a barrier of unavailability. In order for teachers to ask for consultation, they must trust the consultant to be able to help them. For an internal consultant this is easy when meeting the teachers on a day-to-day basis, but it is challenging to the psychologist to keep a neutral view and not get involved in all conflicts in a normal school environment.

Psychologists, as external consultants, have to make a great effort to introduce themselves to teachers and principals. Introduction could mean not just a visit but an offer of workshops or staying for coffee—anything that would make teachers realize that what the consultant has to offer is something they need. This was extensively described in Caplan's (1970) Mental Health Consultation Model. What is considered necessary for introduction may, however, be counterproductive for consultation. As a new consultant, having coffee with teachers in the staff room is highly recommended. After a year or two, however, the staff room may be better avoided in order not to get involved in consultation discussions, which cannot be handled in a professional way during a short break and with a large audience. Issues taken up in the staff room must be handled by setting up new times to consult.

There are several different ways of organizing school psychologists in Sweden. In line with the new Educational Act (Skollagen, 2010, p. 800), there is also a trend to look over the organization of SHW teams. There are conflicting interests. Principals typically want to have the members of the teams employed by the local school, while psychologists want to be employed by the municipality school board in order to keep the role of external consultant. This role, they believe, enables them to enhance consultation services to teachers and to do system-level consultation (Hylander, 2011).

TRAINING, SUPERVISION AND NETWORKING FOR CONSULTATION

When consultation was introduced to preschools, training and supervision in consultation were made available through the municipalities. Professional networks, reflection groups and supervision for psychologists working in preschools helped to support competency and further develop methods and strategies. The Swedish professional network on consultation to preschools became the Swedish basis for international collaboration about consultee-centered consultation, and was responsible for international conferences on consultation. At that time the network consisted of around 100 psychologists with a similar approach to consultation work in preschools.

Today, the picture is somewhat different. Preschools now belong to the same school board as compulsory schools, and few psychologists are employed only to meet the needs of the preschools. Primary and secondary schools typically express their needs in such a way that psychologists tend to be swamped, leaving little time to engage with preschools. One consequence of this development is that there is less psychological consultation work in preschools today. Another consequence is that there are quite a few psychologists in compulsory schools with long experience in preschool consultation work. This experience makes a good base for consulting in compulsory schools.

For a single school psychologist to be able to introduce and anchor consultation as a service to promote well-being, one course in consultation is not enough. There is a need for ongoing training, supervision and networking. Today, a few Swedish universities have consultation courses in the psychology programs. The Swedish Psychological Association offers a course in consultation for licensed psychologists as part of their specialist training, and specialist courses are also introduced at university level. Ongoing professional supervision is an accepted and widely spread professional support system for practicing psychologists in Sweden, and supervision in consultation by experienced psychological consultants is one of many supervision alternatives for Swedish school psychologists.

BARRIERS TO SCHOOL-BASED PSYCHOLOGICAL CONSULTATION IN COMPULSORY SCHOOL

In addition to the barriers to school psychological consultation previously described, a Swedish study (Hylander, 2011) described institutionalized student service routines and teacher expectations as key barriers to a salutogenic approach and the implementation of school psychological consultation. The study showed a vast difference between rhetoric and practice for SHW teams (psychologists, social workers, special education teachers, nurses, doctors and principals). Team members wanted to work in line with promotion of well-being but reported that they kept to traditional roles. They leaned on their traditional and pathogenic methods, such as assessing individual medical, educational, psychological or social difficulties. They had little time to reflect and discuss with each other what was meant by promotion of health and well-being (Hylander, 2011). Institutionalized routines and traditional expectations were some of the reported barriers to a salutogenic approach. The school psychologists reported that they wanted to work with organizational issues and consult with teachers, but their time was spent assessing individual students.

Institutionalized Student Service Routines as Barriers

One reason for keeping to their traditional tasks was that SHW team conferences were spent discussing one individual student after the other. No time was spent on how the interdisciplinary team could fulfill its task of promotion of learning, health and well-being. Also, when discussing individual students, there were few statements suggesting alternative perspectives; instead there was a tendency for consensus, indicating that the different professionals' competencies were not used to clarify the cases. The professionals reported (Hylander, 2011) feelings of loneliness and fear causing conflicts in the team. They thought that if they clearly presented their professional perspectives, other team members would think that they did not want to collaborate and only profile their own professions. Thus, there was a great need for sharing information and negotiating professional roles, tasks and missions in the SHW teams. Without such discussions, the consultative work cannot be understood and appreciated by the interprofessional teams.

Routines that once had been set up to guarantee students the possibility to meet with a psychologist or get help from a special educational teacher became barriers for consultation work (Hylander, 2011). Typically a teacher had to write an intervention program (IP) when they believed that a student had difficulties, and this was reported to the principal. The principal in turn might choose to take the case to a local SHW team meeting, where it was discussed. Thereafter, the case could be sent to a central SHW team for further management, which typically meant a psychological assessment of the child. However, even if teacher consultation became the recommendation from the central team, the teachers did not always accept this. So long a time passed, and the teacher had put so much effort in trying to describe all the difficulties that he or she no longer felt ownership of the problem. The teacher was no longer willing to "just talk about the case" but wanted something concrete to happen with the student. Thus, this routine became a barrier to consultation work because the teacher could not call a psychologist to get consultation right away when a problem appeared. Instead, the case got so well packed and was discussed so far away from the teachers in the classroom that they felt that they did not get any help. Nothing changed in the classroom.

Another barrier was the routine of having the IP written *before* a case was referred to the SHW team, which often left the teacher alone in constructing the IPs. Teachers felt that the IPs were not useful tools but rather dead documents for the principal's filing cabinet (Hylander, 2011).

Professional Expectations as Barriers

The SHW professionals reported that teacher expectations, but also expectations from other members of the team, locked them in in their traditional roles. They all had professional expectations to engage in general promotion for health and well-being, but they expected other professions to stay within their traditional missions. One exception was expectations of the school psychologist. According to the other team members, psychologists were primarily supposed to meet with single students, but secondarily they were expected to consult with teachers. Consultation to teachers was, for principals, seen as a major school psychology service. This was, however, not what psychologists expected to hear. They thought that other professionals would expect them to primarily engage in student assessments. However, much to their surprise, there were several voices from other professions agreeing that assessments took too much time from the psychologist and that psychological competence could better be used in other ways. Thus, it seems that professional expectations as barriers to consultation were as much in the minds of the school psychologists as in the minds of other professionals (Hylander, 2011).

CONCLUSION

Given the emphasis on promotion of well-being in the new Education Act, there is now a renewed opportunity to establish consultation as school psychological service to compulsory schools in Sweden. The principals' responsibilities to lead health promotion in schools have increased, and they need the SHW team to scrutinize existing facilitators and barriers to health promotion work. The prerequisites in the school system are now more favorable to consultation work.

There are, however, still barriers for consultants. There is a lack of consultation training in the psychology programs that needs to be addressed. Also, for consultation to thrive and develop, consultation networks and supervision in consultation are crucial, as psychological consultation requires lifelong learning and reflection on practice. More developmental work and research are also needed to form a solid knowledge base for consultation in schools. More practice in consultation may open up opportunities for more research and a closer link between academic research and school-based consultation evaluations and developmental work.

NOTE

1. In Sweden, early childhood education (nursery school for children aged 1 through 5) is called *preschool*. This term will be used to cover all forms of early childhood education, even if there were prior differences between child daycare and preschool.

REFERENCES

Alzén, B. (2000). *Utvärderingavpsykologiskkonsultation. Resultatavenkätefterettårsanvändning.* [Evaluation of psychological consultation: Results from a questionnaire, used during one year]. Stockholm, Sweden: Stockholm Stad.

Antonovsky, A. (1987). *Unraveling the mystery of health.* San Fransisco, CA: Jossey-Bass.

Antonovsky, A. (1996). The salutogenic model as a theory to guide health promotion. *Health Promotion International, 11,* 11–18.

Brodin, M., & Hylander, I. (1995).*Utvärderingavkonsultationsärenden I Lidingöstadsbarnomsorg.* [Evaluating consultation cases in Lidingö child care and pre-school]. Lidingö, Sweden: LidingöStad.

Bronfenbrenner, U. (1986). Ecology of the family as a context for human development: Research perspectives. *Developmental Psychology, 22,* 723–742.

Caplan, G. (1970). *The theory and practice of mental health consultation.* New York: Basic Books.

Caplan, G., & Caplan, R. B. (1993). *Mental health consultation and collaboration.* San Francisco, CA: Jossey-Bass.

Davies, J., Engdahl, I., Otieno, L., Pramling, I., Siraj-Blatchford, J., & Vallabh, P. (2009). Early childhood education for sustainability: Recommendation for development. *International Journal of Early Childhood, 41,* 113–117.

Dodge, K. A., Greenberg, M. T., & Malone, P. S. (2008). Testing an idealized dynamic cascade model of the development of serious violence in adolescence. *Child Development, 79*, 1907–1927.

Erchul, W. P., & Sheridan, S. M. (Eds.). (2014). *Handbook of research in school consultation: Empirical foundations for the field* (2nd Ed.). New York: Routledge.

Grosin, L. (2002). Rektorer i framgångsrika skolor och deras betydelse för lärarkulturen. (Principals in successful schools and their influence on teacher culture). *Nordic Studies in Education, 22*, 158–175.

Grosin, L. (2011). Effektiva skolor—forskningen om effektiva skolor i relation till anknytningsteori och mentalisering. (Effective schools in relation to attachment theory and mentalization). *Psykisk Hälsa, 4*, 17–23.

Gustafsson, J.-E., Westling, Allodi M., Alin Åkerman, B., Eriksson, C., Eriksson, L., Fischbein, S., . . . Persson, R. S. (2010). *School, learning and mental health: A systematic review*. Stockholm: The Royal Swedish Academy of Sciences, The Health Committee.

Guvå, G. (2001). *Skolpsykologers rolltagande*. (Role taking of school psychologists). (Dissertation). Linköping, Sweden: Linköping University, Department of Behavioral Sciences and Learning.

Guvå, G. (2004). Meeting a teacher who asks for help but not for consultation. In N. Lambert, I. Hylander, & J. Sandoval (Eds.), *Consultee-centered consultation: Improving the quality of professional services in schools and community organizations* (pp. 257–266). Mahwah, NJ: Erlbaum.

Guvå, G., & Hylander, I. (2012). Diverse perspectives on pupil health among professionals in school-based multi-professional teams. *School Psychology International, 2*, 135–150.

Guvå, G., & Hylander, I. (2013). *Psykologisk fallkonsultation*. (Psychological case consultation). Lund: Student litteratur.

Halonen, A., Aunola, K., Ahonen, T., & Nurmi, J. E. (2006). The role of learning to read in the development of problem behaviour: A cross-lagged longitudinal study. *British Journal of Educational Psychology, 76*, 517–534.

Hamre, B. K., & Pianta, R. C. (2001). Early teacher–child relationships and the trajectory of children's school outcomes through eighth grade. *Child Development, 72*, 625–638.

Hattie, J. A. (2008). *Visible learning: A synthesis of over 800 meta-analyses relating to achievement*. London/New York: Routledge.

Hjörne, E., & Säljö, R. (2004). The pupil welfare team as a discourse community: Accounting for school problems. *Linguistics and Education, 15*, 321–328.

Hughes, J. N., Gleasson, K. A., & Zhang, D. (2005). Relationship influences on teachers' perceptions of academic competence in academically at-risk minority and majority first grade students. *Journal of School Psychology, 43*, 303–320.

Hughes, J. N., Loyd, L., & Buss, M. (2008). Empirical and theoretical support for an updated model of mental health consultation for schools. In W. P. Erchul & S. M. Sheridan (Eds.), *Handbook of research in school consultation* (pp. 343–360). New York, NY: Routledge.

Hylander, I. (2000). *Turning processes: The change of representations in consultee-centered-case-consultation* (Dissertation). Linköping, Sweden: Linköping University, Department of Behavioural and Learning sciences.

Hylander, I. (2011). *Professionals' representations of multi professional services to schools*. Final report to the Swedish Research Council, on the "Student Health" project. Stockholm: Karolinska Institutet, Center for Family Medicine.

Hylander, I. (2012). Conceptual change through consultee-centered consultation: A theoretical model. *Consulting Psychology Journal: Practice and Research, 64*, 29–45.

Hylander, I. (2014). Entry-Level activities in system consultation. *Journal of Educational and Psychological Consultation, 24*, 345–353.

Hylander, I., & Guvå, G. (2004). A model for consultation with daycare and preschools. In N. Lambert, I. Hylander, & J. Sandoval (Eds.), *Consultee-centered consultation: Improving the quality of professional services in schools and community organizations* (pp. 65–77). Mahwah, NJ: Erlbaum.

Illback, R. J., & Pennington, M. A. (2008). Organization development and change in school settings: Theoretical and empirical foundations. In W. P. Erchul & S. M. Sheridan (Eds.), *Handbook of research in school consultation* (pp. 225–245). New York, NY: Erlbaum.

Jerome, E., Hamre, B., & Pianta, R. (2008). Teacher–child relationships from kindergarten to sixth grade: Early childhood predictors of teacher-perceived conflict and closeness. *Social Development, 18*, 915–945.

Knotek, S., & Hylander, I. (2014). Research issues in mental health consultation and consultee-centered approaches. In W. P. Erchul & S. M. Sheridan (Eds.), *Handbook of research in school consultation* (2nd ed., pp. 151–179). New York, NY: Routledge.

Lambert, N. M. (1974). A school-based consultation model. *Professional Psychology, 5*, 267–275.

Lambert, N. M., Hylander, I., & Sandoval, J. (Eds.). (2004). *Consultee-centered consultation: Improving the quality of professional services in schools and community organizations*. Mahwah, NJ: Erlbaum.

Masten, A. S., Hubbard, J. J., Scott, D. G., Tellegen, A., Garmezy, N., & Ramirez, M. (1999). Competence in the context of adversity: Pathways to resilience and maladaptation from childhood to late adolescence. *Developmental Psychopathology, 1*, 143–169.

Morgan, P. L., Farkas, G., Tufis, P. A., & Sperling, R. A. (2008). Are reading and behaviour problems risk factors for each other? *Journal of Learning Disability, 41*, 417–436.

Perry, D., Dallas Allen, M., Brennan, E., & Bradley, J. (2010). The evidence base for mental health consultation in early childhood settings: A research synthesis assessing children's behavioral outcomes. *Early Educational Development, 21*, 795–824.

Pianta, R. C. (1999). *Enhancing relationships between teachers and children.* Washington, DC: American Psychological Association.

Pianta, R. C., La Paro, K. M., Payne, C., Cox, M. J., & Bradley, R. (2002). The relation of kindergarten classroom environment to teacher, family, and school characteristics and child outcomes. *The Elementary School Journal, 102*, 225–240.

Pianta, R. C., & Stuhlman, M. W. (2004). Teacher–child relationships and children's success in the first years of school. *School Psychology Review, 33*, 444–458.

Roeser, R. W., Eccles, J. S., & Freedman-Doan, C. (1999). Academic functioning and mental health in adolescence: Patterns, progressions, and routes from childhood. *Journal of Adolescent Research, 14*, 135–174.

Rosenfield, S. (1987). *Instructional consultation.* Hillsdale, NJ: Erlbaum.

Rosenfield, S., Silva, A., & Gravois, T. (2007). Bringing instructional consultation to scale: Research and development of IC and IC teams. In W. P. Erchul & S. Sheridan (Eds.), *Handbook of research in school consultation* (2nd ed., pp. 248–275). New York: Routledge.

Rutter, M. (1983). School effects on pupils progress: Research findings and policy implications. *Child Development, 54*, 1–28.

SBU—Swedish Council on Health Technology Assessment. (2010). *Program förattförebyggapsykiskohälsa hos barn.* [Intervention programs for the prevention of child mental health problems]. Stockholm: SBU. Retrieved from http//www.sbu.se

Sheridan, S. M., & Gutkin, T. (2000). The ecology of school psychology: Examining and changing our paradigm for the 21st century. *School Psychology Review, 29*, 485–502.

Skolverket. (2012). Retrieved from http://www.skolverket.se/statistik-ochutvardering/statistik/forskola/barn-och-grupper

SOU. (2000). *Från dubbla spår till elevhälsa. Slutbetänkande av Elevvårdsutredningen.* (From two strands to student health: Report from the student care investigation). Stockholm: Regeringskansliet.

Utbildnings departementet (Swedish Educational Department). (1994). *Hälsa, lärande och trygghet.* (Health, learning and safety). Regeringens proposition (Governmental proposition) 2002/022:14. Stockholm: Regeringskansliet.

3

REVISITING CANADIAN CONSULTATION MODELS IN SCHOOL PSYCHOLOGY
Just the Same, Only Different

Ester Cole and Judith Wiener

INTRODUCTION

In line with trends toward increased accountability in education and mental health, in this chapter we review Canadian consultation frameworks and applicable research. We describe a Canadian integrative model for comprehensive psychological services in multicultural education systems. The model incorporates primary, secondary, and tertiary prevention for the benefit of school communities and policy makers. It also provides a continuum for divergent direct and indirect services based on theoretical and empirical studies within the consultation literature. Two examples of applications of the model are provided. The first describes multidisciplinary school teams that engage in a consulting role. The second describes online resources as aids for consultative processes in schools and other settings. The chapter concludes with implications for preservice instruction for future practitioners and in-service training for school psychologists seeking to broaden their knowledge and experience in consultative services in education.

THE CANADIAN CONTEXT

Canadian psychology "has a unique character" shaped by its national mosaic (Hadjistavropoulos, 2009, p. 1). The key contextual features include two official languages, English and French, with separate educational practices; a growing and significant population of Aboriginal Peoples, many in remote communities; and high levels of immigration of families who come from diverse countries and cultures and speak many different languages. The Aboriginal population comprises approximately 3.8% of the Canadian population, is younger, and is growing faster than the population of Canada as a whole (Simeone, 2011). Although the Aboriginal population is urbanizing, many live in remote, impoverished Northern communities.

Canada receives approximately 250,000 immigrants and refugees annually, with approximately 20% of the total population born outside the country. Asia was the largest source of immigrants in the last 5 years; there are also large numbers of immigrants from Africa, the Caribbean, and Central and South America. Almost 60% are skilled workers or have their own businesses, and the majority of them have university degrees. Most recent immigrants and refugees live in or near major urban centers (Statistics Canada, 2011). One of the challenges faced by school psychologists is to provide services in a culturally sensitive way for culturally diverse students and their families (Cole, 1998; Geva & Wiener, 2015).

In multilingual societies comprising increasingly diverse cultural communities, children and youth who are at risk for educational underachievement and social maladjustment pose challenges for teachers, administrators, and mental health practitioners. One of the challenges faced by Canadian schools is that they have become sites for intervention with children who have numerous learning and social problems. At the same time, ever-expanding educational goals in an era of budgetary constraints have reinforced the demand for higher accountability practices. Consequently, the pedagogical, social, and budgetary context has become a catalyst for educational reform (Fullan, 2007, 2010). According to Cole (1996), these social demands on education require a change of culture in organizations, including strategic planning, evaluation mechanisms, consultation, and coordinated support services.

There are implications for psychologists in this change of cultures in organizations: they need to be skilled in team building, in working with others to achieve a consensus, and in developing clear mechanisms for communication and consultation. However, school psychologists, whose knowledge and skills can assist in this process, are not always included in the broad discussions that take place to develop policy in Canada (Corkum, French, & Dorey, 2007; Harris & Joy, 2010; Jordan, Hindes, & Saklofske, 2009). In addition, public education is a provincial responsibility; therefore, there are no national policies that pertain to education and the role of school psychologists (Cole, 1998; Hadjistavropoulos, 2009; McIntosh, 2014; Wiener & Siegel, 1992). Moreover, in many public education systems, budgetary demands have resulted in cutbacks to consultative services and have relegated psychologists to the traditional role of providing assessments for special education placement. With growing awareness of needs, it is regrettable that psychologists are not always viewed as playing cost-effective roles as partners in education. Yet, without clear advocacy and a shared vision of the role psychology plays in education, necessary services are likely to diminish or to be reduced to tertiary interventions. Although advocacy by psychology organizations continues to be important, it must be shaped by integrated models of service that are viewed as accountable at the local community level and as central to the goals of education systems (Cole & Siegel, 2003; Manion, 2010; McIntosh et al., 2011; Millar, Lean, Sweet, Moraes, & Nelson, 2013; Schmidt, 2012; Whitley, Smith, & Vaillancourt, 2013).

There is growing evidence, however, that attitudes within psychology itself and within education continue to change. Leaders in education have questioned, over time, whether special education services are the most effective way of dealing with academic underachievement for a heterogeneous population of students (Cole, 1992, 1996; Cole & Brown, 1996, 2003; Lean & Colucci, 2010; Ontario Ministry of Education, 2011; Shapiro, 2008). Additionally, there is skepticism about the diagnostic powers of traditional psychometric assessment (e.g., Kamphaus, 2009; Luther, Cole, & Gamlin, 1996). School psychologists themselves continue to advocate for the opportunity to use a wider range of skills in their work and for better training in a variety of areas related to student and school needs (McCrimmon, Altomare, Matchullis, & Jitiina, 2012; Sandoval, 1996; Ysseldyke et al., 2006). Over the past two decades, publications and conventions (both scholarly and practical) have pointed practitioners in the direction of expanded services.

Organizations such as the Canadian Psychological Association and the National Association of School Psychologists (NASP) continue to play a central role in identifying and improving upon training standards and in providing information to psychologists in education (e.g., Noltmeyer & McLaughlin, 2011; Ysseldyke et al., 2006). Notwithstanding advocacy by psychology organizations, service providers themselves would continue to benefit from exploring avenues for change that will promote cost-effective best practices within a conceptual service model.

INTEGRATIVE MODEL FOR COMPREHENSIVE PSYCHOLOGICAL SERVICES

For many busy school psychologists, the idea of having a service delivery model may seem of relatively little value. Models are abstractions and are therefore inadequate descriptions of everyday life. Yet, most individuals and professional group members have an underlying set of beliefs that govern their professional behavior, and it is thus important to make these beliefs explicit. The following Canadian service delivery model, first published by Cole and Siegel in 1990, evolved from day-to-day practice in elementary and secondary schools. The model is designed to help psychologists gain a better understanding of their own roles and assist in consultation with educators, parents, and other mental health professionals. Finally, the model provides a framework for generating and evaluating alternate methods of service delivery. Since its publication, the model has been taught in graduate programs and discussed in education systems in Canada and elsewhere; for example, Cole has given lectures about this model in several countries (Cole & Siegel, 2003).

The premise of the model is that the ultimate goal of school psychology services is to enhance children's learning and adjustment. Consequently, it is important that services are available to all students and that there are multiple approaches to service delivery (Andrews & Violato, 2003; Fletcher, Coulter, Reschly, & Vaughn, 2004; Fletcher & Vaughn, 2009; Power, 2006, 2008a, 2008b; Schaughency & Ervin, 2006; Thomas & Grimes, 2008; Ysseldyke et al., 2006).

The model is conceptualized as a simple two-dimensional grid (see Table 3.1). The horizontal dimension of the grid elaborates the goals of service delivery as primary, secondary, and tertiary prevention. These concepts are borrowed from the preventative mental health work developed by Caplan (1970). Primary prevention services are provided for the benefit of all students; secondary prevention services are provided for the benefit of students who are at risk; and tertiary prevention services are provided for those who are experiencing significant difficulties with school adjustment. Nastasi (2000) uses the terms *risk reduction* and *early intervention* for secondary prevention and *treatment* for tertiary intervention. Similarly, Lean and Colucci (2010, 2013) introduced a comprehensive structure for integrating community-based service providers and programs into schools. The structure's multitiered framework documents three types of intervention: *universal intervention* (e.g., mental health screening), *targeted intervention* (e.g., parenting groups), and *intense intervention* (such as special education support).

The vertical dimension of the grid, developed by Parsons and Meyers (1984), illustrates that although the goal of educational services is ultimately to benefit students, their needs may sometimes be met most effectively through indirect services to teachers, principals, or the entire school system. That is, rather than services always being

Table 3.1 A Model for Psychological Service in Schools

Goals of Service

Recipients of service	Primary prevention	Secondary prevention	Tertiary prevention
	Identify resources, provide and analyze information; program for all students	Provide information, consult, and program for at-risk students	Provide information, consult, and program for students whose academic and psychosocial difficulties significantly interfere with their adaptation to school
The organization Government, school system, community	Promotion of academic achievement and mental health and well-being by working collaboratively with • Policy makers • Curriculum developers • Designers of web and other media resources • Senior school district administrators Participate on school district research committee	Work collaboratively with school district and community to develop and implement programs for students who are at risk for school failure or mental health challenges such as • Intensive literacy and numeracy instruction • Safe schools/bullying prevention • Transition and integration of immigrants and refugees	Consult with school district regarding development of service delivery models and structures for students with disabilities and disorders Participate on crisis intervention teams and school district identification and placement committees
School staff Teachers/administrators/guidance counsellors Participation on in-school multidisciplinary teams and identification/placement committees Provide professional development workshops Consult to teacher professional learning communities	Consult with school staff regarding fostering academic achievement and emotional and social well-being through evidence-based, whole-classroom programming such as • Implementing a balanced literacy approach • Fostering positive peer relations	Consult with school staff regarding development and delivery of risk reduction programs such as • Family literacy programs for parents who do not speak the dominant language of the country or who have low levels of education • Support to students who are perpetrators or victims of bullying	Consult with school staff regarding accommodations and interventions for students with significant learning and psychosocial disabilities and disorders such as • Autism spectrum disorders, learning disabilities, ADHD, and oppositional and conduct problems

Students/parents Mediated by school staff (administrators, teachers, and guidance counselors)	Consult with individual school staff regarding interpreting results of specific student screening instruments Consult with individual school staff members regarding skill development in specific areas such as classroom management, teaching literacy and numeracy, or fostering positive peer relations Consult with individual school staff members in the development of interventions designed to enhance achievement and well-being such as peer tutoring, conflict mediation, and transition to postsecondary education	Consult with individual school staff regarding providing support for individual students who are at risk for achievement or mental health problems due to factors such as • Transitioning following immigration • Bereavement • Parental separation or divorce • Social and communication challenges • Being a victim or perpetrator of bullying • Homophobia • Test anxiety	Behavioral or conjoint behavioural consultation for individual students with significant learning and psychosocial disabilities and disorders such as autism spectrum disorders, learning disabilities, ADHD, anxiety and mood disorders, and oppositional and conduct problems
Students/parents Direct service	Psychologist delivers workshops to parents or students in a school or school district on topics such as • Positive parenting • Supporting school achievement • Fostering positive peer relationships • Conflict mediation	Individual or group counseling with students who are at risk for achievement or mental health problems due to factors such as • Transitioning following immigration • Bereavement • Parental separation or divorce • Social and communication challenges • Test anxiety	Psychoeducational assessment Group, individual, and family therapy for students with significant achievement or psychosocial disabilities or disorders such as autism spectrum disorders, learning disabilities, ADHD, anxiety and mood disorders, and oppositional and conduct problems

provided directly to students or their parents by the school psychologists or other mental health consultants, they may also be carried out by others, including teachers, with consultation from psychologists or through the impact of services on school personnel or on the school system at large.

The model presented in Table 3.1 is a framework into which most, if not all, activities of school psychologists may be incorporated. Traditional roles, such as student assessments and counseling, fall in the lower right-hand corner of the grid; such roles have the advantage of providing practitioners with firsthand knowledge of student needs but are limiting as to the number of individuals served. Moving upward and to the left, service becomes more indirect and systems oriented. Innovative and divergent services are possible in all roles suggested by the model, and examples have been illustrated in publications over the years (Akamatsu & Cole, 2000, 2003; DiPasquale, 2003; Montgomery, Meyer, & Smart, 2008).

The Role of Consultation within the Model

With an emphasis on preventative services, the model is explicit in identifying a consultative role for the school psychologist as change agent and problem solver. In school systems, psychologists are typically not central to the decision-making process, and therefore, they can effect change through consultative facilitation of decisions made by others. Collaborative consultation provides an effective method for accomplishing this goal; it is a process through which psychologists and educators coordinate their efforts to resolve educational problems by sharing complementary skills and bodies of knowledge (Prince-Embury, 2008; Rosenfield, 2002; Scholten, 2003).

In order for psychologists to function effectively as consultants in this collaborative model, they must avoid presenting themselves as experts or being cast into such a role by educators. Rather, by sharing complementary skills through a collaborative approach, their input is likely to lead to partnerships with educators and thus provide opportunities for role expansion (Andrews & Violato, 2003; Anserello & Sweet, 1990; Cole, 1996; Cole & Brown, 1996; Davison, 1990; Harris & Joy, 2010).

Consultation need not be viewed as an alternative to direct services, such as psychological assessment and individual and group counselling, but as complementary to them. Consultation may lead to more systematic decisions about which and how many students and their families should receive direct services and support for teachers to implement interventions with students. However, once initiated, direct service contacts inevitably result in ideas about what actions can and should be taken. Collaborative consultation then facilitates the implementation of these short-term and long-term interventions (Fagan & Sachs Wise, 2007; Kratochwill, Elliot, & Callan-Stoiber, 2002; Rosenfield, 2002; Schaughency & Ervin, 2006; Ysseldyke et al., 2006).

Prevention is a key feature of the model presented in Table 3.1. Although most school systems engage in prevention activities (Durlak, 2009), even here primary and secondary prevention are not explicit parts of the psychologist's role (Cole, 1992, 1996; Cole & Siegel, 2003). Faced with a high caseloads and too many assessment referrals, psychologists often feel that they simply do not have the time for preventative work or the sanction of educators to become involved in it. Occasionally, preventative programs are implemented because high-level administrators and school principals have identified a particular need. Regrettably, if school psychologists are associated only with a testing role, they may not be thought of as helpful resources available within the system. Furthermore, school districts often choose prevention programs that are not evidence based (Durlak, 2009). If they have the opportunity to be involved in the planning and selection of prevention programs, psychologists, who are trained in research methods and program evaluation, may assist with selection of the most effective programs. Whether such programs are mounted at the system (e.g., crisis intervention teams) or at the school level (e.g., parenting groups, antibullying programs), it is important for psychologists to be assertive about making educators aware of their interest and skills and, if their involvement is requested, to make the time to facilitate the implementation of such programs (see, e.g., DiPasquale, 2003; Ontario Psychological Association, 2013; Psychologists' Association of Alberta, 2010; Ysseldyke et al., 2006).

Since psychologists in schools are in touch on a daily basis with students who have special learning needs, they are in a position to identify recurring patterns of difficulty and to suggest the evidence-based preventative actions that might be taken to deal with them. Providing educators with solid information about the scope of a particular problem is important, although time-consuming. In addition, it will often be necessary to invest time in self-education and identification of complementary resources (Cole & Siegel, 2003).

The multiple options presented in the model are intended to provide a framework for innovation rather than to delineate an ideal service role for psychologists. Individuals who provide services are likely to use the model flexibly in order to promote best practice and achieve a balance of direct and indirect service delivery. Parsons and Meyers (1984) originally suggested that systems-level interventions should be attempted as a first priority because they benefit more people and are therefore more cost efficient. It is likely, however, that such a decision rule may be unrealistic in many cases. Many decision-makers in education may reject psychologists' involvement at this level because they believe that psychologists' competencies are related to the evaluation of individual students and do not include decision-making at the systems level. In identifying service priorities, individual psychologists must take into account service needs identified by educators. Within a particular school community, it is especially important to become familiar with and accept the priorities of the principal, who is the ultimate educational decision-maker in that setting (Cole & Brown, 1996; Jordan et al., 2009; Sladeczek & Heath, 1997). Nevertheless, some principals are not sufficiently familiar with the range of consultation services that psychologists are able to provide. It is therefore important to work with them to increase their awareness of these services and, as a result, expand and reframe their priorities.

CANADIAN APPLICATIONS OF THE INTEGRATED MODEL

Following several years of study, the Mental Health Commission of Canada (MHCC) published its report in 2012. The report included recommendations and strategies that will unfold in the years to come and will involve psychologists in promoting prevention and evidence-based intervention services across the country. In its strategic directions, Priority 1.2 states: "Increase the capacity of families, caregivers, schools, postsecondary institutions and community organizations to promote the mental health of infants, children, and youth, prevent mental illness and suicide wherever possible, and intervene early when problems first emerge" (Mental Health Commission of Canada, 2012).

Implementation of strategies to achieve the laudable early intervention goals of the mental health commission are challenging. Consistent with the direction of the Mental Health Commission, Kutcher and McLuckie (2010) advanced the School-Based Pathway to Care Model which "engages students, teachers, student service providers, parents/families, health care providers, and the wider community through various training programs and both formal and informal linkages between the school, community and health providers" (Kutcher & Wei, 2013, p. 90). Preliminary evaluations have been encouraging with promising outcomes for the model's application in secondary schools for addressing the mental health needs of students. Next we describe two Canadian practical applications that are consonant with the goals of the Mental Health Commission and the School-Based Pathways to Care Model: multidisciplinary teams and website resources.

Multidisciplinary Teams in Canadian Schools

One of the vehicles for service delivery in many North American schools is multidisciplinary school teams. The major function of these teams is to consult with classroom teachers regarding students whom they view as having challenges. Overall, teams are designed to support teachers, administrators, and parents in providing appropriate interventions for students in need of assistance in regular and special education settings (Cole & Brown, 1996, 2003; Cole, Wiener, & Davidson, 1990). These teams are not legally mandated committees whose role is to formally identify students with special educational needs or to place them in special education programs. Advocates of teams highlight the following advantages to this service delivery model: teams encourage sharing of knowledge and resources; group participation often increases acceptance of recommendations made and promotes commitment to outcome; and teams provide appropriate referrals to mental health services and can monitor interventions through cost-effective consultation (Broxterman & Whalen, 2013; Kovaleski, 2002).

The composition of multidisciplinary teams is closely linked to school policies and organizational goals but typically includes school administrators, special and regular education teachers, school psychologists, school social workers, and speech and language pathologists. The roles of members and the functions of teams vary. Teams with broad mandates are more likely, as a result, to address primary, secondary, and tertiary prevention services. Effective teams tend to have several common characteristics, which are highlighted in the literature. These characteristics include clarity of goals and roles, leadership support, effective planning, composition of membership, and team performance (Adelman & Taylor, 2003; Wagner, 2000).

There have been a few evaluations of multidisciplinary teams in Canadian schools (Cole & Brown, 1996, 2003; Davidson & Wiener, 1992; Wiener & Davidson, 1990). Wiener and Davidson found that approximately 13% of a school population was discussed by multidisciplinary school teams. The outcomes for most students discussed by the teams were accommodations in the regular classroom; only 28% of the children discussed by the teams were referred for special education support. Over the 3 years of the study, the rate of referrals for psychological assessments was reduced from 8% to 5%. Teachers and school administrators were highly satisfied with the support they received from the teams in general and the school psychologist in particular (Davidson & Wiener, 1992; Wiener & Davidson, 1990). Qualitative analysis of these data indicated that teachers were satisfied because, as a result of the consultation with the team, they acquired new skills for supporting the students they referred to the teams as well as other students who present with challenges.

Cole and Brown (1996, 2003) specifically examined the effectiveness of the multidisciplinary school team in relation to immigrants and refugee students over a 5-year period. They found that teams were frequently utilized for consultation about immigrant and refugee students due to their common difficulties in coping with adjustment to a new language and culture. About a third of the team members who were surveyed claimed that problems in learning to speak English precipitated student referrals to the team, and about a quarter of the team members surveyed indicated that the challenges of being a refugee precipitated the need for support and team consultation. By using this type of data, school systems can reframe their professional development priorities for staff, create a more systematic link to multilingual and multicultural community services, and implement ecological interventions that support learning and adjustment of students (Cole, 1996, 2003).

It is not yet clear whether the focus of multidisciplinary teams and the work of school psychologists on these teams will change in the context of the MHCC (2012) report and Kutcher's School-Based Pathway to Care Model (Kutcher & McLuckie, 2010; Kutcher & Wei, 2013). Research is required to determine whether teams modify their discussions and activities to promote prevention and treatment of mental health problems and include mental health professionals from the wider community as ongoing members of the team. Table 3.2, developed by the first author and adapted from Cole and Brown (2003), presents an organizer of team characteristics discussed in the literature. Enhancing and inhibiting factors relate to the clarity of the team's goals and roles, leadership support, effective planning, composition of membership, and team performance. This model could provide a framework for change in multidisciplinary teams by explicitly including community organizations and secondary and tertiary prevention in relation to mental health.

Online Resources as Avenues for Consultation

School psychologists, together with other professional groups, have become accustomed to being daily recipients of web-based information. The plethora of offerings varies in quality, accuracy, and originality. However, the public at large and service providers continue to have access to "hands-on" and research publications in multilingual formats. Computer technology has become part of our culture at home, at work, and in school communities. As such, website resources and tools promote professional development options regardless of geographical location and are a time efficient way to link consultation services to knowledge transfer and translation.

In Canada, as in other countries, psychological associations, organizations, and educational systems promote e-learning and web-based communication frameworks and post documents for distribution. This section will highlight three Canadian examples that can enhance consultation services offered by psychologists. The first free website details resources developed by the Psychology Foundation of Canada (2013). The second free online resource, the ABCs of Mental Health, documents the product of a multiyear project with suggested interventions by the Hincks-Dellcrest Centre (2012). The third free online resource, the Balanced Literacy Diet: Putting Research into Practice in the Classroom, was developed by Dr. Dale Willows at OISE/University of Toronto (Willows, 2012). Each of these websites was developed by a team composed of mental

Table 3.2 Characteristics of Multidisciplinary Teams

Enhancing Factors	Inhibiting Factors
1. Goals and roles	
• Goals and roles are clearly defined for team members and invited participants. • Professionals are apprised about the rationale for a particular service model. • Team members have a sense of ownership and are committed to multidisciplinary services. They consider model options. • Summary forms are developed or adapted by the team, following research.	• Team goals and members' roles are unclear to the professionals and the participants. • Different professionals are not sufficiently clear about the team model. • Staff members do not feel supported by their Team. • New members do not receive appropriate orientation regarding the model and its practices and expected outcomes.
2. Leadership support	
• Shared leadership or democratic leadership results in an inclusive atmosphere and following of established guidelines. • Administrative support results in a larger number of consulting relationships, which evolve among participants. • Release time for in-service training is provided for core participants. • Invited members are included on an as needed basis, following consultation.	• Leaderless group results in inefficient decision-making and a lack of focus for activities during meetings and follow-up intervention phases. • Administrative lack of commitment to the team leads to uncertainty and mistrust. • Meetings are held infrequently, and shared decision-making is not promoted. • Clarification of issues is not encouraged, and implementation procedures are fragmented.
3. Regular and efficient meetings	
• Frequent and scheduled meetings allow for a broad range of services. • Goals are discussed and agendas are set by team members. • Individual and group needs are addressed, and multiple recommendations are considered for action plans. • Advance preparation time for staff and computer technology aids are supported. • Discussions are focused and needed documents are available for meetings.	• Infrequently held meetings result in crisis interventions and address only urgent matters or parts of agendas. • Little time is allotted for discussion about group processes or issues of concern. • Meetings focus on reactive agendas. • Communication regarding team dates and agendas are not shared ahead of time. • Discussions are rushed and problems tend to remain unresolved.
4. Team membership	
• Team membership varies according to the objectives it is trying to achieve. • Referring staff are key participants in the appropriate phases of consultation. • Translators/interpreters are arranged as appropriate for family members.	• Core membership varies throughout the year because of poor planning. • Core participants do not include referring sources when appropriate. • Multilingual participants are not invited and/or translators are not provided.
5. Team performance	
• Effective teams ensure democratic and equal participation in the consultation process. • Group dynamics are evaluated, and members review their own role and those of other team participants. • Proper in-service is provided in order to develop skills, including effective communication, prevention strategies, cross-cultural consultation, and collaborative problem-solving. • All members are viewed as bringing different skills and knowledge to the team.	• Cross-disciplinary exchange is not the norm, and conflicts are unresolved. • Lack of proper in-service training leads to ineffective operations, resistance to change, and poor utilization of resources. • Meeting formats are unstable, and consensual plans are not achieved. • Poor verbal and nonverbal communication results in negative emotional reactions, and lack of monitoring of recommendations. • Some team members are not engaged as active participants and are less satisfied with the team process.

health and educational professionals, including a school psychologist and professional web developers. The school psychologist, who was the first author of this chapter, and Dr. Dale Willows from OISE/University of Toronto were key players in the development and dissemination of these primary prevention resources. These websites, however, can be utilized at all levels of the model. They can be used by school psychologists engaging in primary and secondary prevention activities at the organizational and school levels and in consulting with individual teachers. Resources from these websites can also be referred to in psychological reports.

The Psychology Foundation of Canada Website

The Psychology Foundation of Canada (PFC) is a national not-for-profit organization established to share sound psychological knowledge to better people's lives. Its board of trustees includes psychologists and community leaders who advocate for prevention and early intervention services. Its public education programs are designed to support families and are delivered through multiple and diverse partnerships across Canada. The PFC has been active in its participation at conferences, training sessions, and workshops.

One of the foundation's programs is Parenting for Life. The program is designed to promote positive parenting skills and the well-being of families. Over the years, several booklets in English and French have been developed with a steering committee, which mostly included psychologists. To date, over a million booklets have been distributed across Canada to schools, family resource centers, parenting programs, daycares, and clinics. The booklets, which are available on the website, can be shared by school psychologists during team consultations, presentations, family conferences, and meetings with teachers for mediated services. An updated Facilitator's Guide for Parenting the School-Age Child is also available for distribution to professionals.

Each of the booklets addresses familiar topics school psychologists are involved with across the age ranges. Consider, for example, possible uses of the following publications during the consultation process in both elementary and high schools:

- Let's Play! A Child's Road to Learning
- Hands-On Dad: A Guide for New Fathers
- Yes, You Can! Positive Discipline Ideas for You and Your Child
- You and Your Preteen: Getting Ready for Independence
- Focus on Self-Esteem: Nurturing Your School-Age Child
- Kids Can Cope: Parenting Resilient Children at Home and at School
- Straight Talk About Teens: Realistic Ideas and Advice for Parents of Older Teenagers (includes A Teenager's Guide to Parents)

In each of the booklets, the reader receives the following message:

The success of tomorrow's world depends largely on how we live in it today. Building strong, healthy families is the key to our future and the right information at the right time can be a vital support for growing families. Education and skills that enable parents, children and adolescents to grow together, are the foundation we need to give flight to our future.

(www.psychologyfoundation.org)

The ABCs of Mental Health Website

The second Canadian website, the ABCs of Mental Health, provides a comprehensive resource for parents and teachers (www.hincksdellcrest.org/abc). The first author of this chapter was a member of the steering committee that helped shape the conceptual framework of the project and consulted about its developmental phases. The ABCs of Mental Health grew out of the recognition that schools, and those who serve them, are faced by challenges impacted by mental health needs of school age children and youth. In all its phases, this web-based free resource was shaped by ongoing consultations in school systems, sound research, and a collaborative learning process. It is a proactive, easy-to-use, practical program. The rich information included can be used by school psychologists and others for primary, secondary, and tertiary consultation and intervention services.

The first version was released in 2008 and included a teacher resource for children aged 3 to 14. Based on feedback and demand, an extension of the teacher resource resulted in the 2012 version for children and adolescents aged 3 to 18. In addition, a parent resource was also developed based on community consultations. Having both a parent resource and a teacher resource highlights the importance of home–school partnerships and collaborative problem-solving processes.

Over the years, project team members have been mindful of the fact that the ABCs resource will be used both nationally and internationally. As such, information was written in a sensitive, observable, and clear manner rather than using clinical terms. Even the visual aids included aim to be understood in a global and respectful context.

Following consultation and drawing on information from expert advisors, the website posted an introductory general chapter, Mental Health for All Children and Youth, and 10 subject specific chapters: The Worried Child; The Child with Unusual Behaviour; The Child with Poor Social Relations; The Child with Eating Problems; The Defiant or Misbehaving Child; The Angry and Aggressive Child; The Child with Attention Problems; The Self-Harmful Child; The Child with Substance Abuse; and The Sad Child.

In each chapter, observable behaviors are categorized by level of concern and severity and are associated with a specific level of intervention. The "green light" category summarizes behaviors within normal expectations for the child/student. It highlights strategies for promoting good mental health for children/students in the classroom or at home. The second category, "yellow light," describes behaviors that cause concern and warrant further considerations. In consultation, intervention strategies are shared for use by parents and teachers. The third category, "red light," details behaviors that are serious enough to need referral to a mental health specialist. The included intervention strategies require the support of mental health professionals, which may be available in the community.

The ABCs are three steps to consider when working with students who demonstrate troublesome behaviors. *Actions* provide descriptions of behaviors that teachers/parents may find confusing or troubling. *Beliefs* describe possible factors that may be causing or influencing the actions. They are presented under the following headings: (a) biological, congenital, and health; (b) family; (c) disabilities; (d) differences; (e) cultural and/or religion; and (f) trauma, loss, and/or turbulent environment. *Course to Follow* provides tips and ideas for responding to the actions.

Users of the website have quick links to the following:

- *Investigate:* Takes the user straight to the age group of their choice. They can learn about the actions they may see at that stage, and how to understand and respond to these actions.

- *Review a whole chapter:* Allows the reader to deepen their understanding about any of the topics covered in the resource. They can choose to read a particular chapter in its entirety with all age ranges.
- *Behavioural maps:* Allows the user to search key words or to see lists of the behaviors they will find in each chapter.
- *Search:* By entering a word or phrase, the user can quickly search all the chapters in the Parent Resource, Teacher Resource, or both resources to find a specific item of interest.

Psychologists and other support services staff such as social workers, special education teachers, and school administrators were nominated by their school districts to obtain training from the developers of the ABCs of Mental Health. These individuals then trained other school staff in the use of the website. The feedback of the participants was taken into account during the project enhancement phases. Generally, the Steering Committee gathered evidence that the train-the-trainer model was a useful knowledge transfer strategy for participants, with approximately 100 to 250 individuals accessing the site weekly. Overall, the ABCs project has the potential to reach remote areas and at-risk communities in addition to training staff serving large cities.

The Balanced Literacy Diet Website

The third website, the Balanced Literacy Diet, uses a nutritional analogy to provide resources for educators on teaching reading and written language skills to children in kindergarten through grade six. The resources are categorized under various "food groups," such as phonemic awareness, reading fluency and expression, vocabulary, reading comprehension strategies, spelling and word study, and writing processes and strategies. Each section provides reader-friendly recipes for classroom lessons that include written handouts, virtual tours of classrooms, and video clips. These materials can be used by school psychologists conducting workshops on evidence-based practice in the area of literacy and when consulting with individual teachers. Additional sections on teaching reading to English language learners and students with learning disabilities are being added.

Use of Websites by Psychologists in School Consultation

These three websites are examples of web resources that can be used by school psychologists in leadership and consultative positions or in direct service roles. First, psychologists themselves may find them helpful for their own professional development about interventions. Second, they are accessible to parents and teachers because they are written in user-friendly language and do not assume a background in education or mental health. Third, one document on the Psychology Foundation of Canada website has a specific section for adolescents on understanding their parents. Fourth, these websites give service providers and consumers in remote communities information and strategies that might be helpful to them.

IMPLICATIONS FOR PROFESSIONAL TRAINING

The implications of the Integrative Model for Comprehensive Psychological Services (Table 3.1), consistent with NASP's Blueprint III (Ysseldyke et al., 2006), are that school psychologists require complementary skills in consultation; intercultural communication;

individual, group, and family counseling; comprehensive assessment; applied research; and team building. Furthermore, psychologists who work in schools need a broad knowledge base about evidence-based prevention and intervention strategies designed to enhance learning and adjustment of students in the school setting (Durlak, 2009; Kratochwill, Volpiansky, Clements, & Ball, 2007; Lee, Schneider, Davidson, & Robertson, 2012; Linden, Moseley, & Erskine, 2005; Margison & Shore, 2009). Implementation of these strategies involves working collaboratively with educators, mental health practitioners, parents, and the students themselves. Psychologists therefore need to develop the specific interpersonal skills required to work effectively in teams and to create change (Fullan, 2007). The Integrative Model demands a partnership between mental health and education (Nastasi, 2000). Consequently, as discussed by Geva, Wiener, Peterson-Badali, and Link (2003), the overlap between school psychology and clinical child psychology is substantial and should be reflected in training. This overlap includes a solid foundation in developmental psychology and developmental psychopathology; understanding of ethical issues and their application to professional practice; knowledge of jurisprudence pertaining to psychological practice; psychological assessment abilities; formulation of and communication of a diagnosis; core skills for interviewing and therapeutic communication; familiarity with a broad range of psychosocial prevention and intervention programs; communication and counselling skills; skills in consultation and working in multidisciplinary teams; sensitivity to cultural and individual diversity; and program evaluation, research design, and statistics skills.

Given the growth in the Aboriginal population in Canada, the high levels of immigration, and the individual and cultural diversity of the population, it is crucial that both didactic instruction and practicum/internship experiences provide professional training in assessment, intervention, and consultation with culturally and linguistically diverse children, youth, and families. This training should include, among other things, understanding of the typical development of language and literacy skills in second language learners; a deep understanding of the implications of culture, acculturation, and trauma on psychosocial development; risks and protective factors in relation to immigration; and culturally sensitive assessment and intervention strategies (Geva & Wiener, 2015; Wiener & Costaris, 2012). It also involves specific training in interprofessional practice whereby professionals from various disciplines and cultural backgrounds, as well as language and cultural interpreters, consult with each other to enhance skills in working with these diverse populations (Geva, Barsky, & Westernoff, 2000; Geva & Wiener, 2015).

Training in Consultation

Although most school psychology training programs provide a course in consultation, to our knowledge there are no empirical studies that provide evaluations of the efficacy of training practices. The second author of this chapter, however, provides this training for the School and Clinical Child Psychology program at the University of Toronto. Similar to other training programs, this training involves a didactic component, specific skills training, students engaging in case and program consultation in practicum settings, students reflecting on their experiences, and supervision by a licensed school psychologist in the school setting (Hazel, Laviolette, & Lineman, 2010).

The didactic component involves readings and course lectures on effective classrooms and schools and the association of teacher beliefs with their practices (e.g.,

Doll, Leclair, & Kurien, 2009; Ducharme & Schecter, 2011; Gettinger & Callan Stoiber, 2009); consultation models, including collaborative consultation and conjoint behavioral consultation (e.g. Gutkin & Curtis, 2009); and consultation and interprofessional practice in settings with culturally diverse clients (e.g., Geva et al., 2000; Geva & Wiener, 2015). Students learn about primary, secondary, and tertiary prevention models and the factors that are critical for effective implementation of such programs (e.g., Durlak, 2009; Nastasi, 2000).

The specific skills training component includes instruction in classroom observation and teacher interviewing and strategies for effecting educational change. This occurs through case studies, examining videotapes of classrooms, and simulations of teacher interviewing. Because the cultural backgrounds of the students in the program are diverse, they are taught to consult with each other with regard to the cultural issues that they need to be aware of when working with specific children. In their 250-hour school-based practicum, which occurs concurrently with some of the didactic and skills instruction, students are required to undertake at least 20 hours of face-to-face consultation work that is not connected with a psychoeducational assessment. Most implement behavioral or conjoint behavioral consultations with teachers and parents regarding students exhibiting challenging behaviors in classrooms, but some are involved in consulting with regard to school-wide prevention programs.

In addition to receiving ongoing supervision from a school psychologist in the field, they reflect on their own and other students' experiences using a web forum and discussion in class, and they must do class presentations on their experiences. This permits the course instructor to link the didactic and practical components of the course, to scaffold their learning experiences, and to trouble shoot when necessary. Although we attempt to select practicum supervisors who themselves are involved in case and program consultation, the requirement to supervise a graduate student sometimes encourages supervisors to enhance and use their consultation skills and to implement school- and classroom-based prevention and intervention programs. Following the course that mainly focuses on school-based consultation, students use these skills to collaborate with teachers and school staff in relation to an assessment and intervention with a culturally and linguistically diverse child or adolescent in our university clinic. Some students are also involved in a project that provides consultative services to a school in a remote Aboriginal community.

FINAL THOUGHTS

In summary, as education systems become more complex and demands for increased accountability grow, psychologists need to work with educators to help them understand that school psychology is a dynamic profession that can make significant contributions to the development of school communities that provide optimal support of students. To this end, school psychologists need to be more proactive in promoting the concept that psychology in education is not only about services for those experiencing difficulties in mainstream programs but that the profession has a significant role to play in supporting teachers and promoting the academic and social growth of all students. This tall order will likely be achieved by utilizing comprehensive service delivery models and restructuring preservice and in-service training practices that promote inclusiveness and equity of outcomes for the adults of tomorrow.

REFERENCES

Adelman, H. S., & Taylor, L. (2003). Commentary: Advancing mental health science and practice through authentic collaboration. *School Psychology Review, 32,* 53–56.

Akamatsu, T., & Cole, E. (2000). Immigrant and refugee children who are deaf: Crisis equals danger plus opportunity. In K. Christensen (Ed.), *Deaf plus—A multicultural perspective* (pp. 93–120). San Diego, CA: Dawn Sign Press.

Akamatsu, T., & Cole, E. (2003). Deaf immigrant and refugee children: A different kind of multiculturalism? In E. Cole & J. A. Siegel (Eds.), *Effective consultation in school psychology* (2nd revised and expanded ed., pp. 296–321). Toronto: Hogrefe & Huber.

Andrews, J. J. W., & Violato, C. (2003). Contributions to theory, research, and practice of school psychology. *Canadian Journal of School Psychology, 18,* 1–10.

Anserello, C., & Sweet, T. (1990). Integrating consultation into school psychological services. In E. Cole & J. A. Siegel (Eds.), *Effective consultation in school psychology* (pp. 173–199). Toronto: Hogrefe & Huber.

Balanced Literacy Diet: Putting Research into Practice in the Classroom. (2012). Retrieved from http://www.oise. utoronto.ca/balancedliteracydiet/Home/index.html

Broxterman, K., & Whalen, A. J. (2013). *RTI team building: Effective collaboration and data-based decision making.* New York: Guilford.

Caplan, G. (1970). *The theory and practice of mental health consultation.* New York: Basic Books.

Cole, E. (1992). Characteristics of students referred to school teams: Implications for preventive psychological services. *Canadian Journal of School Psychology, 8,* 23–36.

Cole, E. (1996). An integrative perspective on school psychology. *Canadian Journal of School Psychology, 12,* 115–121.

Cole, E. (1998). Immigrant and refugee children: Challenges and opportunities for education and mental health services. *Canadian Journal of School Psychology, 14,* 36–50.

Cole, E. (2003). Violence prevention in schools: Knowledge, skills, and interventions. In E. Cole & J. A. Siegel (Eds.), *Effective consultation in school psychology* (2nd revised and expanded ed., pp. 462–476). Toronto: Hogrefe & Huber.

Cole, E., & Brown, R. (1996). Multidisciplinary school teams: A five-year follow-up study. *Canadian Journal of School Psychology, 12,* 155–168.

Cole, E., & Brown, R. (2003). Multidisciplinary school teams. In E. Cole & J. A. Siegel (Eds.), *Effective consultation in school psychology* (2nd revised and expanded ed., pp. 24–44). Toronto: Hogrefe & Huber.

Cole, E., & Siegel, J. A. (Eds.). (1990). *Effective consultation in school psychology.* Toronto: Hogrefe & Huber.

Cole, E., & Siegel, J. A. (Eds.). (2003). *Effective consultation in school psychology* (2nd revised and expanded ed.). Toronto: Hogrefe & Huber.

Cole, E., Siegel, J. A., & Yau, M. (1992). Multidisciplinary school teams: Perceptions of goals, roles, and functions. *Canadian Journal of School Psychology, 8,* 37–51.

Corkum, P., French, F., & Dorey, H. (2007). School psychology in Nova Scotia: A survey of current practices and preferred future roles. *Canadian Journal of School Psychology, 22,* 108–120.

Davidson, I., & Wiener, J. (1992). Creating educational change: The in-school team. *Exceptionality Education Canada, 1,* 25–44.

Davison, J. (1990). The process of school consultation: Give and take. In E. Cole & J. A. Siegel (Eds.), *Effective consultation in school psychology* (pp. 53–69). Toronto: Hogrefe & Huber.

DiPasquale, G. (2003). Violence prevention in secondary schools: A project for raising awareness and facilitating action. In E. Cole & J. A. Siegel (Eds.), *Effective consultation in school psychology* (2nd revised and expanded ed., pp. 477–507). Toronto: Hogrefe & Huber.

Doll, B., Leclair, C., & Kurien, S. (2009). Effective classrooms: Classroom learning environments that foster school success. In T. B. Gutkin & C. R. Reynolds (Eds.), *The handbook of school psychology* (4th ed., pp. 791–807). New York: Wiley.

Ducharme, J. M., & Schecter, C. (2011). Bridging the gap between clinical and classroom intervention: Keystone approaches for students with challenging behavior. *School Psychology Review, 40,* 257–274.

Durlak, J. A. (2009). Prevention programs. In T. B. Gutkin & C. R. Reynolds (Eds.), *The handbook of school psychology* (4th ed., pp. 905–920). New York: Wiley.

Fagan, T., & Sachs Wise, P. (2007). *School psychology: Past, present and future* (3rd ed.). Bethesda, MD: National Association of School Psychologists.

Fletcher, J. M., Coulter, W. A., Reschly, D. J., & Vaughn, S. (2004). Alternative approaches to the definition and identification of learning disabilities: Some questions and answers. *Annals of Dyslexia, 54,* 304–331. doi: 10.1007/s11881–004–0015-y

Fletcher, J. M., & Vaughn, S. (2009). Response to intervention: Preventing and remediating academic difficulties. *Child Development Perspectives, 3,* 30–37. doi: 10.1111/j.1750–8606.2008.00072.x

Fullan, M. (2001). *Leading in a culture of change.* San Francisco: Jossey-Bass, John A. Wiley.

Fullan, M. (2007). *The new meaning of educational change* (4th ed.). New York: Educators' College Press.

Fullan, M. (2010). *All systems go: The change imperative for whole system reform.* Thousand Oaks, CA: Corwin Press.

Gettinger, M., & Callan Stoiber, K. (2009). Effective teaching and effective schools. In T. B. Gutkin & C. R. Reynolds (Eds.), *The handbook of school psychology* (4th ed., pp. 769–790). New York: Wiley.

Geva, E., & Wiener, J. (2015). *Assessment of culturally and linguistically diverse children and adolescents: A Practitioner's Guide.* New York: Springer.

Geva, E., Wiener, J., Peterson-Badali, M., & Link, N. (2003). Integrating school and clinical child psychology: An innovative model for training school psychologists. In E. Cole & J. A. Siegel (Eds.), *Effective consultation in school psychology* (2nd revised and expanded ed., pp. 107–128). Toronto: Hogrefe & Huber.

Gutkin, T. B., & Curtis, M. J. (2009). School-based consultation: The science and practice of indirect service delivery. In T. B. Gutkin & C. R. Reynolds (Eds.), *The handbook of school psychology* (4th ed., pp. 591–635). New York: Wiley.

Hadjistavropoulos, T. (2009). Canadian psychology in a global context. *Canadian Psychology, 50,* 1–7.

Harris, G. E., & Joy, R. M. (2010). Educational psychologists' perspectives on their professional practice in Newfoundland and Labrador. *Canadian Journal of School Psychology, 25,* 205–220.

Hincks-Dellcrest Centre. (2012). *The ABCs of mental health.* Toronto: Author. Retrieved from www.hincksdellcrest.org/abc

Jordan, J. J., Hindes, Y. L., & Saklofske, D. H. (2009). School psychology in Canada: A survey of roles and functions, challenges and aspirations. *Canadian Journal of School Psychology, 24,* 245–264.

Kamphaus, R. W. (2009). Assessment of intelligence and achievement. In T. B. Gutkin & C. R. Reynolds (Eds.), *The handbook of school psychology* (4th ed., pp. 230–246). New York: Wiley.

Kovaleski, J. F. (2002). Best practices in operating pre-referral intervention teams. In A. Thomas & J. Grimes (Eds.), *Best practices in school psychology—IV* (pp. 645–655). Washington, DC: National Association of School Psychologists.

Kratochwill, T. R., Elliot, S. N., & Callan-Stoiber, K. (2002). Best practices in school based problem solving consultation. In A. Thomas & J. Grimes (Eds.), *Best practices in school psychology—IV* (pp. 583–608). Washington, DC: National Association of School Psychologists.

Kratochwill, T. R., Volpiansky, P., Clements, M., & Ball, C. (2007). Professional development in implementing and sustaining multitier prevention models: Implications for response to intervention. *School Psychology Review, 36,* 618–631.

Kutcher, S., & McLuckie, A. (2010). *Evergreen: A child and youth mental health framework for Canada.* Calgary, Alberta: Mental Health Commission of Canada.

Kutcher, S., & Wei, Y. (2013). Challenges and solutions in the implementation of the school-based pathway to care model: The lessons from Nova Scotia and beyond. *Canadian Journal of School Psychology, 28,* 90–102.

Lean, D. S., & Colucci, V. A. (2010). *Barriers to learning: The case for integrated mental health services in schools.* Lanham, MD: Rowman & Littlefield Education.

Lean, D. S., & Colucci, V. A. (2013). *School-based mental health: A framework for intervention.* Lanham, MD: Rowman & Littlefield Education.

Lee, C. M., Schneider, B. H., Davidson, S., & Robertson, C. (2012). Interprofessional collaboration: A survey of Canadian psychologists and psychiatrists. *Canadian Psychology, 53,* 159–164.

Lewington, J., & Orpwood, G. (1993). *Overdue assignment: Taking responsibility for Canada's schools.* Toronto: Wiley.

Linden, W., Moseley, J., & Erskine, Y. (2005). Psychology as a health-care profession: Implications for Training. *Canadian Psychology, 46,* 179–188.

Luther, M., Cole, E., & Gamlin, P. (Eds.). (1996). *Dynamic assessment for instruction: From theory to application.* Toronto: Captus University Publications.

Manion, I. (2010). Provoking evolution in child and youth mental health in Canada. *Canadian Psychology, 51*(1), 50–57.

Margison, J. A., & Shore, B. M. (2009). Interprofessional practice and education in health care: Their relevance to school psychology. *Canadian Journal of School Psychology, 24,* 125–139.

McCrimmon, A. W., Altomare, A. A., Matchullis, R. L., & Jitiina, K. (2012). School-based practices for asperger syndrome: A Canadian perspective. *Canadian Journal of School Psychology, 27,* 319–336.

McIntosh, K. (2014). Positive behavioral interventions and supports—Soutien au comportement positif (PBIS-SCP) in Canada: Deep history, promising future. *Canadian Journal of School Psychology, 29,* 155–160.

McIntosh, K., Mackay, L. D., Andreou, T., Brown, J. A., Mathews, S., Gietz, C., & Bennett, J. L. (2011). Response to intervention in Canada: Definitions, the evidence base, and future directions. *Canadian Journal of School Psychology, 26*, 18–43.

Mental Health Commission of Canada. (2012). *Changing directions, changing lives: The mental health strategy for Canada.* Calgary, Alberta: Author.

Millar, G. M., Lean, D., Sweet, S. D., Moraes, S. C., & Nelson, V. (2013). The psychology school mental health initiative: An innovative approach to the delivery of school-based intervention service. *Canadian Journal of School Psychology, 28*, 103–118.

Montgomery, J., Meyer, K., & Smart, S. (2008). Book review: Cole, E. & Siegel, J. A. (2003). (Eds.), *Effective consultation in school psychology—2nd revised and expanded edition.* Toronto: Hogrefe & Huber. *Canadian Journal of School Psychology, 23*(2), 231–234.

Nastasi, B. K. (2000). School psychologists as health-care providers in the 21st century: Conceptual framework, professional identity, and professional practice. *School Psychology Review, 29*, 540–554.

Noltmeyer, A., & McLaughlin, C. L. (2011). School psychology's blueprint III: A survey of knowledge, use, and competence. *School Psychology Forum: Research in Practice, 5*, 74–86.

Ontario Ministry of Education. (2011). *Learning for all: A guide of effective assessment and instruction for all students, kindergarten to grade 12.* Toronto: Author. Retrieved from www.edu.gov.on.ca/eng/general/elemsec/speced/learningforall2011.pdf

Ontario Psychological Association. (2013). *Professional practice guidelines for school psychologists in Ontario.* Toronto: The OPA section on Psychology in Education: Author.

Power, T. J. (2006). School psychology review 2006–2010. *School Psychology Review, 35*, 3–10.

Power, T. J. (2008a). Improving intervention effectiveness and efficiency. *School Psychology Review, 37*, 291–293.

Power, T. J. (2008b). Emerging trends for expanding the science base. *School Psychology Review, 37*, 3–4.

Prince-Embury, S. (2008). Translating resiliency theory for assessment and application in schools. *Canadian Journal of School Psychology, 23*, 4–8.

Psychologists' Association of Alberta. (2010). *Position paper: The pivotal role of Alberta school psychology services: A response to Alberta education's setting the direction.* Edmonton: Author. Retrieved from www.psychologistsassociaiton.ab.ca/files/positionpaper.pdf

The Psychology Foundation of Canada. (2013). *Home page.* Toronto: Author. Retrieved from www.psychologyfoundation.org

Rosenfield, S. (2002). Best practices in instructional consultation. In A. Thomas & J. Grimes (Eds.), *Best practices in school psychology—IV* (pp. 609–623). Washington, DC: National Association of School Psychologists.

Sandoval, J. (1996). Becoming indispensable through mental health promotion. In R. C. Talley, T. Kubiszyn, M. Brassard, & R. J. Short (Eds.), *Making psychologists in schools indispensable: Critical questions & emerging perspectives* (pp. 3–7). Washington, DC: American Psychological Association.

Schaughency, E., & Ervin, R. (2006). Building capacity to implement and sustain effective practices to better serve children. *School Psychology Review, 35*, 155–166.

Schmidt, F. (2012). The critical role for psychology in children's mental health system: Being a catalyst to implement and build better interventions. *Canadian Psychology, 53*, 53–62.

Scholten, T. (2003). What does it mean to consult? In E. Cole & J. A. Siegel (Eds.), *Effective consultation in school psychology* (2nd revised and expanded ed., pp. 87–106). Toronto: Hogrefe & Huber.

Shapiro, E. S. (2008). From research to practice: Promoting academic competence for underserved students. *School Psychology Review, 37*, 46–51.

Simeone, T. (2011). *Primer on aboriginal issues.* Retrieved from http://carolynbennett.liberal.ca/files/2010/07/Primer-on-Aboriginal-Issues_EN.pdf

Sladeczek, I. E., & Heath, N. L. (1997). Consultation in Canada. *Canadian Journal of School Psychology, 13*, 1–14.

Statistics Canada. (2011). *Immigration and ethnocultural diversity in Canada.* Retrieved from http://www12.statcan.gc.ca/nhs-enm/2011/as-sa/99-010-x/99-010-x2011001-eng.pdf

Thomas, A., & Grimes, J. (Eds.). (2008). *Best practices in school psychology.* Bethesda, MD: National Association of School Psychologists.

Wagner, P. (2000). Consultation: Developing a comprehensive approach to service delivery. *Educational Psychology in Practice, 16*, 9–18.

Whitley, J., Smith, J. D., & Vaillancourt, T. (2013). Promoting mental health literacy among educators: Critical in school-based prevention and intervention. *Canadian Journal of School Psychology, 28*, 56–70.

Wiener, J., & Costaris, L. (2012). Teaching psychological report writing: Content and process. *Canadian Journal of School Psychology, 29*, 119–135.

Wiener, J., & Davidson, I. F. (1990). The in-school team: A preventive model of service delivery in special education. *Canadian Journal of Education, 15*, 427–444. Retrieved from http://search.proquest.com/docview/618127323?accountid=14771

Wiener, J., & Siegel, L. (1992). A Canadian perspective on learning disabilities. *Journal of Learning Disabilities, 25*, 340–350, 371.

Willows, D. (2012). *The balanced literacy diet: Putting research into practice in the classroom.* Retrieved from http://www.oise.utoronto.ca/balancedliteracydiet/Home/index.html

Ysseldyke, J., Burns, M., Dawson, P., Kelly, B., Morrison, D., Ortiz, S., . . . Telzrow, C. (2006). *School psychology: A blueprint for training and practice III.* Bethesda, MD: National Association of School Psychologists.

4

CONSULTING IN SCHOOL SETTINGS IN AUSTRALIA
Challenges, Positive Development, and Future Opportunities

Terence Bowles

A broad range of factors influence the adoption and practice of school psychology in educational settings (Fletcher et al., 2010), and few have a single profound effect (Cook, Jimerson, & Begeny, 2010). As Farrell noted of school psychology:

> At a time when, in most countries, the profession is experiencing a period of growth and expansion, many problems still remain. Indeed school psychologists themselves devote a great deal of time and space at their conferences and in professional publications to debates about their ongoing role. These debates reflect continuing uncertainty, both within the profession and amongst employers and users of services, about the distinctive nature of the contribution that school psychologists make in supporting children, schools and families.
>
> (2009, p. 74)

So it is in the Australian context, where school psychology practice is informed by the best theory and research in the world, and practice standards are high but the role of school psychologists remains uncertain as school policies and funding arrangements change regularly (Thielking & Jimerson, 2006).

Despite the high quality of the work of psychologists and those involved in psychological consultation, school psychology has some historical and cultural pressures that make it particularly vulnerable. The next decade will see large-scale changes to the way in which psychological services, and consulting specifically, are carried out in Australian schools. This review of psychological consultation in the Australian context will explore future threats to consulting practices, positive developments in school consulting and advanced models of consultation and offer suggestions for future opportunities for school consultation practice. Each of these will be considered in turn after introducing consulting as a central practice in school psychology and a brief outline of the training of school psychologists in Australia.

SCHOOL PSYCHOLOGY IN AUSTRALIA

Training

In Australia, universities follow either the British or the U.S. models of tertiary education, and there are many degree combinations (Australian Psychology Accreditation Council [APACS], 2014, 2015). Undergraduate programs can be general or profession specific with a required 3-year or 4-year sequence, usually with two majors up to the third year and a specialized fourth year. If the program is a general degree, then a sequence comparable to major must be demonstrated to have an accredited undergraduate program. Regardless of the type of program, a major sequence in psychology (e.g., equivalent to 25% of first year, 33% of second year and 50% of third year) of an undergraduate bachelor's degree and honors or fourth year (100% psychology content) in psychology in a rigorously accredited program (APACS, 2015) is necessary to meet the prerequisites to enter the master's level (2 years of 100% psychology content). This is entry level for the profession now.

In Australia, a master's course might be for general practice or specialized into one of nine endorsed areas of practice (previously speciality areas) for which a psychologist might seek registration as a specialist as a health practitioner (APRAH, 2015). The nine endorsed are neuropsychology, clinical psychology, community psychology, counselling psychology, educational and developmental psychology, forensic psychology, health psychology, organizational psychology, and sport and exercise psychology (Australian Health Practitioners Regulation Agency [AHPRA], 2015). Specialist courses and specific content within courses provide an emphasis for each master's program that is accredited and leads to endorsed (specialist) registration. Consultation in school would usually be a one semester course or part of a number of courses in the educational and developmental psychology area.

School psychologist is the term for those practicing psychology in the schools. School psychologists would be able to claim and put after their name that they are a registered educational and developmental psychologist after completing a specialist master's degree. This term is relatively interchangeable with the title of school psychologist. However, not all school psychologists have master's degrees with a specialization in or endorsement as an educational and developmental psychologist. There is no strict requirement that those working as psychologists in schools have endorsement. Some school psychologists may have 4-year training and have had supervision toward registration, another endorsement, or a general master's of psychology degree or D.Ed. or Ph.D. but not the endorsed specialty under registration as an educational and developmental psychologist. This registration allows psychologists to call themselves specialists in educational and developmental psychology. Further, the system of registration is relatively new, and older school psychologists would have been trained under various other systems depending on state requirements at that time.

Further, there are eight states and territories in the Australian federation, and each has their own education systems as well as a large sector of private education providers, the largest of these being religious schools in each state. Each of these providers employ psychologists to perform various duties, from a full range of practice activities to being limited to testing, reporting and advising only. States such as Western Australia provide a substantial amount of psychological support in a very structured manner to schools.

Western Australia provides an excellent example of an integrated system where graduates are trained in practice, services are provided across systems and there are career structures for promotion of psychologists. In Queensland, by contrast, some psychological services are performed by teachers with advanced skills and training.

There is no single way for a graduate to enter the profession. Some may be employed by the education department of the state. Others may be taken up by private providers who contract services to schools. And a large majority will gain employment by working for schools directly. A number of graduates, after working in schools for a short number of years, start their own private practices with various specialties associated with general psychology practice, psychology specific to children and schools, and consulting. As a result of the rigorous requirements to run a program, there are only four universities with such programs, resulting in few educational and developmental psychologists. This, among other problems, is discussed later.

The Definition of School Psychology and the Centrality of Consulting

From an international perspective, school psychology in many countries is experiencing expansion, growth and changes in practice over recent decades. These changes are reflected in the shift from a focus on one-on-one interventions with an individual child to an emphasis on consultation (Farrell, 2009; Farrell, Jimerson, Kalambouka, & Benoit, 2005). Other researchers view the roles of individual work with students and consulting as aspects of the same process,

> characterized as providing individual assessment of children who may display cognitive, emotional, social or behavioural difficulties; develops and implements primary and secondary intervention programs; consults with teachers, parents and other relevant professionals; engages in program development and evaluation; conducts research and helps prepare and supervise others.
>
> (Jimerson, Oakland, & Farrell, 2007, p. 1)

Consistent with the latter definition, consultation may be conceived of as a series of negotiated actions strategically articulating alternatives to prompt movement away from previous states and toward future possible options. In this context, consultation is a process of working through a solution-focused change process, working with the consultee(s) to move from problem to solution through interactions varying in degrees of non-prescriptive direction, within the context, while bolstering and supporting the consultee (Hylander, 2000).

The complexities of consultation reflected in the Australian context fit better with the conceptualization of instructional consultation (IC) and are more focused on instructional practice, learning achievement outcomes and intervention (Rosenfield, 2008). IC has similar features to the strategic approach of the adaptive change model (Bowles, 2006) comprised of process and support factors designed to facilitate effective change. In the IC model there are three components: (1) a consultation *process* in which the relationship between the consultant and consultee is central and the aim is a stage-based, problem-solving approach involving case management and clear communication with the teacher-consultee and consultant; (2) a staged approach to problem-solving with case management, active administration, and clear documentation; and (3) a thorough evaluation of training needs of staff, the implementation and outcomes (Rosenfield,

1995b, 1987, 2008). Importantly, IC teams are multidisciplinary and may be comprised of various specialists drawn together to identify the issues and design an effective intervention. The core of case management is the dyadic relationship between the consultee and the consultant, who work collaboratively together to resolve the problem; providing support to this relationship is the multidisciplinary team (Rosenfield, 2008; 1995b). This comprehensive model is more the approach taken by the best practitioners in Australia. However, there is variability in practice depending on many factors.

In fact, the definition of the work of school psychologists (SPs) and the activity of consulting within the international context is in contrast to the consultation typically carried out by Australian SPs. The scope of the work of Australian SPs has been of interest for many decades and was most recently addressed through the advent of registration of psychologists and the endorsement of educational psychologists as a specialty under Acts of the Australian Parliament (Health Practitioner Regulation National Law Act, 2009 (Vic.) which defined the specialty alongside other health practitioners. However, such definitions do not readily alter the impact of long-term factors that limit best practice in the delivery of psychological services in schools. In this chapter, factors are considered that indirectly and directly impact and challenge SPs' capacities to deliver effective consulting in schools.

There are several challenges that are considered in the early sections of this chapter. First, threats to the practice of school and consulting psychology are considered, followed by a brief review of positive developments that are currently impacting SPs' consulting practices. Finally, the future opportunities that SPs may embrace to enhance the possibility of effectively consulting in schools are considered.

CHALLENGES TO CONSULTING PRACTICE

Currently there are two major threats to consultation in Australian school settings: (1) the length of training and breadth of practice and (2) an aging of the knowledge base or pace of new knowledge and an aging workforce. Each of these threats to the consulting practice in Australian school settings is discussed here.

Length of Training and Breadth of Practice

To practice in a school as a general psychologist, registration as a general psychologist is required (Psychology Board of Australia, 2010a). As previously noted, the pathway for a general psychologist is typically an undergraduate degree with a three-year major in psychology followed by a master's degree with no specialist training or a supervision route with a specialist in educational and developmental psychology (EDP), which requires a master's degree or a D.Psych in an accredited program (Psychology Board of Australia, 2010). Despite these requirements for national registration, different states of Australia have requirements above these related to specialized or further university and other training (Boyle, 2014).

The formal registration process that has been instituted over the past 6 years has had the effect of making SPs with a specialty in EDP exceptionally well qualified at registration to practice. This, in turn, has both positive and some negative consequences. Positively, it means SPs have a breadth of educational, psychological and clinically relevant training. The negative aspects are the cost and intensity of the training, which limit the number of graduates from accredited programs.

This diversity is reflected in the work and research on SPs. The most recent survey of members of the College of Educational and Developmental Psychologists (a group within the major association of psychologists, The Australian Psychological Society; APS, 2015) showed that the competencies and skills utilised most by SP members were associated with psychological assessment. Over 50% of those surveyed were working in private practice, and approximately 15 to 20% were working in the government sector associated directly with education and nongovernment organizations (Fletcher et al., 2010). Thielking and Jimerson (2006) found that Australian SPs and school principals agreed on the work done by SPs as

> IQ assessments (89%); conduct psychological assessments (74%); provide counselling to students (99%); organise group programs for students (88%); provide workshops to teachers about student welfare issues (94%); provide information to teachers about working with students' varying social, emotional and learning needs (99%); be the main referring agent within the school when students' issues are beyond teachers' level of expertise.
>
> (pp. 217–218)

This range of competencies is very large and intersects with consultation on many levels, but it does not specifically mention consultation.

Age of Knowledge and Age of the Workforce

As indicated, Australian psychologists have a wide breadth of training and supervision before practice, a large competency base from which to work and generally a range of tasks to complete. Despite this, much of the work of an SP is taken up with assessments when working in an education context. The work of an SP is considered diverse by the SPs themselves as well as the principals with whom they work (Thielking & Jimerson, 2006). The time taken up writing reports and testing restricts the capacity of SPs to adequately practice as consultants despite the breadth of training, resulting in a problem of the relevance of psychology training over time.

Niemeyer (2012), although referring to U.S. psychologists, suggests that the half-life of knowledge of SPs was 9.33 years and predicted to be 8.2 years in 2022:

> The concept of the "half-life" of professional knowledge has been introduced as an indicator of the obsolescence of professional knowledge over time. It has been defined as the length of time it takes a practicing professional, without any new learning, to become roughly half as knowledgeable or competent to practice, owing to the generation of new knowledge within the field.
>
> (Neimeyer, Taylor, & Rozensky, 2012, p. 364)

This suggests that to meet the needs of a broad role, SPs train for a long time, but the currency of their knowledge is reduced over time. Further, to ensure their knowledge is current, high levels of ongoing professional development must be completed to maintain registration as a psychologist and specialist (Psychology Board of Australia, 2010). While there is little evidence indicating that claims about knowledge redundancy and the effectiveness of training has impacted the work of psychologists, the training of SPs is both a long and costly process, compounded when the breadth of skills, training and knowledge is not mirrored proportionally by the work of SPs.

There are also arguments that the work of SPs could be done by more specifically trained parapsychologists or educators. This is a growing argument within the Australian setting. This trend is manifest in the advent of new, postgraduate courses to train teachers and other professionals to work in school settings from a narrower base of knowledge and a more specific psychological skill set to deal with psychosocial, counseling and problem-solving aspects of intervention. The likelihood of implementing parapsychologists or educators to take on some of the roles and responsibilities of SPs is under consideration.

There are two important points that are impacting this decision. First, nearly 50% of the members of the College of Educational and Developmental Psychologists have approximately 20 years of practice (Fletcher et al., 2010), making this a relatively aging workforce. Compounding this problem is the number of graduates annually. There are four universities with master's programs graduating registered educational psychologists; if each of these is graduating 25 people on average, there are only 100 specialist SPs to enter school service each year. Given this low graduation rate, it is probable that general, clinical psychologists and other professionals will enter schools to practice in the space previously occupied by SPs.

Finally, another issue challenging the prospect of effective practice and consultation is the growing intensification of responsibilities given to SPs by some school principals. This results in more frequent diagnosis of mental illness and identification of social, emotional and learning problems, usually without commensurate adequate increases in resources to deal with them. This is further compounded by the growing trend to contract SPs on a fee-for-service basis rather than keeping SPs as paid school staff. These issues and the uncertainty of tenure of SPs are prompting many SPs to enter private practice (Campbell & Colmar, 2014). The movement of SPs into private practice, however, further reduces the workforce available to perform school and regional consultations.

Each of these considerations is occurring against a background of an absence of understanding of the profession and the growing demands on the SP's role (e.g., limited budget, time and therapy choices, growing costs; Fletcher et al., 2010). This context only intensifies the work pressures, the changes in the nature of the work of SPs and the future (potentially unmet) demands on SPs. This could in turn result in the possible fragmentation of the work role of SPs. The emphasis on assessments and reporting as major functions of the work of SPs also compounds the possibility that others will take consulting and intervention roles after SPs have written reports rather than SPs effectively intervening in line with instructional consultation.

POSITIVE AND POTENTIAL DEVELOPMENTS IN SCHOOL CONSULTING

Despite these issues, there are a number of very positive possibilities for consulting within the Australian context. Foremost among these in the Australian setting are the new trends toward evidence- and outcome-based practice, growing interest in RTI and the place of the consultant, use of strength-based interventions and consulting, and advanced models of consultation. Each of these trends will be discussed in regard to the Australian context.

Evidence- and Outcome-Based Practice

There is a profound and powerful interest in applying new research findings to practice and consultation within the Australian context. This tendency has been growing for a considerable amount of time. The early proponents of this approach coined the term *scientist-practitioners,* adopted for professional psychology at the Boulder Conference in 1949 and widely used in school psychology (Reschly & Ysseldyke, 2002; Stoner & Green, 1992).

There are four important elements that should not be lost in the growing rush to apply research findings. First, theory should not be forgotten in the pressure to provide services that work. In educational settings in Australia, many programs are implemented as a result of research that is not well grounded. Policy based on advice, albeit from experts, has far-reaching implications but does not always include sufficient attention to theoretically informed and replicated research. Second, there is an admission that it is difficult to introduce interventions from research to practice, and consultee-centered consultation has been suggested as a means to facilitate the take-up of new research findings (Kratochwill & Shernoff; Rosenfield, Silva, & Gravois, 2008), as described in the expanding field of implementation science (Forman et al., 2013).

Consistent with previous research, behavioural and functional analysis (n = 1) as a method is useful for working with students needing support because it provides specific programmatic intervention that is evidence-based (Gravois & Rosenfield, 2002). Functional analysis is not used sufficiently as an approach in the Australian context. Functional analysis incorporates the best elements of evidence-based practice in a microprocess: explicit definition of concerns in observable terms, collection of baseline data, specification of measurable goals, specification of intervention components, graphing of data to monitor progress and evaluation of intervention by comparing graphed data to baseline/goals (Donovan & Cross, 2002). As a method, functional analysis provides a valid means of establishing evidence to support the appropriateness and effectiveness of the intervention. Functional analysis and the implementation of interventions based on these principles provide a vehicle for fine-grained skill and competency development as an adjunct to consultee-centered consultation.

Third, early research emphasized the need for published research to be confirmed by practice research, such as single-case study designs (Barlow, Hayes, & Nelson, 1984). Single-subject designs applied by practitioners and consultants are worth encouraging, as the best research has applications that are profound and useful in practice. Also, practitioner research should feedback into funded, generalizable research (see also Chapter 19 of this book).

Fourth, practice, including consultation, needs to inform theory and theory development, ensuring that researchers are involved in the testing of the development of new theoretical arrangements with consultants and other practitioners. Building networks of consultants, researchers and practitioners through local associations is one way in which reflective practice and the integration of new knowledge can occur. Such meetings are common in the Australian context and are required for continued registration. By overlaying a consulting framework to such techniques, school staff, parents and students can benefit from involvement in an observation of the changes affecting the student as well as drawing on this information to provide feedback and inform policy and practice in future.

Growing Interest in RTI and the Place of the Consultant

Alongside the growing interest in evidence-based research is the need to be conversant with response to intervention (RTI) practices, which have been growing within the Australian context. Simply, RTI practices define the specificity and individual level of care provided to students. RTI practices provide the mechanism for applying resources most efficiently; however, careful consultation practices need to strategically accompany RTI to ensure that appropriate case management is achieved. RTI practice provides an alternative to the standard ability–achievement discrepancy approach (Fletcher, Barth, & Stuebing, 2011) or deficit models of problem identification. Instead of assigning a diagnosis, various observations and evidence-based practices can be used to guide instructional practices that systematically address whether adjustment to the curriculum or teaching or demographic factors can be matched to the student's needs prior to, or instead of, assigning a diagnosis (Feifer, 2010). Senior consultant psychologists with specialist training and a breadth of case management experience could be more involved to ensure that RTI, implemented by psychologists new to the profession and teachers, is effectively implemented, managed and resourced appropriately to improve intervention fidelity and effectiveness.

Growing Interest in Strength-Based Interventions and Consulting

In the Australian context, a groundswell of interest has also fostered practices associated with strength-based approaches to intervention (Jimerson, Sharkey, Nyborg, & Furlong, 2004). Strength-based practices and philosophies have been used to inform consultation practices. This, in turn, has prompted a focus on subjective well-being as well as the progress of the development of the individual (Meyers, Meyers, & Grogg, 2004), which is of great interest to consultants within the Australian context. The philosophical shift to strength-based consulting will mean that large portions of the role of educational psychologists will need to grow, such as coaching as an intervention and methods to enhance medium- and high-functioning adolescents. Simultaneously, other aspects of the SPs role, such as testing for funding based on discrepancy and deficit models, may need to diminish. As a result, consultation practices within the Australian context will need to focus on and lead the change in emphasis away from discrepancy- and deficit-based practices to providing evidence-based practices and interventions consistent with strength-based approaches.

Advanced Models Linking Intervention Practices with Consultation

One of the pressing associated problems for school psychologists is managing the balance between the provision of psychological services requiring one-on-one interventions or consultation involving systems and school-level interventions. For example, consultation has a role to play in advocacy, problem-solving and/or diagnosis in RTI. Whether it is policy and identification at tiers 1, 2, and 3 or one-on-one interventions at tier 3 of RTI, consultation knowledge and skills are relevant to both activities. When the skills and competencies are used only at tier 3, there is a danger that the feedback of information that informs policy and organizational learning is lost. Being able to work in-depth, one-on-one for prolonged periods of time with an individual student while providing information to modify the home and school environment in addition to providing information to parents and teachers is a central part of consulting. The focus of this model of intervention is working from the individual to the broader environmental settings. Thus, allowing SPs opportunities to fully engage in consultation roles at multiple levels of schools may appear less efficient, but it may inform multiple practices and inform organizational learning, which leads to far greater efficiencies.

Advanced Models of Consultation Linking Research to Practice

There is a range of models of intervention relevant to consultation that may be employed within the Australian setting. At present there is no one well-accepted, overarching model of consulting. Understanding the various models of consulting in school settings allows SPs to make informed choices.

Models of consultation can be defined in terms of the sphere of their influence. For example, Hazel, Pfaff, Albanes, and Gallagher (2014) investigated the risks associated with year nine students and their educational and psychological needs. This investigation had implications that were influential at the regional, school, year and individual student levels. The data sources that were evaluated by Hazel et al. (2014) included consultation notes, observations, surveys, interviews and district records, in addition to comprehensive consultation involving teachers, teaching teams support staff, school administrators and district personnel. This is a very broad, multilevel impact requiring very different competencies from one-on-one, specialized interventions.

Models can also be determined as a function of the levels of complexity of the process of consulting. For example, Anton-LaHart and Rosenfield (2004) establish that 97% of school psychology consultation instructors indicated that a stage-based approach had been taught, which included reference to the following stages: entry (7%), contracting (56%), problem identification (97%), problem analysis (98%), intervention (97%), evaluation (96%) and closure (3%).

Generic models of change can also inform the practice of consulting in school settings. The Adaptive Change Model (ACM) has been developed from psychological, organizational and general settings in which the management of change is relevant (Bowles, 2006). The stages in this process are openness to opportunity, visualization, planning, action and closure. The three support factors associated with each stage are management of negative emotions, inner drive and social support. These eight stages or factors are known to differentiate people in therapy from a nontherapeutic comparison group, with all eight factors of change indicating higher adaptability to change for the nonclinical respondents (Bowles, 2012).

The ACM is relevant to psychological and school settings as a means of identifying the stage and leading the change process (Bowles & Scull, under review), which is central to the role consultants hold. It also differentiates individual adults who have a preference for contexts where there is stability—a stabilizer group, a group of adaptors who had middle-ranging scores on all eight factors and a group of innovators who have elevated scores on all factors (Bowles & Hattie, 2013). Consultants with such information can help staff responsible for students understand how to effectively assist the student to change, help students to moderate various elements of the change process effectively, and, importantly, assist students to learn to reapply such strategies when required again, for example, assisting a student who has a preference for stability to be more efficient and comfortable with being motivated combined with planning a task and what that might entail. Other examples include helping a student who is innovative (changes a lot) but impulsive to slow down and be more thoughtful and deliberate to curb impulsivity; helping the anxious student who prefers stability to deal with negative emotions and seek help from a teacher (social support) to keep them motivated and focused on task (inner drive) and to limit emoting or overly attending to depressive or demotivating affects (negative emotions). Precisely defining the aspects of interventions and training students to be self-managing and staff to be facilitators in change is a central part of consulting.

As noted by Frank and Kratochwill (2014), "a substantial amount of evidence spanning decades has clearly demonstrated that the quality of the relationship between the consultant and consultee is highly predictive of intervention adoption, implementation quality, and ultimately student outcomes" (2014, p. 26; see also Erchul & Raven, 1997; Gutkin & Curtis, 1999). Assisting the consultee (e.g., the teacher or school staff) to be more adaptive and to adopt practices that focus and refocus on changes for students is central to assisting students. By assisting school staff to apply the elements of the adaptive change model (Bowles, 2006), consultees can adopt practices that strategically and persistently seek opportunities to change the child and their circumstances, imagine, plan, act and define outcomes to the benefit of the child. Consultees can become more experimental, trying and retrying new avenues of intervention, and can be assisted to apply the support factors of the model by consultants. These factors prompt the teacher and school staff to seek social support of every kind (e.g., personal, mentoring, specialist profession) to help them help their student when required, to manage their motivation and inner drive and, finally, to know and own their negative emotions and manage these emotions to the benefit of their student(s) (Bowles & Fallon, 2003). In specific reference to the consultant as a change agent to staff, their approach is a collegial activity comprising a range of skills including coaching, mentoring, facilitating, demonstrating, and never giving up, but ever-exploring new options to facilitate learning for students and teachers.

In sum, when consultation practices are combined with evidence-based methods and models of change and evaluated and applied in conjunction with known methods of intervention, the effectiveness of the change process is accentuated. Within the Australian setting, this level of consultation practice needs to be fostered and evaluated.

While the possibilities noted in the section will have a positive and growing impact on consulting in school psychology in the Australian context over the next several years, there are other further opportunities that are well worth pursuing. These future opportunities are mentioned next.

FUTURE OPPORTUNITIES

There are also many opportunities that will be made available to SPs in relation to consulting practices over the next several decades. These include adapting practices informed by large data sets, taking more leadership roles at the school and regional levels, informing practice with greater cultural diversity and incorporating new technologies.

Big Data

Many of the factors influencing the effectiveness of psychological practice may be small but substantial when applied over large groups of students. Information about such factors is only available through the gathering of large amounts of data or using "big data," that is, when an epidemiological approach to data gathering and analysis is employed. The outcomes would be relevant to policy, system-wide application, cross-disciplinary and multidisciplinary collaboration, and training. This is clearly leading to the development of large-scale datasets and long-term engagement in research; however, the "implications for future school-based consultation is the emerging database about constructive environments and institutions (e.g., communities, families, and schools) that promote outcomes congruent with positive psychology and primary prevention" (Meyers et al., 2004, p. 264). Such an approach would be a major change in direction for school consulting in Australia; however, it would provide evidence-based information currently not available to school consultants.

Leadership Roles: Leading Consultations and Consultation as Leadership

The second area of opportunity, unrelated to the first, is the establishment of career- and course-based pathways linking best practice to consultants in leadership roles. There is a need for a redefinition from a referral-based, individually focused, deficit approach to a service delivery model based on consultation and informed by public health perspectives of multilevel prevention and intervention services. This redefining of the consulting school psychologist's role must integrate systems, schools and services to individuals (Graden, 2004). It would mean that SPs providing consultation would be involved in high-level leadership. This would require integration of services at the national level. In Australia, this would mean building research and networks beyond systemic boundaries/state boundaries, beyond primary-/secondary-level boundaries, beyond sectors—public, private, religious—and, importantly, beyond professional boundaries.

Despite this possibility, leadership, consulting and practice management are not competencies associated with psychological training. Currently there are eight requirements of training for those seeking registration as (school) educational and developmental psychologists in Australia. These are similar to the eight categories defined by Ysseldyke, Burns, and Rosenfield (2009), which specifically relate to the United States but which have relevance internationally. The change to leadership as a role would mean a change to the following current registration requirements to practice in Australia (Psychology Board of Australia, 2010):

- Knowledge of the discipline
- Ethical, legal and professional matters
- Psychological assessment and measurement
- Intervention strategies
- Research and evaluation
- Communication and interpersonal relationships
- Working within a cross-cultural context
- Practice across the lifespan, including leadership in managing psychological interventions when consulting with nonregistered staff and organizations.

Providing training in leadership roles in schools as well as in private practice settings would also mean an expansion to the curriculum at the university level and changes to placement to emphasize the leadership role of the school psychologists as consultants. Alternatively, it is possible that this ninth area of leadership may be better dealt with in conjunction with the development of a postgraduate, postpractice course or refresher for those seeking professional development.

In concluding this section on leadership, it is worth recalling the cautionary words of Graden (2004), who suggests that if SPs' practices continue to focus on assessment, the profession will be marginalized. Graden (2004) suggests that SPs must change to promote reform, work on teams and focus on intervention and prevention practices from a position of leadership. Such leadership roles are consistent with instructional consulting (Rosenfield, 1987) and would allow for a better utilizing of the skills of SPs, but this is not common in the Australian educational context.

Cultural Diversity and Multicultural Consulting

The next opportunity that consultants in psychology and schools can make is to embrace cultural diversity and multicultural consulting. Understanding how people from different cultures approach psychological services and go about help seeking is critical if consulting is to be effective (Hamid, Simmonds, & Bowles, 2009). This will have multiple and long-term benefits for students, their families, their schools and communities, and for the profession. Meyers et al. (2004) maintained that multilevel consultation models need to address children's needs within an ecological context, orienting interventions toward considering the cultural background of those with whom consultants engaged. *Multicultural consultation* is defined as "a culturally sensitive, indirect service in which the consultant adjusts the consultation services to address the needs and cultural values of the consultee, the client, or both" (Tarver, Behring, & Ingraham, 1998, p. 58). The principles that should be embedded within preservice courses and professional development associated with multicultural consultation are described by Ingraham (2000, 2014) as:

- Understanding one's own culture (race, ethnicity, socioeconomic context, acculturation, etc.)
- Understanding the impact(s) of one's own culture on others
- Respecting and valuing other cultures (with some knowledge of the history, values and belief of other cultural groups and models of racial/ethnic/cultural identity)
- Understanding individual differences within cultural groups and the multiple cultural identities prevalent in many individuals
- Cross-cultural communication and multicultural consultation approaches for developing and maintaining rapport throughout consultation
- Understanding cultural saliency and how to build bridges across salient differences
- Understanding the cultural context for consultation (dominant culture, culture of the school or community)
- Multicultural consultation and interventions appropriate for the consultee(s) and client(s).

With increasing levels of migration around the world, there will be a growing need to reemphasize the relevance of consulting with cultural sensitivity while respecting cultural diversity. In the Australian context, racial, cultural and ethnic respect is mandated by law.

New Applications for Technologies

The final opportunity for SPs is the emergence of new technology and its use in practice. The use of new technology for SPs is pertinent in the Australian setting because the majority of Australians have a familiarity with the technology. According to Gilmore, Fletcher, and Hudson (2013), there are several areas in which technology will impact practice and consulting in school settings. For example, the development of apps related to a variety of assistive technologies grows, and they are useful for assisting therapy (Cherniack, 2011), psychoeducational approaches (Warschausky et al., 2012), social skill development through game playing (Danilovic, 2009) and assisting those with disabilities (Lancioni, Sigafoos, O'Reilly, & Singh, 2013). Through being conversant with new technologies, consultants can assist children, their families and teachers to meet the needs of those with whom they work. It is appropriate that SPs endeavor to embrace the use of new technologies as tools that they can utilize with individuals in one-on-one practice and consultation.

Summary of Potential Opportunities

The present review has covered a range of opportunities that will be relevant to SPs over the next several decades. Some of the highlighted opportunities include the emergence of stronger evidence-based consulting, the inclusion of leadership roles for SPs, multicultural consulting and the application of new technologies to consulting practices in Australian school settings. It is necessary that SPs endeavor to embrace these new opportunities in order to maintain and expand the impact and relevance of psychologists in consultation positions.

CONCLUSION AND FUTURE DIRECTIONS

From this outline of pressures on those who practice consulting in schools, it is clear that change is necessary. First, there are serious threats to the continuance and growth of school psychology and consulting practice in the school setting in Australia. Threats in this chapter have been described as issues related to training and practice as well as the age and knowledge base of the workforce currently practicing as SPs. These threats will need to be addressed in the future; otherwise other occupations and professions will adapt to the space for which consulting school psychologists have been trained.

Most noteworthy, after consideration of these threats, is the advent of very positive developments in school consulting. Each of these positive developments has the prospect of strengthening practice and, importantly, improving the outcomes for consultees. Evidence-based practice and attention to RTI will make practice more efficient by targeting interventions more effectively. Strength-based practices again require refocusing to include the broader setting and those working in it, possibly right through to the policy level when attempting to assist the individual. The advanced models of intervention in consultation and links to research through these models will also require a reframing of where the consulting psychologist puts the majority of work time and effort. These developments will place external pressures on psychologists, who will have to continue training and professional development to improve the effectiveness of their practice by including aspects associated with consulting.

Finally, the possibility of embracing future opportunities is a real challenge, as it will require the refocusing and reallocation of resources in addition to changing of roles. The background and training of consulting psychologists working in schools is refocused on policy and leadership and new areas of practice as much as one-on-one intervention and testing. Engaging school psychologists more in the range of consulting activities will better equip educational systems to provide engagement and interventions across educational settings and to students in all the states and territories of Australia. Consulting SPs are also exceptionally well placed to provide leadership and consulting generally, including on matters of cultural diversity and multicultural issues in both the school context and at the community level. SPs should become very conversant with the prospect of technological advancements and the application of such technologies to assist students appropriately and efficiently, either instead of previous evidence-based practices or as adjuncts to such practices. Accommodating these changes and moving to a stronger consulting focus in practice will strengthen the role of SPs in Australia in the future.

REFERENCES

Anton-LaHart, J., & Rosenfield, S. (2004). A survey of pre-service consultation training in school psychology programs. *Journal of Educational and Psychological Consultation, 15,* 41–62.

Australian Health Practitioners Regulation Agency (AHPRA). (2015, October 14). *Endorsement.* Retrieved from http://www.psychologyboard.gov.au/Endorsement.aspx

Australian Health Practitioners Regulation Agency (AHPRA). (2015, October 25). Retrieved from http://www.ahpra.gov.au/Registration/Registration-Process.aspx

Australian Psychological Society (APS). (2015, October 14). *Member group: The APS College of educational and developmental psychology.* Retrieved from https://groups.psychology.org.au/cedp/

Australian Psychology Accreditation Council. (2014). *Australian psychology accreditation council rules for accreditation.* Melbourne: APAC.

Australian Psychology Accreditation Council (APAC). (2015, October 25). Retrieved from https://www.psychologycouncil.org.au/course-search/australia/vic/

Barlow, D. H., Hayes, S. C., & Nelson, R. O. (1984). *The scientist–practitioner: Research and accountability in clinical and educational settings.* New York: Pergamon.

Bell, H. D., & McKenzie, V. (2013). Perceptions and realities: The role of school psychologists in Melbourne, Australia. *The Australian Educational and Developmental Psychologist, 30,* 54–73.

Bowles, T. (2006). The adaptive change model: An advance on the transtheoretical model of change. *The Journal of Psychology: Interdisciplinary and Applied, 140,* 439–457.

Bowles, T. (2012). Developing adaptive change capabilities through client-centred therapy. *Behaviour Change, 29,* 258–271.

Bowles, T., & Fallon, B. J. (2003). The experience of changing and the relationship between changing and coping: An adult perspective. *Australian Journal of Psychology, 55,* 43–50.

Bowles, T., & Hattie, J. (2013). Towards positive adaptive change: The association of three typologies of agency with motivational factors. *Australian Psychologist, 48,* 437–444.

Bowles, T., & Scull, J. (under review). The adaptive change model: A conceptual framework for teaching and consultation in schools.

Boyle, C. (2014). The death of difference: Psychology is psychology. *The Australian Educational and Developmental Psychologist, 31*(2), iii–iv.

Campbell, M., & Colmar, S. (2014). Current status and future trends of school counselling in Australia. *Journal of Asia Pacific Counseling, 4,* 181–197. doi: http://eprints.qut.edu.au/78477/

Cherniack, E. P. (2011). Not just fun and games: Applications of virtual reality in the identification and rehabilitation of cognitive disorders of the elderly. *Disability and Rehabilitation: Assistive Technology, 6,* 283–289.

Coates, D., & Howe, D. (2014). The importance and benefits of youth participation in mental health settings from the perspective of the headspace Gosford youth alliance in Australia. *Children & Youth Services Review, 46,* 294–299. doi: 10.1016/j.childyouth.2014.09.012

Collins, A. S., & Proctor, S. L. (2009). Turning the ideal into reality: Student perspectives on Blueprint III's implications for graduate education in consultation. *Journal of Educational and Psychological Consultation, 19,* 267–274.

Cook, C. R., Jimerson, S. R., & Begeny, J. C. (2010). A model for predicting the presence of school psychology: an international examination of sociocultural, sociopolitical and socioeconomic influences. *School Psychology International, 31*(4), 438–461.

Danilovic, S. (2009). Review of "Autism and second life—An introduction". *Journal on Developmental Disabilities, 15,* 125–129.

Erchul, W. P., & Raven, B. H. (1997). Social power in school consultation: A contemporary view of French and Raven's bases of power model. *Journal of School Psychology, 35,* 137–171.

Farrell, P. (2009). The developing role of school and educational psychologists in supporting children, schools and families. *Papeles del Psicólogico, 30*(1), 74–85.

Farrell, P., Jimerson, S., Kalambouka, A., & Benoit, J. (2005). Teachers' perceptions of school psychologists in different countries. *School Psychology International, 26*, 525–544.

Faulkner, M. (2007). School psychologists or psychologists in schools? *Inpsych, 3*, 1–4.

Feifer, S. (2010). How SLD manifests in reading. In D. P. Flanagan & V. C. Alfonso (Eds.), *Essentials of specific learning disability identification* (pp. 21–41). New York: John Wiley & Sons.

Fletcher, J. M., Barth, A. E., & Stuebing, K. K. (2011). A response to intervention (RTI) approach to SLD identification. In D. P. Flanagan & V. C. Alfonso (Eds.), *Essentials of specific learning disability identification* (pp. 115–143). New York: John Wiley & Sons.

Fletcher, J. M., Bloor, K., Crossman, C., Thornton, J., Briggs, E., Hawkins, T., & Cardwell, K. (2010). Profiling the college of educational and developmental psychologists: An examination of demographics, professional practice, attitudes and professional development preferences. *The Australian Educational and Developmental Psychologist, 27*(1), 1–19. doi: 10.1375/aedp.27.1.1

Forman, S. G., Shapiro, E. S., Codding, R. S., Gonzales, J. E., Reddy, L. A., Rosenfield, S. A., . . . Stoiber, K. C. (2013). Implementation science and school psychology. *School Psychology Quarterly, 28*, 77–100.

Frank, J. L., & Kratochwill, T. R. (2014). School-based problem-solving consultation: plotting a new course for evidence-based research and practice in consultation. In W. P. Erchul & S. M. Sheridan (Eds.), *Handbook of research in school consultation* (2nd ed., pp. 18–41). New York, NY: Routledge.

Gilmore, L., Fletcher, J., & Hudson, A. (2013). A commentary on the current and future status of educational and developmental psychology. *The Australian Educational and Developmental Psychologist, 30*(1), 1–12.

Graden, J. (2004). Synthesis and commentary: Arguments for change to consultation, prevention, and intervention: Will school psychology ever achieve this promise? *Journal of Educational and Psychological Consultation, 15*, 345–359.

Gravois, T., & Rosenfield, S. (2002). A multi-dimensional framework for evaluation of instructional consultation teams. *Journal of Applied School Psychology, 19*, 5–29.

Gutkin, T. B., & Curtis, M. J. (1999). School-based consultation: The art and science of indirect service delivery. In C. R. Reynolds & T. B. Gutkin (Eds.), *The handbook of school psychology* (3rd ed., pp. 598–637). New York: Wiley.

Hamid, P. D., Simmonds, J. G., & Bowles, T. V. (2009). Asian Australian acculturation and attitudes toward seeking professional psychological help. *Australian Journal of Psychology, 61*(2), 69–76.

Hazel, C. E., Pfaff, K., Albanes, J., & Gallagher, J. (2014). Multi-level consultation with an urban school district to promote 9th grade supports for on-time graduation. *Psychology in the Schools, 51*, 395–420.

Health Practitioner Regulation National Law Act 2009 (Vic) No. 79.

Hutton, C., & Gunn, J. (2007). Do longer consultations improve the management of psychological problems in general practice? A systematic literature review. *BMC Health Services Research, 7*, 71–86.

Hylander, I. (2000). *Turning Processes: The Change of Representations in Consultee-Centered Case Consultation.* Linkoping Studies in Education and Psychology No. 74. Linkoping, Sweden: Department of Education and Psychology, Linkoping University, SE 581 83.

Ingraham, C. L. (2000). Consultation through a multicultural lens: Multicultural and cross-cultural consultation in schools. *School Psychology Review, 29*, 320–343.

Ingraham, C. L. (2014). Studying multicultural aspects of consultation. In W. P. Erchul & S. M. Sheridan (Eds.), *Handbook of research in school consultation: Empirical foundations for the field* (2nd ed., pp. 269–291). New York, NY: Routledge.

Jimerson, S. R., Oakland, T. D., & Farrell, P. T. (Eds.). (2007). *The handbook of international school psychology.* Thousand Oaks, CA: Sage.

Jimerson, S. R., Sharkey, J. D., Nyborg, V., & Furlong, M. J. (2004). Strength-based assessment and school psychology: A summary and synthesis. *The California School Psychologist, 9*(1), 9–19.

Kratochwill, T. R., & Shernoff, E. S. (2004). Evidence-based practice: Promoting evidence-based interventions in school psychology. *School Psychology Review, 33*, 34–48.

Lancioni, G. E., Sigafoos, J., O'Reilly, M. F., & Singh, N. N. (2013). *Assistive technology: Interventions for individuals with severe/profound and multiple disabilities.* New York: Springer.

Meyers, J., Meyers, A. B., & Grogg, K. (2004). Prevention through consultation: A model to guide future developments in the field of school psychology. *Journal of Educational and Psychological Consultation, 15*, 257–276.

Neimeyer, G. J., Taylor, J. M., & Rozensky, R. H. (2012). The diminishing durability of knowledge in professional psychology: A Delphi Poll of specialties and proficiencies. *Professional Psychology: Research and Practice, 43*, 364–371.

Psychology Board of Australia. (2010). *General registration standard.* Retrieved from http://www.psychologyboard.gov.au/Standards-and-Guidelines/Registration-Standards.aspx

Psychology Board of Australia. (2015a, October 14). *Areas of practice endorsement.* Retrieved from http://www. psychologyboard.gov.au/Endorsement.aspx

Psychology Board of Australia. (2015b, October 14). *Continuing professional development registration standard.* Retrieved from http://www.psychologyboard.gov.au/Standards-and-Guidelines/Registration-Standards.aspx

Reschly, D. J., & Ysseldyke, J. E. (2002). Paradigm shift: The past is not the present. In A. Thomas & J. Grimes (Eds.), *Best practices in school psychology IV* (Vol. 1, pp. 3–20). Bethesda, MD: National Association of School Psychologists.

Rosenfield, S. (1987). *Instructional consultation.* London: Routledge.

Rosenfield, S. (1992). Developing school-based consultation teams: A design for organizational change. *School Psychology Quarterly, 7,* 27–46.

Rosenfield, S. (1995a). Instructional consultation: a model for service delivery in the schools. *Journal of Educational and Psychological Consultation, 6,* 297–316.

Rosenfield, S. (1995b). The practice of instructional consultation. *Journal of Educational and Psychological Consultation, 6,* 317–327.

Rosenfield, S. (2002). Developing instructional consultants: From novice to competent to expert. *Journal of Educational and Psychological Consultation, 13,* 97–111.

Rosenfield, S. (2008). Best practices in instructional consultation and instructional consultation teams. In A. Thomas & J. Grimes (Eds.), *Best practices in school psychology V* (pp. 1645–1660). Bethesda, MD: NASP.

Rosenfield, S., Silva, A., & Gravois, T. (2008). Bringing instructional consultation to scale: Research and development of IC and IC Teams. In W. Erchul & S. Sheridan (Eds.), *Handbook of research in school consultation: Empirical foundations for the field* (2nd ed., pp. 203–223). New York: Routledge.

Stoner, G., & Green, S. (1992). Reconsidering the scientist-practitioner model for school psychology practice. *School Psychology Review, 21,* 155–167.

Thielking, M., & Jimerson, S. R. (2006). Perspectives regarding the role of school psychologists: Perceptions of teachers, principals, and school psychologists in Victoria, Australia. *Australian Journal of Guidance and Counselling, 16*(2), 211–223.

Warschausky, S., Van Tubbergen, M., Asbell, S., Kaufman, J., Ayyangar, R., & Donders, J. (2012). Modified test administration using assistive technology: Preliminary psychometric findings. *Assessment, 19,* 472–479.

West, J. F., & Idol, L. (1987). School consultation (Part I): An interdisciplinary perspective on theory, models, and research. *Journal of Learning Disabilities, 20,* 388–408.

Ysseldyke, J., Burns, M. K., & Rosenfield, S. (2009). Blueprints on the future of training and practice in school psychology: What do they say about educational and psychological consultation? *Journal of Educational and Psychological Consultation, 19,* 177–196.

5

A MULTILEVEL APPROACH TO SYSTEM-LEVEL CONSULTATION
Critical Components and Transnational Considerations

Chryse Hatzichristou, Aikaterini Lampropoulou,
Georgios Georgouleas, and Spryridoula Mihou

In recent years, traditional school psychological services have proven to be inadequate to respond to the increased challenges present in the school environment. The need for reform has been stressed; several studies in different countries have emphasized that there is a growing number of children with unmet socioemotional and educational needs and that the services provided (e.g., health care, education, juvenile justice and child welfare systems) to them are often inappropriate, insufficient, and poorly coordinated (Hatzichristou, 2011; Oakland & Jimerson, 2007).

Within this context, an effort has been made to provide alternative psychological services in the Greek school communities. Consultation constitutes one of the basic indirect services provided; special emphasis has been given not only to the provision of consultation but to the appropriate training of future school psychologists as well. This chapter presents the multilevel alternative model developed in Greece for combining theory, training, and practice of consultation. This model incorporates the current theoretical approaches and research data into the development and implementation of prevention and intervention programs. In all these programs, consultation is a basic component, and the appropriate training of consultation is considered to be a significant dimension of the described model.

In this chapter consultation is approached at two levels. The first addresses the needs of trainee psychologists, since they will be the providers of consultation. The second one addresses the needs of teachers, since they will be the recipients of consultation services. In addition, a model for consultation training and provision is described. In this context, consultation training issues are discussed by presenting the training process developed at the University of Athens for future consultants. Furthermore, issues regarding the provision of consultation are also developed by presenting two intervention projects: Education of Roma Children and Connecting for Caring Project (that includes the programs Supporting in Crisis, E.M.E.I.Σ. Program, and International Program WeC.A.R.E.).

Consultation training and consultation provision are directly linked in this model because trainees participate in multiple ways in the interventions presented. Training and provision of consultation are interrelated; they constitute the two dimensions of the proposed *synthetic* model in an effort to combine theory and practice and to cover the needs of future school psychologists (and respectively the needs of the school community) in the best possible way.

ALTERNATIVE MODEL FOR THE PROVISION OF SCHOOL PSYCHOLOGICAL SERVICES

During the last two decades, the field of psychology has rapidly expanded in Greece. However, the provision of school psychological services in mainstream public schools is limited, with psychologists mainly working in special education (Hatzichristou & Polychroni, 2014; Hatzichristou, Polychroni, & Georgouleas, 2007). This constituted a challenge to develop an alternative service delivery model that would address the growing and unmet needs of different Greek student population groups (Hatzichristou, 2004, 2011, 2014; Hatzichristou, Lampropoulou, Lykitsakou, & Dimitropoulou, 2010).

The databased model of alternative school psychological services was developed in four phases. The first three phases documented the needs of Greek students, teachers, and families as well as their attitudes toward mental health services and professionals. In Phase 1, an empirical database was developed to describe the profiles of school adjustment and performance of "average" Greek students. In Phase 2, the profiles of at-risk students with unmet needs were explored, and in Phase 3, profiles were developed of the particular needs of specific school districts in communities where various intervention programs were implemented. Throughout the years, each phase was enriched by new research programs and additional goals and with several publications in national and international journals and books (Hatzichristou, 2011).

In the fourth phase, the empirical data derived from the first three phases of the model were integrated into a comprehensive prevention-consultation approach that led to the foundation and development of the Center for Research and Practice of School Psychology (CRPSP) in the Department of Psychology at the University of Athens. The main goals and activities of the CRPSP are (a) promotion of university–school–community partnerships and collaboration; (b) education, preservice and in-service training for graduate students, school psychologists, teachers, and parents; (c) scientific research and publications; and (d) development, implementation, and evaluation of multilevel interventions in the school community (Hatzichristou, 2011; Hatzichristou et al., 2010). Within this context a number of prevention and intervention programs have been developed and implemented in different educational and cultural contexts for the promotion of school resilience, well-being, and crisis management (Hatzichristou, 2014, 2013a; Hatzichristou, Adamopoulou, & Lampropoulou, 2014; Hatzichristou, Lykitsakou, Lampropoulou, & Dimitropoulou, 2010).

Multilevel Approach of School Well-Being: Conceptual Framework

All the activities of the center are developed based on a synthetic approach to school community well-being that has been proposed by Hatzichristou, Lykitsakou et al. (2010). This approach has emerged from the current trends in psychology and school mental health that stress the need to shift away from a focus on individual problems to a focus on positive psychology perspectives and systems interventions that emphasize students' strengths and contextual protective factors (Biglan, Flay, Embry, & Sandler, 2012).

The proposed approach to school community well-being, apart from the systemic approach and the emphasis on positive psychology, incorporates current trends, the latest theoretical approaches, and practice models from resilient, effective schools, schools as caring communities and social-emotional learning literature (Bickel & Beaujean, 2005; Doll, Zucker, & Brehm, 2004; Esquivel, Doll, & Oades-Sese, 2011; Henderson & Milstein, 2008; Kolar, 2011; Kress & Elias, 2006; Luthar, 2006; Masten, 2001, 2011; O'Dougherty & Masten, 2005). Integrating these theoretical components in system-level interventions, schools can enhance resilience and promote positive school climates at all levels. The effective schools model promotes a positive school climate, and schools function as caring communities and provide not only opportunities for learning but also for the development of positive relationships that are important protective factors and contribute to the promotion of resilience (Blum & Libbey, 2004; Masten & Reed, 2002).

This conceptual approach was further developed in an effort to design intervention programs that respond to the immediate needs of the school communities during the economic crisis in Greece. Crisis intervention was included in this approach, and a special emphasis was put on multilevel resilience promotion (individual, classroom, and school level) that can have an important protective effect against life adversities. Within this systemic perspective, teachers can potentially be directed away from a deficit orientation frame to one that recognizes student strengths and contextual protective factors (Morrison, Brown, D'Incau, & O'Farrell, 2006). Figure 5.1 describes the components of the model.

Since consultation constitutes an important dimension of school psychological services, special emphasis has been given to the provision of consultation within the context

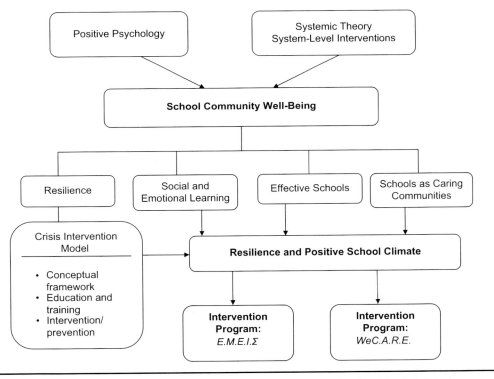

Figure 5.1 Conceptual Framework: Multilevel Approach of Promoting Resilience and Positive Climate in School

of the described model. Consultation in this context has been defined as a "strength-based, cross-system problem solving and decision-making model wherein parents, teachers and other care givers or service providers work as partners and share responsibility" (Sheridan & Kratochwill, 2008, p. 25).

CONSULTATION TRAINING AT THE UNIVERSITY

The provision of consultation has been considered a means for addressing the needs of the school community in a nondirect way and is one of the most important dimensions of a school psychologist's role. Therefore, in order to prepare future school psychologists, there is a special focus on consultation training that includes specialized courses as well as active participation in all interventions developed within the context of the alternative model. The following sections present the University of Athens's Department of Psychology training model and the application of interventions within the paradigm of consultation provision.

Training and continuing professional development have a decisive impact on the specialty definition, the roles of school psychologists, and the nature of psychological services provided in schools (Hatzichristou et al., 2010; Hatzichristou & Polychroni, 2014). Training in consultation is of great importance for future school psychologists, and learning to become a consultant requires much more than just the provision of theoretical models and knowledge. Consultation can be considered as a set of skills that can be learned and applied, but, as Thomas (2004) indicates, consultation can be mainly viewed as an "art, science, craft and profession." This approach reflects the importance and complexity of consultation and at the same time the difficulty of preparing and enabling trainees to become efficient consultants.

Despite the importance of consultation, there is a relative silence regarding consultation training (Rosenfield, Levinsohn-Klyap, & Cramer, 2010). This is further supported by researchers who have identified a lack of literature on consultation training and, especially, on the application of consultation skills by novice school psychologists (Truscott & Albritton, 2011). In addition, the main deficiencies of training programs have been identified: the lack of inclusion of skill application, the focus on multiple theoretical issues rather than on methods to develop competence, and the lack of sufficient supervised practical experience (Anton-Lahart & Rosenfield, 2004; Hazel, Laviolette, & Lineman, 2010; Rosenfield, 2012).

Introductory-Level Undergraduate Courses

The didactic knowledge learned in a university is suggested by Rosenfield (2012) to be a good start, though it is not enough for someone to learn how to become a school consultant. In the University of Athens, Department of Psychology, courses on consultation are introduced in the undergraduate program (Hatzichristou, 2011). Issues about consultation are briefly presented within the context of the introductory course in school psychology, which is required for all psychology major students and is optional for students of other departments (such as philology, English language). In this course (for which the first author is the instructor), issues regarding the definition of the school psychology specialty, the role of the school psychologist, and the provision of school psychological services are presented. Special emphasis is placed on the provision of consultation and the skills of an effective consultant.

A more specialized course on consultation is also provided to students in which consultation theory and practice are further elaborated with the combination of theory presentation and practice experiences. A special chapter on consultation in the *Handbook of*

School Psychology (Hatzichristou, 2011) is provided to students as the basic study material, and a specialized book on psychological consultation and collaboration (Brown et al., 2006) has been translated into Greek.

Graduate-Level Training

At the graduate level, a specialized course on primary prevention and consultation is provided as part of the University of Athens School Psychology Graduate Program. The basic objectives of the graduate course are to provide students with insight into consultation issues and with knowledge and understanding of the relevant theory as well as to provide them with the necessary skills in order to become effective school psychologists. In particular, the main goals of the course are to: (a) train school psychology graduate students in the implementation of consultation; (b) develop in students the ability to use a comprehensive consultation approach in order to implement and achieve positive outcomes; (c) provide students with a solid theoretical background on consultation; and (d) promote their sense of efficacy when applying consultation in their professional contexts. The structure of the course (see Table 5.1) is designed by taking into account the main objectives and the basic issues on consultation training identified in the literature.

Table 5.1 Structure of Consultation Course in the Graduate Program of School Psychology at the University of Athens

Content	• Introduction in consultation • Introduction in the basic models of consultation • Mental health consultation, theory and concepts (i.e., goals, stages, skills, models, sources of difficulties, important issues) • Supervised practice
Purpose/ outcomes	• Acquirement of knowledge and theoretical background • Awareness on multiple consultation issues and application of consultation • Understanding consultation (goals, concepts, difficulties) • Acquirement and application of skills • Application of consultation on the Greek educational setting • Provide the basis for becoming efficient consultants • Enhance students' self-confidence as consultants
Techniques	• Didactic presentation of theoretical issues • Application and demonstration (i.e., practice exercises, tapes) • Participation of students in the training seminars of the interventions developed by Center for Research and Practice of School Psychology (CRPSP) in the Department of Psychology at the University of Athens and attendance of consultation process applied within the context of these sessions • Case studies analysis • Simulation (i.e., role-playing) with feedback from the instructors and the class • Real case application with feedback from the instructors and the class • Supervision
Studying material	• Textbook and articles • Case studies
Assignment	• Presentation of the consultation sessions applied in a real case from the professional setting and analysis based on the theory
Assessment	• Written qualitative evaluation of the process

In short, during this course the most important aspects of consultation are discussed and the most important theoretical approaches and models of consultation are presented, with a special emphasis on mental health consultation. Although all four types of mental health consultation (Caplan, 1970) were presented to students, the main focus of the course was on consultee-centered consultation. The practical aspect of the course includes the following:

- Exercises on the theoretical issues that were discussed in each section
- Simulating and role-playing of consultation with a consultee of their choice (this could be either a colleague or a person of their choice who is a teacher or a parent) The sessions were recorded and then presented to the whole class. Feedback was then provided by the class and the instructors (the main course instructor and an experienced school psychologist with expertise in consultation).
- Supervision for students regarding their consultation practice
- Application of the consultation process to a real case from their internship and a written report. The report includes:
  - short theoretical literature review on consultation
  - descriptions of the detailed sessions
  - analysis of the sessions based on the theory
  - identification of the strengths and weaknesses of their consultation process and justification based on the theory
  - suggestions on what they would alter in the process based on the identified limitations
  - feedback and comments regarding the process and the practical application of consultation.

In addition, all graduate students participated in the training seminars of the interventions, which will be described later in the chapter, in order to gain experience in the practice of consultation. The training activities of the center together with the course provided a unique chance to introduce students to consultation and to provide them with a deeper understanding since they themselves attended the training activities as members of the teachers' groups. Students' participation in the training seminars developed by CRPSP gave them the chance to observe the application of program-centered consultation as well as administrative-centered consultation.

TRAINING TO IMPLEMENT CRITICAL CONSULTATION COMPONENTS

Rosenfield (2012) argues that there are certain basic components that are critical to effective consultation and that novice consultants find difficult to apply. These components include: (a) context understanding; (b) the working relationship between consultant and consultee; (c) communication skills; and (d) a systematic approach to addressing consultee's concerns. This perspective is confirmed by our experience and the work with the students. Most of the students, if not all, express their difficulty in applying these components effectively and with confidence. Therefore, a main priority should be to provide students with supervised practice experience related to these components.

These basic components, along with the most important concepts and stages of mental health consultation, formed the basis for developing the training approach in the University of Athens graduate course as it is described in the following sections.

Introduction to Organization/Understanding School Culture and Context

Within the context of the course, special emphasis was placed on introduction to an organization, since all students were placed in schools during their internships. The first step was the didactic presentation of theory on introduction to organization. In addition, practice exercises were applied, addressing mainly two levels (a) ways of achieving a successful introduction and the main issues to be considered and (b) case studies where students had to identify the ways the consultant tried to understand the working context to identify context issues that the school psychologist failed to recognize and to determine in what ways they became barriers to successful intervention.

Most of the students at this point were in their internships and were already placed in schools. However, on a retrospective basis, students were asked to consider and present: (a) the way they work on the entry stage; (b) what went wrong and what right and what they would do differently; (c) the specific context factors of the school that could influence their interventions; and (d) in what ways these factors interrelated and possibly impacted the case they presented.

Forming a Relationship

The importance of relationships was a matter of concern in the students' training. The simulation practice (role-playing) offered a chance for students to apply their skills for forming a relationship and to gain feedback on their efforts. Furthermore, during the presentation of their consultation on real cases, issues were discussed, such as: (a) in what way they tried to form the relationship; (b) to what extent they thought they had succeeded; (c) what went wrong or right; (d) what things they would do differently; and (e) how they felt the relationship they had facilitated (or did not) the rest of the process. Feedback was then provided by the consultee, in cases of in-class role-playing, as well as by the rest of the class and by the instructors.

Communication Skills

Regardless of what consultation model is applied, a basic component of the consultation process is the communication skills of the consultant (Rosenfield, 2004, 2012). The interaction between consultant and consultee, the mutual communication path, and the communication techniques required are of vital importance. What to say and how to say it has always been the main source of anxiety for consultants. Training should definitely include teaching students the communication skills, but it should also provide the chance to apply them not only in the simulation environment but in real settings. The main areas of concern as identified by Newman (2012) are: (a) using skills covered in coursework; (b) collaborative language; and (c) using nuanced communication skills with a purpose. The university course aims to attend to the specific needs of graduate students in the best way possible through the application of several techniques, such as didactic presentation, book exercises, role-playing, self-monitoring, examples of successful and unsuccessful use of communication skills, and supervised practice.

Stages of Consultation

Assessment

Assessment is the critical stage where the problem is identified and analyzed. Some of the main areas of concern in this stage for novice consultants are lack of academic knowledge related to referrals of learning problems and lack of skill in: (a) clarifying the problem; (b) prioritizing a concern; (c) creating a shared problem frame; and (d) conducting a needs assessment (Newman, 2012). These issues were considered as basic priorities in the course, aiming to strengthen students in their role as consultants. Provision of knowledge through teaching and reading material, in combination with the techniques for practice and supervision, formed the basis for addressing these concerns effectively.

Intervention

Intervention design, implementation, and evaluation are equally important stages for the consultation process. The main areas of concern for novice consultants as identified by Newman (2012) are: (a) lack of knowledge; (b) coordinating interventions and/or resources; (c) interventions that do not match the problem; (d) interventions that are not clearly described; (e) interventions that are not acceptable to the consultee; and (f) interventions that lack treatment integrity in the implementation. In an effort to address these issues and assist students to overcome these barriers, a combination of approaches and techniques was used. Didactic presentation, case studies analysis, book exercises, simulation, and supervised application of consultation were some of the means employed to address these areas of concern within the context of the course.

Supervision

Supervision, one of the most basic techniques and the primary pedagogical tool used by trainers, is an essential facet of training in school psychology. Research shows that consultation practicum experiences and consultation supervision are often absent from many consultation training courses; this has been identified as a significant shortcoming (Newman, 2012; Rosenfield, 2012). There are several techniques used in supervision to support the development of consultation skills of students, such as self-report, case notes, audio and videotaping, and opportunities for reflection. Supervision can focus on the past, the present, and the future and can have the main goals of linking theory with practice, reflecting on actions taken, identifying strengths and weaknesses, promoting students' confidence, and enhancing their future consultation effectiveness. Therefore, supervision was provided to students in multiple situations in an effort to address issues that affect students, such as the feeling of discomfort, the relationship with the supervisor, adequate time, and quality of supervision.

Application on a Real Case

Students were required to conduct a consultation session on a real case of their choice from their internship. They had to record the session and present it to the class. Supervision was provided throughout the process. During the presentations, students have to answer questions that would cover the most significant areas of concern as these are identified in the literature: (a) academic knowledge (how it is reflected in practice); (b) supervision feedback (in order to cover novice consultants need for feedback on what went wrong and what went right); (c) introduction and forming a relationship;

(d) assessment and intervention design; (e) communication skills; (f) identifying and addressing consultees' concerns; and (g) self-assessment (how I see myself as a consultant). Following are some basic questions that students had to answer to cover the these topics:

- How do I feel now after hearing the recording of the process?
- What were my feelings during the process?
- What went wrong or right, and what I would have done differently?
- What model of consultation did I apply?
- What stages did I follow, and how did I try to apply them (in relation to the basic components of consultation presented previously)?
- How effective were the introduction in the organization, the relationship building, the assessment, and the interventions? What made them effective or ineffective?
- What context issues did I identify, and how were they reflected in the way I dealt with them?
- What communication skills did I use? How did they help, and what would I alter?
- What consultee issues discussed in the consultation literature, such as lack of knowledge, lack of objectivity, theme interference did I identify? What made me identify the specific issues, and how did I deal with them?
- Were there any cultural issues?
- How is theory reflected in the session?

At the end of the presentation, feedback was provided by the class and the instructors. Finally, students had to write up the case and its analysis as their final assignment.

Assessing the Course Process

In our continuous effort to improve the course, the students were asked to provide a qualitative assessment of the process, pointing out difficulties, opportunities, and further suggestions. Furthermore, there was an internal assessment among the instructors on the strengths and the weaknesses of the process.

The instructors' perception was that the introduction of consultation process, and especially the practical aspects of the training within the context of the graduate course, was a promising and challenging process. The main weakness of the process was the limited amount of time for the provision of practice and further analysis and supervision for each student. The students' feelings of anxiety in applying and presenting the process to the class were obvious. A further difficulty that was identified was how the students' prior knowledge of behavior modification techniques influenced the process of consultation. Specifically, students tended to provide their solutions to the identified problems; that is, the main focus of their efforts was on providing a direct service solution rather than enhancing teachers' skills. This finding provides new directions regarding students' training and preparation.

The most important strength of the process was the opportunity for practice cases and supervision that gave students chances to reflect on their mistakes and try to improve their practice within the safety of the course and with the support of the instructors. Finally, the presentation and the involvement of the whole class in providing feedback to each consultant, the analysis of each session with a direct connection to consultation theory with the appropriate argument and justification, and the assessment of the process by students themselves were considered assets that were very helpful for developing a deeper understanding and more effective application of consultation.

The most satisfying aspect of this effort was the acknowledgment by the students of the importance of the process and the benefits they gained. They all stressed their anxiety and their feelings of perplexity and embarrassment deriving mainly from their insecurity due to lack of experience in consultation. The dual-level of practice (role-playing and then actual application on real setting), the continuous feedback, and especially the linkage between theory of consultation and their practical efforts made them gain a deeper understanding and become more confident in relation to their role as school psychologists. In their own words:

• "The application of consultation connects theory and practice. The theoretical framework determined the progress of the interview."
• "I have the opportunity to understand the process of consultation, the difficulties and the impact on consultee."
• "Despite the difficulties, the whole process was positive and gave us the chance to put into practice what we were taught."

Finally, as was pointed out by graduate students, there is an apparent need for more courses to cover the array of competencies needed by school psychologists and more opportunities such as the one provided to them for practice based on feedback and supervision.

It is important to note that Greek graduate school psychology students identified common areas of concern that are identified in the relevant literature. It seems that graduate students in school psychology, irrespective of cultural and educational context, share the same needs and express similar concerns and anxieties as novice consultants. This finding can form the basis for the development of a training model that could serve as a guideline for the development of effective and well-structured training courses. Furthermore, combining the different case examples and training models applied in different countries could lead the way to the development of a transnational model of consultation training.

INTERVENTION PRACTICES AND CONSULTATION

The model described in the first section of the chapter has provided the theoretical framework for the development and application of all the activities of the Center for Research and Practice of School Psychology. In the following sections, two examples of intervention projects that have been recently implemented in Greek schools, Education of Roma Children Program and Connecting for Caring Program, are described, placing special emphasis on the consultation process that was applied. The selection of these programs was based on the fact that consultation constituted an important part of the services provided.

Education of Roma Children Program

During the school years 2011 to 2014, the Center for Intercultural Education (KEDA) of the University of Athens (NSRF 2007–2013, Education and Life-Long Learning; Ministry of Education, Life-Long Learning and Religious Affairs) implemented an EU funded project under the title Education of Roma Children. The primary goal of the program is to facilitate access to education for Roma students as well as to support school communities through promoting intercultural understanding, communication, and collaboration. The Center for Research and Practice in School Psychology, in collaboration with KEDA, undertook the task of developing and implementing a multilevel intervention program in order to promote resilience and to provide psychosocial support to the members of the participating schools. In particular, the goals of the intervention program were: (a) needs assessment at individual and system levels; (b) mental health promotion of the members of the school community; (c) promotion of a positive school climate and establishment of intercultural understanding in schools; (d) facilitation of school adjustment of Roma and non-Roma students; and (e) provision of consultation to faculty members and teachers at a school level. In addition to psychosocial interventions, the program included academic interventions in order to support students with learning difficulties (Hatzichristou & Lampropoulou, 2013; Hatzichristou & Lianos, 2013; Hatzichristou & Polychroni, 2013a, 2013b; Lampropoulou & Hatzichristou, 2013). The program had multiple elements.

Participants

There were 57 primary and secondary schools in the first year (14 kindergarten, 36 elementary, 7 high school), 46 schools in the second year (14 kindergarten, 24 elementary, 8 high school), and 50 schools in the third year in Athens and surrounding areas that participated in the program. A criterion for the selection of the schools was the number of Roma students in the schools (percentages ranged from 20 to 80%).

Groups and Areas of Intervention

The intervention team psychologists formed various groups with different tasks: (a) the scientific director and faculty members were responsible for organizing, planning, and implementing the interventions; (b) psychologists' trainers and coordinators provided training and supervision of interventions to the psychologists at schools; and (c) psychologists in the schools applied the interventions in schools and were responsible for actions such as assessment, psychoeducational evaluation, counseling (group or individual), consultation (teachers, administrators, and parents), program implementation in classrooms, and cooperation between schools and families and mental health services (Hatzichristou & Lianos, 2013; Hatzichristou & Polychroni, 2013a, 2013b).

Multicultural Issues

In relation to the specific program, special emphasis was placed on multicultural issues, since the main target group presented special cultural characteristics. Therefore, throughout the process of program development and implementation, the main task was to effectively address all multicultural issues.

Development of the Program Intervention

In order to develop a culturally appropriate program, it was important to use the literature on Roma students as a basic guideline. According to research findings on Roma students, access to education, as well as school adjustment, is a highly complicated issue. Therefore, the availability of school psychological services should aim to reinforce the studying process; lower dropout rates; facilitate school and, more specifically, class adjustment; and facilitate family–school collaboration (Bishop, 2002).

Teacher Training and Intercultural Awareness

An important aspect of the project was the implementation of a primary intervention program titled Social and Emotional Learning in Schools. One of the main goals of this program was to promote social and emotional skills to all students with a special emphasis on diversity issues. School psychologists, in collaboration with teachers, implemented the program.

In order to facilitate the implementation of the specific intervention program, but mainly in an effort to provide teachers with important knowledge and skills, training seminars were held for teachers of all grades. The content of the seminars included issues regarding mental health and resilience, social and emotional development of children, and current trends in school psychology, such as emphasis on system intervention, positive psychology, and social and emotional learning.

Within the context of these seminars, additional emphasis was placed on diversity, that is, helping teachers raise intercultural awareness in school life. Moreover, by presenting the relevant theoretical background to teachers and putting it into practice through experiential activities, they had the chance to understand the concept of cultural diversity, to recognize the role of stereotyping, and to familiarize themselves with the application of specific multicultural approaches to a multicultural class. The process also raised awareness of personal values/diversity in school settings and prevailing biases. Finally, a series of seminars on similar topics were also held for the parents.

Psychological Consultation/Training

Consultation was one of the most frequently provided services within the context of the intervention. Thus, the appropriate preparation of school psychologists was considered important, and for this purpose short-term seminars were held for the program's school psychologists. These seminars aimed to further train psychologists in consultation service delivery and to enhance multicultural-related skills with an emphasis on Roma population.

In addition, all psychologists attended the seminars held for the teachers in order to acquire further knowledge regarding multicultural issues and to have a chance to facilitate their introduction in the schools. It should be mentioned that all school psychology graduate students were expected to attend the seminars, thus providing the opportunity for a successful linking between theory, practice, and training.

Provision of Consultation

Within the context of this intervention program, different types of psychological consultation were conducted.

- *Consultation with teachers/administrators.* Consultation with teachers or administrators was one of the most frequent types of consultation provided by school psychologists. In consultation with the teacher or the administrator, a multicultural consultee-centered consultation was conducted about a Roma student. It is vitally important that teachers and other school personnel begin to recognize and decrease the tendency to filter perceptions through stereotypes, overemphasize culture, or take a color-blind approach (Ingraham, 2000). One of the basic techniques was the provision of information regarding the client's values and cultural beliefs for a better understanding of the interaction between the dominant culture and the client's culture.

- *Consultation with Roma parent.* When working with the parent, the consultee (parent) and the client (student) share a common culture or perspective and the consultant works to find bridges of understanding between the consultant and consultee in order to establish rapport, empathy, and a shared conceptualization of the problem (Ingraham, 2002, 2003, 2004). Consultants should help families gain the knowledge and the skills required to be proactive forces in the educational success of their children. Within the context of the Roma Education Program, this was an important goal of the consultation process.
- *Consultation on systemic issues.* Consultants periodically consult with administrators on systemic issues related to cultural diversity. When culturally diverse students are not meeting school norms on a regular basis, consultants should help administrators look for systemic barriers such as policies, norms, and communication patterns that may be interfering with a high quality education for all children. System-centered (administrative) consultation focuses on school improvement, organizational change, and prevention programming designed to benefit all students (Hylander, 2012).
- *Program-centered consultation.* The implementation of the Social and Emotional Program was an important dimension of the intervention. School psychologists served as consultants to teachers and administrators regarding the implementation of the program whenever they needed help in order to differentiate various activities, since they felt uncertain regarding their ability to implement it.

Supervision

Group supervision of school psychologists was performed on a regular basis. Group supervision meetings are designed primarily for the purpose of discussing cases and developing counseling and consultation skills. When compared to individual supervision, supervisees in group supervision receive considerably more feedback due to the presence of several practitioners rather than just one supervisor. In most cases, this allows supervisees to maximize the amount of benefit that they receive from supervision meetings.

Evaluation

Several areas of the services provided were assessed by using multiple assessment tools. According to our findings resulting from the evaluation of the psychological services that were provided in schools for the first two years, the program was effective and well-accepted by all participants (Lampropoulou & Hatzichristou, 2013).

A detailed database was developed and constantly updated by the school psychologists in order to document the specific activities that were applied. Consultation to teachers was provided at an individual or group level. In total, they performed 1,689 consultation sessions at an individual level and 177 at a group level. Consultation sessions were the largest percentage (41.9%) of services provided to schools within this program (Lampropoulou & Hatzichristou, 2013).

The reduction of these percentages during the second year of implementation may be indicative of increased confidence of the teachers to deal with problems that they faced during the first year. This could be a result of consultation, since the goal was to enhance teachers' skills in order to handle difficulties in their classrooms. The data analysis showed that only 34.9% of the teachers contacted the school psychologists often or very often during the second year. It should also be mentioned that the majority of the teachers were highly satisfied with their collaboration with school psychologists. According to the teachers, their cooperation with the school psychologists helped them to improve their skills in class management, dealing with students' conflicts, and various learning and adjustment difficulties. More important, they stated that they felt more confident and encouraged to keep on with their teaching tasks (Hatzichristou & Lampropoulou, 2013; Lampropoulou & Hatzichristou, 2013).

Connecting for Caring Project

Responding to the current crisis situation in Greece, and with the generous donation of Stavros Niarchos Foundation, the Center for Research and Practice of School Psychology of the University of Athens in cooperation with the Society for School and Family Consultation and Research developed Connecting for Caring (C4C) (www.connecting 4caring.gr). C4C is a multilevel prevention, awareness-building, education, and intervention project that uses a holistic approach to foster positive development, adjustment, and support of children and adolescents in the school and in the family. This project, based on current international and Greek research literature, aims to combine scientific knowledge, research, and practice in order to provide useful knowledge and promote best practices for teachers, parents, administrators, and mental health professionals and to promote best practices for school-age and adolescent children. The optimal goal of this project is to launch national and international networks of resilient schools in these stressful times.

This multilevel project includes intervention programs in Greek schools that: (a) target the entire student population; (b) intend to enhance resilience and self-esteem; (c) strengthen social-emotional skills; and (d) develop a positive school climate and supportive environment in the classroom and the school (Hatzichristou, 2011a, 2011b, 2011c). The first two school-based intervention programs of C4C were the Supporting in Crisis program and the E.M.E.I.Σ.[1] Program.

The E.M.E.I.Σ Program

Aim of the Program

The E.M.E.I.Σ. Program was implemented during the 2012–13 school year in schools of Athens and its surroundings. The main aim of the program was the development of a positive climate in the school environment in order to reinforce individual and group resilience as well as to promote and develop internal strengths, motivation, and skills. At the same time, an important goal of this program was to offer to the teachers an opportunity to strengthen their own resilience and support and empower the students by addressing the intense needs for psychological support that have emerged from the current economic crisis in Greece.

In this program, graduate school psychology students of the Department of Psychology, University of Athens, had the opportunity to apply the consultation process to real cases and participate in the teachers' training seminars and supervision; thus, they were able to practice consultation and gain supervised experience. Students who participated in the teachers' training seminars of the E.M.E.I.Σ Program developed by CRPSP had the chance to observe the application of program-centered administrative consultation, consultee-centered administrative consultation, and consultee-centered case consultation.

Structure of the Program

The theoretical background of the program integrated the literature on resilient classrooms (Doll et al., 2004) and resilient schools (Henderson & Milstein, 1996) with positive school climate (Blum & Libbey, 2004). The program also took into account recent trends in resilience research (Kolar, 2011) as well as in crisis intervention (Brock & Jimerson, 2013; Brock, Sandoval, & Lewis, 2001). Students and teachers had to develop their own school/classroom resilience profiles using a methodology based on the resiliency wheel and the classmaps design (Doll et al., 2009).

The E.M.E.I.Σ. Program included: (a) specialized teacher training seminars, including supervision of the implementation of the program; (b) development and implementation of structured classroom activities; (c) assessment; and (d) a closing ceremony. These activities were implemented:

- at an individual level for each student, with the goal to strengthen and support each child;
- at a classroom level, with the goal to create a positive climate and strengthen/support all the classroom members including the teacher; and
- at a school unit level, with the goal to promote resilience and a positive climate to all members of the school community.

The program included the following five thematic units: (1) practical model of resilience and positive school climate promotion identifying values and goal setting; (2) crisis management in the school community; (3) coping with stress; (4) social skills, conflict resolution, and bullying; and (5) teachers' burn out.

Participants

One hundred twenty-five teachers and 2,500 students from 38 primary schools (1 kindergarten, 17 elementary, 4 special education) and secondary schools (16 junior high) in Athens and surrounding areas participated in the E.M.E.I.Σ. Program.

Psychological Consultation in the E.M.E.I.Σ. Program

The main task of the E.M.E.I.Σ. Program was to conduct program-centered administrative consultation. Program-centered administrative mental health consultation focuses on assessment of mental health aspects of some program or internal functioning of the organization. In this case, the consultant participates in the development of a new program or tries to make existing programs work better (Caplan, 1970; Caplan & Caplan, 1999).

The consultants, who were school psychologists and members of the scientific team of the program, provided a set of recommendations for the development of this preventive mental health program in the schools. They gave to the consultees, who were teachers working in primary and secondary education, general directions for how to implement and improve the efficacy of the program. This kind of consultation took place in groups, similarly to recent projects in other countries (e.g., Hylander, 2012).

Consultee-centered administrative consultation was also conducted in order to improve the professional functioning of teachers in preventive mental health programs implemented in the participating schools. In consultee-centered administrative consultation, the consultant works with the organization's administrative-level personnel to help solve problems in personal management or implementation of organizational policy. The main aim is to help consultees improve problem-solving skills when facing current problems of the organization. The aim here was to improve the teachers' skills to promote mental health in their classes.

Consultee-centered case consultation was also conducted in several cases, especially during the supervision phase. In the consultee-centered case process, the main goal is the improvement of consultee's ability to work on particular cases in the present and cases in the future. The consultant plays the roles of expert and educator. The consultants who were school psychologists and members of the scientific team of the program consulted with teachers on difficulties they encountered with particular students, groups of students, or classes for whom they had responsibility.

Evaluation

Before the implementation of the E.M.E.I.Σ. Program during the academic year 2012–2013, a needs assessment was conducted with the participation of 141 teachers and 683 students from primary and secondary education schools. Teachers' and students' answers were used as a basis for the consultation process.

Analyses show that after the implementation of the program, the intervention group demonstrated higher levels of psychosocial adaptation, resilience, and positive school climate both at individual and group levels. These results were found for both students and teachers. The efficacy of the program was found to be higher in more vulnerable groups of students, such as those who were more concerned with the crisis and those who had lower school achievement. All these results seem to reflect the impact of the different aspects of consultation conducted within the program.

International Program WeC.A.R.E.

The International Program WeC.A.R.E. is a long-distance, web-based program for training teachers on classroom interventions that promote positive climate and resilience in the school community.

Participants

During the 2012–13 school year, the pilot phase took place with 68 teachers from 35 primary and secondary schools and 1,061 students from Greece and Cyprus and Greek students of the second and third generation of immigrants in four countries (United Kingdom, Ireland, U.S., and Belgium). In 2013–14, the main phase was conducted with 134 teachers from 131 primary and secondary schools and 2,060 students from Greece and Cyprus and Greek students of the second and third generation of immigrants in 10 countries (United Kingdom, Germany, Switzerland, Ireland, Ethiopia, Canada, U.S., Sweden, Belgium, and the Netherlands). In the main phase of the program, the intervention was conducted in Greek while a pilot group of teachers from Greece, Belgium, and the U.S. participated as well with the program conducted in English.

The Structure of the Program

The program included the following:

- Distance learning for teachers comprised of four units.
- Class intervention that incorporated: (a) the implementation of activities with the students in class; (b) a common project between classes; (c) the use of the online interactive game "Sailing for Caring," which prompts teachers and students to upload material on the electronic platform based on the implementation of the activities in class while giving them the opportunity to communicate with other classes; (d) uploading material from the program implementation in class; and (e) designing an electronic newsletter titled "The Voice of the Winds" and uploading it on the electronic platform.
- Simultaneous supervision of the implementation of the activities by psychologists carried out through the electronic platform.
- Process and outcome evaluation.

Psychological Consultation in the International Program

Within the context of the program, the psychologists of the scientific team provided supervision on the implementation of the program activities. Psychologists used the electronic platform and organized teleconference meetings with the teachers. During these meetings, the school psychologists conducted e-supervision/consultation as they offered the teachers specific directions on how to implement and improve the efficacy of the program by discussing issues that arose in the classrooms during the activities. Therefore, both consultee-centered case process and program-centered administrative mental health consultations were conducted.

After the implementation of the program, both students and teachers recognized that students' abilities to recognize and express their emotions and their interpersonal relations were improved, and they perceived school climate as more positive. These findings seem to reflect the impact of the different aspects of consultation conducted within the context of the International Program WeC.A.R.E.

TOWARD THE DEVELOPMENT OF A SYNTHETIC MODEL FOR CONSULTATION TRAINING AND CONSULTATION PROVISION AT A TRANSNATIONAL LEVEL

This chapter has outlined an approach to consultation provision and training at the Department of Psychology, University of Athens in Greece, with a goal to combine theory, training, and practice in the most effective way. Therefore, the focus has been mainly on providing consultation knowledge to trainees, developing consultation competence, and employing strategies to support capability in order to provide consultation effectively to school communities.

The effort to develop efficient and effective consultants has a significant value for the Greek educational system since there are no permanent school psychology positions in public schools. The provision of school psychological services in such settings is limited, available only for a short period of time, and mainly provided within the context of EU-funded projects. The focus on consultation training of future school psychologists and the provision of different types of consultation (e.g. group consultation, consultee-centered

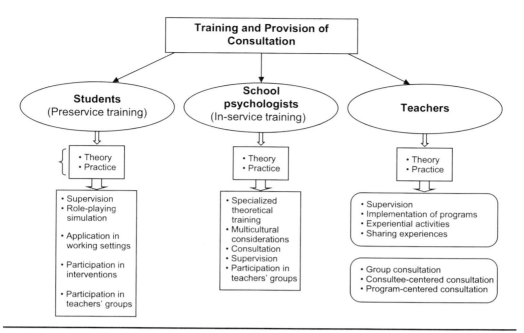

Figure 5.2 Training and Consultation Provision to Graduate Students and Teachers

consultation, and program-centered consultation) that were applied in the interventions described in this chapter emphasize the importance of indirect provision of school psychologists' services (Hatzichristou, 2013b). This effort, which is in accordance with the basic goals of the Center for Research and Practice in School Psychology of the University of Athens, aims to address the needs of school communities and to counterbalance the lack of school psychological services in the Greek public schools. The analysis of the data collected during the evaluation processes regarding the acceptance of the programs and the services provided, as well as the large number of schools and teachers that are willing to participate repeatedly in such activities, is indicative of the effectiveness and the importance of this continuous effort.

The importance of the provision of consultation in school communities, which constitutes a significant dimension of school psychologists' role, illustrates the need for the carefully designed training courses and practices that will lead to the development of efficient consultants. In this chapter, consultation was approached at two levels, providing considerations both for trainee school psychologists (as consultation providers) and for teachers (as consultation recipients) and providing a synthetic model for consultation training and consultation provision (see Figure 5.2).

Psychologists/School Psychologists Trainees (Preservice Training)

Undergraduate Students

With regard to undergraduate students, consultation training (theoretical approach and practice) is provided within the context of various courses where students have the chance to learn about consultation and practice certain consultation skills.

Graduate Students in School Psychology

With regard to graduate students in school psychology, the emphasis was on their training. A training course was provided that: (a) would combine theory and practice; and (b) would cover as much as possible the needs and worries expressed by trainees in most cultural and educational settings. Therefore, a multilevel approach to training was adopted that included both preservice training and participation by students in the in-service training related to the intervention programs.

First, graduate students were given the chance to acquire both theoretical knowledge and practice. The use of various means of didactic and practice techniques aimed at offering students basic theoretical understanding but mainly multiple chances for practice under supervision. The strength of this process was the combination of different practice efforts in various settings with constant self-monitoring, group feedback, and supervision.

Apart from the training process, students also had the chance to have additional training by attending, as members of the group, the seminars provided to teachers that participated in the intervention programs already described. In addition, students were actively involved, both as members of the teachers' group and as members of the scientific team, by participating in reflection meetings that were held after each seminar.

This multilevel approach—the combination of theoretical training, constant practice, and supervision as well as the participation in the actual interventions that were implemented—gave students the chance to engage in consultation and to meet the same needs as expressed by students in other educational contexts.

School Psychologists (In-Service Training)

A multilevel approach was also applied for school psychologists that were involved in interventions that included school visits, as with the Education of Roma Children Program. Most of the school psychologists that participated in this program had graduated from the Graduate Program in School Psychology; therefore, they had already attended the course on consultation. However, short-term training in consultation with a special focus on multicultural issues was offered to all psychologists involved in the program, with an emphasis on various types of consultation that would need to apply. The main focus in this case was the carefully designed supervision that was provided to school psychologists both at individual and at group levels. Supervision and group consultation were provided for all the team members, and these proved to be quite helpful. Finally, in order to enhance the theoretical knowledge and the understanding of the organizations (that is, the schools and the teachers they would work with), school psychologists attended the training seminars held for teachers and participated in the groups they formed.

Teacher Consultation

Consultation was provided to teachers in all the interventions that were described in the chapter. The different forms of interventions, the different needs of teachers, and the differences among school settings led to the provision of different types of consultation. The main domains that contributed to the achievement of consultation goals in direct and indirect ways were the following: (a) the combination of various types of consultation (e.g., program-centered, group consultation, consultee-centered) according to the context and the emerging needs of teachers; (b) teachers' attendance of theoretical presentations on important mental health issues and on their roles as students consultants; (c) teachers' participation in group discussions and experiential activities; (d) the implementation of the programs in the classrooms and feedback from the students; and (e) the supervision teachers received and the chance they had for sharing experiences with their colleagues.

It was most impressive that teachers were empowered in their roles, improved their working skills, and were led to new realizations about their roles as teachers by participating in all other activities apart from the consultation sessions. This was especially the case for the E.M.E.I.Σ. Program, where psychologists did not visit their schools. Teachers acknowledged improvement at both professional and personal levels. As was apparent by the evaluation process, they felt more confident in dealing with difficult situations, especially in these times of economic crisis after the consultation sessions, as they stated in the relevant questionnaires that they had to answer.

In addition, supervision and e-consultation were provided to teachers that participated in the international program *WeC.A.R.E.*, and these gave us the chance to provide services to schools throughout multiple countries. The communication and cooperation with teachers and schools in different countries led to the understanding that, irrespective of country or educational and cultural settings, all school communities share common needs and worries. The needs that were brought up in supervision and consultation sessions were undoubtedly context and school specific, but they had also remarkable similarities for all participants.

The importance and effectiveness of consultation are also reflected in the results from the evaluation process of the interventions. Teachers that participated in all intervention programs were very satisfied with the services provided by school psychologists, stated significant benefits gained by their participation both at professional and personal levels (e.g., "made me a better person," "helped me find ways to make my students cooperate with each other," "conflicts and aggressive behavior were minimized"), and felt more confident to deal with difficult situations in their classrooms. Hence, they addressed school psychologists less and less over time and found the support from school psychologists productive and helpful with regard to teacher–student and teacher–parent relationships (for more results from the assessment of the interventions, see Hatzichristou, Lampropoulou et al., 2010).

Combining theory and practice was the main basis for all the efforts regarding training and provision of consultation. Despite the different target groups that were the focus of the chapter and the differences in goals, needs, and settings, the following common domains can be identified regarding the training approach and consultation provision for students and teachers:

- The main effort was to build an initial theoretical background in order to establish a sound theoretical basis both for teachers and students.
- A needs assessment phase proceeded in each case to cover the unique needs of each group. Concerning school psychology students, the needs assessment had to do with previous experiences of the trainers, assessment data from previous graduate courses, and the relevant literature regarding training and students' expressed needs. As far as teachers are concerned, a needs assessment is conducted prior to interventions with questionnaires aiming to construct school profiles and discover school specific needs.

- Chances for practice were provided both to students and teachers. Role-playing, simulations, and participation in intervention programs were applied to students. Teachers' practice included the implementation of the program and the application of the skills learned through consultation to their students.
- Acknowledgment of the importance of different types of consultation and of supervision was a basic guideline in both cases. Hence, training in all types of consultation for students and provision of all types of consultation (according to needs) for teachers were considered quite important. However, in both cases, supervision was the first priority as the basic "educational" means for supporting both students and teachers.
- All the efforts that were described both for students and teachers had the same goal, that is, to help each professional group become more efficient and effective and to help them improve their working skills for the benefit of the most important members of the school communities: the children.

In this chapter, different dimensions of consultation were presented. The first one was training in consultation in order to help novice consultants become as effective as possible and develop appropriate consultation skills. The second one was related to provision of consultation. Intervention programs were described in which different types of consultation were applied, aiming to address the needs of different groups and populations in schools. The different needs of school communities led to different and multiple goals not only for each intervention program but for the consultation processes as well. Consultation was applied in different settings and with various goals (e.g., multicultural consultation, consultation in times of crisis, and e-consultation). However, in each case, the main concern was to link theory and practice and to respond effectively to the needs of each population we served.

These efforts had, as an additional result, not only an intervention within the context of our cultural and educational setting, but also formed the basis for transnational considerations in developing a model of training and provision of consultation. This can be important since both literature review and our experience during these years verify the fact that, despite the differences of the groups (trainees, students, teachers and parents), they share common needs with similar groups in different countries. The development of a model in training and in provision of consultation could serve as a universal framework of reference and a bridge among psychologists at international and transnational levels in order to develop appropriate and effective training courses and consultation interventions in various contexts.

NOTE

1. Ενδιαφερόμαστε (care), Μοιραζόμαστε (share), Ενθαρρύνουμε (encourage), Ισχυροποιούμαστε (empower), Συμμετέχουμε (participate)

REFERENCES

Anton-Lahart, J., & Rosenfield, S. (2004). A survey of preservice consultation training in school psychology programs. *Journal of Educational and Psychological Consultation, 15*, 41–62.

Bickel, W. E., & Beaujean, A. A. (2005). Effective schools for all: A brief history and some common findings. In C. L. Frisby & C. R. Reynolds (Eds.), *Comprehensive handbook of multicultural school psychology* (pp. 303–328). Hoboken, NJ: Wiley.

Biglan, A., Flay, B. R., Embry, D. D., & Sandler, I. N. (2012). The critical role of nurturing environments for promoting human well-being. *American Psychologist, 67*, 257–271.

Bishop, A. J. (2002). *Mathematical acculturation, cultural conflicts, and transition.* In G. D. Abreu, A. J. Bishop, & N. Presmeg (Eds.), *Transitions between contexts of mathematical practices* (pp. 193–212). The Netherlands: Kluwer Academic Publishers.

Blum, R. W., & Libbey, H. P. (2004). Executive summary. *Journal of School Health, 74*, 231–232.

Brock, S. E., & Jimerson, S. R. (Eds.). (2013). *Best practices in school crisis prevention and intervention* (2nd ed.). Bethesda, MD: National Association of School Psychologists.

Brock, S. E., Sandoval, J., & Lewis, S. (2001). *Preparing for crises in the schools: A manual for building school crisis response teams* (2nd ed.). New York, NY: Wiley.

Brown, D., Pryzwansky, W. B., & Schulte, A. C. (2007). *Ψυχολογική διαλεκτική συμβουλευτική. Εισαγωγή στη θεωρία και την πρακτική εφαρμογή* [Psychological consultation: Introduction to theory and practice]. Scientific Editor of the Greek edition and introduction: C. Hatzichristou. Translation: A. Lampropoulou. Athens: Tipothito.

Brown, D., Pryzwansky, W. B., & Schulte, A. C. (2011). *Psychological consultation and collaboration* (7th ed.). Upper Saddle River, NJ: Merrill.

Caplan, G. (1970). *The theory and practice of mental health consultation.* Prospect Heights, IL: Waveland.

Caplan, G., & Caplan, R. B. (1999). *Mental health consultation and collaboration.* New York, NY: Basic Books.

Doll, B., Kurien, S., LeClair, C., Spies, R., Champion, A., & Osborn, A. (2009). The classmaps survey: A framework for promoting positive classroom environments. In R. Gilman, S. Huebner, & M. Furlong (Eds.), *Handbook of positive psychology in the schools* (pp. 213–227). New York, NY: Routledge.

Doll, B., Zucker, S., & Brehm, K. (2004). *Resilient classrooms: Creating healthy environments for learning.* New York, NY: The Guilford Press.

Dougherty, A. M. (2013). *Psychological consultation and collaboration in school and community settings* (6th ed.). Belmont, CA: Brooks/Cole.

Esquivel, G. B., Doll, B., & Oades-Sese, G. V. (2011). Introduction to the special issue: Resilience in schools. *Psychology in the Schools, 48*, 649–651.

Hatzichristou, C. (2004). Alternative school psychological services: Development of a model linking theory, research, and service delivery. In N. M. Lambert, I. Hylander, & J. Sandoval (Eds.), *Consultee-centered consultation: Improving the quality of professional services in schools and community organizations* (pp. 115–132). Mahwah, NJ: Lawrence Erlbaum.

Hatzichristou, C. (2011). *Σχολική Ψυχολογία* [Handbook of school psychology]. Athens, Greece: Tipothito.

Hatzichristou, C. (Ed. and co-author in each volume). (2011a). *Κοινωνική και συναισθηματική αγωγή στο σχολείο: Πρόγραμμα για την προαγωγή της ψυχικής υγείας και της μάθησης στη σχολική κοινότητα: Εκπαιδευτικό υλικό I: Πρωτοβάθμια εκπαίδευση Νηπιαγωγείο, Α΄, Β΄ Δημοτικού: Θεωρητικό πλαίσιο και δραστηριότητες* [Social and emotional learning in school: Program for the promotion of mental health and learning in the school community (educational material for teachers and students of Grades K-2)]. Athens: Tipothito.

Hatzichristou, C. (Ed. and co-author in each volume). (2011b). *Κοινωνική και συναισθηματική αγωγή στο σχολείο: Πρόγραμμα για την προαγωγή της ψυχικής υγείας και της μάθησης στη σχολική κοινότητα: Εκπαιδευτικό υλικό II: Πρωτοβάθμια εκπαίδευση Γ΄, Δ΄, Ε΄, ΣΤ΄ δημοτικού: Θεωρητικό πλαίσιο και δραστηριότητες.* [Social and emotional learning in school: Program for the promotion of mental health and learning in the school community (educational material for teachers and students of Grades 3–6)]. Athens: Tipothito.

Hatzichristou, C. (Ed. and co-author in each volume). (2011c). *Κοινωνική και συναισθηματική αγωγή στο σχολείο: Πρόγραμμα για την προαγωγή της ψυχικής υγείας και της μάθησης στη σχολική κοινότητα: Εκπαιδευτικό υλικό III: Δευτεροβάθμια εκπαίδευση: Θεωρητικό πλαίσιο και δραστηριότητες* [Social and emotional learning in school: Program for the promotion of mental health and learning in the school community (educational material for teachers and students of secondary education)]. Athens: Tipothito.

Hatzichristou, C. (2013a, July). *Multi-level prevention and intervention programs for supporting children, teachers and parents in times of economic crisis.* Symposium presented at the 35th Annual Conference of the International School Psychology Association, Porto, Portugal.

Hatzichristou, C. (2013b, July). *Training and establishing psychological consultation practices in schools around the world.* Symposium presented at the 35th Annual Conference of the International School Psychology Association, Porto, Portugal.

Hatzichristou, C. (2014, February). *Intervention programs of resilience promotion in stressful times.* Paper Presented at the National Association School Psychology 2014 Annual Convention, Washington, DC.

Hatzichristou, C., Adamopoulou, E., & Lampropoulou, A. (2014). A multilevel approach of promoting resilience and positive school climate in the school community during unsettling times. In S. Prince-Embury (Ed.), *Resilience interventions in diverse communities* (pp. 299–325). New York, NY: Springer.

Hatzichristou, C., & Lampropoulou, A. (2013). Development of a multilevel model of provision of psychological services. In G. Flouris, L. Gioti, C. Parthenis, & E. Miligou (Eds.), *Lifelong education and training of teachers in view of cross-cultural aspect: "Education of Roma Children" as a starting point for new theoretical and empirical approaches* (pp. 113–131). Athens, Greece: Center for Intercultural Education, University of Athens.

Hatzichristou, C., Lampropoulou, A., Lykitsakou, K., & Dimitropoulou, P. (2010). Promoting university and schools partnership: Transnational considerations and future directions. In J. Kaufman & T. Hughes (Eds.), *Handbook of education, training, and supervision of school psychologists in school and community* (Vol. 2, pp. 89–108). New York, NY: Taylor & Francis/Routledge.

Hatzichristou, C., & Lianos, P. (2013, July). *A school-linked university-based model for provision of school psychological services in Greek schools.* Paper presented at the 35th Annual Conference of the International School Psychology Association, Porto, Portugal.

Hatzichristou, C., Lykitsakou, K., Lampropoulou, A., & Dimitropoulou, P. (2010). Promoting the well-being of school communities: A systemic approach. In B. Doll, W. Phohl, & J. Yoon (Eds.), *Handbook of prevention science* (pp. 255–274). New York, NY: Routledge.

Hatzichristou, C., & Polychroni, F. (2013a, April). *Program of psychosocial and academic intervention in school level.* Paper presented at the publicity event of the program "Education of Roma children", Titania Athens Hotel, Athens.

Hatzichristou, C., & Polychroni, F. (2013b, May). *Multilevel intervention model and provision of psychological services: Challenges and Perspectives.* Symposium presented at the 14th Panhellenic Conference of Psychological Research of the Hellenic Psychological Society, Alexandroupolis, Greece.

Hatzichristou, C., & Polychroni, F. (2014). The preparation of school psychologists in Greece. *International Journal of School and Educational Psychology: Special Issue: Academic and Professional Preparation of School and Educational Psychologists: International Perspectives, 2,* 154–165.

Hatzichristou, C., Polychroni, F., & Georgouleas, G. (2007). School psychology in Greece. In S. R. Jimerson, T. D. Oakland, & P. T. Farrell (Eds.), *The handbook of international school psychology* (pp. 135–146). Thousand Oaks, CA: Sage.

Hazel, C. E., Laviolette, G. T., & Lineman, J. M. (2010). Training professional psychologists in school-based consultation: What the syllabi suggest. *Training and Education in Professional Psychology, 4,* 235–243.

Henderson, N., & Milstein, M. (1996). *Resiliency in schools: Making it happen for students and educators.* Thousand Oaks, CA: Corwin Press.

Henderson, N., & Milstein, M. (2008). *Resiliency in schools: Making it happen for students and educators.* (V. Vassara, Trans. of Greek edition; C. Hatzichristou, Ed. of Greek edition). Athens, Greece: Typothito.

Hylander, I. (2012). Conceptual change through consultee-centered consultation: A theoretical model. *Consulting Psychology Journal: Practice and Research, 64,* 29–45.

Ingraham, C. L. (2000). Consultation through a multicultural lens: Multicultural and crosscultural consultation in schools. *School Psychology Review, 29,* 320–343.

Ingraham, C. L. (2002). *Multicultural consultation in schools to support teacher and student success.* Invited workshop at the annual meeting of the National Association of school Psychologists, Chicago.

Ingraham, C. L. (2003). Multicultural consultee-centered consultation: When novice consultants explore cultural hypotheses with experienced teacher consultees. *Journal of Educational and Psychological Consultation, 14,* 329–362.

Ingraham, C. L. (2004). Multicultural consultation: A model for supporting consultees in the development of cultural competence. In N. M. Lambert, I. Hylander, & J. Sandoval (Eds.), *Consultee centered consultation: Improving the quality of professional services in schools and community organizations* (pp. 133–148). Mahwah, NJ: Erlbaum.

Kolar, K. (2011). Resilience: Revisiting the concept and its utility for social research. *International Journal of Mental Health and Addiction, 9,* 421–433.

Kress, J. S., & Elias, M. J. (2006). School based social and emotional learning programs. In K. A. Renninger & I. E. Sigel (Eds.), *Handbook of child psychology* (Child psychology in practice 6th ed., Vol. 4, pp. 592–618). Hoboken, NJ: Wiley.

Lampropoulou, A., & Hatzichristou, C. (2013). Program "Education of Roma children": Data from the implementation of the program of psychosocial intervention. In G. Flouris, L. Gioti, C. Parthenis, & E. Miligou (Eds.), *Lifelong education and training of teachers in view of cross-cultural aspect: "Education of Roma children" as a starting point for new theoretical and empirical approaches* (pp. 565–585). Athens, Greece: Center for Intercultural Education, University of Athens.

Luthar, S. (2006). Resilience in development: A synthesis of research across five decades. In D. Cicchetti & D. J. Cohen (Eds.), *Developmental Psychopathology* (2nd ed., Vol. 3, pp. 739–795). Hoboken, NJ: Wiley.

Masten, A. S. (2001). Ordinary magic. *American Psychologist, 56,* 227–238.

Masten, A. S. (2011). Resilience in children threatened by extreme adversity: Frameworks for research, practice, and translational synergy. *Development and Psychopathology, 23*, 493–506.

Masten, A. S., & Reed, M.-G. J. (2002). Resilience in development. In C. R. Snyder & S. Lopez (Eds.), *Handbook of positive psychology* (pp. 74–88). Oxford, UK: Oxford University Press.

Morrison, G. M., Brown, M., D'Incau, B., & O'Farrell, L. S. (2006). Understanding resilience in educational trajectories: Implications for protective possibilities. *Psychology in the Schools, 43*, 19–31.

Newman, D. S. (2012). Supervision of consultation training: Addressing the content and process concerns of novice consultants. In S. A. Rosenfield (Ed.), *Becoming a school consultant: Lessons learned* (pp. 49–70). New York, NY: Routledge.

Oakland, T. D., & Jimerson, S. R. (2007). School psychology internationally: A retrospective view and influential conditions. In S. R. Jimerson, T. D. Oakland, & P. T. Farrell (Eds.), *The handbook of international school psychology* (pp. 453–462). Thousand Oaks, CA: Sage.

O'Dougherty, M., & Masten, A. S. (2005). Resilience processes in development. In S. Goldstein & R. B. Brooks (Eds.), *Handbook of resilience in children* (pp. 17–37). New York, NY: Kluwer Academic/Plenum Publishers.

Rosenfield, S. (2004). Consultation as dialogue: The right words at the right time. In N. Lambert, I. Hylander, & J. Sandoval (Eds.), *Consultee-centere consultation: Improving the quality of professional services in schools and community organizations* (pp. 337–347). Hillsdale, NJ: Lawrence Erlbaum Associates.

Rosenfield, S. (2012). Introduction: Becoming a school consultant. In S. A. Rosenfield (Ed.), *Becoming a school consultant: Lessons learned* (pp. 1–22). New York, NY: Routledge.

Rosenfield, S., Levinsohn-Klyap, M., & Cramer, K. (2010). Educating consultants for practice in the schools. In E. G. Vazquez, T. D. Crespi, & C. Riccio (Eds.), *Handbook of education training, and supervision of school psychologists in school and community volume 1: Foundations of professional practice* (pp. 259–278). New York, NY: Routledge.

Sheridan, S. M., & Kratochwill, T. R. (2008). *Conjoint behavioural consultation: Promoting family school connections and interventions* (2nd ed.). New York, NY: Springer.

Thomas, G. (2004). A typology of approaches to facilitator education. *Journal of Experiential Education, 27*, 123–140.

Truscott, S. D., & Albritton, K. (2011). Addressing pediatric health concerns through school-based consultation. *Journal of Educational and Psychological Consultation, 27*, 123–140.

Part III

CROSSING CULTURES

6

A TRANSCULTURAL APPROACH TO SYSTEMS-LEVEL CONSULTATION

Bonnie Kaul Nastasi

Developing and sustaining effective consultation relationships across cultural boundaries can pose challenges when working in domestic or international settings. Furthermore, the cultural and contextual considerations increase in complexity as we move from working with individuals or small groups (e.g., client-centered or consultee-centered consultation) to working with systems or organizations. The purpose of this chapter is to describe and illustrate a transcultural model for conducting systems-level consultation that uses a participatory approach to involve stakeholders in the cultural construction of interventions.

Although the model is potentially applicable across a range of goals for consultation, this chapter focuses on consultation for promoting and protecting well-being, with a primary focus on children and adolescents, through systems change. Most importantly, the chapter focuses on engaging in consultation across cultural boundaries in local, national, and regional sectors of the world, thus necessitating an approach that can facilitate the integration of cultural diversity within a given system while negotiating cross-cultural relationships, what Hatzichristou, Lampropoulou, and Lykitsakou (2006) refer to as transcultural, or metacultural, consultation. What distinguishes a transcultural approach from culture-specific or cross-cultural is the focus on integration of diverse perspectives through a co-construction process. In the next section, we explore the conceptual foundations for the proposed transcultural participatory consultation (TCPC) model applied to systems consultation.

CONCEPTUAL FOUNDATIONS OF TRANSCULTURAL PARTICIPATORY CONSULTATION (TCPC)

The development of the TCPC model was an outgrowth of both local and international efforts by the author and colleagues to engage systems (e.g., schools, agencies, communities) in the process of constructing interventions to meet cultural and contextual needs as perceived by stakeholders. In prior work, Nastasi and colleagues have described the Participatory Culture-Specific Consultation Model (PCSC; Nastasi, Varjas, Bernstein, & Jayasena, 2000) and the Participatory Culture-Specific Intervention Model (PCSIM; Nastasi & Hitchcock, 2016; Nastasi, Moore, & Varjas, 2004; Nastasi, Varjas, Sarkar, & Jayasena,

1998). PCSC and PCSIM are applications of a participatory process for development of interventions through partnership with stakeholders with the goal of identifying and addressing cultural and contextual factors in local settings (domestic or international); both embody a "process of consensus building and negotiation of divergent ideas leading to co-construction of change" (Nastasi et al., 2004, p. 37). In both models, the process begins with examining existing theory, research, and practice and proceeds with learning the culture, forming partnerships, identifying goals or problems, and collecting data (formative research) to inform culture-specific hypotheses or conceptual frameworks that in turn influence intervention/program design, implementation, and evaluation. PCSC is a nine-stage process focused on the consultation relationship as a way to address identified problems at client, consultee, or systems levels. The PCSIM is an 11-stage process for engaging stakeholders in development and evaluation of sustainable prevention or intervention programs. The variation in number of phases reflects two differences: (1) creating a separate phase for program adaptation to local context in PCSIM and (2) concluding the cycle with a single phase focused on institutionalization for PCSC compared to two phases focused on capacity building and translation respectively for PCSIM. The variations in part reflect the evolution of our thinking as we applied the models in practice.

The proposed 10-phase transcultural model, TCPC, reflects further evolution and integration of PCSC and PCSIM by: (a) integrating consultation and program development through a participatory research process; (b) maintaining a separate phase for program adaptation to local contexts; (c) concluding the process with one phase that incorporates capacity building, institutionalization, and translation; and (c) highlighting the cultural co-construction process that is fundamental to negotiating across cultural boundaries during consultant–system, consultant–stakeholder, system–stakeholder, and stakeholder–stakeholder interactions. A process of negotiation and consensus building is central to co-construction and requires deliberate attention to the diversity of perspectives, beliefs, experiences, and values of those involved. The complexity of such a process can be overwhelming to the consultant and the target system; parsing this complexity necessitates a scheme for conceptualizing the process. In this section, the conceptual foundations for TCPC are described. In subsequent sections, a scheme for enacting TCPC is described and illustrated.

The conceptual foundations for TCPC include: (a) PCSC (Nastasi et al., 2000) and PCISM (Nastasi et al., 1998, 2004; Nastasi & Hitchcock, 2016) as the bases for defining the participatory approach and program/intervention development; (b) Bronfenbrenner's (1989, 1999) Ecological Systems Theory (EST) as the basis for defining systems; (c) international policies (e.g., UN Convention on the Rights of the Child [Convention], 1989; UN Millennium Development Goals [MDGs], 2000; UN Sustainable Development Goals [SDGs], 2015) as the bases for defining well-being; and (d) social construction theory (Vygotsky, 1978; Wertsch, 1991) as the basis for the process of negotiation and consensus building that we label *cultural co-construction* (Kleinman, Eisenberg, & Good, 1978; Nastasi, Schensul et al., 2015). Furthermore, central to both PCSC and PCSIM are ethnography as the methodology for understanding culture and participatory action research (PAR; Greenwood, Whyte, & Harkavy, 1993; Partridge, 1985) as the research design relevant to TCPC, both of which involve the use of mixed qualitative-quantitative methods.

Culture, Cultural Co-Construction, and Cultural/Intercultural Competence

Relevant to our discussion of transcultural work are the concepts of culture, cultural co-construction, cultural competence, and intercultural competence. These constructs are defined in Table 6.1. As reflected in the definition, *culture* embodies a cognitive-behavioral perspective such that culture influences our interpretations of experiences (cognitions) and our behavior. Culture is considered important to the thinking and behavior of individuals, dyads, and groups, particularly as we endeavor to both understand behavior as researchers and to engage in a co-construction process as consultants or interventionists. *Cultural co-construction* is central to transcultural consultation as one endeavors to interact with consultees across cultural boundaries and to facilitate cross-cultural communication among stakeholders. Moreover, the definition of *cultural competence* is consistent with the concept of *intercultural competence* described by Friedman and Antal

Table 6.1 Definitions of Key Terms Related to Culture and Well-being

Key Term	Definition
	Culture
Culture	"A dynamic system of meanings, knowledge and actions that provides actors collectively, interpersonally, and individually with community-legitimized strategies to construct, reflect upon, and reconstruct their world and experience, and guide behaviour" (Nastasi et al., 2015, p. 96; see also Bibeau & Corin, 1995; Geertz, 1968/1992).
Cultural co-construction	"The process of dialogue among equal partners across class, ethnic/racial, disciplinary, cultural, and other boundaries that integrates knowledge, values, perspectives, and methods derived from all parties, resulting in shared innovation. The co-construction of cultural and other forms of knowledge is an ongoing process that reflects the nature of participatory research and intervention development, and the more dynamic nature of the social construction" (Nastasi et al., 2015, p. 94).
Culture competence	"A set of *problem-solving* skills that includes: (a) the *ability to recognize and understand* the dynamic interplay between the heritage and adaptation dimensions of culture in shaping human behavior; (b) the *ability to use the knowledge* acquired about an individual's heritage and adaptational challenges to maximize the effectiveness of assessment, diagnosis, and treatment; and (c) *internalization* (i.e., incorporation into one's clinical problem-solving repertoire) of this process of recognition, acquisition, and use of cultural dynamics so that it can be routinely applied to diverse groups. . . . It should also be noted that the internalization stage of cultural competence proposed here is akin to Lopez's (1997; Lopez et al., 2002) notion of *shifting cultural lenses* in his model of cultural competence" (Whaley & Davis, 2007, p. 565; emphasis added).
Intercultural competence	"The ability to explore one's repertoire and actively construct an appropriate strategy, . . . [thus] overcoming the constraints embedded in an individual's culturally shaped repertoire, creating new responses, and thereby expanding the repertoire of potential interpretations and behaviors available in future intercultural interactions" (Friedman & Antal, 2005, pp. 74–75).
	Well-being
Individual well-being	Consistent with international policies (UN, 1989, 2000, 2015), encompasses physical, social, psychological (emotional and cognitive), and spiritual components
Interpersonal well-being	Characterized by mutually supportive social interactions and relationships
Collective well-being	Embodies a shared set of norms, values, beliefs, and practices (i.e., culture) that foster a peaceful, safe, and nurturing environment (system, organization)

(2005); both imply the development of a cognitive flexibility that permits interactions across infinite cultural boundaries necessitated by transcultural consultation and development of what Friedman and Antal refer to as a *global identity*.

Well-being: Individual, Interpersonal, Collective

For the purposes of this chapter, *well-being* is broadly defined as encompassing the well-being of both individuals and systems consistent with concepts of: (a) child-friendly/health promoting schools (UNICEF, 2009; WHO, 1998, 2003); (b) positive school climate (Thapa, Cohen, & Higgins-D'Alessandro, 2012), school connectedness (Center for Disease Control and Prevention [CDC], 2009), UN Millennium Development Goals (MDGs; UN, 2000), and Sustainable Development Goals (SDGs; UN, 2015); and (c) Nelson and Prilleltensky's (2005) characterization of well-being at individual, interpersonal, and collective levels. Table 6.1 provides the definitions for individual, interpersonal, and collective well-being relevant to application of TCPC to school and community systems. In the context of schools, for example, promoting well-being includes the promotion of physical health and nutrition, social-emotional and cognitive development, academic achievement, and spiritual well-being at individual (child/adolescent, adult), interpersonal (student–student, student–teacher/staff), and collective (school as an organization/system) levels. Understanding and fostering well-being at multiple levels—individual, interpersonal, collective—requires a systems framework (see also Hatzichristou, Lykitsakou, Lampropoulou, & Dimitropoulou, 2010).

Ecological Systems Theory

Ecological Systems Theory (EST; Bronfenbrenner, 1989, 1999) characterizes the complexity and reciprocity inherent in multilevel systems such as schools or communities. Figure 6.1 depicts the *ecology of the child* (based on EST), which includes the multiple ecological contexts (microsystems) in which the child develops through reciprocal interactions with significant others—family, school, peer group, community (e.g., neighborhood). These contexts are each embedded within a larger context (exosystem) that influences interactions within the microsystem, both directly and indirectly. For example, the interactions of students with teachers in the classroom are influenced by the larger school context. In addition, interactions (mesosystem; depicted by bidirectional arrows) between (school–family) and within (school–district) these systems influence the direct interactions (e.g., student–teacher) within the respective microsystems. Furthermore, the child's ecological system is embedded in a larger macrosystem (e.g., nation, society) that is influenced by multiple factors (e.g., social, political) and reflects collective values, beliefs, and norms. Also relevant to our discussion is the *chronosystem*, which refers to the changes over time for the individual (e.g., developmental changes) or system (e.g., historical changes). The chronosystem is particularly important as one considers the influence of social/cultural/historical changes related to context of interest.

Role of Systems Consultant

As Figure 6.1 indicates, the systems consultant can play a central role in guiding the interactions (mesosystems) between and within specific ecological contexts. Within a transcultural framework, the systems consultant's role is that of a facilitator of communication and negotiation across multiple cultural boundaries (cultural co-construction) with the goal of promoting well-being at individual, interpersonal, and collective levels.

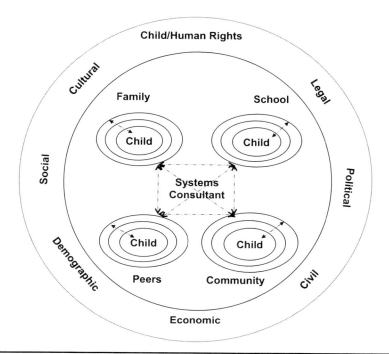

Figure 6.1 The Role of the Systems Consultation in the Ecology of the Child
This figure depicts the child at the center of multiple ecological contexts (microsystems; e.g., classroom, home, playground; see Bronfenbrenner, 1989, 1999) that are influenced by broader contexts that encompass the respective microsystems (exosystems; e.g., school, family, peer group, community); by the interactions within and across systems (mesosystems, e.g., family–school interactions); and by the larger local and global society (macrosystem, reflected in social, political, cultural influences). Unique to this depiction is the central role of the systems consultant as facilitator, through TCPC, of interactions among the key stakeholders in the child's ecology for the purpose of understanding and promoting well-being of the child and the system.

Source: From Nastasi et al. (2004, p. 40). Copyright by the American Psychological Association. Adapted with permission. The use of APA information does not imply endorsement by APA.

For example, systems consultation at the school level requires transcultural communication and negotiation among individual students and peers, teachers, administrators and other school staff; among parents and community members; and with consideration of the larger macrosystem. Effective consultation thus requires a thorough understanding of the diverse cultures within the broad ecological system in order to facilitate the cultural co-construction process. As described and illustrated in the next section, TCPC embodies a research process to facilitate cultural understanding of the ecological system. This understanding of context is especially critical in systems consultation as one attempts to facilitate changes at individual, interpersonal, and systemic levels.

TRANSCULTURAL PARTICIPATORY CONSULTATION (TCPC)

Figure 6.2 depicts the TCPC model. In this chapter, the model is applied to systems-level consultation for the purpose of promoting individual, interpersonal, and collective well-being with a specific system (e.g., school, community). The model, adapted from

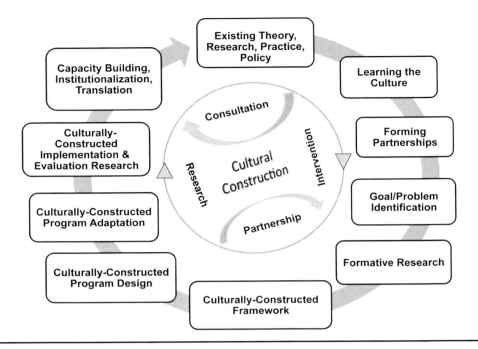

Figure 6.2 Transcultural Participatory Consultation (TCPC)

The TCPC cycle encompasses 10 iterative phases that characterize the process of engaging in the cultural construction of intervention and prevention programs. Central to cultural construction is the facilitation by the systems consultant of partnerships among key stakeholders. This participatory consultation process involves examining existing theory, research, practice, and policy (Phase 1); learning the culture of the target system (Phase 2); establishing partnerships (Phase 3); identifying a shared goal (Phase 4); and conducting formative research (Phase 5) that informs development of a culturally constructed framework (Phase 6) to guide program design, adaptation, implementation, and evaluation (Phases 7–9). The cycle concludes with a phase of capacity building, institutionalization, and translation (Phase 10). Although depicted in 10 phases, the process is iterative such that learning the culture and partnership building continue throughout the cycle, and at any point, stakeholders can return to earlier cycles as deemed relevant (e.g., additional formative research to inform translation).

Source: From Nastasi et al. (2004, p. 54). Copyright by the American Psychological Association. Adapted with permission. The use of APA information does not imply endorsement by APA.

PCSC and PCSIM (Nastasi et al., 2000, 2014), reflects a 10-phase process for developing culturally constructed intervention and prevention programs, in this case to facilitate well-being.

Central to TCPC are *cultural construction, consultation,* and *partnership.* Throughout the TCPC process, key stakeholders are engaged as partners in the process of co-constructing shared understanding and goals, collaborating in the research-intervention process that characterizes program development and evaluation, and ensuring capacity building and institutionalization. The systems consultant plays a central role (see Figure 6.1) in helping to ensure development of partnerships leading to effective co-construction of programs to promote the well-being of individuals and the system.

Also guiding TCPC is the application of an *iterative research-intervention process,* in which research is used to inform development, adaptation, and evaluation of programming. This process is consistent with participatory action research (PAR; e.g., Partridge,

1985), given the focus on the theory-research-practice cycle and the goal of engaging stakeholders to create change they deem relevant to their lives. Although depicted in 10 phases, the research-intervention process is recursive such that partners might return to earlier stages to reformulate goals or engage in additional research to inform program modification or translation. In addition, the focus on partnership and learning the culture is maintained throughout all phases (e.g., adjusting as new partners join the process, maintaining partnerships, and continual attention to in-depth learning about the culture across the system). (Readers interested in more detail about the applied or research aspects of TCPC cycle are referred to Nastasi et al., 2000, 2004; for details about the use of mixed methods research for TCPC, see Nastasi & Hitchcock, 2016.)

Phases of the Process

The TCPC process begins with examining existing theory, research, practice, and policy related to promotion of well-being for individuals and systems (Phase 1). This phase provides both the consultant and consultees with a common knowledge base to frame initial thinking. Consultants are encouraged to share this background information with stakeholders in a format that best meets the needs and expertise of stakeholders (e.g., summarize or provide key articles). For example, the consultant might provide, via handout or presentation, a bulleted list of key findings from research related to the topic of interest. In some instances, school leaders and educators might prefer to see research articles; for example, in one school interested in social-emotional learning as an overarching framework, the principal requested copies of professional literature to be distributed to the leadership team (including the principal) so they have in-depth understanding of the topic and related research. In response, the consultants identified key articles on a periodic basis for the leadership team (e.g., articles on definition of social-emotional competence as discussion of project goals were initiated and examples of effective programs during program design).

Concurrently, the consultant and consultees are engaged in learning the culture (Phase 2) through systematic examination of the "dynamic system of meanings, knowledge and actions that provides actors collectively, interpersonally, and individually with community-legitimized strategies to construct, reflect upon, and reconstruct their world and experience, and guide behaviour" (Nastasi et al., 2015, p. 96). This is best accomplished through the use of ethnographic research methods, which typically include participant observations, interviews, focus groups, and collections of artefacts and permanent products but can also include surveys or questionnaires or other innovative methods (e.g., mixed methods; see Schensul & LeCompte, 1999). The purpose of ethnography is to gain an understanding of culture from the perspectives of its members and as reflected in what they say, do, and produce (Spradley, 1979, 1980). (A detailed description of ethnography is beyond the scope of this chapter. Readers are referred to Schensul & LeCompte, 1999.)

Given the multiple cultural experiences within a given system, Phase 2 requires examination of culture from the perspective of all stakeholder groups. Within a school setting, this might include students, teachers, administrators, health and mental health providers, and secretarial and custodial staff. Consistent with an ecological perspective (see Figure 6.1), Phase 2 would also require understanding culture from the perspectives of families, peers, and community members and examination of culture from a larger macrosystemic focus (e.g., social, political, economic, human rights).

Phase 3 involves development of partnerships with key stakeholder groups such as those identified in Phase 2. These partnerships are expected to frame the cultural construction process and development of culturally constructed well-being programs. The development and maintenance of partnerships requires effective communication and negotiation skills among all parties. The systems consultant, as facilitator of this process, is well advised to institute training and professional development sessions to ensure all stakeholders can participate as equal partners. Such training, of course, is most effectively conducted in collaboration with or by key partners.

Phase 4 involves the identification of a shared goal (e.g., promoting well-being) as defined by the stakeholders/partners. At this stage, stakeholders identify a shared goal based on the outcomes of Phases 1 and 2. The well-being goal identified at this stage can be broadly defined (e.g., physical well-being and/or psychological well-being) as the goals will be further explicated through formative research in the next phase.

Phase 5 is best achieved through a mixed methods research approach (e.g., see Nastasi & Hitchcock, 2016) that includes selected qualitative and quantitative methods. The purpose of formative research is to understand the current status (resources and needs) of the system with regard to the identified goal (e.g., physical and/or psychological well-being). Inherent in the TCPC model is the expectation that formative research findings reflect the multiple perspectives of stakeholders achieved through collaborative decision making about key constructs and relevant data sources and informants, data collection from multiple informants, and collaboration in the analysis and interpretation of data. Within the context of a school, for example, data collection might include interviews, focus groups, surveys, and school record data.

The outcome of formative research is a co-constructed framework (Phase 6) for guiding program design, implementation, evaluation, and capacity building (Phases 7–10). Drawing from prior phases (1–5), the program development team might construct a model that: (a) defines key constructs relevant to physical and psychological well-being; (b) depicts the existing status and connections among physical and psychological well-being and academic performance within the school; (c) describes the individual, interpersonal, and collective factors relevant to well-being for the system; and (d) portrays the respective roles of key stakeholders in the promotion of well-being at individual, interpersonal, and collective levels.

Using the conceptual framework from Phase 6, partners would then engage in a process of culturally constructing a program for promoting well-being (Phase 7), implementing the program and making relevant adaptations to meet population and contextual needs (Phase 8), and implementing a program of research to monitor and evaluate the program (Phase 9). The implementation, adaptation, and evaluation approach should be informed by current research and practice. For example, consistent with current thinking in implementation science (e.g., Helfrich et al., 2010) and mixed methods research (Nastasi & Hitchcock, 2016), evaluation should address both process and outcome variables, make use of mixed (qualitative and quantitative) methods and multiple informants, and contribute to the ongoing adaptation/modification of the program across the system. (For further information, see Nastasi & Hitchcock, 2016.) The goals of evaluation research within TCPC are: (a) to facilitate effective and sustainable programming; (b) inform capacity building, institutionalization, and translation (Phase 10); and (c) contribute to existing theory, research, practice, and policy, thus completing the cycle.

The final phase of TPCP is focused on capacity building, institutionalization, and translation (Phase 10). Although depicted as a culminating phase, efforts to facilitate capacity building and institutionalization are embedded throughout the cycle. For example, capacity building requires that stakeholders/partners develop the necessary skills for continuing a participatory cultural construction approach to program development and evaluation, including translation to other contexts. Thus, the consultant with partners should plan for requisite training in collaboration, research and evaluation, and program development and implementation. Furthermore, engaging administrators and policy makers as partners in the process can help to ensure institutionalization.

The TCPC process has promise for facilitating partnerships across cultural boundaries and developing intervention and prevention programs that are culturally constructed by key stakeholders. Such a process could potentially address issues related to implementation science (e.g., Helfrich et al., 2010) and inform our understanding of the cultural and contextual factors that influence development of effective programs.

Although TCPC is a systematic approach, the complexity of factors related to systems consultation and program development and evaluation pose challenges for any consultant. Examples from research and development projects in which the chapter author has been engaged as a systems consultant (and/or supervising a team of consultants) are used to illustrate the application of TCPC (see Table 6.2). All of these projects have been described in detail in other publications, so the focus in the next section is drawing from those experiences to discuss successes and challenges related to working across cultural boundaries.

Applying TCPC to Systems Consultation for Well-being

Table 6.2 delineates research and development work by Nastasi and colleagues that involved application of a participatory consultation process to facilitate cultural co-construction of intervention and prevention programs related to health and psychological well-being. The collective body of work reflects application of TCPC in schools and communities in South Asia and the U.S. and encompasses child, adolescent, and adult populations. As indicated in the table, the projects spanned several years, illustrating the long-term commitment and multiproject efforts necessary to engage in the TCPC cycle to the point of capacity building, institutionalization, and translation. Because more detailed descriptions can be found in the relevant citations, this section is devoted to discussing issues across projects related to the participatory and transdisciplinary nature of the work, the transcultural negotiation and cultural construction process, and the outcomes of cultural construction for program development.

Participatory and Transdisciplinary Nature of the Work

Characterizing the work across the multiple projects is the development of partnerships with stakeholders from multiple sectors (e.g., family, school, community, health, mental health, research, intervention, university) and across multiple disciplines (e.g., anthropology, education, medicine, psychology, public health, sociology, social work). The management of these relationships required expertise in systems consultation, interpersonal communication, and group process. The transdisciplinary nature of the work necessitated negotiation of diverse perspectives and building consensus regarding research questions, methodology, intervention strategies, and analysis and interpretation of data.

Table 6.2 Examples of Transcultural Systems Consultation for Promoting Well-being

Project location (number of projects, time period)	System focus	Well-being focus	Target population	Partners	Disciplines	Programming outcomes	Relevant citations
Sri Lanka[a] (Central Province) (single project, 1995–1996)	Community	Sexual risk prevention	Adolescents, young adults	Community youth, peer educators, health educators, researchers, interventionists	Anthropology, health, medicine, psychology, sociology	Culturally constructed sexual risk prevention program delivered by peer educators	Nastasi, Schensul et al. (1998–99)
Sri Lanka[b] (Central, Southern, Western provinces) (four projects; 1995–2013)	Schools	Psychological well-being	Children, adolescents	Students, parents, teachers, school administrators, district ministers, policy makers, researchers, interventionists, graduate students and faculty in education and school psychology	Education, school psychology, psychiatry, medicine, sociology	Culturally constructed measures of well-being, culturally constructed psychological well-being promotion programs, adaptation of programs for post-tsunami context, development of teacher and parent education components	Hitchcock, Nastasi et al. (2005), Jayasena, Borja, and Nastasi (2016), Nastasi and Hitchcock (2016), Nastasi, Hitchcock et al. (2010), Nastasi, Hitchcock, Burkholder et al. (2007), Nastasi, Hitchcock, Sarkar et al. (2007), Nastasi and Jayasena (2014), Nastasi, Jayasena, Summerville, and Borja (2011), Nastasi, Moore, and Varjas (2004), Nastasi, Varjas et al. (1998), Nastasi, Varjas et al. (2000)
U.S. (New Orleans)[c] (projects in three schools, 2009–2015)	Schools	Psychological well-being	Children	Students, teachers, parents, school administrators and support staff, researchers, interventionists, graduate students in school psychology; community mental health professionals	Education, school and clinical psychology, social work, counseling	Culturally constructed comprehensive mental health programming, including universal screening and social-emotional learning programs, staff development, secondary and tertiary services, and program evaluation	Bell (2014), Bell, Summerville, Nastasi, MacFetters, and Earnshaw (2015), Bell, Verlenden et al. (2016), Swift (2012, 2015)

[a]For this project, the chapter author served in the role of consultant for development and implementation of the intervention. Relationships and cultural knowledge resulting from this project led to the subsequent school-based research and development projects in Sri Lanka.

[b]These projects were funded with small grants to the PI (Nastasi) from the Society for the Study of School Psychology, Albany State University–New York, Walden University, and Tulane University.

[c]This work reflects university–school partnerships that involve faculty, doctoral students in school psychology, and undergraduates in psychology at Tulane and select elementary charter schools in New Orleans initiated after Hurricane Katrina as schools were reestablished in the city. The formative data collection in one of the schools also contributed to the Promoting Psychological Well-Being Project, a multicountry initiative sponsored by the International School Psychology Association.

This process could prove challenging as experts address conflicting theoretical and methodological perspectives and develop relationships and mutual respect over time. For example, in a research project involving professionals from anthropology, psychology, and medicine (Schensul, Nastasi, & Verma, 2006), the research-intervention team grappled with how to best approach a sexual risk prevention program to be delivered by local doctors: How do we integrate research findings about psychological and cultural factors that influenced sexual risk with current medical practice by biomedical and traditional doctors who are giving minimal attention to psychological and cultural factors? The process of program development required a period of in-depth discussion, debate, and consensus building among the stakeholders to adapt existing medical practice to integrate psychological and cultural considerations. Over time, the partners came to appreciate the importance of the medical, cultural, and psychological perspectives in approaching sexual risk and worked to seamlessly blend the perspectives into a feasible intervention. Moreover, some doctors participating in the project reported extending the integrated approach to assessment, diagnosis, and treatment for all patients.

Particularly working across international borders, electronic communication was critical to supplement periodic face-to-face meetings and could easily lead to miscommunications. Negotiating across both cultural and disciplinary boundaries required attention to meaning as much as language translation. Schensul et al. (2006) provide an in-depth discussion of the challenges related to the intersection of international and interdisciplinary collaboration. For example, in a U.S.–India collaboration (described in Schensul et al., 2006), working across national boundaries required electronic communication, which could lead to misunderstandings; thus, partners had to agree to question each other when misunderstandings occurred or when clarification was needed, whether communicating electronically, by phone, or face-to-face. From this experience, this author learned the importance of being clear about, and routinely asking about, the meaning of common terminology/vocabulary.

In addition to the transdisciplinary collaboration, the participatory nature of TCPC involves the negotiation of perspectives across different stakeholder groups who hold vested interests or resources relevant to program development. The systems consultant plays a key role in facilitating these relationships and interactions, identifying and convening meetings of representatives from different stakeholder groups, ensuring capacity for effective and equitable communication leading to co-construction (e.g., through training in interpersonal communication, negotiation, conflict resolution), facilitating group discussions and meetings of stakeholders, and continuing the process over time until consensus is achieved. Based on experiences from multiple projects cited in Table 6.2, several considerations are warranted:

- Identify a cultural broker who can facilitate selection of appropriate representatives of stakeholder groups, facilitate involvement of local stakeholders, and help to interpret cultural perspectives and experiences.
- Provide opportunities to gather data on the cultural perspectives and experiences of each stakeholder group (e.g., through focus groups and interviews).
- Share de-identified data across stakeholder groups that reflect the points of convergence and divergence and that provides a starting point for planning and negotiation.

- Bring stakeholder groups together periodically to ensure continued involvement and inclusion of multiple perspectives.
- Ensure the inclusion and participation of new members of stakeholder groups (e.g., to address staff turnover in schools).

Transcultural Negotiation and Cultural Construction Process

The development of relationships among stakeholders and across disciplinary groups is critical to engaging in negotiation and co-construction leading to program development. Bell et al. (2015) detail the participatory process and use of formative research to facilitate negotiation of perspectives across stakeholder groups. One strategy we used to accomplish this in a New Orleans School project was to analyze the formative research to identify points of consensus across the major stakeholder groups (students, parents, school staff), looking for complete consensus (all three groups), agreement across two groups (e.g., teachers and parents, but not students), and group-specific findings (e.g., unique to parents). These findings were then shared with all stakeholder groups for discussion and feedback. A team of school leaders (administration, support staff, teachers) used the data to make decisions about next steps. Another example from the same project involved a multiple-session parent group that led to consensus about the needs of students and respective roles of parents and teachers in addressing needs. The parents, in turn, presented the data to school staff with a set of recommendations to which school administration responded positively (see Swift, 2012).

In a second New Orleans school, Swift (2015) convened a series of sessions with teachers and school administrators to explore the teachers' social-emotional competence related to their capacity for supporting students' well-being. This process involved negotiation across multiple cultural perspectives[1] and experiences to identify the needs of staff and inform professional development of teachers. This experience highlighted the need for establishing equitable relationships among teachers and administrators to ensure an effective participatory process. This is an important consideration when bringing together stakeholders with different levels of power and requires skillful facilitation of group process by the consultant and agreement on the part of participants in positions of power (e.g., school administrator in group with teachers). (For further information about facilitating effective group process, see Friend & Cook, 2013.)

In a third New Orleans school, a team of partners was convened to make decisions about goals and formative research and subsequently to develop a plan for school programming based on the outcomes of the formative research (see Bell, 2014). This team included representatives of school administration, teachers, parents, and students. In such instances, advance preparation of student representatives is critical to effective involvement in the team process.

In each of the three schools in New Orleans, engagement in TCPC resulted in program development initiatives related to promotion of student psychological well-being through a comprehensive approach to mental health services (e.g., as illustrated in Bell et al., 2015). The planning involved development of respective program models; program design; professional development of staff; establishing procedures for ongoing data collection to inform adaptation and evaluation; continued consultation with university partners; and, in most instances, enlisting community-based resources to support school programming. Although the process in all three schools was consistent with TCPC, the sequencing and articulation of each phase varied, thus resulting in different culturally constructed programming.

In all three schools, we of course started with building relationships and learning about the school's culture. However, in one school with established mental health programming, we started by working with the team to examine what current programs and related outcome data existed before starting any data collection. The consultation was focused on refining what already existed. In another school with no mental health services, we spent more time coming to an agreement about the need and nature of services. Although the primary administrative consultee agreed with the importance of school-based mental health services, this view was not shared by all in administrative/decision-making roles. So, the initial work was focused on gathering data through qualitative research and universal screening to establish need and develop of a plan for addressing the need. This resulted in first seeking external services to support students' mental health needs for the short term and then later hiring of a social worker and a school psychologist, reflecting the school's commitment to addressing social, emotional, behavioral, and academic needs of students. Furthermore, across the three schools, different universal screening tools and social-emotional learning programs were selected, reflecting differing needs and preferences. In each case, options were shared with staff and selections made following discussion of pros and cons of different approaches for the specific setting. In the next section, we examine the programming outcomes of research and development in Sri Lanka.

Programming Outcomes of Cultural Construction

As noted in the previous section, implementing a consistent process of TCPC across three schools yielded different decisions about programming to meet the respective cultural and contextual needs. To further illustrate this phenomenon, we draw on the school-based work conducted in Sri Lanka. Extensive formative research in several Central Province schools (representing the country's demographics) yielded a culturally constructed conceptual model of psychological well-being, which included culturally valued competencies (defined by child and adult stakeholders), personal and social-cultural stressors, reactions to stress, support systems, cultural norms, and socialization agents and practices (see Nastasi et al., 1998). For example, cultural expectations for academic achievement were reported by students not only as competencies valued by adults and society but also as an important source of stress associated with pressure to achieve and time devoted on evenings and weekends to studying or additional tutoring. An associated stressor was the limited time for recreation (a competency domain valued by students). The emphasis on achievement was related to the limited access to free higher education and the determination of tracking into professions through standardized testing at grades 10 and 12 (an influence of the former status as a British colony).

Furthermore, gender norms became evident in the greater freedom for adolescent boys to go about in the community unchaperoned, whereas girls needed to be chaperoned (perceived by girls as both unfair and a source of stress). In addition, unchaperoned interactions between adolescent boys and girls were prohibited and arranged marriages were the norm. Any unauthorized interactions were subject to disciplinary procedures in school (e.g., if love letters were discovered in a girl's backpack).

The findings informed development of self-report measures of perceived competence (Hitchcock et al., 2005) and stress and coping (Nastasi, Hitchcock, Burkholder et al.,

2007) that reflected the cultural norms and experiences of the target population. For example, in creating the stress and coping measure, scenarios depicting different types of stressors (e.g., school, family, peer group) were created from the formative data (particularly, collective narratives gathered during focus group interviews) and questions related to emotional reactions, coping, and related adjustment problems were created with response options that used language and concepts reflected in the data. In addition, we gave attention to distinctions between stressful situations in which the child could exert some control (e.g., addressing pressures related to academic achievement) and those in which control was limited (e.g., addressing stressors related to cultural norms such as restrictions against interactions between adolescent boys and girls). In the former case, active problem-solving or instrumental support-seeking was possible (e.g., studying more or seeking tutoring to address academic pressures), whereas, in the latter case, strategies for alleviating distress were needed (e.g., talking to a friend to gain emotional support or engaging in relaxation).

In addition, formative research informed the development of a population-level psychological well-being promotion program to be implemented by teachers (Nastasi, Hitchcock et al., 2010). A unique aspect of the program was the use of ecomaps (graphic depiction of self in relationship to others) as stimuli for identifying stressors and support within specific ecological contexts (e.g., school, peer group, family) followed by individual and collaborative problem-solving related to common stressors (e.g., academics, interpersonal conflict). The formative data and initial piloting of intervention strategies revealed that Sri Lankan students consistently described themselves *in relationship to others*; in contrast, the notion of self-awareness and self-development outside of relationships was not valid in the thinking of children or adults.

To address long-term adjustment following the 2014 tsunami (18 months post-tsunami), the initial psychological well-being program was adapted to integrate environmental stressors and increased attention to emotional awareness and regulation (Nastasi et al., 2011). In addition, in response to the reported and observed needs of adults, companion programs for parents were developed to facilitate parental support of child well-being. Analysis of data collected during implementation (e.g., ecomaps and written narratives) revealed that the post-tsunami program provided an opportunity for students to address both developmentally appropriate stressors (e.g., interpersonal conflicts, academic pressure) and tsunami-related stressors (e.g., related to rebuilding, relocation, loss).

Across the projects depicted in Table 6.2, the consistent factor was the transcultural participatory process of consultation and program development. Reflected in the examples is the diversity of populations, contexts, and outcomes of the cultural construction process. Each setting (school, community) was considered to represent a unique cultural context that was better understood by the members of the context (key stakeholders) than by the consultant. Even working within one's own community requires a learning approach to understand the experiences and meanings of the target population and context. In addition, it is likely that one will encounter diverse cultural experiences and perspectives among the stakeholders. Thus, the responsibility of the systems consultant is not only to learn from the stakeholders but also to facilitate shared understanding among stakeholders, whether they are community members or professionals. This learning process is both a challenge and an opportunity to enhance one's own professional expertise as a transcultural consultant and to facilitate action directed by the stakeholders.

Table 6.3 Pedagogical Guidelines for Preparing Consultants in TCPC

Pedagogy to facilitate development of knowledge, beliefs, attitudes, skills, and practices related to engaging as a transcultural consultant in TCPC requires providing the following set of opportunities for learners:

- Opportunities to develop knowledge about participatory (collaborative) models of consultation applied to client, consultee, and organizational/system levels; quantitative, qualitative, and mixed methods applied to ethnography and action research; program development and evaluation models; capacity building (e.g., through staff training and stakeholder empowerment); theory and research related to co-construction of knowledge, effective communication, and culture and intercultural competence
- Opportunities to develop and practice skills/behaviors related to participatory consultation, mixed methods ethnographic and action research, program development and evaluation, capacity building, facilitating co-construction through integration of disparate ideas and consensus building, communicating effectively across cultural boundaries, and self-reflection
- Opportunities to explore and confront existing attitudes and beliefs in order to develop genuine openness to learning from others, valuing of multiple perspectives, willingness to negotiate and reach consensus, commitment to facilitating empowerment of others, and humility with regard to one's cultural competence
- Opportunities to apply and integrate knowledge and skills by engaging in guided/supervised practice in TCPC through school- and community-based projects
- Opportunities to engage in intercultural communication in local communities or across national boundaries through electronic communication or study abroad/exchange programs
- Preparation for reflexive practice and lifelong learning guided by awareness, self-evaluation, and critique and adaptation of beliefs and practices with the goal of ever-expanding intercultural competence and global identity (as described by Friedman & Antal, 2005).

Developing Expertise in TCPC

Effective application of TCPC requires expertise in participatory approaches to consultation, ethnographic and action research, program development and evaluation, capacity building, facilitating co-construction, and intercultural communication. For those interested in using the approach described in this chapter, professional development in these areas is recommended. Table 6.3 provides pedagogical guidelines for professional preparation or development in knowledge, skills, attitudes, beliefs, and practices relevant to engaging in TCPC (see also Nastasi, 2010; Nastasi et al., 2004). The opportunities, listed in Table 6.3, for development of knowledge, skills, attitudes, beliefs, and practices relevant to TCPC can be provided in graduate or postgraduate training in the health, education, and social sciences through coursework and supervised field experiences. Developing expertise in this area is likely to require lifelong commitment to learning and reflective practice across multiple cultures.

CONCLUSIONS

The purpose of this chapter was to describe and illustrate a transcultural approach to systems consultation with a specific focus on developing programs to promote well-being. The goal of the transcultural participatory consultation model (TCPC) is to engage stakeholders as partners in a cultural co-construction process that integrates diverse cultural perspectives and results in a shared set of meanings that in turn influence the thinking and behavior of all participants. The co-constructed system of meaning (culture) then informs the development of intervention programs to facilitate well-being broadly defined (e.g., health, mental health). Critical to this process is the expertise of the systems consultant in developing relationships, convening stakeholders, and facilitating negotiation of perspectives and consensus. The chapter concludes with examples from research and development work of the chapter's author and recommendations for developing expertise relevant to TCPC.

As noted throughout, the TCPC process is complex and recursive. The 10 phases are not typically implemented in a lock-step manner, and consultants will likely need to revisit earlier phases. In addition, the process is typically multiyear and thus requires integration of new partners and new perspectives as programming progresses. The intended outcome of TCPC is development of programs that are culturally constructed (and thus relevant to the target population and context) and adaptable to changing needs of the system. Furthermore, the process is devoted to developing ownership (through participation) and capacity building (through skill development) to facilitate sustainable systemic programming. The application of TCPC to systems consultation for program development has the potential to be rewarding and meaningful for consultants, consultees, and the populations they serve.

NOTE

1. For example, one of the challenges of working in New Orleans public schools post-Katrina is the discrepancy between the cultural experiences of the primarily low socioeconomic status African American children and parents with long family histories in the city who live in communities with high violence rates and the primarily middle to upper-middle class European American population of teachers and administrators who moved to New Orleans from other parts of the country after Katrina and have minimal experience with the culture of the city or the neighborhoods of the students. In addition, schools often had a mixture of the aforementioned new teachers as well as veteran teachers from New Orleans who have in-depth knowledge of the culture of the population.

REFERENCES

Bell, Patrick. (2014, September). *A transformative, participatory approach for social-emotional focused urban school reform* (Unpublished doctoral dissertation). Department of Psychology, Tulane University, New Orleans, LA.

Bell, P. B., Summerville, M. A., Nastasi, B. K., MacFetters, J., & Earnshaw, E. (2015). Promoting psychological well-being in an urban school using the participatory culture specific intervention model. *Journal of Educational and Psychological Consultation, 25*, 1–18. doi: 10.1080/10474412.2014.92995

Bell, P. B., Verlenden, J. M., Swift, A. L., Henderson, H. H., & Nastasi, B. K. (2016). Emic perspectives of risk and support: Voices from lower elementary students in New Orleans, Louisiana, United States of America. In B. K. Nastasi & A. P. Borja (Eds.), *International handbook of psychological well-being in children and adolescents* (pp. 271–290). New York: Springer.

Bibeau, G., & Corin, E. (1995). From submission to the text to interpretative violence. In G. Bibeau & E. Corin (Eds.), *Beyond textuality: Asceticism and violence in anthropological interpretation: Approaches to semiotics series* (pp. 3–54). Berlin: Mouton de Gruyter.

Bronfenbrenner, U. (1989). Ecological systems theory. In R. Vasta (Ed.), *Annals of child development* (Vol. 6, pp. 187–249). Greenwich, CT: JAI Press.

Bronfenbrenner, U. (1999). Environments in developmental perspective: Theoretical and operational models. In S. L. Friedman & T. D. Wachs (Eds.), *Measuring environment across the life span: Emerging methods and concepts* (pp. 3–28). Washington, DC: American Psychological Association.

Center for Disease Control & Prevention. (2009). *School connectedness: Strategies for increasing protective factors among youth*. Atlanta, GA: U.S. Department of Health and Human Services. Retrieved from www.cdc.gov/HealthyYouth

Friedman, V. J., & Antal, A. B. (2005). Negotiating reality: A theory of action approach to intercultural competence. *Management Learning, 36*(1), 69–86. doi: 10.1177/1350507605049904

Friend, M., & Cook, L. (2013). *Interactions: Collaboration skills for school professionals* (7th ed.). Boston: Pearson.

Geertz, C. (1968/1992). *Observer l'Islam. Changements Religieux au Maroc et en Indonésie*. Paris: Éditions de la Découverte.

Greenwood, D. J., Whyte, W. F., & Harkavy, I. (1993). Participatory action research as a process and as a goal. *Human Relations, 46*, 175–192.

Hatzichristou, C., Lampropoulou, A., & Lykitsakou, K. (2006). Addressing cultural factors in development of systems interventions. *Journal of Applied School Psychology, 22*, 103–136.

Hatzichristou, C., Lykitsakou, K., Lampropoulou, A., & Dimitropoulou, P. (2010). Promoting the well-being of school communities: A systemic approach. In B. Doll, W. Phohl, & J. Yoon (Eds.), *Handbook of prevention science* (pp. 255–274). New York, NY: Routledge.

Helfrich, C. D., Darnschroder, L. J., Hagedorn, H. J., Daggett, G. S., Sahay, A., Richie, M., . . . Stetler, C. B. (2010). A critical synthesis of literature on the promoting action on research implementation in health services (PARIHS) framework. *Implementation Science, 5*, 82. doi: 10.1186/1748–5908–5–82

Hitchcock, J. H., Nastasi, B. K., Dai, D. C., Newman, J., Jayasena, A., Bernstein-Moore, R., . . . Varjas, K. (2005). Illustrating a mixed-method approach for identifying and validating culturally specific constructs. *Journal of School Psychology, 43*, 259–278.

Jayasena, A., Borja, A. P., & Nastasi, B. K. (2016). Youth perspectives about the factors that contribute to psychological well-being in Negombo, Sri Lanka. In B. K. Nastasi & A. P. Borja (Eds.), *International handbook of psychological well-being in children and adolescents* (pp. 201–220). New York: Springer.

Kleinman, A., Eisenberg, L., & Good, B. (1978). Culture, illness, and care: Clinical lessons from anthropologic and cross-cultural research. *Annals of Internal Medicine, 88*, 251–258.

Nastasi, B. K. (2010). How much theory do we teach? In E. García-Vázquez, T. Crespi, & C. Riccio (Eds.), *Handbook of education, training and supervision of school psychologists in school and community. Volume I: Foundations of professional practice* (pp. 85–108). New York: Taylor & Francis/Routledge.

Nastasi, B. K., & Hitchcock, J. (2016). *Mixed methods research and culture-specific interventions: Program design and evaluation*. The New Mixed Methods Research Series. Thousand Oaks, CA: Sage.

Nastasi, B. K., Hitchcock, J. H., Burkholder, G., Varjas, K., Sarkar, S., & Jayasena, A. (2007). Assessing adolescents' understanding of and reactions to stress in different cultures: Results of a mixed-methods approach. *School Psychology International, 28*, 163–178.

Nastasi, B. K., Hitchcock, J. H., Sarkar, S., Burkholder, G., Varjas, K., & Jayasena, A. (2007). Mixed methods in intervention research: Theory to adaptation. *Journal of Mixed Methods Research, 1*(2), 164–182.

Nastasi, B. K., Hitchcock, J. H., Varjas, K., Jayasena, A., Sarkar, S., Moore, R. B., . . . Albrecht, L. (2010). School-based stress and coping program for adolescents in Sri Lanka: Using mixed methods to facilitate culture-specific programming. In K. M. T. Collins, A. J. Onwuegbuzie, & Q. G. Jiao (Vol. Eds.), *Toward a broader understanding of stress and coping: Mixed methods approaches: The Research on Stress and Coping in Education Series* (Vol. 5, pp. 305–342). Charlotte, NC: Information Age Publishing.

Nastasi, B. K., & Jayasena, A. (2014). International partnership for promoting psychological well-being in Sri Lankan schools. *Journal of Educational and Psychological Consultation, 24*, 265–282, doi: 10.1080/10474412.2014.929965

Nastasi, B. K., Jayasena, A., Summerville, M., & Borja, A. (2011). Facilitating long-term recovery from natural disasters: Psychosocial programming in tsunami-affected schools of Sri Lanka. *School Psychology International, 32*, 512–532. doi: 10.1177/0143034311402923

Nastasi, B. K., Moore, R. B., & Varjas, K. M. (2004). *School-based mental health services: Creating comprehensive and culturally specific programs*. Washington, DC: American Psychological Association.

Nastasi, B. K., Schensul, J. J., deSilva, M.W.A., Varjas, K., Silva, K. T., Ratnayake, P., & Schensul, S. L. (1998–99). Community-based sexual risk prevention program for Sri Lankan youth: Influencing sexual-risk decision making. *International Quarterly of Community Health Education, 18*(1), 139–155.

Nastasi, B. K., Schensul, J. J., Schensul, S. L., Mekki-Berrada, A., Pelto, B., Maitra, S., . . . Saggurti, N. (2015). A model for translating ethnography and theory into culturally constructed clinical practice. *Culture, Medicine and Psychiatry, 39*, 92–109. doi: 10.1007/s11013–014–9404–9

Nastasi, B. K., Varjas, K., Bernstein, R., & Jayasena, A. (2000). Conducting participatory culture-specific consultation: A global perspective on multicultural consultation. *School Psychology Review, 29*, 401–413.

Nastasi, B. K., Varjas, K., Sarkar, S., & Jayasena, A. (1998). Participatory model of mental health programming: Lessons learned from work in a developing country. *School Psychology Review, 27*, 260–276.

Nelson, G., & Prilleltensky, I. (2005). *Community psychology: In pursuit of liberation and well-being*. New York, NY: Palgrave Macmillan.

Partridge, W. L. (1985). Toward a theory of practice. *American Behavioral Scientist, 29*, 139–163.

Schensul, J. J., & LeCompte, M. D. (Eds.). (1999). *Ethnographer's Toolkit, Volumes 1–7*. Walnut Creek, CA: AltaMira Press.

Schensul, S. L., Nastasi, B. K., & Verma, R. K. (2006). Community-based research in India: A case example of international and interdisciplinary collaboration. *American Journal of Community Psychology*, pp. 1–17, [online version]. doi: 10.1007/s10464–006–9066-z. Retrieved from http://dx.doi.org/10.1007/s10464–006–9066-z

Spradley, J. P. (1979). *The ethnographic interview*. New York: Holt, Rinehart, & Winston.

Spradley, J. P. (1980). *Participant observation*. New York: Holt, Rinehart, & Winston.

Swift, Allisyn L. (2012, April). *Parental stress and socialization practices of Black parents: Qualitative research and analyses to inform interventions* (Unpublished master's thesis). Department of Psychology, Tulane University, New Orleans, LA.

Swift, Allisyn L. (2015, March). *Toward a local model of teacher professional development for social-emotional learning for elementary teachers of urban minority youth* (Unpublished doctoral dissertation). Department of Psychology, Tulane University, New Orleans, LA.

Thapa, A., Cohen, J., Higgins-D'Alessandro, A., & Gaffey, S. (2012). *School climate research summary: August 2012*. New York: National School Climate Center.

UNICEF. (2009). *Child-friendly schools manual*. Geneva: UNICEF. Retrieved from http://www.unicef.org/publications/index_49574.html

United Nations (UN). (1989). *Convention on the rights of the child*. Retrieved from http://www2.ohchr.org/english/law/crc.htm

United Nations (UN). (2000). *Millennium development goals*. New York: Author. Retrieved March 30, 2015, from http://www.un.org/milleniumgoals/

United Nations (UN). (2015). *Sustainable development goals*. New York: Author. Retrieved October 1, 2015, from http://www.un.org/sustainabledevelopment

Vygotsky, L. S. (1978). *Mind in society: The development of higher psychological processes*. Cambridge, MA: Harvard University Press.

Wertsch, J. V. (1991). *Voices of the mind: A sociocultural approach to mediated action*. Cambridge, MA: Harvard University Press.

Whaley, A. L., & Davis, K. E. (2007). Cultural competence and evidence-based practice in mental health services: A complementary perspective. *American Psychologist, 62*, 563–574. doi: 10.1037/0003–066X.62.6.563

World Health Organization (WHO). (1998). *WHO's global school health initiative: Health-promoting schools*. WHO/HPR/HEP/98.4. Geneva: WHO. Retrieved January 18, 2014, from http://www.who.int/school_youth_health/media/en/92.pdf?ua=1

World Health Organization (WHO). (2003). *Creating an environment for emotional and social well-being: An important responsibility of a health-promoting and child friendly school*. WHO Information Series on School Health, Document 10. Geneva: Author. Retrieved October 6, 2015, from http://www.who.int/school_youth_health/resources/information_series/en/

7

NAVIGATING THE CULTURAL COMPLEXITIES OF SCHOOL CONSULTATION WITH CONTEMPORARY FAMILIES IN A GLOBALIZED WORLD

Candice A. Hughes

The socially situated nature of consultation makes the variable of human diversity immediately relevant to its practice and investigation.

(Clare, 2002, p. 252)

A diversity-focused conceptual framework and navigational mindset can facilitate the work of school professionals engaging in consultation practices regarding school referral concerns for the diverse range of students and their families they will encounter in their professional work. It is advisable to do so from a conjoint consulting perspective, in which the consultant works together with school professionals and the parent(s) and/or other caregivers to inform, shape, and implement each stage of the consultation process (Sheridan & Kratochwill, 2007). Inclusion of the parent(s) or other significant family members/caregivers as consultees is vital, because they have the knowledge base about the family's diversity background and lived experiences that will be invaluable to resolving school concerns about their child.

However, the ability to skillfully navigate the stages of multicultural consultation can be the Achilles' heel of the work of a school consultant when confronted with the many cultural, intercultural, and diversity scenarios that can present themselves in school settings, making it difficult to know where to begin, with whom, why, and how. Inadequate approaches to addressing pertinent issues of culture and diversity for specific cases can result in ineffective resolution of presenting concerns and increase the probability of a longer-term negative impact for the focal student, family, and even the school community. In contrast, intentional focus on the role of culture and diversity in presenting problems that the consultant addresses with consultee(s) can both enhance the problem resolution as well as carry the potential to transform the overall learning experience for the student and the relationship of the family with the school community (Masten, 2014; Zirkel, 2008).

School communities can also be seen as places where families and school professionals may encounter one another across cultural/diversity divides, often with different expectations for how to interact in mutually accommodating and/or adaptive ways regarding one or more of the features of schooling in these settings (Li & Vasquez-Nuttall, 2008; Nastasi, 2005; Zirkel, 2008). Such encounters may trigger different types of responses and consequences for the participants involved.

This chapter focuses on the students and their families who comprise the increased diversity of educational communities in the world—who they are, their key characteristics, and the types of issues and challenges that constitute their lived experiences. Further, it highlights the potential for growth and resiliency that they have when culturally sensitive consultation practices lead to insights and strategies that meet their normative as well as unique needs in the educational community where these children attend school.

DEFINITION OF HIGHLY DIVERSE SCHOOL SETTINGS

The reader is invited to zoom in and visualize a classroom, one that could be located anywhere in the world. It is characterized by the label of "highly diverse" with regard to the students who enter it on a daily basis during a school year. The label of "highly diverse" has many meanings based on the classification system used, such as:

- The racial/ethnic/cultural mixture of the students and any other category of diversity to which they belong
- The migration pathways that they and their families have traveled (e.g. refugee, immigrant, expatriate, sojourner, international adoptee)
- The unique labels that have been assigned to them in contrast to "nondiverse" or "mainstreamed" students (e.g., first or second generation, limited English proficiency [LEP], culturally linguistically diverse [CLD], bilingual or bicultural, child of color, transnational/third-culture kid [TCK]/global nomad, and the rapidly increasing numbers of children identified as multiracial and/or multiethnic)
- The reality that some children in this classroom will have lesser-valued status and access to opportunities in the society where this school is located on the basis of their skin color, ethnicity, socioeconomic status, religion, sexual orientation, gender identity, and ability versus disability status
- The fact that the family history timelines for some of these children will have added to their unique diversity status because of additional experiences used to define them within the contexts of where they have lived (e.g., trauma and PTSD, victimization by violence and/or war, bullying, trafficking, or terrorism), as well as family life status (e.g., divorce, parental and/or sibling incarceration, drug addiction, or mental illness).

This complex scenario, while not yet the norm for the majority of classrooms in the U.S. and other countries, is a growing phenomenon in the contemporary world of schooling. The rapidly changing demographic mixtures of students, families, and even school professionals have led to highly multicultural and diverse educational communities in many places in the world (Li & Vazquez-Nuttall, 2009; Munz, 2013).

Creating Sense from Complexity: An Organizational Framework
for Consulting with Diverse Families

In a primarily monocultural school setting, a school consultant would presumably have the cultural competence to work effectively with professional colleagues and a child's primary parents or caregivers because of shared backgrounds regarding one or more of the standard diversity categories. However, once one or more of these diversity features vary from one's known cultural referent perspective, the consultation begins to increase in complexity due to the number of diversity variables present as well as the interactive effects that can exist between them.

For example, consider a consultation meeting where four adults (consultant, teacher, parents) come together to consult about the school concerns of the focal student. Assume that all share similar values and beliefs with respect to race/ethnicity, nationality, socio-economic level, ability, gender, sexual orientation, religion, and age. One might then anticipate that there may be a high likelihood of shared perceptions, assumptions, and expectations regarding this student as well as an efficient resolution of the presenting concern via the collaborative consultation process.

In contrast, consider a consultation meeting with four adults who represent one or more forms of diversity. The child's mother is African American and Baptist and the father is from Mexico and is Roman Catholic, the teacher is an Asian American male, and the school consultant is a white European background female who self-identifies as bisexual. What are the potential cultural and diversity variables that might add complexity to this consultation meeting? Will it be differences in participant expectations regarding school performance and/or behavior? Might it be previous life experiences for some of the people at the table who have personally experienced educational inequities when they attended school or within the larger society? Will it be differences in culturally based communication and emotional expressiveness styles? What else might be operative in this situation? And, most important, how successful will this consultation meeting prove to be in forming the next steps for the child in question if these cultural variables are not recognized and incorporated within the fabric of the meeting?

The conceptual organizational framework presented in Figure 7.1 provides three analytical dimensions of culture and diversity in school communities to incorporate in

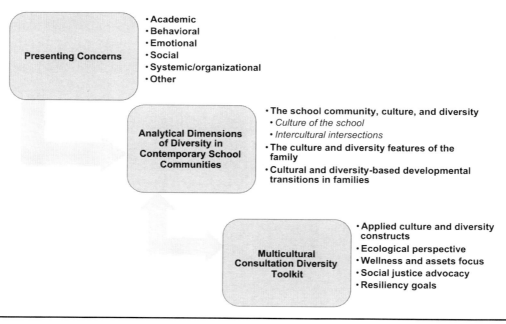

Figure 7.1 An Organizational Framework for School Consultation with Diverse Families

one's consultation work with students for whom culture and/or diversity factors may be relevant to resolving their school referral concerns. This consultative process includes identification of the presence or influence of these dimensions regarding the school-related problem of the student, assessment of their relevance to the focal student concerns, consideration of their role in intervention planning, and their incorporation in ways of evaluating the efficacy of the intervention and the fidelity of its implementation.

A toolkit utilizing primary concepts of professional theories and models via proactive questioning and a range of activities and strategies to obtain needed answers is included in this model for use by the consultant in incorporating the three analytical diversity dimensions as relevant throughout the stages of the consultation case.

Analytical Dimensions of Diversity in Contemporary School Communities

Consultation cases regarding students from diverse backgrounds generally occur because of a schooling concern in the academic, behavioral, emotional, or social domains. These concerns are likely to be embedded in a cultural and/or intercultural context that will need to be addressed during the consultation stages for them to be resolved. When this occurs, the consultant should work to address this situation throughout the consultation process with the parents, school professionals, and other community members who may have a role in the intercultural intersections that may have occurred. This section describes three broad analytical dimensions presented in Figure 7.2 of a consultation framework to guide a school consultant's identification and incorporation of the multiplicity and complexity of school, community, cultural, and individual family diversity factors in addressing the school concerns about a student for whom these may be relevant.

Diversity Dimension One: The Culture of the School and the Phenomenon of Intercultural Intersections in the School Community

When working as a school professional during these current times, it is highly likely that even without leaving the school buildings where one's work is geographically located it will be necessary to functionally cross cultural/diversity borders. In fact, where most

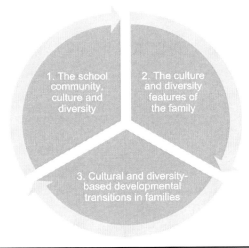

Figure 7.2 Three Dimensions of Diversity in Contemporary School Communities

people in a school community were once more alike than different, it appears that we are fast approaching a point in time where members of many school communities may be more different than alike on one or more of the basic categories of diversity—race, ethnicity, age, ability, gender, sexual orientation, religion, and socioeconomic status.

The Culture of the School

Schooling, the process of providing children with learning experiences, exists around the world and generally encompasses several key generic features that will vary by the culture of the society in which it takes place. These features include: (a) the mission or philosophy of the schooling; (b) an organizational structure that can range from one that is informal and loosely developed to highly formalized and very structured; (c) a curriculum of what is to be learned, instructional practices for that to occur, and expected student learning behaviors to demonstrate their acquisition of knowledge and skills that have been taught; (d) norms for the formation and maintenance of relationships within the context of the schooling environment; (e) normative communication patterns between various school community members; (f) expectations for emotional expressiveness and behavioral conduct; and (g) typical problem-solving strategies when issues arise.

Therefore, a beginning point for a diversity-focused consultation case is to consider where the schooling is taking place for the student and/or family of concern (Le, Lai & Wallen, 2009; Zirkel, 2008). One facet includes the unique cultural manifestations of these generic schooling features in individual school buildings that generally mirror the philosophies, values, and expectations for education of the larger society in which they are situated. Further, a school building is embedded in a larger educational community comprised of students, families, and school professionals who each are representatives of their own cultural group membership. Some represent the mainstream societal culture and other members are from diverse backgrounds.

Parents from other cultures frequently lack the knowledge and skills to effectively navigate the culture of their child's new school and the community in which it is embedded (Copeland & Bennett, 2001; Nastasi, 2005). Instead, they bring with them knowledge and expectations of schooling based on their own educational experiences in their home countries and/ or other countries where they may have lived during their developmental years. Alternatively, they may bring no prior knowledge of schooling because either they spent their childhood as refugees with no access to education or they held minority statuses in their own home countries that barred their participation in any type of school experience. As a result, they may be challenged in their abilities to be of assistance to their children with school assignments, with collaborating with school professionals when a schooling issues emerge for their children, and with their relationships with other families in the school community.

Schools as Places of Intercultural Intersections

How to navigate the cultural and diversity differences that may exist within a school community and to create a sense of unity or inclusiveness can be challenging when families and school professionals encounter each other. Further, it can be complex to work with these cultural differences as a consultant when difficulties arise for students and their families. To do so, it is important to understand the unique culture of the school as a societal institution, recognize the differential experiences of participating in the school community for families based on their diversity statuses, and anticipate the likelihood of a continuum of different types and degrees of intensity of intercultural intersections between the school community members.

Navigation of these intersections is a function of the intercultural sensitivity and competencies of school community members who are traversing them. Table 7.1 presents a continuum of categories of intersections that may occur when the pathways of school community members with differing cultural or diversity-based worldviews cross, physically or metaphorically.

Table 7.1 Categories of Intercultural Intersections in Contemporary School Communities

Categories	Description
Transformative	These intersections represent spaces where those coming together with different worldviews do so with complementary goals, proactive orientations, and the intercultural competencies to know how to navigate them for a positive outcome for all involved (Zirkel, 2008). *Example:* A parent group working to raise funds for playground equipment solicits, respects, and acts upon input from all members, mainstreamed and diverse alike, to yield a decision that reflects more than one single perspective.
Bumps and bruises	These events tend to be momentary, episodic ones representing brief cultural misunderstandings, misattributions, or microaggressions (Sue & Capodilupo, 2008) or simply mainstreamed school community members ignoring the presence of those who represent diversity when passing each other in the same space. Often not registered cognitively by the dominant, mainstreamed group members, they often are experienced emotionally by those who feel targeted by these encounters that are too often not addressed by anyone. Instead, they serve as intercultural stressors that, when too many occur, can add to a level of tension and stress between community members. Further, those who perceive their status as being targeted and devalued experience heightened apprehension, making them feel unsafe and unwilling to approach others about their concerns. Community members who feel marginalized can be the ones who have the most perceptive observations of what is transpiring regarding certain issues. Because their input is not sought and/or dismissed, valuable insights that would lead to a more transformative solution are not obtained (Clare, 2002). *Examples:* The parent who is a member of a specific ethnic group in the school community who is interrupted when trying to talk in a meeting of parents finds herself misunderstood when she tries to present an idea to other parents and feels targeted by subtle forms of criticism directed toward her ethnicity by a school professional. The context of a consultation meeting can also serve as an example of this type of intercultural intersection. School professionals may not be attuned to the cultural features and meanings of the behaviors and language of the culturally diverse parents attending this meeting. This may result in a situation in which these parents feel devalued by the perceived attitudes and/or observed behaviors toward them by the professionals in the room (Clare, 2002).
Collisions	These occur when there is an intense clash of diversity-based differences and those caught in the intersection experience significant emotions and/or negative outcomes. *Examples of impact:* Overrepresentation in special education, school suspensions, failing grades, exclusion and/or alienation from the school community, or significant community dissension and a need to address social inequities in the community (Zirkel, 2008).
Educational tragedies	Unfortunately, some experiences in school intercultural intersections result in total failure for one or more parties who are involved (Zirkel, 2008). These can be manifested by parental refusal to communicate or collaborate with school professionals about their child, student absenteeism and dropouts, bullying and violence, gang enrollment, addiction choices, and even suicide. *Example:* Phoebe Prince, an Irish immigrant newcomer, took her life in 2010 after countless incidents of bullying by other students at the school she attended in South Hadley, Massachusetts (Bennett, 2011). She did not receive cultural orientation and acculturation support to help her acculturate to the social norms of her new school and likely prevent the bullying she experienced.

Navigating these intersections successfully requires core multicultural knowledge and competencies by all members of the school community. Family members from other cultures, as part of their acculturation, will need information and instrumental support to learn how to function in the new school setting in their respective roles as students, parents, and school community members. Together, all community members must become cognizant of how worldviews relative to their own subgroup may differ from those of other cultural groups to facilitate the successful navigation of intercultural intersections when they occur. Consultants can serve as ideal navigational pilots for this process in a school community.

Diversity Dimension Two: The Culture and Diversity Features of the Family

There are generic dimensions of family life that are almost universal as they can be observed with families in most locations in the world. These include: (a) fundamental beliefs and values; (b) organizational structures; (c) family member roles; (d) operational rules; (e) internal relationship patterns; (f) communication styles; (g) problem-solving patterns; and (h) ways of connecting to the larger community and society. How these are manifested will vary by a family's cultural and diversity group membership and its core values, attitudes, expectations, and worldview (Balcazar & Qian, 2000; Falicov, 2003; McGoldrick, 2003; Patterson & Saxton, 2013). It is advisable to read professional literature that focuses on culture-specific groups (e.g., Hispanics, African Americans, Asian Americans) represented in contemporary schools (Patterson & Sexton, 2013) when preparing to engage in consultation regarding school concerns about a child who is a member of any one these groups. The consultant will find this information useful to help formulate questions and hypotheses to guide one's work with the focal child of the consultation case.

Table 7.2 presents several types of circumstances for families for which cultural and/or diversity features have a significant role. During the consultation process, the consultant

Table 7.2 Variations of Diversity Dynamics for Nonmainstreamed Families

Focus	Comment
Core family cultural features based on their diversity category membership(s)	The consultant seeks information about the key cultural features for the diversity categories that represent the family that may play a role in the school-based concerns addressed during the consultation process (Patterson & Sexton, 2013). For example, it may be important to ascertain the hierarchy and function of different roles in the family, particularly with how rules are made and who makes the major decisions. This can be very critical when working with families from specific cultures in which males have a privileged, dominant status and with those from different cultural religious affiliations that have specific rules for behaviors, many of which are gender based.
Migratory impact on core cultural features of families	It is vital to explore if, and how, the key features of the core family dimensions may have been modified during their cultural transition journey and exposure to one or more different cultures (Balcazar & Qian, 2000). A common example is change in gender roles, especially for women who move from male dominant cultures to more gender-balanced ones. Another involves changes in parenting behavior after exposure to the practices of mainstreamed parents in the new host country and others from different countries living there.

(Continued)

Table 7.2 (Continued)

Focus	Comment
Intergenerational differences within diverse families	Intergenerational differences often emerge in families with parents who have migrated to a new culture yet still maintain many of the cultural behaviors of their passport country; whereas their children, who are born and raised in the new country, are exposed to both their home and larger societal cultural values and expectations. This often leads to their children feeling caught between the cultural expectations of their parents and the influences of the country in which they were raised, a fact that can create significant family stress (Balcazar & Qian, 2000). One example relates to family rules where adolescent Hispanic females often struggle with feeling overprotected compared to their non-Hispanic female friends whose parents allow them greater independence outside the family home.
Intersectionality of diversity categories for family units and members	It is also important for the school consultant to identify the impact of intersectionality that may exist in the presence of two or more diversity categories in a family. An example is a highly religious family with a child who has self-identified as having a homosexual orientation. It will be important to explore with the parents their worldview about each of these intersecting diversity categories, religion and sexuality, and the challenges that may exist for them in accepting their child's sexual orientation.
Role in intercultural intersections for family members in the school community	The diversity features of family life may also be contributing factors when problematic intercultural intersections occur between members of different families and/or school professionals in the school community (Zirkel, 2008). Common examples include when parents clash over child behavior expectations during play dates or between teacher and parents about an appropriate bedtime for a child to be able to function in school the next day.
Relevance to changing diversity compositions of family units	The increasing number of family units founded by parents who are from different cultural or diversity backgrounds is resulting in home environments with a blend of multiple cultural, racial, ethnic, religious, and other diversity categories (Brown, 2009; Gates, 2013; McCarthy, 2007). This creates an additional complexity as the parent must choose how to incorporate their individual culturally driven worldviews into both their relationship and the various dimensions of the family unit that they lead.

should be alert and responsive to whether, and to what degree, one or more of these situations apply to the focal child's family and have a role in triggering, sustaining, or resolving the school referral concern(s).

Diversity Dimension Three: Cultural and Diversity-Based Developmental Transitions in Families

The school consultant should attend to the types of unique developmental transitions that some families and their members may experience because of one or more of the following reasons: (a) the children are experiencing the normative process of individual identity development along with a developmental trajectory linked to the particular racial, ethnic, or other diversity category to which they belong; (b) members of the family are developing a bicultural or multicultural identities by virtue of prolonged exposure to multiple cultural influences; and/or (c) they are experiencing the dynamics of cultural transition due to their migration from another country.

Racial/Ethnic Identity Developmental Transitions

Several theorists have focused on the stages of differential developmental experiences of youth based on their race and/or ethnicity (Balcazar & Qian, 2000; Martin & Nakayama, 2008; McDermott & Samson, 2005; Pedersen, 2000; Pumariega & Rothe, 2010; Sue & Sue, 2008; Williams, 2009). These theories focus on how societal cultural socialization patterns, majority versus minority group members' differences in lived experiences, and core developmental processes (cognitive, social, emotional) combine to move an individual through a series of stages that shape how they view themselves as members of their racial/ethnic group versus those of other racial/ethnic groups. Cognitive dissonance and associated behavioral challenges are common experiences during this journey of racial/ethnic identity development. Challenges and complexities encountered by the growing numbers of multiracial/ethnic children in their identity development journey may differ from those from a single racial/ethnic background, a topic receiving increased scholarly attention (Williams, 2008).

A student's behaviors at the stage of cognitive dissonance may mirror challenging social-emotional behaviors representative of various types of differential diagnoses (e.g., ADHD, oppositional defiant disorder, bipolar disorder). School consultants are cautioned to remain alert to whether these behavioral concerns may actually be manifestations of this type of developmental trajectory, one that would warrant a different type of supportive response for the student (Williams, 2009).

Multicultural Individual Identity Development

There are also children of families whose life experiences have resulted in their development of a multicultural identity because of prolonged exposure to multiple cultures and/or routine and frequent boundary crossing between two or more different cultural environments. They are able to understand and function in more than one culture on an interchangeable basis (McDonald, 2011) because they have developed intercultural and cross-cultural competencies and often the ability to speak more than one language. These students often include: (a) international adoptees whose adoptive families intentionally incorporate features of the child's biological home culture into the family life; (b) second-generation children who daily cross cultural borders between a family life based on the key cultural features of their parents' native culture and the larger societal culture of their family's new host culture; and (c) global nomads or TCKS (third-culture kids) whose childhoods have been spent in and shaped by one or more cultures outside their passport culture (Balcazar & Qian, 2000; McDonald, 2011; Pollock & Van Reken, 2001). It is important to recognize that there may be specific developmental characteristics for these children very much associated with their unique life experiences that have resulted in their multicultural identities.

Family Migratory Cultural Transition Journeys

The world is currently experiencing the largest international migration of individuals and families since World War II because of natural disasters, global instability, and warfare (Cohen & Sirkeci, 2011; Hadid & Krauss, 2014). The unprecedented surge of unaccompanied minors seeking to enter the United States resulted in a crisis of how to respond to these youth (Negroponte, 2014). Globally, boatloads of refugees have experienced desperate plights in their search for new countries to take them in, a dire humanitarian crisis with serious political and economic implications for the countries where they are seeking asylum (Townsend & Oomen, 2015).

Therefore, it is highly likely that a consultation case could involve, in addition to the presenting school-based concerns, cultural transition issues and challenges for a family who has entered the school community from another country. Three key sets of variables important to address when working with families that have migrated to a new country include: (1) the migratory pathway; (2) three broad tasks of cultural relocation—adaptation, acculturation, and achievement of role requirements; and (3) stages of cultural transition core issues.

1. *Migratory pathways*: Families can be in cultural transition via a broad range of pathways, including refugee, immigrant, international adoptees, expatriate, repatriates, sojourner, native-born regional transfer students, and those who go back and forth between country-based geographical locations such as migrant workers and military members. Family members may travel together on these pathways or they may be separated, sometimes by choice and other times forcibly. Common features and critical differences exist for these transitional pathways with regard to migratory decisions, dynamics, challenges, and tasks for the different routes they take (Cohen & Sirkeci, 2011). For example, refugee pathways often include significant trauma, a prolonged migratory journey, and significant dependency on others for survival and support (Nugent & Roberts, 2013; Pumariega & Rothe, 2010). Immigrant pathways are usually chosen in search of a better life, but often with limited financial and other resources when reaching targeted destinations (Balcazar & Qian, 2000; Pumariega & Rothe, 2010). In contrast, sojourners, such as international exchange students and expatriates, who have moved for career purposes, often do so with more support and services during their cultural transition journey.

2. *Core cultural transition tasks*: Irrespective of their migratory pathway, family members must simultaneously focus on three core tasks during their cultural transition journeys. The first is *adaptation*, the process of coping with the key psychosocial challenges commonly found in cultural transitions, such as loss of identity and contact with important people, pets, and material possessions. These families are on migratory journeys that involve psychosocial dynamics that may continue for several months, sometimes even years, after they have physically relocated to the school community where their children attend school. Handling the psychosocial stressors and, for some, trauma that can be part of the transition journey can create emotional challenges for both the family unit and its respective members (Foster, 2001; Pumariega & Rothe, 2010). In fact, sometimes the adaptive coping strategies of a migratory family member can resemble the symptomatology of more pathological states such as PTSD, depression, anxiety, or ADHD. In such instances, it is important to proceed with caution before making a differential diagnosis by first ruling out the role of normative adaptive cultural transition behaviors.

   The second core task is *acculturation*, the process of learning how to settle in to a new country in ways that meet the societal norms for behavior, language, and other expectations (Berry, 2002). This involves learning the language, norms, and values of the culture to which one has relocated, while at the same time letting go of some of the cultural values, beliefs, and behaviors associated with one's home or passport culture (Chieh & Vazquez-Nuttall, 2009). This can be a highly challenging process, one which can be carried out in multiple ways, such as through integration, assimilation, isolation, and marginalization (Berry, 2002). It can be very dependent on individual and family choices regarding residential location decisions, new language acquisition, and connections with both one's own cultural referent groups and with members of the new culture. A significant factor is the degree of receptivity by the host, or new society, to the cultural group to which the family belongs (Berry, 2002; Schwarz, Unger, Zamboanga, & Szapocznik, 2010). Internal family dynamics can often develop in the form of *acculturative stress* (Balcazar & Qian, 2000), which can sometimes lead to significant changes in the core family cultural features as well as psychological coping problems for one or more members via a process known as *acculturative family distancing* (Pumariega & Rothe, 2010). Additionally, a history of previous significant stressors for the family can further corrode its ability to function in its new setting and significantly contribute to the acculturation challenges being experienced (McCubbin, McCubbin, Thompson, & Thompson,1998). These family dynamics may play a significant role in presenting concerns and thus are important for the consultant to ascertain and work to address during the consultation process.

Finally, family members must learn how to engage in the *achievement* behaviors for their designated roles, such as parent, child, sibling, spouse, employee, and student in their new residential culture. This involves awareness and knowledge of the behavioral norms for these specific roles in the new cultural setting and demonstrating them per these expectations. This can be stressful when a significant learning curve is required and when cultural mentors are not available to provide information and/or support that would be helpful. For example, parents may feel that they are "parenting between cultures" as they feel caught between how they might respond parentally to a specific issue in their home country versus what is required in their new country. Children also can feel caught between two cultures and it does not take long for a student to feel confused, lost, and alienated from a sense of belongingness when experiencing a mismatch between one's learned student behaviors and the new ones that need to be acquired in a new setting.

3. *Stages of cultural transition*: A migratory cultural transition involves not a singular event but a series of stages marked by specific tasks that can present significant psychosocial challenges for the family unit and its individual members (Pollock & Van Reken, 2001; Pumariega & Rothe, 2010). All family members generally go through these stages, but they tend to do so at their own individual paces. These stages include: (a) *involvement*, the premigratory stage wherein one feels a member of community and knows how to function in it; (b) *disengagement*, where one must let go of a known life style in order to move to a place that is foreign; (c) *transition*, the period of time between disengaging and resettling into a new place; (d) *entry*, a very sensitive stage of moving into a community where there is the possibility of either acceptance or rejection by those who already belong there; and (e) *reengagement*, achievement of an acculturated status and inclusion in the new residential community (Pollock & Van Reken, 2001).

Table 7.3 Transition Stage Features for Different Migratory Pathways

Migratory pathways	Predeparture stage	Transition stage	Entering stage
Refugees and asylum seekers	• Violence, political instability, natural disaster • Abrupt departure with no certainty of destiny or destination	• Multiple relocations; refugee camps • Loss of meaningful belongings • Separation from loved ones • Dependency on others for survival	• Limited time of instrumental assistance • Lack of host culture language • Degree of community readiness and receptivity for their arrival • PTSD frequently present and needs to be addressed
Immigrants	• Economic challenges in home country trigger for decision to leave • Legal or illegal status decision • Leaving known life behind • Entire or partial family leaves	• Parents busy with organizing next steps • Reliance on others to reach destination • Many steps to final destination • Uncertain status with law • Language issues • Family members often separated	• Peer reactions to newcomer • Degree of societal tolerance and openness in host culture • Victimization • Social justice inequities • Continuation of contact with home country members and friends • Ambivalent mindset regarding becoming a member of new host country
Sojourners, expatriates, study abroad, seasonal workers, military members	• Work or educational reasons for decisions • May or may not be voluntary • Varying control over how and when • Assistance often available	• Parents busy with transition tasks • Variance in length of transition time • Family members can be separated because of different role demands • Changes and different levels of connection and contact for family members	• Awareness and intercultural skills regarding new setting and peer culture • Host culture attitude toward foreigners • Status and role of sojourner • Avoids movement to next stage in anticipation of reentry to home culture

Table 7.3 introduces some of the key dynamics for each of the three primary categories of migration pathways. The combination of these dynamics may contribute to significant changes in the dimensions of family life, which may result in dysfunctional outcomes for the family as a unit and/or for individual members. Therefore, these should be taken into account regarding focal school concerns when making any diagnostic or intervention decisions for the diverse student during the consultation process.

A Professional Toolkit for Consulting with Diverse Students and Families

To incorporate the three analytical diversity dimensions in consultation cases, the school consultant is advised to employ a toolkit based on five recommended professional theories and models when consulting about students for whom diversity factors may have a role in their school-based concerns. A range of applied tools representative of these

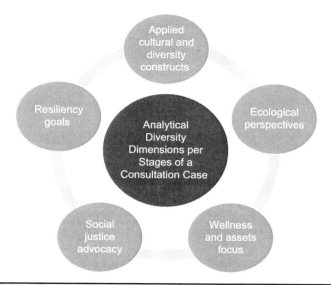

Figure 7.3 Multicultural Consultation Diversity Toolkit

theories and models has been and continues to be developed. They include assessment interviews, questionnaires and inventories; contextual and social mapping techniques; observational systems; and projective, experiential, and other creative strategies. Selective use of these tools in the various stages of consultation can address questions pertaining to each of the diversity dimensions that may be relative to the presenting school concerns about students for whom culture and diversity factors are important factors in their lives. Optimally, their use will yield valuable information that can enhance intervention decisions and effectively resolve presenting concerns for a student. Figure 7.3 illustrates the five recommended theories and models for formulating guiding questions to appraise the relevance of the three analytical diversity dimensions during each stage of a multicultural consultation case.

Applied Cultural and Diversity Constructs

Central to the work of addressing diversity in school settings is the need for the consultant to have a basic knowledge of core cultural constructs and their applications when diversity factors are present for a focal child or children. Three very important constructs from the intercultural field provide a foundation for approaching one's consultation work with cultural sensitivity and competence: 1) the term "culture", 2) the metaphor of the cultural iceberg, and 3) the construct of worldview.

Defining the term *culture*

The word ***culture*** as it relates to the focus of this chapter refers to "an organized set of thoughts, beliefs, and norms for interaction and communication for a specific population of individuals, all of which may influence cognitions, behaviors, and perceptions" (Ingraham, 2000, p. 325). These specific populations may be constituted of people representing one or more of the major categories of diversity (e.g., race/ethnicity, religion,

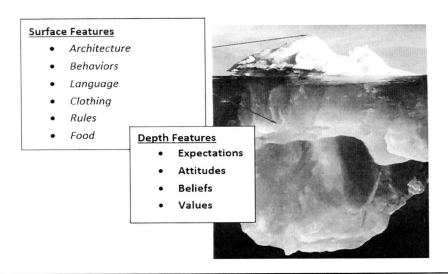

Figure 7.4 The Cultural Iceberg Analogy

socioeconomic status, age, gender, sexual orientation, ability) as well as those involving other groups of people that share common features (e.g., nationality, homeless, adoptees, military families).

Metaphor of the cultural iceberg

The metaphor of the "cultural iceberg" (Figure 7.4) was first introduced by Hall (1973) as a way to visually depict that a culture, whether of groups of people or of societal institutions, can be described as having surface features (e.g., language, clothing, behaviors, architecture) that are visible above the water line and experienced when observing and/or interacting with representatives of that culture. However, as with an iceberg, the most significant aspects of a culture are invisible and exist below the surface as depth features that serve as drivers of visible surface features. These depth features are the values, beliefs, and expectations that exist for a given culture, that is, what the group members and institutions hold dearest, what directly influences their assumptions and expectations for most facets of life experiences, and what is manifested in the visible features and behaviors one encounters when interacting with individuals from the cultural group. These surface features can include what one sees (e.g., architecture, clothing), experiences (e.g., food, music, films, news), and what happens in interpersonal interactions (e.g., communication styles and use of language, patterns of emotional expression and conflict management, relationship features).

Developing a worldview

Individuals are generally socialized during their developmental years as members of one or more categories of diversity, beginning with the direct influence of their families and then extending to the institutional and societal influences encountered as they move through the journey of life (Harro, 2000; Pumariega & Rothe, 2010). An individual's cumulative cultural socialization as well as unique personal experiences evolve into a *worldview* that is often similar to others in their cultural or diversity group(s) that can be defined by how one perceives, reflects, and acts upon encounters with others who differ from oneself in one or more "cultural/diversity" categories (Kolko-Rivera, 2004).

Ecological Perspective

In his groundbreaking work, Bronfenbrenner (1979, 1986) posited that an individual and/or family unit can be conceived as developing and functioning within an ecological network that ranges across five different levels of connectedness and influences. This model can serve as a tool to explore how the lived experiences and contexts of a student's family with a diverse status may relate to identified school concerns as well as contribute to the development and implementation of interventions during the consultation process (Balcazar & Qian, 2000; Li & Vazquez-Nuttall, 2009).

Following are descriptions of the five levels of Bronfenbrenner's model and suggested ways in which they can be applied when consulting with referral concerns involving diverse students and their families:

- *The microsystem*: the individual and the specific settings, such as family, school, peers, health professionals, and religious group, with which the person most frequently interacts and is influenced. It is important to consider how the various cultural and diversity features represented within this space for diverse families may differ from that of nondiverse families in the school community.
- *The mesosystem:* the space between the microsystem and the larger exosystem in which relationships exist in connection to the individual and family system with others outside that sphere. Important considerations here are both the existing and potential relationships with other members of the school community as well as other types of relationships that diverse families may establish outside of the school community that affects their overall functioning.
- *The exosystem:* the various individuals, groups, organizations, and facilities within the proximity of the microsystem with which the diverse individual and family are likely to have a range of relationships, both direct and indirect, or none at all. These can include social services, community members, local political organizations, mass media, and industry. Important considerations are similarities and differences in the cultural features of the school as an institution and the cultural characteristics of the other members of the school and larger community in relationship to the focal diverse family with which one may be working.
- *The macrosystem:* represents the cultural features that encompass belief systems, values, and norms of the larger society, both at the community level and nationally, in which diverse families are situated as well as the referent distant macrosystems that are specific to their own cultural/diversity category with which they identify. Important is the degree to which these macrosystems present concordance or dissonance for diverse family units relative to their societal status, intergenerational values and behavior choices, and acculturation choices if they have a migration history.
- *The chronosystem:* represents the timeline of events, including those of the larger society and/or at the global level that may have had an impact on the life experiences of a diverse student and his/her family. This layer, one that cuts across all the

other layers, can be very critical for certain diverse families, especially those who have migrated from another country and those who have been targeted by acts of intolerance because of the societal status and/or category of diversity to which they belong.

Nastasi states (2005), "multicultural consultation requires a critical focus that extends beyond the family and includes understanding the culture of schools and individual consultants." (p. 116). This is further reinforced by Li and Vazquez-Nuttall (2009, p. 5), who wrote that "all levels of the ecological system need to be considered in order to understand a problem in consultation."

For example, consider the elementary-aged child who has recently immigrated with his family to the United States. The pivotal concern is his unpredictable loss of behavioral control when triggered by certain school setting stimuli. Using an ecological perspective when consulting with his parents, a map can be created of the locations of: (a) his primary sources of influence, interaction, support, and guidance; (b) adverse individual and group triggers for his behaviors; and (c) the identification of possible gaps in home and community support and guidance. As the consultation case progresses, this ecological map for the child and family can continuously be revised by identifying and creating alternative individuals and activities for the child to experience. Perhaps steps can be taken to link him to a local children's sports or scouts group with whom he can learn alternative behaviors to those he manifests within his school classroom. Additionally, the student's mother may be invited to participate in a psychoeducational group to help her better understand how to effectively parent her son within the existing behavioral norms of the school community. In doing so, the ecology of the student's life, as well as that of his family, becomes richer due to an increase of the number and strength of connections to draw upon as sources of support.

Wellness and Assets Focus

A pathological focus regarding school concerns does not enlighten ways in which to address the challenges that diverse families and their members may be experiencing. Instead, a more positive orientation provides hope by engaging with family members to help them identify their wellness features and assets despite the challenges that they experience and to help them set goals for what needs to change on behalf of their child's school functioning. Further, diverse family members may perceive a focus on strengths and assets by a consultant working with them as far less threatening, especially if they are from other cultures and have had very limited and/or previously negative experiences working with school personnel with regard to their children and family matters.

The Wellness Model by Myers and Sweeney (2005) helps consultants work with diverse students and families to identify the degree to which 17 dimensions of wellness grouped into 5 broad categories (the essential self, the social self, the coping self, the creative self, and the physical self) are present in their lives. This information can be gathered via a wellness interview or questionnaire in order to gain a perspective of the strengths, social assets, and resources the child and family members have that can be helpful for both understanding and resolving the presenting school concerns.

For example, when conducting a wellness interview, one focus is on the dimension of "social self." The individual is asked to rate one's level of satisfaction with friendships on a scale of low to high and to provide examples of the types of social interactions typically engaged in as well as the ways in which they create positive feelings for him or her. This information can be useful for identifying the degree of social connectedness or assets that exists for the child and/or family members in the school community as well as the types of social relationships that they may find most appealing to help them establish.

It may be likely that children from diverse family backgrounds may experience differences in this social self dimension from the mainstreamed students that are relevant to the presenting concern, such as cultural differences in interpersonal and communication behaviors that influence friendship development and peer conflict resolution. Alternatively, the child may have many friends who share a similar cultural background, and this may be a social support asset to draw upon to help resolve the presenting concern for this child.

Social Justice Advocacy

It is important for the school consultant to be alert to the presence of social justice issues with consultation cases involving children from diverse families that may be relevant to the school concerns, particularly if they serve to impede a child's access to full equitable opportunities and/or social inclusion in the school community (Li & Vazquez-Nuttall, 2009). Ideally, diverse students and their primary caretakers will be motivated to share this type of information. However, there will be families who are guarded and even strongly resistant to doing so. They may have experienced prior social justice inequities in connection with education, which have left them distrustful of school personnel. The consultant is advised to proceed with caution and respect when working with these students and parents. This may mean the need to schedule multiple meetings to build a working relationship with them by demonstrating interest and empathy in learning about their lived experiences as diverse members of the school community. Doing so will help to build a communication bridge that fosters the ability to learn what they need to feel safe and included and to collaborate with them on the needs and concerns of their child.

The complexities of the lived experience for many diverse families in school communities can be adverse for a number of reasons. For families with a minority and/or targeted social status, key social justice issues (e.g., privilege, social inequities, discrimination, racism) must be seriously weighed regarding their contribution to presenting school concerns about a child (Balcazar & Qian, 2000; Li & Vazquez-Nuttall, 2009; McIntosh, 1998; Pumariega & Rothe, 2010; Sue & Capodilupo, 2008; Zirkel, 2008).

Most countries have differentiated levels of privilege and inclusion that are representative of the values, norms, expectations, and worldviews of a society's majority group. These can vary along each of the key categories of diversity—race, ethnicity, age, gender, religion, ability, sexual orientation, and socioeconomic status. Children and their families belonging to groups seen and/or treated as marginalized and inferior too often are: (a) the focus of inequities in terms of available resources in their school communities and residential neighborhoods; (b) labeled as deviant by the standards of the larger society and thus overly likely to be placed in special education and/or for the family members to rejected by other community members; (c) afforded harsher punishments than other students for infractions; (d) targeted for bullying and/or peer exclusion; (e) the targets of discrimination; (f) have a higher risk to drop out of school; and (g) likely to succumb to peer pressures for gang memberships and violent behavior (Miranda, Boland & Hemmeler, 2009; Shriberg, 2009).

The school consultant needs to encourage a candid sharing of these experiences of social injustice by family members/caretakers and collaborate with them about ways in which to address their grievances. Gorski and Pothini (2014) have developed an equity literacy framework that incorporates four key skills: (1) recognizing, (2) responding to, (3) redressing bias and inequities in school settings for targeted community members, and (4) creating and sustaining unbiased and equitable learning environments. The model employs a multistep analytical case study approach that can be incorporated into the stages of a consultation case in which a social justice issue is relevant. These steps include: (a) identify the key social justice concern; (b) ascertain the potential perspectives of all involved in the situation; (c) determine what would be an equitable outcome or goal for the student or the family; and (d) select the process by which equity goals can be achieved.

Resilience Goals

Resilience refers to the "capacity to rebound from adversity strengthened and more resourceful. It is an active process of endurance, self-righting and growth in response to crisis and challenge" (Walsh, 1998, p. 4). A resiliency lens helps identify how to use the strengths and resources of a diverse family and its members to manage and/or develop alternative coping strategies regarding the stressful and uncertain conditions that may exist for them in a school community (Bai & Repetti, 2015; Masten, 2014; Masten & Monn, 2015). With such families, school consultants should incorporate a focus on resiliency-building goals, strategies, and support mechanisms to assist students and their families in overcoming critical challenges and to become more empowered in the process (Bai & Repetti, 2015; Davidson, 2014; McCubbin et al., 1998; Simon, Murphy, & Smith, 2005; Walsh, 1998, 2003). Fortunately, a growing number of initiatives and programs exist that have been developed to aid school consultants in helping members of diverse families become more resilient (Balcazar & Qian, 2000; Brown, 2009; Li & Vazquez-Nuttall, 2009; Nugent & Roberts, 2013; Pumariega & Rothe, 2010; Zirkel, 2008).

A Navigational Framework to Address Dimensions of Diversity in School Consultation Cases

The school consultant can use the information provided in this chapter to develop a planning rubric to serve as a navigational map for a consultation case focusing on the school concerns of a child with a diverse family background. The knowledge and skills provided by the toolkit of five professional theories and models can guide the development of questions that focus on the role of the three analytical dimensions during each stage of a consultation case for students for whom diversity may be a factor regarding their school-based concerns. The degree of detail for a consultation planning rubric will very much depend on the relevance of the three diversity dimensions for the focal child of a diverse family to the type and complexity of the presenting school concern(s).

A variety of professional tools and strategies can be employed to obtain responses to these questions that have been placed on the navigational rubric. Some will be generic, such as interviews, observations, questionnaires, and other types of assessment tools and approaches that serve to yield data for the questions. Others may be specific to the theory or model used, such as the concentric circles of Bronfenbrenner's ecological model (Bronfenbrenner, 1979) and the Wellness Evaluation of Lifestyle Inventory (Myers & Sweeney, 2005). Additionally, family timelines, genograms, sociograms, projective techniques, drawings and photography, and other creative options can serve to enhance the type of cultural/diversity information obtained in separate meetings with a focal child and family members or in conjunction with consultation meetings and related activities.

Table 7.4 presents an example of a navigational planning rubric for investigating the role of the first dimension, the culture of the school and intercultural intersections in the school community, during the initial stage of a consultation case. It demonstrates the guiding questions these professional theories and models can yield.

Table 7.4 Navigational Rubric Sample for Dimension One: The Culture of the School and the Phenomenon of Intercultural Intersections in the School Community
Consultation Stage One:
Referral Clarification & Assessment for a Behavioral Concern

Toolkit theories and models	Consultation questions to address regarding school concern(s) of focal child
Cultural and diversity constructs	• What cultural or diversity features represented in the dimensions of schooling in this educational community are relevant to the school concern for the focal child? • Does the school concern involve school community intercultural intersections?
Ecological perspectives	• What are the contextual triggers for the concern about this child in this school community? What contextual features of this school community serve to prevent the occurrence of the concern? • Where is the concern about this child manifested in the context of the school community? Where is it not being manifested? • Who in the school community is involved regarding this concern, why, and at what level of appropriateness or impact?
Wellness and assets focus	• What is the norm in this school community for wellness and how does this focal child compare to this norm? • What is the norm for ways of establishing and maintaining wellness behaviors and social assets in this school community? To what degree is the focal child following this norm or using a different approach?

Social justice advocacy	• Which of the following patterns are present in this school community and to what extent might they be relevant for the concern of the focal child?
	  • Norms regarding privilege for specific groups of student
	  • Inequities regarding discipline
	  • Inequities regarding entry and/or exclusion into specific classes or activities
	  • Issues of intolerance and targeted discrimination

Resiliency goals	• How are students and their families encouraged in this community to achieve success, including overcoming obstacles, via resiliency building? • What are seen as appropriate personal resiliency development goals to strive for in this school community?

SUMMARY AND RECOMMENDATIONS

This chapter has provided a conceptual navigational framework in which to address the increasing complexities of the diverse families that are joining school communities in countries throughout the world. Three analytical diversity dimensions have been presented as a guide for the consultant when working with these families with regard to school focal concerns for their children: (1) the culture of the school community and intercultural intersections that exist within it, (2) the culture and diversity features of these families, and (3) diversity-driven developmental transitions. A toolkit using five professional theories and models has been recommended to facilitate the school consultant's navigational exploration of these diversity dimensions for ascertaining their contribution to the existence of the school concern about a focal child and/or its resolution. These toolkit theories and models include cultural and diversity constructs, ecological systems theory, social justice advocacy principles, positive psychology and the wellness model, and resilience research.

REFERENCES

Bai, S., & Repetti, R. L. (2015). Short-term resilience processes in the family. *Family Relations, 64*, 108–119.

Balcazar, H., & Qian, Z. (2000). Immigrant families and sources of stress. In P. C. McKenry & S. J. Price (Eds.), *Families & change: Coping with stressful events and transitions* (pp. 359–377). Thousand Oaks, CA: Sage Publications.

Bennett, J. (2011, April 17). Phoebe Prince: Should school bullying be a crime? *Newsweek*. Retrieved from http://www.newsweek.com/2010/10/04/phoebe-prince-should-bullying-be-a-crime.html

Berry, J. W. (2002). Conceptual approaches to acculturation. In K. Chun, P. Organista, & G. Marin (Eds.), *Acculturation* (pp. 17–37). Washington, DC: APA.

Bronfenbrenner, U. (1979). *Ecology of human development*. Cambridge, MA: Harvard University Press.

Bronfenbrenner, U. (1986). Ecology of the family as a context for human development. *Developmental Psychology, 22*, 723–742.

Brown, M. R. (2009). A new multicultural population: Creating effective partnerships with multiracial families. *Intervention in School and Clinic, 45*, 124–131.

Chieh, L., & Vazquez-Nuttall, E. (2009). School consultants as agents of social justice for multicultural children and families. *Journal of Educational and Psychological Consultation, 19*, 26–44.

Clare, M. M. (2002). Diversity as a dependent variable: Considerations for research and practice in consultation. *Journal of Educational and Psychological Consultation, 13*, 251–263.

Cohen, J. H., & Sirkeci, I. (2011). *Cultures of migration: The global nature of contemporary mobility*. Austin, TX: The University of Texas Press.

Copeland, A. P., & Bennett, G. (2001). *Understanding American schools: The answers to newcomers' most frequently asked questions*. Brookline, MA: The Interchange Institute.

Davidson, T. (2014). STRENGTH: A system of integration of solution-oriented and strength-based principles. *Journal of Mental Health Counseling, 1*, 1–17.

Falicov, C. J. (2003). Immigrant family processes. In F. Walsh (Ed.), *Normal family processes* (3rd ed., pp. 280–300). New York: Guilford Press.

Foster, R. P. (2001). When immigration is trauma: Guidelines for the individual and family clinician. *American Journal of Orthopsychiatry, 71*, 153–170.

Gates, G. M. (2013). *LGBT parenting in the United States*. The Williams Institute. Retrieved from http://williamsinstitute.law.ucla.edu/wp-content/uploads/LGBT-Parenting.pdf

Gorski, P. C., & Pothini, S. G. (2014). *Case studies on diversity and social justice education*. New York: Routledge.

Hadid, D., & Krauss, J. (2014, June 20). For the first time since WWII, there are more than 50 million refugees. *The Huffington Post*. Retrieved from http://www.huffingtonpost.com/2014/06/20/world-refugee-day_n_5514414.html

Hall, E. T. (1973). *The silent language*. New York: Anchor Books Editions.

Harro, B. (2000). The cycle of socialization. In M. Adams, W. J. Blumenfeld, R. Castaneda, H. W. Hackman, M. L. Peters, & X. Zuniga (Eds.), *Readings for diversity and social justice* (2nd ed., pp. 45–51). New York: Routledge.

Ingraham, C. L. (2000). Consultation through a multicultural lens: Multicultural and cross-cultural consultation in schools. *School Psychology Review, 29*, 320–343.

Kolko-Rivera, M. E. (2004). The psychology of worldviews. *Review of General Psychology, 8*, 3–58.

Li, C., & Vazquez-Nuttall, E. (2009). School consultants as agents of social justice for multicultural children and families. *Journal of Educational and School Consultation, 19*, 26–44.

Martin, J., & Nakayama, T. (2008). Identity development. In J. Martin & T. Nakayama (Eds.), *Experiencing intercultural communication* (3rd ed., pp. 105–118). New York: McGraw-Hill Companies, Inc.

Masten, A. S. (2014). *Ordinary magic—Resilience in development.* New York: The Guilford Press.

Masten, A. S., & Monn, A. R. (2015). Child and family resilience: A call for integrated science, practice, and professional training. *Family Relations, 64*, 5–21.

McCarthy, Kate. (2007). Pluralist family values: Domestic strategies for living with religious difference. *The ANNALS of the American Academy of Political and Social Science, 61*(1), 187–208.

McCubbin, H. I., McCubbin, M. A., Thompson, A. I., & Thompson, E. A. (1998). Resiliency in ethnic families: A conceptual model for predicting family adjustment and adaptation. In H. I. McCubbin, E. A. Thompson, A. I. Thompson, & J. E. Fromer (Eds.), *Resiliency in native American and immigrant families* (pp. 3–48). Thousand Oaks, CA: Sage Publications.

McDermott, M., & Samson, F. L. (2005). White racial and ethnic identity in the United States. *Annual Review of Sociology, 31*(1), 245–262.

McDonald, K. E. (2010). Transculturals: Identifying the invisible minority. *Journal of Multicultural Counseling and Development, 38*, 39–50.

McGoldrick, M. (2003). Culture: A challenge to concepts of normality. In F. Walsh (Ed.), *Normal family processes* (3rd ed., pp. 235–259). New York: Guilford Press.

McIntosh, P. (1998). White privilege: Unpacking the invisible knapsack. In M. McGoldrick (Ed.), *Re-visioning family therapy: Race, culture, and gender in clinical practice* (pp. 147–152). New York, NY: The Guilford Press.

Miranda, A. H., Boland, A., & Hemmeler, M. (2009). Understanding privilege in America. In J. M. Jones (Ed.), *The psychology of multiculturalism in the schools: A primer for practice, training, and research* (pp. 67–82). Bethesda, MD: NASP Publications.

Munz, R. (2013). *Demography and migration: An outlook for the 21st century.* Migration Policy Institute. Retrieved from http://www.migrationpolicy.org/research/demography-and-migration-outlook-21st-century

Myers, J. E., & Sweeney, T. J. (2005). *Counseling for wellness: Theory, research, and practice.* Alexandria, VA: American Counseling Association.

Nastasi, B. (2005). School consultants as change agents in achieving equity for families in public schools. *Journal of Educational and Psychological Consultation, 16*, 113–125.

Negroponte, D. V. (2014, July 2). The surge in unaccompanied children from Central America: A humanitarian crisis at our border. *Brookings.* Retrieved from http://www.brookings.edu/blogs/up-front/posts/2014/07/02-unaccompanied-children-central-america-negroponte

Nugent, N., & Roberts, S. (2013). *Child and adolescent refugees: From surviving to thriving.* The Brown University Child and Adolescent Behavior Letter. Rhode Island: Bradley Hospital.

Patterson, T., & Sexton, T. (2013). Bridging conceptual frameworks: A systemic heuristic for understanding family diversity. *Couple and Family Psychology: Research and Practice, 2*, 237–245.

Pedersen, P. (2000). Developing a cultural identity. In P. Pederson (Ed.), *A handbook for developing multicultural awareness* (3rd ed., pp. 61–82). Alexandria, VA: American Counseling Association.

Pollock, D. C., & Van Reken, R. (2001). *Third culture kids: The experience of growing up among worlds.* Boston, MA: Nicholas Brealey North America.

Pumariega, A. J., & Rothe, E. (2010). Leaving no children or families outside: The challenges of immigration. *American Journal of Orthopsychiatry, 80*, 505–515.

Schwarz, S. J., Unger, J. B., Zamboanga, B. L., & Szapocznik, J. (2010). Rethinking the concept of acculturation: Implications for theory and research. *American Psychologist, 63*, 237–251.

Sheridan, S., & Kratochwill, T. (2007). *Conjoint behavioral consultation: Promoting family-school connections and interventions* (2nd ed.). New York: Springer.

Shriberg, D. (2009). Social justice and school mental health: Evolution and implications for practice. In J. M. Jones (Ed.), *The psychology of multiculturalism in the schools: A primer for practice, training, and research* (pp. 49–66). Bethesda, MD: NASP Publications.

Simon, J. B., Murphy, J. J., & Smith, S. M. (2005). Understanding and fostering family resilience. *The Family Journal: Counseling and Therapy for Couples and Families, 13*, 427–436.

Sue, D. W., & Capodilupo, C. M. (2008). Racial, gender, and sexual orientation microaggressions: Implications for counseling and psychotherapy. In D. W. Sue & D. Sue (Eds.), *Counseling the culturally diverse: Theory and practice* (5th ed., pp. 105–130). Hoboken, NJ: Wiley.

Sue, D. W., & Sue, D. (2008). Racial/cultural identity development in people of color. In D. W. Sue & D. Sue (Eds.), *Counseling the culturally diverse: Theory and practice* (pp. 233–258). Hoboken, NJ: John Wiley & Sons, Inc.

Townsend, J., & Oomen, C. (2015). *Before the boat: Understanding the migrant journey.* Migration Policy Institute Europe. Retrieved from http://www.migrationpolicy.org/research/boat-understanding-migrant-journey

Walsh, F. (1998). *Strengthening family resilience.* New York: The Guilford Press.

Walsh, F. (2003). Family resilience: Strengths forged through adversity. In F. Walsh (Ed.), *Normal family processes: Growing diversity and complexity* (3rd ed., pp. 399–423). New York: The Guilford Press.

Williams, R. F. (2009). Black-white biracial students in American schools: A review of the literature. *Review of Educational Research, 79,* 776–804.

Zirkel, S. (2008). Creating more effective multi-ethnic schools. *Social Issues and Policy Review, 2,* 187–241.

8

FOUNDATIONS FOR CONSULTATION IN EDUCATIONAL SETTINGS WITH SECOND LANGUAGE LEARNERS

Samuel O. Ortiz and Kristan E. Melo

School-based consultation is an indirect problem-solving and decision-making model that is designed to identify and clarify primary needs of the student/client and then develop, implement, and evaluate appropriate strategies for intervention. It requires the cooperative efforts of a consultant (i.e., the specialist) and consultees (teachers, parents, caregivers), and it focuses on addressing the needs of a client (often, a student) via intervention implemented through the consultee (Sheridan, Holmes, Coutts, & Smith, 2012). One best practice model, referred to as *instructional consultation*, is delineated by an instructional "triangle" that emphasizes the working consultation relationship in which, rather than looking for intrinsic deficits, a student's academic problems are conceptualized by focusing on the interaction between: (a) the student's current skill level; (b) the instructional strategies being used; and (c) the actual task the student is expected to perform (Rosenfield, 2008). Within this model, effective consultation is likely to result when careful attention is paid to salient variables operating within any or all of the components, that is, characteristics that may be important and unique to the student, the type of instruction being delivered, or the task at hand. In that regard, the process of consultation may be subject to specific types of issues and problem conceptualizations for some students that might not occur with other students. This model provides a unique lens through which to conceptualize consultation for second language learners (SLLs).[1]

One essential aspect to consider when engaging in a consultative relationship is the native language of the student. For example, if the student is not a native speaker of the language in which formal education is typically delivered (i.e., a second language learner), then the expected academic progress may become confounded by the fact that the student is learning a new language at a point later than that of his or her same-age peers who have all been learning it since birth. In other words, native and nonnative speakers of the instructional language who normally begin schooling at the same chronological age, may bring with them the same relative level of maturation, but not necessarily the same level of and language proficiency. There is no difficulty in the case of the former, who will receive instruction via the native language and in a manner specifically designed to support and foster development in that language—a language they currently speak and comprehend quite well and which has been in development for their entire lives. In contrast, while the SLL will often receive the very same instruction, it may represent an entirely new and initially incomprehensible language that they must first learn and in which they must become highly proficient before they can begin to benefit from instruction in that language.

The educational implications of this rather straightforward but often misunderstood duality are described well by Goldenberg (2008), who notes that SLLs "face the double challenge of learning academic content and the language of instruction simultaneously" (p. 8). Consequently, underperformance of SLLs when compared to native speakers is, unfortunately, the norm. Using statistics from the U.S. as an example, on the 2007 National Assessment of Educational Progress, SLLs scored considerably lower than their non-SLL counterparts. In that year, fourth-grade SLL students scored about 36 points below native English speakers in reading and 25 points below in math (Goldenberg, 2008). Examination of the gaps among eighth graders showed a similar pattern—42 points lower in reading and 37 points lower in math. Further evaluation of this gap with NAEP data from 2004 and 2008 reveals a similar pattern where in 2004 the gaps between U.S.-based SLLs and native English speakers in reading achievement were 31 points in fourth grade, 41 points in eighth grade, and 42 points by twelfth grade. Rather than closing the gap, and despite the implementation of both higher standards and stricter accountability methods via the 2001 No Child Left Behind Act, the differences in reading in 2008 were 30 points in fourth grade, 45 points in eighth grade, and 52 points by twelfth grade.

SLLs thus bring unique challenges to the consultation process that must be well understood and carefully accommodated within the consultation instructional triangle if there is to be any reasonable expectation of success. This is the main issue that forms the focus of the current chapter: In what manner might the process of consultation, within the context of the instructional triangle, be adjusted or altered so as to best suit the specific needs of SLLs? We begin with a discussion of multicultural consultation as proposed by Ingraham (2000) and then extend this discussion to working with SLLs and focus on understanding their academic development. We then discuss issues unique to SLLs in regard to possible target areas for consultation, which include various aspects of achievement, intervention, and behavior.

MULTICULTURAL CONSULTATION

At some point in their careers, school psychologists will inevitably engage in consultation services with individuals whose cultural identities and experiences are different than their own. In such cases, school psychologists, in accordance with various standards (e.g., AERA, APA, & NCME, 2014; APA, 1990, 2002; NASP, 2000, 2010) need to be aware of and address any unique cultural issues that may arise and which may influence the manner or nature of the delivery of consultation (and other) services. In response to these largely aspirational guidelines, Ingraham (2000) proposed a set of guidelines for multicultural consultation to be used as a framework to enhance existing consultation models. Ingraham (2000) proposed that, when multicultural consultation is deemed necessary, it is the consultant's duty to consider the influences that differences in culture impart to each person and to make appropriate adjustments to practice that will develop and maintain rapport with and engender a better understanding of the consultee(s) and client(s) and their needs.

Ingraham (2000) defined culture as an organized set of thoughts, beliefs, and norms for interaction and communication within a specific group of people that can be influenced by race, ethnicity, language, socioeconomic status, age, educational attainment, sexual orientation, spirituality, professional role, and level of acculturation. As defined, it is important to recognize that multicultural consultation thus includes consultation triads where all members may be from one particular ethnic group but differ in terms of educational attainment. Thus, it would be too restrictive and narrow to apply multicultural consultation only to those cases where at least one member of the triad is a member of a different ethnic or racial group than the other members because such a definition of culture is far too limited (Ingraham, 2000). In multicultural consultation, both individual differences (e.g., religion, sexual orientation, language) as well as broader, socially based differences (e.g., race, ethnicity, gender, class, socioeconomic status) are considered together so as to prevent either overemphasizing or deemphasizing the influence of all types of cultural underpinnings in the process. For a complete review of Ingraham's framework, please refer to Chapter 16 in this book.

While the issues described are certainly an essential conceptual framework for multicultural consultation practice that is appropriate, effective, and as nondiscriminatory as possible, the major focus has been primarily on establishing positive relationships between members of the consultation triad. However, positive relationships alone are not enough to ensure success and efficacy in service delivery. For example, in the case of SLLs, school psychologists need to have specific knowledge regarding how cultural, experiential, and developmental issues affect school-based learning and particularly expectations around rates of progress and age- or grade-related levels of attainment. Such knowledge does not form a common or routine focus in school psychology training, and its lack could have significant implications regarding the success or failure of consultation efforts. In cases where cultural differences are less obvious, the knowledge necessary for effective consultation practice may go completely overlooked. Differences that are subtle are no less important than those that are apparent, and they are no less potentially detrimental to a consultant's best efforts. Too often, culture has been treated as if it referred only to race or ethnicity (Ortiz, Flanagan, & Dynda, 2008). Although this represents the traditional definition of the concept, it has become too outdated to apply broadly enough or accurately in present day society where differentiation among human beings occurs on a much wider range of dimensions and characteristics than ever before. For this reason, culture is best understood as a combination of all the factors that have played a significant role in the development of one's own identity, beliefs, attitudes, values, worldview, and biases.

It is clear that effective service delivery also requires knowledge that is particular to the constellation of idiosyncratic cultural differences present in any given consultation triad. And, whereas recognition of differences when working with SLLs has never been a major obstacle, the knowledge necessary to promote success beyond the formation of solid working relationships remains problematic. The goal of this chapter is to provide just this type of knowledge, specific to consultation with SLLs in any country and culture that will further enhance the process, its appropriateness, and ultimately its likelihood of success.

CULTURAL AND LINGUISTIC ISSUES IN CONSULTATION

The questions regarding the manner in which cultural and linguistic factors influence academic learning and become salient considerations in consultation with SLLs are complex. Both factors are often viewed in oversimplified ways: culture is examined primarily in light of acculturative processes in which an individual begins an integrative (sometimes assimilative) journey from their own culture into the majority culture; language is viewed merely as an issue of the student's degree of proficiency in the instructional language. SLL students who are being raised at home in one culture but are expected to learn and function within a different one face a balancing act that has significant bearing on development of ethnic self-identity, belonging, behavior, values, attitudes, and so forth (Ortiz et al., 2008). Without question, the psychosocial development of SLLs will be best understood when viewed within the context of these different and often competing and conflicting forces in the student's life. But for reasons to be discussed, these factors tend to have comparatively less direct influence on academic learning.

Conversely, language proficiency is at present well-known to be and readily recognized as an obstacle to school-based learning. But the impact of language difference on learning often ends right there under the mistaken notion that once a child reaches an arbitrarily set threshold of language proficiency in the second language, they are capable of meeting the same standards and expectations for same-age or same-grade native speakers of that language. The mistaken and discriminatory aspects of such beliefs tend to go unrecognized.

The main error in these views is largely the same. With respect to culture, it is not that there is a difference per se that will affect learning, but rather that the process of learning about a new culture is, itself, a developmental process. That is, there is a sequential nature to the development and acquisition of acculturative knowledge (knowledge that differs from that which is being absorbed at home and from the student's parents). With respect to language, there is also a sequential aspect to its development and acquisition, but there is a vast difference between language that is sufficient for general social conversation and the language that is demanded within an academic setting. When no cultural or linguistic differences are present, both of these processes develop linearly and naturally and are tied directly to age, with academic expectations also increasing linearly with age and grade. With SLLs, however, both processes, by definition, are not tied strictly to the student's age or grade because the learning of either one did not begin at birth. Further, the total amount of time, experience, and opportunity to learn them is always less, sometimes much less, than that of their same-age and same-grade peers. Failure to apprehend the concept that learning (but also behavior and socioemotional functioning) is rooted in basic aspects of development is likely to result only in inappropriate and ineffective consultation efforts.

CULTURAL FACTORS AND SLLS

Recommendations and guidelines regarding methods for developing cultural competence, particularly as related to understanding and appreciating the attendant beliefs, values, or attitudes from one culture or another, have been provided elsewhere (e.g., Gravois & Rosenfield, 2006; Ingraham, 2000; Ortiz, 2006; Ortiz & Gardner, in press) and will not be repeated here. Rather, multicultural consultation with SLLs will need to concern itself with the way in which acculturative knowledge is acquired and how this process goes awry for those who are not native speakers of the instructional language. Thus, the focus here will be on delineating the developmental nature of acculturative learning and how this, and not "culture" per se, is of paramount concern in consultation that centers around enhancing and improving a student's learning, including issues related to problematic behavior or social emotional development in the school setting.

The process of acquiring the basic knowledge of a culture typically begins at birth. Parents will, of course, transmit to their child the cultural knowledge they possess while the child remains at home. When the parents' culture is the same as the residential culture in which the child is being raised, the opportunities for acquisition of cultural knowledge are increased. What a child should know—that is, what facts they should have internalized, what objects and artifacts they ought to recognize, what things they are likely familiar with—is all known and understood so well that it forms the basis of potential assessments at any given age.

Likewise, when a child begins formal education, typically in kindergarten at the age of 5, if the school is rooted in the mainstream culture (e.g., public school system), it will also provide new and enhanced opportunities for the acquisition of ever higher levels of culture-specific knowledge. From the beginning, the school setting places its own expectations on what cultural knowledge is valued and what is expected to be learned and by what age. This is usually understood as the difference between what is learned incidentally, just by being exposed to people and things, as opposed to what is learned formally through direct and explicit instruction. Learning to read, write, and do mathematics and later instruction on subjects ranging from geography to science to history all represent culturally bound information valued by the majority culture and taught for the express purpose of imbuing each and every student with such knowledge. When parents are from a culture that is not the same as the mainstream one in which they are raising their child (a very common and typical situation for immigrant children and parents), the child begins by learning cultural knowledge that is specific to the parents' own culture. The parents are generally not equipped to immediately switch to teaching or transmitting much of a culture they know little about themselves. Therefore, the opportunities for the child to acquire the knowledge rooted in the majority culture is rather limited, even when the child and parents reside full time in that culture.

The main opportunity for SLL children to begin significant acquisition of cultural knowledge often starts when they enter kindergarten and receive formal education. Like their same-age, native language speaking peers, they too will have about 7 hours a day to learn about the new culture and internalize knowledge specific to it. Consider, however, that when SLL children go home or when school is not in session, the opportunity for exposure and the learning it promotes essentially ceases, whereas for native speakers, the opportunities for incidental learning at home and the parental transmission of cultural knowledge continue. For SLLs, opportunities in the community and outside the home are comparatively limited in that the child's parents are unlikely to have all the requisite cultural knowledge about the majority culture themselves let alone the time or ability to transmit it to their children. Because the parents themselves were raised in their own native culture and have spent a lifetime acquiring and internalizing the unique aspects of it, their native culture has likely engendered a deep sense of comfort and familiarity in them. Therefore, it is this body of cultural knowledge, not the mainstream's, that will be naturally transmitted to their children.

When culture is viewed erroneously as a mere difference in race or ethnicity, the obvious discrepancy in learning versus learning opportunities gets obscured and will tend to penalize SLLs. Schools often view their curricula as sacrosanct, especially in the current age of international educational performance comparability (e.g., TIMSS, PISA) and the increased emphasis on accountability often via mass testing and assessments. Thus, SLLs will invariably be expected to meet the proficiency and learning standards that match their grade, often irrespective of how long they have been learning the language in which they are being taught or tested. An SLL who begins school at any age has learned less about the culture (regardless of the reasons), which may have negative consequences (e.g., academic retention, dismissal, failure), particularly with respect to incidental learning experiences and incidental knowledge. SLLs who start school at the age of 5 will only have approximately 1 academic year (10 months) to acquire knowledge that their peers have now amassed over the course of 6 full years (72 months).

The same can be said with respect to formal, academic-based learning. While it is true that both groups (SLLs and native speakers) have had the same amount of exposure to instruction (10 months), SLLs come in with less knowledge to begin with. In the vast majority of cases, they also do not have sufficient development and proficiency in the instructional language such that they might benefit from the instruction to the same extent and to the same degree as their age-matched peers. This issue will be further discussed in the following section, but it is important to note that neither the comparability in age nor the relatively equivalent exposure to formal instruction should be assumed to result in comparable levels or expectations of development and achievement. It is perhaps even more disconcerting to recognize that, as each year passes, the incidental learning opportunities and experiences of native speaking children will always be greater than that of SLLs, such that SLLs' exposure to these experiences can never actually reach the same level as their age- or grade-related peers throughout the entire length of formal education. This is not to say that the educational attainment of all children is foreclosed but more that the success of less-resilient children and the vast majority of them who are simply "average" in terms of innate ability remains at significant risk for academic failure.

LANGUAGE ACQUISITION AND SLLS

Unlike acculturative knowledge, there is general recognition that language proficiency is an important issue in the learning and academic achievement of SLLs. This is quite correct, of course, but the manner in which language acquisition influences actual academic performance is not a common topic in the training of all educational professionals, particularly school psychologists, counselors, administrators, and even many teachers. The basic issue, as already described, is that SLLs begin learning the language of instruction at a point other than birth. Ordinarily, language development is closely tied to an individual's age. For example, the relative ages at which children are able to recognize phonemes in the parents' native language, produce their own sounds, speak their first words, use basic grammatical constructions, employ appropriate pragmatics in conversation, and so forth are very well-known (Fromkin, Rodman, & Hyams, 2013). The milestones are similar regardless of the parents' native language or culture. In short, language development follows a very predictable pattern that is measured by degrees of proficiency that are tied to approximate chronological ages and that have been classified into four distinct descriptive categories. These stages are described in the following section.

Language Acquisition

All individuals, whether learning their first language from birth or a second language at some point other than at birth (or simultaneously with the first language) go through various stages of acquisition (e.g., Fromkin et al., 2013; Krashen, 1982). Even in the absence of cultural or linguistic differences as discussed thus far, school professionals will benefit from understanding each stage as it has particular relevance in the delivery of effective consultation services. A lack of awareness regarding how much language a child has acquired risks delivery of services that are either inappropriate or unlikely to be effective due to a mismatch between the child's proficiency and that required by the task.

The first stage of language acquisition, *preproduction/comprehension*, is sometimes called the "silent period," where the individual concentrates completely on figuring out what the new language means without worrying much about speaking or production skills (Fromkin et al., 2013). In this phase, receptive comprehension is paramount and actual speech is limited. Communication, depending on age, is primarily of a nonverbal fashion that includes listening, pointing, matching objects, drawing figures, proximity to desired objects or objectives, choosing from various options, pantomiming, and acting out what they want to say. Consider that even from birth, infants remain in this stage for only about a year or up until they begin to produce actual verbalizations and words with meaning to facilitate further comprehension (Fromkin et al., 2013). If the language being learned is a second language and occurs at a point later than birth, say at age 5 for an SLL that just entered school, the amount of time in this stage would be correspondingly less. And in well-educated adults with appropriate development in another language, this period would be considerably shorter if not nearly absent altogether in an immersive experience.

During the second stage of language acquisition, *early production*, speech begins to emerge naturally, but the primary linguistic process continues to be the development of listening comprehension and understanding (Fromkin et al., 2013). In this phase, an individual's speech will contain a significant number of grammatical and syntactical errors. Pragmatics are basic, and vocabulary is still extremely limited. Typically, the progression into the phase of speech production is accompanied by the ability to answer yes/no questions; list short, basic words (e.g., I, a, me); give one word answers; produce two-word strings (e.g., "I jump"), and produce short phrases (e.g., "he come here") (Fromkin et al., 2013). As with the prior stage, the amount of time it takes to reach this level is relatively short, as evidenced by the fact that 2-year-olds are considered to be well within this stage.

By the time an individual reaches the third stage, *speech emergence,* sentences have become longer and more complex, and they contain a wider range of vocabulary (Fromkin et al., 2013). The grammar and syntax have improved markedly, the more obvious errors have decreased, and more subtle errors are also declining slowly. Individuals at this stage begin to easily use three-word or longer sentences and short phrases, eventually moving to actual comprehensible dialogue and longer phrases. At this stage, speech has become productive enough to be considered representative of early or beginning fluency in the language. Further development includes the ability to engage in extended social discourse, complete verbal sentences where appropriate, and retell narratives with clarity and accuracy.

By the time an individual reaches the fourth stage, *intermediate fluency*, there has been sufficient exposure to adequate social language models and opportunities to interact with other fluent speakers such that full capability in terms of receptive understanding and expressive ability has been achieved (Fromkin et al., 2013). At this level, an individual has excellent listening comprehension skills and is quite capable of understanding virtually anything he or she may hear in general conversation, with notable exceptions in more culturally bound parts of speech such as humor, idioms, and colloquialisms. At this stage, the individual's speech contains even fewer grammatical errors, and those that do remain are more subtle and less obvious.

It is important to note here that linguists are not concerned with academic learning or the demands of school as related to specific and more advanced aspects of language (e.g., technical vocabulary, debate skills, verbal reasoning, logic). Rather, for linguists, the term *intermediate fluency* refers to a level of proficiency that is commensurate with the average speaker of that language in such a way that permits meeting basic needs and fulfilling virtually any purpose within normal social interaction. For example, the individual can easily ask for directions, express various needs (e.g., hunger, sadness, excitement), communicate intentions and thoughts, and hold normal conversations. By the time a child is 5 years old, they are well into this stage and quite comfortable and capable in using the language even in the classroom setting and with only a rudimentary, but solid, grammatical framework. A summary of the four stages of language acquisition is provided in Table 8.1 for easy reference.

It seems clear that knowledge of these stages has implications for the development and implementation of various instructional strategies and expectations of performance for children, particularly SLLs. Whatever is planned in terms of consultation must take into account the SLL's current stage of language acquisition. Consultants can informally assess language level in a number of ways, including via interview of

Table 8.1 The Stages of Language Acquisition

Preproduction/Comprehension (no BICS)

Sometimes called the silent period, where the individual concentrates completely on figuring out what the new language means without worrying about production skills. Children typically may delay speech in L2 from one to six weeks or longer.

- Listen, point, match, draw, move, choose, mime, act out

Early Production (early BICS)

Speech begins to emerge naturally, but the primary process continues to be the development of listening comprehension. Early speech will contain many errors. Typical examples of progression are

- Yes/no questions, lists of words, one word answers, two word strings, short phrases

Speech Emergence (intermediate BICS)

Given sufficient input, speech production will continue to improve. Sentences will become longer and more complex and there is a wider vocabulary range. Numbers of errors will slowly decrease.

- Three-word strings and short phrases, dialogue, longer phrases
- Extended discourse, complete sentences where appropriate, narration

Intermediate Fluency (advanced BICS/emerging CALP)

With continued exposure to adequate language models and opportunities to interact with fluent speakers of the second language, second language learners will develop excellent comprehension and their speech will contain even fewer grammatical errors. Opportunities to use the second language for varied purposes will broaden the individual's ability to use the language more fully.

- Give opinions, analyze, defend, create, debate, evaluate, justify, examine

Source: Information from Krashen, S.D. (1982). *Principles and practice in second language acquisition.* New York: Pergamon Press.

the consultee or parents about the English language capabilities of the child, observing the child in social situations where English is being spoken, and having a conversation in English with the child. If the child is receiving second language instruction and services, it may be possible to review any test scores that could illuminate progress and current proficiency. By considering the SLL's current level of proficiency, school psychologists can offer linguistically and developmentally appropriate consultation services.

Were this the entire extent of language development, the task might seem rather easy. The reality is that being able to converse in a language for social purposes is simply not enough for the purposes of achieving school success. SLLs have been exposed to and have experience with more than one language. In most cases, this means the degree of development they possess in each one is unlikely to be equal or balanced. Typically, the SLL's native language (L1) is better developed by virtue of having had the greatest opportunities, interaction, and exposure for its development relative to the second language (L2). Were SLLs only expected to function within social settings, the relative discrepancy in proficiency would ultimately work itself out. But SLLs, like most children, go to school where they are expected to learn more than just incidental cultural knowledge. They are, in fact, expected to develop formal academic knowledge and advanced linguistic capabilities that are the very hallmarks of an education. Therefore, educators expect a much higher standard for language development than linguists. It is this difference in proficiency that is critical for the provision of appropriate consultation services.

BICS versus CALP

One of the first researchers to wrestle with the distinction between language proficiency sufficient for social purposes versus academic success was Cummins (1984), who developed the concepts of basic interpersonal communication skills (BICS) and cognitive academic language proficiency (CALP). Cummins' intent was to conceptualize the difference between language proficiency that represents the linguists' views of fluency from language proficiency as viewed by educators who expect increasingly higher levels of fluency as a student progresses from grade to grade. Although both types of proficiency are continua in their own right, in that there is a range of development in each one, they are interrelated and overlap. For example, when instruction begins in the native language at the typical age of 5, eventual academic fluency in the native language is simply built upon the foundations provided by the social language fluency brought naturally to the educational setting.

In general, BICS refers to the ability to effectively communicate one's basic needs and wants and the ability to carry on basic interpersonal conversations without the need for or any regard to formal instruction—social language (Cummins, 1984). Cummins noted that the development of BICS for SLLs takes only about 1 to 3 years, depending on the age of the individual, with younger children typically taking somewhat longer than older ones. In many ways, BICS is comparable to the third and fourth stages of language development such that individuals at the intermediate fluency stage can be said to possess intermediate to advanced BICS (See Table 8.1).

BICS fluency is insufficient for the purposes of long-term academic success. As Cummins (1984) notes, CALP only develops in response to formal education, and it does not begin to emerge as a distinct level of proficiency until after about 5 to 7 years of such formal instruction, or essentially around the time an individual has become literate. That is, by the time the curricula in most schools are shifting away from basic skills instruction (approximately kindergarten to third grade) to focus on more conceptual development (about fourth grade on up), early CALP has begun to form and emerge. It is important to recognize that CALP does not constitute an either/or existence but is also a continuum of proficiency such that it is reasonable to describe it in terms of its own stages, for example, early, intermediate, and advanced. Not only does Cummins' notion of CALP fit nicely with the structural changes that are typical of education across the early elementary gradespan, it also provides an elegant explanation regarding the trouble that besets SLLs who are expected to develop both types of proficiency.

In general, CALP refers to the ability to communicate thoughts and ideas with clarity and efficiency as well as the ability to carry on advanced interpersonal conversations and use language for academic purposes. Therefore, CALP includes the internalization of technical and domain-specific vocabulary, verbal reasoning skills including deduction and induction, debating skills, and advanced application of grammatical, syntactical, and pragmatic language skills. In brief, CALP is the ability to think critically in a language and use it in the service of and promotion of further learning. The common educational refrain related to the shift in the late elementary school curriculum, described as moving from "learning to read" to "reading to learn," is a fair description of and an indirect acknowledgment of the emergence of early CALP. Because structured education progresses from one grade to the next with corresponding increases in expectations of learning and attainment, academic problems may result if the expected level of CALP is not developed by the expected grade.

This is precisely the situation in which SLLs often find themselves and why their academic achievement is placed at significant risk that increases with advancement in grade. The failure to understand the development of proficiency in the language of instruction as extending beyond the ability to simply speak, listen, read, or write means that SLLs are being asked to reach the same level of CALP as their native-speaking peers but within a shorter period of time (i.e., about 4 years versus 9 years). To condense 9 years of language development supported by 4 years of formal instruction and learning into a 4-year period without the benefit of any prior development in the instructional language is simply not a reasonable expectation or one that can be overcome by most SLLs, even those with average ability (Thomas & Collier, 2002).

Cummins (1984) invoked his BICS and CALP concepts to fit within a second language learning framework that he called the *developmental interdependence hypothesis* and by which he also sought to explain factors that predict academic success for SLLs. What Cummins hypothesized is that when a student has developed CALP, it provides a foundation that permits the transfer of skills via the "common underlying proficiency" that is shared between any two languages. That is, if an individual has developed language fluency to the point that early CALP has begun to emerge, then learning a second language is facilitated since the individual need not relearn the rudimentary aspects of academic language; they only need to apply those skills in a different language. To do so, only BICS-level instructional language is necessary since the grade-related academic skills are in fact already possessed by the student and the only obstacle is one of comprehension—something that is readily managed in 1 to

3 years of development in social language. Conversely, an individual who has not yet developed CALP, presumably because they have not yet reached the fourth or fifth grade or because they have had limited, interrupted, or no prior schooling at all, has no CALP skill that can be transferred; thus, instruction cannot immediately focus on academic content but must first attend to the basics of social language in terms of developing speaking and listening skills. With sufficient time and opportunity, the development of advanced CALP may follow for individuals with such backgrounds, but it seems highly improbable given that the process would add a minimum of 5 years of schooling and extend K–12 education to about age 23.

While it appears that Cummins is correct in his developmental interdependence hypothesis, his model is more descriptive than explanatory. A closer look at his hypothesis reveals that the reasons for both effective linguistic transfer and lack thereof can be traced to the developmental trajectories of both of the individual's languages and their interaction with the parallel processes occurring in instruction and cognitive development.

PARALLEL PROCESSES IN DEVELOPMENT AND LEARNING

To fully understand how cultural and linguistic factors affect student learning, one must understand that language, cognition, and instruction are parallel developmental processes occurring at the same time and in concert with each other. For the most part, the development across these three domains is rather consistent, and the parallel aspect of development is known and accommodated across all three. For example, the teaching of readiness skills occurs at the point in a preschooler's life when it is believed they are ready for it in terms of language and cognitive development, sometimes irrespective of known milestones and significant normal variability in such a young population. Nevertheless, the entire formal education system is predicated upon the provision of classroom instruction that is at least believed to be developmentally appropriate for any given age or grade, SLL and otherwise. These parallel processes are illustrated in Figure 8.1.

However, for the SLL, such instruction may not be nearly as appropriate as it may seem, because the instruction is predicated on an assumed level of comparable experience, exposure, and proficiency typically shared by those of the same age—in short, similar development. When instruction is given in the same language the child has learned, as is the case with native speakers of the instructional language, the entire process of development remains parallel and proceeds according to age- and grade-based expectations. When the process of development is set askew because the language of instruction does not match the native language of a student entering school, development for SLLs is put off kilter and can no longer remain in alignment with expectations that are appropriate only for native speakers. In a strict sense, for instruction to be effective it must match the actual level of development of the student with respect to the language being used. That is, if instruction is delivered in the native language and development is most advanced in that language, the greatest educational benefit is derived. If instruction is delivered in the second language, as is typical for SLLs in mainstream public schools, the benefit will be reduced considerably since the proficiency in the language is insufficient and does not match the expectations of the instruction.

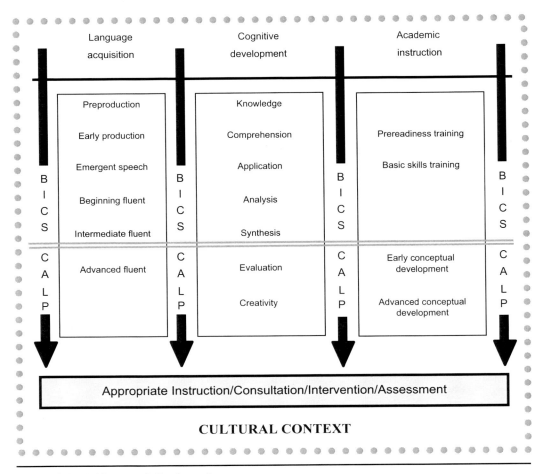

Figure 8.1 Parallel Processes in Development

IMPLICATIONS FOR INTERVENTION

In an ideal situation, SLLs should receive linguistically appropriate instruction in their second language upon entering school. Many schools, in fact, do offer SLLs a type of instructional support service that is designed primarily to promote basic language development and often includes little, if any, core instruction. These linguistically superficial services are typically offered for a limited period of time (e.g., 45 minutes) every day or several times a week, sometimes less, and are decontextualized in that they are rarely connected to the curriculum. But even under the best of circumstances and with careful attention to providing content-based language instruction, by definition, SLLs do not bring the usual 5 or so years of language development before beginning formal schooling in the language of instruction like native speakers do. And because schools cannot, of course, simply wait for 5 years to begin teaching content to students who nevertheless do not yet comprehend the language in which the content is being taught, such services will generally result in little more than a Band-Aid fix for a problem that goes much deeper (Goldenberg, 2008, 2013; Thomas & Collier, 1997, 2002).

Schools are sometimes aware of the mismatch between age and language development of SLLs, but they must also wrestle with concerns that arise from the emotional and physical consequences of placing older children in classes with much younger ones, difficulties in finding qualified teachers, limited funding for appropriate curricula, worries about poor student performance on mandated tests and assessments used to evaluate accountability, and a host of other practical concerns. Moreover, SLLs differ widely in their language proficiency and not all will need or require instruction that is below their actual chronological age. As Cummins noted, individuals who have received solid native language instruction up to about the fourth grade are likely to have little difficulty with learning academic content in any other language because, as stated previously, they only need to learn to apply the skills they acquired in their native language to the second language. Conversely, those who do not receive such instruction are placed at much greater risk for academic difficulties (Goldenberg, 2008).

Implications for Consultation

Consultants need to help the consultee recognize that the degree to which the relationship and interaction between language, cognition, and instruction has or has not remained parallel is the most appropriate context for understanding prior and current academic performance. Measurement of any abilities, skills, or knowledge or any sample of behavior collected via one language does not necessarily correspond equally to the individual's abilities, knowledge, or behavior that might be collected via the other language. When conceptualizing SLLs learning or behavior problems within a consultation process, consultants must seek to understand the factors that have influenced all three major aspects of development and in both languages so that reasonable expectations of performance can be established separately for each language in which the individual may receive services.

As long as the processes—that is, language acquisition, general cognitive development, and academic development/instruction—all remain parallel, efforts in assessment and instruction remain appropriate and effective. That is, when development has not been interrupted or altered by circumstance, expectations regarding performance (as measured by tests), delivery of grade-level instruction, and proposed interventions will be appropriate and nondiscriminatory.

For SLLs, difficulty tends to arise pursuant to a circumstantial alteration in the parallel structure of the developmental processes because, unlike cognitive development, an individual can begin a new, second developmental process in language at any point in life. A mismatch thus occurs whereby an SLL who is 8 years old has had 8 years of language development, but only 3 of those have been in the school's instructional language. Furthermore, even those 3 years were only partially in the instructional language since schooling does not occur every day of the year. This means that the vast majority of an SLLs language development (which is in L1) is summarily dismissed and formal instruction begins in a language (L2) in which the SLL has comparatively little and well below age-expected development. Perhaps even more worrisome is that because the instruction occurs in L2 upon entering school, the student's development in L1 does not progress much beyond that which with they entered. And despite the fact that kindergarten-level instruction may be characterized as being relatively simple, it is nevertheless predicated upon possession of a level of proficiency in the instructional language that must be at least at the early fluency stage. Because an SLL, by definition, does not yet have that level of proficiency, they are unable to fully comprehend the instruction and are therefore very unlikely to benefit much, if at all, from it. The mismatch between language proficiency and formal instruction can also exist in the opposite manner such that an individual who is very proficient in the instructional language does not need or require instruction to be given at any level below their development.

In summary, the difficulty in consultation regarding the learning patterns of SLLs revolves around the fact that when they enter school, there is a very high probability that they will face the double challenge of learning academic content rendered in a language they cannot understand well or at all while at the same time being expected to learn to speak and comprehend the language (Goldenberg, 2008, 2013). Therefore, decisions regarding interventions, educational programming, expectations of performance, and other potential considerations for consultation must be made in light of the degree to which this unreasonable expectation has created inhibiting circumstances that are potentially too severe for even an average student to overcome. The following sections will highlight various issues that may influence delivery of consultation services with respect to target areas that include academic achievement, intervention/response to intervention, and behavior.

TARGET FOR CONSULTATION: ACADEMIC ACHIEVEMENT

A goal of consultation should be to educate others regarding the fact that academic underperformance by an SLL may well be the unfortunate result of the educational system's inability to properly accommodate individuals whose language development has not remained parallel to chronological age. In addition to providing education for those in the consultation process, school professionals may then use the same information with which to assist in developing appropriate and effective academic instruction and interventions for SLLs. This information was highlighted best by Thomas and Collier (1997, 2002) whose data, summarized in Figure 8.2, clearly show that whether academic performance ever reaches grade-level expectations depends directly on the type of program an SLL receives.

In their longitudinal outcome study of various types of educational programs commonly employed with SLLs in the U.S., Thomas and Collier (2002) demonstrated that programs that provided the greatest amount of native language (L1) instruction produced the best outcomes in achievement in English (L2). Conversely, the programs that provided the greatest amount of instruction in English (or in English only, L2) produced the worst outcomes in English (L2). For example, students in "dual-language" or "dual immersion" programs in which the goals are bilingualism and biliteracy built through instruction in both languages through about sixth grade, results on average in academic performance across all areas of about 20 percentile ranks above the average performance of monolingual English speakers (70th percentile rank/61st NCE versus 50th percentile rank/50th NCE). In stark contrast, students in typical English-as-a-second-language (ESL) pullout programs (taught only in English) end up 39 percentile ranks below the average of monolingual English speakers (11th percentile rank/24th NCE). Thus, instructional programming alone accounts for a difference of up to 59 percentile ranks (approximately equal to the difference between standard scores of 108 and 81, respectively), a difference of nearly two standard deviations solely as a function of type of educational program. Although the studies by Thomas and Collier (1997, 2002) are based

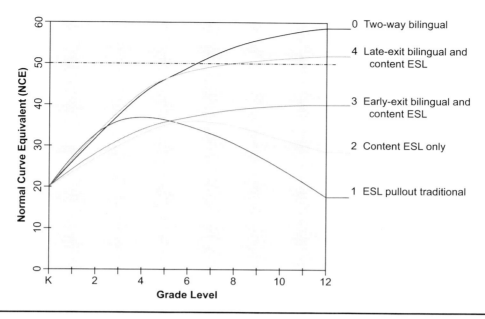

Figure 8.2 General Pattern of SLL Student Achievement on Standardized Tests in English

Source: Adapted from Thomas, W. P. & Collier, V. P. (1997). Language minority student achievement and program effectiveness. Washington DC: National Clearinghouse for Bilingual Education.

on nonnative English speakers in the U.S., the pattern of results can be generalized to other countries, cultures, languages, and schools (Cummins, 1982). Language and cognitive development have many "universal" aspects, and their interaction with formal instruction, in whatever language or culture, remains sufficiently invariant to allow cross-cultural application (Fromkin et al., 2013).

The implications of educational programming and its interaction with cognitive and academic development are crucial in regard to the provision of effective consultation services, particularly as related to instruction for SLLs. As Thomas and Collier (1997) noted, typical SLLs who begin school about 30 NCEs behind their native speaking peers in achievement (and many are much further behind) are expected to learn at "an average of about one-and-a-half years' progress in the next six consecutive years (for a total of nine years' progress in six years—a 30-NCE gain, from the 20th to the 50th NCE) to reach the same long-term performance level that a typical native-English speaker ... staying at the 50th NCE)" (p. 46). In other words, SLLs must make 15 months of academic progress in each 10-month school year for 6 straight years, which represents a rate of learning that is one and a half times faster than the average native speaking student. There simply aren't many SLLs who will meet with either ease or success in overcoming such a challenge. Therefore, goals for consultation involving SLLs who are underperforming academically should include education for all participants on the nature of typical SLL academic learning and progress, understanding the importance of language proficiency level and second language acquisition to instruction, and the need for modifying instruction so as to be as comprehensible to SLLs and at their respective level of linguistic and cognitive development.

TARGET FOR CONSULTATION: RESPONSE TO INTERVENTION

Another common target in the consultation process involves academic intervention, particularly within a response to intervention (RTI) or multitiered support system (MTSS) framework. It has long been assumed that RTI/MTSS will automatically benefit SLLs because it avoids the suggestions of bias associated with standardized, norm-referenced tests. For example, in describing a basic three-tier RTI model, Kovaleski and Prasse (2004) asserted that one of the potential benefits was "increased fairness in the assessment process, particularly for minority students."

Unfortunately, a careful review of current and prior research on this issue suggests that this premise appears to be a bit more wishful thinking than reality (Vanderwood & Nam, 2007). In 1995, Baker and Good investigated the reliability, validity, and sensitivity of English curriculum-based measure (CBM) passages, a standard RTI assessment, with bilingual Hispanic students and concluded that it was as reliable and valid for them as for native English speakers despite the presence of differential growth rates. The fact that there were differential growth rates seemed not to deter the researchers in making their claims. In fact, such a finding strongly suggested that some factor was present that was preventing the existence of similar growth rates for both groups—as would be expected. Similarly, Gersten and Woodward (1994) suggested that CBM could be used to develop growth rates for SLLs (which is true) but then erroneously suggested that SLL students generally continue to make academic progress toward grade-level norms, whereas SLL students with learning disability do not. The fallacy in this statement should be evident in light of the previous discussion regarding academic outcomes and their relation to instructional language and educational program.

But there are also other issues that school professionals must understand so as to ensure that intervention attempts, even within an RTI/MTSS framework, are developed and offered in such a way that they will be as appropriate and provide every chance of success as is reasonably possible.

In a typical three-tier RTI/MTSS system, students receive what is believed to be evidence-based instruction in a large group or classroom setting and are screened on a periodic basis to identify those who may need additional support. This segment usually represents about 5 to 10% of the students. The main issue for SLLs is the basic idea that forms the foundation of RTI/MTSS, which specifies that children should receive instruction that has been empirically validated to be effective. In the case of SLLs, any educational program other than two-way bilingual and late-exit bilingual would be a violation of this basic premise, since early-exit bilingual and second language support programs have been empirically validated as being ineffective for SLLs (Thomas & Collier, 1997, 2002). Thus, how can an RTI/MTSS model be implemented with any credibility at all if the major principle on which it is founded is not or cannot be met?

Intervention within an MTSS/RTI model must be viewed in light of the fact that the SLL may not be receiving an appropriate education; any lack of response to intervention is likely attributable more to this fact than to any other. No matter how well-designed or effective instruction might be, it simply cannot make up for deficiencies in educational pedagogy. Specifically, any RTI/MTSS that focuses on teaching SLLs to read in their second language should also emphasize teaching an SLL to read in their native language, since proficient reading skills in the native language boost reading achievement in the second language (Goldenberg, 2008).

Tier 2 is often employed when a student does not make adequate progress in the core curriculum and is placed in a smaller group situation to intensify the instruction.

Consultation services at Tier 2 must ensure that effective instruction is provided to the target student in small groups, and it must measure the effects of the instruction on the student's performance. An important key for services at this level is to ensure that members of the RTI/MTSS team recognize that what works with native-speaking students will not necessarily work with SLLs, as Vanderwood and Nam (2007) caution that very little data exist about the effectiveness of the vast majority of treatment/intervention protocols with EL learners.

Another important issue for school psychologists to consider is the meaning of "what works" in relation to empirical validation. When an intervention program is described as being empirically or scientifically validated, it merely indicates that within the context of experimental conditions, on average, the group of children who received the intervention improved academically more than another group that did not receive the intervention. However, this does not mean that *all* children benefited or improved or that all children will learn via that technique. In addition, it does not mean that it is even the best technique available. With respect to SLLs, it should be noted that no matter how effective or successful the intervention may have been shown to be (due to developmental reasons discussed previously), it will not allow SLLs to "catch up" to their native-speaking peers. Interventions can be shown to be evidence-based in that they will "work" for SLLs, but it does not mean they will enable them to reach classroom, school, or district-wide aim lines or expectations within the school year due to the gradual nature of progress for SLLs who are learning in a second language.

Figure 8.3 provides a hypothetical illustration of the problems inherent in determining what actual "response to intervention" is for SLLs and what is not. The illustration shows an example of what would be an aim line for words read correctly per minute (WRCPM), which would be established by a typical screening performed on

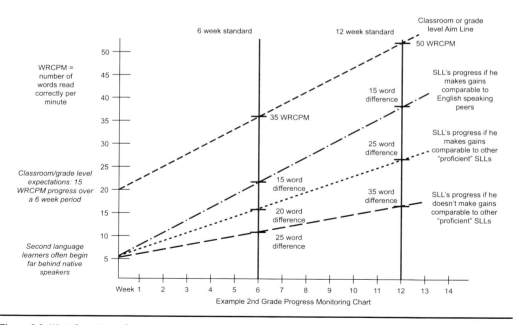

Figure 8.3 What Constitutes Response to Intervention for Second Language Learners?

the entire class that includes a mixture of SLLs but is primarily native language (L1) speakers. Let us assume that the developers of the hypothetical intervention program indicate that it will increase WRCPM by 15 words every 6-week period. Thus, if the classroom aim line begins at 20 WRCPM and progresses accordingly, students should be at 50 WRCPM by the end of the 12th week of intervention. Recall, however, that SLLs rarely start at the same point as native speakers for all the reasons discussed previously. Thus, is it unlikely that the average SLL is at 20 WRCPM. Rather, it is far more likely that the average SLL is well below that—in this example, we will say they are on average at only five WRCPM. Once the intervention begins, three general outcomes are possible. The first is shown by the line with long dashes separated by a single dot. In this example, an SLL makes 15 WRCPM each 6-week period. In every way, this student is responding very well to the intervention and is making exactly the same rate of progress as any other student. However, he or she remains 15 WRCPM behind at each marking period—that is, progress is not being made toward the aim line, and as long as the learning remains at that rate, the student will never actually reach it. Such a failure to make progress toward the aim line has often been alluded to, erroneously of course, as being indicative of a learning disability, and as such, an SLL student with this pattern may well be misidentified as learning disabled when in reality they are learning and responding quite well.

This initial scenario likely represents the best case since it is not reasonable to expect that SLLs would make the same rate of progress as native speakers as research indicates that there tends to be differential rates of growth. Accordingly, a more reasonable expectation is provided by the second line (dotted) which shows an SLL who is able to make gains that would be considered comparable to other SLLs (e.g., 10 WRCPM each marking period), but which is now five words less than that of native speakers. This student ends up at 20 words below the aim line target at the first marking period and 25 WRCPM below at the second. The longer the progress is monitored, the more clear it becomes that, despite the apparent progress, the SLL is slowly getting further and further behind his or her peers. As before, this pattern of performance is very likely to be misconstrued as a failure to respond to intervention, when in fact the student is benefitting as much as could be reasonably expected and in a manner that is developmentally appropriate for students with similar developmental backgrounds.

The third line (long dashes only) shows progress that an SLL might display if the gains are not quite comparable to other SLLs and instead only manages to make five WRCPM increases every marking period, rather than 10, which would put him or her at 25 WRCPM below the aim line after 6 weeks and 35 WRCPM behind after 12 weeks. In this case, some might argue that if this progress is indeed less than what other SLLs make, it would constitute sufficient evidence to suggest that the he or she is learning disabled. On the other hand, it might simply be the progress for a student with low average ability, not necessarily a disability. Or, what if the SLL only arrived recently in the country and had been receiving instruction for only a year or two? What if this is a student with interrupted formal education (SIFE)? In fairness, although the rate of progress is not as much as other SLLs, the student is still demonstrating a good response to the intervention because the WRCPM are in fact increasing, albeit slowly.

When any student reaches Tier 3 within an RTI/MTSS framework, the focus is on increasing the intensity of the interventions once again to the point that it may be delivered on a one-to-one basis and more often. The same issues that were discussed as part of Tier 2 intervention are much the same for Tier 3. What is or is not RTI is not as clear for SLL students as it may be for native speakers whose developmental trajectories can be easily identified and quantified. As should be obvious, there are many factors that might best explain such a pattern, and their presence may well mitigate what constitutes RTI or lack thereof (Esparza Brown & Ortiz, 2014). Knowledge of the research in this area, combined with an understanding of the educational implications of language difference, is the only way school professionals will be able to provide appropriate and effective consultation services.

TARGET FOR CONSULTATION: BEHAVIOR

School professionals who engage in consultation activities will very likely find themselves in situations where the focus of the consultation process centers on a student's behavior. It might seem odd to think that behavioral issues could differ for one student versus another student simply on the basis of a language difference. Nevertheless, SLLs have experiences that are most assuredly not the same as those experienced by monolingual, native (L1) speakers. This means that school professionals must be able to recognize those situations in which linguistic (and possibly cultural issues) play a role in understanding the nature and extent of an SLL's behavior.

Perhaps the most prominent manner in which language differences affect behavior, particularly in the classroom, involves the fact that the comprehension and receptive comprehension of SLLs are by definition not as good as those of a native speaker. Thus, all types and kinds of difficulties may arise due to either a lack of successful communication or misunderstandings. Table 8.2 provides a list of behaviors and characteristics that are often closely associated with deficits in attention and hyperactivity. The column on the right, however, provides an explanation regarding why limited comprehension might manifest itself in exactly the characteristic associated with it.

Table 8.2 Classroom Behaviors and Performance of Second Language Learners

Characteristics and behaviors often associated with various learning problems	Common SLLs actions during classroom instruction that may mimic various disorders or cognitive deficits
Slow to begin tasks	SLLs may have limited comprehension of the classroom language such that they are not always clear on how to properly begin tasks or what must be done in order to start them or complete them correctly.
Slow to finish tasks	SLLs, especially those with very limited English skills, often need to translate material from English into their native language in order to be able to work with it and then must translate it back to English in order to demonstrate it. This process extends the time for completion of time-limited tasks that may be expected in the classroom.
Forgetfulness	SLLs cannot always fully encode information as efficiently into memory as monolinguals because of their limited comprehension of the language, and they will often appear to be forgetful when in fact the issue relates more to their lack of proficiency with English.

(Continued)

Table 8.2 (Continued)

Characteristics and behaviors often associated with various learning problems	Common SLLs actions during classroom instruction that may mimic various disorders or cognitive deficits
Inattentiveness	SLLs may not fully understand what is being said to them in the classroom, and consequently they don't know when to pay attention or what exactly they should be paying attention to.
Hyperactivity	SLLs may appear to be hyperactive because they are unaware of situation-specific behavioral norms, classroom rules, and other rules of social behavior.
Impulsivity	SLLs may lack the ability to fully comprehend instructions, so they display a tendency to act impulsively in their work rather than following classroom instructions systematically.
Distractibility	SLLs may not fully comprehend the language being spoken in the classroom and therefore will move their attention to whatever they can comprehend, giving the appearance of being distractible.
Disruptiveness	SLLs may exhibit disruptive behavior, particularly excessive talking—often with other ELLs, due to a need to try to figure out what is expected of them or due to frustration about not knowing what to do or how to do it.
Disorganization	SLLs often display strategies and work habits that appear disorganized because they don't comprehend instructions on how to organize or arrange materials and may never have been taught efficient learning and problem-solving strategies.

For example, the very first row lists "slow to begin tasks," something commonly seen in classrooms from a variety of children. If the student is an SLL, it is possible that their comprehension of the instructions as conveyed by the normal classroom language of the teacher is limited, thereby causing a reduction in clarity and comprehension of the assigned task or the manner in which to begin it or what materials are required. Very often, teachers take for granted the level of their language in the classroom, and when students are at the grade or age-expected level of development, this is rarely a problem. For SLLs, it cannot be presumed that they have such development, particularly as they move up in grades and the language of the teacher increases accordingly and the need to explain ever more complex subject matter becomes commonplace. In general, SLLs may be slow to begin or finish tasks and may appear to be forgetful, inattentive, impulsive, distractible, disruptive, and disorganized primarily as a function of limitations in comprehension. It is difficult to know when to pay attention or what precisely to pay attention to if you cannot understand well what is being said in the first place. While it is possible that a student exhibiting these types of behaviors and characteristics may actually have a disability of some sort, the idea that the student lacks developmentally appropriate language skills that result in limited comprehension of directions, lack of familiarity with situation-specific behavioral norms, and agitated efforts to seek comprehensible input in unintentionally disruptive ways cannot be easily discounted or ignored (Ortiz & Dynda, 2008).

Another often overlooked but important factor in an SLL's behavior involves the process of acculturation, which can take many paths but also has a common set of experiences. For example, children that move to a new country at an early age or who are born there tend to find themselves in situations where there is conflict between their heritage culture and the new culture in which they reside (Ortiz, 1999). Making the decision to try to "fit in" and identify with the new culture, seek to maintain a balance and become bicultural, or reject any part of the assimilation process and remain staunchly identified to the heritage culture are all legitimate dilemmas that SLLs face and native speakers rarely do. Thus, questions regarding development of a comfortable ethnic self-identity, feelings of school and neighborhood membership, and the struggle in balancing potentially conflicting values, attitudes, and beliefs within the home against those within society may all affect the behavior of SLLs in the schools (Ortiz & Dynda, 2008). As such, it is imperative that teachers understand the unique effects of culture and language on SLLs' performance, so as not to conclude incorrectly that such behavior is maladaptive or indicates disability or dysfunction when there is none. In the consultation process, reframing the behavior for the teacher, educating the student regarding prevailing behavioral norms, and recognizing the student's need for increased comprehensible input are all critical issues that will benefit from careful exploration within the consultation triangle.

SUMMARY

On the surface, consultation activities that involve SLLs seem relatively straightforward. Certainly, the need to recognize that when any member of the consultation triangle brings a degree of diversity to the process, nearly all aspects of service delivery need to be carefully considered. Effective consultation in multicultural settings has largely focused on the development of positive relationships, which stems from recognition, respect, and affirmation for a wide variety of individual characteristics that consultation team members possess. And while the creation of positive relationships and the building of good working relationships are crucial to the process, ultimate success will necessitate a more dynamic view of the interaction involving cultural and linguistic differences in every aspect of the consultation process. One of the most important considerations in providing effective and appropriate consultation services rests on the development of a fairly extensive knowledge base regarding the impact of cultural and linguistic differences on educational achievement and classroom performance.

This chapter attempted to clarify this issue by discussing a framework that specifies the relationship among linguistic, cognitive, and academic development as unfolding in a parallel manner that integrates the way in which learning takes place. Development is a key concept in understanding what is appropriate to expect from SLLs, why they perform and behave the ways they do, what this means, and what is necessary to ensure that services are delivered in a way that is appropriate and most likely to lead to success. Likewise, effective consultation will require considerable knowledge of the manner in which first and second languages are learned and the interaction between language development and the instructional language. It was shown that the longer an SLL is educated in their native language (L1), the better they will do academically in the second language (L2). In similar fashion, albeit more tragically, the less native language instruction an SLL receives, the worse they will likely do academically (on average) in the second language. While these notions are simple, the developmental mechanism by which they operate is a bit more complex. Thus, having a firm grasp on developmental issues will be a fundamental component of the knowledge base needed to guide effective service delivery.

In sum, multicultural consultation goes beyond being "sensitive" to others who are different from ourselves. It is a matter that is neither based exclusively on race nor confined to ethnic, cultural, gender, socioeconomic status, sexual orientation, or religious issues. In most cases, however, effective multicultural consultation requires a much greater depth of knowledge regarding the manner in which culture, language, and cognition all interact in predictable ways that can either significantly enhance or greatly inhibit learning, academic performance, and behavior.

NOTE

1. There are various ways of identifying nonnative speakers of a language who are in the process of learning a second or even a third language. Because of the international focus of this chapter and volume, we have decided to use SLL as a generic reference to any individual in any situation who has not been learning the instructional language since birth and for whom the instructional language does not match the heritage language. This designation is primarily for the sake of clarity and is not intended to be or offered as standard nomenclature.

REFERENCES

American Educational Research Association, American Psychological Association, & National Council on Measurement in Education. (2014). *The standards for educational and psychological testing.* Washington, DC: Author.

American Psychological Association. (1990). *Guidelines for providers of psychological services to ethnic, linguistic, and culturally diverse populations.* Washington, DC: Author.

American Psychological Association. (2002). Ethical principles of psychologists and code of conduct. *American Psychologist, 57,* 1060–1073.

Baker, S. K., & Good, R. H. (1995). Curriculum-based measurement of English reading with bilingual Hispanic students: A validation study with second grade students. *School Psychology Review, 24,* 561–578.

Cummins, J. (1984). *Bilingual and special education: Issues in assessment and pedagogy.* Avon, England: Multilingual Matters, Ltd.

Esparza Brown, J. E., & Ortiz, S. O. (2014). Interventions for English language learners with disabilities. In J. T. Mascolo, D. P. Flanagan, & V. C. Alfonso (Eds.), *Essentials of planning, selecting and tailoring intervention.* New York: Wiley & Sons, Inc.

Flanagan, D. P., Ortiz, S. O., & Alfonso, V. C. (2013). *Essentials of cross-battery assessment* (3rd ed.). New York: John Wiley.

Fromkin, V., Rodman, R., & Hyams, N. (2013). *An Introduction to Language* (10th ed.). Boston, MA: Wadsworth.

Gersten, R., & Woodward, J. (1994). The language minority student and special education: Issues, themes and paradoxes. *Exceptional Children, 60,* 310–322.

Goldenberg, C. (2008). Teaching English language learners: What the research does—and does not—say. *American Educator, 32*(2), 8–23, 42–44.

Goldenberg, C. (2013). Unlocking the research on English learners: What we know—and don't yet know—about effective instruction. *American Educator, 37*(2), 4–11, 38–39.

Gravois, T. A., & Rosenfield, S. (2006). Impact of instructional consultation teams on the disproportionate referral and placement of minority students in special education. *Remedial and Special Education, 27,* 42–52.

Ingraham, C. L. (2000). Consultation through a multicultural lens: Multicultural and cross-cultural consultation in schools. *School Psychology Review, 29*(3), 320–343.

Kovaleski, J. F., & Prasse, D. P. (2004, February). Response to instruction in the identification of learning disabilities: A guide for school teams. *NASP Communiqué, 32*(5), 159–161.

Krashen, S. D. (1982). *Principles and practices in second language acquisition.* New York: Pergamon Press.

National Association of School Psychologists. (2000). *Professional conduct manual.* Bethesda, MD: Author.

National Association of School Psychologists. (2010). *Model for comprehensive and integrated school psychological services, NASP practice model overview [Brochure].* Bethesda, MD: Author.

Ortiz, S. O. (1999). You'd never know how racist I was, if you met me on the street. *Journal of Counseling and Development, 77*(1), 9–12.

Ortiz, S. O. (2001). Assessment of cognitive abilities in Hispanic children. *Seminars in Speech and Language, 22*, 17–37.

Ortiz, S. O. (2006). Multicultural issues in working with children and families: Responsive intervention in the educational setting. In R. B. Menutti, A. Freeman, & R. W. Christner (Eds.), *Cognitive behavioral interventions in educational settings: A handbook for practice* (pp. 21–36). New York: Brunner-Routledge Publishing.

Ortiz, S. O., & Dynda, A. M. (2008). Issues unique to English language learners. In R. J. Morris & N. Mather (Eds.), *Evidence-based interventions for students with learning disabilities and behavioral challenges* (pp. 321–335). New York, NY: Routledge/Taylor & Francis Group.

Ortiz, S. O., Flanagan, D. P., & Dynda, A. M. (2008). Best practices in working with culturally and linguistically diverse children and families. In A. Thomas & J. Grimes (Eds.), *Best practices in school psychology V* (pp. 1721–1738). Washington, DC: National Association of School Psychologists.

Ortiz, S. O. & Gardner, K. (in press). The Culturally Competent School Psychologist. In M. T. Terjesen and M. Thielking (Eds.) *The Australian Handbook of School Psychology*. NY: Springer Books.

Rosenfield, S. (2008). Best practice in instructional consultation and instructional consultation teams. In *Best Practices in School Psychology V* (pp. 1645–1660). Washington, DC: National Associations of School Psychologists.

Sheridan, S. M., Holmes, S. R., Coutts, M. J., & Smith, T. E. (2012). *Preliminary effects of conjoint behavioral consultation in rural communities* (CYFS Working Paper No. 2012–8). Retrieved from the Nebraska Center for Research on Children, Youth, Families and Schools website: cyfs.unl.edu

Thomas, W. P., & Collier, V. P. (1997). *Language minority student achievement and program effectiveness*. Washington, DC: National Clearinghouse for Bilingual Education.

Thomas, W. P., & Collier, V. P. (2002). *A national study of school effectiveness for language minority students' long-term academic achievement*. Santa Cruz, CA: Center for Research on Education, Diversity, & Excellence.

Vanderwood, M. L., & Nam, J. E. (2007). Response to intervention for English language learners: Current developments and future directions. In S. R. Jimerson, M. K. Burns, & A. M. VanDerHeyden (Eds.), *Handbook of response to intervention: The science and practice of assessment and intervention* (pp. 408–417). New York, NY: Springer Science+Business Media, LLC.

9

THE ENTRY PROCESS IN INTERNATIONAL SYSTEMIC SCHOOL CONSULTATION

Abigail Harris and Mio Ueda

Systemic consultation has been defined as a collaborative, problem-solving process in which the client is a system (or element of a system) and the consultees are stakeholders in the system (Harris, 2007). Whether the client is a country's entire educational system (e.g., Department of Education [DOE]) or some element(s) within the system (e.g., the curriculum, assessment, or training unit within the DOE; an internationally funded educational reform program; or a specific school), systemic consultation provides a unique opportunity for school consultants to serve as change agents. The consultant focuses on analyzing the system and identifying power hierarchies, alliances, strengths, values, norms, and cultural influences as the basis for facilitating sustainable systemic changes. Assessment and data-based decision-making support this process (Conoley, 1981; Curtis, Castillo, & Cohen, 2008; Harris, 2007). This chapter describes the entry and problem identification processes in cross-cultural systemic consultation focused on supporting educational reform within developing country contexts.

Systemic consultation draws elements from consultee-centered consultation as described by Caplan (1970) and elaborated by Lambert (2004) and others. Unlike a medical model of consultation, where the consultant investigates the symptoms, diagnoses the "illness," and prescribes a treatment or remedy, systemic consultation as used in this chapter refers to a collaborative process that supports a nonhierarchical relationship between the consultant and other partners in the problem-solving or reform effort. An important goal of the systemic consultation is strengthening local capacity to support the sustainability of improvements. This involves recognizing the expertise of the consultees (e.g., local educators and policy makers), fostering local ownership of the process, and working to empower local stakeholders to lead rather than take a backseat to the "expert consultant" (Lambert, 2004).

The stages in systemic consultation in an international context are similar to those discussed in other models of school-based consultation (Brown, Pryzwansky, & Schulte, 2010; Meyers, Parsons, & Martin, 1979). One potential difference is the iterative nature of the process. For example, *entry* and *problem identification* (PI) are used to establish the parameters of the consulting relationship. The consultant focuses on data gathering and building rapport with and consensus among relevant stakeholders regarding the focus of the consultation. It is typically after this focus is defined that a contractual relationship is established. However, even after a contract has been signed, consultants continue the entry process as they engage with new stakeholders and strive for a workable partnership. Perhaps because of the multiple consultees in systemic consultation, the stages are less clearly delineated than in consultation with only one or two consultees.

Similarly, *problem analysis* (PA) and *intervention* may be combined because the iterative process of data gathering, sharing, and consensus building provides a mechanism for supporting local problem-solving capacity. A major goal for the consultant is to foster the engagement and empowerment of the consultees to address the current issues and to be better prepared to address similar challenges in the future (Conoley, 1981; Curtis, Castillo, & Cohen, 2008; Lambert, 2004); thus, PA continues after interventions are implemented. The *evaluation* stage is used to assess the impact and effectiveness of the interventions and the consultation process. Finally, there may be an *adaptation* stage whereby adjustments to the interventions or availability of consultant services are made in order to enhance effectiveness or sustainability.

Box 9.1 provides an overview of key activities in systemic consultation in an international context. It extends earlier work on systemic reform in the U.S. (Comer, Haynes, Joyner, & Ben-Avie, 1996; Harris, 2007; Sarason, 1996) and was developed by the first

---

Box 9.1 Key Activities in Systemic Consultation in an International Context

Entry

Negotiate scope of work and terms of the relationship.

Begin establishing mutual rapport and trust.

Problem Identification

Gather data related to the educational system.

>   Review school census information (class size, school structure).

>   Investigate availability of testing results—international, national, regional, school/classroom.

>   Review curriculum documents (scope and sequence, textbooks, teacher training information).

>   Make school visits and observe in classrooms.

>   Identify relevant legal regulations.

Gather data related to the consultation process.

>   Analyze the power structures (governmental, program, covert, etc.).

>   Identify local norms for communication.

>   Identify individuals and/or coalitions supportive, resistant, or indifferent to change.

>   Recognize cross-cultural influences and potential biases.

Assess resource constraints and opportunities.

Relationship and consensus building with key stakeholders—fostering local ownership.

Problem Analysis and Intervention

Gain authorization of political and educational leaders.

Ensure compliance with legal regulations.

Conduct research to guide decision-making and serve as baseline for monitoring effectiveness (curriculum-based measurement, observation, focus groups, etc.).

Facilitate iterative process of gathering data, shared reflection, consensus building.

>   Promote ongoing engagement and empowerment of local educators.

>   Conduct small-scale pilot evaluation of potential interventions.

Plan for scaling up and optimizing sustainability.

Emphasize ongoing local capacity strengthening.
Evaluation
Collect data to evaluate effectiveness.
Identify unintended consequences.
Reflect on consultation process.
Adaptation, Replication, and Scaling Up
Foster sustainability.

author based on over two decades of consultation experiences in nine different countries in the Caribbean, Central America, and Africa. Typically, the focus of the consultation was providing technical assistance and expertise to educators and policy makers in a country seeking to improve some aspect of its educational system. Most often, the funding was provided under the auspices of one of the international banks (e.g., World Bank, International Development Bank), a contractor for the United States Agency for International Development (USAID), or directly by an educational program or agency within the country.

The first author's entrée into international work came when she was asked by a colleague from the World Bank to provide technical assistance related to assessment of learning and the examination systems in Jamaica (Lockheed & Harris, 2005). Then, during the 1990s she worked in Ghana and Malawi as part of the Improving Educational Quality Project (see www.ieq.org). There the focus was collaborating with local educators to conduct research to guide and improve the implementation of USAID funded initiatives within the country as well as to generate and share knowledge between countries. Subsequently, she worked in El Salvador and Egypt where her role involved assisting local educators within the respective Ministry of Education (MOE) with implementation of classroom-level continuous assessment in grades one through six. Typically she was involved with a U.S. contractor in the initial project proposal development or she was recruited after the project was funded. In Jamaica, Honduras, and El Salvador, she was contracted by a local program after the initial funding period had ended. This chapter draws on those experiences.

ENTRY AND PROBLEM IDENTIFICATION

Typically in the international development context, entry and problem identification are intertwined. *Entry* refers to "the process whereby a consultant comes into contact with, and begins the analysis of problems presented by members of the organization when the intent of the consultant is to provide consultation service to the organization" (Pipes, 1981, p. 11). Although it is not uncommon for systemic consultants to work as change agents within the systems where they are employed (see advantages and disadvantages of internal and external consultants in Brown et al., 2010; Pipes, 1981), the literature on systemic consultation typically assumes that the consultant is someone from outside the system (e.g., Caplan & Caplan, 1993; Connell & Klem, 2000; Gallessich, 1981, 1986). When the consultant is brought in from outside the system, the entry period is used to negotiate the parameters, rules, and conditions of the relationship (typically described in a contractual agreement) and to begin the process of establishing mutual rapport and trust. Negotiating the parameters includes identifying and exploring the "problem" or areas in need of improvement for which the consultant is being recruited.

In some instances, the recruiting or contracting agency has defined the skills and activities that are expected of the consultant. In other instances, the consultant is brought into the process at the time that a proposal or project is being developed and the consultant's roles are not as well defined. In either case, one of the ethical responsibilities of consultants is to recognize the boundaries of their competence and any potential limitations or biases that could affect the services they offer (American Psychological Association, 2002).

During the entry stage, it is important for consultants to be clear on the relevant principles that guide the services they provide. To illustrate this point, Box 9.2 provides an example of principles that have guided the first author's consulting in her work in several different countries where she was asked to provide technical expertise in assessment and monitoring of children's learning. The principles have been drawn from research on effective instructional practices.

Evidenced-based guiding principles such as these provide a framework to use when negotiating the level of effort required for a task or deliverable defined by the contracting agency. For instance, it may seem to be a fairly straightforward task to prepare a pre–post test to measure the learning outcomes of implementing an intervention. However,

Box 9.2 Examples of Guiding Principles Related to Assessment and Evaluation

---

1. **An effective educational system has alignment between the learning objectives, the teaching process (methods and materials), and the evaluation process (Nitko & Brookhart, 2010).**

| Sequenced learning objectives → | Teaching methods | → | Assessment and evaluation process |
| | Educational materials | | |

Optimally, the learning objectives are carefully sequenced and ultimately lead to learning goals or competencies that are valued by the country. The sequence of objectives is defined such that learners develop knowledge and skills in an orderly fashion. In the U.S., federal funding to states is linked to having approved state standards, and typically the state standards or learning benchmarks are linked to approved curricula and to statewide assessments (U.S. Department of Education, 2011).

2. **The evaluation process (e.g., how students and teachers are "graded" and the examination system) can sabotage or support learning** (Au, 2007; Lockheed & Wagemaker, 2013). For example, in Jamaica, the Common Entrance Exam, a high stakes test that was used until 1999 to determine selection for secondary school, included subtests in math, English, and mental abilities. Although science and social studies were part of the national curriculum, virtually no classroom attention was given to these areas because they were not covered on the exam. When the content of the exam changed to include broader curricular coverage, teachers adjusted their teaching. The evaluation process went from one that sabotaged or undermined the national curriculum to one that supported it (Barnes, 2000; Lockheed & Harris, 2005; Ministry of Education, Youth & Culture, 2007).

3. **When used effectively, evaluation can support every aspect of learning.** Assessment and evaluation results provide teachers, teacher trainers, and curriculum developers with information to better match instruction to the learner. Appropriately matched instruction leads to greater student success (Nitko & Brookhart, 2010). Student success is motivating for the teacher and the student (Covington, 1992; Schunk, Meece, & Pintrich, 2013). Evaluation that provides evidence of student success (and challenges) facilitates a continued instructional match and enhances student learning (Rosenfield, 1987, 2008; Ysseldyke & Christenson, 2002).

---

writing test questions is very different from developing a contextualized evaluation strategy that is consistent with the local culture and supports the desired learning and goals.

To illustrate, as part of the entry stage of consultation in Equatorial Guinea (EG; for more information see www.guineaecuatorialpress.com/?lang=en), the contracting agency[1] provided the first author with a scope of work that included a list of proposed tasks and deliverables as well as the level of effort (number of days of work) that the agency assumed would be required by the consultant to complete the work. Proposed activities included developing a strategy for evaluating and certifying the teachers being trained in the Diplomado Program (Ginzberg et al., 2012) and conducting a baseline study of the academic skills of first- and second-grade students. Since the activities and deliverables in the original scope of work appeared more ambitious than the allotted time, it was important to detail for the contracting agency the proposed services and activities. The defining principles were useful in conceptualizing the work and describing to the contractor the steps that would be required. The negotiated consequence was that an experienced school psychologist was added to the consulting team (Harris, Acevedo, Rodriquéz, & Edú Ndong, 2010). As this example illustrates, consultants need to enter the negotiation process with an understanding of the work that is being requested. They also need to conceptualize the work within a framework that incorporates the tenets of successful consultation and includes evidenced-based guiding principles.

DATA GATHERING ABOUT THE COUNTRY AND ITS EDUCATIONAL SYSTEM

Consultants need knowledge about the context in which the work will be performed. Ideally, the consultant is familiar with the country (or specific region within a country) and has an understanding of its systems, values, cultural norms, resources, and so on. Unfortunately, at the time of the initial consulting negotiations, this is often not the case. Nonetheless, consultants can take advantage of online resources to learn more about the country or region. For many countries, there are official government sponsored websites. A good example is the website of the MOE of El Salvador (www.mined.gob.sv). In addition, the U.S. State Department website (www.state.gov) provides regularly updated information on U.S. relations with countries around the world, and the Centers for Disease Control and Prevention website (wwwnc.cdc.gov/travel) provides up-to-date information about health risks and needed immunizations. In addition, there are several valuable online databases that provide current demographic information as well as country-level and regional information on key indicators of health and education. Box 9.3 lists some of these resources and the kinds of data they provide.

International testing programs designed to measure and track student achievement (such as those listed in Box 9.4) may provide additional information about an unfamiliar educational system. Similar to the National Assessment of Educational Progress (NAEP) in the U.S., the programs are not used for individual student certification or selection. Instead, they provide criterion-referenced information about student skill levels and monitoring information related to how skills and performance change over time, as well as country-level performance comparisons. Results from these assessments may be informative if the country of interest participated. Although the number of participating developing countries has increased in recent years (largely due to financial support and external pressure from international donor agencies; Lockheed, 2013), it

Box 9.3 Examples of International Databases/Statistics

UNESCO Institute for Statistics (UIS): Main source of education data for leading reports and databases, including Education For All (EFA) Global Monitoring Report (UNESCO); World Development Indicators (World Bank); Human Development Report (UNDP); State of the World's Children (UNICEF); Millennium Development Goals (MDG). Produces, analyzes, and develops indicators for effective policymaking and to monitor emerging issues in education.
http://www.uis.unesco.org/Pages/default.aspx

ChildInfo: UNICEF's database for global monitoring of Millennium Development Goals (MDGs). Provides statistical information to monitor the situation of children and women worldwide through Multiple Indicator Cluster Survey (MICS).
http://www.childinfo.org

World Inequality Database on Education (WIDE): Provides comparative data from Demographic and Health Surveys and Multiple Indicator Cluster Surveys on the impact of factors associated with inequality and to inform public and international policies. Launched by EFA Global Monitoring Report.
http://www.education-inequalities.org

EDSTATS: World Bank database with extensive query and search capabilities by country, topic, and so forth.
http://data.worldbank.org

Education Policy and Data Center (EDPC): A research unit within FHI 360 that serves as a resource for education data and reports (issues and trends in education specific to country) with a primary focus on low and middle income countries. Cross-country comparisons (across 10 dimensions) as well as country-specific data are made accessible.
http://www.epdc.org

Box 9.4 International Educational Assessment Programs

The International Association for the Evaluation of Educational Achievement (IEA) conducts global comparative studies in education to identify the impact of policies and practices on the educational system of different countries. Assessments are standardized in multiple languages for administration and benchmarking.
http://www.iea.nl/data.html

The Trends in International Mathematics and Science Study (TIMSS) provides countries with information to improve teaching and learning in mathematics and science. It assesses math and science achievement every 4 years at the fourth and eighth grades. It includes information about the availability of resources and the quality of curriculum and instruction.
http://timssandpirls.bc.edu/timss2011/international-database.html

The Progress in International Reading Literacy Study (PIRLS) is an international reading assessment of fourth grade students that takes place every 5 years. For developing countries, the pre-PIRLS assessment was used to assess children's basic reading skills (needed for PIRLS), which utilizes shorter and less difficult texts.
http://timssandpirls.bc.edu/pirls2011/international-database.html

The Programme for International Student Assessment (PISA), launched by the Organization for Economic Co-operation and Development (OECD) in 1997, evaluates education systems around the world by assessing 15-year-olds' competencies in reading, math, and science every 3 years.
http://www.oecd.org/pisa/aboutpisa/

The Programme for International Assessment of Adult Competencies (PIAAC), launched by OECD, assesses and surveys cognitive and workplace competencies among adult populations. The first report was published in 2013 and contained results from 33 participating countries. http://www.oecd.org/site/piaac/surveyofadultskills.htm

Student Achievement in Latin America and the Caribbean (SERCE) is an UNESCO-sponsored assessment of third and sixth grade student achievement in math, language, and natural science. (Spanish). http://www.unesco.org/new/en/santiago/education/education-assessment/second-regional-comparative-and-explanatory-study-serce/

is mostly the more technologically developed countries that have participated in these international testing efforts. Also, for some of the countries that have participated, the results need to be interpreted carefully. For example, when access to education is limited, the students who are tested may represent only a small proportion of the age cohort. Or, there may be other measurement limitations related to the curriculum match and range of skills tested (Lockheed & Wagemaker, 2013).

Often, a bit more investigative work is needed to gather detailed information about the educational system: its historical roots, its political and curricular initiatives, and the cultural and societal factors that affect access to primary and secondary education as well as educational quality and learning outcomes. Some useful resources are listed in Box 9.5. The list is not intended to be exhaustive but rather provides examples of where valuable information about a country can be uncovered. For example, by locating the country of interest on the website for the U.S. Agency for International Development (USAID; www.usaid.gov), a consultant can determine whether the country has received funding from this source and the kinds of initiatives and programs that have been supported.

Often the education system in a developing country has been modeled after the country that most recently wielded influence over the country's governance. For example, long after Ghana, Malawi, and Jamaica were no longer governed by the British Commonwealth, the educational systems in these countries evidenced many similarities with the British system, including similar educational terminology and an exam system modeled after the Common Entrance Exam. Similarly, EG and many Latin American countries have been influenced by Spain. Often local educators have traveled on scholarships to Spain to complete graduate studies, and the curricular materials used in the schools provide evidence of Spanish influence (e.g., references to funding and technical support from Spain). A common language background facilitates the transfer. In El Salvador, recent educational reforms focused on "competencies" were modeled after reforms in Spain and were largely driven by a consultant brought in from Spain to lead the process (Zabala & Arnau, 2007).

Similarly, examining local teacher training materials and textbooks often reveals the funding source and a hint of the methodological philosophy behind the materials. For example, current USAID educational funding policy focuses on early grade reading using a phonics-based approach, with effectiveness being determined largely by oral reading rates (https://www.usaid.gov/what-we-do/education/all-children-reading). For consultants who have the opportunity to work in a country with an MOE receiving USAID educational funding, the curricular

Box 9.5 Major Types of Funding Sources and Examples

Multilateral Donor Organizations: Partnership organizations that receive funding from multiple sources and administers aid to recipient countries or programs.

United Nations Funds and Programmes: UN Children's Fund (UNICEF), UN Entity for Gender Equality and the Empowerment of Women (UN-Women). Supports research, policies and services targeted to improving conditions and opportunities for women and children. http://www.unicef.org; http://www.unwomen.org

United Nations Specialized Agencies: UN Educational, Scientific and Cultural Organization (UNESCO); International Monetary Fund (IMF); World Bank Group. coalition of donor organizations and banks that support international development. http://en.unesco.org; http://www.imf.org; http://www.worldbank.org

Global Partnership for Education (GPE): Formerly known as the Education for All-Fast Track Initiative (EFA FTI). Represents partnerships and mutual collaboration with international agencies, banks, donor countries, private sectors, and civil society organizations that provide developing countries with the resources and supports needed to strengthen and implement education plans. The online database provides information needed to monitor progress and identify emerging issues in countries. http://www.globalpartnership.org

Bilateral Donor Organizations: Assistance given directly by donor government to a recipient country. The donor government may provide this assistance directly to the recipient government or to nongovernmental institutions operating in the recipient country.

United States Agency for International Development (USAID): Within the education sector, USAID endorses three goals: improvement of early grade reading, improvement of workforce development programs, and accessibility to education in crisis and conflict-affected countries. http://www.gov.uk/government/organisations/department-for-international-development

United Kingdom Department for International Development (DFID): Official development agency of the UK that provides aid to developing countries to promote quality child education and access to conflict states and marginalized populations. http://www.gov.uk/government/organisations/department-for-international-development

Regional Banks: Similar to international lending organizations but with a regional focus.

African Development Bank (AfDB): AfDB aims to reduce poverty and improve the quality of life in African countries by providing funding to public and private projects and programs. http://afdb.org

Asian Development Bank (ADB): ADB facilitates the economic and social development of countries in Asia and the Pacific through loans and grants to both public and private sectors. http://www.adb.org

Non-governmental Organizations (NGOs): Organizations that are typically not affiliated with any government and are usually but not always nonprofit; they often receive funding to provide services (e.g., implement a program) either locally, nationally, or internationally.

OxFam International: Consists of 15 organizations working in more than 90 countries with the aim to reduce poverty and support the rights of individuals. http://www.oxfam.org

Save the Children: International NGO that promotes children's rights and provides relief to children in developing countries affected by war, poverty, and other conflicts. http://savethechildren.org

options likely will be constrained by the programmatic and accountability requirements of the funding agency.

Educational trends seem to migrate through countries linked by a common language. A good example is Escuela Nueva Unitaria (Mogollón, Solano-Mogollón, & Flórez, 2011), which originally was developed and implemented in Colombia in the 1970s to better serve multigrade classrooms in rural areas. The basic model has been replicated in various formats throughout Latin America (e.g., Solano-Mogollón & Mogollón, undated) and now EG as well. In sum, consultants who take the time to research and become familiar with the historical and recent influences on the country's educational philosophies and trends will be better able to contextualize current concerns.

Gathering information about an unfamiliar educational system can be a daunting task. Often there are legal documents that prescribe what will be taught, who has access to schooling, and so on. Sometimes there is a nationalized curriculum that may or may not be aligned with what actually happens in classrooms. What occurs in rural or less resourced schools can be completely different from what happens in urban or private schools. Also, in many countries there are examination systems and/or discriminatory practices that are used to control the flow of students to secondary and tertiary education (King & Hill, 1993; Lewis & Lockheed, 2006). Guiding principles such as those outlined in Box 9.2 are useful because they provide a framework for soliciting information and organizing what is made available.

DATA GATHERING RELATED TO
THE CURRICULUM AND LEARNING

Unlike the U.S., where only recently has there been a strong initiative for a "national curriculum" (i.e., Common Core State Standards Initiative; www.corestandards.org), many smaller countries such as Guatemala (www.mineduc.gob.gt/portal/index.asp), Jamaica (www.moe.gov.jm/curricula), and El Salvador (www.mined.gob.sv/index.php/index.php/component/jdownloads/viewcategory/18.html) have adopted national learning goals and curriculum standards that are available on their websites. Many African countries have adopted national curriculum objectives and written textbooks to align with the objectives. Obtaining copies of available materials is useful. If copies are not readily attainable from MOE officials, it is possible that they are unavailable or are in limited supply for local educators as well. Outdated or unavailable materials may hint at a lack of alignment between national learning objectives and available classroom materials.

Language Policy

When reviewing materials, it is useful to consider whether the available teaching manuals and textbooks are written in languages consistent with the country's language policies. Many countries with multiple indigenous languages have adopted policies to help children transition to a national language. For example, in Ghana, where English is the official language, there are over 50 reported indigenous languages. From 1974 until 2002, the official policy was for a Ghanaian language to be used as the medium of instruction for grades one through three with a transition to English in grade four. The policy changed in 2002, stipulating that the medium of instruction for all grades should be English (Owu-Ewie, 2006). A complicating factor is that some indigenous languages are not written languages and have not been standardized. In some countries (such as Peru, Guatemala, and many African countries) educational materials are available in a few indigenous languages, but the teachers may or may not be fluent in or able to read these languages (Bamgbose, 1991; Chilora & Harris, 2001; Owu-Ewie, 2006). The consultant may not have the language skills to evaluate the instructional materials, but considering the alignment between language policy, resources, and practice is valuable.

Exams and Evaluation: Alternative Drivers of the Curriculum

In many countries, exams are used as gatekeepers for moving ahead in the educational system, ultimately controlling access to quality education. High-stakes tests can drive the curriculum because teachers and parents feel pressure to prepare their students for the exam, often at the expense of teaching children skills not covered in the exam (Au, 2007; Lockheed & Wagemaker, 2013). The "curriculum express," as termed by Rosenfield (1987), often dictates a fast-paced instructional process that leaves many students behind. Knowing about the existing exams in a country (i.e., the role these exams play and their alignment with the curriculum) is important to understanding the potentially competing demands on the instructional process.

It also is important to investigate local assessment norms, especially those related to evaluation and grading. For example, every country has its own traditions, even to the point of defining what percentage is required for passing. In some countries, the tradition is to consider 60% a passing grade. In Equatorial Guinea, 50% is the tradition. Proposing a different scale would be breaking the norm. While not impossible, it would likely create an unnecessary hurdle.

Observing in Classrooms

Ultimately, observing in classrooms is one of the richest sources of information about a country's educational system. While it is useful to request visits to an array of schools (urban, rural, typical, atypical), the sites chosen for visits may be limited by logistical concerns such as proximity, availability of translators (if needed), ease of obtaining MOE approvals, and so on. Observations need to be filtered through this lens. Accompanying local stakeholders on school visits provides an opportunity for the partners to share an understanding of classroom conditions (e.g., availability of desks, protection from adverse weather, adequacy of lighting, presence of student learning materials, teaching and discipline practices). Asking children to read from their class notes or exercise books the neatly copied lessons can reveal that a child has excellent penmanship but limited decoding or reading comprehension skills. Asking teachers how they keep track of student progress can expose an elaborate system of continuous assessment or complete reliance on end-of-term tests. This firsthand experience allows consultants to correct their misperceptions and gain insight into the day-to-day reality in the classroom. It also provides an opportunity to rely on and highlight the expertise of local educators.

Some examples illustrate the potential discrepancies between data in the central offices of the MOE and the reality in the classroom. In Ghana, the textbook-to-student ratio provided by the MOE seemed reasonable, but a few visits to schools provided a different story. Few textbooks were visible, and almost none were in the hands of students (Harris, Okyere, Mensah, & Kugbey, 1997). A follow-up investigation revealed that the textbooks had been delivered to the schools, but most were stored in a secure location such as a locked cupboard or the chief's house. Interviews revealed that teachers believed they would be held accountable if any books were lost or damaged. To avoid having to pay for lost or damaged books, teachers kept only a few for use in the classroom. Subsequently, the Ghana Education Service issued a policy statement clarifying that teachers would not be held accountable for textbook damage from normal wear and tear. The statement directed teachers to assign books to students and to hold parents accountable for lost books. Although subsequent school visits indicated that more textbooks were visible in the classroom, teachers reported anecdotally that some parents had returned the books to avoid a possible penalty.

In Jamaica, a qualitative follow up to an econometric study (Lockheed & Harris, 2005) indicated that some prescient school directors held a proportion of the books aside because they recognized a historical pattern of late textbook delivery at the beginning of each school year. By holding some aside, they ensured that some books would be available for use the following year. Thus, classroom observations that had suggested an unfavorable textbook-to-student ratio were reinterpreted based on the interviews with school directors and "reframed" as proactive school leadership.

DATA GATHERING RELATED TO THE CONSULTATION PROCESS

Relationship building includes identifying relevant stakeholders and trying to understand and analyze the communication norms within the culture. One challenge for the consultant in cross-cultural consultation is establishing a nonhierarchical relationship with consultees. As Caplan (1970) pointed out, "Whatever the type of consultation . . . the ideal consultation relationship is one of *coordinate interdependence,* in which each side both gives to and takes from the other" (p. 80). To foster this kind of relationship, the consultant needs to understand and respect the local channels and norms for communicating.

Often in international consultation, the contracting agency and the consultees are expecting the consultant to follow a medical model: the "expert" consultant studies the symptoms, provides a diagnosis, and prescribes what needs to be done. While this approach may be what is expected, it reinforces an inherent power differential that can be difficult to overcome. At least two status characteristics present obstacles to a coordinate relationship: the consultant is touted as the expert (with the educational degrees, consulting fees, and a title to prove it), and aspects of the consultant's social status (e.g., race, economic background, country of origin) may be considered by at least some of the consultees as higher than their own. The consultant's own internal biases and/or desire to demonstrate expertise may interfere as well.

Another factor working against a nonhierarchical relationship relates to host country perceptions that the consultant represents the funding source. This power differential was particularly evident when the first author was consulting for an international bank. She was recruited to support collaborative problem-solving within a MOE assessment unit and to be a resource on technical measurement issues, but at least initially she was perceived by local staff to be an auditor (someone sent to make sure the money was spent as intended). Building trust in this context was extremely difficult, and it was only after an extensive amount of time working side-by-side with staff in the unit, wrestling with the complexities of the tasks, that she truly felt welcomed and valued.

Power differentials such as these are counterproductive to building a nonhierarchical relationship and fostering local ownership and sustainability. These circumstances make Caplan's "one-downmanship" strategies (Caplan & Caplan, 1993) an essential part of the consultant's interpersonal awareness and skills. Sensitivity to the ways in which status, respect, and esteem are communicated in the specific culture is vital if the consultant is to "answer deference with deference, both in his tone of voice and in his attention to the opinions and comfort of the consultee" (p. 75).

Deciphering local power hierarchies—both official and unofficial—can be key to making the contacts necessary for building constituents' support for activities that come out of the consultation process (e.g., data collection, interventions, policy changes). In many countries, leadership in the MOE is made by political appointment and selection is influenced by the ruling political party. Sometimes there is a permanent secretary or department head whose position is relatively stable, and only the top positions, such as the cabinet member or minister, change following an election (e.g., U.S., Jamaica). In other countries, it is common for many professionals and nonprofessionals to be replaced (e.g., Equatorial Guinea, El Salvador, and Honduras). Consultants working in countries where political parties wield strong influence need to recognize the fluidity of the system. Following an election, a consultant may need to start the rapport-building process with a new set of stakeholders. Also, when there are changes at the top, a consultant or a reform project that is too closely aligned with one political party can lose favor (including access to leaders or schools) and government support.

Along with identifying key stakeholders, an effective consultant is attentive to local norms for communicating. For example, in many countries, meetings with government officials begin with sometimes lengthy social exchanges that often include refreshments and a gracious hospitality event. Consultants who attempt to be efficient and quickly launch into business-related concerns might be viewed as "foreign" and rude. Also, they will miss valuable opportunities to learn about the local cultural norms and values as well as the unique perspective of the host(s).

Awareness of cultural differences related to time is critical to effective planning. Any efficiency that may be gained by setting meetings back-to-back is lost when a delay in one meeting causes the cancellation of the later meeting. Some causes of delay can be anticipated (midday prayers or lengthy meals), whereas others seem more random (power outages, traffic gridlock) but are nonetheless predictable.

Similarly, there are rules and norms for visiting schools and interacting with educators and parents. Permission for a school visit generally begins with securing the support as well as a formal letter of introduction from the MOE, followed by a visit to the district office, and subsequently a visit to the school director. Each of these visits provides an opportunity to gain insights about the local culture and perspectives and to communicate the importance of the officials' contributions. Also, in some countries (e.g., Ghana and Malawi), a school visit may include a prior visit to the local chief or a visit with the school's parent committee. Overlooking this process—and the respect for local authorities that it implies—is a missed opportunity for greater cross-cultural understanding, and it can result in significant delays or even cancellation of the work.

NEGOTIATING A WORKABLE PARTNERSHIP

As mentioned earlier, the entry and problem identification stages often occur in the context of preparing a contractual relationship between the organization seeking services and the consultant. One scenario would be if the consultant were negotiating directly with the government agency or program (e.g., the assessment unit in the MOE wants technical help in introducing continuous assessment). Alternately, and more typical, is the situation in which an NGO in the donor country has been contracted to work with the host (receiving) country to implement a reform. The NGO, hopefully in collaboration with stakeholders in the host country, seeks and negotiates the consultant's services. While the contract is with the NGO, the host country often controls the work visas, local resources, access to stakeholders, and so on. Thus, fostering a workable partnership includes identifying the relevant stakeholders and, if possible, soliciting their active engagement in the entry and negotiation process.

There are several key elements to a workable partnership. Principally it is important to reach shared clarity about the goals and to articulate expectations. This is true for any consultation relationship, whether contractual or less formal. Typically, the expectations include specific tasks/activities (often with defined intermediate tasks), deliverables, deadlines, and contingencies. The responsibilities of the agency (kind and level of support to the consultant) and of the consultant need to be clearly identified. Many times the agency will expect the consultant to agree to a confidentiality clause, thereby limiting the publication of evaluation or research findings. An explicit understanding of the ownership of products (e.g., curricular or teacher training materials developed under the leadership of the consultant) is important as well. Ultimately, the success of the partnership and the continuity of mutual trust are facilitated by shared expectations.

Care should be taken to incorporate some flexibility and opportunities for adjustments in partnership obligations. A rigid schedule is likely to pressure the consultant into jumping too quickly to adopt emerging ideas. When there is premature closure, the result is likely to be fragmented and lack the ownership that comes from a more deliberate and participatory process. Often a phased approach protects both the consultant and the contractor. While the early activities and deliverables are clearly defined, the activities and services for subsequent stages (e.g., implementation of interventions) are less defined. A phased approach allows the interventions to be developed and refined as a series of progressive approximations that are more likely to reflect multiple inputs and to garner the support of a broader base of stakeholders (Caplan & Caplan, 1993).

TIPS FOR ENTERING THE INTERNATIONAL CONSULTING ARENA

Breaking into the field of international consulting can be challenging. Until a consultant has demonstrated competence in working effectively in the international context, recruiters are hesitant to assume the transferability of a consultant's skills to a different context. Another frequently mentioned concern is whether the consultant has the adaptability to adjust to the different and sometimes trying conditions in the developing world. There are a variety of ways to help allay these concerns.

One way consultants can establish and demonstrate their competence is through seeking experience working for an NGO with overseas projects. Exposure to the grant writing and project implementation processes helps consultants develop and articulate expertise relevant to the international context. Applying for funding to teach or conduct research overseas through programs such as the U.S. Fulbright Program (http://us.fulbrightonline.org) is another option, but typically priority is given to applicants with established relationships in the receiving country. Finally, programs such as the Save the Children SUPERS project are targeted to young professionals. Save the Children solicits research support typically from graduate students (with faculty mentors) to evaluate and improve their programs and in exchange they provide limited funding, technical support, and access to project data (SUPER: Save-University Partnerships for Education Research; www.savethechildren.org).

To reduce concerns about adaptability, a prospective consultant can gain international experience in the Peace Corp teaching English overseas or participating in service learning internships. Even working successfully with immigrants in the U.S. provides some evidence of the consultant's exposure to different cultures and economic conditions. Demonstrating fluency in languages beyond English is another potential asset.

Last, participation in international professional associations such as Division 52 of the American Psychological Association, the Comparative and International Education Society (CIES; www.cies.us/), and discipline-specific associations such as the International School Psychology Association (ISPA; www.ispaweb.org/) provides valuable exposure to current projects and issues as well as networks of colleagues engaged in international work.

SUMMARY

In this chapter, we've covered some basics for successful entry and problem identification when using consultee-centered systemic consultation to improve educational quality in an international context. In reviewing the process, we've identified some of the challenges unique to working in an unfamiliar system or culture and some of the resources that can help consultants work to bridge the gaps. Fortunately, as pointed out by Lambert (2004), the consultant doesn't need to enter with all the answers:

> The experienced consultant has developed a keen sense of the importance of recognizing the expertise of the consultee. This would be reflected in types of questions asked, redirection of requests for advice, clarification of what has been attempted, and exploration of the resources available. . . . A joint solution of the consultee's work problem results from the reciprocal nature of the consultee-centered process.
>
> (p. 15)

Instead, systemic consultants need a clear understanding of the boundaries of their competence and a recognition that successful consultation depends upon exploring and analyzing the system's barriers and enhancers of change. It also requires a keen sensitivity to and genuine respect for cross-cultural differences that affect the consultation relationships. As Conoley (1981) noted, "the best consultants have a careful knowledge of the recipients of change, clear concrete objectives, collaborative working styles, and most importantly, an openness to the unlikely" (p. 10).

NOTE

1. Academy for Educational Development (now FHI-360) is a U.S.-based company that had received funding from the HESS Corporation to team with EG to implement several national educational reform efforts, including implementation of an "active schools" approach in the primary schools, a teacher training certification program for over 1,000 untrained teachers (Diplomado), and a school census/information system to support national policy decisions.

REFERENCES

American Psychological Association. (2002). *Ethical principles of psychologists and code of conduct.* Retrieved from http://www.apa.org/ethics/code/index.aspx?item=5

Au, W. (2007). High-stakes testing and curricular control: A qualitative metasynthesis. *Educational Researcher, 36,* 258.

Bamgbose, A. (1991). *Language and the nation: The language question in sub-saharan Africa*. Edinburgh: Edinburgh University Press.

Barnes, C. (2000, March) New test of ability for high school entry in the Caribbean. *World Education Forum*. Retrieved from http://www.unesco.org/education/wef/en-news/caribbean2.shtm

Brown, D., Pryzwansky, W. B., & Schulte, A. C. (2010). *Psychological consultation and collaboration: Introduction to theory and practice* (7th ed.). Boston, MA: Allyn & Bacon.

Caplan, G. (1970). *The theory and practices of mental health consultation*. New York: Basic Books.

Caplan, G., & Caplan, R. B. (1993). *Mental health consultation and collaboration*. San Francisco: Jossey-Bass.

Centers for Disease Control and Prevention. Retrieved from http://wwwnc.cdc.gov/travel

Chilora, H., & Harris, A. M. (2001). The role of teacher's home language in mother tongue policy implementation: Evidence from IEQ research in Malawi. In J. F. Pfaffe (Ed.), *Local languages in education, science and technology*. Zomba, Malawi: Centre for Language Studies, University of Malawi. Arlington, (Based on paper presented at the 44th annual meeting of the Comparative and International Education Society, March 2001). Retrieved from http://www.ieq.org/pdf/Investigating_Role_Language.pdf

Clay, M. M. (1979). *Reading: The patterning of complex behavior*. Portsmouth, NH: Heinemann.

Comer, J. P., Haynes, N. M., Joyner, E. T., & Ben-Avie, M. (1996). *Rallying the whole village*. New York: Teachers College Press.

Common Core State Standards Initiative. Retrieved from http://www.corestandards.org

Connell, J. P., & Klem, A. M. (2000). You can get there from here: Using a theory of change approach to plan urban educational reform. *Journal of Educational and Psychological Consultation, 11*, 193–120.

Conoley, J. C. (1981). The process of change: The agent of change. In J. C. Conoley (Ed.), *Consultation in schools: Theory, research, procedures* (pp. 11–34). New York: Academic Press.

Covington, M. V. (1992). *Making the grade: A self-worth perspective on motivation and school reform*. Cambridge: Cambridge University Press.

Curtis, M. J., Castillo, J. M., & Cohen, R. M. (2008). Best practices in system-level change. In A. Thomas & J. Grimes (Eds.), *Best practices in school psychology V* (pp. 887–901). Washington, DC: National Association of School Psychologists.

DeAngelis, T. (2013). Traumatic stress in a violent world. *APA Monitor, 44*(8), 38.

Gallessich, J. (1981). Organizational factors influencing consultation in schools. In M. J. Curtis & J. E. Zins (Eds.), *The theory and practice of school consultation* (pp. 149–158). Springfield, IL: Charles C. Thomas.

Gallessich, J. (1986). *The profession and practice of consultation: A handbook for consultants, trainers of consultants, and consumers of consultation services*. San Francisco: Jossey-Bass.

Ginzberg, M., Rodriguez, J. V., Edú Ndong, A., Bourdon, C. H., Hamm, T. C., Grajeva, E., . . . Tubman, W. (2012). Different approaches, different outcomes: Professional development of teachers in the political context of Equatorial Guinea. In M. Ginzberg (Ed.), *Preparation, practice and politics of teachers: Problems and prospects in comparative perspectivs* (pp. 49–78). Istanbul: Sense Publishers. ISBN: 978 94 6209 0774 (ebook).

Harris, A. M. (2007). Systemic consultation in a multilingual setting. In G. B. Esquivel, E. C. Lopez, & S. G. Nahari (Eds.), *Handbook of multicultural school psychology*. Hillsdale, NJ: Lawrence Erlbaum.

Harris, A. M., Acevedo, M., Rodriquéz, J. V., & Edú Ndong, A. (2010). Destrezas básicas en lecto-escritura y matemáticas. In *Estudios Sobre Calidad Educativa* (pp. 1–76). Bata, Guinea Equatorial: Programa de Desarrollo Educativo de Guinea Ecuatorial (PROGEGE), Republica de Guinea Ecuatorial.

Harris, A. M., Okyere, B., Mensah, A., & Kugbey, H. (1997). *What happens to the textbooks?* Arlington, VA: Institute for International Research. (Available in English and Spanish). Retrieved from http://www.ieq.org/pdf/textbooks.pdf

King, E. M., & Hill, M. A. (Eds.). (1993). *Women's education in developing countries: Barriers, benefits and policies*. Baltimore: Johns Hopkins University.

Lambert, N. M. (2004). Consultee-centered consultation: An international perspective on goals, process, and theory. In M. N. Lambert, I. Hylander, & J. H. Sandoval (Eds.), *Condultee-centered Consultation* (pp. 3–19). Mahwah, NJ: Lawrence Erlbaum.

Lewis, M. A., & Lockheed, M. E. (2006). *Inexcusable absence: Why 60 million girls aren't in school and what to do about it*. Washington, DC: Center for Global Development.

Lockheed, M. E. (2013). Causes and consequences of international assessments in developing countries. In H. Meyer & A. Benavot (Eds.), *PISA, power and policy: The emergence of global educational governance* (pp. 163–184). [Oxford Studies in Comparative Education]. Oxford: Symposium Books.

Lockheed, M. E., & Harris, A. M. (2005). Beneath education production functions: The case of primary education in Jamaica. *Peabody Journal of Education, 80*(1), 6–28.

Lockheed, M. E., & Wagemaker, H. (2013). International large-scale assessment: Thermometers, whips, or useful policy tools. *Research in Comparative and International Education, 8*, 296–306. Retrieved from http://dx.doi.org/10.2304/rcie.2013.8.3.296

Meyers, J., Parsons, R. D., & Martin, R. (1979). *Mental health consultation in the schools.* San Francisco: Jossey-Bass.

Ministry of Education, Youth and Culture. (2007). *National assessment programme.* Retrieved from http://www.moec.gov.jm/divisions/ed/assessment/nap.shtml

Mogollón, P., Solano, M., & Flórez, A. (Eds.). (2011). *Active schools: Our convictions for improving the quality of education.* Washington, DC: FHI360.

Nitko, A. J., & Brookhart, S. M. (2010). *Educational assessment of students* (6th ed.). Englewood Cliffs, NJ: Pearson.

OECD Programme for International Assessment (PISA). (2009). Retrieved from http://www.pisa.oecd.org/

Owu-Ewie, C. (2006). The language policy of education in Ghana: A critical look at the English-only language policy of education. In J. Mugane, J. P. Hutchison, & D. A. Worman (Eds.), *Selected Proceedings of the 35th Annual Conference on African Linguistics* (pp. 76–85). Somerville, MA: Cascadilla Proceedings Project. Retrieved from www.lingref.com

Pipes, R. B. (1981). Consulting in organizations: The entry problem. In J. C. Conoley (Ed.), *Consultation in schools: Theory, research and practice* (pp. 11–33). New York: Academic Press.

Progress in International Reading Literacy Study. Retrieved from http://timss.bc.edu/pirls2011/countries.html

Rosenfield, S. A. (1987). *Instructional consultation.* Hillsdale, NJ: Lawrence Erlbaum.

Rosenfield, S. A. (2008). Best practices in instructional consultation. In A. Thomas & J. Grimes (Eds.), *Best practices in school psychology V* (pp. 1645–1660). Washington, DC: National Association of School Psychologists.

Sarason, S. B. (1996). *Revisiting "The culture of the school and the problem of change".* New York: Teachers College Press.

Save the Children. SUPER: Save-university partnerships for education research. Retrieved from http://www.savethechildren.org/site/c.8rKLIXMGIpI4E/b.6196513/

Schunk, D., Meece, J. R., & Pintrich, P. R. (2013). *Motivation in education: Theory, research and applications* (4th ed.). Upper Saddle River, NJ: Pearson.

Solano-Mogollón, M., & Mogollón, O. (undated). *Leo y escribo. Escuela Nueva Unitaria—2º grado.* Guatemala: Ministerio de Educación de Guatemala. Proyecto Fortalecimiento de la Educación Básica.

Student Achievement in Latin America and the Caribbean (SERCE). Retrieved from http://www.llece.org/public/component/option,com_publicaciones/task,ver/id,6/Itemid,6/lang,en/

TIMSS & PIRLS International Study Center. (2011). *Countries participating in PIRLS 2011.* Retrieved from http://timss.bc.edu/pirls2011/countries.html

UNESCO Institute for Statistics (UIS). Retrieved from http://www.uis.unesco.org/Pages/default.aspx

UNESCO Institute for Statistics (UIS). 2004. *Global education digest 2004.* Montreal: UIS.

UNESCO Institute for Statistics (UIS). 2006. *Global education digest 2006.* Montreal: UIS.

U.S. Agency for International Development (USAID). Retrieved from http://www.usaid.gov/what-we-do/education/improving-early-grade-reading

U.S. Department of Education. (2011). *Race to the top fund.* Retrieved from http://www2.ed.gov/programs/racetothetop/index.html

U.S. Department of State. (2011). *Bureau of African affairs: Background note: Equatorial Guinea.* Retrieved from http://www.state.gov/r/pa/ei/bgn/7221.htm

Ysseldyke, J., & Christenson, S. (2002). *Functional assessment of academic behavior: Creating successful learning environments.* Longmont, CO: Sopris West.

Zabala, A., & Arnau, L. (2007). *11 ideas clave. Cómo aprender y enseñar competencias.* Barcelona, España: Editorial Graó.

10

INTERNATIONAL COLLABORATION TO DEVELOP A SCHOOL PSYCHOLOGY TRAINING PROGRAM IN VIETNAM

Kimberly S. Kassay and Mark D. Terjesen

INTRODUCTION

This chapter presents the consultative work that contributed to the development of a school psychology training program at Hanoi National University of Education (HNUE) in Vietnam. The program represents the collaborative work of many professionals whose individual contributions collectively established the first formal training program of its kind in the country. In addition to their efforts, the training program was simultaneously shaped by the international professional context of which it is a part, the unique national culture within which it emerged, and its local professional context. These influences will be described and related to the favorable conditions and societal needs for school psychologists and a formal training program to prepare such professionals. Finally, the process aimed at developing the school psychology training program and the outcomes associated with the program will be described.

INTERNATIONAL SCHOOL PSYCHOLOGY

Today many countries around the world have *school psychologists*. Although they may use different titles and have slightly different job descriptions, they share the same professional purpose as psychological service providers in schools with the overarching goal of improving children's quality of life (International School Psychology Association [ISPA], n.d.a) and providing society with similar services (Jimerson, Skokut, Cardenas, Malone, & Stewart, 2008). Variations of school psychological service provision models have developed in different countries based on specific needs, cultural climates, and local advances in the field of psychology, yet a common profession can be distinguished throughout the world today (Oakland, 2007).

The profession of school psychology is shaped by its educational, economic, geographical, and demographic contexts (Farrell, Jimerson, & Oakland, 2007). Countries that have more highly developed and legally mandated education systems, especially those that provide special education services to students with academic, behavioral, emotional, and social difficulties, generally have greater need and provide more support for school psychological services and thus have more advanced fields of school psychology (Farrell et al., 2007). A country's economy also has a great impact on the development of the profession, as the number of school psychologists in a country is positively associated with its gross national product (GNP). In addition, school psychologists in low GNP countries tend to have less professional preparation, which may be related to the fact that the profession of psychology is less developed in low GNP countries, fewer psychology master's programs exist, and psychology is not as specialized as it is in high GNP countries (Oakland, 2007). Further, a country's geography and demographics can affect the field of school psychology because communication, regulation, and mobility are more difficult in large and sparsely populated countries (Farrell et al., 2007). As a result, the growth of the profession is facilitated in more industrialized countries where a greater part of the population lives in urban settings (Farrell et al., 2007).

Recently, a special issue of the *International Journal of School and Educational Psychology* (Oakland & Hatzichristou, 2014a) examined school psychology programs globally and some of the country-specific processes and factors that influenced the development of school psychologist training and preparation. Oakland and Hatzichristou (2014b) offer a review of issues to consider in preparation of school psychologists, including international issues and conditions that may impact preparation. They describe the influence of economic and regional and national agencies external to the field that may also have an impact on the training of school psychologists. These variables will be considered below in the development of school psychology in Vietnam.

DEVELOPMENT OF SCHOOL PSYCHOLOGY IN VIETNAM

The conditions in Vietnam have influenced how the profession of school psychology has developed. Advances in the education system (Ministry of Education and Training [MOET], 2003) created a need for school psychological services, and a rapidly growing economy has provided resources to support such social reforms (World Bank, 2007). The country's low GNP and primarily agricultural society were also factors that needed to be considered as the profession expanded. In addition, the history and professional development of other countries provided valuable lessons that guided the emerging profession of school psychology in Vietnam as well as the development of the training program at HNUE.

Profile of Vietnam

The Socialist Republic of Vietnam is a geographically diverse nation in Southeast Asia. Today, with a population of over 92 million, Vietnam is the 15th most populous country in the world (Central Intelligence Agency, 2014). Traditional Vietnamese culture built around agriculture and communes is still present, though it is blended with modern technology and international culture (Ashwill & Thai, 2005; Embassy of Vietnam, n.d.). This integration of traditional societal emphasis with more modern and global perspectives has impacted many areas, among them education and children's healthy development.

Vietnamese culture is seen as a strong, long-lasting indigenous culture that has been influenced by that of foreign nations that neighbored or at times controlled the country (Ashwill & Thai, 2005; Embassy of Vietnam, n.d.). Following reunification in 1975, a period of social and economic hardship ensued (Ashwill & Thai, 2005). By 1986, inflation rates soared and the government launched an all-round renovation program. The program was successful at bringing the country out of socioeconomic crisis by decentralizing political regulation, accepting international aide, and transitioning to an open market economy, all within the confounds of the Communist Party's overarching control (Bondurant, Henderson, & Nguyen, 2003; Clarke, Gayfer, Landymore, & Luttrell, 2007). Economically, the program appears to have made impressive achievements, lowering poverty rates from 58% in 1993 to 20% in 2010 (World Bank, 2014). Recently, Vietnam was still considered a low-income developing country; however, it has now attained lower-middle income country status (World Bank, 2014). With the economic change, it would stand to reason that this has had a positive impact on other areas of life within Vietnam, among them education.

One of the ways that Vietnam has achieved such success and plans to continue to advance the country into the future is through education reform. Vietnam reforms have made five years of primary education compulsory, built new schools, and set standards for teachers and textbooks (World Bank, 2007). The Ministry of Education (MOET, 2003) views educational development as a means by which to launch Vietnam into the global market. The importance of education cannot be overstated in Vietnam. Its inclusion in the Constitution as a "primary national priority" (National Assembly, 2001, p. 7) highlights this point.

The Need for a School Psychology Training
Program in Vietnam

The fact that Vietnamese society was experiencing rapid economic growth (World Bank, 2007), political reform (Embassy of Vietnam, n.d.), and social changes, including universalizing education (MOET, 2003), a shift towards urbanization (Bondurant et al., 2003), and increasing communication with and participation in the international community (Ashwill & Thai, 2005), created a need and context for the development of the school psychology profession. Public officials as well as practitioners in Vietnam recognized the need for a school psychology training program and also identified their country's readiness for such a program to be developed (Applied Psychology Section, 2007). The move to universalize education, specifically, created a need for professionals who could meet the diverse needs of children who previously would not have been seen by the school system, including ethnic minorities, the poor, and disabled children.

Despite concerted efforts to universalize primary education, many children in remote areas, as well as some urban centers, especially ethnic minorities, remain uneducated in Vietnam (MOET, 2003). In addition, the quality of the education received by many is weak, as there is a shortage of qualified teachers, school facilities, and modern teaching materials (MOET, 2003). This situation further demonstrates a need for trained professionals to advocate for the rights of a vulnerable population of children, consult with teachers who may not have been properly trained, and provide academic, behavioral, or social-emotional interventions to children who are not being or have not been educated appropriately or who may experience behavioral and/or social-emotional difficulties.

The current state of mental health services, especially those available for children, in Vietnam is not very advanced, although a need for them certainly exists (Schirmer, Cartwright, Montegut, Dreher, & Stovall, 2004). In a large-scale investigation of mental health functioning among Vietnamese children, Weiss et al. (2014) reported that approximately 12% of the population is in need of mental health services. Mental health care is typically reserved for only the most severe of mental disorders, such as schizophrenia, epilepsy, depression, substance abuse, and brain injuries (Schirmer et al., 2004). Few treatment options exist for those suffering from mental illness, and current resources are not adequate to meet the need (Weiss et al., 2012).

In sum, a need for psychological services for people of all ages in Vietnam existed and the need was not being adequately met in the existing primary care mental health system, so changes were needed. In a system where all children are required to attend school, few mental health service options exist, and there may be a stigma attached to mental illness, schools are a place where children experiencing emotional, behavioral, and/or social difficulties can be identified and treated in an environment that is not threatening to children or their families. With the development of the education system and the financial resources invested in the growth and education of children in Vietnam, having well-trained professionals with psychological and educational expertise who can meet children's academic and social-emotional needs in a school setting could be an efficient approach to meet these goals. Such professionals would need to be formally trained; hence, a need for a school psychology training program in Vietnam exists.

Higher Education and the Training of Psychologists in Vietnam

It appears that higher education has a particularly salient role in Vietnam's modernization program, as it prepares individuals to take the lead in the country's professional development. Undergraduate, master, and doctorate programs are designed to train graduates to not only succeed in their careers but also to identify areas in need of further development and take steps necessary to advance their fields and their country (MOET, 2003).

According to the MOET (2003), there are two key pedagogical institutions in Vietnam, one in Ho Chi Minh City and one in Hanoi; the aim of these universities is to train graduates to be at the forefront of their fields and to be teachers of students of all educational levels. HNUE was the first university to train teachers in Vietnam. Established in 1951, it remains as the premier pedagogical institution in the country.

In 1965, the Department of Psychology and Education (DPE) was formed at HNUE (Hanoi National University of Education, n.d.). The DPE is currently divided into seven sections or specialty areas (Hanoi National University of Education, 2007). The most recently added section is the Applied Psychology Section (APS), which was founded September 27, 2006 (Applied Psychology Section, 2007).

Prior to the consultative work to modify psychology training at HNUE that will be described in this chapter, HNUE offered an undergraduate degree program in psychology and education (4 years), master's degrees in psychology or education (2 years), and doctorate degrees in psychology or education (4 years). The majority, though not all, of the DPE faculty earned master's or doctorate degrees in basic psychology (such as developmental or personality psychology) or education; further, many of the faculty members had studied abroad, often citing Russia as a primary influence in their training (Hanoi National University of Education, 2007).

The Emerging Field of School Psychology in Vietnam

Although prior to the establishment of the program at HNUE there were no formal school psychology training programs in Vietnam, there were professionals who performed functions of school psychologists in school settings (Applied Psychology Section, 2007). This is consistent with a number of countries (Jimerson et al., 2008). These professionals regularly engaged in "cognitive and academic assessment, collaboration with the community to provide support to the whole family of the students with learning or behavioral difficulties, and collaboration with local hospitals, especially psychiatric hospitals, in referring and assessing students with disabilities" (Le, 2009, p. 17).

However, Do (2006) (as cited in Le, 2009) found that most of these professionals performing psychological services in the schools graduated in programs unrelated to school psychology. This made the delivery of school psychological services highly variable and may also not allow for effective intervention. For example, the DPE of HNUE began a program to provide school psychological services to students in two high schools in Hanoi in December 2004 with financial support from the United Nations Children's Fund (UNICEF) (Applied Psychology Section, 2007). The program was intended to be a pilot program for future school psychologists in Vietnam and to inform the development of school psychology training at HNUE (Applied Psychology Section, 2007). Yet without formal training in the assessment, consultation, and therapeutic techniques they were using, communication with the practitioners indicated that they were aware that they were not providing their clients with the most appropriate and effective services to meet their educational, mental health, and professional needs.

The practitioners' experiences served as additional incentives to the plan to develop a formalized school psychology training program at HNUE. Based on consideration of current educational and mental health needs and consultation with national and international professionals, the MOET recognized that in order to better serve the students and teachers at these schools as well as those of other schools throughout Vietnam, formal professional training was needed for school psychologists (Applied Psychology Section, 2007). In 2006, the DPE of HNUE was selected by the MOET to establish the first school psychology training program in Vietnam, and it was hoped that the program would be a model that other institutions in Vietnam could use to guide their own development of similar training programs in the future (Applied Psychology Section, 2007).

Stages of Program Development

The consultative steps involved in the development of the first formalized training program in school psychology in Vietnam involved faculty and administrators from both HNUE and St. John's University (STJ), as well as other governmental and nongovernmental organizations (NGOs) that began in the spring of 2007. The model of consultation that guided the development of the training program was organizational in nature and followed the work of Nastasi, Varjas, Bernstein, and Jayasena (2000). The organizational model has been used in school settings when introducing school-wide interventions and response to intervention (RTI) (Erchul & Young, 2014) to allow for school psychologists to communicate their knowledge and skills in a planned, systemic process to have an impact on a larger number of individuals. This model was chosen because it incorporates several theoretical viewpoints and involves the introduction of principles into the organization to allow implementation of new programs (Illback, 2014). Organizational development of the school psychology program would then allow the DPE at HNUE (consultee) to prepare professionals to engage in school psychology practice and assist those parents, students, and teachers (clients).

The Participatory Culture-Specific Consultation (PCSC) model proposed by Nastasi and colleagues (Nastasi et al., 2000) was helpful in its focus on the identification of the culture-specific needs of both the individuals and systems in which they exist.

Nastasi and colleagues describe the process of PCSC as a series of both formal and informal interactions with consultees and representatives of organizations/systems. The importance of evaluation of the process of implementation is stressed. Promotion of ownership and empowerment of stakeholders and sustainability of efforts within the institutions are also emphasized. The stages described next reflect the organizational and participatory components in the development of the school psychology program in Vietnam.

Stages of Consultation

Preplanning and Contracting Stage

The first stage of the program development was the preplanning stage during which the DPE at HNUE contemplated the development of a school psychology training program at their university. Between 2004 and 2006, the need for professional school psychologists in Vietnam was discussed among the DPE faculty and administration at HNUE. They considered this need, along with the resources available to begin the first formal training program in the country, to decide if it was desirable and feasible to establish such a program (Applied Psychology Section, 2007).

Consultation among the MOET, NGOs, and STJ administrators (deans and department chairpersons) led the faculty and administration at HNUE to take steps to determine the need for a program, obtain permission from the MOET, obtain financial support from NGOs, and evaluate the practicality of establishing the program within HNUE. STJ had become involved in working with HNUE through some collaborative education programs that focused on biology and sociology. Early discussions to enter into a collaborative and consultative relationship between HNUE and STJ began at the individual level between HNUE and STJ administrators and then led to the development of a memorandum of understanding to formally establish a professional relationship between the universities. This was an important early step in that it established expectations for the collaboration and clarified roles and expectations of each party. The development of a consultation contract is an essential component in the process of consultation (Zins & Erchul, 2002). This reduced the likelihood of any disruption in the collaborative relationship and also provided support from the administration of HNUE for the efforts that were to be undertaken. The early success (i.e., exchange programs, invited lecturers, research collaboration) of the work among the biology and sociology department provided a structure and reinforcement for expansion of the relationship between the universities. This desired expansion led to collaboration in the development of the school psychology training program.

Planning Stage

The second stage was the planning stage, which began with the development of the Applied Psychology Section (APS) of the DPE in 2006 (Applied Psychology Section, 2007) and ended before formal preparation of the APS faculty began in the summer of 2008. This stage had an overarching goal of planning for the development of a university program that could begin training school psychologists. As it was to be the first school psychology training program in Vietnam, the faculty and administrators at HNUE did not have any clear models in their country to follow and decided to reach out to international colleagues. Given the already existing relationship with the administration of STJ, the faculty and administrators at HNUE contacted the school psychology training program at STJ to assist them in the development of a school psychology training program. Through a number of online lectures for APS faculty and small group meetings related to the field of school psychology, the faculty and administrators of HNUE and STJ faculty started to build professional relationships and discussed working together to develop the school psychology program at HNUE and the field of school psychology in Vietnam.

Building upon the more general MOU between the universities, the agreement to extend the work together toward the development of a school psychology training program was viewed as the next step in this partnership. The work would be in a very different area than previously, and biology and sociology had already existed within HNUE. Development of a specialized training program such as school psychology led to 10 days of consultative meetings among the HNUE and STJ individuals in January 2008 at HNUE, with approximately 8 hours of meetings daily. The authors of this chapter, along with another STJ faculty member and doctoral candidate in school psychology, traveled to Vietnam to meet with all of the newly created APS faculty members, the DPE chair and vice chair, the president of HNUE, and representatives from UNICEF and Vietnam Veterans of America Foundation (VVAF), who provided administrative and financial commitments to the program's development. The faculty and administrators at HNUE had prior relationships with these NGOs and reached out to them to determine their interest in possibly sponsoring these programs. Additional electronic correspondence occurred between the parties for the months leading up to the meetings as well as after they took place. These 10 days of consultative meetings were conducted to discuss the needs of the developing program and field training guidelines, curriculum recommendations, practical training issues, and plans for the preparation of the APS faculty. Training and fieldwork guidelines from professional school psychology organizations (e.g., International School Psychology Association, n.d.b; NASP, 2008; Ysseldyke et al., 2006) and fieldwork guidelines were reviewed, and an in-depth review of the STJ curricula and training program was discussed. Representatives of the NGOs attended some of the planning and summary meetings and then made a commitment for support to the collaborative project.

Cultural Considerations

All agreed that it would be a mistake to take the STJ model that was successful in the U.S. and mirror it in Vietnam without considering the unique cultural and linguistic variables as well as some of the practical needs for implementing a program. Attention to relevant multicultural considerations, such as current economic and educational developments as well as cultural values such as collectively serving the national interest, occurred here and are consistent with the establishment of a partnership as proposed by Harvey and Struzziero (2008) and Nastasi et al. (2000). As such, this dialogue was bidirectional and involved sharing information and brainstorming solutions to best meet the needs of the profession in Vietnam. In sum, the STJ representatives served as organizational and systemic consultants to the HNUE program in a manner consistent with the Illback (2014) and Nastasi et al. (2000) PCSC models described earlier. They provided the HNUE representatives with information, engaged in open dialogue, and made recommendations for the program; however, the HNUE faculty and administration made all final decisions regarding the program's development. Further, the STJ representatives also engaged in consultation in a manner that was consistent with the PCSC model in that psychological theory and research guided the planning, data and consultees' experiences helped define/describe the problems, and culture-specific considerations were offered to assist in program development.

DESIGNING THE PROGRAM

The focus of the consultative meetings over those 10 days in January was how best to build the school psychology training program at HNUE, considering the needs determined in the preplanning stage, the perceptions of the APS faculty, the resources that were available, the practical component (i.e., appropriately trained faculty, obtaining administrative approval) of developing a training program, as well as what is considered best practice in development of a training program (Brown, 2008; Cunningham & Oakland, 1998; Lopez & Bursztyn, 2013). This proved to be among the more challenging consultative areas because there was no model of the development of a school psychology training program in a similar region and there were limited resources available in Vietnamese (i.e., textbooks, research, testing instruments). Particular emphasis was placed on discussion of curriculum development, course selection and sequence that considered the aforementioned training standards that would fit within their educational model, the incorporation of practical experiences throughout the training program, and obtaining teaching materials such as textbooks, journal articles, and training videos. Given the consultants' familiarity and access to U.S.-based resources, the majority of the resources came from the United States, but additional areas of support and research came from Australia, China, Great Britain, France, Norway, and Russia. For example, some APS faculty members shared that they had attended training workshops internationally and had obtained training materials from those countries. Several important discussions during the consultative meetings shaped the formation of the school psychology program at HNUE.

There was an initial discussion during the meetings about developing a mission statement as a way of stating the purpose of the program so that the university community, professional colleagues, potential students, and the public would be aware of the need for a program and what the focus of it would be. The mission statement developed at the consultative meetings combined aspects of the STJ school psychology program mission, the HNUE philosophy, and National Association of School Psychologists (NASP) and ISPA training standards. The mission statement that was drafted on January 7, 2008, is as follows:

> The mission of the HNUE School Psychology Program is to prepare Vietnamese students for the profession of school psychology as defined by international standards. The primary goal of the program is to prepare practitioners and scholars (trainers and researchers) whose activities promote the psychological and educational development and well-being (mental health and socialization) of diverse children and youth to assist their functioning in society. These goals will be in consideration of the unique needs of the Vietnamese educational system, children, and families.

Degree Level and Course Sequence

A substantial portion of the discourse during the consultative meetings surrounded decisions on degree level and related course selection and sequence. The STJ representatives discussed and recommended a master's-level program that would train students who already had a bachelor's degrees in psychology and/or education. This was based on the training standards for the professional practice of school psychology in the United States and international data that indicated that 55% of the countries surveyed offered training at the master's level (Jimerson, Oakland, Renshaw, Fraser, & Ruderman, 2010) along with the fact that HNUE currently offered master's level training in special education.

The HNUE representatives asserted a preference for training students initially at the bachelor's level to be school psychologists. They proposed a program in which students would take general HNUE course offerings in education and psychology in their first 2 years and specialize in school psychology in their final 2 years in the program. This preference was based on knowledge of the intentions of the HNUE higher-level administration as well as considerations of the cultural context, specifically a culture where few are able to attain graduate degrees and the professional practice of psychology is still emerging. As such, course sequences were developed at the bachelor's and master's levels so that both were available for the HNUE administration to review when they made their decision of degree level of the program. Discussions of course selection for the program included the current STJ and HNUE course offerings, NASP and ISPA training standards, the MOET's mandatory curriculum, and needs for school psychologists in Vietnam. The eventual decision was made to begin the curriculum at the bachelor's level.

Practice Experiences

A major issue that arose during the consultative meetings was how practical experiences would be arranged for students in the training program. All parties agreed that opportunities for students to practice the professional skill sets they were learning in their courses would be essential; however, where these experiences would take place and who would supervise these experiences needed to be determined. It was discussed and agreed that students could initially practice in the counseling rooms of pilot program schools in Hanoi affiliated with HNUE and be supervised by the HNUE professors who were providing services in those schools. In addition, HNUE was in the process of building a training clinic on campus that would eventually serve as a setting for practical training experiences. Further, it was recognized that the first cohorts of students to go through the program would be able to later serve as supervisors for future students in the program. The initial supervisors would be professionals with master's degrees in psychology, education, or special education, and they would to participate in the trainings offered by HNUE prior to serving in a supervisory role. One specific aspect of the trainings that will be discussed focused on effective training and supervision in fieldwork experiences. It was agreed that participation in this training would enhance the quality of the learning experience of the students when they have their fieldwork placements.

Training Materials

Discussions of how to obtain necessary and appropriate training materials also took place during the consultative meetings. Members of the school psychology program at STJ shared sample syllabi from STJ courses and additional training programs as well as sample lectures with their HNUE colleagues. These could be reviewed by the HNUE faculty as they developed their course syllabi and lectures. The program leaders assisted faculty members who had more difficulty in reading content in English. Once course needs were established, ways to translate critical books and articles would be determined. A critical piece of this collaborative program was the agreement to start translation, cultural adaptation, and standardization of a variety of psychological measures; this program is ongoing and will also be reviewed later.

Development of Faculty Training Model

Finally, discussions of how best to prepare the HNUE faculty to teach and supervise their students in school psychology were held during the consultative meetings. Collaborative ideas generated included: (a) videoconferencing with STJ faculty and students as well as other experts in the field; (b) providing the HNUE with professional literature; (c) hiring visiting lecturers/supervisors; (d) sending select HNUE faculty members to be formally trained in the U.S.; and (e) holding workshops to train the HNUE future trainers. HNUE and STJ faculty determined through the consultative meetings that the HNUE faculty would need advanced training in the core areas of school psychology in order to begin to train students to become school psychologists in Vietnam.

To this end, it was decided to plan an intense training program to take place during the summer of 2008. The structure, content, and schedule of the training courses were determined through correspondence between HNUE and STJ representatives leading up to the summer of 2008. The discussion focused on the needs of the HNUE faculty, standard school psychology training domains, how learning outcomes would be achieved, as well as practical issues such as financial constraints, cultural/language differences, and scheduling conflicts.

To inform the selection of training courses and topics covered in the training courses, a needs assessment was developed for the HNUE faculty that asked them to rate their level of knowledge of school psychology topics, how important they believed each topic would be to their developing school psychology training program, and how interested they were in learning more about each topic on a Likert scale. A brief description of the major areas of practice and training of school psychologists was provided (International School Psychology Association, n.d.b; NASP, 2008; Ysseldyke et al., 2006) prior to their completion of the survey. The survey also asked them to rate how relevant different childhood disorders and conditions would be to the profession of school psychology in Vietnam.

Results of the needs assessment may be seen in Kassay (2011), and the data provided helped guide the training courses in 2008. Overall, ratings of perception of understanding were slightly greater than the midpoint of the Likert scale, indicating that the APS faculty perceived themselves to have a moderate level of understanding of the training domains. Ratings of perception of importance for the development of the school psychology training program and interest in further learning were higher, indicating that the APS faculty considered all of the training domains very important and were very interested in learning more about each of the training domains. This collection of data to guide planning and decision-making is consistent with the needs assessment task within organizational consultation (Illback, 2014). These results were taken into consideration during the planning of the advanced training courses in school psychology. By identifying perceived gaps in knowledge and training, as well as areas of perceived importance for training in consideration of the Vietnamese culture, these data allowed for some collaborative prioritizing as to what to initially develop and implement.

Preparation, Implementation, and Evaluation Stage

The next stage of the consultation included preparation, implementation, and evaluation of the program; this stage has been occurring since the summer of 2008. The primary goal of this stage was to adequately prepare a training program and faculty and supervisors that would be able to train professional school psychologists in Vietnam. This stage began with the advanced training courses in school psychology that were held at HNUE during the summer of 2008. The advanced training courses in school psychology were developed to train the APS faculty in core areas of school psychology in order to prepare them to teach and supervise the students of the new school psychology training program at HNUE.

Professional Training of Faculty

The consultative approach taken to prepare the HNUE faculty through the use of advanced training courses in school psychology was quite rigorous, with lengthy discussion as to the best approach to follow to increase the likelihood of success (i.e., competent faculty to teach in the program). The courses were designed to provide the participants with a general understanding of broad competency areas of school psychologists and serve as a foundation for the participants to build upon as they advanced their knowledge and skills as leaders in the emerging field of school psychology in Vietnam. The academic backgrounds of the APS faculty members were taken into account as the training courses were planned, as were their self-identified strengths and weaknesses on the needs assessment. The APS faculty's priorities and expectations for the profession of school psychology in Vietnam, as identified on the needs assessment, were also incorporated into the training courses.

The program for the advanced training courses was developed through the collaboration between a team of HNUE and STJ representatives; however, UNICEF, the L & L Organization, and the VVAF also provided financial support for the program. The two primary leaders were Dr. Terjesen from STJ and Dr. Thu from HNUE. The final program consisted of 3-week intense trainings, during which the participants took two 18-hour training modules per week for a total of six training modules. Each week consisted of 5.5 training days; generally days were broken into two 3.5 hour sessions, alternating between modules. The training modules taught were: (a) Evidence-Based Psychological Interventions: Individual and Group Therapy; (b) Academic Assessment and Intervention; (c) Evidence-Based Psychological Interventions: School-Based Screening and Universal Approaches; (d) Personality Assessment: Linking Data to Guide Counseling and Intervention; (e) School-Based and Mental Health Consultation; and (f) Supervision in School Psychology: Supervising Assessment and Therapy Practica and Interns. Each of the modules had a practical component in which participants either observed or conducted an administration of a psychological assessment or role-played counseling, consultation, and supervision.

Discussion of the theoretical underpinnings of each content area was integrated with consideration of cultural and linguistic variables. As an example, there was consideration of common parenting practices within the Vietnamese culture because that would relate to parenting interventions for children with ADHD. Feedback as to content and style as they relate to professional practice within the Vietnamese culture was quite extensive. As an example, in the Evidence-Based Psychological Interventions module, participants commented on the positive aspect of the opportunity to practice doing a functional behavioral assessment and on the structure of the cognitive behavioral model for intervention that was observed during the demonstration. More specifically, the ABC model of Rational Emotive Behavior Therapy (REBT; Bernard, Ellis, & Terjesen, 2005) that was demonstrated in the training was something that they thought was practical and direct, which were things that they valued. Participants who attended all six of the advanced modules and completed the competency examinations received certificates authorized by STJ and HNUE that attested to their qualifications as school psychologists and lecturers/supervisors of school psychology in Vietnam.

The instructors of the advanced modules were selected by STJ consultants based on their areas of specialization. The instructors represent a diverse group of faculty members/school psychologists from STJ, Pace University, the University of California Santa Barbara, and public school districts. All of the instructors had experience teaching and/or supervising at a graduate level. Instructors were provided with the results of the needs assessment to inform their training module preparation before they traveled to Vietnam. Based on input from the HNUE faculty, instructors were asked to include didactic teaching methods, group discussion, and practical experiences, when applicable.

Although the primary language of all of the training participants was Vietnamese, none of the instructors were able to speak in Vietnamese. To overcome this language barrier, all training materials were translated, and a translator was present in every training session. The translators were university faculty members and program participants who were compensated for their work. Instructors prepared PowerPoint presentations, training materials, and exams in advance of their sessions and all were translated for the participants. Prior to instruction, each of the instructors was sent background information about Vietnam, the current state of school psychology in Vietnam, and issues in Vietnam that may be related to their instructional area. They all participated in a conference call about preparation for instruction and working with the HNUE faculty. Lectures and training discussions were translated as they occurred.

Participants

The program for the advanced training modules was originally planned for the faculty of the DPE at HNUE; however, the Vietnamese faculty who served in the consultee roles recognized that there was a need for other professionals working with children in Vietnam to receive training. Inviting outside professionals to collaborate and share resources was also consistent with the missions of many of the organizations supporting the program. As such, the DPE faculty informed colleagues from all over Vietnam of the program and invited them to attend.

The final composition of 33 participants was diverse; they ranged in province of origin and professional background. More detail as to the demographics of the participants is available from Kassay (2011). Interestingly, 51.5% of had doctoral degrees; further, 71% of the participants reported that their highest degree was in psychology, 22.6% in education, and 6.5% in counseling. Participants reported working in many related areas of psychology with some serving multiple roles (i.e., working as a professor as well as a school psychologist). Overall, 47.1% reported that they were employed as psychology professors, 25% worked as psychologists (not in a school setting), 43.8% worked as counselors, and 20.6% worked as school psychologists. Twenty-nine participants completed the advanced training program and received certificates endorsing their qualifications as school psychologists and lecturers/supervisors of school psychology in Vietnam.

Evaluation of Training Outcomes

In order to evaluate the effectiveness of the advanced training modules and determine areas in which the APS faculty members required further training and development, a Likert-style questionnaire of perception of understanding, ability to apply, and ability to teach school psychology knowledge and skills was administered prior to, immediately following, and approximately 1 year after the advanced training modules were held. The questionnaire was based on the learning objectives proposed by the instructors on their module syllabi. Participants responded to identical questions at each of the three time points. Comparisons of school psychology knowledge and skills based on the subject areas of the modules were made at different time points, and results of those that completed the questionnaires indicated that knowledge and skills increased in all domains between pre- and posttraining and pretraining and 1-year follow-up. Effect size was calculated using Cohen's d. Table 10.1 presents the results of the t-tests and effect size calculations. While there were no significant differences in school psychology knowledge and skills between posttraining and follow-up, knowledge and skills increased in all domains between pre- and posttraining and pretraining and follow-up.

Table 10.1 Comparisons of School Psychology Knowledge and Skills between Pretraining, Posttraining, and 1-Year Follow-Up of the Summer 2008 Advanced Training Courses

School psychology domain	Comparison	t-value	df	p-value	Cohen's d
Individual and group therapy	Pre/post	−2.854	19	.010*	−.640
	Pre/follow-up	−2.352	10	.041*	−.709
	Post/follow-up	.056	8	.957	.019
Cognitive assessment and interventions	Pre/post	−1.884	19	.075	−.441
	Pre/follow-up	−1.590	10	.143	−.489
	Post/follow-up	.610	8	.559	.207
Personality assessment: linking data to guide counseling and intervention	Pre/Post	−2.544	19	.020*	−.570
	Pre/follow-up	−2.907	10	.016*	−.922
	Post/follow-up	−.213	8	.293	−.071
School-based screening and universal approaches	Pre/Post	−2.037	19	.056	−.457
	Pre/follow-up	−3.974	10	.003*	−1.258
	Post/follow-up	−1.126	8	.293	−.320
Consultation	Pre/post	−1.666	19	.112	−.373
	Pre/follow-up	−1.921	10	.084	−.600
	Post/follow-up	.371	8	.720	.124
Supervision	Pre/post	−1.946	18	.067	−.032
	Pre/follow-up	−2.570	10	.028*	−.778
	Post/follow-up	−.191	8	.853	−.064

Note: Negative Cohen's d and t-values indicate an increase in school psychology knowledge and skills through the advanced training courses.
*p < .05

Ongoing Professional Development

Program collaborators understood that appropriate and thorough training and development of the HNUE faculty could not be accomplished only through time-limited formal training events such as workshop courses. As such, continuing professional development in the form of access to professional literature, colleague mentoring, ongoing topic-specific trainings, and practical experiences was planned and began after the advanced training courses in 2008. To assist in the ongoing development of the program, APS faculty members were able to consult with the American professors who taught their advanced training courses and STJ school psychology faculty members via electronic mail for assistance regarding any of these responsibilities or for professional advice on issues that might arise during teaching of the school psychology courses. Further, efforts were made to establish a colleague mentoring program such that APS faculty members would be partnered with school psychology professors in the United States who specialize in the content areas that they were teaching to serve as professional support as well as to provide ongoing problem-solving assistance. The intention was for American professors to also be able to share content-related readings, videos, and their own training materials with the APS faculty through their mentoring relationships.

This proved challenging for a few reasons. First, there were practical challenges in terms of time of day of the training, with Vietnam having 11 or 12 hour time differences, some language barriers among participants, and some technological difficulties (e.g., poor Internet connectivity). This somewhat hindered the success of this mentoring aspect of the program. Second, some of the APS faculty members expressed a preference for more information dissemination on specific topic areas rather than an opportunity for discussion of issues related to problem-solving when it came to instructional or supervision methodologies or service provision. In hindsight, perhaps collaboratively establishing more clearly the expectations of these mentoring relationships along with identifying technological resources for support would have been more beneficial.

Additionally, HNUE decided to send a member of their faculty to STJ in 2008 to be trained in the school psychology doctoral program, and this faculty member earned his doctorate in the APA and NASP accredited STJ school psychology program in January 2014. His training was supported by HNUE, STJ, and the MOET, which reflected the emerging national support for the development of the field of school psychology in Vietnam.

As applied psychology and school psychology in particular are emerging fields in Vietnam, field-specific professional literature was not available to the APS faculty members and was seen as a barrier to program and professional growth. It was determined that having access to professional literature would be critical for the APS faculty to expand their foundational school psychology knowledge, develop specialized topics of interests, and stay current on advances in the field. Administrators at STJ agreed to provide 11 APS faculty members with access to the STJ library, which has access to numerous electronic databases and professional journal subscriptions. In addition to library access, the faculty of the STJ psychology department shared new and used textbooks, training videos/DVDs, and assessment materials with their HNUE colleagues. English-speaking APS faculty members assisted their colleagues who were unable to utilize the resources without translation.

Summer 2009 Training

Ongoing communication among the STJ consultants and HNUE consultees led to the determination that more direct training was needed to build upon the summer 2008 advanced training courses and continue to develop the APS faculty as they prepared their school psychology training program. Specifically, both the STJ consultants and APS faculty thought it would be beneficial to give the APS faculty direct experience of psychological service models in the United States. The DPE sent a group of faculty members to STJ to receive further training and practical experiences before they started to teach the first HNUE school psychology students in the fall of 2009. A program of site visits, lectures, graduate courses, and social/cultural experiences was planned for the nine DPE faculty members. Four faculty members participated for 2 weeks, four faculty members participated for 2 months, and one faculty member participated for 6 months.

A Likert-style questionnaire was developed that asked the DPE faculty planning to attend the program in 2009 to rate their level of understanding and interest in further learning of each of the ISPA training domains. This questionnaire was designed around the ISPA training domains because they represent the competencies that ISPA deems critical for school psychologists internationally. Perception of level of understanding was moderately low across the training domains and interest in further learning was relatively high, indicating that the DPE faculty perceived a need for further training to develop their level of understanding and had an interest in doing so.

The STJ consultants arranged a total of 19 site visits to schools and mental health care settings in summer 2009 to give DPE consultees the opportunity to observe how psychological services are provided to children in a variety of settings in New York. Although not necessarily representative of how psychological services are provided to children across the United States, urban and suburban sites were chosen to give the participants more diverse experiences. In addition, a total of twenty-four 2-hour lectures were held to provide the participants with in-depth information in specialized topics. The lectures afforded the participants with opportunities for discussions with professors and practitioners with a wide range of areas of expertise. Some of these discussions lead to plans to collaborate on cross-cultural research projects, including studies of personality, anger, and parenting as well as agreements to collaborate on the translation and standardization of assessment measures (Del Vecchio, Jerusalmi, & Terjesen, 2015; Mooney, 2014; Nicolai, 2014). Participants also had the opportunity to audit the STJ graduate courses in psychology that were being offered during their stay. Finally, social and cultural events were planned for the DPE faculty for the purposes of networking with international colleagues and learning about the cultural context of the field of school psychology.

Two Likert-style questionnaires were developed and administered to the participants upon completion of the summer 2009 program to evaluate its effectiveness in preparing the HNUE faculty in important school psychology domains as defined by ISPA. Due to the small sample sizes and differences in their length of stay in the U.S., tests of statistically significant differences would not be meaningful and were not analyzed. A general trend can be seen in the data, with all participants' perceptions of understanding of the ISPA training domains increasing from before to after the summer 2009 program.

DEVELOPING ASSESSMENT RESOURCES FOR VIETNAM

Providing translated, standardized, valid, reliable, and culturally appropriate measures of cognitive abilities, academic achievement, and social-emotional functioning is important to the development of the field of school psychology in Vietnam. Faculty and students from HNUE, STJ, and the Worldwide Orphan Foundation (WWO) have been collaboratively working on translating and collecting standardization data on various assessment tools with support from test publishing companies, HNUE, and Psi Chi. At present, contracts have been signed with test publishing companies for the translation, standardization, and Vietnamese production of the Conners Comprehensive Behavior Rating Scales (CCBRS), Conners 3, Autism Spectrum Rating Scales (ASRS), Child Behavior Checklist (CBCL), and Bayley Scales of Infant Development. Other measures have being translated and piloted through collaborative relationships with individuals from STJ and HNUE.

CURRENT STATE OF THE HNUE SCHOOL PSYCHOLOGY PROGRAM

Consultation with the APS occurred with regard to decisions about the degree level of the program, the sequence of courses and practical training experiences that will be requirements of the program, and the criteria for selecting students to accept into the program. While ultimately these decisions were the responsibility of the APS, the STJ consultants provided multiple models and approaches and discussed the strengths and limitations of various models.

HNUE decided to begin to train students at the bachelor's level in psychology with a specialization in school psychology in the 2008–2009 academic year. The first cohort of 18 students who were accepted into the school psychology program matriculated in September 2008, and these students graduated in the summer of 2012. While the second cohort dropped in terms of overall number (12 students), subsequent years showed significant interest in the profession with incoming cohorts of 37 (2010), 25 (2011), 37 (2012), 31 (2013), 31 (2014), 28 (2015), and 49 (2016) students. A total of 129 students have graduated the program with BAs in school psychology as of 2016. The program director estimates that approximately two-thirds of the graduates from 2008 through the 2012 incoming classes now have jobs as school psychologists with some variability in title.

Students applying to HNUE request entrance to the program and then take the national examination; students who pass the examination are accepted into the program. The application to acceptance ratio was approximately 17 to 1 as of the 2010 enrollment.

Students in the school psychology program take compulsory university courses and general psychology courses in their first 2 years of study. They go on to take specialized courses in school psychology beginning in the second semester of their second year of study. In total, they take 61 credits of required psychology/school psychology coursework and 18 credits of electives in school psychology. Practical experiences begin during students' training in the second semester of their third year and are the focus of their final year of study, as students are required to complete a year-long professional practicum. Practical experiences occur at the counseling rooms of the HNUE-affiliated high schools, local schools, and the HNUE counseling center. The program has students complete their practica at the various locations, supervised by onsite practitioners, and they return to the HNUE for supervision from the program faculty.

There is considerable diversity in the number of practica sites that they have for their students, including both schools and counseling centers. Some of the supervisors at these sites are graduates of the program, which was an initial objective discussed during the developmental stage of the program.

The faculty at HNUE has a preliminary plan to start the process for a master's degree program in school psychology by the fall of 2018. In Vietnam, master's programs typically have 1 year of study and 1 year of work on a thesis. Preliminary consultation has begun to assist in the development of the program at the master's level. There has been discussion about having two "tracks" of the program: one for students who have graduated from their program and another for students who have psychology degrees without a school psychology focus.

CHALLENGES IN CONSULTATION AND PROGRAM DEVELOPMENT

The biggest challenge faced during the consultation to develop the HNUE school psychology program is that it pioneered the field in Vietnam. As with any introduction of a field, the program has had to break some new ground and overcome multiple difficulties along the way. Without any in-country models to follow, the DPE faculty has had to conduct extensive research and run pilot projects, consult with international colleagues, create standards, and make programmatic decisions without the benefit of past precedents. They have also had to establish a need for its work and inform others of its mission in order to receive and maintain the support of the MOET, HNUE, and the public.

Lack of Faculty and Resources

The next challenge that the program has faced is the lack of trained faculty and specialized training materials and professional tools, including course syllabi and lectures, textbooks, professional literature, assessment tools, and intervention programs. Efforts have been made to assist faculty in the development of course syllabi and lectures through consultative meetings, advanced training courses, and ongoing mentoring webinars. An important aspect of each of these efforts has been work with the APS faculty to consider what makes cultural sense and to work with them on developing assessment, consultative, and intervention resources that consider the role of culture and language. This work continues as the program develops, and faculty members continue to teach more advanced school psychology courses. Textbooks and professional literature have been made available to the APS faculty by STJ sharing academic materials, STJ providing access to its online database, and colleagues posting information on the School Psychology Vietnam website.

However, this too is limited, as this information is all in English and represents select areas of training with minimal consideration of the Vietnamese language and culture. Efforts by the APS faculty to identify individuals who are able to read and communicate in English to be "leaders" in specific aspects of the training program have been met with some positive results. As an example, one APS faculty member has been identified as the "personality assessment" leader. He collects the information in this area, translates it, considers the role of culture, and shares it with his colleagues and students.

Need to Develop Tools and Interventions

Assessment tools and interventions pose a greater challenge because they require substantial work to translate, modify, standardize, and publish in another culture (Achenbach & Rescorla, 2006). Collaborative research projects have begun between HNUE, STJ, and test publishers to this end, but they need to continue into the future. In Vietnam, there are very few indigenous questionnaires (Leung & Wong, 2003). This has led to a lack of culture-specific items and constructs. Recently, Dang, Weiss, Pollack, and Nguyen (2012) adapted the first standardized intelligence test (WISC-IV) for use in Vietnam. As professional tools for school psychologists generally did not exist in Vietnam and are not easily created, much work is still needed in this area to develop professional tools that are available in Vietnamese and are culturally appropriate. Translating measures without taking into consideration possible cultural differences with regard to item content or wording is an area that would benefit from being addressed (International Test Commission (ITC), 2005). A natively developed measure may be more appropriate to capture the true levels of functioning and adequately represent the constructs in question in consideration of the Vietnamese culture. A challenge here is the sheer size and costs in undertaking such an endeavor. As the program continues to develop, consideration of allocation of resources for this purpose may be warranted.

Development of Practice Experiences

Arranging practical training experiences for students in the program is another ongoing challenge that has been identified. Balancing the need for practical training experiences with good supervision for these placements is a challenge for any type of developing applied program, especially where school psychology is not a formalized profession and adequately trained site supervisors are not readily available.

Continued Development of School Psychology at HNUE and in Vietnam

As previously described, a great deal of work in the development of the HNUE school psychology program is ongoing. This includes continuing to provide the APS faculty with access to professional literature through library access, mentoring webinars, and consultation as needed. Communication with the faculty from STJ and HNUE led to a number of considerations for how this program development could have been enhanced. For example, greater opportunities for technological sharing of resources and face-to-face interactions for longer periods of time would have been advantageous, and efforts to provide this are ongoing.

In addition, collaborative research projects aimed at the translation and standardization of measures of cognitive abilities, academic achievement, and social-emotional functioning are progressing, and it is believed that these will be quite helpful to the development of the program and the profession. Current projects involve translating measures into Vietnamese and modifying them to make them culturally appropriate. However, as mentioned earlier, future advances should include building measures within the Vietnamese culture rather than adapting only American measures.

To date, research efforts have focused on the development of assessment tools. Future research may want to explore the need and adaptation of empirically supported interventions for different presenting problems. It will be important to examine the effect of culture on the targeted emotional and behavioral problems because that will impact the acceptability and efficacy of interventions. It is likely that some interventions will translate more easily into another culture than others; some symptom presentations may have more universal maintaining mechanisms, whereas others would be found to be more culturally bound. It is also likely that this line of research will reveal a need for new Vietnamese-specific interventions for children facing emotional and behavioral difficulties.

Prior to the development of the school psychology program at HNUE, behavioral and emotional needs of children were identified in Vietnam, and the MOET determined that services were needed. However, trained professionals were limited in the country, leading various individuals to perform some functions of school psychologists without adequate skills and knowledge to do so (Applied Psychology Section, 2007; Le, 2009). HNUE's school psychology training program was the first established in Vietnam, but since 2006, other Vietnamese universities have begun to prepare similar programs.

While HNUE was building its school psychology training program, another group of Vietnamese practitioners was in communication with other American and international school psychologists. These professionals, with similar aims and motivations as those from HNUE and STJ, came together in August 2009 in Hanoi to hold the first official school psychology conference in Vietnam. This conference was organized by Vietnamese American school psychologist Dr. Phuong Le of California State University Long Beach (USCLB) and Chapman University (CU). Over 150 Vietnamese, American, and Australian professionals attended the conference (M. Hass, personal communication, September, 2010; http://michaelrhass.wordpress.com). Representatives from HNUE were in attendance and had the opportunity to come together with colleagues to work on their collective goal: to develop the field of school psychology and provide mental health services to children in schools in Vietnam. This meeting lead representatives from Vietnamese and American institutions to form the Consortium to Advance School Psychology-Vietnam (CASP-V), which was officially established with an MOU effective in February 1, 2010 (CASP-V, 2010). The stated primary purpose of CASP-V is "to establish the discipline and profession of school psychology in Vietnam and promote the adoption of the highest quality education and practices in school psychology" (CASP-V, 2010, p. 2).

CONCLUDING THOUGHTS

Because the HNUE program was the first formal university-based training program in school psychology in Vietnam, it is expected that the addition of other programs will enhance the provision of psychological services to children in schools. Future directions for the field of school psychology in Vietnam should include constant reevaluations of the developing training programs and school psychology practice in the country and dissemination of new information. This will serve to inform the leaders in the field and allow for the training programs and practitioners to adapt to the developing standards of best practices of school psychology training and practice in Vietnam. This consultative process and product provided the program developers with insight into considerations for the successful development of programs internationally.

REFERENCES

Applied Psychology Section. (2007, July). *Training course for future lecturers and supervisors in school psychology.* Hanoi, Vietnam: Hanoi National University of Education, Department of Psychology and Education.

Ashwill, M. A., & Thai, N. D. (2005). *Vietnam today: A nation at a crossroads.* Boston, MA: Intercultural Press.

Bernard, M. E., Ellis, A., & Terjesen, M. D. (2005). Rational emotive behavior approaches to childhood disorders: History, theory, practice and research. In A. Ellis & M. E. Bernard (Eds.), *Rational emotive behavior approaches to childhood disorders* (pp. 3–84). New York: Springer.

Bondurant, A., Henderson, S., & Nguyen, C. Q. (2003, September). *Addressing the reproductive health needs and rights of young people since ICPD: The contribution of UNFPA and IPPF. Vietnam country evaluation report.* Retrieved August 22, 2008, from http://www.unfpa.org/monitoring/country_evals/vietnam/vietnam_countryeval.pdf

Central Intelligence Agency. (2014). Vietnam. In *The World Factbook.* Retrieved February 14, 2014, from https://www.cia.gov/library/publications/the-world-factbook/geos/vm.html

Clarke, J., Gayfer, J., Landymore, P., & Luttrell, C. (2007, May). *Country programme review: Vietnam* (Department for International Development Evaluation Report EV673). Retrieved August 22, 2008, from www.dfid.gov.uk/aboutdfid/performance/files/ev673-summary.pdf

Consortium to Advance School Psychology-Vietnam. (2010). *Memorandum of understanding.* Vietnam: Author.

Cunningham, J., & Oakland, T. (1998). International school psychology association guidelines for preparation of school psychologists. *School Psychology International, 19,* 19–30.

Dang, H. M., Weiss, B., Pollack, A., & Nguyen, M. C. (2012). Adaption of the Wechsler Intelligence Scale for Children-IV (WISC-IV) for Vietnam. *Psychological Studies, 56,* 387–392.

Del Vecchio, T., Jerusalmi, D., & Terjesen, M. D. (2015). Psychometric characteristics of the Parenting Scale in a Vietnamese sample. *International Journal of Psychology.* doi: 10.1002/ijop.12242

Embassy of Vietnam. (n.d.). *Learn about Vietnam.* Retrieved August 22, 2008, from http://www.vietnamembassy-usa.org/learn_about_vietnam/

Erchul, W. P., & Young, H. L. (2014). Best practices in school consultation. In P. L. Harrison & A. Thomas (Eds.), *Best practices in school psychology: Data-based and collaborative decision making* (pp. 449–460). Bethesda, MD: National Association of School Psychologists.

Fagan, T. K., & Wise, P. S. (2007). *School psychology: Past, present, and future* (3rd ed.). Bethesda, MD: National Association of School Psychology.

Farrell, P. T., Jimerson, S. R., & Oakland, T. D. (2007). School psychology internationally: A synthesis of findings. In S. R. Jimerson, T. D. Oakland, & P. T. Farrell (Eds.), *The handbook of international school psychology* (pp. 501–509). Thousand Oaks, CA: Sage Publications.

Hanoi National University of Education. (n.d.). Retrieved August 22, 2008, from http://www.hnue.edu.vn/portal/page/portal/dhsphn_en/about_us

Hanoi National University of Education. (2007, October 15). *Department of psychology and education.* Retrieved August 22, 2008, from http://www.hnue.edu.vn/portal/page/portal/dhsphn_en/newsdetail?item_id=420702&p_details=1

Harvey, V. S., & Struzziero, J. A. (2008). *Professional development and supervision of school psychologists* (2nd ed.). Bethesda, MD: National Association of School Psychologists.

Illback, R. J. (2014). Organization development and change facilitation in schools: Theoretical and empirical foundations. In W. P. Erchul & S. M. Sheridan (Eds.), *Handbook of research in school consultation* (2nd ed., pp. 276–303). New York, NY: Routledge.

International School Psychology Association. (n.d. a). *About ISPA.* Retrieved September 1, 2008, from www.ispaweb.org/t3.html

International School Psychology Association. (n.d. b). *International guidelines for the preparation of school psychologists.* Retrieved June 7, 2009, from http://ispaweb.org/Documents/International%20Guidelines%20for%20the%20preparation%20of%20school%20psychologists.htm

International Test Commission (ITC). (2005). *International guidelines for adapting tests.* Downloaded electronically on May 10, 2013, from www.intestcom.org/itc_projects.htm

Jimerson, S. R., Oakland, T. D., & Farrell, P. T. (2007). Introduction to the handbook of international school psychology. In S. R. Jimerson, T. D. Oakland, & P. T. Farrell (Eds.), *The handbook of international school psychology* (pp. 1–4). Thousand Oaks, CA: Sage Publications.

Jimerson, S. R., Oakland, T. D., Renshaw, T. L., Fraser, S., & Ruderman, M. (2010). *Prevalence and characteristics of school psychology programs around the world*. International Institute of School Psychology. Retrieved from: http://mina.education.ucsb.edu/jimersen/ISSP/SPIS_brief_training_programs41610SRJ.pdf

Jimerson, S. R., Skokut, M., Cardenas, S., Malone, H., & Stewart, K. (2008). Where in the world is school psychology? Examining the evidence of school psychology around the globe. *School Psychology International, 29*, 131–144.

Jimerson, S. R., Stewart, K., Skokut, M., Cardenas, S., & Malone, H. (2009). How many school psychologists are there in each country of the world? International estimates of school psychologists and school psychologist-to-student ratios. *School Psychology International, 30*, 555–567.

Kassay, K. S. (2011). *Development of a training program in school psychology in Vietnam* (Unpublished Doctoral Dissertation). St. John's University, Queens, NY.

Kassay, K. S., Terjesen, M. D., Nguyen, S., Nguyen, H., Phan, L., Hoang, P., et al. (2010). Preparation of faculty for a school psychology program in Vietnam. *International Psychology Bulletin, 14*, 21–23.

Le, P. N. (2009). Gap analysis of Vietnamese student counselors' knowledge competencies. *Dissertation Abstracts International: Section A. Humanities and Social Sciences, 70*(8-A), 2903.

Leung, P. W. L., & Wong, M. M. T. (2003). Measures of child and adolescent psychopathology in Asia. *Psychological Assessment, 15*, 268–279.

Lopez, E. C., & Bursztyn, A. M. (2013). Future challenges and opportunities: Toward culturally responsive training in school psychology. *Psychology in the Schools, 50*, 212–228. doi: http://dx.doi.org.jerome.stjohns.edu:81/10.1002/pits.21674

Ministry of Education and Training. (2003, November 20). *Vietnam education and training directory*. Retrieved March 15, 2007, from http://en.moet.gov.vn

Ministry of Education and Training. (2009, October 29). *Report of the development of higher education system, the solutions to ensure quality assurance and improve of education quality* (Resolution No. 760/BC-BGDDT). Retrieved February 14, 2014, from http://en.moet.gov.vn/?page=6.13&view=19831

Mooney, J. (2014). *Validation of the Conners Comprehensive Behavior Rating Scale (CBRS) and Conners Early Childhood (EC) with a Vietnamese population* (Unpublished Doctoral Dissertation). St. John's University, Queens, NY.

Nastasi, B. K., Varjas, K., Bernstein, R., & Jayasena, A. (2000). Conducting participatory culture-specific consultation: A global perspective on multicultural consultation. *School Psychology Review, 29*, 401–413. Retrieved from http://search.proquest.com.jerome.stjohns.edu:81/docview/219646184?accountid=14068

National Assembly of the Socialist Republic of Vietnam, Tenth Legislature, Tenth Session. (2001). *1992 constitution of the socialist republic of Vietnam: As amended 25 December 2001* (Resolution No. 51–2001-QH10). Retrieved October 1, 2008, from http://www.vietnamlaws.com/freelaws/Constitution92(aa01).pdf

National Assembly of the Socialist Republic of Vietnam, Eleventh Legislature, Seventh Session. (2005). *The education law* (Law No. 38/2005/QH11). Hanoi, Vietnam: Author.

Nicolai, L. (2014). *Examining the role of irrational beliefs and automatic thoughts in predicting affect and behavior among students in Vietnam* (Unpublished Doctoral Dissertation). St. John's University, Queens, NY.

Oakland, T. D. (2007). International school psychology. In T. K. Fagan & P. S. Wise (Eds.), *School psychology: Past, present, and future* (3rd ed., pp. 339–365). Bethesda, MD: National Association of School Psychology.

Oakland, T. D., & Hatzichristou, C. (2014a). International perspectives on academic and professional preparation of school and educational psychologists: Introduction to a special issue of the International Journal of School & Educational Psychology. *International Journal of School & Educational Psychology, 2*, 150–153.

Oakland, T. D., & Hatzichristou, C. (2014b). Professional preparation in school psychology: A summary of information from programs in seven countries. *International Journal of School & Educational Psychology, 2*, 223–230.

Oakland, T. D., & Jimerson, S. R. (2007). School psychology internationally: A retrospective view and influential conditions. In S. R. Jimerson, T. D. Oakland, & P. T. Farrell (Eds.), *The handbook of international school psychology* (pp. 453–462). Thousand Oaks, CA: Sage Publications.

Schirmer, J. M., Cartwright, C., Montegut, A. J., Dreher, G. K., & Stovall, J. (2004). A collaborative needs assessment and work plan in behavioral medicine curriculum development in Vietnam. *Families, Systems, & Health, 22*, 410–418.

Schirmer, J. M., & Le, N. H. (2002). The Vietnam family medicine development project: A cross-cultural collaboration. *Families, Systems, & Health, 20*, 303–310.

Tran, T. L. T. (2010). *History of establishing and implementing the first training program on school psychology in Vietnam*. Paper presented at the Second International Conference on School Psychology in Vietnam, Hue, Vietnam, January 2010.

Weiss, B., Dang, M., Trung, L., Nguyen, M. C., Thuy, N. T. H., & Pollack, A. (2014). A nationally representative epidemiological and risk factor assessment of child mental health in Vietnam. *International Perspectives in Psychology: Research, Practice, Consultation, 3*(3), 139–153. doi: 10.1037/ipp0000016

Weiss, B., Ngo, V. K., Dang, H. M., Pollack, A., Trung, L. T., Tran, C. V., . . . Do, K. N. (2012). A model for sustainable development of child mental health infrastructure in the LMIC world: Vietnam as a case example. *International Perspectives in Psychology: Research, Practice, Consultation, 1*, 63–77. doi: 10.1037/a0027316

World Bank. (2007, February). *IDA at work: Vietnam: Laying the foundation for steady growth.* Retrieved August 25, 2008, from http://www.worldbank.org/ida/resources/ida-vietnam.pdf

World Bank. (2014). *Vietnam.* Retrieved February 14, 2014, from http://www.worldbank.org/en/country/vietnam

World Health Organization. (2005). Viet Nam. In *Mental Health Atlas 2005* (pp. 504–506). Geneva: Author.

Ysseldyke, J., Burns, M., Dawson, P., Kelley, B., Morrison, D., Ortiz, S., . . . Telzrow, C. (2006). *School psychology: A blueprint for training and practice III.* Bethesda, MD: National Association of School Psychologists.

Zins, J. E., & Erchul, W. P. (2002). Best practices in school consultation. In A. Thomas & J. Grimes (Eds.), *Best practices in school psychology IV* (pp. 625–643). Bethesda, MD: National Association of School Psychologists.

11

SCHOOL CRISIS CONSULTATION
An International Framework

Stephen E. Brock and Shane R. Jimerson

SCHOOL CRISIS CONSULTATION: AN INTERNATIONAL FRAMEWORK

This chapter discusses how the PREP<u>a</u>RE model of school crisis prevention and intervention (Brock et al., 2009, 2015) can be employed internationally as a framework for school crisis consultation. The PREP<u>a</u>RE model provides a flexible framework for school crisis prevention, preparedness, response, and recovery that can be used in a variety of different school environments. Although originally developed for use in the public schools of the United States, its prevention and preparedness elements have recently been adapted by Jimerson and colleagues (Jimerson, 2012, 2013a, 2013b; Jimerson, Brown, & Shahroozi, 2012; Jimerson, Brown, Shahroozi, Watanabe, & Brown-Earl, 2012; Jimerson & Shahroozi, 2012) for use in a variety of international school contexts. This chapter begins with an overview of the PREP<u>a</u>RE model, then examines cross-cultural considerations in school crisis consultation, and finally discusses how each element of PREP<u>a</u>RE can be used in school crisis consultations.

THE PRACTICE OF SCHOOL CRISIS CONSULTATION USING THE PREP<u>a</u>RE MODEL

The PREP<u>a</u>RE model of school crisis prevention and intervention employs elements of both mental health and behavioral consultation. According to Kratochwill (2008), although differences exist between these consultation models, both employ the special problem-solving knowledge of the consultant within a triadic relationship (see Erchul & Sheridan, 2014, for a review of contemporary research in school consultation). As illustrated in Figure 11.1, this type of triadic relationship typically finds a crisis intervention specialist (e.g., school psychologist) in the role of the consultant, adult caregivers (e.g., administrators, teachers, or parents) in the role of consultees, and the student with coping challenges in the client role. However, in some cases the consultee may be a school administrator and the client an adult school staff member (e.g., a classroom teacher who is experiencing coping challenges).

In Figure 11.1, the line leading directly from the consultant to the client illustrates that this model of crisis intervention consultation can include the provision of direct

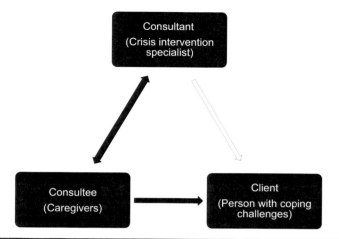

Figure 11.1 The Triadic Crisis Intervention Consultation Relationship

services by the crisis intervention specialist when the needs of the person in crisis exceed those that can be met by natural caregivers (e.g., parents and teachers). In other words, while many of the activities that take place under the umbrella of PREP$_a$RE find the crisis intervention specialist providing indirect consultation services, the model dictates the use of direct mental health crisis intervention when indicated (e.g., when the student or school staff member experiences severe psychological traumatization). Yet even with these relatively intense and potentially highly directive crisis intervention services (offered by the crisis intervention specialist directly to the client who is in crisis), a basic problem-solving orientation is the primary vehicle through which support is offered. This problem-solving approach is consistent with the school-based problem-solving consultation process involving: (a) relationship building; (b) problem identification; (c) problem analysis; (d) intervention implementation; and (e) program evaluation (Frank & Kratochwill, 2014).

As illustrated in Figure 11.2, the PREP$_a$RE stands for prevent, reaffirm, evaluate, provide and respond, and examine. To the extent it is possible to do so, the model asserts that the crisis consultant should assist the school in preventing those crises that can be avoided and in preparing for those that either cannot be or are not prevented. Next, the crisis response consultant strives to help the school ensure that objective physical safety is reaffirmed and, furthermore, that students perceive the school environment as safe and secure. Evaluation of psychological trauma risk is the next step or element of the PREP$_a$RE model, and this involves the identification of mental health crisis intervention needs. Initially this "psychological triage" is offered as an indirect service with the crisis consultant gathering data from consultees. However, it is emphasized within the PREP$_a$RE model that such triage is a process not an event, and as the crisis response consultant directly interacts with students (i.e., provides direct mental health crisis intervention assistance) he or she personally assesses these needs and makes more refined mental health referral decisions. From the evaluation of psychological trauma, the PREP$_a$RE model directs the crisis response consultant to begin to provide crisis interventions and, in doing so, meets students' psychological needs. To the extent it is appropriate to do so,

P	Prevent crisis events
R	Reaffirm physical health and perceptions of security and safety
E	Evaluate psychological trauma risk
P a R	Provide interventions and Respond to psychological needs
E	Examine the effectiveness of crisis prevention and intervention

Figure 11.2 The PREPaRE Acronym Represents a Flexible, Sequential, and Hierarchical Set of Crisis Interventions

Source: Adapted from Brock et al. (2009, p. ix)

the PREPaRE model emphasizes providing such services indirectly via crisis consultation with the parents and teachers who are the student's primary caregivers. Finally, the model requires the crisis consultant to assist the school in examining the effectiveness of existing crisis prevention strategies, crisis preparedness efforts, and the effectiveness (Brock et al., 2009).

In addition to the special subject matter knowledge of crisis prevention and intervention required of the crisis consultant (which the PREPaRE workshops provide), it is also important to acknowledge that effective communication skills are essential to crisis consultation (not to mention their importance in those situations where the consultant is called on to provide direct crisis intervention services; Rosenfield, 2004). Perhaps most important, the ability to help the consultee (and in the case of direct services, the client) identify and prioritize crisis-generated problems is essential. Often when consultees (e.g., parents, teachers, and administrators) struggle to find ways to help students recover from their crisis exposures, crisis-generated problems are viewed as a vague collection of competing needs. Consequently, the consultant will need to help the consultee specifically identify the coping challenges generated by the crisis event and then help prioritize them. Challenges that involve physical safety should be identified for the consultee as the primary concerns, followed in order by ways to minimize crisis exposure, determining the level of crisis response required, evaluating individual psychological trauma risk, and then providing crisis interventions (Brock et al., 2009).

Identifying and prioritizing crisis challenges are facilitated by use of the listening skills (e.g., clarifying, paraphrasing, and perception checking) described in helping skills literature (Rosenfield, 2004). When employing these skills, it is important for the consultant to recognize that to the extent the consultee is affected by the crisis event, he or she is likely to find his or her working memory overloaded by event details, thus leaving relatively little working memory available to process guidance offered by the consultant. Given this reality, the listening skill of perception checking is critical, and the consultant should be prepared to restate and rephrase guidance offered. In doing so, it will be important to acknowledge for the consultee how difficult it is to process such guidance in crisis situations so as to assertively avoid giving the impression that the consultee is being judged for "not listening." Role-play can be helpful in developing these skills, and such practice is a standardized element of the PREPaRE curriculum's *Workshop 2: Crisis Intervention and Recovery* (Brock, 2011).

In addition to the basic communication skills described, it is also essential for the international crisis consultant to have special knowledge of the child's unique perspective of the crisis event. In particular, when preparing to provide these services in international contexts, the crisis consultant must attend to not only the child's individuality but also to the social, cultural, and political contexts within which they live (Jones, 2008). Jones (2005), for example, reports that for Kurdish children from Northern Iraq living in temporary camps or shelters, they were most fearful of being bitten by "scorpions and snakes" (p. 269). Jones goes on to report:

> For the most part, in the 11 sites that I assessed, children made little reference to the wars that had displaced them. Their worries and fears centred on the everyday hazards and the discomforts of their current lives: fights, discrimination, beatings, mines, snakes and scorpions, heat, dust, noise, dirt, dangerous roads, sickness, the absence of space to study and, universally, the lack of space to play.
>
> (p. 269)

In other words, the international crisis consultant should not rigidly adhere to preconceived views regarding the crisis problems affecting children. Rather, they should strive to understand the context of the child when facilitating problem-solving. In the following paragraphs we provide further discussion of this essential knowledge.

Cultural and Contextual Considerations in School Crisis Consultation

Tarver and Ingraham (1998) defined multicultural consultation as "a culturally sensitive, indirect service in which the consultant adjusts the consultation services to address the needs and cultural values of the consultee, the client, or both" (p. 58). Ingraham (2014) highlights the importance of the multicultural aspects of consultation, including the organized thoughts, beliefs, and norms for interaction and communication that may influence cognitions, behaviors, and perceptions. As Soo-Hoo (1998) emphasized, understanding a person's perspective involves understanding his or her cultural, sociopolitical, and psychological contexts. This is particularly salient when considering the diverse populations served by a crisis consultation system. For instance, there may be different languages, races, ethnicities, and cultural backgrounds among consultants, consultees, and clients (Ingraham, 2014).

As student populations and communities vary, it is important that professionals involved in school crisis prevention, preparedness, response, and recovery are sensitive to cultural and contextual considerations (Brock, Reeves, & Nickerson, 2014; Hatzichristou, Jimerson, Reeves, Brock, & Nastasi, 2010). Whereas the general PREPaRE principles are applicable across diverse cultures and contexts, it is imperative that professionals consider those factors most relevant within the local context (e.g., customs, traditions, cultural norms, cultural expectations, and beliefs about mourning or receiving psychological support services). Awareness and sensitivity to these contextual considerations is important both within and across countries, states, and provinces because children and families within a given geographic location will not all share homogeneous cultures.

Case Examples

The following discussion provides two brief case examples to illustrate previous efforts to use the PREPaRE model during school crisis consultation in diverse regions of the world.

Greece

Early efforts to utilize the core principles of PREPaRE school crisis consultation internationally involved collaborations between Shane Jimerson, Stephen Brock, and Chryse Hatzichristou (e.g., Brock & Jimerson, 2008; Jimerson, 2008; Jimerson & Brock, 2008). These efforts built upon the foundation of local expertise and systems that had been previously developed. For instance, after the September 1999 earthquake in Athens, Greece, a crisis intervention program was implemented in schools (Hatzichristou, 2008) for the students to understand the natural disaster, exchange experiences, describe and express their emotions, and feel empowered. (The same program was also implemented following the 2007 wildfires in Peloponnese.) The psychoeducational interventions were designed to meet the needs of students within the classroom setting and were implemented by school psychologists in collaboration with trained teachers (Brock, Sandoval, & Lewis, 2001).

Through communications and collaborations, the PREPaRE school crisis prevention, preparedness, intervention, and response workshops were developed specifically for use in the Greek context. For example, the PREPaRE materials were initially infused with many examples and references to many educational infrastructures that are unique to the United States context (e.g., federal and state laws pertaining to school crisis plans; guidelines from the U.S. Department of Education; alignment with the incident command system required for emergency responders in the U.S.; modifications to language, such as *principal, superintendent,* and *school board,* and terms that may not be relevant within another educational system). Thus, there were extensive efforts to remove these specific referents and include language and examples that would be particularly salient within the Greek context.

Because the United States has extensive diversity, the importance of cultural and contextual considerations was already included within PREPaRE; however, further efforts were made to highlight cultural and contextual considerations particularly salient in Greece (e.g., considerations about the specific cultural heritage, spiritual beliefs, recent events such as previous wildfires and earthquakes that impact the coping of children and families within the local context). These workshops established the foundation for further local refinement and application of PREPaRE school crisis consultation within the local context by including numerous professors and professionals throughout Greece; more recently, Stephen Brock and Melissa Reeves presented contemporary PREPaRE workshops (Brock & Reeves, 2009).

The infrastructure for education systems varies, and as a result there are different consultation approaches found across these systems. Hence, an emphasis on organizational consultation (Illback, 2014) was particularly important when developing PREPaRE school crisis consultation in Greece. PREPaRE school crisis consultation is relevant to all forms of crisis prevention, preparedness, response, and recovery, such as with wildfires and student/teacher loss, which have been particularly historically relevant in Greece; recently this required local adaptations to support students, families, and school communities amidst the significant economic crisis (Hatzichristou, Adamopoulou, &

Lampropoulou, 2014; Hatzichristou, Issari, Lampropoulou, Lykitsakou, & Dimitropoulou, 2011; Hatzichristou et al., 2012).

Japan

Another illustration of using the PREP<u>a</u>RE school crisis consultation framework internationally emerged following the massive magnitude 9.0 Great East Japan earthquake that occurred near the northeast coast of Honshu, Japan, on March 11, 2011. This event triggered a tsunami that tragically destroyed, damaged, and displaced many coastal villages. The earthquake also damaged the Fukushima Dai-ichi Nuclear Power Plant, and thousands of residents in the region were evacuated as authorities worked to prevent a nuclear meltdown at those facilities. Heavy casualties and extensive damage were caused by this series of disasters. Over half a million residents were left homeless, and millions were without electricity or water for weeks following the earthquake and associated tsunami. Hundreds of thousands of residents were displaced or relocated, and over 20,000 persons died. For weeks there were widespread concerns regarding water and food contamination and the potential spread of disease. Children in the impact zones and communities throughout the country were in need of immediate and long-term support.

In the immediate aftermath, colleagues in the Japanese Association of Educational Psychologists and the Japanese Association of School Psychologists collaborated with colleagues from the United States' National Association of School Psychologists (e.g., Jimerson & Watanabe, 2011). Many of the basic principles of the PREP<u>a</u>RE school crisis consultation were immediately employed (e.g., reassuring safety and security, psychoeducation outreach and resources for professionals and families [Saeki, Ishikuma, Watanabe, & Jimerson, 2011a, 2011b, 2011c, 2011d; Saeki, Watanabe, & Jimerson, 2011a, 2011b]; processes for psychological triage).

However, the scope of the tragic events and the local cultural contextual considerations warranted special attention. For instance, many of the local support systems and educational infrastructures (including school professionals, schools, and even communities) were displaced, which complicated the immediate, short-term, and long-term support efforts typically afforded with PREP<u>a</u>RE school crisis consultations. The events also prompted further interest among educational psychologists and other school-based professionals to develop more robust preparedness and response infrastructures to support students, staff, and families. Shane Jimerson collaborated with Yayoi Watanabe and other colleagues in Japan to present the PREP<u>a</u>RE school crisis consultation framework with an emphasis on relevant cultural and contextual considerations (e.g., sensitivity to the representation of mental health supports among populations that do not historically embrace such psychological services; emphasis on existing established community support networks; attending to the guidelines for crisis preparation and response prepared by the Ministry of Education, Culture, Sports, Science and Technology; sensitivity to the salience of the recent 9.0 Great East Japan earthquake; addressing the needs of both Japanese students and specific minority populations from China, Korea, and other countries; Jimerson, 2013a, August).

Awareness of Culture and Context

Consistent with Ingraham (2014), the authors' experiences with the PREP<u>a</u>RE model in both Greece and Japan emphasized the importance of considering the multicultural aspects of consultation. As was discovered during these consultations, there were various systems level, cultural level, and contextual factors that were particularly relevant to providing school crisis consultation. Consultants need to understand that while the school crisis consultation principles are commonly applicable across many diverse contexts, the processes, timelines, and specific strategies must be responsive to the local context. Preparation and planning efforts within a given context are invaluable in helping to determine the local cultural and contextual considerations in advance of any prevention and response efforts. This awareness was an important antecedent to the international version of the PREPaRE curriculum.

The International Version of PREPaRE

During the past 3 years, Shane Jimerson has led collaborative efforts with international colleagues to develop an international version of PREPaRE specifically refined to provide a flexible framework for school crisis prevention, preparedness, response, and recovery that can be used in schools around the world. The experiences described previously in collaborating with colleagues in Greece and Japan, and additional collaborations with colleagues from over 50 countries, informed the development of the international version of PREPaRE. Revisions emphasized eliminating phrasing examples that were unnecessary and only relevant to specific contexts in the world, and they also enhanced examples illustrating key considerations across diverse contexts and cultures. For example, some countries have existing national emergency response infrastructures and protocols; however, invoking one system for all countries is not appropriate. Thus, modifications were made in the international version to highlight the relevant content without specifying the governing agency and also noting that alignment with existing emergency response infrastructures is critical for school-based professionals. This international curriculum has been presented and piloted in multiple countries during recent years, including Bangladesh, Canada, Japan, and Jamaica (e.g., Jimerson, 2012; Jimerson, 2013b, July; Jimerson et al., 2012; Jimerson, & Shahroozi, 2012). The next phase of efforts will focus on making the crisis response and recovery elements of the PREPaRE curriculum available internationally.

THE PREPaRE MODEL

We now discuss how each element of PREPaRE can be used in school crisis consultations. For an additional contemporary description of these activities the reader is referred to Brock et al. (2014).

Crisis Prevention

School crisis consultation begins with efforts to prevent crises from occurring in the first place and finds the crisis consultant working directly with a school principal and/or school safety and crisis team (who would be considered the consultees). When approaching this critical task, it is important for the crisis consultant to acknowledge that different schools in different parts of the world will face different crisis events and potential natural disasters (Jimerson et al., 2012). Thus, it is important that this element of school crisis consultation begins with assessment of the specific risks and strengths of a school context (or school system) and then employs specific and targeted crisis prevention efforts. Consequently, the consultant must have special knowledge of how to conduct both needs assessments or school safety audits and of a range of crisis prevention programs (Reeves, Kanan, & Plog, 2010; Brock et al., 2009).

The PREPaRE workshop titled *Crisis Prevention and Preparedness: Comprehensive School Safety Planning,* also known as Workshop 1 (Jimerson et al., 2013; Reeves et al., 2011), offers a "School Building Vulnerability Assessment" (Skalski, 2006) and a "Comprehensive School Safety Team Checklist" that may be especially helpful tools for school crisis consultants. The PREPaRE model also advocates for a range of crisis prevention strategies and emphasizes the need to ensure both physical and psychological safety. The former can be facilitated by knowledge of Crime Prevention through Environmental Design (Crowe, 2000; Crowe & Zahme, 1994; Robinson, 1996), and the latter requires a general understanding of how to facilitate a positive school climate, social-emotional learning, and a variety of internal and external sources of resiliency (Brock et al., 2009; Reeves et al., 2011).

Crisis Preparedness

Also considered to be a primary school crisis consultation task, crisis preparedness strives to ensure that the school (or school system) is ready to respond to those crises that cannot be, or are not, prevented. Here the crisis consultant again works directly with a school principal and/or the school safety and crisis team. The importance of these activities is emphasized by the fact it is not a question of *if* a school will be exposed to a crisis but rather *when* a school crisis event will occur. As was the case for crisis prevention, when approaching this task, the crisis consultant needs to acknowledge that different schools in different parts of the world will need to have greater or lesser degrees of preparedness for specific crisis events. In other words, school crisis consultants should not simply help schools prepare for general crisis events; they should strive to help schools prepare for the specific types of crises a particular school is most likely to face (e.g., particular types of natural disasters, potential human generated crises, suicide, homicide). However, at the same time, consultants need to recognize that crises are by definition unpredictable, and consequently the crisis plans they help schools develop must be flexible enough to be useful when addressing a broad range of crises.

Again, the PREPaRE workshop titled *Crisis Prevention and Preparedness: Comprehensive School Safety Planning* (Jimerson et al., 2013; Reeves et al., 2011) offers resources that can help the school crisis consultant facilitate school crisis preparedness. As was mentioned, the model offers the "School Building Vulnerability Assessment" (Skalski, 2006) that will be helpful as the school crisis consultant helps the school to identify the specific types of crises it needs to be prepared to address. The model also advocates for a range of crisis preparedness activities and offers guidance on how to develop, implement, and maintain school safety and crisis response teams. It also offers an examination of several different special considerations in crisis preparedness (e.g., addressing special needs students, memorials, cross-cultural issues, and working with the media; Brock et al., 2009). From the PREPaRE model the crisis consultant will find "Emergency Protocols, Drills, Exercises, and Procedures" (Cherry Creek School District, 2007; Federal Emergency Management Agency, 2003; Reeves et al., 2010; U.S. Department of Homeland Security, 2007) especially helpful while assisting the school to be better prepared to address crises.

Reaffirming Physical Safety

Common sense dictates that the immediate response to a crisis event is to ensure physical safety and, in doing so, to mitigate the risk of physical (and psychological) trauma (Haskett, Schott, Nears, & Grimmett, 2008; Hobfoll et al., 2007). As was the case with the crisis prevention and preparedness tasks, reaffirming objective physical safety typically finds the crisis consultant working directly with a school principal and/or school safety and crisis team. Obviously, such objective physical safety is prerequisite to recovery.

A special circumstance that the crisis consultant needs to be prepared to address is the instance where objective safety cannot be restored (e.g., in the case of ongoing war or threat of terrorist attacks). In such a situation the school crisis response strives to give students at least some sense of control. This may involve teaching students what they can do to minimize the risk of harm and best ensure their safety. Doing so will lessen the event's potential to generate psychological trauma, as the more controllable students view the event to be, the lower will be the degree of traumatic stress (Saylor, Belter, & Stokes, 1997). In the instance where school attendance itself would be dangerous (e.g., due to ongoing threats), virtual or online schools may be an option for maintaining some sense of routine and teaching students while at the same time better ensuring student safety.

Reaffirming Perceptions of Safety

In addition to offering guidance that helps to ensure objective physical safety, it is important for the crisis consultant to direct school administration and the school safety and crisis response teams to ensure that student perceptions of safety (i.e., their beliefs that crisis-related dangers have terminated) are also reaffirmed. In particular, it will be important to make concrete for students the actions that adults are taking on their behalf to make certain they are safe. Critical to the successful communication of these actions is how adults are reacting to the crisis, as there is an association between these reactions and traumatic stress among children. Children's exposure to adult traumatic stress reactions correlates with their own traumatic stress (Landolt, Vollrath, Timm, Gnehm, & Sennhauser, 2005; Ostrowski, Christopher, & Delahanty, 2007). Regardless of how it is reaffirmed, the belief that dangers associated with the crisis event have ended is necessary before mental health crisis intervention and recovery can begin (Barenbaum, Ruchkin, & Schwab-Stone, 2004; Brown & Bobrow, 2004).

Returning to school and reestablishing familiar rituals and routines can be important to ensuring student perceptions of safety. Of course if the school environment is not safe, this will not be possible, and in these instances the crisis consultant might suggest the use of either alternative (and physically safe) school sites or the use of online or virtual schools.

Evaluating Psychological Trauma Risk

After safety has been reaffirmed, the next crisis response task is to conduct a psychological triage of school community members who have been exposed to the crisis. Initially, this task finds the crisis consultant gathering information from consultees (e.g., caregivers) and other sources regarding crisis details and the degree to which individuals were personally exposed to the crisis (physical and/or emotional proximity to the event) and/or have preexisting personal vulnerabilities (e.g., mental illness, trauma history, developmental immaturity, limited social support resources) that will make it more difficult for them to cope with crisis-generated challenges. Referred to as *primary triage,* this initial risk screening is used to make initial mental health crisis intervention treatment decisions (Brock et al., 2009).

As the crisis intervention progresses, the next level of triage (*secondary triage*) continues to find the crisis consultant gathering information from consultees regarding how individuals are coping with crisis-related problems. However, it is at this point that the crisis response consultant may have begun to provide direct services, and from these client contacts additional information is gathered about the mental health crisis intervention treatment priorities and needs. Finally, the process of psychological triage concludes with what is referred to in the PREPaRE model as *tertiary triage.* This is the level of treatment decision-making wherein psychotherapy treatment referrals (of the most severely traumatized of individuals) are made (Brock et al., 2009).

Especially relevant to this volume's international theme is the PREPaRE model's acknowledgment that crisis consultants must have a basic understanding of the cultural and contextual factors that influence the display of crisis reactions. Simply put, what might be a common display of psychological distress in one culture may be atypical in another culture (Sandoval & Lewis, 2002). Klingman (1986), for example, in describing the interventions conducted by crisis workers as they notified parents of a school bus accident, stated that cultural awareness

> proved valuable in that they were prepared for various culturally based manifestations of traumatic grief reactions, and thus refrained from requesting the use of sedatives in cases in which the parents' reactions to a death notification on the surface seemed extreme but were in line with their cultural norms.
>
> (p. 55)

Likewise, cultural and contextual factors such as those described by Jones (2008, 2005) will also influence potential support strategies. Thus, to conduct triage and successfully make crisis intervention treatment decisions, cultural competence is critical.

The PREPaRE workshop titled *Crisis Intervention and Recovery: The Roles of School-Based Mental Health Professionals,* also known as workshop 2 (Brock, 2011), offers resources that can help school crisis consultants facilitate the process of psychological triage. For example, the model offers "Primary Risk Screening," "School Crisis Intervention Referral," and "Psychological Triage Summary Sheet" forms (Brock et al., 2009; Brock et al., 2001) that are helpful as the crisis consultant helps the school to match individual needs to specific types of crisis interventions.

Providing Interventions and Responding to Mental Health Needs

Providing mental health crisis interventions is the next element of the PREPaRE model. Three general classes of crisis intervention are offered, and from least to most directive they are: (1) reestablishing social support, (2) psychological education, and (3) psychological interventions. The specific interventions associated within each of these intervention groupings are offered in Table 11.1 (Brock et al., 2009).

Decisions regarding which interventions are provided to individuals are based upon the psychological triage discussed in the preceding section. To the extent it is possible to do so, the crisis consultant maintains the traditional consultant–consultee relationship and, only in instances wherein the client is severely traumatized will he or she leave this

Table 11.1 General Classes and Specific Types of PREPaRE Crisis Interventions

	General Classes of Crisis Intervention		
	Reestablish social support	**Psychological education**	**Psychological intervention**
Specific types of crisis interventions	• Reunite with primary caregivers • Reunite with peers and teachers • Return students to familiar environments/routines • Facilitate community connections • Empower caregivers with crisis recovery information	• Informational documents • Caregiver trainings • Classroom meetings • Student psychoeducational groups	• Classroom-based crisis intervention • Individual crisis intervention • Psychotherapy

Source: Brock et al. (2009).

role and provide direct mental health services to the client. As a rule, it is possible for the first two groups of crisis intervention (i.e., "reestablishing social support" and "psychological education") to be provided as indirect services by the consultant. Conversely, the class of interventions referred to as "psychological interventions" often requires the training and skills of a mental health professional and are thus frequently provided as a direct service by the crisis consultant.

Again, when it comes to the provision of mental health crisis intervention services, cultural competence is essential. To begin with, an understanding of culturally specific crisis recovery resources is necessary. Regarding the first class of crisis interventions (i.e., reestablishing social support), cultures vary in terms of the type and amount of social support they tend to offer. For example, Chen, Kim, Mojaverian, and Morling (2012) report that European Americans appear to provide more emotion-focused support than problem-focused support, and the Japanese exhibit the opposite pattern. Similarly, the first author's own anecdotal observations suggest that, by virtue of their promotion of the extended family, some cultures have broader and potentially more resilient social support networks. For example, the traditional Greek family often finds grandparents, godparents, and aunts/uncles to be important members of the family. Conversely, families located in western parts of the United States, where individuals tend to be more geographically dispersed, may find such resources limited to the nuclear family. In other words, the crisis consultant might expect to make use of naturally occurring social support systems to a greater extent in some contexts than in others.

In addition, there may be interactions between crisis type, cultural norms, and the availability of social support resources. For example, when it comes to the crisis of suicide, some cultures have more restrictive attitudes toward this act than do others (Jordan, 2001; Roberts, Lepkowski, & Davidson, 1998). Among groups wherein the act of suicide is more taboo, social support will be less available and consequently there will be a greater need for more direct crisis intervention services. Knowledge of these cultural attitudes and contextual considerations is important to the crisis consultant as he or she determines the extent to which direct crisis intervention services will need to be provided.

Finally, it is important to acknowledge that the acceptability of mental health services, and consequently the provision of direct mental health crisis intervention, can vary from group to group (Kouyoumdjian, Zamboanga, & Hansen, 2003; Kung, 2004). Within settings wherein asking for and/or receiving mental health services is less acceptable, the crisis consultant will want to ensure that naturally occurring social support resources have been exhausted before considering direct forms of crisis intervention. At the same time, the crisis consultant will need to acknowledge that individuals in need of direct and professional mental health crisis intervention may be more reluctant to ask for such assistance.

Again, the PREPaRE workshop titled *Crisis Intervention and Recovery: The Roles of School-Based Mental Health Professionals* (Brock, 2011) offers resources that can help the school crisis consultant facilitate the provision of mental health crisis interventions. Among the resources offered by the model are a "Sample Classroom Meeting Script and Outline" (Brock et al., 2009), "Stress Management Resources and Adaptive Coping Strategies" (Brock, Jimerson, & Zatlin, 2003), and "A Lesson Plan for Use by a Crisis Intervention Team Member when Conducting a Student Psychoeducational Group" (Brock et al., 2009). In addition, it presents a number of psychological first aid resources developed by Brymer et al. (2006).

Examining the Effectiveness

The final element of the PREPaRE model directs the crisis consultant to assist the consultee (i.e., the school principal and/or the school safety and crisis team) in examining the effectiveness of crisis prevention, preparedness, response, and recovery efforts. The importance of doing so is emphasized by the fact that each and every crisis event is unique and thus presents the consultee with a learning opportunity. Both PREPaRE workshops (Brock, 2011; Reeves et al., 2011) offer resources that can help the school crisis consultant facilitate the evaluation of crisis prevention, preparedness, response, and recovery. Among these resources are a "Questionnaire for Examining the Crisis Team's Immediate Response and Longer-Term Recovery Efforts" (Brock et al., 2009), "Interview or Focus Group Questions Used to Evaluate the Process of Crisis Response and Recovery Implementation" (Brock et al., 2009), and "Checklist: Evaluating the Crisis Response—After Incident Report (Process Analysis)" (Reeves et al., 2010).

CONCLUDING COMMENTS

The efforts to develop the PREPaRE school crisis consultation framework for use in countries around the world have been consistent with a collaborative participatory process for facilitating the development of acceptable, socially valid, effective, and sustainable programs in creating culturally specific school-based mental health programs and services (Nastasi, Vargas, Bernstein, & Jayasena, 2000; Nastasi et al., 2000). In addition to crisis content-specific knowledge/skills (prevention, preparedness, response, recovery; Brock et al., 2015), consultants also need to develop effective communication and listening skills as they are used in the consultation process (e.g., clarifying, paraphrasing, and perception checking; Rosenfield, 2004). Additionally, knowledge of problem-solving consultation processes (Frank & Kratochwill, 2014), systems and organizational considerations (Illback, 2014), and sensitivity to cultural and contextual considerations (Ingraham, 2014) are all essential aspects of the PREPaRE school crisis consultation framework. Throughout the world, it is apparent that there is an ongoing need for school crisis prevention, preparedness, response, and recovery activities, and the PREPaRE school crisis consultation framework may be used and adapted internationally.

REFERENCES

Barenbaum, J., Ruchkin, B., & Schwab-Stone, M. (2004). The psychosocial aspects of children exposed to war: Practice and policy initiatives. *Journal of Child Psychology and Psychiatry, 45,* 41–62. doi: 10.1046/j.0021-9630.2003.00304.x

Brock, S. E. (2011). *Workshop 2: Crisis intervention and recovery: The roles of school-based mental health professionals.* Bethesda, MD: National Association of School Psychologists.

Brock, S. E., & Jimerson, S. R. (2008, April). *School crisis response and intervention.* Workshop presented at University of Athens, Athens, Greece.

Brock, S. E., Jimerson, S. R., & Zatlin, R. (2003, June). *Certification of advanced training and specialization in crisis intervention skills and strategies.* Workshop presented at the California Association of School Psychologists' Summer Institute, Lake Tahoe, CA.

Brock, S. E., Nickerson, A. B., Reeves, M. A. L., Conolly-Wilson, C., Jimerson, S. R., Pesce, R. C., & Lazzaro, B. (2015). *School crisis prevention and intervention: The PREPaRE model* (2nd ed.). Bethesda, MD: National Association of School Psychologists.

Brock, S. E., Nickerson, A. B., Reeves, M. A. L., Jimerson, S. R., Lieberman, R. A., & Feinberg, T. A. (2009). *School crisis prevention and intervention: The PREPaRE model.* Bethesda, MD: National Association of School Psychologists.

Brock, S. E., & Reeves, M. A. L. (2009). *Crisis intervention & recovery: The roles of school-based mental health professionals.* Invited speakers: S. E. Brock & M. A., Reeves, Chair: C. Hatzichristou. Organized by the Graduate Program in School Psychology and the Center of Research and Practice of School Psychology, National and Kapodistrian University of Athens in collaboration with the Division of School Psychology of the Hellenic Psychological Society, Athens, Greece, March 28–29, 2009.

Brock, S. E., Reeves, M. A. L., & Nickerson, A. B. (2014). Best practices in school crisis intervention. In P. Harrison & A. Thomas (Eds.), *Best practices in school psychology: System level services* (pp. 211–230). Bethesda, MD: National Association of School Psychologists.

Brock, S. E., Sandoval, J., & Lewis, S. (2001). *Preparing for crises in the schools: A manual for building school crisis response teams* (2nd ed.). New York, NY: Wiley.

Brown, E. J., & Bobrow, A. L. (2004). School entry after a community-wide trauma: Challenges and lessons learned from September 11th, 2001. *Clinical Child and Family Psychology Review, 7,* 211–221. doi: 10.1007/s10567-004-6086-9

Brymer, M., Jacobs, A., Layne, C., Pynoos, R., Ruzek, J., Steinberg, A., . . . Watson, P. (2006). *Psychological first aid: Field operations guide* (2nd ed.). Rockville, MD: National Child Traumatic Stress Network and National Center for PTSD. Retrieved from http://www.nctsn.org/nccts/nav.do?pid=typ_terr_resources_pfa

Chen, J. M., Kim, H. S., Mojaverian, T., & Morling, B. (2012). Culture and social support provision: Who gives what and why. *Personality and Social Psychology Bulletin, 38,* 3–14. doi: 10.1177/0146167211427309

Cherry Creek School District. (2007). *Emergency response/crisis management training.* Workshop presented to staff as part of a Title IV Safe and Drug Free Schools Grant, Greenwood Village, CO.

Crowe, T. D. (2000). *Crime prevention through environmental design: Applications of architectural design and space.* Boston, MA: Butterworth-Heinemann.

Crowe, T. D., & Zahme, D. L. (1994, Fall). Crime prevention through environmental design. *Land Development,* 22–27. Retrieved from http://www.popcenter.org/Responses/closing_streets/PDFs/Crowe_Zahm_1994.pdf

Erchul, W. P., & Sheridan, S. M. (2014). *Handbook of research in school consultation* (2nd ed.). New York, NY: Routledge.

Federal Emergency Management Agency. (2003). *Emergency management institute independent study: Exercise design.* Washington, DC: Author.

Frank, J. L., & Kratochwill, T. R. (2014). School-based problem-solving consultation: Plotting a new course for evidence-based research and practice in consultation. In W. P. Erchul & S. M. Sheridan (Eds.), *Handbook of research in school consultation* (2nd ed., pp. 18–39). New York, NY: Routledge.

Haskett, M. A., Scott, S. S., Nears, K., & Grimmett, M. A. (2008). Lessons from Katrina: Disaster mental health services in the Gulf Coast region. *Professional Psychology: Research and Practice, 39,* 93–99. doi: 10.1037/0735-7028.39.1.93

Hatzichristou, C. (Ed.). (2008). Στήριξη των παιδιών σε καταστάσεις κρίσεων [Supporting children in crisis]. Center for Research and Practice of School Psychology, University of Athens. Athens, Greece: Τυπωθήτω.

Hatzichristou, C., Adamopoulou, E., & Lampropoulou, A. (2014). A multilevel approach of promoting resilience and positive school climate in the school community during unsettling times. In S. Prince-Embury & D. H. Saklofske (Eds.), *Resilience interventions in diverse communities* (pp. 299–325). New York, NY: Springer.

Hatzichristou, C., Issari, P., Lampropoulou, A., Lykitsakou, K., & Dimitropoulou, P. (2011). The development of a multi-level model for crisis prevention and intervention in the Greek educational system. *School Psychology International, 32,* 464–483.

Hatzichristou, C., Jimerson, S., Reeves, M., Brock, S., & Nastasi, B. (2010). *Cross-cultural and cross-national considerations in crisis intervention (NASP special session).* Symposium presented at the 41st Annual Convention of National Association of School Psychologists, March 1–6, Chicago, USA.

Hatzichristou, C., Kati, A., Lykitsakou, K., Lampropoulou, A., Dimitropoulou, P., Yfanti, T., . . . Georgouleas, G. (2012). *Διαχείριση Κρίσεωνστη Σχολική Κοινότητα* [Crisis intervention in the school community]. Athens, Greece: ipothito.

Hobfoll, W. E., Watson, P., Bell, C. C., Bryant, R. A., Brymer, M. J., Friedman, M. J., . . . Ursano, R. J. (2007). Five essential elements of immediate and mid-term mass trauma intervention: Empirical evidence. *Psychiatry: Interpersonal and Biological Processes, 70,* 283–315. doi: 10.1521/psyc.2007.70.4.283

Illback, R. J. (2014). Organization development and change facilitation in school settings: Theoretical and empirical foundations. In W. P. Erchul & S. M. Sheridan (Eds.), *Handbook of research in school consultation* (2nd ed., pp. 276–303). New York, NY: Routledge.

Ingraham, C. L. (2014). Studying multicultural aspects of consultation. In W. P. Erchul & S. M. Sheridan (Eds.), *Handbook of research in school consultation* (2nd ed., pp. 323–348). New York, NY: Routledge.

Jimerson, S. R. (2008, April). *An overview of school crisis preparedness, prevention, and intervention: The PREPaRE model.* International Symposium Entitled: "Crisis Management: Prevention and Intervention in the Community", C. Hatzichristou (Chair). Organized by the Graduate Program in School Psychology and the Center of Research and Practice of School Psychology, National and Kapodistrian University of Athens, April 4, Megaron Plus, Athens, Greece.

Jimerson, S. R. (2012, April). *School crisis prevention & intervention: The International PREPaRE model.* Workshop presented for College of Humanities, Behavioural and Social Sciences, Northern Caribbean University, Jamaica.

Jimerson, S. R. (2013a, August). *PREPaRE international: School crisis prevention, preparedness, and intervention curriculum.* Invited presentation at the Annual Convention of the Japanese Association of Educational Psychologists. Tokyo, Japan.

Jimerson, S. R. (2013b, July). *International PREPaRE: School Crisis Prevention, Preparedness, and Intervention Curriculum.* Presented at the Annual Convention of the International School Psychology Association, University of Porto, Porto, Portugal.

Jimerson, S. R., & Brock, S. E. (2008, April). *Crisis prevention, preparedness, intervention & recovery: The PREPaRE model of school crisis response.* Invited speakers: S. R., Jimerson & S. E. Brock, Chair: C. Hatzichristou. Organized by the Graduate Program in School Psychology and the Center of Research and Practice of School Psychology, National and Kapodistrian University of Athens in collaboration with the Division of School Psychology of the Hellenic Psychological Society, Athens, Greece, April 5–6, 2008.

Jimerson, S. R., Brown, J. A., Saeki, E., Watanabe, Y., Kobayashi, T., & Hatzichristou, C. (2012). Natural disasters. In S. E. Brock & S. R. Jimerson (Eds.), *Best practices in school crisis prevention and intervention* (2nd ed., pp. 573–596). Bethesda, MD: National Association of School Psychologists.

Jimerson, S. R., Brown, J. A., & Shahroozi, S. R. (2012, September). *International PREPaRE: School crisis prevention and intervention curriculum: Highlights and updates.* Paper presented at the California Association of School Psychologists Conference, Costa Mesa, CA.

Jimerson, S. R., Brown, J. A., Shahroozi, S. R., Watanabe, Y., & Brown-Earl, O. (2012, July). *International PREPaRE: A global school crisis prevention and preparedness curriculum.* Paper presented at the International School Psychology Association Conference, McGill University, Montreal, Canada.

Jimerson, S. R., & Shahroozi, S. R. (July, 2012). *International PREPaRE: School crisis prevention and preparedness: Comprehensive school safety planning.* Workshop presented at the International School Psychology Association Conference, McGill University, Montreal, Canada.

Jimerson, S. R., & Watanabe, Y. (2011). Inspirational international response. *Communique, 40*(4). Bethesda, MD: National Association of School Psychologists. Retrieved from http://www.nasponline.org/publications/cq/40/4/inspirational-international-response.aspx

Jones, L. (2005). Soapbox: A letter from Northern Iraq, 2003. *Clinical Child Psychology and Psychiatry, 10,* 266–272. doi: 10.1177/1359104505051215

Jones, L. (2008). Responding to the needs of children in crisis. *International Review of Psychiatry, 20,* 291–303. doi: 10.1080/09540260801996081

Jordan, J. R. (2001). Is suicide bereavement different: A reassessment of the literature. *Suicide & Life-Threatening Behavior, 31*, 91–102. doi: 10.1521/suli.31.1.91.21310

Klingman, A. (1986). Emotional first aid during the impact phase of a mass school disaster. *Emotional First Aid, 3*, 51–57.

Kouyoumdjian, H., Zamboanga, B. L., & Hansen, D. J. (2003). Barriers to community mental health services for Latinos: Treatment considerations. *Clinical Psychology: Science and Practice, 10*, 394–422. doi: 10.1093/clipsy/bpg041

Kratochwill, T. R. (2008). Best practices in school-based problem-solving consultation: Applications in prevention and intervention systems. In A. Thomas & J. Grimes (Eds.), *Best practices in school psychology V* (pp. 1673–1688). Bethesda, MD: National Association of School Psychologists.

Kung, W. W. (2004). Cultural and practical barriers to seeking mental health treatment for Chinese Americans. *Journal of Community Psychology, 32*, 27–43. doi: 10.1002/jcop.10077

Landolt, M. A., Vollrath, M., Timm, K., Gnehm, H. E., & Sennhauser, F. (2005). Predicting posttraumatic stress symptoms in children after road traffic accidents. *Journal of the American Academy of Child & Adolescent Psychiatry, 44*, 1276–1283. doi: 10.1097/01.chi.0000181045.13960.67

Nastasi, B. K., Vargas, K., Bernstein, R., & Jayasena, A. (2000). Conducting participatory culture-specific consultation: A global perspective on multicultural consultation. *School Psychology Review, 29*, 401–413. Retrieved from www.nasponline.org

Nastasi, B. K., Vargas, K., Schensul, S. L., Silva, K. T., Schnesul, J. J., & Ramayake, P. (2000). The participatory intervention model: A framework for conceptualizing and promoting intervention acceptability. *School Psychology Quarterly, 15*, 207–232. doi: 10.1037/h0088785

Ostrowski, S. A., Christopher, N. C., & Delahanty, D. L. (2007). Brief report: The impact of maternal posttraumatic stress disorder symptoms and child gender on risk for persistent posttraumatic stress disorder symptoms in child trauma victims. *Journal of Pediatric Psychology, 32*, 338–342. doi: 10.1093/jpepsy/jsl003

Reeves, M. A., Kanan, L., & Plog, A. (2010). *Comprehensive planning for safe learning environments: A school professional's guide to integrating physical and psychological safety: Prevention through recovery.* New York, NY: Routledge Publishing.

Reeves, M. A., Nickerson, A. B., Conolly-Wilson, C. N., Susan, M. K., Lazzaro, B. R., Jimerson, S. R., & Pesce, R. C. (2011). *Workshop 1: Crisis prevention and preparedness: Comprehensive school safety planning.* Bethesda, MD: National Association of School Psychologists.

Roberts, R. L., Lepkowski, W. J., & Davidson, K. K. (1998). Dealing with the aftermath of a student suicide: A T.E.A.M. approach. *NASSP Bulletin, 82*, 53–59. Retrieved from http://bul.sagepub.com/content/82/597/53.abstract

Robinson, M. B. (1996). The theoretical development of CPTED: 25 years of responses to C. Ray Jeffery. In W. Laufer & F. Adler (Eds.), *Advances in criminological theory* (Vol. 8). New Brunswick NJ: Transaction Publishers. Retrieved from http://web.archive.org/web/20040908004516/http://www.acs.appstate.edu/dept/ps-cj/vitacpted2.html

Rosenfield, S. (2004). Consultation as dialogue: The right words at the right time. In N. M. Lambert, I. Hylander, & J. H. Sandoval (Eds.), *Consultee-centered consultation: Improving the quality of professional services in schools and community organizations* (pp. 337–347). New York, NY: Erlbaum.

Saeki, E., Ishikuma, T., Watanabe, Y., & Jimerson, S. R. (2011a). *Identifying severely traumatized children: Tips for parents and educators* (also available in Japanese). Bethesda, MD: National Association of School Psychologists. Retrieved from www.nasponline.org

Saeki, E., Ishikuma, T., Watanabe, Y., & Jimerson, S. R. (2011b). *Quick facts and tips: Crisis reactions* (also available in Japanese). Bethesda, MD: National Association of School Psychologists. Retrieved from www.nasponline.org

Saeki, E., Ishikuma, T., Watanabe, Y., & Jimerson, S. R. (2011c). *Quick facts and tips: Risk factors for trauma reaction* (also available in Japanese). Bethesda, MD: National Association of School Psychologists. Retrieved from www.nasponline.org

Saeki, E., Ishikuma, T., Watanabe, Y., & Jimerson, S. R. (2011d). *Quick facts and tips: Tips for supporting children and youth* (also available in Japanese). Bethesda, MD: National Association of School Psychologists. Retrieved from www.nasponline.org

Saeki, E., Watanabe, Y., & Jimerson, S. R. (2011a). *Times of tragedy: Preventing suicide in troubled children and youth—Tips for parents and schools* (also available in Japanese). Bethesda, MD: National Association of School Psychologists. Retrieved from www.nasponline.org

Saeki, E., Watanabe, Y., & Jimerson, S. R. (2011b). *Times of tragedy: Preventing suicide in troubled children and youth—Tips for school personnel or crisis team members* (also available in Japanese). Bethesda, MD: National Association of School Psychologists. Retrieved from www.nasponline.org

Sandoval, J., & Lewis, S. (2002). Cultural considerations in crisis intervention. In S. E. Brock, P. J. Lazarus, & S. R. Jimerson (Eds.), *Best practices in school crisis prevention and intervention* (pp. 293–308). Bethesda, MD: National Association of School Psychologists.

Saylor, C. F., Belter, R., & Stokes, S. J. (1997). Children and families coping with disaster. In S. A. Wolchik & I. N. Sandler (Eds.), *Handbook of children's coping: Linking theory and intervention* (pp. 361–383). New York, NY: Plenum.

Skalski, S. (2006). *School building vulnerability assessment.* Denver, CO: Department of School Psychology, University of Colorado, Denver.

Soo-Hoo, T. (1998). Applying frame of reference and reframing techniques to improve school consultation in multicultural settings. *Journal of Educational and Psychological Consultation, 9,* 325–345. doi: 10.1207/s1532768xjepc0904_3

Tarver, B. S., & Ingraham, C. L. (1998). Culture as a central component to consultation: A call to the field. *Journal of Educational and Psychological Consultation, 9,* 57–72. doi: 10.1207/s1532768xjepc0901_3

United States Department of Homeland Security. (2007). *Homeland security exercise and evaluation program (HSEEP).* Washington, DC: Author. Retrieved from https://hseep.dhs.gov/pages/1001_HSEEP7.aspx

Part IV

IMPLEMENTING CONSULTATION
SERVICES IN THE SCHOOLS

12

CONSULTATION AND THE ROLE OF THE SCHOOL PSYCHOLOGIST
Barriers and Opportunities

Peter Farrell and Kevin Woods

INTRODUCTION

The view that the work of school psychologists[1] would be more effective if they increased the amount of time they spent on school-based consultation is not new. Indeed, discussions on the importance of consultation in providing effective mental health services for children and adults go back several decades (see Caplan 1963, 1970), and it is this pioneering work that is often seen as the stimulus for school psychologists to adopt these approaches. Following Caplan's seminal publications, there followed a number of papers on the development of the profession of school psychology that discussed the rationale for and described different approaches to consultation, and these often included evaluations of its impact (see, e.g., Medway, 1979).

This has led to a plethora of publications that have stressed the need for school psychologists to adopt school-based consultation as their principal method of working. These include papers emanating from the 2002 Futures Conference (Dawson, et al., 2004) that were strongly supported by Curtis, Grier, and Hunley (2004). They reinforce points made in an earlier paper (Sheridan & Gutkin, 2000) and urge school psychologists to move away from "medical" models of service delivery and to adopt systems-based approaches that emphasize collaborative problem-solving and consultation, a view which is also reinforced by Ehrhardt-Padgett, Hatzichristou, Kitson, and Meyers (2004) and Erchul and Martens (2010). Similar pleas are made from school psychologists working in other countries. For example, Hatzichristou (2002) and Kikas (1999), referring to the developing role of school psychology in Estonia and Greece, respectively, stress the need for school psychologists to adopt consultative approaches to their work.

There are also several accounts in the UK of educational psychologists adopting consultation as their principal method of working (see, e.g., Cording, 2011; Kennedy, Cameron, & Monsen, 2009; Kennedy, Frederickson, & Monsen, 2008; Wagner, 2008). These papers reflect the acceleration in interest in consultative approaches that took place in the UK during the 1990s as the impact of government legislation on special educational needs created increasing demands for educational psychologists to respond to individual child referrals. In short, consultation was attractive because it supported educational psychologists to better manage increasing caseloads (Forrest, Hinnigan, Keenaghan, & Owen, 1992).

Despite the large volume of literature and expressed benefits of school-based consultation, some writers have commented that relatively few school psychologists appear to be working in this way (see, e.g., Ahtola & Niemi, 2013; Bartolo, 2010; Curtis, 2002; Curtis et al., 2004; Hosp & Reschly, 2002; Reschly, 2000). Indeed, in a recent survey, Castillo, Curtis, and Gelley (2012) report that approximately 10% of the members of the National Association of School Psychologists (NASP) spend their time in individual consultation and 6% in systems-level consultation activities, with the majority of their time devoted to special education–related activities.

In this chapter, we discuss some of the subtle and often unspoken barriers that may have prevented school psychologists from abandoning traditional and predominantly individual-assessment focused ways of working. Following a brief review of the definition of consultation as it may apply to the work of the school psychologist, we consider some of the reasons why school psychologists have difficulties in adopting consultative approaches and offer some promising ways forward. Although the main focus is on the work of school psychologists in the UK and the U.S., implications for the development of school psychology services in other countries are also considered.

DEFINING CONSULTATION IN RELATION TO THE WORK OF SCHOOL PSYCHOLOGISTS

There are a number of definitions of the term *consultation*. In the "Instructions for Contributors" to the journal of *Educational and Psychological Consultation*, for example, consultation is described quite simply as "a process that facilitates problem solving for individuals, groups and organisations." Several authors elaborate this broad definition. For example, Wagner (2000) refers to consultation as being a "collaborative and recursive process that combines joint problem exploration, assessment, intervention and review" (p. 11). Some consultative approaches adopt particular theoretical perspectives, for example, interactional and systemic (Osborne, 1994), psychodynamic (Caplan, 1970) or process orientation (Farouk, 2004). Others have developed models such as behavioral consultation (Kratochwill & Bergan, 1993), instructional consultation (Rosenfield, 2002), problem-solving consultation (Kratochwill & Pittman, 2002), and responsive system consultation (Denton, Hasbrouck, & Sekaquaptewa, 2003; Hughes, Hasbrouck, Serdahl, Heidgerken, & McHaney, 2001).

Some years ago, Gutkin and Curtis (1982) concluded that there were nine key characteristics of school consultation: (1) a greater emphasis on direct work with adults rather than children/young people; (2) a trusting relationship between consultant and consultee; (3) neither consultant nor consultee has power over the other; (4) the consultee is actively involved; (5) consultees have the right to accept or reject suggestions made by the consultant; (6) the relationship is voluntary; (7) the consultation is confidential; (8) the focus is on work-related problems; and (9) the consultant has the dual roles of remediation and prevention. More succinctly, Strein, Cramer, and Lawser (2003) define consultation as "models or specific practices of individual, group or organizational consultation in the schools, including in-service training for staff" (p. 424).

Although there are differences in emphasis, definitions of consultation have much in common. Essentially, they stress that school psychologists can enhance their impact on helping children and young people if they increase the time they spend with the consultee (typically a teacher or related professional) and less time in direct work with children. To do this effectively, it is important for them to have a detailed knowledge of the system where children live and work (school, family, and community), to develop mutually supportive trusting relationships with people who are part of the system, and to work jointly with all relevant parties adopting a problem-solving framework. Through working in this way, schools psychologists should empower teachers and others to become more effective practitioners, and hence they will have a more potent impact on helping vulnerable children and their families, including those from diverse and multicultural communities, than they would if they worked solely with individual children.

Despite the considerable degree of congruence in the definitions of the consultation approach, there does not appear to be a clear statement of work that is *not* consultative. The assumption appears to be that the traditional role of the school psychologist, that is, one that does not involve consultation, is to carry out an individual assessment of a child who has been referred as being a "problem," to inform the parents and the teachers of the findings, and to make recommendations. These findings and recommendations are typically based on the results of a range of diagnostic procedures, often psychometric tests, which are designed to find out what is "wrong" with the child. This, it appears, is the very antithesis of the consultative approach.

In practice, of course, it is relatively rare for a school psychologist to work in such a way. Those who adopt this "traditional" approach would normally discuss the child's difficulties with the teachers and parents, and they would seek their views on different ways in which the child might be helped; good practice indicates that they would not rely solely on the results of the psychometric assessments. In this sense, there is always likely to be a client-centered consultative element to the work of the most traditional school psychologist who works in an individual referral-based system. Hence, it is slightly simplistic to say that a school psychologist either works in a consultative way or does not. In reality, school psychologists probably use consultative methods to some extent in all their work, but their commitment to and confidence in using this approach may vary considerably.

This discussion indicates that definitions of consultation in relation to the work of school psychologists are on a continuum. On the one side, school psychologists who spend the majority of their time working with children who have been referred to them because they have difficulties in learning and/or behavior will still use consultation in their discussions with teachers and the children's parents. On other side, a school psychologist may choose to work predominantly with teachers and other school staff and rarely with individual children. As a result of these consultations, these staff will feel empowered to work more effectively with the children, and because the school psychologist is working with the school system, such changes are more likely to be sustainable. It is our impression that publications in the U.S. and elsewhere on school psychology practice in consultation have adopted the latter side of the continuum as the preferred model (see, e.g., Burns, 2004; Dennis, 2004; Farouk, 2004; Kennedy et al., 2009; Larney, 2003; Perez-Gonzalez, Garcia-Ros, & Gomez-Artiga, 2004; Sheridan, Clarke, & Burt, 2007).

In relation to the extent to which school psychologists have incorporated consultation into their everyday practice, surveys on the work of school psychologists in the U.S. suggests that they still spend relatively little time on this activity. Hosp and Reschly

(2002), for example, found that school psychologists spent from 50 to 66% of their time on formal psychoeducational evaluations and around 25% of their time on consultation-related activities. These findings were little different from those of an earlier survey (Reschly, 2000) and are supported by Curtis (2002).

From an international perspective, the International School Psychology Association (ISPA) survey on the role of school psychologists in different countries (Jimerson et al., 2004) found that school psychologists in five countries only spent between 5% and 20% of their time in consultation-related activities. In a more recent study, Jimerson, Oakland, and Yu (2010) found that although school psychologists from 48 countries who took part in their survey commented that consultation with administrators was part of their work, very few used this approach to bring about organizational or systems change, a key objective of school-based consultation; the vast majority devoted the bulk of their time to individual counseling with children and young people and to individual psychological asessments using IQ tests.

In relation to the United Kingdom, evidence of the extent to which educational psychologists have incorporated consultation into their everyday work is more encouraging. Several educational psychological services promote consultation as the principal approach underpinning their work (see websites for the following local authorities in the UK: Aberdeen City Council, 2012; the London Borough of Richmond, 2011; Southwark Council, 2011). These developments are reflected by Dunsmuir, Brown, Iyadurai, and Monsen (2009) and Leadbetter (2006) who suggest that, over the past two decades, most educational psychology services in the UK have incorporated consultative principles into their ways of working. A number of other British psychologists (for example, Gillies, 2000; Turner, Robins, & Doran, 1996; Wagner, 2000; Watkins, 2000) offer examples of consultation in action in UK psychological services. However, Cording (2011), while acknowledging this literature, found that many educational psychologists were unclear about whether they had the skills and expertise to work effectively using consultation and that they felt under pressure from teachers to adopt more traditional approaches.

SOME BARRIERS TO CONSULTATION FOR THE SCHOOL PSYCHOLOGIST

The general conclusion from the publications referred to in the previous section is that, despite a clear professional view of the positive value of consultative approaches in school psychology practice, there is evidence suggesting that school psychologists may still be reluctant to embrace the approach. In this section, we discuss some of the interconnected barriers that may be preventing school psychologists from working in this way.

School Psychologists: Victims of their History?

There is undoubtedly a strong influence of history upon the current work landscape and job roles of any profession. With this in mind, it has to be remembered that the profession of school psychology is still relatively new. In the UK, psychological services only began to be established in the 1960s. At the time of the Summerfield report (Department of Education and Science, 1968), there were as few as 350 educational psychologists in England and Wales. In order for the profession to grow, it was important to establish some key tasks that could only be done by educational psychologists and which were in demand from parents, teachers, doctors, and other related professionals. In the UK, two such tasks emerged that were closely related to each other: the administration of individual intelligence (IQ) tests and the assessment (evaluation) of children requiring special educational provision. The impact of these tasks on the role and work of school psychologists around the world is considered next.

Developments in our understanding of intelligence—in particular its relation to academic achievement and, most important, the development of instruments to measure intelligence—closely mirror the growth in the profession of school psychologists. The origins of such instruments were quintessentially psychological, and hence it seemed logical that it should be psychologists who should use them in applied settings such as schools and hospitals. As an emerging profession, it was crucial to identify a task that could only be performed by someone in that profession, and IQ testing provided the perfect example. Here was a practical method of applying psychology that was seen to be of value to schools, parents, and doctors and which was derived from the discipline of psychology. It was therefore a task that should rightly be carried out by trained psychologists. In the UK, this position was greatly strengthened by an agreement that individually administered IQ tests should be "closed," that is, they were only for use in clinical settings by appropriately trained applied psychologists. Hence, IQ testing was something that no other professional could do—a truly distinctive task and one which therefore greatly contributed to the development and identity of the profession (see Farrell, 2010, for a more detailed discussion of this issue).

A second key distinctive task for educational psychologists in the UK and for school psychologists in the U.S. was the assessment of pupils who may require special educational provision. This also has its origins in the growth in the importance of IQ testing. Organizations such as the World Health Organization gave credibility to the importance of the IQ by labelling children with different degrees of learning difficulties based on their IQ score (WHO, 1968). Thus, school psychologists could test the child and assign a label that would have direct implications for educational provision. All of this was enshrined in legislation and, without the involvement of the school psychologist, the child might not receive the services that were thought to be needed. Again, this role has been hugely influential in defining the role of school psychologist and in stimulating the growth in numbers entering the profession. Furthermore, it has helped employers to develop a clear understanding about what they can expect from the school psychologist.

Hence, the rapid development of the profession of school psychology can, to a great extent, be explained by school psychologists being assigned a unique role in IQ testing and special education assessments. As Reschly (2000) points out, without these tasks being assigned to school psychologists, the profession would not have become so well established so quickly. Yet proscribing the role of the school psychologist to these specific tasks may be counterproductive to the development and operation of consultative approaches to services to schools and families. Arguably, these tasks are rooted in the medical model, emphasizing a summative rather than formative role, where problems are seen to be centered within the child and where they can be explored through the psychologist working in a separate room, testing the child, and using the results to predict educational performance. This way of working tends to ignore the contribution that the school or family can make toward causing the problem in the first place and toward prevention and intervention for individuals, groups, families, and communities.

In addition, the findings and implications of the psychometric tests results tend to be accepted as valid.

Despite the wealth of recent literature that is critical of the role of IQ testing (see, e.g., Farrell, 2010; Restori, Gresham, & Cook, 2008), of the relevance of the medical model, and of the effectiveness of special education provision (Sheridan & Gutkin, 2000), evidence from studies referred to earlier (Curtis et al., 2004; DfEE, 2000; Jimerson et al., 2004; Jimerson & Oakland, 2010) indicates that school psychologists still spend the bulk of their time undertaking formal special education evaluations. Similarly, in relation to approaches to psychoeducational assessment, a number of studies have also shown that school psychologists are reluctant to abandon traditional IQ testing (see, e.g., Burns, 2004; Shapiro, Angello, & Eckert, 2004). Studies in the UK (Farrell, Harraghy, & Petrie, 1996; Rees, Rees, & Farrell, 2003) also suggest that IQ testing remains a core part of the educational psychologist's role.

It is difficult to resolve this paradox. On the one hand, most recent literature on the developing role of school psychologists is extremely critical of IQ testing, the medical model of working, and gate-keeping roles in special education assessments. Alternatives that are based on consultative approaches are advocated strongly. Yet school psychologists seem reluctant to change their practices. Are we as a profession partly to blame for this? In order to establish our credentials as a new profession in the early days, we stressed the fact that we were the *only* people who had the expertise and training to administer IQ tests and to use the findings to make recommendations for special education. Are school psychologists, who have been brought up in this tradition, reluctant to move forward and to abandon some of their traditional practices for fear that they will be losing their professional identity and distinctive role? And, furthermore, if they lose distinctive role, might schools and local authorities no longer feel the need to employ them? Hence a fear of the consequences of breaking away from traditional roles can represent a major barrier to change.

The Social Context in Which School Psychologists Work

School psychologists do not work in a vacuum. Through their work in schools and with local authorities, they have to be mindful of the needs and wishes of employers, teachers, and other professional staff. To question these people and to challenge their views could result in the school psychologists' advice being ignored and, in exceptional circumstances, to their services being terminated. Schools usually refer a child to a school psychologist because they think there is something "wrong" with him or her, for example, thinking that the problem is located within the child's personality or lack of intelligence. Through working directly with the child, the school psychologist is colluding with this initial view and may be masking, or playing down, other issues that might well be affecting the child's performance, for example, the poor quality of teaching, the management in the school, or chaotic relationships in the family. All these factors may be known to the school psychologist, but, because of the nature of the working relationship with the school, where the focus is on the referred child, the school psychologist may be reluctant to mention them.

This, of course, can be a key barrier to consultation, as the basis of the school psychologist's involvement is to respond to the referral of an individual pupil causing concern to the school. Both the teachers and the school psychologist may feel comfortable within this role because it causes minimum threat to their working relationship as the center of attention is on the referred child. In consultation, the focus of the work is likely to be on the school, the relationships between the teachers, the curriculum, and so on. An open and frank discussion of these issues involving several people can, quite understandably, leave school staff feeling threatened and under scrutiny, and the school psychologist may not want to engage in such discussions for fear that their relationship with the school will be put at risk.

This problem may be exacerbated when the school directly employs the school psychologist or when there is a competitive market for providing school psychological services. In the present English context, the majority of psychological services are directly purchased by (traded to) schools and so customer satisfaction may, notwithstanding the maintenance of ethical standards, affect how and which services are delivered by educational psychologists (Woods, 2014). It is in the nature of the school psychologist's work that the needs of the employer may not always coincide with the needs of the client (child). It is possible, for example, that the outcomes of a consultation approach would be to highlight the inadequacies in a school that certain key staff may be unwilling to acknowledge. These staff can therefore put pressure on the school psychologist to explain a child's problem in terms of his or her "unsolvable" problems that could only be helped by placement in a special school. Once again, in cases such as these, school psychologists may be unwilling to confront the school about the real problem (something within the school), as it may make it harder for them to work effectively with the school in the future and the school may consider employing another school psychologist. This makes it difficult for the school psychologist to move toward working in a consultative way. The net result of all this is that the school may carry on as before, the child is removed to another school, and the school psychologist colludes with acknowledged poor practice in the school.

This discussion indicates that the social context in which school psychologists work inevitably means that they have to be mindful of the views of other professional colleagues, some of whom may be in positions of power, for example, staff in schools and local authorities. These professionals may not be interested in engaging in joint problem-solving with the psychologist and may feel uncomfortable with the suggestion that they, themselves, are contributing to the creation and maintenance of children's problems. In response to this pressure, school psychologists may be unwilling to address those issues and will instead focus their attention, using traditional approaches, on those with the least power: the child and family.

The Role of the Professional Associations

In a seminal chapter on international school psychology, Oakland (2000) makes the point that a key part of establishing effective school psychology services in any country lies in the development of strong national associations. In the UK, for example, the Association of Educational Psychologists (AEP) and the Division of Educational and Child Psychology (DECP) have played major roles in establishing the profession. The same can be said of the National Association of School Psychologists (NASP) and Division 16 of the American Psychological Association (APA) in the U.S. All these organizations can be called upon to represent the profession by governments and other national bodies, and they all write policy documents and position papers on the development of the profession. In addition, they publish high quality professional journals and run annual conferences.

There are, however, some interesting potential dilemmas that are associated with having strong professional associations for school psychologists when at the same time they are being encouraged to develop more consultative approaches. One of the key roles of any professional association representing school psychologists is to set clear boundaries that depict who can and cannot enter the profession, the knowledge and skills that school psychologists should possess on completing their training programs, and the range of work that they should normally undertake. As the profession became established in the UK, the AEP and the DECP were successful in stipulating these requirements. In so doing, they restricted entry to the profession to applicants with clearly defined preentry qualifications, and they reinforced the view that there are some key tasks that should only be carried out by educational psychologists. Some of these key tasks focused on the individual assessment (evaluation) of children who may have special educational needs and for whom additional resources may be needed. There is an implication that this was the *only* role that the associations stated should be solely restricted to school psychologists.

In contrast, neither the AEP nor the DECP in the UK has stipulated that a key and distinguishing role for school psychologists is in working in a consultative capacity and that no other professional should be permitted to work in this way. If a school or local authority invited nonpsychologists to work as consultants in a school to work on, for example, the development of behavior-management programs or mental health prevention, the professional associations representing school psychologists would not state that this role was the sole prerogative of their members. If, however, the school or local authority suggested that another professional (e.g., a support teacher) should carry out individual assessments on children and make recommendations for special educational provision, it is likely that the AEP and the DECP would protest vehemently and state that this was a distinctive skill that could *only* be done by an educational psychologist.

This suggests that the role the professional associations are the most keen to protect is that associated with traditional work: individual psychoeducational evaluations (assessments). Other work, including consultative approaches, seems to be less precious. In this context, is it surprising that some school psychologists are reluctant to move toward working more consultatively?

Expertise Needed for School Psychologists to Work Consultatively

A final factor that may act as a barrier to school psychologists adopting school-based consultation as their principal method of working lies in the knowledge and expertise needed to work effectively in this way.

Essentially, to be an effective consultant, school psychologists need to have skills and knowledge in two complementary areas. First, and perhaps foremost, they need to possess expert knowledge and skills in the field of school psychology theory and practice. Teachers and other school staff would not consult with a school psychologist unless they felt that these professionals possessed expert knowledge in, for example, children's development and learning, approaches to overcoming literacy difficulties, classroom management, various therapeutic approaches, and many other areas. After all, these topics form the basis of the curriculum in professional training programs for school psychologists. Indeed, the initial request for a consultation meeting is almost always related to a child's (or a group of children's) problems with learning and behavior. For example, a teacher may wish to consult with a school psychologist about approaches to tackling bullying in schools or effective approaches to support children with disabilities in a mainstream classroom. The school psychologist should possess knowledge and expertise in each of these areas on which they would draw during the consultation process.

The second key prerequisite area for effective school-based consultation relates to interpersonal skills. These include the ability to work effectively with other adults, to share expertise, to facilitate during meetings, to empower others to come to decisions, to synthesize complex and sometimes contradictory information, and to help the consultees formulate a plan of action. Hence, in contrast to "traditional" work in which school psychologists spend the bulk of their time in a separate room working with an individual child often out of sight from other adults, school-based consultation is more of a public activity. The school psychologist is working directly with one or more adults, many of whom may be older and more experienced practitioners, and some may hold entrenched views about the problem being discussed and/or about the competence (or incompetence) of the school psychologist! Hence, the arena in which school-based consultation takes place is more complex and potentially more threatening to the school psychologist than the tradition of working alone with a child in a separate room. Is it surprising, therefore, that the newly qualified school psychologist (probably in their mid-20s) embarking on their new career and anxious to please teachers and other school staff, many of whom have been working in the school for several years, will spend the bulk of their time responding to teachers' requests for them to work with children on a one-to-one basis? And, once they begin working in this way, it is harder to change their practice and to increase the amount of time they spend on school-based consultation.

OVERCOMING BARRIERS TO CONSULTATION

In the light of the previous discussion, it is important to address the question of how school psychologists can enhance their role in school-based consultation. In this section, three factors will be considered, each of which throws some light on how or whether the profession might widen its scope to deliver a consultative mode of service delivery that is effective in supporting children, schools, and families, including those from diverse and multicultural communities.

A Continuum of Service Delivery

First, given the emphasis that school psychologists currently appear to place on traditional ways of working and the implied support that this enjoys from the professional associations, it is important to ask whether school psychologists can and should work in both ways. Can we give a consistent message to a school if we accept individual referrals but at the same time plan consultation activities with the school staff? To many, the straightforward answer to this question is yes. There is nothing incompatible about the school psychologist emphasizing the two approaches at the same time in the same school. Indeed, we would argue that the question of whether to work consultatively and more directly with school staff and parents or whether to devote considerable amounts of time to direct work with children may be a false dichotomy. School psychologists understand fully the importance of the child's school and family contexts and that these settings offer the greatest potential to bring about change for the child. At the same time, school psychologists have expert knowledge and skills in child development, family systems, adult–child interactions, group processes, child and adult well-being, communication skills, and general problem-solving. School psychologists are expected to bring this expertise to bear in school- and family-based consultation in ways that are both credible and ethical. To do this may well require individual assessment, observation, and sometimes direct intervention by the school psychologist; there is nothing essentially "medical" or "within child" about the school psychologist bringing information, gathered firsthand and purposively, to the school-based or family-based consultation (see also Jones, 2003). To rely solely on secondhand information provided by a teacher may be unreliable, even unethical, since the school psychologist's expertise clearly brings additional insights on child-related concerns to teachers, parents, and other professionals.

This view that individual child assessment work can be incorporated within a school-based consultation model has been adopted by some educational psychology services in the UK (Aberdeen City Council, 2012; Kelly, 2008; the London Borough of Richmond, 2011; Southwark Council, 2011). These services have adopted consultation approaches with all their schools and have attempted to abandon traditional individual referral-based approaches altogether. This does not, of course mean that school psychologists in these services do not work with individual children and, on occasion, carry out IQ assessments (i.e., work in a "traditional way") as part of a special educational evaluation. However, the origin of the referral is different; the child's family, teachers, and the school psychologist will have discussed and monitored the problem for some time, a number of approaches will have been tried and evaluated, and, at some stage in this process, all those involved will have agreed that it would be helpful for the school psychologist to see the child individually and that information gained in this way would contribute to the problem-solving process. This way of working, it is argued, combines the best of the traditional approach within a consultation framework, provided the emphasis is on the contribution that all involved can make toward the prevention and alleviation of all the problem areas that have been highlighted. And, moreover, the problems associated with the child who is assessed are seen in the context of wider problems throughout the classroom or the school (e.g., lack of support staff, the need to buy new materials), and these issues should also be addressed alongside any intervention strategy to help the individual child.

This approach to school psychology practice closely resembles Caplan's client-centered consultation (Caplan, 1970), in which the primary focus is on helping the child. But the expectation is that through this process, the teacher will learn skills and gain confidence that will enable him or her to help other children with similar problems.

The Psychological Foundations of Consultation

The second issue concerns the nature of the consultation activity itself. There is a great deal that is "psychological" in consultation (Kennedy et al., 2008; Wagner, 2008), so school psychologists, with their training and experience, are in an excellent position to be able to carry out this activity effectively. As we have discussed, in addition to the expertise in children's learning and behavior that a school psychologist brings to a consultation meeting, the consultant needs to possess excellent interpersonal and facilitatory skills and a high level of professional credibility among those with whom he or she is consulting, all of which are psychological in nature.

There are, for example, psychological theories about group dynamics (Lewin, 1947), organization development (Bradford & Burke, 2005), and the management of change (Goddard & Bohac-Clarke, 2007) that can be applied in consultation work. There are also theories in social psychology (Bandura, 1977) that are relevant. Finally, there are psychological theories that inform the consultation process itself. Among these, socio-cultural activity theory (Daniels, 1993; Engestrom, 1987, 1999) provides a useful founda-tion that underpins school psychologists' approaches to consultation. Indeed, Leadbetter (2004) draws on this theory to interpret school psychologists' consultations in schools. She shows how Engeström's conceptual models form a basis for analyzing consultation meetings in relation to coordinated, cooperative, and communicative systems.

There is therefore an abundance of psychological theory that informs the effective use of consultation, and hence school psychologists should feel confident that they possess the prerequisite academic background that legitimizes their use of this approach.

Training

Finally, and perhaps most important, there is the issue of training. To be an effective consultant, a school psychologist needs experience, expertise, and, above all, credibil-ity among those with whom he or she consults. Trainers of school psychologists need to introduce students to various theoretical approaches to consultation and give them opportunities to practice their consultation skills on their practicums and internships. School psychologists who are well-trained in consultation skills are much more likely to engage in the practice and be more comfortable in addressing all of the issues/barriers that are discussed in this chapter.

Not surprisingly, therefore, regulatory bodies and professional organizations that have developed standards of training and practice in school psychology (e.g., the UK Health and Care Professions Council, 2009; ISPA, 2014; NASP, 2010) all include sections on the theory and practice of consultation. These documents also include the full range of knowledge and skills that school psychologists should possess on completing their training program, of which consultation is only one part. Trainers of school psycholo-gists therefore face a continuing challenge to provide comprehensive coverage of all areas of the curriculum on what are always extremely intensive training programs.

However, given the typical age range of the school psychologist in training (mid-20s), it is easy to understand how trainers might feel more comfortable focusing on teaching them to work with individual children using psychometric-based approaches at the pos-sible expense of their training in consultation. As discussed earlier in this chapter, this activity is more private and one over which the young and inexperienced school psy-chologist may feel he or she has more direct control. There is also some evidence from the U.S. that supports the view that coverage of consultation is not all that extensive in school psychology training programs (Alpert & Taufique, 2002; Anton-LaHart & Rosen-field, 2004; Hazel, & Laviolette Lineman, 2010; Truscott & Albritton, 2011).

Because school psychology services continue to stress the importance of consultation as a key part of their service delivery, it is incumbent upon trainers to ensure that new entrants to the profession are adequately equipped to work in this way. As indicated in this chapter, there are a number of publications that illustrate how school psychologists can improve their skills in consultation, and a recent book (Rosenfield, 2012) contains several chapters that discuss how school psychologists can become effective school-based consultants. This body of work can also be used to inform continuing professional devel-opment opportunities for school psychologists. Despite some of the challenges referred to by Newman, Salmon, Cavanaugh, and Schneider (2014), it is vitally important for school psychologists to improve their knowledge and skills in consultation, to embed this training in sound theoretical foundations that can be the bedrock for the development of effective practice, and to provide them with the confidence they need to move forward.

CONCLUSION

Interest in consultation approaches to the work of school psychologists is not new. Nevertheless, the available evidence suggests that they are reluctant, or unable, to embrace fully this way of working and still tend to spend the bulk of their time engaged in more traditional, child-focused work. It is possible, of course, that surveys of school psychology practice have oversimplified the dichotomy between both approaches and that further research may provide a more accurate picture of the range of working practices that they adopt.

Nonetheless, there are clear barriers to the development of consultative approaches to school psychology practice. These barriers have their origins in our history, the social context in which school psychologists work, in the messages emanating from professional associations, and in the confidence and competence that school psychologists feel that they possess in order to undertake what is arguably a more demanding approach to the work. However, the profession has expanded considerably over the years, and the demand for school psychology services continues to grow. In this context, the climate for further development and the extension of consultative approaches to the work of school psychologists has never been better.

NOTE

1. Throughout this chapter, we use the term *school psychologist* when referring to trained psychologists who work with children, schools, and families. However, in some countries, notably the United Kingdom (UK), the term *educational psychologist* is used. Hence, when referring to research and practice that is specifically related to the UK, we refer to educational rather than school psychologists.

REFERENCES

Aberdeen City Council. (2012). *Educational psychology service consultation model.* Retrieved February 4, 2014, from http://www.aberdeencity.gov.uk/education_learning/schools/educational_psychology/scc_eps_consultation_model.asp

Ahtola, A., & Niemi, P. (2013). Does it work in Finland? School psychological services within a successful system of basic education. *School Psychology International, 35,* 136–151.

Alpert, J., & Taufique, S. (2002). Consultation training: A field in need of review, revision, and research. *Journal of Educational and Psychological Consultation, 13,* 7–11.

Anton-LaHart, J., & Rosenfield, S. (2004). A Survey of preservice consultation training in school psychology programs. *Journal of Educational and Psychological Consultation, 15,* 41–62.

Bandura, A. (1977). *Social learning theory.* Englewood Cliffs, NJ: Prentice Hall.

Bartolo, P. (2010). Why school psychology for diversity? *School Psychology International, 31,* 567–580.

Bradford, D. L., & Burke, W. W. (Eds.). (2005). *Organization development.* San Francisco: Pfeiffer.

Burns, M. K. (2004). Using curriculum-based assessment in consultation: A review of three levels of research. *Journal of Educational and Psychological Consultation, 15,* 63–78.

Caplan, G. (1963). Types of mental health consultation. *American Journal of Orthopsychiatry, 33,* 470–481.

Caplan, G. (1970). *The theory and practice of mental health consultation.* New York: Basic Books.

Castillo, J. M., Curtis, M. J., & Gelley, C. (2012). School psychology 2010: Demographics, employment, and the context for professional practices—Part 1. *NASP Communiqué, 40,* 28–30.

Cording, J. (2011). *A study of educational psychologists' use of consultation and users' views on what a service should deliver.* (Unpublished doctoral thesis). Exeter, England: School of Education, University of Exeter.

Curtis, M. J. (2002). *The changing face of school psychology: Past, present and future.* Keynote address to The Future of School Psychology 2002 Invitational Conference, Indianapolis, IN.

Curtis, M. J., Chesno Grier, J. E., & Hunley, S. A. (2004). The changing face of school psychology: Trends in data and projections for the future. *School Psychology Review, 33,* 49–67.

Daniels, H. (1993). *Charting the agenda: Educational activity after Vygotsky.* London: Routledge.

Dawson, M., Cummings, J. A., Harrison, P. L., Short, R. J., Gorin, S., & Palomares, R. (2004). The 2002 multisite conference on the future of school psychology: Next steps. *School Psychology Review, 33,* 115–126.

Dennis, R. (2004). So far so good? A qualitative case study exploring the implementation of consultation in schools. *Educational Psychology in Practice, 20,* 17–29.

Denton, C. A., Hasbrouck, J. E., & Sekaquaptewa, S. (2003). The consulting teacher: A descriptive case study in responsive systems consultation. *Journal of Educational and Psychological Consultation, 14,* 41–73.

Department of Education and Science (DES). (1968). *Psychologists in the education services* (The Summerfield Report). London: HMSO.

DfEE. (2000). *Educational psychology services (England): Current role, good practice and future directions.* The Report of the Working Group. London: HMSO.

Dunsmuir, S., Brown, E., Iyadurai, S., & Monsen, J. (2009). Evidence-based practice and evaluation: From insight to impact. *Educational Psychology in Practice, 25,* 53–70.

Ehrhardt-Padgett, G. N., Hatzichristou, C., Kitson, J., & Meyers, J. (2004). Awakening to a new dawn: Perspectives of the future of school psychology. *School Psychology Review, 33,* 105–115.

Engestrom, Y. (1987). *Learning by expanding: An activity-theoretical approach to developmental research.* Helsinki: Orienta-Konsultit.

Engestrom, Y. (1999). Innovative learning in work teams: Analysing cycles of knowledge creation in practice. In Y. Engestrom, R. Miettinen, & R. L. Punamaki (Eds.), *Perspectives on activity theory* (pp. 377–407). Cambridge: Cambridge University Press.

Erchul, W. P., & Martens, B. K. (2010). *School consultation: Conceptual and empirical bases of practice.* New York: Springer, Verlag.

Farouk, S. (2004). Group work in schools: A process consultation approach. *Educational Psychology in Practice, 20,* 207–220.

Farrell, P. (2010). School psychology: Learning lessons from history and moving forward. *School Psychology International, 31*(6), 581–598.

Farrell, P., Harraghy, J., & Petrie, B. (1996). The statutory assessment of children with emotional and behavioural difficulties. *Educational Psychology in Practice, 12,* 80–85.

Forrest, J., Hinnigan, M., Keenaghan, L., & Owen, A. (1992). CSD: An innovatve style of service delivery. *Educational Psychology in Practice, 8*(3), 166–171.

Gillies, E. (2000). Developing consultation partnerships. *Educational Psychology in Practice, 16,* 33–39.

Goddard, J. T., & Bohac-Clarke, V. (2007). The cycles of school change: Toward an integrated developmental model. *The Journal of Educational Thought, 41,* 105–124.

Gutkin, T., & Curtis, M. (1982). School-based consultation: Theory and techniques. In T. Gukin & C. Reynolds (Eds.), *The handbook of school psychology* (pp. 224–278). New York: Wiley.

Hatzichristou, C. (2002). A Conceptual framework for the evolution of school psychology: Transnational considerations of common phases and future perspectives. *School Psychology International, 23,* 266–282.

Hazel, C., Laviolette, G., & Lineman, J. (2010). Training professional psychologists in school-based consultation. *Training and Education in Professional Psychology, 4,* 235–243.

Health and Care Professions Council. (2009). *Standards of education and training.* Retrieved September 16, 2014, from http://www.hcpcuk.org.uk/assets/documents/1000295EStandardsofeducationandtraining-from September2009.pdf

Hosp, J. L., & Reschly, D. J. (2002). Regional differences in school psychology practice. *School Psychology Review, 31,* 11–30.

Hughes, J. N., Hasbrouck, J. E., Serdahl, E., Heidgerken, A., & McHaney, L. (2001). Responsive systems consultation: A preliminary evaluation of implementation and outcomes. *Journal of Educational and Psychological Consultation, 12,* 179–201.

ISPA—International School Psychology Association. (2014). *ISPA accreditation standards.* Retrieved September 16, 2014, from http://www.ispaweb.org/accreditation/

Jimerson, S. R., Graydon, K., Farrell, P., Kikas, E., Hatzichristou, S., Boce, E., & Bashi, G. (2004). The international school psychology survey: Development and data. *School Psychology International, 25,* 259–286.

Jimerson, S. R., Oakland, T., & Yu, R. (2010). *Assessments, interventions and conceptual foundations used by school psychologists around the world.* International Institute of School Psychology, University of California, Santa Barbara. Retrieved November 23, 2016, from http://mina.education.ucsb.edu/jimerson/IISP/SPIS_Brief_on_Assessments,_Interventions_&_Conceptual_Foundations_6.25.2010SRJ.pdf

Jones, R. J. (2003). The construction of emotional and behavioural difficulties. *Educational Psychology in Practice, 19*, 147–157.

Kelly, B. (2008). Perspectives on applying educational psychology. In B. Kelly, L. Woolfson, & J. Boyle (Eds.), *Frameworks for practice in educational psychology: A textbook for trainees and practitioners* (pp. 7–21). London: Jessica Kinglsey.

Kennedy, E. K., Cameron, R., & Monsen, J. (2009). Effective consultation in educational and child psychology practice: Professional training for both competence and capability. *School Psychology International, 30*, 603–625.

Kennedy, E. K., Frederickson, N., & Monsen, J. (2008). Do educational psychologists "walk the talk" when consulting? *Educational Psychology in Practice, 24*, 169–187.

Kikas, E. (1999). School psychology in Estonia: Expectations of teachers and school psychologists versus reality. *School Psychology International, 20*, 103–115.

Kratochwill, T. R., & Bergan, J. R. (1993). *Behavioural consultation in applied settings.* New York: Plenum.

Kratochwill, T. R., & Pittman, P. H. (2002). Expanding problem-solving consultation training: Prospects and frameworks. *Journal of Educational and Psychological Consultation, 13*, 69–95.

Larney, R. (2003). School-based consultation in the United Kingdom: Principles, practice and effectiveness. *School Psychology International, 24*, 5–19.

Leadbetter, J. (2004). The role of mediating artefacts in the work of educational psychologists during consultative conversations in schools. *Educational Review, 56*, 133–145.

Leadbetter, J. (2006). Investigating and conceptualising the notion of consultation to facilitate multi-agency work. *Educational Psychology in Practice, 22*, 19–31.

Lewin, K. (1947). Frontiers in group dynamics: Concept, method and reality in social science; social equilibria and social change. *Human Relations, 1*, 5–41.

London Borough of Richmond. (2011). *Educational Psychology Service.* Retrieved February 4, 2014, from http://www.richmond.gov.uk/educational_psychology_service

Medway, F. J. (1979). How effective is school consultation?: A review of recent research. *Journal of School Psychology, 17*, 275–282.

NASP—National Association of School Psychologists. (2010). *Standards for graduate preparation of school Psychologists.* Bethesda, MD: National Association of School Psychologists.

Newman, D. S., Salmon, D., Cavanaugh, K., & Schneider, M. F. (2014). The consulting role in a response-to-intervention context: An exploratory study of instructional consultation. *Journal of Applied School Psychology, 30*, 278–304.

Oakland, T. (2000). International school psychology. In T. Fagan & P. Wise (Eds.), *School psychology: Past, present & future* (pp. 355–382). Bethesda, MD: National Association of School Psychologists.

Osborne, E. (1994). The teacher's view: Working with teachers out of school setting. In E. Dowling & E. Osborne (Eds.), *The family and the school* (pp. 102–112). London: Routledge.

Perez-Gonzalez, F., Garcia-Ros, R., & Gomez-Artiga, A. (2004). A survey of teaching perceptions of the school psychologist's skills in the consultation process: An exploratory factor analysis. *School Psychology International, 25*, 30–41.

Rees, C., Rees, P., & Farrell, P. (2003). Methods used by psychologists to assess pupils with emotional and behavioural difficulties. *Educational Psychology in Practice, 19*, 203–214.

Reschly, D. J. (2000). The present and future status of school psychology in the United States. *School Psychology Review, 29*, 507–522.

Restori, A. F., Gresham, F. M., & Cook, C. R. (2008). "Old habits die hard": Past and current issues pertaining to response-to-intervention. *The California School Psychologist, 1*, 10–23.

Rosenfield, S. (2002). Developing instructional consultants: From novice, to competent, to expert. *Journal of Educational and Psychological Consultation, 13*, 97–111.

Rosenfield, S. (Ed.). (2012). *Becoming a school based consultant: Lessons learned.* New York: Routledge.

Shapiro, E. S., Angello, L. M., & Eckert, T. L. (2004). Has curriculum based assessment become the staple of school psychology practice? An update and extension of knowledge, use and attitudes from 1990–2000. *School Psychology Review, 33*, 249–258.

Sheridan, S. M., Clarke, B. L., & Burt, J. D. (2007). Conjoint behavioural consultation; or: what do we know and what do we need to know. In W. P. Erchul & S. M. Sheridan (Eds.), *Handbook of research in school consultation* (pp. 171–202). London: Routledge.

Sheridan, S. M., & Gutkin, T. B. (2000). The ecology of school psychology: Examining and changing our paradigm for the 21st century. *School Psychology Review, 29*, 485–502.

Southwark Council. (2012). *Consultation: Educational psychology.* Retrieved February 4, 2014, from http://www.southwark.gov.uk/info/200335/pupil_health_and_wellbeing/956/educational_psychology/2

Strein, W., Cramer, K., & Lawser, M. (2003). School psychology research and scholarship: USA status, international explorations. *School Psychology International, 24*, 421–436.

Truscott, S. D., & Albritton, K. (2011). Addressing pediatric health concerns through school-based consultation. *Journal of Educational and Psychological Consultation, 21*, 169–174.

Turner, S., Robins, H., & Doran, C. (1996). Developing a model of consultancy practice. *Educational Psychology in Practice, 12*, 86–93.

Wagner, P. (2000). Consultation: Developing a comprehensive approach to service delivery. *Educational Psychology in Practice, 16*, 9–18.

Wagner, P. (2008). Consultation as a framework for practice. In B. Kelly, L. Woolfson, & J. Boyle (Eds.), *Frameworks for practice in educational psychology: A textbook for trainees and practitioners* (pp. 135–178). London: Jessica Kingsley Publishers.

Watkins, C. (2000). Introduction to the articles on consultation. *Educational Psychology in Practice, 16*, 5–8.

WHO. (1968). *Organisation of services for mentally retarded, fifteenth report of the WHO expert committee on mental health, WHO technical report*. Serial 392. Geneva: World Health Organisation.

Woods, K. (2014). "In this together": Developing university-workplace partnerships in initial professional training for practitioner educational psychologists. In O. McNamara, J. Murray, & M. Jones (Eds.), *Teacher learning in the workplace: Widening perspectives on practice and policy. Part 2: Insights from practice across professions and nations* (pp. 87–101). London: Springer.

13

THINKING *IN* THE BOX

A Tool for Promoting Innovative Problem-Solving in Israeli School Psychology Services

Sharone L. Maital

INTRODUCTION

Coming up with innovative and creative solutions to a problem is often regarded as thinking "out of the box," that is, thinking in new and unconventional ways. In fact, many innovative responses to difficult problems reflect thinking within the box. The box represents binding constraints that cannot be ignored, such as demands for particular types of service, lack of sufficient resources, time constraints, and lack of training in alternative approaches to service delivery. The approach to dealing with such constraints presented in this article suggests that the box *itself* may often promote creative solutions. These solutions are innovative not because they are completely new but because they are new ways of resolving problems that had not been previously considered. Innovative ideas are more likely to be stimulated under conditions such as times of crisis, when easy answers are not readily available, or when budgets shrink and professional resources are limited.

In this article, I present a tool adapted from management consulting (Drucker, 1994) to help examine Israeli school psychologists' ideas about services that they provide, particularly systems-level consultation. The tool was used in group meetings with Israeli school psychologists to stimulate innovative thinking about how to overcome constraints and encourage more widespread use of systems thinking and consultation at the local level. It was also presented as a tool that could be used by the psychologists in later organizational consultations with school staff. The questions in the protocol were also used to examine nationally sponsored innovations in providing school psychology services.

ORIGINS OF MH CONSULTATION IN ISRAEL

In some sense, mental health (MH) consultation was first conceived and implemented by Gerald Caplan (1970) as an innovative response to constraints. *Consultation* is defined here broadly as an indirect process of providing psychological services aimed at both resolving existing problems and preventing future difficulties. The story of the development of MH consultation by Caplan in the late 1940s and early 1950s while working in Israel may be told as a tale of the life-line of innovative thinking about mental health services. Caplan and his small staff of psychologists and social workers at the Mental Health and Child Guidance Center of Hadassah Hospital in Jerusalem were confronted with the need to help large numbers of immigrant refugee children who had arrived alone and were placed in residential institutions throughout the country (run as boarding schools). In addition to the challenges of moving to a new culture, many of the children arrived after having had stressful experiences, and they exhibited serious emotional difficulties that made it hard for them to adjust. Yet few were so disturbed that they needed to be removed from the school system.

When he arrived in Israel in 1948, Caplan found a system that put a high priority on diagnosis and direct treatment of the children's difficulties. However, it was impossible to provide the needed direct services to each child with the limited resources available. There were too few qualified mental health professionals and there were also logistic limitations. As a result, he developed his well-known methods for providing psychological consultation to the educational staff (Caplan, 1970).

Despite the effectiveness of Caplan's innovative (at the time) approach, it was met with resistance by administrators and educators as well as mental health workers who were used to traditional methods of direct, individual therapy. Notably, after he left for Harvard University in 1952 to establish the Community Mental Health Program there (Cutler & Huffine, 2004), the Mental Health Center in Jerusalem reverted to a medical model and an individual focus. One might conjecture that this was in part due to the influence of European psychoanalytic views on the training and practice of psychology in Israel. It may have also reflected an ever-present demand by stakeholders for direct services to children with difficulties (Farrell, 2010). Nevertheless, Caplan's ideas about MH consultation were subsequently widely adopted and adapted in school psychology practices around the world, including in Israel (e.g., Cohen & Osterweil, 1986; Erchul, 2009; Hatzichristou, 2004; Lambert, 2004; Meyers, Parsons, & Martin, 1979).

A Brief History of School Psychology in Israel

School psychology services in Israel were initially organized and administered as local clinics serving schools in a particular municipality. Toward the end of the 1960s, the services were brought under the umbrella of a National Educational Psychology and Counseling Services Department (known by the Hebrew acronym *Shefi*) within the Israel Ministry of Education. Subsequently, school psychology (known in Hebrew as *educational psychology*) services have been established in most of the local and municipal councils throughout the country. Today there are about 3,200 school psychologists working in 257 city and local councils (*"Odot Agaf Psychologia,"* n.d.). The National Department, Shefi, is responsible for overseeing and advancing professional practices through policy directives and in-service training. The daily administration and provision of services is semi-autonomous at the local level, leading to variability in actual practices across the country.

Beginning with the earliest independent school psychology services under local auspices, there were prominent school psychologists who saw the advantages of intervening at a school-wide level and helping teachers and parents by providing consultation rather than just testing and placing children with special needs (Benyamini, 1982; Raviv, 1985). When Shefi was established as a national department within the Ministry of Education, these early school psychologists influenced the official emphasis on systems interventions, particularly in response to crisis situations (Stein, 2007). Current guidelines for Israeli school psychology practice place a high priority on providing consultation and adopting an ecosystemic focus in helping children, their families, and their teachers ("Mitveh Hasherut Hapsihologi Hinuhi," 2010).

Concomitantly, state specialist licensing in school (educational) psychology requires proficiency in psychotherapy with children as well as skills in consultation and systems-level intervention (Israel Ministry of Health, 2015). Thus, many Israeli school psychologists, who have been trained in traditional clinical methods, are pulled toward clinical practice along with their work in the schools. Despite licensing requirements, some suggest they are often not as well trained in consultation and systems-level intervention (Stein, 2007). Moreover, in Israel, as elsewhere in the world, there is an ongoing demand for clinically oriented services that focus on individual assessment, diagnosis, psychotherapeutic treatment, and placement of school children experiencing difficulties in special education programs. Thus, a combination of training, demand for clinical services, and state regulations preserves a degree of ongoing tension between reliance on a medical model and greater emphasis on consultation, especially at a systems level (Levinson, 1999; Maital & Shalhevet Kaniel, in press; Stein, 2007).

To some extent, these tensions between systems and individual intervention have been addressed in projects sponsored at a national level by the leadership of the Israeli school psychology services. Many programs are based on integrating consultation with school staff, multidisciplinary collaboration, and individual, short-term therapy. These programs, implemented at a local level by school psychologists, often with additional funding, focus on areas such as reducing school bullying and violence and helping schools cope with children with learning difficulties, ADHD, abuse, and trauma. They are aimed at both treating individuals with difficulties and preventing mental health problems at a systems level. The need for more training in systems approaches is addressed in part by providing in-service courses associated with each project.

Nevertheless, school psychologists need to think innovatively about reconciling the competing demands and constraints they face not only in terms of national policy but also with respect to demands at the local level. Moreover, the 21st century is characterized by rapid changes in society and technology that impact schools. The goal of the tool presented here was to guide an ongoing examination of the "theory of providing services" held by Israeli school psychologists themselves. The encouragement of bottom-up innovation is an important complement to top-down innovative leadership.

The Current Challenge

The story of the development of mental health consultation in Israel illustrates the ongoing tension and constraints faced by school psychologists in Israel, as elsewhere in the world (e.g., Farrell, 2010). They are caught between demands for clinical practice, including assessment (and the allure of clinical work) and training based primarily on a medical model, and recognition of the need for consultation practices and working with others in the educational system in order to efficiently meet increasing demands for services with limited resources. Recognition of the need for a systemic focus is reinforced by the local community base of school psychologists in Israel and their enlistment to provide wide-scale crisis intervention and prevention services.

Thus, there is an ongoing need for a process for examining how we can promote and provide systems-level school psychology services and overcome constraints. The tool for thinking "in the box" is presented in the following section as a means for conducting such a process. I then show how it was applied with several groups of psychologists with the aim of promoting creative and innovative solutions in providing school psychology services in Israel. Finally, I discuss the responses of the psychologists in the field with respect to ideas about the theory of school psychology services reflected in discussions at national leadership conferences (held each summer over the last decade) and in public documents from the Ministry of Education, Department of Educational Psychology and Counseling Services. In concluding, the wider applicability of tools for encouraging consultation and a systems orientation in school psychology will be discussed.

TOOLS FOR SYSTEMS THINKING

The chains of habit are too light to be felt, until they are too heavy to be broken.
Warren Buffet (Buffet & Clark, 2006)

Changing the ways in which school psychology is practiced is not an easy task. It requires systematic examination of the assumptions that lie behind many professional activities. Peter Drucker, a leading business consultant, once observed that organizations get into trouble *not because* they do the right things wrong, but because they *continue to do* the wrong things expertly (Drucker, 1994). School psychology services in Israel appear to face similar difficulties. Many school psychologists are quite expert (and comfortable) engaging in traditional roles involving psychological testing, diagnosis, and individual therapy. Requirements for expertise in these roles are clearly defined, and this is often the basis for more remunerative private practice work compared with systems-oriented consultation in the public sector.

A key first step toward innovative solutions that can help reconcile ongoing constraints and meet changing needs is to challenge our basic assumptions. We often look to processes such as brainstorming to generate new ideas beyond the boxes that constrain us. However, as noted, there will always be some constraints within which innovation may occur. We need to consider which constraints are self-imposed and dispensable and which are binding. The method for thinking innovatively, "in the box," presented in this chapter is adapted from Drucker's (1994) theory of business, which guides managers through a series of structured questions that challenge every basic assumption. The goal is to help school psychologists to look inward and examine how changing key assumptions can lead to new alternatives for providing psychological services. The aim is not to produce innovations that are completely new, never yet conceived, but rather to encourage ideas that had not been previously considered seriously by the participants.

Drucker (1994) suggests that each organization has a theory of providing services. A theory of the organization, Drucker explains, has three parts. First, there are assumptions about the context: society, stakeholders, and technology. These are assumptions about what the organization is paid to do. Second, there are assumptions concerning the organization's specific mission. These define what the organization considers to be meaningful results. Third, there are assumptions about the key abilities or "core competencies" needed to accomplish the organization's mission. These assumptions define areas in which an organization must excel in order to maintain leadership. Building a clear and valid theory of an organization requires conscious reflection and needs to be reevaluated periodically.

Drucker (1994) proposed a protocol to guide the process of rethinking and reinvention. It has been adapted here to guide the examination of school psychology services. The protocol includes questions for each of four factors associated with developing a theory of an organization: (1) assumptions about the social context in which services are provided and the changes occurring therein; (2) assumptions about the specific mission of school psychology services; (3) assumptions about the core competencies needed to fulfill that mission; and (4) questions that help summarize and test the resulting general theory of providing school psychology services. The process begins by asking about the widest social context and then zooms in toward more specific aspects of the organization and its capabilities. Finally, it requires "zooming out" again to integrate the results of the process. The questions in each domain appear in Table 13.1.

Table 13.1 Theory of School Psychology Services

1. Assumptions about the social context
- *What are our assumptions about society and social forces and how they are changing?*
- *What are our assumptions about our stakeholders and our clients and their values and behaviors? How well do we understand them? How will these changes impact our services?*
- *Who are our competitors, present and future? How do we identify them? How well do we know them?*
- *What are our assumptions about key technologies and methodologies? Do we identify disruptive technologies (ways of providing services that are at present far from perfect but may be widely used in the future)?*
- *How do our services create value? What is unique?*
- *Which of these assumptions is crucial for our strategies for providing services?*

2. Assumptions about the specific mission of school psychology services
- *How does our organization "make a difference" in society at large? Do we have an impact on the economy?*
- *How do we measure success?*
- *What drives behavior in school psychology services?*
- *What does the organization believe is its mission (reason for existence)?*
- *Which of these assumptions is crucial for our strategies for providing services?*

3. Assumptions about core competencies needed to accomplish the mission
- *What are our assumptions about the core competencies needed to achieve our mission?*
- *What must we excel at in order to succeed and achieve or maintain excellence in providing services?*
- *What are our assumptions about our key strengths and weaknesses?*
- *Which of these assumptions is crucial for our strategies for providing services?*

4. Testing the theory of providing school psychology services
- *Do our assumptions fit reality with regard to education and society, mission, and core competencies? Why or why not? How do we test these assumptions regularly?*
- *Which of the assumptions are doubtful, and how will this affect our current strategy for service provision?*
- *Should our strategy be altered in light of our reexamination of our theory of service provision?*
- *Are the assumptions in the three key areas properly aligned (internally consistent)?*
- *Do we constantly challenge every service, method, procedure, and routine?*
- *If we were not providing our current range of services, what would we do differently, what areas would we enter, and what areas would we choose to leave? Which of the services we provide have a high impact on the well-being of children and the educational system and therefore deserve more time and resources, and which have low impact and hence deserve less time and fewer resources?*

CASE STUDIES APPLYING THE DRUCKER PROTOCOL
WITH SCHOOL PSYCHOLOGISTS

In this section I describe how the questions in the protocol developed by Drucker (1994) were used in focus groups with Israeli school psychologists at three levels of service: a group of directors of local, community-based school psychology services; a group of staff psychologists from a medium-size regional clinic; and a group of staff psychologists from a small regional clinic. The directors' group was comprised of eight participants in an ongoing group of local directors of school psychology services that meets monthly to discuss dilemmas in providing services and applying national educational policies in each of the directors' respective municipalities. The directors are all senior school psychologists certified as supervisors in school psychology. The services they direct range in size from medium (about 15–20) to small (4–5) staffs of school psychologists who service the local schools from preschool through high school in Israel.

The two groups of staff psychologists, one from a large regional council (with 15 psychologists) and another from a smaller local council (with 5 psychologists), were both more heterogeneous and included school psychologists at various levels of training, from senior staff members trained in supervision to beginning psychologists. Regional councils in Israel aggregate a number of semi-autonomous communities for purposes such as education and other public services. The psychologists all provided services in schools (including special education) for children ranging in age from preschool to age 18 in the different communities making up their respective districts. In both cases, the focus group meetings were conducted during a weekly staff meeting.

The focus groups were initiated following the publication (in April 2010) of the new guidelines for school psychology services by the National Department of School Psychology Services (Shefi) and efforts to encourage implementation at the local level. As noted previously, these guidelines included a mandate for increased systems level consultation but also advocated allocating time for individual therapy with children.

The groups were conducted by the author in coordination with the regional head of the school psychology services to encourage the discussion at the regional and local level. Toward the end of the year (May and June 2010), a 2.5-hour session was devoted to examining each group's theory of school psychology services. All participants were aware of the new guidelines prior to the group meetings.

Each meeting began with a presentation and discussion of Drucker's "theory of service" protocol by an outside expert in management consulting. From the outset, participants were informed that, based on the protocol, they would be asked to critically examine their assumptions and seek alternatives for providing school psychology services. For the directors' group, discussions (and often complaining) about constraints and conflicting demands on school psychology services are a common theme in their meetings. The participants reacted enthusiastically to the topic of innovation in services and the protocol. They also asked to present the protocols within their individual psychological services for discussion among staff members. In the groups of staff psychologists, despite differences in level of training, the participants were familiar with one another and they all actively contributed to the discussion and provided varied perspectives.

A Comparison of Key Responses to the Protocol by the Three Groups

The key responses provided by each of the three groups concerning their assumptions about school psychology services are presented in Table 13.2. These are presented following the outline of the protocol. Common themes across the groups are listed in bold in the table.

Social Context of School Psychology Services

With respect to the social context, the groups all focused on assumptions based on their perception of constraints that were imposed by the context on optimal provision of services. As might be expected, the directors' group was more aware of political aspects of the context as it related to the mission of the school psychology services. They focused on assumptions about reduced resources for public services, pressures to increase efficiency, and the effect of the entry of NGOs to provide services on a contract basis. Staff psychologists from the smaller local council also noted pressures by the council to reduce expenses as well as measure output, along with increased encouragement of the use of private psychological services and other resources. The staff psychologists from the larger regional council were somewhat less concerned about external constraints. They were more focused on the immediate context and assumed that there were endless needs

Table 13.2 Assumptions about School Psychology Services

Staff in a Large Regional Council	Staff in a Small Regional Council	Directors of School Psychology Services
Context		
• **Reduced public resources and entry of NGOs** • Pressure to increase efficiency	• **Reduced resources drive need to increase efficiency** • **Differences among local communities in use of services** • Multiple stakeholders and consultees	• People in need of help will seek it • **Endless needs and problems to be solved** • **Differences among schools and communities** • Need for outreach if need for help is not recognized
Mission (goals)		
• **Change focus from "fixing" the child to influencing the context** • Gain political influence • Specialization among psychologists • Field-based theory of parenting	• **"Bridge" among various professionals and agencies** • **Balance needs of the system and needs of individuals** • **Provide easily accessible and convenient services**	• Client satisfaction with psychological help and support • **Provide accessible and convenient services**
Core competencies		
• **Continuous learning** • Political skills	• Leadership skills • **Broad, multidisciplinary knowledge** • **Up-to-date knowledge of assessment and intervention techniques**	• **Up-to-date knowledge of intervention techniques** • Flexibility and adaptability to changing context

and demands by school personnel for school psychology services focused on children and their families, requiring that the psychologists themselves better define the limits of the services they wished to provide. Staff psychologists in both the smaller regional council and the larger one also noted the unique and varied challenges to children and their families in the different communities within their councils. Those from the smaller regional council also assumed that the small, close-knit communities demand greater coordination among more stakeholders than in city schools.

Notably, in discussing the context of services, all the groups related to the tension between demands to help children based on a traditional, medical model focused on individuals and their difficulties and constraints resulting from limited time and demands for increased efficiency. Various forces in the context were viewed as counter to psychologists' assumptions about the core value of school psychology services as providing solutions to children's problems and being able to follow individual children and their development over the course of their schooling based on both individual and systems-level interventions.

The Mission and Goals of School Psychology Services

Overall, in considering the assumptions expressed regarding the mission of school psychology services, it would appear that the goals of providing mental health services focused on individual children and families are constrained by many of the contextual conditions. In line with their views of the context, the directors examined assumptions associated with the need to gain political influence and to influence the educational system proactively, moving away from a child-oriented medical model toward more systems-wide interventions. The staff psychologists were more focused on goals associated directly with client satisfaction. For both groups, this related to providing convenient and accessible services for children with difficulties and their families. The staff from the larger regional council noted that this often involved acting as "firefighters" called in to help school staff resolve acute problems. For the smaller group, the goal was one of better integrating and balancing the needs of individual children with more systemic intervention. In keeping with this, they noted their goal of coordinating among the various professionals and different agencies providing services to the children and their families.

Core Competencies of School Psychologists

With respect to their assumptions about core competencies, the groups all noted assumptions about the need for ongoing training, especially with respect to intervention techniques. While they all mentioned core competencies in systems-level consultation in some form, there were differences in the areas seen as most important to develop. The directors' group focused on the need for political skills needed to gain influence and consult at a systems level. This area was perceived as a weakness not only for directors but also among school psychologists in general. They also noted the need for advanced training, particularly with respect to the need for specialized services, such as psychotherapy within the schools, and both individual- and systems-level interventions with abused children and children with behavior problems. The psychologists from the smaller regional council suggested that core competencies should include the skills in working with interdisciplinary teams and leadership and having a wide range of expertise in multiple areas. Areas noted included family therapy, use of alternatives to formal psychological assessment, and consultation. In this respect, they were more similar to the directors' group than the staff psychologists from the larger regional council. The latter group did note the need for awareness of what is transpiring at a systems level, the ability to present themselves to the public, and the ability to gain authority and flexibility in adapting to a changing environment. However, these were perceived as secondary corollaries of more traditional core competencies of professional psychologists: ability to listen, empathy, sensitivity, responsiveness, and up-to-date knowledge about intervention.

Generating Innovative Ideas

The innovative ideas for providing services are presented in Table 13.3. In trying to elicit innovative resolutions to the constraints that the groups perceived, there were few truly innovative ideas about alternative ways to provide school psychology services. Rather, there were proposals for small, incremental changes that might lessen some of the constraints. All the groups suggested changing the balance to reduce time devoted to psychological assessment, allowing greater emphasis on direct treatment of children, consultation, and intervention. The directors suggested devoting more time to systems-level consultation with school principals and political leadership in order to influence changes in policy. All the groups raised the possibility of outsourcing psychological testing for special education placement in order to enable them to devote more time to both direct interventions and consultation. Staff from the psychological services in both localities suggested they should work on promoting public recognition of school psychology as a profession devoted primarily to providing mental health services that help students overcome social, emotional, and behavioral difficulties that interfere with functioning in school and prevent further difficulties.

With respect to broadening the range of services provided and the associated competencies of school psychologists, the directors' group suggested enabling psychologists to work in teams, possibly using technology to create virtual teams in order to maximize the impact of professional specialization. The psychologists from the smaller local council also proposed that they take on the role of making mental health–related information more widely available through articles in local media, lectures for parents and educational staff, and use of web-based platforms as an efficient alternative to time invested in individual interventions. This was one of the more innovative suggestions.

Table 13.3 Ideas for Changes in Providing School Psychology Services

Directors of school psychology services	Staff in a small regional council	Staff in a large regional council
• Teams—working together in one school • Use of technology to create virtual teams • Documentation and sharing of new ideas • Work with principals and local officials to influence policy	• Increasing efficiency to reduce testing and increase consultation and intervention • Outsourcing assessments • Activities to increase visibility of services • Multiple ideas for small, incremental changes	• Leaving the clinic room and joining the system leads to change in the balance between testing and intervention • Need to influence policy and work on visibility and "branding" of services

In seeking innovative ideas for providing school psychology services, the psychologists from the larger regional council had greater difficulty and even expressed some resistance. One participant even raised the question of why one should assume a need to think about change. The view expressed by a consensus of participants was that "if there is no need for continually consulting with us (the school psychology service), this is a sign we have not positioned ourselves and have not made ourselves sufficiently visible, as school psychologists." They expressed the view that they had little control over their ability to become more involved in consultation roles, especially at the systems level. In general, participants in this group perceived themselves as already flexible and able to reinvent their work in response to change. However, in practice, it was hard for them to present new ideas for making changes from "within the box." It is difficult to discern the source of the attitude of those in this group, but it is perhaps associated with the fact that they were less concerned with constraints or pressures from the social context of their services and therefore felt less need to change the way in which they were providing services.

INNOVATIVE IDEAS ABOUT SCHOOL PSYCHOLOGY SERVICES: THE NATIONAL LEADERSHIP PERSPECTIVE

At the national level, a leadership conference attended by approximately 200 psychologists has been convened each summer for over a decade. The participants include the national leadership (the chief psychologist and deputy chief psychologist for the national department of school psychology services, Shefi, and all regional psychologists and their deputies), representatives of the local school psychology services (mainly directors of services or psychologists in leadership positions nominated by the regional psychologists in each region of the country), and psychologists from different parts of the country who participate in standing, special interest forums throughout the year. The conferences were initially modeled after the Conferences on the Future of School Psychology in the United States sponsored by a coalition of national school psychology organizations. The goal of the Israeli conference each year has been to present lectures on current issues facing school psychology in Israel and to encourage discussions about the need for continuing change, often encouraging innovative ideas. While the conferences did not use the Drucker protocol, many of the discussions and subsequent position papers and directives address similar questions concerning key assumptions about Israeli school psychology services. The ideas and programs promulgated at the national level can be contrasted with the responses of the staff psychologists and their directors in the field during the focus group sessions.

Social Context

What have been the assumptions about the social context represented at the national conferences? A key assumption relates to the recognition that there is a need for continuous reexamination of the services provided by school psychologists. For example, the conference in 2010 was titled "Innovation in School Psychology: The National and Regional Perspective" (Tzameret, 2010). A keynote lecture at that conference by Professor Shlomo Maital, a management expert, directly addressed the need for "benchmarking" of best practices both within Israel and abroad and developing creative ideas within constraints. Israeli school psychologists are faced with multiple demands and changing needs. These include dealing with the need for ongoing crisis response, diverse school populations with respect to ethnic and religious backgrounds and special needs, helping children at risk and who have suffered abuse, and remaining up to date by participating in in-service training. The participants in the focus groups noted some of these needs. Others were overlooked, possibly because they are taken for granted as part of the social context and referred to by the shorthand "diversity in the schools and communities."

Mission

With respect to the mission of school psychology services in Israel, support for a systems perspective and interventions based on consultation have been expressed repeatedly by psychologists in national leadership positions. A further assumption about the mission of school psychological services that emerged from the conferences is that school psychologists are in a position to lead in providing school-based mental health services ranging from systems-level prevention to interventions based on consultee-centered consultation and psychotherapy. This in keeping with definitions of psychotherapy as a range of interventions focused on improving psychological strengths and helping overcome difficulties (e.g., Roth & Fonagy, 2006; Weisz & Gray, 2008). There is growing evidence that even very brief psychotherapeutic intervention (3–10 sessions) can have lasting effects (Abbass, Kisely, Rasic, Town, & Johansson, 2015). While there is some overlap in defining *counseling* and *psychotherapy,* in Israel, the latter term is preferred in referring to psychological interventions. Counseling is widely used to refer to the work of educational counselors who are oriented toward empowering and helping clients achieve their goals (Kaplan, Tarvydas, & Gladding, 2014).

Core Competencies

With respect to core competencies, there were repeated discussions about the need to encourage school psychologists to remain up to date with respect to evidence-based practices and to ensure a high level of training among psychologists with different training backgrounds. Israel is a country that has absorbed professionals in psychology from many countries and differing professional psychology backgrounds. Due to demand for school psychologists, many enter the field in need of further training in order to qualify for specialist licensure. An innovative solution that grew out of discussions at some of the early conferences involved the establishment in 2005 of an Institute for Advanced Post-graduate Studies in School Psychology under the auspices of the Department of Educational Psychology and Counseling Services. The institute administers in-service, postgraduate courses for school psychologists (at all levels, from novices to experts and supervisors) working in the local services throughout the country. At later conferences, participants and members of interest group forums, some of which were established following discussions at leadership conferences, were involved in writing documents such as standards for psychological assessments of children with special needs (Standartim L'haaracha Psychologit L'vaadot al pi Hok, 2007), a model for the work of school psychologists in kindergarten classes (Sherut Psychologi B'ganey Hayeladim: T'fisa teoretit V'Kavim Manchim L'avoda, 2013), and a forthcoming edited volume with articles reflecting best practices in Israeli School Psychology (Maital & Shalhevet Kaniel, 2017).

Revamping Practice

With respect to the tension between practices based on a systems focus and reliance on consultation and the demands for psychological assessment, discussions at the conferences from 2005 contributed to a revamping of the national Guidelines for School Psychology Services ("Mitveh Hasherut Hapsihologi Hinuhi", 2010). The earlier guidelines were defined as a "basket of services." During initial discussions about revising the "basket," there were some who expressed satisfaction with the status quo and proposed only small changes in the list format. However, after many discussions and debates, new guidelines, issued as a Ministry of Education directive, were developed.

The new guidelines are conceptually organized and advocate a holistic, ecosystemic, developmental perspective with an associated emphasis on early identification of difficulties, prevention and promotion of resilience, as well as crisis intervention. In implementing the guidelines, school psychologists are expected to give high priority to systems-level as well as consultee-centered consultation and intervention programs. However, the guidelines also continue to require involvement with individual children with difficulties, conducting psychological assessments, making recommendations for special education placement, and providing short-term psychotherapy. This may contribute to the sense of psychologists in the focus groups presented here that there is an ever-present tension between demands for special education gatekeeping and their roles as consultants responsible for systems interventions and prevention.

Recent intervention protocols for children at risk reflect an attempt to involve school psychologists in providing services that integrate consultation at the systems level, consultee-centered work, and individual interventions. The protocols for working with children with emotional difficulties from high-risk families or children with ADHD call for work within a multidisciplinary team involved in consultation to school principals and staff as well as group and individual therapeutic work with parents and the children ("Hatohnit Haleumit", 2014). School psychologists participating in the programs are afforded pay for additional hours of work required. This may help mitigate some of the tension in moving toward more systemic and integrated services. But experience in the field suggests that some school principals (and teachers) remain interested primarily in the additional, direct services for the children and resist consultation for themselves or the educational staff.

Another possible resolution to the constraints stemming from the assumption that school psychologists provide a multifaceted set of services is the attempt to reduce the amount of formal psychological testing required for special education services ("Yisum Hok Hinuh Meyuhad," 2014). Current guidelines allow greater reliance on initial assessment of children experiencing difficulties by documenting their response to interventions within the classroom. This, in turn, may encourage greater reliance on consultation to teachers, particularly with respect to instructional practices rather than formal testing. However, it is not clear whether Israeli school psychologists have sufficient tools and training to systematically observe and document learning and instructional practices.

DISCUSSION: CONSULTATION AND THE CHANGING ROLE OF SCHOOL PSYCHOLOGISTS IN ISRAEL AND THE WORLD

The Israeli school psychologists at the various levels of service generally concurred that both consultee-centered consultation and systems interventions are key to their mission of providing mental health services in educational settings. This is parallel to the position presented over the years in the professional literature by leaders of school psychology from other Western countries (e.g., Adelman & Taylor, 1998; Conoley, Conoley, & Reese, 2009; Gutkin, 2012; Hatzichristou, 2004; NASP, 2010; Nastasi, 2004; Sheridan & Gutkin, 2000). For example, Nastasi (2004) was among those who called for a paradigm shift from a clinically oriented medical model focused on the individual to a public health model focused on improving the psychological well-being of all children as part of the educational process.

Bradley-Johnson and Dean (2000) suggest that the calls for role change in the direction of wider-scale reliance on consultation and indirect, systemic intervention is not new. Yet, there appears to be little evidence for widespread adoption of the suggested change (Bradley-Johnson & Dean, 2000; Conoley et al., 2009). A notable exception is reports on the development of a broader, systemic approach to providing school psychology services in Greece (e.g., Hatzichristou, 1998; Hatzichristou & Lampropoulou, 2004; Hatzichristou, Lykitsakou, Lampropoulou, & Dimitropoulou, 2010). The process of developing a consultation based, systemic model led by Hatzichristou and her colleagues may have been more easily accepted due to the fact that it was implemented along with the introduction of services in schools that did not have a tradition of working with more medically oriented school psychology services. No doubt, the careful integration of data-based needs assessment to define critical needs of students, families, and schools with a problem-solving model to identify threats and opportunities for implementation and leadership by a university-field partnership are also important components (Hatzichristou, Lampropoulou, Lykitsakou, & Dimitropoulou, 2010).

Many experts have noted the difficulties and constraints involved in changing school psychologists' roles to promoting mental health and working at systems levels. What is the source of this difficulty? One source of difficulty suggested by the responses of the Israeli school psychologists may be the perceived complexity of the needs within the social context in which they provide services. Especially among the Israeli staff psychologists, there was concern about the constraints inherent in the associated expectation that they fulfill multiple roles. There was a sense that they were thinking within a more limited box and hence had more difficulties generating creative and innovative ideas for change compared with their colleagues at the national level. Similarly, in addressing the reluctance of school psychologists around the world to adopt new roles, Farrell (2010) suggested that when faced with a shortage of psychologists relative to high demands for multifaceted services, many school psychologists take a path of least resistance and fulfill the roles most widely expected of them: testing and making placement recommendations.

Braden, DiMarino-Linnen, and Good (2001) suggest that concerns of stakeholders (such as policy makers and politicians, the business community, and even the media) with visible proof for maximizing students' academic achievement have led to an emphasis on standards and testing. In this respect, concerns about lack of sufficient training needed for advocacy and gaining political influence mentioned by the Israeli school psychologists, particularly the directors of services, may be a salient constraint that needs to be addressed in ways that go beyond challenging their assumptions and encouraging innovative solutions. They suggested a need to "rebrand" school psychology services, that is, to create and market a clear, easily distinguishable identity that can promote stakeholders' acceptance of a changed role for school psychologists (Andreasen & Kotler, 2003). Interestingly, parents in the U.S. were reported to be more in tune with humanistic goals of promoting a holistic view of children's well-being and integrating health promotion within educational settings, in keeping with views of experts in school psychology (Braden et al., 2001).

To overcome this difficulty, more extensive training in leadership skills and use of organizational consultation have been recommended in order to promote the needed changes at organizational (within schools) and interagency levels of the system (Meyers, Meyers, Graybill, Proctor, & Huddleston, 2012; Nastasi, 2004). It is important that psychologists gain a more in-depth understanding of organizational change as well. Kotter (2011) noted that often there is insufficient recognition that change is a process involving a series of steps that can take time. Skipping stages may contribute to difficulties in implementing change. For example, Kotter noted the need to begin from a sense of urgency. This sense of urgency may explain Caplan's initial success in introducing consultation in Israel when there were few professionals to meet needs. Today, despite pressures, there may be less of a sense of urgency among Israeli school psychologists given the relatively high ratio of psychologists to students. Jimerson, Stewart, Skokut, Cardenas, and Malone (2009) reported that Israel has one of the highest ratios of psychologists to students of 48 countries surveyed in 2007.

Other stages involve developing a vision and a coalition in support of change, plans for removing obstacles to the new vision, and providing some immediate experiences of success. Notably, psychologists at the national level may feel less bound by insurmountable constraints in advocating change in the direction of encouraging systems consultation. This may be due to the fact that the national leadership feels more empowered to influence policies and can surmount constraints more easily than staff psychologists.

With respect to removing obstacles, Drucker (1994) suggested that in order for companies to do new things, they would first have to free time and resources for innovation by abandoning old things (Edersheim, 2006). As noted previously, in Israel, advocacy of role change toward increased engagement in consultation and promotion of mental health at the systems level led only minimally to more limited responsibilities for psychological assessments for special education eligibility and individual interventions. Similarly, careful examination of Nastasi's (2004) list of "potential roles for school psychologists in systems change and capacity building for mental health promotion" (p. 301) shows that, along with many innovative roles involving consultation at the school and inter-agency levels of educational systems, the list includes such items as providing individual or group counseling for at-risk or identified students. It may be that experts and leaders in school psychology in Israel, and around the world, need to carefully consider how increasing reliance on consultation and preventive services can be achieved by abandoning some of the traditional practices rather than adding to or changing the order of priorities. Moreover, a sense of urgency for changing practices and gaining wider support from stakeholders should be an important consideration.

A further constraint on changing the role of school psychologists stems from resistance of school psychologists themselves and a lack of sufficient training in organizational consultation (Braden et al., 2001; Meyers et al., 2012). Farrell (2010) suggests that one source of resistance may be concern about losing the distinctive role of school psychologists, that is, psychological assessment (especially IQ testing). As noted, other experts emphasize the need for more extensive training and ongoing supervision of school psychologists in organizational consultation and systems intervention. The rebranding of school psychology services can also help define systems-level consultation as a distinctive role of school psychologists.

The in-depth examination of the responses of the sample of Israeli school psychologists in the field as compared with the national leadership suggests an additional source of difficulty in gaining wider adoption of consultation to the system. It would seem that as much as there are very real, external constraints to be overcome, the *salient perception* of constraints precludes truly innovative thinking "within the box," as found among the staff members of Israeli school psychology services. Clearly, in Israel, as elsewhere, constraints such as lack of sufficient training and scarce resources need to be addressed. Even when Israeli school psychologists gain basic skills in consultation in the course of gaining licensure, they expressed a need for further, ongoing training, especially in systems-level consultation and social and political influence processes. The experience in adapting Drucker's tool to encourage examination of the psychologists' assumptions about school psychology services suggests that, along with the need for greater attention to salient difficulties in leading change within organizations, there may be significant resistance to change within the psychologists themselves.

In his classic article, Argyris (1991) suggested that often well-educated and highly committed professionals who are assumed to be good at learning may actually have difficulty. He proposes that most are experts at problem-solving that involves identifying and resolving external difficulties. However, they have much greater difficulty looking inward and examining their assumptions. Frequently, professionals have a history of success in their work, and when this is the case, Argyris suggests, they are likely to become defensive and focus on external constraints rather than their own beliefs. This may help explain the focus of many of the Israeli school psychologists on external constraints in response to the Drucker protocol.

Similarly, Kegan and Lahey (2001) note that often, even when people have gained the skills required and express support for changes in their roles, they may experience difficulty due to energy devoted to "hidden competing commitments." These are subconscious (or at least unaddressed) goals or beliefs that are counter to a desired change and that are supported by one's core beliefs. Kegan and Lahey present examples of hidden assumptions concerning need for control or fear of not succeeding in resolving a problem. I would hypothesize that psychologists, trained to seek intrapsychic factors in individual difficulties, may assume that reliance on systems-level consultation may not really resolve psychological difficulties. They may believe that they would "miss" the real source of difficulty and not treat it or resolve the problem.

Kegan and Lahey (2001) propose a three-stage process of examining difficulties with change that is suitable for ongoing psychological supervision that may accompany acquiring skills in consultation. This includes questioning to uncover "competing commitments," examination of the commitments to determine the underlying core beliefs, and then challenging the core beliefs and changing behavior as might be done in a cognitive behavioral intervention. Notably, leaders and supervisors in an organization are also susceptible to such difficulties in implementing change, requiring that they too engage in an ongoing process of self-reflection or work in small groups where it is safe to be vulnerable.

A CONCLUDING NOTE

In sum, it would appear there is a need for tools that can help psychologists examine their assumptions and develop innovative ideas, together with stakeholders, about implementing changes in their roles. Conoley and Gutkin (1995) are widely quoted as observing that psychology suffers not from "lack of good science" but from "a science devoted almost exclusively to answering the wrong sets of questions" (p. 210). The similarity to Drucker's insight about businesses experiencing difficulties because they continue to do the wrong things expertly is striking (Drucker, 1994). Drucker's solution was to develop a tool for "thinking in the box," which was presented here. Closer examination of the Israeli experience with respect to promoting role change and encouraging systems consultation suggests that all school psychologists need further opportunities to thoroughly and safely examine and question their assumptions, including consideration of which roles can be abandoned, in order to find innovative solutions within the framework of the box.

The literature from management consultation on change suggests that a single focus-group session is not sufficient to promote innovative ideas for providing school psychology services based on systems consultation. Rather, it requires ongoing supervision along with gaining a wider range of skills in systems consultation. Moreover, it requires that school psychologists become committed and empowered to lead organizational changes, including influencing the expectations of key stakeholders concerning measurement of educational outcomes and children's well-being.

REFERENCES

"360, Hatohnit Halumit L'yiladim V'noar B'sikun" [Hebrew] [National Project for Children and Youth at Risk]. (2014). *Project listings (updated): (Hebrew): Inter-departmental offices, Government of Israel*. Retrieved May, 2014, from http://www.molsa.gov.il/ProjectShmid/IndexedProjects/Pages/IndexedProjects_Page1.aspx.

Abbass, A., Kisely, S., Rasic, D., Town, J. M., & Johansson, R. (2015). Long-term healthcare cost reduction with Intensive Short-Term Dynamic Psychotherapy in a tertiary psychiatric service. *Journal of Psychiatric Research, 64*, 114–120.

Adelman, H. S., & Taylor, L. (1998). Mental health in schools: Moving forward. *School Psychology Review, 27*, 175–190.

Andreasen, A. R., & Kotler, P. (2003). *Strategic marketing for nonprofit organizations* (pp. 44–53). Upper Saddle River, NJ: Prentice Hall.

Argyris, C. (1991). Teaching smart people how to learn. *Harvard Business Review, 69*, 3–15.

Benyamini, K. (1982). The four clients of the school psychologist. *School Psychology International, 3*, 15–22.

Braden, J. S., DiMarino-Linnen, E., & Good, T. L. (2001). Schools, society, and school psychologists: History and future directions. *Journal of School Psychology, 39*, 203–219.

Bradley Johnson, S., & Dean, V. J. (2000). Role change for school psychology: The challenge continues in the new millennium. *Psychology in the Schools, 37*, 1–5.

Buffett, M., & Clark, D. (2006). *The Tao of Warren Buffett: Warren Buffett's words of wisdom: Quotations and interpretations to help guide you to billionaire wealth and enlightened business management*. New York: Simon and Schuster.

Caplan, G. (1970). *The theory and practice of mental health consultation*. New York: Basic Books.

Cohen, E., & Osterweil, Z. (1986). An "issue-focused" model for mental health consultation with groups of teachers. *Journal of School Psychology, 24*, 243–256.

Conoley, C. W., Conoley, J. C., & Reese, R. J. (2009). Changing a field of change. *Journal of Educational and Psychological Consultation, 19*, 236–247.

Conoley, J. C., & Gutkin, T. B. (1995). Why didn't—Why doesn't—School psychology realize its promise? *Journal of School Psychology, 33*, 209–217.

Cutler, D. L., & Huffine, C. (2004). Heroes in community psychiatry: Professor Gerald Caplan. *Community Mental Health Journal, 40*(3), 193–197.

Drucker, P. F. (1994). The theory of the business. *Harvard Business Review, 72*(5), 95–104.

Edersheim, E. H. (2006). *The definitive Drucker: Challenges for tomorrow's executives*. New York, NY: McGraw Hill.

Erchul, W. P. (2009). Gerald Caplan: A tribute to the originator of mental health consultation. *Journal of Educational and Psychological Consultation, 19*, 95–105.

Farrell, P. (2010). School psychology: Learning lessons from history and moving forward. *School Psychology International, 31*, 581–598.

Gutkin, T. B. (2012). Ecological psychology: Replacing the medical model paradigm for school-based psychological and psychoeducational services. *Journal of Educational and Psychological Consultation, 22*, 1–20.

Hatzichristou, C. (1998). Alternative school psychological services: Development of a databased model. *School Psychology Review, 27*, 246–259.

Hatzichristou, C., & Lampropoulou, A. (2004). The future of school psychology conference: A cross-national approach to service delivery. *Journal of Educational and Psychological Consultation, 15*, 313–333.

Hatzichristou, C., Lampropoulou, A., Lykitsakou, K., & Dimitropoulou, P. (2010). Promoting university and schools partnership: Transnational considerations and future directions. In J. Kaufman & T. Hughes (Eds.), *The handbook of education training and supervision of school psychologists in school and community* (pp. 79–108). New York: Routledge.

Hatzichristou, C., Lykitsakou, K., Lampropoulou, A., & Dimitropoulou, P. (2010). Promoting the well-being of school communities: A systemic approach. In B. Doll, W. Phohl, & J. Yoon (Eds.), *Handbook of prevention science* (pp. 255–274). New York: Routledge.

Israel Ministry of Health. (2015). *Instructions and Forms for the Process of Specialization in Educational Psychology*. Retrieved from http://www.health.gov.il/English/Services/MedicalAndHealthProfessions/Psychology/Expert_Psychologist/Pages/Educational_Psychology.aspx

Kaplan, D. M., Tarvydas, V. M., & Gladding, S. T. (2014). 20/20: A vision for the future of counseling: The new consensus definition of counseling. *Journal of Counseling & Development, 92*(3), 366–372.

Kegan, R., & Lahey, L. (2001). The real reason people won't change. *Harvard Business Review, 79*(10), 85–92.

Kotter, J. P. (2011). Leading change: Why transformation efforts fail. In J.C. Wood & M.C. Wood (Eds.), *On change* (pp. 1–16). Cambridge, MA: Harvard Business Review Press.

Lambert, N. M. (2004). Consultee-centered consultation: An international perspective on goals, process, and theory. In N. M. Lambert, I. H. Hylander, & J. H. Sandoval (Eds.), *Consultee-centered consultation: Improving the quality of professional services in schools and community organizations* (pp. 3–19). Mahwah, NJ: Lawrence Erlbaum Associates, Inc.

Levinson, S. (1999). Psihologia B'ma'arehet Hahinuh B'yisrael. In A. Peled (Ed.), *Yovel L'ma'arehet Hahinuh B'yisrael*. [Hebrew]. [Psychology in the educational system in Israel]. In A. Peled (Ed.), *Fifty years of the educational system in Israel* (Vol. 2, pp. 685–700). Jerusalem: Israel Ministry of Education.

Maital, S. L., & Shalhevet Kaniel, R. (in press). Hitpatchut Hapsihologia Hahinuhit B'yisrael [Hebrew]. [The development of educational psychology in Israel]. In S. Maital & R. Shalhevet Kaniel (Eds.), *Sugiot B'psihologia Hinuhit B'yisrael* [Handbook of school psychology in Israel]. Jerusalem, Israel: Psychological and Counseling Services Department, Israel Ministry of Education.

Meyers, A. B., Meyers, J., Graybill, E. C., Proctor, S. L., & Huddleston, L. (2012). Ecological approaches to organizational consultation and systems change in educational settings. *Journal of Educational and Psychological Consultation, 22*, 106–124.

Meyers, J., Parsons, R. D., & Martin, R. (1979). *Mental health consultation in the schools*. San Francisco: Jossey-Bass.

"Mitveh Hasherut Hapsihologi Hinuhi" [Hebrew], [Guidelines for Educational Psychology Services]. (2010). *Psychological and Counseling Services Department, Israel Ministry of Education*. Retrieved from http://cms.education.gov.il/EducationCMS/Applications/Mankal/EtsMedorim/3/3-7/HoraotKeva/K-2010-8a-3-7-61.htm

Nastasi, B. K. (2004). Meeting the challenges of the future: Integrating public health and public education for mental health promotion. *Journal of Educational and Psychological Consultation, 15*, 295–312.

"Odot Agaf Psyihologia." (n.d.) [Hebrew]. [About the Psychology Department], *Psychological and Counseling Services Department, Israel Ministry of Education*. Last retrieved May 15, 2014, from http://cms.education.gov.il/EducationCMS/Units/Shefi/gapim/psychology/

Raviv, A. (1985). School psychology in Israel. *Journal of School Psychology, 22*, 323–333.

Roth, A., & Fonagy, P. (2006). *What works for whom? A critical review of psychotherapy research*. New York, NY: Guilford Press.

Sheridan, S. M., & Gutkin, T. B. (2000). The ecology of school psychology: Examining and changing our paradigm for the 21st century. *School Psychology Review, 29*, 485–502.

Sherut Psychologi B'ganey Hayeladim: T'fisa Teoretit V'Kavim Manchim L'avoda. [Hebrew] [Psychological Services in Preschools: Theoretical Perspectives and Guidelines for Practice]. (2013). *Psychological and counseling services department, Israel ministry of education*. Last retrieved September 10, 2014, from http://meyda.education.gov.il/files/shefi/model_avoda.pdf

Standartim L'haaracha Psychologit L'vaadot al pi Hok [Hebrew]. [Standards for Psychological Assessment for Statutory Hearing Committees]. (2007). *Psychological and counseling services department, Israel ministry of education*. Retrieved from http://cms.education.gov.il/EducationCMS/Units/Shefi/mediniyut/HanchayotVeNehalim/StandartimVaadodHok.htm

Stein, B. (2007). School Psychology in Israel. In S. R. Jimerson, T. D. Oakland, & P. T. Farrell (Eds.), *The handbook of international school psychology* (pp. 189–198). Thousand Oaks, CA: Sage Publications. Last retrieved April 15, 2015, from http://faculty.education.ufl.edu/toakland/schoolpsychologyinternationally.pdf

Tzameret, K. (2010). [Hebrew], [Leadership conference, Summer, 2010]. *Shefi, Department of Psychology and Counseling Services, Israel Ministry of Education*. Retrieved from http://cms.education.gov.il/educationcms/units/shefi/gapim/psychology/peilut/tzameret2010.htm

Weisz, J. R., & Gray, J. S. (2008). Evidence-based psychotherapy for children and adolescents: Data from the present and a model for the future. *Child and Adolescent Mental Health, 13*(2), 54–65.

"Yisum Hok Hinuh Meyuhad" [Hebrew]. [Application of the Special Education Law]. (2014). *Directive of the Israel ministry of education*. Retrieved May, 2014, from http://cms.education.gov.il/EducationCMS/Applications/Mankal/EtsMedorim/1/1-2/HoraotKeva/K-2014-5-1-1-2-42.htm

14

DEALING WITH DIFFICULTIES
The Strategies of Instructional Consultants in Hong Kong

Shui-fong Lam

INTRODUCTION

At the turn of the millennium, the Hong Kong government initiated a large-scale reform that has long-term impact on many areas of education, including curriculum, admission system, education structure, and assessment mechanism (Education Commission, 2000). Like the many large-scale education reforms that have been launched since the 1990s in Western countries (Fullan, 2000), the education reform in Hong Kong is driven by a strong demand from society that students learn how to meet the challenges of a knowledge-based and fast-changing society.

Difficulties in Implementing Curriculum and Special Education Reform

The many changes, particularly those in curriculum, have direct and immediate implications for classroom practices. A key feature of the curriculum reform in Hong Kong is a paradigm shift from teacher-centered approaches to student-centered approaches. To equip students with skills in critical thinking, collaboration, communication, and problem-solving, teachers are encouraged to use more student-centered teaching approaches, such as project-based learning. These approaches are unfamiliar to many teachers in Hong Kong who were taught by traditional approaches. Tse, Lam, Lam, and Loh (2005) showed that, although student-centered approaches are officially recommended, many teachers still rely heavily on teacher-centered approaches to explain teaching materials to students. To cope with the rapid changes induced by the reform can be stressful for many teachers. Lee, Tsang, and Kwok (2007) found that teachers in Hong Kong report more job-specific stressors and have higher prevalence rates of generalized anxiety disorder and major depressive episodes than members of the general population.

The stress for Hong Kong teachers does not only come from the education reform but also from the unprecedented movement toward inclusive education that was launched since 1997, when the government implemented a pilot project, the Whole School Approach to Integration (Education Bureau, 2010). Teachers now have more students with special needs in their classrooms. Currently, 31,390 students with special needs are enrolled in regular primary and secondary schools in Hong Kong, making up 5.2% of the student population (Education Bureau, 2013). Although inclusive education has been implemented for more than a decade, many teachers still feel that they are not prepared for it.

Many, even those who were trained recently, still feel stressed and have concerns about having students with disabilities in their classes (Forlin & Chambers, 2011).

A survey of 219 school principals (Department of Psychology, 2001) has confirmed that schools in Hong Kong have difficulties with curriculum innovations and coping with student diversity. More than 70% of the respondents in that survey reported that they had difficulties in these two areas. Most importantly, about half of the respondents reported that school-based support in these two areas was inadequate.

Consultation on Instruction

In the context of education reform, school consultation, particularly consultation on instruction, may be an invaluable support to teachers (Wizda, 2004). Ysseldyke and Geenen (1996) posit that consultation, as an indirect service to students through empowering teachers, may help education reform produce promising outcomes for all students in need of assistance. In consultation, a consultant (specialist) and consultees (teachers) form a cooperative partnership and engage in a systematic problem-solving process with the goal to promote students' well-being and performance through enhancing the consultee systems (Gutkin & Curtis, 1999; Kratochwill, 2008; Sheridan, Richard, & Smoot, 2000). While school consultation may cover many aspects of students' well-being and performance, consultation on instruction has a focus on learning and the academic achievement of students. When Hong Kong teachers are faced with the challenges of curricular reform and inclusive education, consultation on instruction may provide them with useful support.

Difficulties Implementing Consultation in Practice

Despite consultation appearing to be efficacious, many researchers have pointed out that its potential as a tool for both preventing and solving problems is far from being realized in actual practice (Bramlett & Murphy, 1998; Conoley, Conoley, & Reese, 2009; Gonzalez, Nelson, Gutkin, & Shwery, 2004; Knoff, 2013). Many teachers are not receptive to consultation, although they may be stressed out by the difficulties in their classrooms. When consultation does not work, it is not uncommon for consultants to attribute the failure to teacher resistance (Gorges, Elliott, & Kettler, 2004). The most often cited causes of failure are teachers' inflexibility and poor motivation (Margolis, Fish, & Wepner, 1990; Schultz, Reisweber, & Cobb, 2007).

The emphasis on teachers' personal traits as a cause of failure may be a sign of the fundamental attribution error, a tendency to place an undue emphasis on internal characteristics to explain other people's behaviors, rather than considering external factors (Krull, 2001).

The causes for the failure of consultation can be multifaceted, with some related to consultees, some to consultants, and some to the environment. Even teacher resistance, a cause that is attributed to consultees, has many causes itself. Gonzalez et al. (2004) identified nine causes of teacher resistance to school consultation. Only three are associated with teachers (e.g., teacher efficacy) and the rest with the consultant (e.g., the consultants' interpersonal skills), organization (e.g., principal support), or situation (e.g., adequacy of time available for consulting). Nevertheless, most consultants attribute resistance primarily to the consultees rather than to themselves or the environment

(Gorges et al., 2004). The consultants' deemphasizing of the other causes is a self-serving bias that is harmful to the building of collaborative partnership between the consultants and the consultees.

To realize the promise and potential of consultation on instruction as a support to teachers during an era of education reforms, there is a need to study the obstacles with a comprehensive view of the causes that extends beyond self-serving bias. Without an accurate understanding of the obstacles, it is impossible to come up with the right strategies to overcome them. One objective of the current study is to address this concern.

Overview of the Study

The study reported in this chapter is aimed at understanding how instructional consultants in Hong Kong perceive the difficulties in consultation on instruction[1] during the education reform that has set off an avalanche of innovative practices in instruction. This is a qualitative study that documented their opinions as voiced in focus group discussions. To avoid fundamental attribution errors, a special effort was made to structure the discussion so that the instructional consultants had to pay attention to the difficulties caused by the school systems and themselves. After the difficulties were identified, the instructional consultants were asked to brainstorm solutions to these difficulties.

A second objective of the present study was to document the strategies they deemed efficacious. The opinions of the instructional consultants in Hong Kong could be a useful reference for their counterparts in the other parts of the world where demand for innovative changes in teaching and learning is also enormous.

METHOD

Participants

The participants were 45 instructional consultants from a division in the Education Bureau of the Hong Kong government. Over 90% of the instructional consultants in this division were included. This division supported schools in the implementation of curriculum policies and innovations. Most of the consultants in this division were in the age range of 30 to 45 years. The ratio of female to male was about 2 to 1. All the instructional consultants had teaching qualifications and some years of work experience as school teachers before they joined the division in the Education Bureau.

One of the tasks of these instructional consultants was to develop, experiment, and disseminate effective curriculum practices in local schools. As government employees, they solicited collaboration from some schools and worked with the teachers there to try out innovative curriculum practices, such as project-based learning. The schools and teachers were identified through the network of the regional offices in the Education Bureau. With reference to the three-tiered service delivery model proposed by Ysseldyke et al. (2006), the work of these instructional consultants was mostly at a universal level or at a targeted level. As they were not school psychologists, they did not take case referrals. Their major duty was to provide consultation to teachers on innovative curriculum practices that would improve all students' competence. They work side by side with teachers to solve the problems and difficulties in instructions.

Although most of them did not have preservice training in consultation, they received on-the-job training in consultation after they had joined the Education Bureau. The training was in form of an apprenticeship supplemented with continuing professional development workshops or seminars. In the apprenticeship, they learned from their supervisors or senior colleagues in school consultation. In professional development workshops or seminars, the instructors were experienced instructional consultants or professors with relevant expertise from higher education institutes. These supervisors and instructors have diverse orientations and backgrounds. The consultation models they adopt may include client-centered, consultee-centered, or process-centered models. Nevertheless, many of them may be identified as adopting an eclectic model. The skills they teach include communication skills, team-building skills, collaboration skills, problem formulation, and resolution skills.

Procedures

The opinions of the instructional consultants were collected in a staff development workshop conducted by the author. The focus of the workshop was the difficulties in consultation on instruction and how to deal with them. The three-hour workshop had two major activities. In the first half of the workshop, the participants were divided into three groups with 15 people in each group. They identified the difficulties they had encountered in instructional consultation. Each group listed their opinions on flip chart paper and presented them to the other groups at the end of the discussion. In the second half of the workshop, the participants brainstormed solutions to the difficulties they had identified. They also wrote their opinions on flip chart paper and presented them at the end of the discussion.

Difficulties in the EPS Framework

To facilitate the discussion, a framework was provided to the participants. Each group of participants was asked to identify difficulties from three sources: (1) difficulties arising from the environment or systems, (2) difficulties arising from people, and (3) difficulties arising from themselves. With this EPS framework (environment, people, self), the participants were able to minimize fundamental attribution errors and achieve a more comprehensive view of their predicament in consultation. Environment, people, and self were discussed in this order so that the participants did not need to discuss the difficulties caused by themselves or other people first. The purpose of this arrangement was to minimize any self-defensiveness and finger-pointing.

Strategies in the EPS Framework

The EPS framework was used again when the participants brainstormed the strategies that would address the difficulties they had identified. They were asked to come up with solutions to the difficulties that arose from environment, people, and themselves. To facilitate a more in-depth discussion of strategies, the three groups were randomly assigned to focus on one of the three categories of difficulties. The first group focused on the environment, the second on people, and the third on the self.

RESULTS

Categorization of the Opinions

As the EPS framework was employed in the discussion of both the difficulties and strategies, the participants' opinions were reported and summarized according to the three categories in the framework: environment, people, and self.

Difficulties Arising from the Environment
Lack of Physical Space

Two groups pointed out that lack of physical space for meetings was a pressing concern. Hong Kong is an overcrowded metropolis in which school buildings are usually very compact. Almost all the rooms in a school building are occupied during the daytime. The participants found it difficult to have a quiet place where they could meet with teachers.

Lack of Time

Two groups said that teachers did not have the time to work with them. In Hong Kong, the workload of teachers is usually very heavy. On average, each teacher has to teach 30 class periods or more weekly. They do not have time, energy, or motivation to start new projects or try new measures. The participants pointed out that even when teachers were engaged in a school-based curriculum change despite all the heavy workload, they did not have time to reflect on their experience.

Lack of Flexibility in the Systems

All three groups thought that many schools in Hong Kong were very rigid. For example, they said that some schools demanded all classes in the same grade to abide by the same curriculum and the same examination paper. Deviation from the standard policy was not tolerated. It thus allowed little room for experimentation of new teaching methods or curriculum.

Lack of Research Support

The participants in one group were particularly concerned about the lack of research support for some innovative instructional practices. They pointed out that there were no ready answers for many problems in education. For example, they were not sure what strategies would be effective in dealing with student diversity in Hong Kong, but they were supposed to give advice to teachers about this.

Difficulties Arising from People
Weak Leadership in School

All three groups pointed out that in some schools leadership was problematic. Some principals invited instructional consultants to their schools without obtaining prior consent from the teachers involved. Thus, the consultation was imposed on these teachers and alienated them even before any consultation took place. When democratic participation was missing, teachers responded with passivity and did not feel that they should participate actively in the process.

Unrealistic Expectation of Ownership

Participants in one group said that some teachers expected that instructional consultants would solve their problems for them. These teachers hoped that consultants would provide them with clear guidance or even implement the projects or measures for them. They vested the consultants with the ownership of the new teaching practices. If the consultants did not want to take up ownership and implement everything, the teachers would feel that the consultants were not helpful. When the consultants were left alone to develop projects or measures with little input from the teachers, these projects or measures were usually deemed to be unfit for the school. As a result, the teachers would dismiss the innovations, saying that these measures were unpractical. Even if the innovations were successful, the teachers would be less likely to continue the efforts after the consultants had left their schools.

Tension among School Personnel

Two groups pointed out that tension among school personnel posed a threat to their work. This problem was particularly serious in schools with weak, poor, or rigid leadership. The instructional consultants were easily caught in the middle of the bickering.

Lack of Communication and Trust

Two groups brought up the issue of inadequate communication and trust between instructional consultants and teachers. The instructional consultants were considered outsiders who only paid visits to schools occasionally. It was not easy for them to establish rapport with teachers. Some teachers might feel being evaluated and monitored when the consultants tried to help them. The support from the consultants was not necessarily perceived in a positive light.

Lack of Support from Parents

Two groups pointed out that parents might sometimes be a hindrance to school-based innovations in the curriculum. The participants found that some parents would query any endeavors that deviated from the tradition. For example, they would ask why there was so little drilling or why their children were not required to learn by rote.

Lack of Shared Vision

Participants in one group said that the principals, teachers, and instructional consultants might not share the same vision of a certain teaching practice or even of education in general. For example, some principals might see their students achieving academic excellence in public examinations as the ultimate goal. Their performance-oriented mindset was incompatible with inclusive education. The students with special needs would be considered a hindrance to the actualization of their ultimate goal of achieving academic excellence in public examinations. It would be very difficult for instructional consultants, as outsiders, to change the mindset of such principals.

Difficulties Arising from Consultants Themselves
Lack of Knowledge

All three groups admitted that they did not know the answers to many problems in teaching and learning. They themselves might not be sure which strategies could achieve a certain school-based innovation.

Lack of Preparation

All three groups admitted that they might not have time to catch up with the rapid changes in the education system and to equip themselves for the school-based innovation that they were assigned to facilitate.

Lack of People Skills

Participants from one group said that they were not skillful enough to negotiate a reasonable working relationship with principals and teachers. This difficulty was most serious in the schools with poor leadership and intense interpersonal conflicts.

Lack of Competencies in Fostering System Change

Participants from one group brought up the issue of system change. They thought that they were not competent to make changes in school culture. This difficulty was particularly evident in the schools with poor leadership and rigid traditions. As outsiders, they had no legitimacy to intervene. For example, they could not really say anything about democratic participation in the schools where they served.

Strategies for Addressing Difficulties Arising from the Environment

Reengineering

To create time and space for teachers, the participants suggested that they could help the schools to conduct business process reengineering (BPR) (Accounting and Information Management Division, 1997). BPR is a technique in the business sector that helps companies to fundamentally rethink how they do their work in order to cut operational costs and improve services. The participants borrowed this technique from the business sector and suggested that before starting a new teaching project, school personnel should reflect on whether they could cancel any existing but futile projects. Without cutting excessive workload, the participants thought that it was unfair and impractical to add more work to teachers' current workloads. The instructional consultants could work with school personnel to examine whether there was anything the school should not keep on doing and whether there was anything the school should do but had not done. The things that they should not do any more they should *stop* doing, and the things that they should do but had not done they should *start* doing. They could also examine whether there was anything they were doing too much or too little. The things they were doing too much they should *scale down*, and the things that they were doing too little they should *scale up*. For example, when consultants and teachers found that they were doing too much on the refinement of direct instruction but too little on the experimentation of constructivist approaches, they would scale down the former and scale up the latter.

Right Timing for Intervention

The participants suggested that if a school was not ready for a new teaching project, they should wait for the right timing. It did not help if the school imposed support on the teachers who did not think they needed this assistance as the innovations would only end up being mere formalities that would hurt rather than help. The participants suggested that it would be better for instructional consultants to wait until the teachers felt the need for support. One of them jokingly said that they would not have to wait too long before the teachers felt the need for support because the education system in Hong Kong was constantly in crisis. That was particularly true ever since Hong Kong had launched the large scale education reform in 2000. For example, the change of assessment mechanism in public examinations has forced teachers to master new concepts and skills in assessment.

Flexibility in the Systems

To deal with the rigid school systems, the participants suggested that they should work with both school administrators and teachers to bring about some flexibility. They thought that they could not ignore the obstacles in the systems, and that they might need to start with small changes to gain the blessing of school administrators for flexibility in the systems. For example, if the school administrators gave the green light to implement different curricula for different groups of students in the same grade, there would be more possibilities for experimentation with differentiated instruction that caters to student diversity (Landrum & McDuffie, 2010; Reis, McCoach, Little, Muller, & Kaniskan, 2011; Tomlinson, 2001).

Action Research

The participants were aware of the fact that it was impossible to have ready answers to all the problems in education. They thought that it would be all right for them not knowing all the solutions as long as they did not give up the continuous search for solutions. They came to an understanding that knowledge could be generated from the empirical studies conducted by researchers in universities as well as from the action research done by them and by teachers during their experimentation with various innovative teaching practices. On the one hand, they thought that it was important to pay attention to the findings of researchers in universities. On the other hand, they thought that they could also contribute to the accumulation of knowledge by doing small-scale research as part of their practice.

Strategies for Addressing Difficulties Arising from People

Working on School Leadership

The participants argued that it was legitimate for them to influence the leadership of the schools that they served because factors in the systems, such as democratic participation, would definitely enhance, moderate, neutralize, or even counteract their efforts. They suggested that they should not only work with the teachers in the trench but also with the principals in the commander's office. If they could reinforce the leadership of the schools and gain support from the administrators, there would be more chance for innovative teaching practices to be successful. One participant made a playful remark that the principal was usually the "loneliest" person in a school. Therefore, it would not be too difficult for instructional consultants to form alliances with a principal if they could provide him/her with support. Other participants suggested that instructional consultants could work as a bridge between principals and their teachers. They might be able to facilitate communication and harmonious relationships among school personnel if they could tactfully handle the needs of different parties.

Partnership and Ownership

The participants said that the problems in leadership, partnership, and ownership were intricately related to one another. If democratic participation was present in school culture, it would be easier for teachers to own the new teaching project because they took part in it voluntarily. When they did not vest instructional consultants with ownership of the innovation, it would be easier for them to form a genuine partnership with instructional consultants. The participants suggested that to form a genuine partnership with teachers, they should insist on the implementation of an action research paradigm. This means that all team members, including instructional consultants, should be equal partners in the quest for solutions to problems. These problems might include those related to the lack of support from parents. As a team, instructional consultants and teachers should take measures to win the acceptance of parents for innovative practices.

Strategies for Addressing Difficulties Arising from Consultants Themselves
Continuous Professional Development

The participants felt that it would be all right for them not knowing the answers to many problems in education. They thought that this would be all right as long as they could continuously build up their knowledge base. While they acknowledged that they might lack competence in many areas, they believed that skills in consultation were acquired through experience, training, and supervision instead of something that was inborn. They felt that they could learn these skills either by attending courses or by examining their actual work experience with their supervisors.

Peer Coaching

Some participants thought that it was important for instructional consultants to learn from one another. They felt that through peer coaching and by supporting one another and sharing experience and resources, they could enhance their competence.

DISCUSSION

With the EPS discussion framework, the participants were able to go beyond self-serving bias and could achieve a more balanced and comprehensive view of the difficulties they encountered in instructional consultation. Instead of blaming teachers for most of their difficulties, they were able to see their own share in their predicament. Most important, they were aware of how systems might facilitate or hinder their work. This comprehensive understanding provided them with a solid foundation for developing appropriate strategies to deal with the difficulties.

Systems-Based Service Delivery

To address the difficulties arising from the environment, the participants proposed four strategies: (1) helping the school to conduct business process reengineering so as to create time and space for teachers; (2) waiting for the right time for intervention; (3) working with the administrators to induce flexibility in the systems; and (4) engaging in action research. These strategies are in line with the systems-based service delivery model proposed by Ysseldyke et al. (2006). Human development occurs in a nested arrangement of systems, each contained within the next (Bronfenbrenner, 1977). The dynamics and relationships in these systems have a significant impact on human development. Schools and classrooms are some of these systems that affect learning and development in diverse and complex way. To make consultation efficacious, consultants must understand how school systems work and make use of this knowledge to help organize the systems in ways that promote student learning. Reengineering, appropriate timing, flexibility, and action research are promising strategies for addressing the difficulties arising from the systems. When implemented tactfully with deliberation, it is possible to transform the school systems and make them receptive to innovative changes in teaching practice (Lam, Yim, & Lam, 2002).

To address the difficulties arising from people, the participants proposed two strategies that are also systems based: (1) enhancing the school leadership and (2) insistence on the action research paradigm so that consultants and consultees are equal partners in the problem-solving process. It is noteworthy that the participants were able to get away from a finger-pointing mentality when they brainstormed the strategies for addressing the difficulties arising from people. Although they realized that some difficulties were related to people, they chose to work on the systems that kept people from displaying problematic behaviors. They directed their strategies to the systems instead of the behaviors of teachers. To make it easy for teachers to participate, they thought it was important to work with school administrators so that the systems would be conducive to teachers' participation. To administratively impose a certain innovative practice onto teachers without considering the obstacles they encounter in the systems will only alienate them. It is a wise maneuver for the instructional consultants to give up the *administratively imposed* type of change for the *organizationally induced* type of change. Grimmett and Crehan (1992) point out that the latter type of change is a top-down program-solving approach to school improvement "through careful manipulation, not of teachers' practices and behaviors, but of the environment within which teachers live and work and have their professional being" (p. 70). This approach is consistent with the systems-based service delivery model proposed by Ysseldyke et al. (2006).

Action Research Paradigm

Action research is a form of collective self-reflective enquiry undertaken by participants in social situations (Altrichter, Kemmis, McTaggart, & Zuber-Skerritt, 1991). It is an alternative approach to traditional social science research in that the findings gained from the research are not only for the advancement of knowledge in the field but also for the immediate improvements during and after the research process (Burns, 2007; James, Milenkiewicz, & Bucknam, 2007). Twice the participants mentioned action research as a strategy: once to address the difficulties related to the environment and once to address the difficulties related to people. When it was mentioned the first time, it was meant to address the lack of empirical evidence for the effectiveness of some innovative teaching practices. When it was mentioned the second time, the focus was no longer on the research findings but was meant to address the difficulties in partnership and ownership.

During consultation it seems to be legitimate for consultants to take up the role of expert when teachers invite them to do so. If they do not play such a role, teachers may see them as unhelpful. However, once consultants accept such an invitation, teachers will look to them for guidelines and instructions. The ownership of the innovations will then shift to the consultants. To tackle this embarrassing dilemma, the participants of this study advocated for an action research paradigm.

In an action research team, all the members are equal partners in search of solutions to a problem. Both the consultants and the teachers are experts in their own right. Like the blind men who examined an elephant in the Indian parable, each party in the consultation has only a small piece of information. They would not have the full picture of the situation unless they were able to pool their information together. The consultants may have knowledge about the new instructional practices, but it is the teachers who have the knowledge about their students and the feasibility of such practices in their school systems. To seek and try out solutions together, the two parties must share their expertise on an equal footing.

Development Partnership versus
Implementation Partnership

With reference to the advocacy for an action research paradigm, advice from Biott (1992) may be insightful. He suggests that consultants adopt a *development* partnership instead of an *implementation* partnership during the consultation. As equal partners to develop new solutions for a certain problem, consultants should use the strategies of asking, inquiring, discussing, and developing instead of giving, telling, showing, and implementing. The former set of strategies is consistent with the action research paradigm in which the consultants do not have all the answers to the problem. If they already have all the answers, they do not need to engage in action research with the teachers. They could simply tell the teachers what to do. Telling the teachers what to do is an implementation model in which the teachers implement the plan handed down by the consultants. This is a risky model because any plan without input from the teachers is susceptible to failure. The participants of the current study had a poignant analysis of this problem when they mentioned the difficulties of partnership and ownership. They were aware of the importance that teachers should have ownership of innovative practices.

The advocacy for an action research paradigm has another implication for the consultant–consultee relationship. As they are equal partners in action research, their focus is on problem-solving so that student learning will be enhanced. Although it is the goal of consultation to improve staff competence as a route to positive student outcomes, it is better to let the teachers know that the focus is on problem-solving rather than on enhancing their competence, since emphasis on enhancing the teachers' competence may have a condescending connotation that leads to the teachers becoming self-conscious about their competence. This self-consciousness is unfavorable for the collaborative partnership between the consultants and the consultees. Once the teachers are concerned whether their competence measures up to the standards held by the consultants, they will be on guard and self-defensive. In contrast, if they know that the consultants are their partners in search for answers to the problems that hinder their students' learning, they will be more receptive to the collaboration. Although the competence of the teachers will be enhanced at the end of the consultation, it is unwise to put the teachers' competence up front as the focus in the consultation. The chances to have a development partnership instead of an implementation partnership will be slim if the teachers feel any condescending attitudes from the consultants.

Professional Development of
Instructional Consultants

In the EPS discussion framework, the difficulties arising from the consultants themselves were discussed last. To address these difficulties, the participants proposed two strategies: (1) engagement in continuous professional development and (2) involvement in peer coaching. After they had identified the difficulties related to the environment and to other people, they were less defensive and more willing to admit their own inadequacies.

They acknowledged the importance of continuous professional development and the need for peer coaching in their daily practice. Their advocacy of peer coaching is commendable because peer coaching has a tremendous impact on the transfer of knowledge and skills from a staff development course to real-life practice (Lam & Lau, 2008).

Contributions

The current chapter presents the opinions of a group of instructional consultants in Hong Kong regarding the difficulties and the corresponding solutions in instructional consultation. As the study was conducted in the midst of large-scale education reform in Hong Kong, the opinions of these consultants are likely to be of use to consultants in other countries who are facing similar challenges brought about by education reforms. Their opinions may shed light on the work of other consultants who are struggling with similar difficulties during a time of rapid change.

The present study adopted the EPS discussion framework and enabled the participants to go beyond the fundamental attribution error—that is, blaming the consultees—so as to hold a more balanced and comprehensive view of their difficulties. They could see how components in the school systems interacted and affected their work in diverse and complex ways. As a result, they were able to address the difficulties with a systems-based service delivery model. They adopted systems-oriented strategies not only for the difficulties arising from the environment but also for the difficulties arising from people. It is easy for people-related difficulties to trigger a finger-pointing mentality. Nevertheless, after the participants had considered the difficulties and strategies related to school systems, they were able to generalize their systems thinking to the difficulties related to people. They continued to use a systems approach to deal with the people problem. Instead of trying to manipulate the teachers' practice and behaviors, they indicated their intention to manipulate the systems that had tremendous impacts on the teachers' practice and behaviors.

Limitations and Future Directions

Despite the above contributions, the present study has some obvious limitations. First, the number of participants was small ($n = 45$) and the generalizability of the findings may be limited. Future studies may consider replicating the study with more participants in other agencies apart from the Education Bureau. Second, the participants were instructional consultants who only provided consultation at a universal level or at a targeted level (Tier 1 or Tier 2 services). In the school system in Hong Kong, only school psychologists, social workers, and student guidance personnel take case referrals. Because the instructional consultants in this study did not take case referrals, their opinions could not be generalized to an intensive level (Tier 3 service). It is unknown to what extent the difficulties and strategies they identified are relevant to consultation that involves individual students who are referred for assistance. Future studies may consider recruiting the other helping professionals who provide Tier 3 services (e.g., school psychologists) as participants so that the difficulties and strategies related to all three levels of service could be explored. Third, there was no follow-up investigation to examine the effectiveness of the solutions generated in the current studies. It is unclear how useful these strategies were in coping with the difficulties in consultation. It is worthwhile for future studies to evaluate the effectiveness of these strategies.

Last, the present study only examined the perspective of the consultants. The opinions of the consultees are missing. As the Indian parable of the blind men and the elephant implies, it is important to see the reality from different perspectives. It will be worthwhile for future studies to examine the opinions of consultees regarding the difficulties and solutions in instructional consultation.

CONCLUSION

The present study documented the opinions of a group of Hong Kong instructional consultants on the difficulties of their work. It also documented their suggestions for strategies to address these difficulties. Because the study was conducted during a large-scale education reform that had affected many areas in Hong Kong education, the opinions of these consultants are a potential valuable reference for consultants facing similar challenges as a result of education reforms in other parts of world.

NOTE

1. The consultation in the present study refers to the consultation offered to teachers by consultants on instruction in general. It is not the same as the specific instructional consultation in Rosenfield's model (2008). The latter is a collaborative problem-solving model that focuses on communication skills, contracting process, and other aspects that are not embedded in the consultation on instruction investigated in the present study.

REFERENCES

Accounting and Information Management Division, United States General Account Office. (1997). *Business process reengineering assessment guide*. Retrieved from http://www.gao.gov/assets/80/76302.pdf

Altrichter, H., Kemmis, S., McTaggart, R., & Zuber-Skerritt, O. (1991). Defining, confining or refining action research? In O. Zuber-Skerritt (Ed.), *Action research for change and development* (pp. 3–9). Hants: Avebury.

Biott, C. (1992). Imposed support for teachers' learning: Implementation or development partnership? In C. Biott & J. Nias (Eds.), *Working and learning together for change* (pp. 3–18). Philadelphia: Open University Press.

Bramlett, R. K., & Murphy, J. J. (1998). School psychology perspectives on consultation: Key contributions to the field. *Journal of Educational and Psychological Consultation, 9*, 29–55.

Bronfenbrenner, U. (1977). Toward an experimental ecology of human development. *American Psychologist, 32*, 513–531.

Burns, D. (2007). *Systemic action research: A strategy for whole system change*. Bristol: Policy Press.

Conoley, C. W., Conoley, J. C., & Reese, R. J. (2009). Changing a field of change. *Journal of Educational & Psychological Consultation, 19*, 236–247. doi: 10.1080/10474410903106836

Department of Psychology, University of Hong Kong, and Division of Educational Psychology, Hong Kong Psychological Society. (2001). *Report on the survey of the school-based professional support services to primary school*. Hong Kong: Author.

Education Bureau. (2010). *Operation guide on the whole school approach to integrated education*. Retrieved from http://www.edb.gov.hk/attachment/en/edu-system/special/support/wsa/IE_Guide_English_19-11-13.pdf

Education Bureau. (2013). *Figures and statistics*. Retrieved from http://www.edb.gov.hk/en/about-edb/publications-stat/figures/index.html

Education Commission. (2000). *Learning for life, learning through life: Reform proposal for the education system in Hong Kong*. Hong Kong: Government Printer.

Forlin, C., & Chambers, D. (2011). Teacher preparation for inclusive education: Increasing knowledge but raising concerns. *Asia-Pacific Journal of Teacher Education, 39*, 17–32. doi: 10.1080/1359866X.2010.540850

Fullan, M. (2000). The return of large-scale reform. *Journal of Educational Change, 1*, 5–28.

Gonzalez, J. E., Nelson, J. R., Gutkin, T. B., & Shwery, C. S. (2004). Teacher resistance to school-based consultation with school psychologists: A survey of teacher perceptions. *Journal of Emotional and Behavioral Disorders, 12*, 30–37. doi: 10.1177/10634266040120010401

Gorges, T., Elliott, S. N., & Kettler, R. J. (2004). Resistance: Experienced and novice consultants' interpretations and strategies for addressing it in behavioral consultation interviews. *Canadian Journal of School Psychology, 19*, 1–32. doi: 10.1177/082957350401900101

Grimmett, B. L., & Crehan, E. P. (1992). The nature of collegiality in teacher development: The case of clinical supervision. In M. Fullan & A. Hargreaves (Eds.), *Teacher development and educational change* (pp. 56–85). London: Falmer Press.

Gutkin, T. B., & Curtis, M. J. (1999). School-based consultation theory and practice: The art and science of indirect service delivery. In C. R. Reynolds & T. B. Gutkin (Eds.), *The handbook of school psychology* (3rd ed., pp. 598–637). New York: John Wiley & Sons.

James, E. A., Milenkiewicz, M. T., & Bucknam, A. (2007). *Participatory action research for educational leadership: Using data-driven decision making to improve schools.* Thousand Oaks: Sage.

Knoff, H. M. (2013). Changing resistant consultees: Functional assessment leading to strategic intervention. *Journal of Educational & Psychological Consultation, 23*, 307–317. doi: 10.1080/10474412.2013.845496

Kratochwill, T. R. (2008). Best practice in school-based problem-solving consultation: Applications in prevention and intervention system. In A. Thomas & J. Grimes (Eds.), *Best practices in school psychology V* (pp. 1673–1688). Bethesda, MD: The National Association of School Psychologists.

Krull, D. S. (2001). On partitioning the fundamental attribution error: Dispositionalism and the correspondence bias. In G. B. Moskowitz (Ed.), *Cognitive social psychology: The Princeton symposium on the legacy and future of social cognition* (pp. 211–227). Mahwah, NJ: Lawrence Erlbaum Associates.

Lam, S.-F., & Lau, W.-S. (2008). Teachers' acceptance of peer coaching: Impact of collegiality and goal orientation. *Journal of School Connection, 1*, 3–24.

Lam, S.-F., Yim, P.-S., & Lam, T. W.-H. (2002). Transforming school culture: Can true collaboration be initiated? *Educational Research, 44*, 181–195.

Landrum, T. J., & McDuffie, K. A. (2010). Learning styles in the age of differentiated instruction. *Exceptionality, 18*, 6–17. doi: 10.1080/09362830903462441

Lee, S., Tsang, A., & Kwok, K. (2007). Stress and mental disorders in a representative sample of teachers during education reform in Hong Kong. *Journal of Psychology in Chinese Societies, 8*, 159–178.

Margolis, H., Fish, M., & Wepner, S. B. (1990). Overcoming resistance to prereferral classroom interventions. *Special Services in the Schools, 6*, 167–189.

Reis, S. M., McCoach, D. B., Little, C. A., Muller, L. M., & Kaniskan, R. B. (2011). The effects of differentiated instruction and enrichment pedagogy on reading achievement in five elementary schools. *American Educational Research Journal, 48*, 462–501. doi: 10.3102/0002831210382891

Rosenfield, S. (2008). Best practice in instructional consultation and instructional consultation teams. In A. Thomas & J. Grimes (Eds.), *Best practices in school psychology V* (pp. 1645–1659). Bethesda, MD: The National Association of School Psychologists.

Schultz, B. K., Reisweber, J., & Cobb, H. (2007). Mental health consultation in secondary schools. In S. W. Evans and M. D. Weist (Eds.), *Advances in school-based mental health interventions: Best practices and program models* (Vol. 2, pp. 1–20). Kingston, NJ: Civic Research Institute.

Sheridan, S. M., Richard, J. R., & Smoot, T. Y. (2000). School consultation. In A. E. Kazdin (Ed.), *Encyclopedia of psychology* (pp. 167–170). New York: Oxford University Press.

Tomlinson, C. A. (2001). *How to differentiate instruction in mixed-ability classrooms.* Alexandria, VA: Association for Supervision and Curriculum Development.

Tse, S. K., Lam, W. I., Lam, Y. H., & Loh, E. K. Y. (2005). *Learn to read: The performance of Hong Kong primary 4 pupils in PIRLS 2001.* Hong Kong: Hong Kong University Press.

Wizda, L. (2004). An instructional consultant looks to the future. *Journal of Educational & Psychological Consultation, 15*, 277–294. doi: 10.1207/s1532768xjepc153&4_5

Ysseldyke, J. E., Burns, M., Dawson, P., Kelley, B., Morrison, D., Ortiz, S., . . . Telzrow, C. (2006). *School psychology: A blueprint for training and practice III.* Bethesda, MD: National Association of School Psychologists.

Ysseldyke, J. E., & Geenen, K. (1996). Integrating the special education and compensatory education systems into school reform process: A national perspective. *School Psychological Review, 25*, 418–430.

Zuber-Skerritt, O. (Ed.). (1991). *Action research for change and development.* Hants: Avebury.

15

ECOLOGICAL CONSULTATION AS A MEANS TO PROMOTE CHILD RIGHTS

Cynthia E. Hazel

ECOLOGICAL CONSULTATION AS A MEANS TO PROMOTE CHILD RIGHTS

School-based consultation can perpetuate inequities and privileges, or consultation can be one of our most powerful tools to promote liberation, empowerment, and social justice (Clare, 2009; Pearrow & Pollack, 2009; Sander, 2013). Too often, school-based consultation is conceptualized as a consultant working with a consultee (most often a teacher or a parent) to change the behavior of a student (or small group of students) toward something that is found more tolerable by the adult. In contrast, broader conceptualizations of consultation view systems change, prevention, and strengthening supports for all students as goals of consultation in addition to problem remediation (McNamara, 2014; Meyers, Meyers, & Grogg, 2004).

However, even these broader conceptualizations of consultation rarely integrate the rights of children. The Convention on the Rights of the Child (CRC) (United Nations [UN], 1990) stated that all children deserve protection and have the same rights. However, societies privilege some groups over others and have structured educational institutions to perpetuate social inequities. Educational policies and practices continue to privilege the rights of some groups of students over others (Shriberg & Desai, 2014).

This becomes starkly evident at the secondary level where we see that obtainment of a secondary-level education varies greatly for students, depending on personal, school, and community demographic variables. The opposite of disproportionality would be zero correlation: there would be no relationship between children's demographic, neighborhood, school, or national characteristics with educational outcomes, postsecondary opportunities, and health. Zero correlation would be the embodiment of all children's rights being protected equally. It is beholden upon consultants working in schools to challenge disproportionality and work to ensure equal protection of rights for all children.

This chapter outlines how the practice of school-based ecological consultation can promote social justice and the rights of all children. The chapter begins with a review of the CRC applied to educational practices. It then defines socially just psychological and educational practices informed by the CRC. Ecological consultation is presented as a means to promote all students' rights. The chapter presents two case studies of ecological consultation with an urban district and secondary school administrators in a United States city to promote socially just, equitable educational opportunities for all students.

CONVENTION ON THE RIGHTS OF THE CHILD AND EDUCATION

The CRC was adopted by the UN General Assembly in 1989 (UN, 1990). The CRC was the product of 10 years of collaboration between leaders in governments, nongovernmental organizations, human rights advocates, health and development experts, and educators (United Nations International Children's Emergency Fund [UNICEF], 2014). Now, over 25 years later, it is lauded as the most highly ratified human rights treaty in history (UNICEF, 2014). The International School Psychology Association (ISPA) is strongly committed to the promotion of children's rights. As stated in its mission statement:

> ISPA is strongly committed to improving healthy development and quality of life for children everywhere. ISPA has thus made children's human rights a high priority in its international work during the last decade and will maintain this emphasis in the future. For this purpose, ISPA has initiated and collaborated with international endeavors that benefit children or hold a genuine promise to do so. The involvement of school psychology at the national level will significantly strengthen many of these projects.
>
> (ISPA, n.d.)

The CRC contains 41 articles defining and outlining the rights of children. The Preamble references earlier child human rights treaties, including the Declaration of the Rights of the Child, which states that children, due to their physical and mental immaturity, need special safeguards and care. The Preamble also identifies that "in all countries in the world, there are children living in exceptionally difficult conditions, and that such children need special consideration" (1990, p. 1). The UNICEF (2014) summary of the CRC states:

> The Convention establishes in international law that States Parties must ensure that all children—without discrimination in any form—benefit from special protection measures and assistance; have access to services such as education and health care; can develop their personalities, abilities and talents to the fullest potential; grow up in an environment of happiness, love and understanding; and are informed about and participate in, achieving their rights in an accessible and active manner.

The rights outlined in the CRC have been organized into four categories: (1) guiding principles, (2) survival and development rights, (3) protection rights, and (4) participation rights (UNICEF, 2011). The right to education is considered a survival and development right. Taken together, the CRC recognizes that childhood is a special and vulnerable time, and there are some children with particular vulnerabilities (due to circumstances or individual needs); however, children are also people who are entitled to human rights and privileges. Therefore, there is a tension between protecting (and deciding for) children and promoting children's rights to self-determination (Lansdown, Jimerson, & Shahroozi, 2014).

Although the full CRC provides critical guidance for protecting and promoting the rights of children (defined as persons up to the age of 18) in all settings (including in educational settings), Articles 28 and 29 are most specific to education. Article 28 states that "States Parties recognize the right of the child to education" (p. 8), which shall include free and compulsory primary education, various forms of secondary education (such as general and vocational), and taking measures to encourage regular attendance and reduce drop-out rates. Specific to secondary educational opportunities, Article 28 of the CRC (UN, 1990) states that countries should make secondary education available and accessible to every student (UN, 1990, p. 8). Whereas Article 28 stipulates the types of education that should be available to all children, Article 29 outlines critical educational content:

> States Parties agree that the education of the child shall be directed to:
> (a) The development of the child's personality, talents and mental and physical abilities to their fullest potential;
> (b) The development of respect for human rights and fundamental freedoms, and for the principles enshrined in the Charter of the United Nations;
> (c) The development of respect for the child's parents, his or her own cultural identity, language and values, for the national values of the country in which the child is living, the country from which he or she may originate, and for civilizations different from his or her own;
> (d) The preparation of the child for responsible life in a free society, in the spirit of understanding, peace, tolerance, equality of sexes, and friendship among all peoples, ethnic, national and religious groups and persons of indigenous origin;
> (e) The development of respect for the natural environment. (p. 9)

The CRC states that all children are entitled to a broad and comprehensive education that emphasizes respect for diversity and the ability to promote equity. Nations should ensure educational success of all children and give attention to those vulnerable to nonattendance and noncompletion. Vulnerable children include those deprived of protective family environments, children who are refugees, children of minority ethnic status, and children with disabilities (UNICEF, 2011).

Placed in the broader context of the CRC, schooling should promote children's wellbeing (Kosher, Jiang, Ben-Arieh, & Huebner, 2014). In order to do this, schooling and education must address students' (a) provisional rights (being easily accessible to all children, providing opportunities to meet basic needs, and fostering learning, development, health, and overall well-being); (b) protection rights (being free of physical, mental, or other dangers); and (c) participation rights (allowing students, individually and collectively, to contribute to decisions made about them and dispute actions that they perceive as unjust, discriminatory, or abusive) (Kosher et al., 2014; Lansdown et al., 2014). Participation rights require special attention from educational officials as schools are "characterized by a societal context where adult authority and power is almost absolute" (Kosher et al., 2014, pp. 11–12).

Although the CRC places the responsibility for protecting children's rights on nations, it will be through school, family, and community partnerships that these rights are realized: "the school is the only government agency through which the Convention can be applied to the life and development of virtually all children across the majority of their developmental period, directly and indirectly, in a pervading manner" and "psychologists who practice in schools are the primary child development and learning experts in that environment" (Hart & Hart, 2014, p. 7). Further, "school psychologists are uniquely qualified and positioned at the intersection of school, family, and community to promote and protect child rights" (Nastasi & Naser, 2014, p. 37). Therefore, there is a seminal and critical role for psychologists working in schools to consult with and build collaborations between all individuals integral to a child's development to promote equitable outcomes for children.

SOCIALLY JUST PSYCHOLOGICAL AND EDUCATIONAL PRACTICES

Practitioners can attend to individual children's rights but still remain blind to how systems perpetuate social inequities (Shriberg & Desai, 2014). For this reason, Prilleltensky and Nelson (2002) contend that psychologists working to promote equal protection of all children's rights must concern themselves with power, well-being, oppression, and liberation. Power can be used to oppress, or to resist marginalization and strive for liberation. Well-being is greatly affected by institutions that control resources and environments and the individuals with the power within those institutions. Oppression, the abuse of power, is characterized by asymmetric power relations and rooted in domination and subordination. Domination is maintained through having control of others' access to material resources and encouraging self-deprecating beliefs in the oppressed. Oppression is maintained through either being unable to resist domination or believing that one is unable to resist successfully. Only through awareness of oppression can individuals and groups begin to challenge structures that support domination and subordination.

Few educational communities have placed a critical lens upon themselves to ask how oppression is perpetuated in its systems and how this disadvantages groups of children and then worked to eradicate domination. However, the CRC asks nations and the global community to do just that. Social justice is defined as a process and goal that seeks liberation for all members of a society:

> The goal of social justice is full and equal participation of all groups in a society that is mutually shaped to meet their needs. Social justice includes a vision of society in which the distribution of resources is equitable and all members are physically and psychologically safe and secure.
>
> (Bell, 2013, p. 21)

When *society* is replaced with *school* or *schooling,* we have a vision of liberation through education that is highly compatible with the CRC. Freire (2003) argued that when education is practiced as a liberatory praxis, all members are both students and teachers, and all members experience growth. Applying critical theory to psychological practice in schools, Prilleltensky and Nelson (2002) challenge us with the following:

> The fundamental question that the critical psychologist practicing in the school must ask himself or herself is: "Am I working for the school as an agent of social control, or am I working with disadvantaged children and families for personal, educational, and social change?"
>
> (p. 93)

It has been argued that practicing psychology in schools is the optimal mental health position for promoting social justice agendas (Gutkin & Song, 2013). However, realizing the potential to increase equity of opportunities and outcomes will require adopting an ecological orientation to our practice (Williams & Greenleaf, 2012). Further, resistance that will result in liberation will require that we collaborate with others. Therefore, consultation becomes a critical tool for promoting the educational rights of all children.

ECOLOGICAL CONSULTATION AS A MEANS TO PROMOTE ALL CHILDREN'S EDUCATIONAL RIGHTS

Consultation designed to impact the whole school is often referred to as organizational, ecological, or systems-level consultation. In this chapter, the term *ecological consultation* will be used. Meyers, Proctor, Graybill, and Myers (2009) state that the goal of ecological consultation is "to strengthen the overall functioning of the system with positive effects for its members, particularly students" (p. 921). Ecological consultation is grounded in ecological theory, which states that all behaviors are a result of current and prior behavior–environment interactions (Bandura, 1977; Bronfenbrenner, 1979). Ecological consultation operates from three assumptions: (1) children are inseparable from their surrounding environments, (2) problems represent a mismatch between systems demands and child behavior, and (3) collaborative consultation is imperative for successful ecological interventions (Ysseldyke, Lekwa, Klingbeil, & Cormier, 2012). Whereas school-based ecological consultation was originally focused on problem remediation, in recent years ecological perspectives have stressed of the importance of prevention, health promotion, and public health (Trickett & Rowe, 2012).

Intentional systems change in schools is not easy. Granger (2002) summarized the findings on intentional change, highlighting the importance of relationships and ongoing support:

- Knowledge about new ways of achieving goals is a useful component, but not enough to ensure that change will occur.
- We like to learn about new practices from people we trust.
- Interventions that fit with existing practices, are relatively simple, and are seen as improvements on the status quo are more easily adopted.
- Change is unlikely to occur without dissatisfaction with the status quo and the knowledge, skills, and resources to support the change.
- The more complex and nuanced the issue, the more local ownership and an iterative process are needed to create desirable change.

In a synthesis of the literature on implementation, Fixsen, Naoom, Blasé, Friedman, and Wallace (2005) found that after initial training on an evidence-based practice or program, consultation and coaching were critical to support successful implementation. It is imperative that the consultant has a clear, detailed vision of the ecological change toward which the system is moving and the steps of intervention implementation necessary to realize that change (Fixsen et al., 2005; Forman et al., 2013). As sagely stated by Hall and Hord (2015),

> A major reason that widespread change often occurs only modestly across a school/ district is that the implementers, change facilitators, and policymakers do not fully understand what the change is or what it will look like when it is implemented in the envisioned way.
>
> (p. 56)

Although all aspects of an intervention or change cannot be preplanned, planning for change is critical to the future success of any endeavor. The Knoster Model of Managing Complex Change (Knoster, Villa, & Thousand, 2000) states that there are five critical aspects to realizing change: (1) vision, (2) skills, (3) incentives, (4) resources, and (5) an action plan. Without vision, a change effort will result in confusion. Without the necessary skills, a change effort will result in anxiety. Without incentives, a change effort will result in resistance. Without the needed resources, a change effort will result in frustration. Understanding implementation science is particularly salient for psychologists consulting in schools due to the importance of increasing the effective use of evidence-based interventions, the diverse populations within school communities, and the significance of school-level organizational characteristics (such as leadership models, culture, and climate) (Forman et al., 2013).

An early model of ecological consultation that was concerned with challenging educational inequalities was advocacy consultation; more recently, social justice consultation has been discussed. Further, proponents of comprehensive school-based mental health services have argued for the adoption of a public health approach. Each of these consultation approaches will be reviewed next.

Advocacy Consultation

In 1981, Conoley coined the term *advocacy consultation*; advocacy consultation is concerned with the law, media, organizing people, writing persuasively, and negotiation and confrontation. The advocate-consultant will organize activities such as demonstrations, letter writing, public hearings, fact-finding forums, symbolic acts, community education, lobbying, and boycotts. Conoley recommends that those directly affected (e.g., students, family members, and teachers) should be the face of these activities (i.e., the ones to speak to the media and gatekeepers about their concerns and requests). She also states that the advocate-consultant can provide mediation between groups experiencing conflict. Conoley concludes:

> Advocacy consultation is a way to use the present difficulties of a group in effecting long-range preventative change. Once involved, we will lose our detachment. We will be angry. We will feel helpless in the face of overwhelming difficulties. However, it is possible that such involvement will put us on the cutting edge of efforts aimed at improving the human condition.
>
> (p. 177)

Absolutely, this work is not easy. But, it is tremendously powerful to conceptualize consultation as a liberatory practice.

Social Justice Consultation

Defining consultation practice from a social justice lens, Shriberg and Fenning (2009) state,

> A social justice framework combines empirically based practices and active consideration of the social, environmental, political, and cultural context in which these practices are implemented at both the macrolevels and microlevels. School consultants will strive both to find areas of common ground among people and to identify and support that which makes us different. School consultants do this toward the end of finding just solutions to challenging problems and opportunities facing individuals and schools, with particular attention to students and families who have been disenfranchised through larger systemic and institutional biases and barriers. School consultants will strive to bring their training, experiences, and talents to bear toward actively resisting the status quo in schools and institutions when these actions result in the perpetuation of injustice.
>
> (pp. 4–5)

For consultation to be empowering to students, teachers, and families (who are often disempowered by the hierarchical norms of schools), we need to provide consultees with the knowledge and skills to think critically about the systemic inequities in their school and collaboratively develop strategies to challenge these institutions (Pearrow & Pollack, 2009). Clare (2009) and Sander (2013) provide key questions for socially just consultation:

- Who is excluded in your school?
- Who is privileged by the curriculum, pedagogy, and epistemology of the school?
- How is the school funded?
- Whose ethnic/racial identities/worldviews/gender roles/sexual orientations/gender identities dominate your school?
- Who are the traditional healers/cultural consultants for school community members whose cultures are different from your own?
- What issues of school oppression are regularly addressed and which are not by those in power?
- How are decisions made in your school?
- Whom do you want as allies inside and outside the school?
- What are the barriers and fears to cultural and systemic change in your school?

Social justice consultation requires increasing our professional role to include advocacy and other forms of social action. Promoting the educational rights of all children compels us to *work for* those who the current systems discriminate against; consultation will allow us to *work with* these partners (Conoley, 1981; Sander, 2013).

Public Health Problem-Solving Model

Concerned that individual-focused services are both ineffectual and reactive, some psychologists who work in schools have advocated for adopting a public health perspective to the provision of services in schools (e.g., Doll & Cummings, 2008; Hess, Short, & Hazel, 2012). As stated by Hess et al. (2012):

> The challenge for our educational system is to find a framework of service that incorporates strategies for supporting healthy social-emotional development for all children, providing targeted, evidence-based services for children who need higher levels of support, and incorporating and aligning these services to be congruent with the context of schools and the goal of increased academic achievement.
>
> (p. 15)

The Public Health Problem-Solving Model (PHPSM) is a means by which to meet this challenge. The PHPSM is a collaborative problem-solving consultation model from a public health lens. The PHPSM is designed to provide population-based services that promote health and prevent illness rather than focusing on problem remediation. The PHPSM stresses the importance of building collaborative partnerships within schools and between the school system, families, and community agencies. The stages are as follows:

1. *Problem identification through applied epidemiology*: During the problem identification phase, both risk and protective factors for all students are identified. This information used to generate hypotheses about the relationships between protective factors, risk factors, and outcomes for students at all levels of need.
2. *Problem analysis of risk and protective factors*: Given the preliminary hypotheses from the problem identification phase, the consultant works with consultees to collect data on all ecological systems' risk and protective functions for the target condition: personal, peer, school, family, and community.
3. *Define risk and protective factors in the child-environment interaction*: The third phase moves from data collection to defining the interactions that are promoting or hindering the desired outcomes for students. A logic model is used to define the interventions and implementation requirements to achieve the desired outcomes.
4. *Ecological plan implementation*: Plan implementation includes mapping the intervention(s), communicating about the intervention(s) with the broader community, and providing skills training to consultees as needed. As the plan is implemented and refined, the consultant continues to collaborate with the various parties.
5. *Monitor and evaluate outcomes*: Monitoring and evaluating outcomes includes capturing the implementation process as well as client outcomes. Process evaluation is particularly important in the PHPSM because it is hard to directly capture prevention outcomes. Outcome evaluation, similar to the whole process, should consider impacts on all students and the systems of which they are a part across levels of need.

The PHPSM provides a framework from which to consult with schools to realize the rights of all children, as outlined in the CRC (UN, 1990).

CASE STUDIES: ECOLOGICAL CONSULTATION TO PROMOTE CHILDREN'S EDUCATIONAL RIGHTS

This chapter will document two examples of ecological consultation using the PHPSM with schools and district personnel to affect systems-level change that promotes social justice by increasing equitable access to educational opportunities. Both consultations were conducted with an urban school district that wanted to increase its on-time high school graduation rates in schools and communities that had historically graduated only 50% of their students on time.

High school graduation rates are an example of educational inequities that violate the CRC. The Directorate for Education and Skills, within the Organization for Economic Co-operation and Development (OECD), publishes an annual analysis of internationally comparable educational outcome indicators for 44 countries. Although it is arguable that these 44 countries (the 34 member countries and 10 others from whom educational statistics are available) may provide greater educational opportunities for their citizens than the nations that are not included, the annual Education at a Glance report provides the most comprehensive and timely report through which to understand global educational trends. In 2012, the average international on-time high school graduation rate was 85%, and the average with an additional 2 years was 87% (OECD, 2014). Korea had the highest percentage of citizens who graduated from high school on time (95%), whereas Luxembourg had the lowest (40%). In the United States, 85% of students completed high school on time.

Historically, the United States had much higher high school graduation rates than most nations. For instance, when looking at adults between ages 55 and 64, 90% of United States adults have a high school education, whereas the international average is only 64% (OECD, 2014; Stetser & Stillwell, 2014). But whereas other nations have prioritized education for all citizens and increased their high school graduation and postsecondary educational obtainment rates, the United States rates have only risen modestly (Stetser & Stillwell, 2014), and educational obtainment for students in United States has been outpaced by many nations that have made education a priority (Darling-Hammond, 2010; Gamoran, 2013; OECD, 2014). Not only are graduation rates not keeping up with the increases seen in other nations, but socioeconomic differences in performance are greater in the United States than in any other nation (Chapman, Laird, & KewalRamani, 2010), and these performance differences are continuing to grow (Putnam, 2015).

Graduation and dropout rates vary sharply by student race, economic status, living arrangements, and identification for special education in the United States. For poor minority students in urban districts, on-time high school graduation rates are estimated to be 50% (Darling-Hammond, 2010). In many urban locations, low-income and minority students attend dropout factories; that is, schools with graduation rates of 50% or less (Balfanz, Bridgeland, Moore, & Hornig Fox, 2010). Representing approximately 10% of all high schools, dropout factories are responsible for half of the U.S. students who drop out of school. Not only are inequitable educational opportunities provided to students based on neighborhood demographic features, such as poverty and predominant ethnicity, but also within U.S. high schools students are segregated and treated differently. The most recent national statistics are that about 72% of youths with disabilities complete high school (with a diploma or certificate of completion) (U.S. Department of Education, 2005). However, only 56% of students who qualify for special education with an emotional disturbance will graduate from high school. Similarly, only 50% of students in foster care will complete high school by age 18 (Foster Care and Education, 2014). The shocking statistics of graduation disparities suggest that the U.S. educational system is violating the educational rights of poor students, racial and ethnically diverse students, students with special needs, and students with fewer family supports. The PHPSM offers psychologists a means to work with school personnel to challenge educational inequities and promote the rights of all students.

Consultation to Support the Transition from Middle School to High School

For this consultation case, I was approached by a district administrator who wanted to improve ninth grade outcomes by focusing on the middle school to high school transition; this became known as the *Transition Initiative*. Although dropping out of school is often a long-term process with indicators evidenced by elementary or middle school (Balfanz et al., 2010; Finn, 1989; National Research Council & Institute of Medicine, 2004), the transition from middle school to high school is a pivotal time in the lives of youth. A student's level of success in ninth grade often predicts his or her likelihood of graduating from high school (Allensworth & Easton, 2007).

This multiyear consultation occurred with district personnel and six schools: three middle schools and three high schools. I was the primary consultant at the district level. Under my supervision, graduate students in school psychology consulted with the faculty at each school. At each school, the consultees included a building administrator, counselor, psychologist, and teachers. The Transitions Initiative consultation spanned approximately 6 years. See Table 15.1 for an overview of the consultation activities for the first 3 years, which involved the piloting of the Transitions Initiative at one school. The following 3 years repeated the activities of the pilot site, but now at six schools.

When the consultation began, the district administrative structure had recently been reorganized to combine support for all secondary schools into one department. Further, this department was now charged with promoting students' postsecondary readiness. Historically, some administrators had supported middle schools and others had supported high schools. Therefore, when the consultation began, there was no formalized communication between the middle and high school personnel. Further, there was no standardized means to assess a student's probability of graduating from high school on time or to track his or her progress toward this goal. At the district level, no one had been responsible for or accountable to the students and their families. The district administrators enlisted my consultation services to promote student-centered practices and collaboration.

The PHPSM consultation led to collaborations between district administrators, school personnel, and community partners. Through multiple iterations and years of collaborating, the consultees defined the middle to high transition as comprised of three stages:

1. *Preparation for the transition:* actions taken during or prior to the spring of the student's last year in middle school
2. *During the transition:* actions taken during the summer between middle and high school
3. *After the transition:* actions taken after the student has started high school.

For students to successfully transition from middle to high school, all three phases of the transition needed to be considered and each student provided with appropriate

Table 15.1 Transition Initiative Consultation Timeline

Year	Consultation with district	Consultation with school administrators and support staff	Training and supervision of students	Student role
1	• I start meeting with a district partner about mutual interest in student school engagement. • I receive internal grant to hire graduate students. • Based on report from Johns Hopkins regarding district graduation rates, the middle to high school transition is identified as critical point to intervene (Stage 1: Problem Identification).			
2	• District partner and I start planning for Transitions Initiative. • District partner recruits one high school to pilot the Transitions Initiative. • District partner receives grant to implement Transitions Initiative. • Upper-level district administrator is impressed with pilot school's risk and protective factor analysis and has similar reports created for all high schools.	• District partner and I meet with principals and assistant principals at possible pilot schools and identify one that has need and resources. • I consult with building administrators and district data support personnel to define risk and protective factors for ninth grade students at pilot school (Stage 2: Problem Analysis). • Building administrators identify support staff and teachers to provide leadership for Transitions Initiative. • District partner, building administrator, support staff, teacher representatives, and I meet during spring semester and summer to create a model for change (Stage 3: Child–Environment Interaction).	• Students are trained to administer the Student School Engagement Measure (SSEM). • Four students who have completed the consultation courses and have an interest in systems consultation are recruited for next year's implementation. • Students are trained in district initiatives and pilot site needs by district partner. • Students are further trained in ecological change and project by me.	• Students administer the SSEM at three middle schools

Table 15.1 (Continued)

3			
• I consult at least monthly with district partner and other district support personnel regarding data reports. • From this, three district-wide student risk reports are created and disseminated. • District data personnel train administrators on the use of the student risk reports. • District partner and I present results from pilot year to district administrators (Stage 5: Monitor and Evaluate Outcomes). • Plans are made to expand Transition Initiative to a total of three middle schools and three high schools (including pilot site).	• District partner, students, building administrator, support staff, PLC team representatives, and I meet weekly to discuss Transitions Initiative implementation (Stage 4: Ecological Plan Implementation). • I consult with district and building administrators at least monthly to problem-solve implementation challenges. • Students and I present evaluation report to all faculty and staff who work with ninth grade students (Stage 5: Monitor and Evaluate Outcomes).	• I observe and mentor students during the weekly school leadership meetings. • I meet with students weekly to provide supervision and mentoring on their consultation cases and consultation skill development. • Six students who have completed the consultation courses and have an interest in systems consultation are recruited for next year's implementation (each will have one school to consult with). • Students are trained in district initiatives and pilot site needs by district partner. • Students are further trained in ecological change and project by me.	• Students administer SSEM for all incoming freshmen at pilot school. • Students are assigned as the consultant to one PLC; they provide group consultation weekly and individual consultation as needed (Stage 4: Ecological Plan Implementation). • Students and I create a comprehensive report regarding (a) students' entering risk levels, their engagement, and their ninth grade success; (b) student success by various PLC teams; and (c) needs of the various PLC teams (Stage 5: Monitor and Evaluate Outcomes).

supports. Based on their data collection, literature review of best practices, and clinical experiences, the consultees developed a best practices checklist for student transitions from middle to high school. This checklist included interventions to support academic, social, and behavioral student outcomes across levels of need as well as team and collaboration activities. See the Appendix for the checklist that was developed.

An example of a practice that was implemented was an annual spring district-wide meeting of all middle school and high school counselors; as students from one middle school often went to multiple high schools, this district-wide meeting allowed the middle school counselors to explain to the counselors at the receiving high schools the services and needs of various students. The middle and high school counselors have found this meeting extremely helpful and now contact each other as needed beyond this annual event.

Another example was a high school that implemented a freshman mentoring and tutoring program to increase the number of high school students with passing course grades. For students who did not have passing grades, an adult became their mentor and met with the student before or after school and helped students understand how to be academically successful (such as turning in assignments and studying for tests) and helped with academic content.

In order to have meaningful data that could be used to understand student needs and track progress, I helped the district consultees design three electronic "dashboard" student tracking tools: (1) indicator of risk (a cumulative score based on math grades, English grades, attendance, and discipline infractions) for incoming seventh- through ninth-grade students; (2) on track to graduation status report for all high school students at the end of each grading period (based on accrued credits toward graduation requirements); and (3) a constantly updated risk report for all high school students (based on current grades, attendance, and behavior infractions).

This ecological PHPSM consultation has resulted in greater collaboration within and across schools, useful tools for school teams to make data-based decisions on how promote the development of all students, and the means to identify students at risk of failing during the middle to high school transition so that they can intervene to prevent this outcome. Through this coordinated effort, the district saw freshman student high school attendance rates increase, and more students ended their first year of high school on track for on-time high school graduation. This reduced disproportionality and promoted the educational rights of all students as outlined in the CRC (UN, 1990).

Consultation to Provide Targeted Supports
to Struggling Secondary Schools

In contrast to the previous case study, this consultation is still in its infancy, having spanned only 1 year at the point of this writing. I consulted with the same district administrator. In this PHPSM consultation, the district administrator enlisted my consultation after identifying that individual secondary schools would benefit from various levels of district support; however, she felt that the district's current identification of schools' needs and provision of supports was reactive and nonsystematic. Applying a multitiered system of support model to all middle and high schools in the district, we identified schools that were successful with most of their students with universal district supports, schools that could benefit from targeted supports, and schools that needed intensive district supports. As there were programs in place to support the schools with intensive needs, we focused on the schools that were in the targeted zone and currently receiving no additional district supports. Some of these schools had consistently had mediocre student outcomes and some were seeing declining student outcomes, enrollment, or both.

The pilot high school was identified as being in decline, both in student outcomes and enrollment. Student enrollment was continuing to diminish as fewer students choose to come to the school from further neighborhoods and students who lived proximally to the school often selected to attend less convenient but for many reasons more desirable high schools. Within the school, the high school operated as two distinct schools: about a third of the students (469 students) participated in the international baccalaureate (IB) program, whereas most students (984 students) were enrolled in the general curriculum. The district had implemented the IB program many years ago to attract diverse, academically successful students from around the district to the high school. The IB curriculum is designed to offer an internationally standardized college-preparatory curriculum (IB, n.d.). Often referred to as *magnet programs,* the district had implemented specialized curricula (such as IB) in schools in low-income neighborhoods to encourage voluntary desegregation (Mickelson, Bottia, & Southworth, 2012). To be in the IB program, students had to apply and admission was competitive; although students from around the district attended, most were affluent and White. The general curriculum was largely populated by students from the neighborhood who were predominantly poor, and many were students of color. The overall high school graduation rates were higher than the district average. However, this was because the IB program had a nearly 100% on-time high school graduation rate. For the general curriculum students, the on-time high school graduation rate was about 50%.

In my consultation with the school's assistant principal and mental health providers (school counselor and psychologist), they identified that they wanted to increase attendance as a means of addressing inequities in student outcomes. Under my supervision, graduate students in an organizational consultation course served as consultants to the school consultees. See Table 15.2 for the consultation activities to date. The consultees had identified that they had two primary attendance problems: (1) students who did not come to school and (2) students who came to school but did not attend classes. They wanted to learn more about the variables that affected students' coming to school and attending classes.

The first step was to investigate student characteristics and attendance patterns. Attendance patterns did not vary by gender but were correlated to ethnicity and race (poverty data were not available); for instance, 83% of White students had strong attendance, whereas only 58% of Hispanic and Black students had strong attendance. Overall, students in the IB program evidenced much stronger attendance rates and better grades than students not in the IB program. Although attendance was positively correlated to grades, some students in the general curriculum had strong attendance rates but were still failing most or all of their courses. Through the consultation, two main needs were identified: (1) to improve attendance for some students and (2) provide greater academic supports for the students who attended regularly.

The consultation helped the district and building staff to realize that White students and students attending the IB program were much more likely to graduate from high

Table 15.2 Consultation to Provide Targeted Supports to Struggling Secondary Schools

Year	Consultation with district	Consultation with school administrators and support staff	Training and supervision of students	Student role
1	• I consult with a district partner in applying an MTSS model to secondary schools; some schools are identified as being able to flourish with *universal* supports, some need more targeted supports, and some need intensive supports. • We focus on schools identified as needing targeted supports (Stage 1: Problem Identification).	• District partner and I begin meeting monthly with pilot high school assistant principal, school counselor, and school psychologist. • Through our consultation and analysis of school data, school staff identify that attendance is the risk and protective factor that they would like to first address (Stage 2: Problem Analysis). • We agree that graduate students from my organizational consultation class will consult with them regarding attendance.	• Twenty-six graduate students studying school psychology and research methods and statistics enroll in the 10-week organizational consultation course; school psychology students are required to have taken a prior consultation course. • Based on the identified attendance needs, students are divided into seven teams. • I meet weekly in class with students as a whole group and in their small groups, as well as outside and via email.	• Students meet with school partners and learn about their perceptions of student attendance needs (Stage 2: Problem Analysis). • Students collect additional preliminary data and present proposals to school staff (Stage 3: Child–Environment Interaction). • Students, in consultation with key school personnel, complete seven projects (Stage 4: Plan Implementation): • Analysis of attendance patterns by student demographic characteristics. • Analysis of attendance patterns by teachers and subjects. • Recommendations on increasing student engagement and student–teacher relationships. • Inventory of community resources to support student attendance. • Create a survey to be administered in the fall regarding student perceptions of the school. • Create and administer a survey for students who attend school but not classes. • Inventory of funding sources that support attendance initiatives. • Students present findings in an interactive forum to interested district and school community members (Stage 5: Monitor and Evaluate Outcomes).
2	• I continue to consult with district partner on how best to support schools with targeted needs (Stage 2: Problem Analysis for the district consultation).	• Based in part on students' organizational consultation findings, the district forms a community workgroup to plan the reenvisioning of the school that integrates all students in the curriculum and does not include an IB program (Stage 1: Problem Identification for the school consultation).		

school on time and be prepared for postsecondary success. The discovered inequities confirmed for the district and building administrators that the part IB, part general curriculum was not meeting the needs of most students. The inequities at this school parallel national trends where it has been found that the internal organization of schools with "partial magnets" results in students in the magnet programing being isolated from the larger student population (Mickelson et al., 2012) and can have detrimental impact on the academic success of students in the nonmagnet programs (Neild, 2004). The district administrators launched a series of community forums; the ultimate decision was to eliminate the IB curriculum. Instead, the school would offer multiple rigorous academic pathways with particular attention to school climate and student-centered pedagogy. This has been labeled the ONE School redesign. Currently, the school is continuing to engage the community in the redesign planning with multiple committees meeting frequently to envision how the school will be configured. I continue to consult with the district and school personnel as they work with their community to envision the school's redesign. The intent of the redesign is that the school will more equitably meet the educational needs and rights of all students, in keeping with the CRC. This consultation case study exemplifies how an initial consultation can highlight a larger systemic inequity or inefficiency that must be addressed if all students, faculty, and staff are to function to their capacity.

CONCLUSION

The CRC states that all children are entitled to have their rights protected and promoted. These rights include the right to an education that promotes each child's personality, talent, and mental and physical development to his or her fullest potential. Children should not be discriminated against based on ability or disability, gender, ethnicity and culture, or family attributes. Further, education should prepare students to be global citizens with an awareness and appreciation for their culture, the environment, and people from whom they are dissimilar.

Schools can be locations where children's rights are equitably addressed and promoted. Far too often, schooling serves to perpetuate social hierarchies and inequities. This chapter highlighted the educational inequities in secondary educational outcomes. These inequities often originate in preprimary and primary educational environments and continue in tertiary educational opportunities. Internationally, national on-time high school graduation rates range from 40 to 95%. Within nations, on-time high school graduation rates also have huge variability. Inequities in on-time high school graduation rates are in direct violation of the CRC right to nondiscrimination (UNICEF, 2011). All persons involved with children and schooling should be outraged that many educational institutions continue to promote, rather than fight, violations of children's rights.

Consultants who practice in schools have a unique opportunity and the moral imperative to challenge social injustices and promote the development of all students. A consultant who is working toward social justice for children will pay attention to power, well-being, oppression, and liberation as practiced or experienced by individuals and by systems. Promoting educational equity through consultation requires us to use an ecological lens to assess and address student outcomes. Often, how to achieve social justice in schools is much less clear than the aspiration to do so (Shriberg & Desai, 2014).

Implementation research provides important guidance to move successfully from desire to action.

One of the most powerful means of facilitating systems change to promote the development of all students is collaborative, ecological consultation. This chapter presented a public health model of ecological consultation intended to promote positive development, reduce risks for negative outcomes, and ameliorate deficits. Ecological consultation has the potential to be one of the best psychological tools for promoting social justice. However, when practicing consultation, it is important to critically examine one's own practice and biases. As school psychology is practiced and school psychologists work in increasingly diverse settings, this becomes even more imperative and raises this question: "Is the expansion of school psychology across the globe leading to the importation of White, male, Christian, heterosexist, Western privilege, or will school psychology be able to adapt to the needs, values, and added opportunities/benefits of different cultures and countries?" (Shriberg & Desai, 2014, p. 12). Ecological consultation, practiced in collaboration with many partners across groups and communities, offers the opportunity to promote voices that have often been ignored and realize children's rights to development, protection, and participation (UNICEF, 2011) in educational settings.

REFERENCES

Allensworth, E. M., & Easton, J. Q. (2007). *What matters for staying on-track and graduating in Chicago public high schools: A close look at course grades, failures, and attendance in the freshman year*. Chicago, IL: Consortium on Chicago School Research at the University of Chicago.

Balfanz, R., Bridgeland, J. M., Moore, L. A., & Hornig Fox, J. (2010). *Building a grad nation: Progress and challenge in ending the high school dropout epidemic*. Washington, DC: Civic Enterprises, Everyone Graduated Center at Johns Hopkins University, & America's Promise Alliance.

Bandura, A. (1977). *Social learning theory*. Englewood Cliffs, NJ: Prentice-Hall, Inc.

Bell, J. (2013). Understanding Adultism: A key to developing positive youth-adult relationships. In M. Adams, W. J. Blumenfeld, C. Castaneda, H. W. Hackman, M. L. Peters, & X. Zuniga (Eds.), *Readings for diversity and social justice* (3rd ed., pp. 542–549). New York, NY: Routledge.

Bronfenbrenner, U. (1979). *The ecology of human development: Experiments by nature and design*. Cambridge, MA: Harvard.

Chapman, C., Laird, J., & KewalRamani, A. (2010). *Trends in high school dropout and completion rates in the United States: 1972–2008* (NCES 2011–2012). Washington, DC: National Center for Education Statistics, Institute of Education Sciences, U.S. Department of Education. Retrieved from http://nces.ed.gov/pubsearch

Clare, M. M. (2009). Decolonizing consultation: Advocacy as the strategy, diversity as the context. *Journal of Educational and Psychological Consultation, 19*, 8–25.

Conoley, J. C. (1981). Advocacy consultation: Promises and problems. In J. C. Conoley (Ed.), *Consultation in schools: Theory, research, procedures* (pp. 157–178). New York, NY: Academic Press, Inc.

Darling-Hammond, L. (2010). *The flat world and education: How America's commitment to equity will determine our future*. New York, NY: Teachers College Press.

Doll, B., & Cummings, J. A. (2008). *Transforming school mental health services: Population-based approaches to promoting the competency and wellness of children*. Bethesda, MA: NASP Publications & Thousand Oaks, CA: Corwin Press.

Fixsen, D. L., Naoom, S. F., Blasé, K. A., Friedman, R. M., & Wallace, F. (2005). *Implementation research: A synthesis of the literature*. Tampa, FL: University of South Florida.

Forman, S. G., Shapiro, E. S., Codding, R. S., Gonzales, J. E., Reddy, L. A., Rosenfield, S. A., . . . Stoiber, K. C. (2013). Implementation science and school psychology. *School Psychology Quarterly, 28*(2), 77–100.

Freire, P. (2003). *Pedagogy of the oppressed*. New York, NY: The Continuum International Publishing Group, Inc.

Gamoran, A. (2013). Inequality is the problem: Prioritizing research on reducing inequality. In L. Neier (Ed.), *Annual report* (pp. 6–15). New York, NY: William T. Grant Foundation.

Granger, R. C. (2002). Creating the conditions linked to positive youth development. *New Directions for Youth Development, 95*, 149–164.

Gutkin, T. B., & Song, S. Y. (2013). Social justice in school psychology: A historical perspective. In D. Shriberg, S. Y. Song, A. H. Miranda, & K. M. Radliff (Eds.), *School psychology and social justice: Conceptual foundations and tools for practice* (pp. 15–28). New York, NY: Routledge.

Hall, G. E., & Hord, S. M. (2015). *Implementing changes: Patterns, principles, and potholes* (4th ed.). Upper Saddle River, NJ: Pearson.

Hart, S., & Hart, B. (2014). Children's rights and school psychology: Historical perspective and implications for the profession. *School Psychology International, 35*, 6–28.

Hess, R. S., Short, J. R., & Hazel, C. E. (2012). *Comprehensive children's mental health services in schools and communities: A public health problem-solving model.* New York, NY: Routledge.

International Baccalaureate. (n.d.). *About the IB's programmes.* Retrieved from http://www.ibo.org

International School Psychology Association (ISPA). (n.d.). *Mission statement.* Retrieved from http://www.ispaweb.org/about-ispa/mission-statement

Knoster, T., Villa, R., & Thousand, J. (2000). A framework for thinking about systems change. In R. Villa & J. Thousand (Eds.), *Restructuring for caring and effective education: Piecing the puzzle together* (pp. 93–128). Baltimore, MD: Brookes.

Kosher, H., Jiang, X., Ben-Arieh, A., & Huebner, E. (2014). Advances in children's rights and well-being measurement: Implications for school psychologists. *School Psychology Quarterly, 29*, 7–20.

Lansdown, G., Jimerson, S. R., & Shahroozi, R. (2014). Children's rights and school psychology: Children's right to participation. *Journal of School Psychology, 52*(1), 3–12.

Legal Center for Foster Care and Education. (2014). *Research highlights on education and foster care.* Retrieved from http://www.fostercareandeducation.org/NationalWork/NationalWorkGroup.aspx

McNamara, K. (2014). Best practices as an internal consultant in a multitiered support system. In P. L. Harrison & A. Thomas (Eds.), *Best practices in school psychology: Data-based and collaborative decision making* (pp. 553–568). Bethesda, MD: National Association of School Psychologists.

Meyers, J., Meyers, A. B., & Grogg, K. (2004). Prevention through consultation: A model to guide future developments in the field of school psychology. *Journal of Educational and Psychological Consultation, 15*, 257–276.

Meyers, J., Proctor, S. L., Graybill, E. C., & Myers, A. B. (2009). Organizational consultation and systems intervention. In T. B. Gutkin & C. R. Reynolds (Eds.), *The handbook of school psychology* (4th ed., pp. 921–940). Hoboken, NJ: John Wiley & Sons, Inc.

Mickelson, R. A., Bottia, M., & Southworth, S. (2012). School choice and segregation by race, ethnicity, class, and achievement. In G. Miron, K. Welner, P. H. Hinchey, & W. J. Mathis (Eds.), *Exploring the school choice universe: Evidence and recommendations* (pp. 167–192). Charlotte, NC: Information Age.

Nastasi, B., & Naser, S. (2014). Child rights as a framework for advancing professional standards for practice, ethics, and professional development in school psychology. *School Psychology International, 35*, 36–49.

National Research Council & the Institute of Medicine. (2004). *Engaging schools: Fostering high school students' motivation to learn.* Washington, DC: National Academy Press.

Neild, R. C. (2004). The effects of magnet schools on neighborhood high schools: An examination of achievement among entering freshman. *Journal of Education for Students Placed at Risk, 9*, 1–21.

OECD. (2014). *Education at a glance 2014: OECD indicators.* OECD Publishing. Retrieved from http://dx.doi.org/10.1787/eag-2014-en

Pearrow, M. M., & Pollack, S. (2009). Youth empowerment in oppressive systems: Opportunities for school consultants. *Journal of Educational and Psychological Consultation, 19*, 45–60.

Prilleltensky, I., & Nelson, G. (2002). *Doing psychology critically: Making a difference in diverse settings.* New York, NY: Palgrave Macmillan.

Sander, J. B. (2013). Consultation and collaboration. In D. Shriberg, S. Y. Song, A. H. Miranda, & K. M. Radliff (Eds.), *School psychology and social justice: Conceptual foundations and tools for practice* (pp. 225–243). New York, NY: Routledge.

Shriberg, D., & Desai, P. (2014). Bridging social justice and children's rights to enhance school psychology scholarship and practice. *Psychology in the Schools, 1*, 3–14.

Shriberg, D., & Fenning, P. (2009). School consultants as agents of social justice: Implications for practice: Introduction to the special issue. *Journal of Educational and Psychological Consultation, 19*, 1–7.

Stetser, M., & Stillwell, R. (2014). *Public high school four-year on-time graduation rates and event dropout rates: School years 2010–11 and 2011–12.* First look (NCES 2014–391). U.S. Department of Education. Washington, DC: National Center for Education Statistics.

Trickett, E. J., & Rowe, H. (2012). Emerging ecological approaches to prevention, health promotion and public health in the school context: Next steps from a community psychology perspective. *Journal of Educational and Psychological Consultation, 22*, 125–140.

UNICEF. (2011). *Convention on the rights of the child: Guiding principles: General requirements for all rights.* Retrieved from http://www.unicef.org/crc/files/Guiding_Principles.pdf

UNICEF. (2014). *Convention on the rights of the child FAQs and resources*. Retrieved from http://www.unicef.org/crc/index_30225.html?p=printme

United Nations: Office of the High Commissioner for Human Rights. (1990). *Convention on the rights of the child*. Retrieved from http://www.ohchr.org/Documents/ProfessionalInterest/crc.pdf

U.S. Department of Education. (2005). *Facts from NLTS2*. Washington, DC: Author.

Williams, J. M., & Greenleaf, A. T. (2012). Ecological psychology: Potential contributions to social justice and advocacy in school settings. *Journal of Educational and Psychological Consultation, 22*, 141–157.

Ysseldyke, J., Lekwa, A. J., Klingbeil, D., & Cormier, D. C. (2012). Assessment of ecological factors as an integral part of academic and mental health consultation. *Journal of Educational and Psychological Consultation, 22*, 21–42.

APPENDIX
Middle School to High School Transition Inventory

This inventory is intended to provide high school personnel and teams with an opportunity to reflect on current practices that are specific to ninth grade success. Because the transition to ninth grade incorporates supporting eighth graders preparing to enter high school as well as providing additional supports for some students as they prepare for tenth grade, this inventory encompasses the spring semester of eighth grade through the summer prior to tenth grade.

Next to each best practice, please check the box that you feel best represents your CURRENT implementation of the following.

Middle school–high school coordination (spring of eighth grade year)	Well established	Somewhat established	Not at all established	Notes
Diverse articulation activities. Develop a variety of activities with your key feeder middle school including school visits, open houses, and time for students and/or parents to shadow.				
Student engagement assessment. Schools use a self-reporting instrument (either existing or self-generated) to learn more about student engagement styles and student interests (clubs, sports, hobbies, etc.).				
Matching incoming student interests with HS activities. Eighth graders are made aware of extracurricular opportunities and admission criteria and processes and are encouraged to preregister for at least one extracurricular activity.				
Personnel meeting. Provide explicit and clear information about academic expectations for entering HS by having middle and high school personnel come together to learn about one another's curriculum. This includes defining what skills/knowledge students will need to be able to do well in core classes, including but not limited to literacy, vocabulary, comprehension, and math skills.				

(Continued)

(Continued)

	Well established	Somewhat established	Not at all established	Notes
Mental health staff meeting. Determine time for middle school and high school professional support staff (counselors, deans, advisors, psychologists, social workers, etc.) to meet for a full day to review incoming student plans and information.				
Long-term planning. Involve various stakeholders (parents, students, counselors, school psychologists, etc.) in helping students to develop academic and life goals in the eighth grade for up to 5 or 6 years into the future. Keep these plans in the students' files and refer to them each term when the student registers for courses to help him/her see the relevance in current course work.				
Family involvement. Keep families well informed of the transition process and allow families to have input into the curricular and course selections for their students.				
Risk report. High school uses middle school history to respond proactively to specific needs of incoming ninth graders. This may include establishing specific intervention classes for subpopulation groups, working with students and parents to establish high school goals and monitoring strategies, and assigning a staff member as responsible for providing individualized support for students for whom it might be especially beneficial.				
Summer programs				
Ninth grade academy. Entering ninth graders begin school early and take a number of different courses to help them prepare for entering high school. Courses may include academic, behavior, and social/emotional support. Upperclassmen may be involved in a variety of ways.				
Intensive support. During the summer, there are opportunities for students entering school who are behind in their academic skills to have additional and intensive support in small groups. May include partnering with outside community agencies or hiring teachers.				
Peer mentors. Exemplary upperclassmen participate in the summer transition programs for course credit. They can be assigned to different classes and even help teach classes on introduction to high school.				
Family involvement. Keep families well informed of the summer academy objectives, and allow families to have input into the curricular and course selections for their students.				

(Continued)

	Well established	Somewhat established	Not at all established	Notes
Adaptable programs. Assess the success of orientation programs by surveying students, parents, and teachers about their experiences, and then change the programming based on feedback as well as other information gathered surrounding changing contexts over time. Student engagement measures can be used to generate orientation planning ideas.				
Structures to support freshman transition (ninth grade academic year)				
Advisories. Freshmen and/or sophomores have an assigned staff person in the school who meets with a small group of students (10–20) at least twice a week for 30 minutes. Focus of advisories is on positive relationship building, tracking grades, and attendance. The advisor also provides parents with one adult in the school who serves as an advocate for their child. Information that should be gathered, especially with highly diverse populations, includes the language used at home, family history of school dropout, and whether students have after-school employment or other significant responsibilities.				
Academy team structures. Schools identify a team of strong teachers to teach in freshmen teams to increase personalization and relationship building. Cross-disciplinary teams meet weekly to discuss and strategize around students. Teams are held responsible for the progress of their students.				
Freshmen hall. An area in the building is established where freshmen teachers and classes are all/mostly located to increase accountability and relationship development.				
Ninth grade center. Identified and specific place in the school for students, parents, and teachers to meet. This can also serve as a tutoring and resource center.				
Separate lunch period for freshmen. Freshmen only lunch period to help minimize student truancy.				
Flexible scheduling. Schedule allows for students to have longer blocks of time for learning and to accommodate nontraditional student needs.				
Positive behavior support system. School-wide expectations for positive student behavior have been developed by teachers, staff, students, and parents. These expectations are clearly articulated and known, and students and adults are reinforced for displaying positive behaviors. Align behavioral policies across schools within a district. Responses to behavioral infractions include restorative justice, as less punitive policies have been found to decrease withdrawal rates.				

	Well established	Somewhat established	Not at all established	Notes
Use of ongoing data. School staff track attendance, behavior, and academic course performance on a regular basis. This can include teachers, professional support staff and administration. Based on student data, interventions are matched and tracked.				
Small learning communities/academics. Each student has the same four core classes with the same teachers, but not necessarily in the same order, to encourage greater support of all students.				
Extended learning opportunities. Structured and required time is established for students to receive additional help from teachers. Possible structures may include office hours for teachers, a mandatory study hall, or after-school course work.				
Common planning time for teachers. Time is built into the master schedule to allow for daily planning for like-subject teachers to create lessons and analyze data. A separate time exists for academy teachers to identify common problems and discuss solutions—discipline, special needs for specific students on a weekly basis. Ideally, common planning is for both academy teams and subject teams.				
Freshmen seminar classes. Specialized introduction to high school classes are offered during first semester to all or a subpopulation of students to smooth the transition to high school. Curriculum can include study skills, organizational support, note taking, and character building lessons.				
Academic intervention classes. Classes are during the same period of the day and provide opportunities for students to get additional help and support. Opportunities exist for upperclassmen to participate in peer-mentoring roles during these classes.				
Ninth grade support staff. The school has identified specific people in the building to provide additional support for ninth graders. These include, but are not limited to, assistant principal, guidance counselor, parent coordinator, student advisor, and administrator attendance liaison.				
Institute a no-zero policy. Require that all students need to complete work and demonstrate competency in classes. Work with teachers to understand and adjust grading policies as needed. Students are required to complete all work and structures are provided for students who are missing assignments. Teachers and students are held accountable for all students performing to expectations.				

(*Continued*)

	Well established	Somewhat established	Not at all established	Notes
Extra time, extra help. Offer tutoring during and after school with support from community and business partners and university partnerships. Have an assigned staff person responsible for coordinating the program and aligning it with academic classes.				
College prep. Require that all students must stay after school to complete missing school work. College prep refers to emphasizing the importance of assignments and homework completion as a critical step in preparing them for college. Teachers keep track of student's homework completion rates and follow-up with students who are not completing homework assignments, including asking how much time they spend on homework on average. Parents are involved in homework completion planning.				
Culturally responsive teaching and curriculum. Teachers understand the acculturation process and the cultural backgrounds of their students. Curriculum utilizes an additive model of acculturation that encourages students to maintain their native language and values while also becoming accustomed to mainstream culture. Pedagogy integrates and utilizes students' values and knowledge.				
Strong academic curriculum. Offer advanced-placement courses and/or other challenging courses. Instill and maintain an academic focus in students. Increase students' exposure to core academic courses.				
Relationships. Develop positive, caring, and trusting relationships with students that help them feel connected to school. This can be done through offering students assistance with personal problems, providing more personal attention in class, and holding high expectations for students. Students who enter high school without many peer friendships are provided extra supports.				
School/classroom organization. Ensure that all classrooms have strong organizational processes established. Maximize structural stability for ninth grade students by maintaining schedules and teachers as much as possible.				
Community involvement. Partnerships are developed with community agencies, faith organizations, local businesses, and civic groups. Establish connections with community resources such as local colleges, volunteer organizations, and mental health services to work with students both during school and after school. This can help students to link educational achievement to their own future opportunities and receive critical intervention services when school staff is overwhelmed.				

(*Continued*)

	Well established	Somewhat established	Not at all established	Notes
Family involvement. Family participation is encouraged in many ways including celebratory and fun activities, voice in school management and decisions, and student goal-setting. Families know who to contact and how to access information about their student's progress. Events are scheduled at various times so that families with nontraditional schedules can also be accommodated and involved in their students' educational experiences. Parents are provided with resources for how to encourage their children, help with homework, and get involved at school. Families in need of intensive services are assigned a mentor to work with them for an extended period of time (at least 2 years).				
Student voice. Give students choices and autonomy in selecting their educational paths (i.e. course selection, assignment selection, etc.) Teach students how to set goals and self-monitor progress toward intervention outcomes and future career aspirations.				
Credit recovery. For students that did not pass all fall semester courses, there is a means for students to complete or recover credit for those courses.				
Attendance expectations. Attendance expectations are made clear and absences are followed up on daily. There is a means for students to complete work and receive missed instruction, such that they are able to participate in their classes after an absence.				
Mentors. Students who appear less connected to school or who would benefit from a positive role model are provided with a community mentor.				
Structures to support on-track status (summer after ninth grade academic year)				
Intensive support. During the summer, there are opportunities for students who are behind in their academic skills to have additional and intensive support in small groups. May include partnering with outside community agencies or hiring teachers.				
Professional interest development. Summer opportunities (through school or community partnerships) are available to students to develop interests and talents.				
Credit recovery. For students that did not pass all needed ninth grade courses, there is a means for students to complete or recover credit for those courses.				

Part V

EDUCATING EFFECTIVE CONSULTANTS

16

TRAINING AND EDUCATION OF CONSULTANTS
A Global Perspective

Colette L. Ingraham

Learning to become an effective consultant is a complex and ongoing task. For both consultants-in-training (CITs) and experienced consultants alike, there are many issues, dynamics, challenges, and styles to consider, and each new consultation case brings its own learning opportunities. The purpose of this chapter is to present models and practices for the development of professionals to become effective consultants in the schools and communities they serve. While there is research on the teaching of consultation skills within a specific model (e.g., see Sheridan, Clarke, & Ransom, 2014, for an excellent review of conjoint behavioral consultation research studies), empirical research on the teaching of consultation processes is much more limited. This chapter will: (a) summarize some of the research on consultation education and training, including consultation context, focus, processes, and issues faced by consultation educators; (b) focus explicitly on consultation in cross-cultural and systemic contexts and the additional training needed for mastery; (c) present a developmental model, from novice to professional integration, that articulates global competencies and instructional approaches for consultation professional growth; (d) describe a training activity with data on its use; and (e) suggest directions for future research.

INTRODUCTION TO CONSULTANT TRAINING AND EDUCATION

For over the past 40 years, school psychology educators have been discussing key issues and different aspects of school-based consultation. In an issue of the *Journal of Educational and Psychological Consultation* devoted to training, J. Meyers (2002) reflected on his 30 years in teaching consultation and presented suggestions for those providing consultation training. He emphasized the indirect and prevention focus of consultation from individual to systems levels of intervention. Meyers proposed that the content of coursework in school-based consultation should attend to levels of consultation and have an emphasis on indirect services and prevention, problem-solving stages, interpersonal process skills, and group and individual consultation formats. He called on consultation educators to support students in linking theory to practice, to conduct more research on the training of consultation, and to be models by studying uses, processes, and outcomes of consultation within the university. Given the prevalence of consultation in national professional standards, such as in Ireland, the U.K., and the U.S., and the increases in transnational work, it is incumbent to prepare a new generation of consultation educators who can design and support the learning of consultation in ways that are consistent with regional, national, and global needs.

The Context for Learning Consultation

There is a great deal of variety in how consultation is learned in different regions, nations, and the settings in which consultation education and training take place. In some countries, consultation is learned through in-service training. For example, in Sweden, consultation is a specialty area that is learned after one has been educated and enters the profession as a psychologist (see Hylander, 2012). In Sweden, psychologists may acquire advanced training in consultation while they are working as psychologists; thus, the consultation education comes after they have attained expertise and experiences as practicing psychologists. As one might imagine, the preparation of experienced psychologists to add consultation to their professional practice is quite different from students learning consultation as a course in their graduate education. Gravois, Knotek, and Babinski (2002) described a model for educating practitioners as members of instructional consultation teams that may be useful to trainers designing training experiences for those who have already completed their university studies, although as demonstrated in Newman, Salmon, Cavanaugh, and Schneider (2014b), research with practicing consultants can be complex and challenging.

For other countries, such as the U.S., consultation skills are part of the national standards for school psychology and are part of graduate education. In these programs, consultation is often taught through a discrete graduate course or courses and may be supervised as part of applied practice in practicum or internships (Anton-LaHart & Rosenfield, 2004; Hazel, Laviolette, & Linemen, 2010). Even though this consultation education takes place within the context of graduate education, there is great variation in how these graduate programs teach consultation, as will be illustrated later in this chapter.

The Focus of Consultation Learning

A second issue involves the focus of the consultation—which model or models are taught and with what depth. Here, educators will make decisions regarding the scope and depth of the consultation education. How much time is allocated to focused learning of consultation (number of hours, courses)? Does one teach a variety of different consultation models or focus on a specific model with greater depth? If a range of models is taught, are skills for using these models taught, or is the focus more on the theory with limited time for teaching the skills and supervising practice? For example, texts such as Brown, Pryzwansky, and Schulte (2011) include chapters on differing consultation models—mental health, cognitive-behavioral, solution-focused, and systems consultation—and then include attention to the stages and processes and consultation with particular types of consultees. When multiple models are taught, how does the consultant learn which models to use in which circumstances (Ingraham, Flanagan, Oka, & Truscott, 2011)?

Some authors combine different models and offer their own integrated model. For example, Conoley and Conoley (1992) proposed an ecological model of consultation. Gutkin and Curtis (2009) referred to ecological consultation (and related terms in earlier publications) to characterize school-based consultation with "the hope of underscoring the significance of mutual and reciprocal systemic interactions between micro-, meso-, exo- and macro-environments" (p. 611). Erchul and Martens (2012) integrated aspects of behavioral and mental health consultation into a practice-oriented approach. J. Meyers (2002) described his model of "mental health consultation that uses a combination of psychodynamic, cognitive-behavioral and ecological principles within a constructivist framework that seeks to empower the consultee" (p. 36).

Other consultation resources focus on a specific model of consultation and go into greater depth regarding the theory, research, and practice of that model. Sheridan and Kratochwill (2007) provided an excellent presentation of conjoint behavioral consultation; Rosenfield and Gravois (1996) and Gravois et al. (2002) focused on instructional consultation; and Lambert, Hylander, and Sandoval (2004) and Sandoval (2014) concentrated on consultee-centered consultation. For trainers who know what model they want to emphasize, each of these texts provides valuable resources for educating future consultants.

Research indicates that most U.S. school psychology programs have one course in consultation. Hazel et al. (2010) studied course syllabi among participating APA-approved school psychology programs and reported that 68% offered one course dedicated to consultation. The Anton-LaHart and Rosenfield (2004) study of school psychology programs found that 63% of specialty level programs and 71% of doctoral level programs had one course in consultation. Additionally, 21% of specialist-level programs and 8% of doctoral programs did not have a separate course but taught consultation as part of one or two other courses, and 10% of specialist-level and 25% of doctoral programs had two or more separate courses in consultation. The models most often used in preservice education were behavioral (91%), mental health (59%), instructional (53%), and organizational (52%), with many programs teaching multiple models. Time in training spent on topics varied greatly, with more emphasis on theoretical/conceptual and intervention development and very little on multicultural skills. In fact, 76 to 80% of the responding programs reported that they devoted 0 to 10% time on multicultural skills during their one or two consultation courses. This is consistent with the gap between professional standards and training described in Newell et al. (2010), and readers are encouraged to read their recommendations for future directions.

The Processes and Stages of Learning Consultation

The processes used to teach consultation can vary too, partly due to differences in depth and partly due to their emphasis on differing processes and stages in the learning progression. There are various models for professional development of educators and consultants, and many include similar components. In research with inservice training with teachers, Joyce and Showers (1980) found that the most effective training activities are "those that combine theory, modeling, practice, feedback, and coaching to application" (p. 385). Rosenfield (2002) built on work by Joyce and Showers (1980) and outlined a consultation training model for Instructional Consultation (IC). The IC training model has four training stages or levels of impact: (1) awareness and understanding, (2) skill acquisition, (3) application of skills, and (4) advanced skill development. Gravois et al. (2002) and Newell and Newman (2014) adapted the IC model with levels of impact whereby the first level is awareness and the second level is conceptual understanding, with the remaining three levels consistent with the ones described in previous publications: skill acquisition, application of skills, and advanced skill development.

While many consultation educators write about the stages of consultation, others focus more on the processes and dynamics that occur between a consultant and consultee (e.g., Hylander, 2004, 2012). I believe that education in and supervision of consultation *stages and processes* are important to prepare consultants to work within and across cultures, systems, and nations. To give attention to global perspectives in the education and training of consultants, a model for Consultation Learning and Development (CLAD) is presented later in this chapter. It is a framework to consider in educating consultants with global perspectives who are prepared to consult across cultures, contexts, and countries.

Issues Faced by Consultation Educators

Those teaching consultation face a range of issues in designing their consultation education experiences. Some of the major issues faced include what to teach, how to balance theory/practice, conceptual/skill development, and how to support and assess learning. A. Meyers (2002) wrote about some of these dilemmas as she prepared to teach her first consultation course. J. Meyers (2002) built on his 30 years of teaching consultation and addressed topics such as the content of consultation, how to link consultation theory with practice, and issues that have created challenges to trainers. Both authors discussed the dilemmas consultation educators face, such as how to balance didactic and practice components of consultation training. Rosenfield (2002) offered a model of consultant development that moves from novice to competent to expert instructional consultation, and Newell and Newman (2014) wrote an excellent summary of some of the unanswered questions that plague consultation trainers. Finally, Hatzichristou, Lampropoulou, Georgouleas, and Mihou (Chapter 5 in this volume) developed a multilevel approach that connects consultation training and practice.

In addition to the consultant education issues described, educators preparing consultants with global competencies need ways to develop and build cross-cultural knowledge and skills among consultants. What are the knowledge, skills, and beliefs that contribute to successful consultation across different cultures and perspectives? How can consultants acquire the expertise and dispositions needed for work with diverse consultees and clients? There is very little published to support consultant educators in designing and guiding learning in these areas.

Helping Consultants Develop Nonthreatening Expertise and Dispositions

Competent consultants need knowledge, skills, practices, and dispositions that make them valuable resources for consultees. Additionally, the goal is to prepare consultants with dispositions that invite consultees to participate in the consultation process and leave with new conceptualizations and strategies to address challenging situations.

A. Meyers (2002) wrote about her process of making educational and design decisions as she prepared to teach her first consultation class. Through the use of Collins's work with Black feminist epistemology (as cited in A. Meyers, 2002), A. Meyers outlined considerations for developing consultants based on an emphasis on lived experiences, dialogue to check for meaning, an ethic of caring, and an ethic of personal accountability. Meyers highlights some of the relational aspects of effective consultation and the dilemma educators and trainers face—how to help consultants become nonthreatening experts.

Consultant educators in a global world are advised to support consultants to develop confidence in their expertise while maintaining openness to the knowledge, perspectives, and approaches of others. Multicultural consultation (Ingraham, 2000) attends to the consultant and consultee needs for development of knowledge, skills, perspective, and confidence. J. Meyers (2002) supports learners in developing their own ideas about consultation and encourages them to develop and try out methods for implementing them. Maintaining a degree of flexibility and innovation in how we teach consultation can support new scholars and practitioners to find intriguing questions to investigate and to develop a level of ownership in consultation.

CROSS-CULTURAL AND SYSTEMIC CONTEXTS FOR CONSULTATION: ADDITIONAL TRAINING NECESSARY FOR MASTERY

The need for research and models for consultation training is amplified in the areas of cross-cultural, multicultural, transnational, and systems-level consultation (e.g., Clare, 2009; Hatzichristou et al., Chapter 5, this volume; Ingraham, 2000, 2017; Ingraham & Meyers, 2000; Nastasi, Moore, & Varjas, 2004), models that hold promise for developing global perspectives in the education of consultants. Effective consultation in these models requires knowledge and skill in basic consultation as well as additional expertise to work with the complexities of differing cultures, perspectives, languages, nations, and levels of service delivery inherent in systems-level, cross-cultural, and transnational consultation. Knowledge and skills in consultation through interpreters are important for any psychologist who works within a multilingual context (see Lopez, 2008, for additional resources), as is the case in many schools today. Utilizing culturally responsive consultation (see Knotek, 2102), decolonizing consultation (Clare, 2009), and consultation matched with the cultural perspectives of participants is critical when working cross-culturally and within heterogeneous systems (Ingraham, 2000, 2003; Nastasi et al., 2004; Nastasi, Varjas, Bernstein, & Jayasena, 2000).

At this point in the field, while additional research is being conducted, we can consider what is known about multicultural training in school psychology and explore how this might inform the preparation of consultants. Rogers (2005) summarized key findings from three studies of exemplary models of multicultural training in psychology graduate programs in the U.S., especially those in school psychology. She identified four characteristics of the multicultural curricula and training environments that were found in the exemplary programs she investigated: (1) employment of an integration model of multicultural training that embeds multicultural perspectives throughout the curriculum, (2) exposure of students to a diverse clientele during applied training, (3) emphasis on diversity issues in research training, and (4) assessment of cross-cultural knowledge on comprehensive examinations. These highlights of exemplary multicultural training programs may be useful in considering what helps prepare school psychologists for consultation with a global perspective. Specifically, for training and education of consultants, we can use integration models of training that embed global perspectives throughout the curriculum, not just as an added focus.

Tendency to Seek Consultees Congruent with Consultant's Worldview and Perspectives

It is important for CITs to have experiences with consultees with perspectives different from their own. Yet, with whom does a CIT typically practice consultation? I have found that as CITs seek cases to practice their emerging consultation skills, there is a tendency to select consultees who hold perspectives and use communication styles similar to the consultant. It is much harder to try a developing skill in situations where one is less assured that there will be rapport and shared understandings with the consultee. While working with culturally similar consultees may be useful in first developing consultation skills, to develop competence with cross-cultural consultation, work with more challenging cases is necessary to prepare consultants for the realities of practicing in a diverse world.

Maital (2000) referred to the notion of *reciprocal distancing* to describe the phenomenon when consultees who hold beliefs different from their clients seek to conceptualize them as unwilling or resistant rather than owning some responsibility for the schism between consultant and consultee. In her work with consultants in Israel, she points to the consultant's efforts to externalize or explain away consultees who are not responsive to their consultation rather than looking to see what they might do differently.

It is possible that this notion also applies to consultants who want to work with people like them and avoid those with differing worldviews, perspectives, values, and communication styles. Consultants gravitate to those with whom they have similarities that make rapport building, communication, and patterns more familiar and fluid. It takes more effort to practice consultation skills with consultees who hold divergent perspectives from the consultant. It takes a great deal of support for CITs to move out of their comfort zone and to risk practicing a new skill, especially practicing it with someone who comes from a different value systems and/or communication style. In workshops, I have referred to this as a *reframing of consultee resistance*. I tell CITs that what they may perceive as resistance is often the consultant's cue to try something different, an alternative approach, more rapport development, or communication styles and conceptual paradigms more aligned with the consultee's perspectives. It is not the time to label the consultee as resistant, which does nothing to rebuild the rapport.

Developing global perspectives to consultation necessitates knowledge and skills for consultation with those who are dissimilar from the consultant. This calls on consultant educators to develop or use methods for exposing their trainees to people who hold worldviews, communication styles, and perspectives different from their own. They will also need to use training methods that help CITs move beyond their own lived experiences to open them to thinking from different paradigms, perspectives, and styles. With my colleague Evelyn Oka, we developed a multiyear collaboration where we put our CITs in contact with one another, using technology to help them expand the scope of diversity and perspectives with which they are in contact (Ingraham & Oka, 2013; Oka & Ingraham, 2013) as they learn consultation. Through use of Skype, video conferencing, and online chats, we conducted real-time, carefully designed cross-cultural activities across our two classes in two different universities. This approach has much promise for global efforts to prepare consultants because of the potential for using technology for transnational collaborations.

CONSULTATION LEARNING AND DEVELOPMENT (CLAD): A DEVELOPMENTAL MODEL FOR CONSULTANT PROFESSIONAL GROWTH

The CLAD model for consultant professional growth, outlined in Table 16.1, is a way to connect the stages and processes of consultation training previously identified (e.g., Newell & Newman, 2014; Rosenfield, 2002) with the additional complexities of cross-cultural,

Table 16.1 Consultation Learning and Development (CLAD): Stages and Topics in Learning Consultation with a Global Perspective

Learning stage	Topics learned
1. Conceptual understanding	What is consultation, how it is used, and what are its basic goals? Issues of learning, development, behavior, social justice, culture, and privilege.
2. Theories informing consultation	Theories underlying a specific model or approach (e.g., behavioral, social learning, constructivism) and theories of developing cultural proficiency, cultural pluralism, and attention to ecological influences.
3. Research about consultation processes and outcomes	May include empirical studies, evidence-based interventions, case studies, and narrative reports of various aspects of the consultation process with diverse participants. Examine the outcomes of multicultural and transnational consultation at individual to systems levels.
4. Skill acquisition and practice	Training-based exercises or practice of consultation skills, role-play, scenarios that include global perspectives, power differentials, and cross-cultural interactions involving participants with diverse worldviews.
5. Supervised practice in school or community	Consultation with authentic, diverse cases in the context of practice. Supervision and feedback on recorded sessions, including ecosystemic issues of culture, national and cultural identities, communication styles, worldviews, social locations, and perspectives that may arise.
6. Advanced practice/integration in-service delivery	Advanced development of consultation skills, analysis of consultation cases, supervision, and proficiencies in more complex issues such as cross-cultural, transnational, and systems-level consultation.

systemic, and transnational consultation. The six-stage CLAD model includes different stages and learning activities that go from beginning to learn about consultation to demonstrated competence in applied settings. Like the models by Joyce and Showers (1980), Newell and Newman (2014), and Rosenfield (2002), the CLAD model includes stages for skill acquisition and practice, supervised practice and feedback, and coaching for application in real settings. Additionally, CLAD includes specific cross-cultural content and global perspectives.

The CLAD model differs from previous models in two important ways. One difference is that the CLAD model includes greater attention to differing perspectives in the beginning stages, which is critical when working across cultures, paradigms, and perspectives. Here is where the differences between ethnocentric, multicultural, and global paradigms can be introduced:

• *Ethnocentric paradigms* are ones located within the worldview of a specific ethnicity or cultural belief system. For example, a school that is on vacation during the celebration of Christmas (i.e., refers to the "Christmas vacation") locates this school within a paradigm of Christian tradition (or perhaps earlier Pagan practices). This perspective works when others share the same religious paradigm, but it is not inclusive of Islam, Judaism, Hinduism, or other religious belief systems.

Non-Christian families may feel marginalized by calling the vacation the "Christmas break."

- *Multicultural paradigms* are those that attend to notions of pluralism, differing cultures and belief systems, and how these intersect in cross-cultural interactions. A school that takes a "winter break" at the end of December is using a more multicultural paradigm that is not grounded in a specific religious belief system. It is more multicultural than a "Christmas break," but it is not aligned with international and global differences about which months in the calendar represent the season of winter (e.g., north and south of the equator).
- *Global paradigms* are those that include multicultural and cross-cultural paradigms and add a component of transnational interaction, whereby those involved may be working across language, cultural, political, ethnic, and national differences and complexities. Perhaps calling the same vacation the "December break" might be more inclusive of different religious practices as well as international contexts in both the northern and southern hemispheres where December could be the winter or summer season.

These examples do not preclude those celebrating an important religious tradition from publically referring to Christmas, or Yom Kippur, or Ramadan, and so forth. It simply recognizes the pluralism of belief systems among those in the school's community. When all members of a community share a common paradigm, there is nothing wrong with calling the break by a term that connects with all the residents' belief systems. However, when efforts are made to adopt a global paradigm, then the lens through which one perceives the events at the end of December can matter.

Attention to issues of pluralism, power differentials, ecological influences, and social justice are included in these early stages where the theories and paradigms shape our understanding. The assumptions and theories embedded in one's conceptualization of psychological issues are important to explore (see Henning-Stout, 1994; Ingraham, 2000; Ingraham & Oka, 2006; Nastasi et al., 2004; Tarver-Behring & Ingraham, 1998). A second difference is that issues of culture, paradigm, and perspective are infused throughout the stages.

Six Stages of the CLAD Model

Stage 1

In CLAD, the first stage is developing *conceptual understanding* about what consultation is, how it is used, and what are its basic goals. Theories and issues about learning, development, behavior, social justice, culture, and privilege are fundamental in how and what we develop as conceptual understanding. This may be accompanied by a discussion of the assumptions, parameters, or characteristics of consultation. For example, Conoley and Conoley (1992) identified important parameters of consultation: the consultee initiates the service; the consultee has freedom to accept or reject consultation; the relationship is confidential, collaborative, and coordinate and deals only with professional problems; and the focus is on prevention. It is usually considered an indirect form of service delivery because the consultant works with the adults who are responsible for the clients, most often children and youth. Brown et al. (2011) and others have expanded the earlier definitions of consultation to include consultation initiated by either consultee or consultant, and the consultant may have some involvement with the client.

Stage 2

The second stage of CLAD is about the *theories that inform consultation*. In a global perspective of consultation training, it is also important to explore the underlying assumptions and beliefs that create the theory of consultation; thus, the CLAD model goes into more depth and detail in the early stages to develop shared understandings and concepts. It is important for consultants to understand the theories upon which their consultation models and practices are grounded, because each involves assumptions about the topics for consideration, the epistemology leading to hypothesis development, the questions asked during consultation, and the interventions that may be developed. Learners may be exposed to the different theories of development, behavior, social learning, and motivation as they apply to each model, as well as theories for developing cultural proficiency, pluralism, and attention to ecological and systemic influences.

Different theories involve different assumptions, and the theories that serve as the foundation for consultation are reflective of the paradigm from which one is operating. For example, learners taught ecological models of human development and constructionist perspectives may look for different characteristics in behavior and interpersonal relationships, such as the interconnected influences of the family, school, and community, whereas these would be less the focus in a behaviorist approach. The same is true for the different models of consultants and the basic theories that undergird them. For instance, behavioral consultation builds on the principles of human behavior and behavioral change, foundational principles underlying conjoint behavioral consultation (Sheridan & Kratochwill, 2007), and problem-solving consultation (Kratochwill, 2008). Consultee-centered consultation, a more recent variation of mental health consultation, focuses on the intersection of relationships and psychological mindedness, giving attention to cognitive, affective, and motivational components of consultation (e.g., Lambert, 2004; Newman, Ingraham, & Shriberg, 2014a; Sandoval, 2014). Participatory culture-specific consultation (e.g., Nastasi et al., 2000; 2004) includes discussion of the theories related to participatory and mixed-methods research designs and how to use these to develop mental health programs that are specific for the cultures of the populations served.

Stage 3

In the third stage of consultation learning, *research about consultant processes and outcomes*, there are great differences with how much research findings are emphasized in the training of consultants. Some texts focus specifically on the empirical bases and research informing consultation in their country. Erchul and Sheridan (2014) edited an excellent collection of primarily U.S. research findings about a wide range of consultation topics. In their book, the purpose is more to present thorough discussions of the available research rather than to focus on the skill development of future consultants. Some books emphasize learning a specific model of consultation and integrate research findings as they relate to that specific model. Examples include: Rosenfield's (2012) case studies using instructional forms of consultee-centered consultation; Sandoval's (2014) step-by-step guide to consultee-centered consultation; and Sheridan and Kratochwill's (2007) articulation of conjoint behavioral consultation. Consultants trained with global perspectives may need to learn about research grounded in ecological, behavioral, relational, cross-cultural, and organizational theories.

Some consultation education ends at this point, with the main emphasis on consultation theory, whereas other approaches continue into skill acquisition and supervised practice. Anton-LaHart and Rosenfield (2004) studied preservice consultation training and supervision and found that responding graduate programs spent more time on theoretical and conceptual aspects of consultation and less on consultation skill development. There was great variation in how skills were developed and supervised through graduate coursework; only 14% of the programs required weekly or biweekly taping of consultation sessions, and supervisors reviewed tapes in only 9% of those. They found that "43% of the responding programs did not provide any type of regular supervision to consultation students during coursework activities," and "32% of responding programs did not provide any type of regular supervision during practicum" (p. 53).

Stage 4

Stage four of CLAD involves *skill acquisition and practice* through training activities such as role-plays, scenarios, and other exercises. Skills in communication, interpersonal relationships, and problem-solving are all central to effective consultation. Some programs embed into the coursework activities to help CITs develop and practice defined skills. For example, trainers may develop activities to help CITs learn to ask open-ended questions, listen to consultees, practice active listening and summarizing, and exploring perspective-taking and related skills (e.g., Gravois et al., 2002; Ingraham, 2002; Ingraham & Sandoval, 2008; Sandoval, 2014; Sheridan & Kratochwill, 2007). Additionally, educators can help consultants learn cross-cultural skills to communicate with those from differing perspectives, to understand their own culture(s) and how others perceive them, and to navigate across differences related to communication style, culture, national origin, language, and perceived power.

Stage 5

The fifth stage is *supervised practice in school or community*. In this stage, CITs conduct consultation sessions under close supervision in their school settings. Gravois et al. (2002) wrote about the importance of coaching as consultants are practicing skills to provide feedback and promote professional reflection during practice; they described methods of online and face-to-face coaching. Providing feedback to recorded or live consultation sessions is critical for consultants to learn to improve their skills, but supervision of recorded consultation sessions is not as common as one might hope. For example, in the Anton-LaHart and Rosenfield (2004) study, the form of supervision varied greatly, ranging from individual to group supervision with and without recoded consultation sessions. In fact, 40% of responding programs conducted weekly or biweekly supervision without recording. Only 8% of programs included weekly supervision of recorded consultation sessions in coursework or in practicum, and only 2% included biweekly review with supervisors of recorded sessions. Thus, while feedback on real consultation cases is important for the development of effective consultation skills, few U.S. graduate programs are providing this with regularity and depth. Yet, to develop skills for cross-cultural work with diverse consultees, this is exactly the kind of preparation that is needed.

Stage 6

The sixth stage of CLAD is *advanced practice and integration into service delivery*. Here reflective practice and supervision focus on more complex issues of consultation, such as cultural and contextual influences, consultee resistance or defensiveness, consultant theme interference, and overcoming strong belief systems, racism, or color-blind perspectives. These are issues that can arise in cross-cultural consultation where the consultation participants may come from diverse worldviews, perspectives, and belief systems. It takes specialized training to address cross-cultural issues in service delivery (e.g., see Ingraham, 2000, 2003; Newell et al., 2010; Tarver Behring, Cabello, Kushida, & Murguia, 2000). Newell (2010) found that cultural responsiveness to multiracial cases was missing in the problem conceptualization of consultants in a multiracial context. With close supervision and explicit training in cross-cultural consultation, however, CITs are able to address some of these complex issues, but integration of these topics into effective consultation practice takes time and feedback (e.g., Ingraham, 2003).

Rosenfield (2002) refers to this stage as *advanced skill development* where consultant proficiency and expertise are developed further. In her consultation sequence, advanced students engage in supervision of novice consultants as part of developing proficiency at this stage. This advanced stage goes beyond listening to recorded consultation sessions and can focus on subtleties in the relationship development, communication patterns, and dialogues of consultants and consultees. Moreover, this stage should include training in supervision of consultants (see Newman, 2012; Newell & Newman, 2014), although that is not yet prevalent in many training programs (Anton-LaHart & Rosenfield, 2004).

The CLAD model includes attention to consultation development and learning from the initial stages of learning about consultation to the deeper integration of complex consultation knowledge and skills into professional practice in real school settings. Similar to recommendations for infusing multicultural perspectives throughout multicultural training in school psychology (e.g., Lopez & Bursztyn, 2013; Newell et al., 2010; Rogers, 2005), global and transnational perspectives for consultation are infused within each of the six stages of the CLAD model. Great attention to the first three stages is important for consultants working across different countries and cultures because cultures and individuals may hold very different understandings of the purpose and goals for consultation and the theoretical underpinnings that determine what is considered and how. It is also important to devote additional emphasis to coaching consultants in strategies to address racism, color-blind paradigms, and ethnocentrism, as these areas can be challenging for consultants (Ingraham, 2003). While a complete articulation of the education and training of consultants with global perspectives is beyond the scope of this chapter, I hope I have identified some key issues for readers to consider.

PREPARING CONSULTANTS TO WORK ACROSS DIFFERENT WORLDVIEWS AND PERSPECTIVES

As I talk with consultation educators at various universities and in other countries, I am often asked how a trainer can challenge the perceptions and worldviews of CITs so that they can begin to understand how to work effectively with persons with vastly differing perspectives. I believe this may relate to what A. Meyers (2002) wrote about helping consultants develop nonthreatening expertise and dispositions. I have developed several activities to support CITs in exploring their own worldviews and how they might differ from their consultees' (e.g., see Ingraham, 2016), and with my students we have shown the relationships of worldviews with cross-cultural consultation (e.g., Ingraham et al., 2007; Ingraham, Ortega, Medina, Ikeda, & Fis, 2009). In this chapter, I have chosen to describe one activity in detail because it has proven so valuable in helping consultants begin to understand how paradigms can impact their consultation relationship with consultees. The activity broadens CIT and practitioner perspectives and abilities to work with people different from them. This will prepare them to work with more heterogeneous populations from a more global, versus parochial, perspective.

In cross-cultural interactions, and even in cross-communication styles within our own cultures, there are some clear differences that can challenge rapport and communication. I have found that discussing Hall's (1976) work offers a useful platform to begin exploring how one's communication style can impact their consultation effectiveness. Hall described how people from different cultures could use differing styles of communication, called *context communication*, and how cultures can have high-context (where extensive knowledge of the culture is needed to interpret meaning of communications) and low-context (where the message is straightforward and does not necessitate knowledge of the culture to infer meaning) emphases. Elsewhere, I explained Hall's work with high- and low-context cultures and messages (Ingraham, 2006) and its application for the consultation process (Ingraham, 2002, 2014).

In a global perspective for consultation training and education, the high- versus low-context communication may be related to cultural, national, and/or personality factors. As consultants are prepared to work across cultures, they need to learn about their own culture(s) and worldview(s) and how they may be perceived by those from different cultures and values (see Ingraham, 2000). This is critical as consultants traverse cultural contexts and work with members of differing cultures and communication styles.

I developed an activity called Direct versus Indirect Communication Styles to help consultants learn about their own communication style preferences and how these intersect with persons using different styles of communication. For about 15 years, I have been using this activity in preservice and in-service training as a means to open consultant awareness to communication style differences and to prepare them to develop more successful consultation relationships. I describe the activity in this chapter because I have found it to be a valuable tool to deepen understanding and empathy about how one's interpersonal style, whether based on cultural context or personality factors, is perceived by others of differing perspectives. The affective reactions of people when they encounter a style divergent from their own can be intense and can jeopardize relationships and consultation. This activity makes more transparent the affect, assumptions, and preferences of persons with different communication styles and strategies to bridge across the differences.

Our ultimate goal is to develop ways to communicate, build rapport, and share understanding across different cultures, communication styles, and perspectives. The training goals of the Direct versus Indirect Communication Styles activity are to develop awareness, understanding, and empathy and then to practice skills in crossing communication styles that will lead to more effective communication with persons using different styles. When I use this training activity, consultants and CITs become aware of the impact of their own styles on others who prefer a different style, and they can get coaching to practice approaches to help them expand their communication repertoires to include bridging strategies to build connections with persons who use very different styles of communication.

Direct vs. Indirect Communication Styles: An Activity

Conceptual Background

Provide a brief presentation on communication styles and Hall's (1976) high- and low-context communication work. This will give participants an understanding of different ways and reasons for our use of one style versus another. I typically do this with a 15-minute PowerPoint presentation, discussion, and examples of high- and low-context communication. There are situational, contextual, and cultural reasons that a style might be preferred in a given situation, and people generally use differing styles depending on their preferences and the perceived demands of a given situation. This activity takes about 90 minutes and necessitates a skilled facilitator to lead it. It is important to allow enough time to process and debrief with participants during and after the experience, to offer new ways to reframe their thinking and beliefs, and to teach and practice strategies to bridge across communication style differences.

Introduction to Activity

Say to participants: "We are going to do an activity that focuses on our preferred communication styles and what can happen when we are communicating with a person with a different style. Ultimately, we want to learn to bridge across communication styles so that we can establish effective communication with people, no matter what their style preferences are. There are times when we each use one style or the other, as we just saw in the presentation, so many of us use a combination of styles. *For today*, I want you think of communication styles as on a continuum from extremely direct to extremely indirect. Many of us are somewhere along the continuum in the middle zone, but for today, I want you to pick one end of the continuum or the other. Think about which end of the spectrum is more familiar or comfortable to you when you are consulting with a person in your school setting. For today, you are going to be a spokesperson for one end of the continuum or the other, so that you will be representing people who have even more of a direct or indirect style than you do. This will help us learn what can happen when the two styles are prevalent within a given conversation. So for today, pick if you will be a spokesperson for the very direct or very indirect styles of communication."

Allow participants a short period to decide which style they will represent for today's activity. Ask the group to divide into two groups, with one group representing the direct style of communication and the other group representing the indirect style of communication. Once participants have organized their seating into the two groups (best if on opposite sides of the room to support the group cohesion), say that each group will work as a team to develop responses to four questions, and then they will share them with each other to help them better understand each communication style.

Say to participants: "Please establish a group recorder so we can share your thinking. First identify some of the *values and behaviors* typical of your communication style (very direct or very indirect). Create a list. I will circulate between the groups." Give groups about 10 minutes (or when both groups have finished) to discuss their group's communication style, including the values and behaviors that are typical of persons using that style. This time will allow them to explore the ways persons from their communication style think and feel and will help solidify their group process.

Say to participants: "Okay, the second questions is: What are some of the things about the other style of communication (direct or indirect) that are irritating or bothersome to your style? What bugs you about those using that other style?" Again, give groups 5 to 10 minutes to reflect and develop a list. The groups will probably become more animated. Remind them that their job is to represent those who are very far into the communication style of their group; therefore, honest answers will be most useful to the whole group. Encourage groups to express their real sentiments.

Say to participants: "The third question is: When someone is strongly taking the other style of communication, how do you feel as you try to talk with them?" Again, give groups 5 to 10 minutes to reflect and develop a list of responses for this question. Once both groups have developed a working list, continue to the fourth question.

Say to participants: "So when you are communicating with the person who is far to the end of the continuum with the other communication style, what do you wish the person using the other style would do to make your communication smoother? I wish they would just_____." This will probably not require as much time.

Groups may feel nervous about sharing, especially if participants know each other before starting the activity. Remind them that this is a unique opportunity to learn perspectives about things we typically do not discuss. Say, "as we share, listen with an open heart so we can truly understand the different perspectives." Allow groups to take turns in sharing their responses to each question. I often start with the indirect group because the direct groups typically want to go first, and the activity is designed to heighten awareness of how the styles intersect and can collide. I explain this to the groups. Indirects share responses to the first item; then, ask directs, "Is there anything you want them to clarify or you don't understand?" Allow the indirects to explain more fully if needed. Then ask the directs to share their responses to the first item while the indirects listen and then have a chance to ask clarifying questions.

Follow this turn-taking process between groups until both groups have shared responses to all four items. There may be tension in the room as participants realize that there is intensity to these styles and feelings. Typically, I follow this with examples of what happens when a person with an indirect style interacts with a person with a direct style and vice versa. For example, as the direct communicator becomes increasingly frustrated with the longer narrative of the indirect communicator, they tend to revert even more into their direct style, further leading the indirect communicator to shut down, become offended, or feel frustrated to the point where they are not sure what to say. As the indirect communicator is faced with a very direct communicator, they may give subtle cues that they want to use a more indirect style, but the direct communicator often does not recognize these subtle cues, and misunderstanding and frustration ensue. In either case, the result is to further fragment rapport and understanding rather than to build effective communication.

Often, I ask the groups to stop and notice who is in each group to see if there are clear patterns with those who have chosen to be in one group or the other. I ask and then let the groups take time to explore each hypothesis: "Is there a gender difference? Is there a racial difference? An age difference? Cultural, ethnic, or national origin difference?" As I have done the activity many times, I have found that there is often not a definite way to predict what kinds of individuals self-select for each group. Then I ask, "Well, is there a familial difference? How many of you have a sibling or family member who gravitates towards the 'other' style of communication from you?" Usually most people can identify a family member with the different style. I conclude with, "So there is no right or wrong style, these are just differences we are likely to see in the schools where we are working and as school psychologists, and we should be prepared to communicate well with persons of either style. Next, we are going to explore some strategies for you to reach out to a consultee of the 'other' style to build positive rapport and communication."

I follow this awareness with a set of activities designed to help each style of communicator learn how to intermittently or, when necessary, reach out in the communication style of the other to rebuild rapport. We practice skills in cross-communication style dialogue. For example, when the direct communicator is frustrated and feels the indirect communicator shutting down or withdrawing from engagement, stepping back and asking a gentle, indirect-style question may help draw out the indirect communicator. For the indirect communicator who is sensing that the direct communicator is losing interest or getting frustrated, asking a short, direct question that asks the direct communicator's thoughts about the key issues is likely to engage them more actively in the dialogue. We also talk about the dilemma when both communicators are using the same style and how that can affect the consultation process.

Recently, I have asked each group to prepare a "tip sheet" of notes to help someone from a different communication style better connect with them. On these tip sheets, each group lists suggestions to help a person better communicate with members of their communication style. Following creation of the tip sheets, we engage in practice in communicating across styles. I invite a volunteer from each group to role-play a consultant or consultee who is firmly grounded in one communication style. The consultant, with coaching and use of the tip sheet, tries to ask a question of the consultee using the style more aligned with the consultee's style and is presumably different from the consultant's usual style. The groups provide feedback to the consultant on whether their questions might feel acceptable with a person of their style. Consultants get practice in shifting styles to reach out to consultees in the consultee-compatible style with feedback from the groups. The facilitator's skills in creating a supportive atmosphere and mediating differences are critical here.

I conclude with encouragement that learning the other style may be difficult and will take practice. What the participants can do to support each other is to recognize when their colleague is trying to use a less familiar style and offer encouraging feedback that builds confidence and skill. For groups with whom I have continued contact, such as those in a class or workshop series, we revisit the topic in a subsequent session. I ask if anyone had experience with observing the style differences and trying to use some of the strategies we discussed. Invariably, there are multiple examples of how the concepts were applied to communications in their work and interpersonal relationships.

I have been using this activity for the past 15 years and have found many similarities in the responses of the differing communication styles. Table 16.2 shows responses that were generated by members of each communication style group. The data for this table were collected from four different cohorts of my school psychology students. All students were in their second year of the school psychology graduate program and were enrolled in a required course (consultation or family-school collaboration). Group sizes ranged from 5 to 12 people, and although each cohort included males and females of diverse ethnic identities and native languages, the self-selection of individuals to each group did not result in meaningful differences in group composition according to gender, age, race, nationality, or ethnicity. Their responses were generated to the open-ended questions, and they did not have access to the responses of previous years' students; thus each cohort provided their comments independently of each other. For analyses, only responses that were generated by 50% or more of the same communication style groups are shown, along with those responses generated by 75% and 100% of the cohorts.

Table 16.2 Percentage of Direct and Indirect Groups That Generated Responses Aligned with Each Theme, Reported for Each of Four Questions

Direct Communication Group Responses	Indirect Communication Group Responses

Q1: Identify some of the values and behaviors typical of your communication style (very direct or very indirect).

Responses	Responses
100%	**100%**
• Forthcoming, quick to provide suggestions, actively engaged, proactive, stand up for yourself	• Understanding, empathetic, empathy • Hear different perspectives, considerate of others' values and opinions, want to listen to the other person, constantly take others' perspective • Listen, good listeners, polite • Try not to offend, choose our words carefully, mindful, don't want to offend, we choose our battles wisely, imply rather than say it directly
75%	**75%**
• Vocal, first to speak, talkative, initiate the conversation • Honest, value honesty, keep it real, telling the truth • Confident • Difficult to intimidate, confrontation is a positive and necessary thing, okay with getting *no* for an answer	• Time to build rapport, building rapport, comfort, observant of person's demeanor (body language, nonverbal), mindful of what people need without them having to ask • Respectful, respect • Collaborative • Look at various angles, provide examples, analytical
50%	**50%**
• Goal oriented • Get to the point, don't beat around the bush • Strong personalities • Straightforward, answers to the point • Natural leaders, leadership roles • Good advocates, advocating for yourself and others • Concise/clear • Efficient/competent • Effective communication to understand the problem, share your thoughts more easily • Genuine/authentic, openness/integrity • What I said is what I meant—don't infer, less self-monitoring, independent • Risk taker, open to critique, resilient • Invested, hardworking • Solution comes quicker, time management	• Nonjudgmental, take time before making judgments • Not overbearing or intimidating, less threatening • Pick up or observant of nonverbal communication

Q2: What are some of the things about the other style of communication (direct or indirect) that are irritating or bothersome to your style? What bugs you about those using that other style?

100%	**100%**
• Time wasted; you assume they don't have an opinion if they don't state it, so you can go for weeks without knowing there is a problem • Timid, insecure, not speaking up for themselves, intimidated, lack of confidence • Long conversation, wordy, throwing in a bunch of irrelevant information, lack of focus, take longer to communicate, talk forever without making a point • Safe, reserved, evasive, avoiding confrontation	• Egocentric, self-absorbed, come off with "I'm right" attitude, comes off as one-sided • Intimidating, intimidates me, makes us feel like we need to defend ourselves • Dominant, they dominate the situation, controlling, bossy, pretentious • Overrides other person's opinions/personal experiences, cut you off before you can say something, don't allow you to speak, pushy, don't agree to disagree, attitude—have to have the last word

Table 16.2 (Continued)

Direct Communication Group Responses	Indirect Communication Group Responses
	• Not tactful, hurtful and not open-minded, moody/grumpy, inconsiderate, invalidating, unapologetic • Dogmatic, opinions are set in stone, oblivious to situation and people, might not be listening, not flexible, not open to others' ideas
75% • Stammering over words, babble, confusing • Appear incompetent, lack of life skills, ill-prepared • Avoidant, can't trust them, will talk to peers rather than directly to the person	**75%** • Rude, blunt, can be perceived as rude • Insensitive
50% • Wishy-washy, spineless • Passive • Weak	**50%** • Impulsive • Stubborn • Emphasize their own points, their ideas are more important, may impose their values • Snappy, they make snap judgments • Unaware of how others respond to what they're saying, don't think before they speak

Q3: When someone is strongly taking the other style of communication, how do you feel as you try to talk with them?

100% • Pushy, burden, pick up their slack/work, superior, coming off as rude, how it's perceived	**100%** • Defensive, defensive/put your guard up, makes us more oppositional, defensive, and protective
75% • Anxious, uncomfortable • Frustrated • Impatient, wasting my time, I am wasting my time • Confused, loss of control/no direction, zone out of the conversation	**75%** • Get away from them, get away, want to run away • Attacked, threatened, scared • Shut down, detached or distant, avoidant, want to tune it out so you're not affected by it, disregarded • Inferior, insecure, less value, ignored
	50% • Hurt, hurtful • Frustrated • Annoyed • Rushed • Get to the boiling point, worried about escalating, have to contain ourselves from becoming a monster

Q4: So when you are communicating with the person who is far to the end of the continuum with the other communication style, what do you wish the person using the other style would do to make your communication smoother? "I wish they would just_____."

	100% • Check in with the other person, consider other people's feelings, be less selfish, give the other person time
67%[1] • Be honest • Get to the point • Take a stand, be willing to disagree, effectively communicate needs • Just get it off your chest, spit it out—just do it	**75%** • Take a different perspective, reframe what they're saying, be more flexible, accept differences • Just chill! Relax, take a yoga class and relax • Be conscious of nonverbals, communication styles
	50% • Listen, take the time to listen • Shut up

[1] For question 4, one of the four groups did not get to this question, so there were only three sets of group responses; thus responses generated by two of the three groups are shown with 67%. There were no items shared by all three direct communication groups.

After collecting the data, responses were coded into themes. Table 16.2 presents participant responses that were grouped into each theme. For example, for the first item, "Identify some of the values and behaviors typical of your communication style," all four cohorts of indirect communication generated responses worded as understanding, empathic or empathy; therefore, these are listed as the first bullet/theme under the 100% criterion. Three of the four indirect groups listed collaborative, which is why this is shown as a bullet in the 75% criterion group. In reading the responses for how the direct and indirect groups responded to each question, the reader is able to see the descriptive words used by the respondents and to form an impression regarding the perceptions of that group about themselves and toward the other communication style. This may assist trainers in anticipating responses that may arise and in preparing for skilled facilitation. Although the data in Table 16.2 were generated by CITs, the results are very similar with what practicing school psychologists report when I have done the activity at NASP or other professional workshops.

SUGGESTIONS FOR FUTURE RESEARCH

Several scholars have noted the lack of recent research on consultation training at both the preservice and inservice levels (e.g., Anton-LaHart & Rosenfield, 2004; Hatzichristou et al., Chapter 5, this volume; Hazel et al., 2010; J. Meyers, 2002; Newell & Newman, 2014; Rosenfield, 2012). Research is needed on the learning, practicing, training, and outcomes of consultation, and this need is evident across several models of consultation (e.g., behavioral, mental health, instructional, consultee-centered, multicultural, systems-level consultation). Some attention has been given to the development and supervision of consultants. For example, Rosenfield (2002) described a developmental progression, Newman (2012) presented results of a grounded theory study of preservice consultation supervision, and Newman et al. (2014b) discussed the challenges of conducting research with practicing consultants. Newell and Newman (2014) studied consultation training research across a variety of studies and models and concluded that there are three interrelated pressing research agendas: (1) identifying and evaluating consulting competencies, (2) understanding how CITs develop from novice to competent consultants, and (3) analyzing the impact of consultants' competence on consultee and client outcomes. Clearly, researchers of consultation training have multiple directions and topics to pursue.

There are many needs for future research regarding the models, processes, and outcomes of consultation training (J. Meyers, 2002; Newman, 2012; Rosenfield, 2002). Lopez and Bursztyn (2013), Newell et al. (2010), and Rogers (2005) called for future research in many areas of multicultural school psychology, including the training of school psychologists with the knowledge and skills to competently serve the diverse student body of today's schools. With the scarcity of research on consultation training and the even greater absence of research on preparing professionals with global competencies, there is room for numerous types and methods of research. Studies of cross-cultural and systemic training within a specific culture and/or across cultures will help inform the preparation of consultants for a more global context. For example, researchers could use the CLAD's six-stages of consultation learning and development to study different ways for preparing consultants within both preservice and in-service contexts. Researchers working in this area will need to be well versed with a variety of methodologies to best document the complexities of cross-cultural, systemic, and global consultation (for examples, see Ingraham, 2003, 2014; Knotek, 2012; Lopez, 2008; Nastasi et al., 2004; Newell, 2010).

There are numerous questions to explore, such as: How much and what kinds of training experiences show promising results for preparing consultants with global perspectives? What competencies are most salient in preparing globally thinking consultants? What curricular approaches support consultants in learning the complexities of cross-cultural, systemic, and transnational consultation? What similarities and differences are found in the group patterns of indirect and direct communication seen in the data from this author's work when compared with data from other trainers? When exposure to diverse cultures and perspectives is limited by geography or by the cultural lens of the dominant narrative, how can consultants broaden their perspectives to prepare them for work with culturally divergent consultees? How does the cross-cultural proficiency of the consultant affect the processes and outcomes of consultation?

There are multiple intriguing paths to explore, and there is room for a multitude of researchers to work in this area. The field of multicultural school psychology has grown within the past two decades, and there are now numerous resources to inform research and practice. It is time to build a body of research using global perspectives in educating consultants to guide the preparation of consultants for tomorrow's schools and cultural contexts.

REFERENCES

Anton-LaHart, J., & Rosenfield, S. (2004). A survey of preservice consultation training in school psychology programs. *Journal of Educational and Psychological Consultation, 15,* 41–62.

Brown, D., Pryzwansky, W. R., & Schulte, A. C. (2011). *Psychological consultation and collaboration: Introduction to theory and practice* (7th ed.). Upper Saddle River, NJ: Pearson.

Clare, M. M. (2009). Decolonizing consultation: Advocacy as the strategy, diversity as the context. *Journal of Educational and Psychological Consultation, 19,* 8–25.

Collins, P. H. (2000). *Black feminist thought: Knowledge, consciousness, and the politics of empowerment* (2nd ed.). New York: Routledge.

Conoley, J. C., & Conoley, C. W. (1992). *School consultation: Practice and training* (2nd ed.). Boston: Allyn & Bacon.

Erchul, W. P., & Martens, B. K. (2012). *School consultation: Conceptual and empirical bases of practice* (3rd ed.). New York: Springer.

Erchul, W. P., & Sheridan, S. M. (Eds.). (2014). *Handbook of research in school consultation: Empirical foundations for the field* (2nd ed.). New York: Routledge/Taylor.

Gravois, T. A., Knotek, S., & Babinski, L. M. (2002). Educating practitioners as consultants: Development and implementation of the instructional consultation team consortium. *Journal of Educational and Psychological Consultation, 13,* 113–132.

Gutkin, T. B., & Curtis, M. J. (2009). School-based consultation: The science and practice of indirect service delivery. In T. B. Gutkin & C. R. Reynolds (Eds.), *The handbook of school psychology* (4th ed., pp. 591–635). Hoboken, NJ: John Wiley & Sons.

Hall. E. T. (1976). *Beyond culture.* Garden City, NY: Anchor Press/Doubleday.

Hazel, C. E., Laviolette, G. T., & Linemen, J. M. (2010). Training professional psychologists in school-based consultation: What the syllabi suggest. *Training and Education in Professional Psychology, 4,* 235–243.

Henning-Stout, M. (1994). Consultation and connected knowing. *Journal of Educational and Psychological Consultation, 5,* 5–21.

Hylander, I. (2004). Analysis of conceptual change in consultee-centered consultation. In N. M. Lambert, I. Hylander, & J. H. Sandoval (Eds.), *Consultee-centered consultation: Improving the quality of professional services in schools and community organizations* (pp. 45–61). Mahwah, NJ: Erlbaum.

Hylander, I. (2012). Conceptual change through consultee-centered consultation: A theoretical model. *Consulting Psychology Journal: Research and Practice, 64,* 29–45.

Ingraham, C. L. (2000). Consultation through a multicultural lens: Multicultural and cross-cultural consultation in schools. *School Psychology Review, 29,* 320–343.

Ingraham, C. L. (2002, February). *Multicultural consultation in schools: Strategies for supporting teacher and student success*, full-day workshop for the National Association of School Psychologists, Chicago, IL. Audiotape set available through NASP.

Ingraham, C. L. (2003). Multicultural consultee-centered consultation: When novice consultants explore cultural hypotheses with experienced teacher consultees. *Journal of Educational and Psychological Consultation, 14*, 329–362.

Ingraham, C. L. (2006). Context communication. In Y. Jackson (Ed.), *Encyclopedia of multicultural psychology* (pp. 110–111). Thousand Oaks: Sage.

Ingraham, C. L. (2014). Studying multicultural aspects of consultation. In W. P. Erchul & S. M. Sheridan (Eds.), *Handbook of research in school consultation: Empirical foundations for the field* (2nd ed., pp. 323–348). New York: Routledge/Taylor & Francis Group.

Ingraham, C. L. (2016). Educating and training consultants for multicultural practice of consultee-centered consultation. *Journal of Educational and Psychological Consultation*. Retrieved December 5, 2016, from http://dx.doi.org/10.1080/10474412.2016.1174936

Ingraham, C. L. (2017). Multicultural process and communications issues in consultee-centered consultation. In E. C. Lopez, S. H. Nahari, & S. L. Proctor (Eds.), *Handbook of multicultural school psychology: An interdisciplinary perspective* (2nd ed., pp. 77–93). New York: Routledge/Taylor & Francis Group.

Ingraham, C. L., Flanagan, R., Oka, E., & Truscott, S. (2011, February). *School-based consultation (SBC) in an evolving world of practice.* Paper presented at the annual convention of the National Association of School Psychologists, San Francisco.

Ingraham, C. L., Lai, F., Mohammed, C., Medina, A., Ikeda, M., Ortega, L., & Zacky, D. (2007, March). *Worldview and cross-cultural consultation: Responsiveness to diverse perspectives.* Paper presented at the annual convention of the National Association of School Psychologists, New York, NY.

Ingraham, C. L., & Meyers, J. (Eds.). (2000). Multicultural and cross-cultural consultation in schools: Cultural diversity issues in school consultation. [Special issue], *School Psychology Review, 29*(3).

Ingraham, C. L., & Oka, E. R. (2006). Multicultural issues in evidence-based intervention. *Journal of Applied School Psychology, 22*, 127–149.

Ingraham, C. L., & Oka, E. R. (2013, August). *Promoting cultural proficiency and conceptual change through web-based learning communities.* Poster presented at annual conference of American Psychological Association, Honolulu, HI.

Ingraham, C. L., Ortega, L., Medina, A. P., Ikeda, M., & Fis, F. (2009, March). *Advances in cross-cultural consultation: Using worldview as a transformative lens.* Paper presented at the annual conference of the California Association of School Psychologists, Riverside, CA.

Ingraham, C. L., & Sandoval, J. H. (2008, February). *Using questions to foster conceptual change in consultee-centered consultation.* Mini-skills workshop at the annual convention of the National Association of School Psychologists, New Orleans.

Joyce, B., & Showers, B. (1980). Improving inservice training: The messages of research. *Educational Leadership, 37*, 379–385.

Knotek, S. E. (2012). Using culturally responsive consultation to support innovation implementation in a rural school. *Consulting Psychology Journal: Practice and Research, 64*, 46–62. doi: 10.1037/a0027993

Kratochwill, T. R. (2008). Best practices in school-based problem-solving consultation: Applications in prevention and intervention systems. In A. Thomas & J. Grimes (Eds.), *Best practices in school psychology V* (pp. 1673–1688). Bethesda, MD: National Association of School Psychologists.

Lambert, N. M. (2004). Consultee-centered consultation: An international perspective on goals, process, and theory. In N. M. Lambert, I. Hylander, & J. H. Sandoval (Eds.), *Consultee-centered consultation: Improving the quality of professional services in schools and community organizations* (pp. 3–19). Mahwah, NJ: Erlbaum.

Lambert, N. M., Hylander, I., & Sandoval, J. H. (Eds.). (2004). *Consultee-centered consultation: Improving the quality of professional services in schools and community organizations.* Mahwah, NJ: Erlbaum.

Lopez, E. C. (2008). Best practice in working with school interpreters. In A. Thomas & J. Grimes (Eds.), *Best practices in school psychology V* (pp. 1751–1769). Bethesda, MD: The National Association of School Psychologists.

Lopez, E. C., & Bursztyn, A. B. (2013). Future challenges and opportunities: Toward culturally responsive training in school psychology. *Psychology in the Schools, 50*, 212–228. doi: 10.1002/pits.21674

Maital, S. L. (2000). Reciprocal distancing: A systems model of interpersonal processes in cross-cultural consultation. *School Psychology Review, 29*, 389–400.

Meyers, A. (2002). Developing nonthreatening expertise: Thoughts on consultation training from the perspective of a new faculty member. *Journal of Educational and Psychological Consultation, 13*, 55–67.

Meyers, J. (2002). A 30-year perspective on best practices for consultation training. *Journal of Educational and Psychological Consultation, 13*, 35–54.

Nastasi, B. K., Moore, R. B., & Varjas, K. M. (2004). *School-based mental health services: Creating comprehensive and culturally specific programs.* Washington, DC: American Psychological Association.

Nastasi, B. K., Varjas, K., Bernstein, R., & Jayasena, A. (2000). Conducting participatory culture-specific consultation: A global perspective on multicultural consultation. *School Psychology Review, 29,* 401–413.

Newell, M. L. (2010). The implementation of problem-solving consultation: An analysis of problem conceptualization in a multiracial context. *Journal of Educational and Psychological Consultation, 20,* 83–105. doi: 10.1080/10474411003785529

Newell, M. L., Nastasi, B. K., Hatzichristou, C., Jones, J. M., Schanding, G. T., & Yetter, G. (2010). Evidence on multicultural training in school psychology: Recommendations for future directions. *School Psychology Quarterly, 25,* 249–278. doi: 10.1037/a0021542

Newell, M. L., & Newman, D. (2014). Assessing the state of evidence in consultation training. In W. P. Erchul & S. M. Sheridan (Eds.), *Handbook of research in school consultation* (2nd ed., pp. 421–449). New York: Routledge/Taylor & Francis Group.

Newman, D. S. (2012). A grounded theory study of supervision of preservice consultation training. *Journal of Educational and Psychological Consultation, 22,* 247–279. doi: 10.1080/104/10474412.706127

Newman, D. S., Ingraham, C. L., & Shriberg, D. (2014a). Consultee-centered consultation in contemporary schools. *Communiqué, National Association of School Psychologists, 42*(6), 14–17.

Newman, D. S., Salmon, D., Cavanaugh, K., & Schneider, M. F. (2014b). The consulting role in a Response-to-Intervention context: An exploratory study of instructional consultation. *Journal of Applied School Psychology, 30,* 278–304. doi: 10.1080/15377903/2014/924456

Oka, E. R., & Ingraham, C. L. (2013, January). *Promoting cultural competence through web-based learning communities.* Poster presented at annual conference of National Multicultural Summit, Houston, TX.

Rogers, M. R. (2005). Multicultural training in school psychology. In C. Frisby & C. R. Reynolds (Eds.), *Comprehensive handbook of multicultural school psychology* (pp. 993–1022). Hoboken, NJ: John Wiley & Sons.

Rosenfield, S. A. (Ed.). (2002). Developing instructional consultants: From novice to competent to expert. *Journal of Educational and Psychological Consultation, 13,* 97–111.

Rosenfield, S. A. (2012). *Becoming a school consultant: Lessons learned.* New York: Routledge.

Rosenfield, S. A., & Gravois, T. A. (1996). *Instructional consultation teams: Collaborating for change.* New York: Guilford.

Sandoval, J. H. (2014). *An introduction to consultee-centered consultation in the schools: A step-by-step guide to the process and skills.* New York: Routledge/Taylor & Francis Group.

Sheridan, S. M., Clarke, B. L., & Ransom, K. A. (2014). The past, present, and future of conjoint behavioral consultation research. In W. P. Erchul & S. M. Sheridan (Eds.), *Handbook of research in school consultation* (2nd ed., pp. 210–247). New York: Routledge/Taylor & Francis Group.

Sheridan, S. M., & Kratochwill, T. R. (2007). *Conjoint behavioral consultation: Promoting family-school connections and interventions* (2nd ed.). New York: Springer.

Tarver Behring, S., Cabello, B., Kushida, D., & Murguia, A. (2000). Cultural modifications to current school-based consultation approaches reported by culturally diverse beginning consultants. *School Psychology Review, 29,* 354–367.

Tarver Behring, S., & Ingraham, C. L. (1998). Culture as a central component of consultation: A call to the field. *Journal of Educational and Psychological Consultation, 9,* 57–72.

17

PROFESSIONAL TRAINING AND DEVELOPMENT IN CONSULTATION

From Knowledge to Competence and Capability in Educational and Child Psychology Practice in the UK

Emma Kate Kennedy, Sandra Dunsmuir, and R.J. Cameron

INTRODUCTION

The challenge of connecting the "ivory tower" of academic knowledge to the "earthen trench" of professional practice has been a long-standing problem for a range of applied psychology disciplines. This is a symbiotic relationship—without knowledge from reflective practice, academic learning becomes esoteric; without scientific theory and enquiry, professional practice develops into folk psychology. Integration of psychological theory, research and practice enables the "diffusion, dissemination and processes of change in movement toward effective implementation [of empirically validated research]" (Flaspohler, Meehan, Maras, & Keller, 2012, p. 430). Researchers and practitioners need to know "what kinds of interventions work under optimal, university-based, research-laboratory-style conditions . . . [and are] palatable, feasible, durable, affordable, and sustainable in real-world settings" (Jensen, Hoagwood, & Trickett, 1999, p. 207). Lowman (2012) argued that psychologists working within a consultation framework not only required well-developed knowledge but also had an important role as scientist-practitioners in linking practice with research and theory. Relatedly, Newell and Newman (2014) argue that if applied psychological practice is guided by scientific research, then training (including training in consultation) should be the same.

How to prepare consultants effectively is a task of considerable importance for university training courses, professional bodies and those working in the field. It is also an issue for employers and, most significantly, for those receiving psychological services. Alongside their values, personal experiences and working contexts, "the degree of training that . . . [psychologists] receive, or don't receive, creates . . . variation at the actual practice level" (Gravois, 2012, p. 84). This chapter outlines an approach to teaching consultation on a professional training doctorate for educational and child psychologists (ECPs) in the United Kingdom. It focuses on consultation *knowledge* to be shared with trainees, how they develop consultation *competence* (utilizing knowledge to achieve positive outcomes for clients) over time and how they employ strategies to support *capability* (the adaptation of practice to new problems, changing circumstances and fresh research evidence from the psychology evidence base).

The chapter begins with a consideration of the contribution of consultation within applied psychology practice and how a consultant can make a distinctive, but complementary, contribution to partnerships of professionals working in different settings. It briefly considers various consultation models prevalent in the UK and then goes on to describe the University College London (UCL) approach to consultation training. This includes a focus on consultation competencies and examples of teaching methods, protocols and processes for intervention planning and evaluation. It also highlights how diverse elements of the curriculum need to be synthesized in order to support students' developing understandings of the integration between research, theory and practice when developing competence. Finally, the concept of capability is examined with particular emphasis on coaching, supervision, feedback and reflection in continuing professional and personal development.

ACQUIRING THE UNDERPINNING KNOWLEDGE

All applied psychologists face the twin challenges of relating the carefully executed and rigorously scrutinized academic theory and research with the urgent, multilayered and complex demands of real-world practice. High quality professional practice involves the employment of psychology in creative and innovative ways to

- Attend to the various contexts within which children and young people are developing
- Develop insights into complex problem situations which occur in these environments
- Provide help that meets the myriad needs of people that have resulted from such problem situations.

Cameron (2006) has argued that there are five factors that make the applied psychologist's approach to consultation different from that of other practitioners:

1. Adopting a psychological perspective on the nature of human problems
2. Drawing on the psychology knowledge base to uncover mediating variables that potentially explain why and how certain events are related
3. Unravelling problem dimensions using sophisticated models, navigating through a sea of complex human data and providing useful maps of the interaction between individual factors and aspects of their living and learning environments
4. Selecting and adapting information from the research and theoretical database to recommend evidence-informed strategies for change
5. Promoting innovative concepts underpinned by psychological research and theory that enable clients to spot potential opportunities for positive change.

MODELS OF CONSULTATION

Along with timing and structures, consultation models are of concern to those delivering training (Newell & Newman, 2014). The latter is relevant to the knowledge component in that initial training courses may consider focusing either on one particular model and teaching to proficiency level or on content and processes that are more generic (Hazel, Laviolette, & Lineman, 2010; Rosenfield, Levinsohn-Klyap, & Cramer, 2010). In their review of school-based consultation service delivery, Gutkin and Curtis (2009) identified three major models of consultation—ecological, mental health and organizational—each of which has developed further since then (Erchul & Sheridan, 2014). In the UK, research on practicing ECPs use of consultation has identified a variety of models in use, the most frequently cited based on problem-solving frameworks (Kennedy, Frederickson, & Monsen, 2008).

One UK model developed by Wagner (1995, 2000) has proven to be influential, as demonstrated by the number of psychology services that adopted it for use in their own contexts (Dennis, 2004; Gillies, 2000; MacHardy, Carmichael, & Proctor, 1995; Munro, 2000). Wagner highlighted a number of psychological approaches (e.g., personal construct psychology, symbolic interactionism, systems thinking) influencing her model. She argued against the use of such terms as *consultant* and *consultee* (because of power and expert status implications) as well medical, pathologizing and within-child constructs that emphasized deficits rather than strengths (Wagner, 2008). She outlined key principles for practice—constructive, comprehensive, self-reflexive and transparent—that led to the development of flexible consultation scripts that in turn provided consultants with a structure within which to operate.

ACQUIRING COMPETENCE IN CONSULTATION

There have been moves toward competency-based training across professions and disciplines more generally (see Fouad et al., 2009; Klose, Plotts, & Lasser, 2012); consultation is no different. Woodruffe (1993) described competencies as dimensions or behavioral repertoires that underpin competent performance. This definition is extended by Epstein and Hundert (2002) as "the habitual and judicious use of communication, knowledge, technical skills, clinical reasoning, emotions, values and reflection in daily practice for the individual and community being served" (p. 226). Developing a curriculum for initial professional training involves the identification of the requisite knowledge novice consultants need, the provision of sufficient and appropriate practice opportunities to progress to competency and agreement on how knowledge and skill can be assessed at the performance level.

It is important to distinguish between competence and performance in professional educational psychology. Performance is an indication of competence, but we can never be certain that in a particular situation a student's performance is representative of their full competence (Resnick & Resnick, 1992). An individual's competence describes what he or she is able to do ("shows how") and their performance describes what they actually do ("does") in practice. Miller's (1990) competence model in Figure 17.1 illustrates the distinction between knowledge ("knows" and "knows how") and the more practical skills required in competent professional practice.

Kennedy, Cameron and Monsen (2009) applied and expanded this model to consultation training, arguing that an appropriate consultation curriculum includes the "knowledge aspects of consultation content (cognitive components), skill aspects (behavioural components) and attitudes/values (affective components)" (p. 610). Trainee

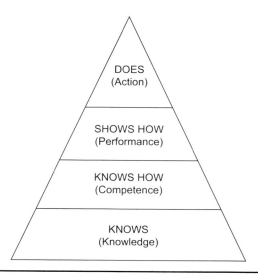

Figure 17.1 Miller's (1990) Model of Knowledge and Skill Development

consultants have to take into account a significant spectrum of knowledge when consulting, such as:

- The model of consultation they are applying
- Child and adolescent development, including atypical development
- The diversity of developmental tasks across cultures, as well as gender, religious, sexuality and socioeconomic variations
- Individual and systemic risk and protective factors, possible assessment tools and related evidence-based interventions.

Critical to the consultant's success in accessing and making sense of this multilayered information are interpersonal and relationship skills. In turn, drawing on such knowledge and skills requires an overarching framework (including key attitudes/values) that must be aspired to in the range of interpersonal activities undertaken during consultation. These include, but are not limited to, utility, authenticity, equity, sensitivity and collaboration.

A CURRICULUM FOR COMPETENCE
Professional Standards
External professional, credentialing and regulating bodies have a central role in defining the core curriculum content of professional training programs. In the UK, the British Psychological Society (BPS) Division of Educational and Child Psychology Training Committee (DECPTC) has recently specified revised standards for educational psychology training in England, Northern Ireland, and Wales for 3-year professional doctoral training. Learning about consultation is an established core requirement, and the guidance stipulates a series of consultation competencies that must be achieved by the end of

training (DECPTC, 2015). Similarly, the Health and Care Professions Council (HCPC)[1] has stated that all educational psychologists in professional practice should achieve the proficiency standard of "be[ing] able to conduct consultancy and [to] understand the theoretical basis of, and the variety of approaches to, consultation and assessment in educational psychology" (p. 17).

What Is to Be Taught?

The UK situation on consultation training has much in common with the U.S., in that practice is largely justified by limited, outdated work that is lacking in methodological rigor (Newell & Newman, 2014). Over a decade ago, in a special issue of *Educational Psychology in Practice*, Watkins and Hill (2000) outlined the principles and values underpinning one approach to professional training in consultation, which was important since Anton-LaHart and Rosenfield (2004) indicated that a course faculty's theoretical orientation influenced the models of consultation taught. Watkins and Hill argued that the aim of their course was to "develop systemic psychological thinking, especially the three Cs: contexts, cycles and connections" (2000, p. 49). ECP trainees were encouraged to:

- Not only reflect on classroom contexts but the working context of the ECP and the service from which they came
- Explore the cyclical relationships between key people in a system and not to adopt causal, uni-directional thinking about such relationships
- Seek connections between various developmental domains (cognitive, social and emotional) and various levels of working (group, family, school).

More up-to-date studies drawing on the variety of theoretical approaches adopted by the initial training courses are required.

How Consultation Is Taught

Evans, Grahamslaw, Henson, and Prince (2012) collated the views of recently qualified ECPs in England, Wales and Northern Ireland who had completed training in 2009 and 2010. All had received professional training in consultation, but little was stated about *how* this had been done. In the U.S. literature, there has been reference to specific pedagogies used in consultation training such as, for example, readings, class discussions, use of training manuals, instructor or videotaped modelling, rehearsal, role-play, computer simulation, supervision, performance feedback and student self-monitoring (Newell, 2012; Newell & Newman, 2014). Less evident in the literature are robust enquiries into whether such teaching methods are effective in producing competent consultants. As Henning-Stout (1999) stated, in the majority of cases "the relationship between pedagogy and learning has been left unexplored . . . [and] little insight has been provided in to how [trainees] navigate academic content, instructional formats and evaluation criteria to construct their own functional consultation skills" (p. 74).

DEVELOPMENT OF CONSULTATION COMPETENCE— AN ENGLISH PRESERVICE MODEL

Consultation trainees in the initial doctoral training program at UCL are taught the specific skills key to managing consultations at all stages of the problem-solving process

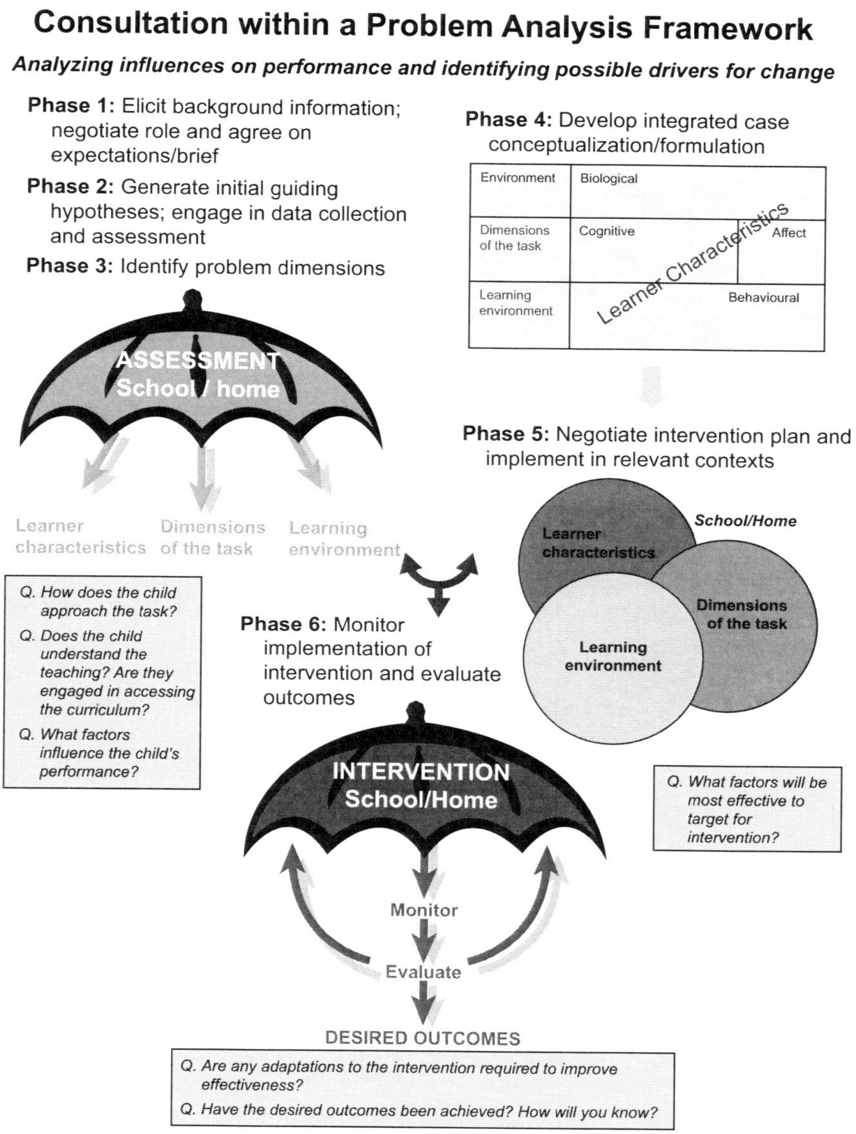

Consultation within a Problem Analysis Framework

Analyzing influences on performance and identifying possible drivers for change

Phase 1: Elicit background information; negotiate role and agree on expectations/brief

Phase 2: Generate initial guiding hypotheses; engage in data collection and assessment

Phase 3: Identify problem dimensions

Phase 4: Develop integrated case conceptualization/formulation

Environment	Biological	
Dimensions of the task	Cognitive	Affect
Learning environment	*Learner Characteristics*	Behavioural

ASSESSMENT
School / home

Learner characteristics | Dimensions of the task | Learning environment

Q. How does the child approach the task?

Q. Does the child understand the teaching? Are they engaged in accessing the curriculum?

Q. What factors influence the child's performance?

Phase 5: Negotiate intervention plan and implement in relevant contexts

Learner characteristics | School/Home | Dimensions of the task | Learning environment

Phase 6: Monitor implementation of intervention and evaluate outcomes

Q. What factors will be most effective to target for intervention?

INTERVENTION
School/Home

Monitor

Evaluate

DESIRED OUTCOMES

Q. Are any adaptations to the intervention required to improve effectiveness?

Q. Have the desired outcomes been achieved? How will you know?

Figure 17.2 The UCL Approach to Consultation within the Problem Analysis Framework

(see Figure 17.2 for a diagrammatic representation of the framework used). Consultation is construed as a core competence that is reinforced across different course elements and synthesized with learning to use a problem analysis framework, a meta-conceptual map to guide thinking and action. This approach shares common features with other problem-solving consultation models (e.g., Kratochwill, 2008).

The UCL framework highlights the complexity of the problem analysis process and the range of core professional competencies required for effective practice. Identification of competencies is a prerequisite to assessing trainee learning outcomes. Staff on the

Table 17.1 Examples of UCL Functional Competency Statements Relating to Consultation

Applies psychology in interviewing and consultation skills	Applies psychology in assessment and intervention skills	Oral communication skills	Service delivery and systems working
Provides evidence of preplanning and clear interview structure Negotiates and contracts role and establishes agreed objectives and expectations with consultees Uses accessible dialogue Closes interviews appropriately, summarizing information and explaining what will happen next Critically evaluates consultations with teachers and parents	Generates plausible initial guiding hypothesis informed by psychological theory and research Identifies problem dimensions that are justifiable conceptually Draws on assessment information to develop an integrated case conceptualization and intervention plans Negotiates implementable action plans with consultees Establishes agreed criteria for evaluation (quantitative/qualitative) and sets up monitoring arrangements Evaluates outcomes and communicates back to consultees	Communicates psychological knowledge and interpretations in an accessible manner, adapting information to the audience Succinctly presents the key points of psychological case conceptualization with key client groups and colleagues Takes into account the communication needs and views of others Demonstrates communication relevant to age, stage and developmental needs of children and young people	Critically evaluates school systems and structures within schools and settings Critically evaluates a range of facilities and special provision offered by placement local authority Critically evaluates a range of EP practice Demonstrates an understanding of the range of roles and responsibilities of staff working within partner services

UCL program defined competency statements through surveys and consultations with key stakeholders (university tutors, practicing educational psychologists, service managers and so on), deriving both foundational and functional competencies (Rodolfa et al., 2005). Foundational competencies underpin core functions of psychological practice and involve the application of scientific principles and awareness of ethical and diversity issues, including the capacity to understand in a multicultural context the impact of power, discrimination and oppression and the ability to work with these issues psychologically. Trainee psychologists have to be provided with opportunities to appreciate societal diversity and the contributions of different sociocultural groups as well as the development of skills in fostering inclusive practices. Functional competencies are evident in a psychologist's professional performance. Competencies relating to consultation within the UCL competency framework are shown in Table 17.1.

The Problem Analysis Process

The problem analysis process, which has been further developed and reviewed in the context of applied professional practice (e.g., Annan et al., 2013; Monsen & Frederickson, 2008; Monsen & Woolfson, 2012), represents the assessment-formulation-intervention-evaluation cycle within a six-phase process. Students are encouraged to gather consultee perspectives and to ask questions relating to alterable environmental/contextual factors that could be adapted to promote the client's learning and well-being. Difficulties or concerns are assumed to represent complex sets of conceptual and interpersonal interactions, the resolution of which draw heavily on consultative skills such as information processing, problem identification, analysis and hypothesis testing (Annan et al., 2013).

Trainees who learn to apply this model effectively develop—jointly with clients, their families and the practitioners working with them—comprehensive problem formulations that in turn lead to effective interventions and positive outcomes. The framework advocates an ecological approach and promotes reflection on the social, political, economic and cultural factors relevant across phases. Also highlighted in Figure 17.2 is the blend of key elements of learning across the curriculum, for example, application of the Interactive Factors Framework (IFF) in Phase 4. The IFF:

- Represents what is known about an individual's unique pattern of strengths and needs
- Provides a significant degree of conceptual space for the environmental factors that are possibly acting upon the problem situation, as well as potential interventions to address concerns
- Generates working hypotheses about what are complex and ill-defined problem situations
- Represents these hypotheses in a simple, visual fashion that emphasizes the interactive nature of person and environment (Frederickson & Cline, 2009).

Instructional Strategies

Key teaching strategies include role-play and opportunities for supported practice on placements. There is widespread use of video, a medium that captures verbal and non-verbal information facilitating student analysis of content. In contrast with research indicating that only 17% of trainers required audio-recording consultations and only 9% of those reviewed their recordings with a supervisor (Anton-Lahart & Rosenfield, 2004), a robust emphasis is placed on video-recording consultations and the provision of feedback (tutor and peer). Self-assessment using the competency framework is also encouraged (see Belar et al., 2001), as this has been shown to enhance learning and performance and support the maintenance of competence across a professional career.

This process assists trainees in identifying examples of their performance that they consider to have been particularly effective in eliciting important information, building rapport, communicating effectively, developing/extending the case formulation and so on. Bandura's (1997) social learning theory suggests it is crucial that positive elements of the consultation are identified in supervised video analysis, as this increases self-efficacy of learners. However, there are also opportunities to identify elements of the consultation that went less well as the basis for consideration of adapted or alternative ways to manage consultations in the future. Video feedback functions as a catalyst for critical self-reflection and provides a tool to stimulate supervisory discussions (Kimbrough, Davis, & Wickersham, 2008).

Evidence-Informed Practice and Action Planning

UCL places a significant weight on trainees being aware (and making use) of the evidence of "what works" in applied psychology. Alongside the increasing acknowledgment that educational psychologists need to be critical reviewers of up-to-date relevant research,

Box 17.1 UCL Consultation Action Planning Protocol

1. Develop an understanding of the context in which the intervention will be implemented (e.g., systems, structures, policies, politics, recording).
2. Find out about available resources (e.g., books, equipment, staffing [e.g., teaching assistant time], space).
3. Decide who to negotiate the intervention with (e.g., with an individual, with a group).
4. Aim to work with high status individuals—those who have a strong interest in success, those who have track records; those who exert a high degree of influence in the context, and so on.
5. Assess the consultees' beliefs, values and existing level of knowledge and understanding of potential solutions/interventions.
6. Establish common goals/objectives.
7. Negotiate an action plan: aim to elicit potential solutions/interventions from the consultee (to encourage ownership and increase likelihood of implementation), use solution-focused questioning, be prepared to make recommendations yourself, develop a collection of resources that can be shared/circulated, elicit consultees views and encourage active evaluation of suggestions.
8. Once an intervention has been agreed, guide the discussion toward the details of implementation (e.g., who, what, where, when procedures).
9. Ensure that the consultee considers the plan to be manageable.
10. Agree on implementation and monitoring process for feedback/learning conversations (e.g., internal [daily intermittent schedule carried out by high status personnel], external [e.g., ECP]).
11. Plan for trouble-shooting—what to do if there are difficulties with implementation, a lack of progress, resistance (active or passive), lack of commitment to agreed objectives.
12. Make arrangements for evaluation (how [e.g., goal attainment scaling], by whom, when), and feedback and future planning.

they also must transport the evidence and apply it in the unique cultural contexts of schools (Forman et al., 2013; Thigpen, Puddy, Singer, & Hall, 2012). Trainees are taught to not only think analytically about the available evidence underpinning practice but also to consider which practices lead to intervention implementation (Noell & Gansle, 2014). The nature and importance of consultation intervention planning should not be underestimated (Annan et al., 2013; Kelly, 2006). Protocols that support consultants-in-training with accounting for factors such as performance feedback, consultee self-efficacy and degree of fit with the child's ecosystem are of substantive benefit. When consulting on possible interventions, the training program model encourages active and collaborative action planning approaches with key stakeholders in the client's life, adopting the role of "transfer and change agents" (Dunsmuir & Kratochwill, 2013). The action planning protocol outlined in Box 17.1 has been developed for this purpose.

Assessment of Competence

The challenge of developing appropriate assessment measures has been recognized not only in consultation training but also in the competency-based movement more generally (Kaslow et al., 2009). A range of assessment methods is used at UCL to appraise consultation competence. Miller's (1990) framework, shown in Figure 17.1, provides the rationale for the range of assessments utilized. The essential underpinning of competence in consultation is a systematic appreciation of the theoretical and evidence base of the approach; in the Miller framework, this is the "knows" level (referring to the recall of facts, principles, theories, etc.). Knowledge is assessed in part through written examinations that employ problem-solving questions to assess factual knowledge applied to case scenarios. The structure of these examinations incorporates elements of the second part of Miller's framework, the "knows how" level, where trainees must provide coherent and defensible responses to common problems encountered in day-to-day practice. Also included at the knows how level are written case reports, enabling trainees to demonstrate integration of psychological theory, research and practice and critical reflection on consultation competence following the problem analysis framework.

The third level of the Miller (1990) model, "show how," has been developed further through the use of simulations or demonstrations of skills in controlled settings. Trainees simulate and video record consultation practice. This is used for self-assessment, peer review and university tutor formative assessment. The final level in Miller's (1990) framework is "does", originally referring to what "the graduate *does* when functioning independently in a clinical practice" (p. S63). At UCL, these include observation of and feedback to the trainee consulting in live situations on real problem situations by university tutors and fieldwork supervisors, who also complete competency evaluation ratings. Trainees themselves undertake critical analysis of consultations through reflective reviews of consultation transcripts. These are presented in placement portfolios for assessment by external examiners.

This multiplicity of formative and summative assessment approaches is congruent with reports provided by other training providers (Kaslow et al., 2009). In common with UCL's approach, where assumptions are not made about professional competence based solely on client outcomes, Alpert and Taufique (2002) argue against trainees solely being evaluated in this way. For a range of different reasons (e.g., the variation in contexts and degree of "difficulty" presented by them, the complexity of the presenting problem situation and so on), assessment based on client outcomes may be considered to lack reliability and validity (Kennedy et al., 2009). However, trainees include an element of child- and family-level outcomes analysis in evaluations of their work. To ensure greater fairness and equity in judging competence, it is essential to provide a prescriptive set of fieldwork tasks to trainees, fieldwork supervisors and university tutors and ensure repeated opportunities for liaison between the university, placement and student. It is also necessary to ensure that supervisor feedback and trainee self-reflection are included alongside outcomes data; the portfolio-based approach plays an important role in this regard.

MOVING FROM COMPETENCE TO CAPABILITY: CONTINUING EDUCATION FOR THE PROFESSIONAL

Fraser and Greenhalgh (2001) argue that "in today's complex world we must educate not merely for competence but for capability (the ability to adapt, to change, generate new knowledge, and continue to improve performance)" (p. 799). This is a longer-term goal of training—the generalization and adaptation of learning—supporting self-directed learners who critique their own practice and engage in lifelong professional and personal development activities. Published work on consultation training in the postqualification period is limited (Newell & Newman, 2014), but studies have highlighted the significance of the practice context of the qualified psychologist in the earthen trench of practice (Newell, 2010).

In the UK, postqualification training is of interest to both practitioners and employers, especially in relation to the continuing professional development (CPD) required to ensure consultation capability. For the purposes of this chapter, the HCPC definition of CPD is used: "a range of learning activities through which . . . professionals maintain and develop throughout their career to ensure that they retain their capacity to practise safely, effectively and legally within their evolving scope of practice" (2014, p. 6). Of course, it is one thing to learn how to consult within the relatively secure and supportive boundaries of the initial training program; it is more of a challenge to transfer knowledge and skills flexibly and adapt these effectively in the workplace. This section explores this issue further, including the constraints on CPD as well as the key roles of supervision, coaching and feedback in ensuring capability after initial training.

Consultation Practice in the Current UK Context

This chapter is being written at a time of significant national and local change for ECPs, where economic recession and government education ideology have had important practical implications for the day-to-day work of practitioners. Their ability to effectively apply their consultation competence is affected by increasingly constrained budgets and a political narrative espousing schools as the commissioners or purchasers of psychological services that they feel they most need, rather than to accept those provided by public services. Such constraints are not confined to the UK. Gravois (2012) in the U.S. has commented that "any service that cannot be effectively articulated, capably trained, or sufficiently researched is subject to the axe" (p. 85). Furthermore, much as training courses may advocate a wider vision of practice, it appears that some ECPs continue to perform roles within schools that, as in the U.S., are "more focused on securing services for struggling students rather than primarily being consultants to teachers . . . to be . . . blunt, very few professionals get hired to be consultants in schools" (Gravois, 2012, p. 83). Finally, it may be difficult for employers to consistently and coherently identify individual (and subsequently team) consultation CPD needs, since this process is often more dependent on the self-assessment of the practitioner and possible feedback from service users (if available) than would be the case for a trainee.

Outcome Measurement in Competent Consultation

Consultants operating at an advanced level of proficiency include arrangements for monitoring and reviewing progress, as well as evaluation methods, in the intervention planning stage of their consultation. Outcome-based evaluation aims to fulfill multiple purposes and assists the experienced consultant, the consultee, the client and any relevant others to know if the intervention was effective and to consider whether a different approach is needed. Outcomes can be evaluated through the use of goal or target-based measures, for example, goal attainment scaling (Rosenfield, Gravois, & Silva, 2014), or variants such as the Target Monitoring and Evaluation system (TME) (Dunsmuir, Brown, Iyadurai, & Monsen, 2009) and the Student Documentation Form (Rosenfield, 2014; Rosenfield et al., 2014). These are highlighted because of the documented relationship between the graphing and maintenance of visual data representation and enhanced intervention implementation.

Competent consultants also actively draw the consultee into the definition of targets for the intervention and the evaluation of effectiveness. Standardized measures may be used to ascertain the difference in scores obtained when preintervention measures are obtained with data collected postintervention. Qualitative data may be gained by seeking a range of perspectives (including child, parent and teacher) using semistructured interview formats. Ideally, a combination of approaches is drawn upon to ensure the reliability and validity of information gathered. Management of the practitioner has a role to play in ensuring monitoring and evaluation processes are embedded in day-to-day work as well as making the links between this work and the CPD experiences that would be of most benefit to them.

COACHING AND SUPERVISION: THE IMPORTANCE OF FEEDBACK AND REFLECTION

The work of Joyce and Showers is often mentioned in relation to the implementation of CPD activities (e.g. Joyce & Showers, 2002; Showers & Joyce, 1996). They found that while there were limitations to how much learning transfer took place following conventional staff development activities (with as few as 10% of participants implementing what they had learned), coaching and supervision had a significant positive impact on the application of skills in the workplace. In the context of consultation training postqualification, conventional training opportunities for practitioners wishing to develop their consultation skills are patchy—where there may be a range of accredited, postqualification short and long courses in various assessments/interventions, once initial training is completed, in-service consultation training in the UK is relatively limited.

The Joyce and Showers typology of training methods and consequent impact on practice is significant for in-service training planning, especially if coaching and supervision of practice are likely to lead to the flexible application and adaptation of skills. For example, coaching is a key element of the in-service consultation training model outlined by Gravois, Knotek, and Babinski (2002), where both online and onsite face-to-face approaches were utilized. Strategies included the consultants themselves being coached with structured observation and reviews of audiotaped consultations by an experienced coach with feedback provided to the consultant. While in need of further investigation to determine the impact on the development of consultation skills, Gravois and colleagues have outlined an exciting and innovative pathway for experienced practitioners to develop consultation capability.

Coaching

In the context of developing consultation capability, coaching refers to an active, relationship-based and developmental strategy enabling a coachee to fulfill goals relating to enhanced performance and growth (see Figure 17.3 for one such model). Because

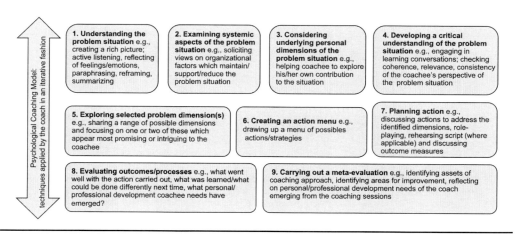

Figure 17.3 A Coaching Model for Consulting Psychologists in Applied Practice

Source: Adapted from Cameron and Monsen (1998)

coaching and supervision are both characterized by relationships between individuals, it is important to make a clear distinction between the two. Coaching is a strategy that may be employed by a multitude of individuals with an emphasis on the coachee's acquisition of new knowledge and skills—an educative or developmental aspect. Supervisors, however, must always remain vigilant regarding the professional regulation and ethical standards of their supervisees as well as employ other behaviors that account for the broader remit of supervision—the reflective and personal aspects.

Coaching can facilitate goal achievement through adequate exploration of the constraints underpinning work-based problem situations and on the identification and implementation of defined behaviors to address these. Effective coaching models review the implementation of these proposed solutions and support reflection on what worked and what has been learned (Cameron & Monsen, 1998). While the evidence base is emerging rather than established (Neufeld & Donaldson, 2012), coaching has been shown to have positive impact across a range of factors such as communication, team working, facilitating change in others, meta-cognition, goal attainment and enhanced insight (Grant, 2003; Ravitz et al., 2013; Sue-Chan & Latham, 2004; Timmerman, 2013).

Further research is required to determine which models of coaching applied in what ways have the greatest impact in developing consultation capability. Central to the Cameron and Monsen model of coaching is the use of critical or accessible dialogue, which is considered essential in developing consultation capability (Cameron & Monsen, 1998; Frederickson & Monsen, 2002). Here the coach infers, advocates and enquires throughout their provision of feedback to the coachee. Built on the work of Chris Argyris, Donald Schön and Viviane Robinson, accessible dialogue enhances the accuracy, relevance and usefulness of the information shared between both parties (Monsen & Frederickson, 2002) (see Figure 17.4 for an example).

Such dialogue moves beyond open and honest communication because it is explicitly rooted in defined governing variables and accounts for complex inferential cognitive processes. Employing accessible dialogue while coaching provides multiple opportunities

Say what you think (advocate) *versus hide what you think*	**e.g. I would like to discuss with you the middle phase of that consultation as I think you missed an opportunity to pick up on some resistance to the problem analysis**
Say why you think it (infer) *versus believe in the absolute correctness of your views, no reason(s) or example(s) given, overconfidence in the worth of your views*	**e.g. The teacher stopped making eye contact with you, put her pen down, shuffled papers and interrupted you several times. You didn't stop and ask her whether there was an issue or what she thought about your formulation. You gave her more examples of evidence that supported your position and then said "Okay, so let's think about what to do next."**
Check out your understanding (inquiry) *versus hide your views from public testing, expectation that others know what you think*	**e.g. Do you remember it this way? Do you think you missed this opportunity to talk about what the teacher was thinking or feeling at that time?**

Figure 17.4 Example of Accessible Dialogue

for learning conversations to take place. In such conversations, the coach uses relevant data about the consultant's practice and adopts an "inquiry habit of mind" in the context of a respectful and challenging coaching relationship (Earl & Timperley, 2009). This supports the avoidance of activity traps where coach and coachee move too quickly to "doing," feeling busy and industrious without actions being sufficiently grounded in pertinent evidence (Katz, Earl, & Ben Jaafar, 2006).

Supervision in Professional Practice

While supervision is a term commonly used across a range of different fields, it may be erroneously used by different people in different contexts to describe different but related activities (e.g., personal development, active case management). It is essential that practicing psychological consultants, their supervisors and managers understand these differences. Usefully, the BPS DECP (2010) has provided educational and child psychologists with supervision guidelines. These guidelines recognize that line management coexists but is clearly distinct from professional supervision (the personal and professional development of the individual). In models of service delivery where the line management function has been separated from the professional supervisory one, it is critically important that an effective three-way communication system is in place, especially in relation to ongoing professional development needs (e.g., in some "matrix" models, the budget for professional development sits with the line manager not the professional supervisor). Feedback on the effective provision of consultation, especially where there are concerns about practice, have to be appropriately shared between the manager, supervisor and supervisee through agreed on and appropriate processes.

Fuggle, Dunsmuir and Curry (2013) highlight the distinction between the supervisory relationship and other interactions like coaching. Long considered a considered a critical reflective space for practicing psychologists, supervision involves a triadic relationship between the supervisee, supervisor and the client. Within this relationship, the "supervisee offer[s] an honest and open account of their work and . . . the supervisor offers feedback and guidance which has the primary aim of facilitating the development of the supervisee's . . . competencies, but also ensures they practice in a manner which conforms to current ethical and professional standards" (Roth & Pilling, 2007, p. 4). In this definition, supervision is explicitly linked to competency, and indeed Stoltenberg (2005) has argued that the process of supervision may be the most important mechanism in the acquisition of competence.

Feedback in Coaching and Supervision

Archer (2010), writing about the education of health professionals, argued strongly for the central role of feedback, where "information about previous performance is used to promote positive and desirable [cognitive, technical and professional] development" (p. 102). For consulting ECPs and those who employ them, maximizing the opportunities for the provision of effective feedback is crucial in the development of capability. Whether coaching, supervision or a mixture is employed, it is the feedback provided to the practitioner, as well as the quality of relationship between individuals, that is most critical (e.g., Gravois et al., 2002; Heckman-Stone, 2004; O'Donovan, Halford, & Walters, 2011; Rosenfield, 2002). Indeed, it is difficult to discuss one (feedback) without the other (the relationship within which the feedback occurs), as they are interactive and interdependent. For example, some supervisors "attempt to protect the supervisory relationship and the supervisee's self-esteem to such an extent that negative feedback was too indirect to be comprehended by supervisees" (Heckman-Stone, 2004, p. 25).

This inhibits the provision of feedback from being a genuine opportunity for learning because it fails to "respect the capacity of all involved to learn and improve" (Earl & Timperley, 2009, p. 10). Muse and McManus (2013) have identified other related issues within supervision, especially any kind of evaluative work the supervisor attempts to complete, where factors such as the likeability of the practitioner and their performance in other areas may influence the supervisor. Feedback must be linked to professional behaviors that are within the control of the receiving practitioner, be amenable to change and be offered in a sequence designed to enhance realistic self-evaluation (Farnill, Gordon, & Sansom, 1997). Schein (1999) offers a number of feedback principles which may be usefully employed in this context.

All of this raises questions for service managers and employers. For example, do supervisors/work-based coaches supporting ECP consultants have the requisite skills in providing feedback? How do employers judge these skills? Are there related CPD needs for the supervisor/coach in providing feedback and in building effective relationships? Do current models of coaching and supervision ensure that feedback, especially constructively critical feedback, is provided in a clear and accessible way? How do supervisors appropriately provide feedback on consultant performance (which is more often based on secondhand reports of treatment rather than direct observation), especially when practitioners may fail to disclose essential information from their interaction with clients and consultees (e.g., Ladany, Hill, Corbett, & Nutt, 1996)? Are those receiving feedback provided with preparatory time to consider and agree how they will interpret and apply what has been shared?

The Importance of Critical Reflection

Schön (1983) highlighted that the capacity to reflect on action was a hallmark of capable professional practice. He was particularly concerned with the messy and ill-defined real-life situations faced by applied practitioners; while knowledge (content) deficiencies may be more easily rectified in such situations, competence (process) deficiencies are more subtle and complex. Sometimes these deficits stem from an overreliance on experience in which "experts" may be more likely to seek substantiation of their current knowledge rather than actively consider other possibilities. Lichtenberg (1997) has written on the issues presented by experienced practitioners holding inaccurate or biased views of clients and engaging in faulty reasoning regarding their concerns. For example, he argued that confirmatory bias has been identified in a number of studies of clinical judgments where practitioners tended to "seek out information about clients in a manner that is consistent with and supportive of the counselor's prior beliefs or assumptions about the client" (Lichtenberg, 1997, p. 227). Similarly, Senge et al. (1994) highlighted how dysfunctional beliefs can hinder or stifle both organizational and individual development (see Table 17.2).

Reflective practitioners explore their practices with a view to understanding process as well as outcome. They not only ask themselves what happened but also why, how and now what? They consider personal as well as professional dimensions of their practice, and they recognize that reflection leads to enhanced self-efficacy. Some of the superordinate skills in the reflective process include valuing the irritating, discomforting or mismatching factor; spotting subtle opportunities for change; noting emerging sequences

Table 17.2 Potential Dysfunctional Beliefs Affecting Development

Common beliefs	Possible constraining behaviors that can result from these beliefs
I am my position.	My colleagues should respect my judgment.
The enemy is "out there."	Within-team problems can be ignored at the present.
The illusion of taking charge	I can sort out this big issue on my own.
The fixation on events	The restructuring of our team will sweep away some of the historical difficulties that we have faced.
Insensitivity to gradual decay	My previous history as a successful practitioner should not be challenged.
The delusion of learning from experience	My 20 years as a practitioner enable me to tackle most problems.
The myth of the management team	The management team can sort out this big issue while I get on with my everyday work.

Source: Adapted from Senge (1994)

Box 17.2 Reflective Questions to Consider after a Particularly Satisfying/Unsatisfying Consultation Encounter

> What made me feel so satisfied/dissatisfied with the outcome?
> Were others as satisfied/dissatisfied as I was?
> What made it turn out so well? What made it turn out so badly?
> When did it start to go well? When did it start to go wrong?
> What particular strengths did I employ? What particular weaknesses can I identify?
> What psychological theory and research did I draw upon?
> What psychological theory and research could I have drawn upon?
> What general themes emerge from this reflection activity?
> What (if anything) would I do differently next time?

and themes; and understanding the importance of the statement "we see things not as they are but as we are" (see Box 17.2 for some questions that are likely to encourage the reflection process). Above all, embracing a reflective stance involves becoming comfortable with complexity, tension and uncertainty.

CONCLUDING COMMENTS

More than a decade ago, Fraser and Greenhalgh (2001) argued that in addition to competence in professional practice, another dynamic for continuing professional development had emerged—*capability*—the characteristic which enables a practitioner to adapt effectively to constant change. Trainees need to begin their professional careers having developed core *knowledge* and professional *competence* in order to become capable practitioners. While some professional associations internationally have broadly defined competencies in consultation, this has only occurred in the UK context in 2015. Now that training providers have a coherent set of cognitive, affective, behavioral and social competencies associated with effective performance provided by the national professional body, we are now in a better position to further pursue research agendas as outlined by Newell and Newman (2014), such as developmental approaches to consultation training. Furthermore, creative, innovative opportunities to engage in in-service learning partnerships between those based in universities and those working in applied contexts could enhance the capability of those working in a broad range of educational settings.

Practicing ECPs could research their own consultation practices both to improve their performance and to broaden the existing knowledge base through enquiry grounded "in the perspectives of practitioners who use consultation" (Meyers, 2002, p. 44), not the academic community alone. With the capacity to extend application of psychology—in identification, assessment, intervention planning and evaluation of the problems experienced by children, young people, their families and staff working with them—consultation can provide the mechanism to stimulate positive change through the symbiotic relationship between the ivory tower and earthen trench.

NOTE

1. The HCPC is the regulatory body for a number of professions (including practitioner psychologists) that was set up to protect the public. The council maintains a register of practitioners who meet prescribed training, professional skills, behavior and health standards.

REFERENCES

Alpert, J. L., & Taufique, S. R. (2002). Consultation training: 26 years and 3 questions. *Journal of Educational and Psychological Consultation, 13*(1–2), 13–33.

Annan, M., Chua, J., Cole, R., Kennedy, E. K., James, R., Markúsdóttir, I., . . . Shah, S. (2013). Further iterations on using the problem analysis framework. *Educational Psychology in Practice, 29*(1), 79–95.

Anton-LaHart, J., & Rosenfield, S. (2004). A survey of preservice consultation training in school psychology programs. *Journal of Educational and Psychological Consultation, 15*, 41–62.

Archer, J. C. (2010). State of the science in health professional education: Effective feedback. *Medical Education, 44*, 101–108.

Bandura, A. (1997). *Self-efficacy: The exercise of control.* New York: Freeman.

Belar, C. D., Brown, R. A., Hersch, L. E., Hornyak, L. M., Rozensky, R. H., Sheridan, E. P., . . . Reed, G. W. (2001). Self-assessment in clinical health psychology: A model for ethical expansion of practice. *Professional Psychology: Research and Practice, 32*, 135–141.

BPS. (2006). *Division of educational and child psychology quality standards for educational psychology services.* Leicester: BPS.

BPS. (2010). *Division of educational and child psychology professional supervision: Guidelines for practice for educational psychologists.* Leicester: BPS.

British Psychological Society [BPS] Division of Educational and Child Psychology Training Committee (2015). *Standards for the accreditation of educational psychology training in England, Northern Ireland & Wales.* Leicester: BPS.

Cameron, R. J. (2006). Educational psychology: The distinctive contribution. *Educational Psychology in Practice, 22*, 289–304.

Cameron, R. J., & Monsen, J. J. (1998). Coaching and critical dialogue in educational psychology practice. *Educational and Child Psychology, 15*, 112–126.

Dennis, R. (2004). So far so good? A qualitative case study exploring the implementation of consultation in schools. *Educational Psychology in Practice, 20*, 17–29.

Dunsmuir, S., Brown, E., Iyadurai, S., & Monsen, J. (2009). Evidence-based practice and evaluation: From insight to impact. *Educational Psychology in Practice, 25*, 53–70.

Dunsmuir, S., & Kratochwill, T. (2013). From research to policy and practice: Psychologists as agents of change. *Educational and Child Psychology, 30*, 60–71.

Earl, L. M., & Timperley, H. (2009). Understanding how evidence and learning conversations work. In L. M. Earl & H. Timperley (Eds.), *Professional learning conversations: Challenges to using evidence for improvement* (pp. 1–12). London: Springer.

Epstein, R. M., & Hundert, E. M. (2002). Defining and assessing professional competence. *Journal of the American Medical Association, 287*, 226–235.

Erchul, W. P., & Sheridan, S. M. (2014). The state of scientific research in school consultation. In W. P. Erchul & S. M. Sheridan (Eds.), *Handbook of research in school consultation* (2nd ed., pp. 3–17). New York: Routledge.

Evans, S. P., Grahamslaw, L., Henson, L., & Prince, E. (2012). Is restructured initial professional training in educational psychology fit for purpose? *Educational Psychology in Practice, 28*, 373–393.

Farnill, D., Gordon, J., & Sansom, D. (1997). The role of effective feedback in clinical supervision. *Australian Journal of Clinical & Experimental Hypnosis, 25*, 155–161.

Flaspohler, P. D., Meehan, C., Maras, M. A., & Keller, K. E. (2012). Ready, willing, and able: Developing a support system to promote implementation of school-based prevention programs. *American Journal of Community Psychology, 50*, 428–444.

Forman, S. G., Shapiro, E. S., Codding, R. S., Gonzales, J. E., Reddy, L. A., Rosenfield, S. A., . . . Stoiber, K. C. (2013). Implementation science and school psychology. *School Psychology Quarterly, 28*, 77–100.

Fouad, N. A., Grus, C. L., Hatcher, R. L., Kaslow, N. J., Hutchings, P. S., Madson, M. B., . . . & Crossman, R. E. (2009). Competency benchmarks: A model for understanding and measuring competence in professional psychology across three levels. *Training and Education in Professional Psychology, 3*(4, Suppl.), S5–S26.

Fraser, S., & Greenhalgh, T. (2001). Coping with complexity: Educating for capability. *British Medical Journal, 323*, 799–803.

Frederickson, N., & Cline, T. (2009). *Special educational needs: Inclusion and diversity* (2nd ed.). Berkshire: Open University Press.

Frederickson, N., & Monsen, J. J. (2002). Consultant problem understanding as a function of training in interviewing to promote accessible reasoning. *Journal of School Psychology, 40*, 197–212.

Fuggle, P., Dunsmuir, S., & Curry, V. (2013). *Cognitive behaviour therapy with children, young people and families*. London: Sage Publications.

Gillies, E. (2000). Developing consultation partnerships. *Educational Psychology in Practice, 16*, 31–37.

Grant, A. M. (2003). The impact of life coaching on goal attainment, metacognition and mental health. *Social Behaviour and Personality, 31*, 253–263.

Gravois, T. A. (2012). Consultation services in schools: A can of worms worth opening. *Consulting Psychology Journal: Practice and Research, 64*, 83–87.

Gravois, T. A., Knotek, S., & Babinski, L. M. (2002). Educating practitioners as consultants: Development and implementation of the instructional consultation team consortium. *Journal of Educational and Psychological Consultation, 13*, 113–132.

Gutkin, T. B., & Curtis, M. J. (2009). School-based consultation: The science and practice of indirect service delivery. In T. B. Gutkin & C. R. Reynolds (Eds.), *The handbook of school psychology* (4th ed., pp. 591–635). New York: Wiley.

Hazel, C. E., Laviolette, G. T., & Lineman, J. M. (2010). Training professional psychologists in school-based consultation: What the syllabi suggest. *Training and Education in Professional Psychology, 4*, 235–243.

Health and Care Professions Council (HCPC). (2014). *Continuing professional development and your registration*. London: HCPC.

Heckman-Stone, C. (2004). Trainee preferences for feedback and evaluation in clinical supervision. *The Clinical Supervisor, 22*, 21–33.

Henning-Stout, M. (1999). Learning consultation: An ethnographic analysis. *Journal of School Psychology, 37*, 73–98.

Jensen, P. S., Hoagwood, K., & Trickett, E. J. (1999). Ivory towers or earthen trenches? Community collaborations to foster real-world research. *Applied Developmental Science, 3*, 206–212.

Joyce, B., & Showers, B. (2002). *Student achievement through staff development* (3rd ed.). Alexandria, VA: Association of Supervision and Curriculum Development.

Kaslow, N. J., Grus, C. L., Campbell, L. F., Fouad, N. A., Hatcher, R. L., & Rodolfa, E. R. (2009). Competency assessment toolkit for professional psychology. *Training and Education in Professional Psychology, 3*(4, Suppl.), S27–S45.

Katz, S., Earl, L. A., & Ben Jaafar, S. (2006). *Networking schools for learning*. Thousand Oaks, CA: Corwin Press.

Kelly, B. (2006). Exploring the usefulness of the Monsen problem-solving framework for applied practitioners. *Educational Psychology in Practice, 22*, 1–17.

Kennedy, E. K., Cameron, R. J., & Monsen, J. J. (2009). Effective consultation in educational and child psychology practice: Professional training for both competence and capability. *School Psychology International, 30*, 603–625.

Kennedy, E. K., Frederickson, N., & Monsen, J. J. (2008). Do educational psychologists "walk the talk" when consulting? *Educational Psychology in Practice, 24*, 169–187.

Kimbrough, S., Davis, J., & Wickersham, L. (2008). The use of video feedback and semi-structured interviews for reflection among pre-service teachers. *Journal of Education and Human Development, 2*(2), 1–12.

Klose, M. L., Plotts, C., & Lasser, J. (2012). Participants' evaluation of consultation: Implications for training in school psychology. *Assessment & Evaluation in Higher Education, 37*, 817–828.

Kratochwill, T. R. (2008). Best practices in school-based problem-solving consultation: Application in prevention and intervention systems. In A. Thomas & J. Grimes (Eds.), *Best practices in school psychology V* (pp. 1673–1688). Bethesda, MD: National Association of School Psychologists.

Ladany, N., Hill, C. E., Corbett, M. M., & Nutt, E. A. (1996). Nature, extent, and importance of what psychotherapy trainees do not disclose to their supervisors. *Journal of Counselling Psychology, 43*, 10–24.

Lichtenberg, J. W. (1997). Expertise in counselling psychology: A concept in search of support. *Educational Psychology Review, 9*, 221–238.

Lowman, R. L. (2012). Frontier no more: International consulting skills as necessary minimal competencies for consulting psychologists. *Consulting Psychology Journal: Practice and Research, 6*, 338–343.

MacHardy, L., Carmichael, H., & Proctor, J. (1995). *School consultation: It don't mean a thing if it ain't got that swing.* Aberdeen: Aberdeen City Council.

Meyers, J. (2002). A 30 year perspective on best practices for consultation training. *Journal of Educational and Psychological Consultation, 13*, 35–54.

Miller, G. E. (1990). The assessment of clinical skills/competence/performance. *Academic Medicine, 65*(Suppl.), S63–S67.

Monsen, J. J., & Frederickson, N. (2002). Consultant problem understanding as a function of training in interviewing to promote accessible reasoning. *Journal of School Psychology, 40*, 197–212.

Monsen, J. J., & Frederickson, N. (2008). The Monsen et al. framework problem solving model ten years on. In B. Kelly, L. Woolfson, & J. Boyle (Eds.), *Frameworks for practice in educational psychology: A textbook for trainees and practitioners* (pp. 69–93). London: Jessica Kingsley.

Monsen, J. J., & Woolfson, L. (2012). The role of executive problem solving frameworks in preparing for effective change in educational contexts. In B. Kelly & D. Perkins (Eds.), *The Cambridge handbook of implementation science for educational psychology* (pp. 132–149). Cambridge: Cambridge University Press.

Munro, E. (2000). Angles on developing consultation: First steps to making consultation our own. *Educational Psychology in Practice, 16*, 53–58.

Muse, K., & McManus, E. (2013). A systematic review of methods for assessing competence in cognitive-behavioural therapy. *Clinical Psychology Review, 33*, 484–499.

Neufeld, B., & Donaldson, M. (2012). Coaching for instructional improvement: Conditions and strategies that matter. In B. Kelly & D. F. Perkins (Eds.), *Handbook of implementation science for psychology in education* (pp. 373–391). Cambridge: Cambridge University Press.

Newell, M. L. (2010). Exploring the use of computer simulation to evaluate the implementation of problem-solving consultation. *Journal of Educational and Psychological Consultation, 20*, 228–255.

Newell, M. L. (2012). Transforming knowledge to skill: Evaluating the consultation competence of novice school-based consultants. *Consulting Psychology Journal: Practice and Research, 64*, 8–28.

Newell, M. L., & Newman, D. (2014). Assessing the state of evidence in consultation training: A review and call to the field. In W. P. Erchul & S. M. Sheridan (Eds.), *Handbook of research in school consultation: Empirical foundations for the field* (2nd ed., pp. 421–449). New York: Taylor & Francis/Routledge.

Noell, G. H., & Gansle, K. A. (2014). Research examining the relationships between consultation procedures, treatment integrity and outcomes. In W. P. Erchul & S. M. Sheridan (Eds.), *Handbook of research in school consultation* (2nd ed., pp. 386–408). New York: Routledge.

O'Donovan, A., Halford, W. K., & Walters, B. (2011). Toward best practice supervision of clinical psychology trainees. *Australian Psychologist, 46*, 101–112.

Ravitz, P., Lancee, W. J., Lawson, A., Maunder, R., Hunter, J. J., Leszcz, M., . . . & Pain, C. (2013). Improving physician–patient communication through coaching of simulated encounters. *Academic Psychiatry, 37*, 87–93.

Resnick, L. B., & Resnick, D. P. (1992). Assessing the thinking curriculum: New tools for educational reform. In B. Gifford & M. O'Connor (Eds.), *Changing assessments: Alternative views of aptitude, achievement and instruction* (pp. 37–75). London: Kluwer Academic Publishers.

Rodolfa, E. R., Bent, R. J., Eisman, E., Nelson, P. D., Rehm, L., & Ritchie, P. (2005). A cube model for competency development: Implications for psychology educators and regulators. *Professional Psychology: Research and Practice, 36*, 347–354.

Rosenfield, S. (2002). Developing instructional consultants: From novice to competent to expert. *Journal of Educational and Psychological Consultation, 13*, 97–111.

Rosenfield, S. (2014). Best practices in instructional consultation and instructional consultation teams. In A. Thomas & P. Harrison (Eds.), *Best practices in school psychology: VI* (pp. 1645–1660). Bethesda, MA: National Association of School Psychologists.

Rosenfield, S., Gravois, T., & Silva, A. E. (2014). Bringing instructional consultation to scale: Research and development of instructional consultation and instructional consultation teams. In W. P. Erchul & S. M. Sheridan

(Eds.), *Handbook of research in school consultation: Empirical foundations for the field* (2nd ed., pp. 248–275). New York: Taylor & Francis/Routledge.

Rosenfield, S., Levinsohn-Klyap, M., & Cramer, K. (2010). Educating consultants for practice in the schools. In E. Vasquez, T. D. Crespi, & C. Riccio (Eds.), *Handbook of education, training and supervision of school psychologists in school and community* (pp. 259–278). New York: Routledge.

Roth, A. D., & Pilling, S. (2007). *The competences required to deliver effective cognitive and behavioural therapy for people with depression and with anxiety disorders.* London: Department of Health.

Schein, E. (1999). *Process consultation revisited.* Reading, MA: Addison-Wesley.

Schön, D. (1983). *The reflective practitioner: How professionals think in action.* London: Temple Smith.

Senge, P. M. (1994). *The fifth discipline: The art and practice of the learning organization.* New York: Doubleday.

Showers, B., & Joyce, B. (1996). The evolution of peer coaching. *Educational Leadership, 53,* 12–16.

Stoltenberg, C. (2005). Enhancing professional competence through developmental approaches to supervision. *American Psychologist, 60,* 857–864.

Sue-Chan, C., & Latham, G. P. (2004). The relative effectiveness of external, peer, and self-coaches. *Applied Psychology, 52,* 260–278.

Thigpen, S., Puddy, R. W., Singer, H. H., & Hall, D. M. (2012). Moving knowledge into action: Developing the rapid synthesis and translation process within the interactive systems framework. *American Journal of Community Psychology, 50,* 285–294.

Timmerman, G. M. (2013). Developing clinical nurse specialist students' coaching skills for facilitating lifestyle change. *Clinical Nurse Specialist, 27,* E19.

Wagner, P. (1995). *School consultation: Frameworks for the practising educational psychologist.* London: Kensington and Chelsea Psychology Service.

Wagner, P. (2000). Consultation: Developing a comprehensive approach to service delivery. *Educational Psychology in Practice, 16,* 9–18.

Wagner, P. (2008). Consultation as a framework for practice. In B. Kelly, L. Woolfson, & J. Boyle (Eds.), *Frameworks for practice in educational psychology* (pp. 139–161). London: Jessica Kingsley.

Watkins, C., & Hill, V. (2000). On consultation and beginner educational psychologists. *Educational Psychology in Practice, 16,* 47–52.

Woodruffe, C. (1993). What is meant by a competency? *Leadership & Organization Development Journal, 14,* 29–36.

18

COMPLICATING THE THINKING OF TRAINEE CONSULTANTS IN CONSULTEE-CENTERED CONSULTATION

Frank C. Worrell, Jessica Ernandes Naecker, Christine E. Gerchow, Chloe Green, Claire E. Kunesh, and Anna Casey

There are several major models of consultation in the literature, including behavioral consultation (Kratochwill & Bergan, 1990; Sheridan, 1997), mental health consultation (Caplan & Caplan, 1999), instructional consultation (Rosenfield, 1987; Rosenfield & Gravois, 1996), and organizational development (Anderson, 2011). Although the school psychology program at University of California (UC), Berkeley, introduces its students to all of the models, the students are trained primarily in consultee-centered consultation (CCC; Lambert, Hylander, & Sandoval, 2004; Sandoval, 2014), one type of mental health consultation. In this chapter, we describe the rationale for this model, the way the model complements the theoretical focus of the program, and the utility of the model for training consultants across national and cultural contexts. Johannessen (2004) described consultation as complicating the thinking of the consultee, and we see our goal as complicating the thinking of the consultant in training.

THE UC BERKELEY TRAINING MODEL

UC Berkeley is located in the San Francisco Bay Area, and our students are exposed to a wide range of urban and suburban districts and a diverse set of students and school contexts. These extremes can result in students working with highly qualified teachers in well-resourced schools as well as less effective teachers in schools with very few resources. One can argue that teachers in these settings should be treated differently. We would argue that any differences in treatment should not be predicated on a restriction of autonomy for some and an enhancement of free will for others (Kelman, 1965; Sandman & Munthe, 2010); rather, much as we do with students, the program deems it important to meet teachers where they are and "promote the enhancement of freedom of choice" for the consultee (Kelman, 1965, p. 46).

Additionally, the theoretical foundation of the program is developmental and constructivist in orientation, and the program stresses the importance of prevention and early intervention. Thus, students are encouraged to be *school* psychologists and not just *special education* psychologists and to engage with teachers about students whose problems have not yet become serious enough to warrant a psychoeducational evaluation, with an ideal being that an evaluation will never be necessary. CCC stresses a nonhierarchical relationship (Sandoval, 2014) with both parties bringing expertise to the table. Importantly, CCC is well suited for consultants and consultees who differ in nationality, cultural backgrounds, and attitudes (Hatzichristou, 2004; Hylander & Guvå, 2004; Ingraham, 2000, 2004; Lambert, 2004).

The students begin learning to consult in the first semester of their second year while taking a seminar in consultation and after exposure to curriculum-based measurement and developmental theories focused on childhood and adolescence in year 1. Although the consultation seminar is only one semester long, the students have a two-semester consultation practicum in which they practice consultation with two different teachers. At the same time that they begin to engage in supervised consultation experiences, they are also being trained in assessment and prevention. This parallel process is deliberate, as we want the students to bring their knowledge of theoretical perspectives into the consultation relationship with the consultee and not their expertise in assessment or intervention processes. More specifically, we do not want specific techniques in which they will clearly be experts relative to teachers to become a barrier or a crutch while *learning to consult*. In this way, consultation is learned as a *process* and *intervention* in its own right.

The program recognizes that students will need more expertise than they currently have as they begin the process. Thus, in addition to participating in the consultation seminar, students receive on a weekly basis two sets of supports on campus. First, they receive *supervision* from program faculty who review their consultation logs and make suggestions for ways to proceed or suggest resources that the students can use. Second, they receive *consultation* every week—that is, the students are *consultees* with a faculty member consultant. Thus, students are engaged in three professional roles simultaneously: they are consultants to two teachers, supervisees to a faculty member (receiving direct guidance), and consultees to other faculty members (receiving CCC), and they experience the differences between consultation and supervision in real time. Students continue in their roles as both supervisees and consultees to faculty members for four additional semesters through the completion of their school-based internship, with the expectation that they will also be engaging in consultation as a standard part of their professional practice. In this way, students learn about and experience the process of consultation from the perspective of consultant and consultee for 3 years.

COMPLICATING THE THINKING OF CONSULTANT TRAINEES

Consultation involves a relationship that is developed between a consultant and one or more consultees, and it is predicated on effective and genuine communication and the sharing of knowledge. Moreover, in addition to the general principles that underlie consultation more generally (e.g., consultation involves a consultant, consultee, and client; consultation focuses on the professional work problems of the consultee), there are several principles that underlie CCC specifically (e.g., the consultant and consultee need to engage in active reflection to resolve the problem; Lambert, 2004). Like psychotherapy, talking is an integral part of the process, and talking is also important in reflecting changes in how the consultation problem is being conceptualized. Johannessen's (2004) metaphor of complicating thinking provides one lens into the process of CCC. Sandoval (2004, 2014) highlighted the importance of conceptual change in thinking, and Newell

(2012) suggested that one goal of training student consultants is moving them from knowledge to skill. All of these analogies speak to the importance of the training model as a tool for moving the consultant trainee from novice to initiate and ultimately to master.

To make explicit this idea of complicating the trainee consultant's thinking, in week 3 of the semester, before they have started their consultation placements, students are required to create a conceptual map explicating their current understanding of consultee-centered consultation and provide a written explanation of their conceptual map. At the end of the semester, students are asked to revise their conceptual maps based their increased knowledge base, their experiences with their consultees, and their participation in their supervision sessions and sessions as consultees. In their end of the semester write-up, students are asked to use the initial and revised maps to reflect upon how their understanding of consultation has changed over the semester (see Sandoval, 2004, for how these maps can be used to evaluate changes in consultees' conceptualization after consultation).

In this section, we present conceptual maps and reflections from the five student co-authors on this paper to illustrate how the trainee consultees move from a more naive to a more sophisticated understanding of consultation across the first semester. We present both the initial and the final maps as well as the students' reflections on why they changed the maps. Although our students will not be expert consultants for some time, and perhaps never during their time as students, the program's goal is for students to continue to reflect on consultation and their development as consultants throughout their practice (Garcia, 2004). Before presenting the five case studies (see also Rosenfield, 2012), we briefly describe Hylander's (2004, 2012) description of conceptual change in CCC because several of the case studies refer to this model.

Hylander's Notion of Conceptual Change

In 2004, Hylander described the process of conceptual change in CCC. Using qualitative data—focus groups, interviews, audiotaped consultation sessions, responses to open-ended questions—from 23 experienced consultants and a grounded theory analytic strategy, she argued that consultation involves *presentations* (what is said by the consultee and consultant) and *representations* (what the consultee and consultant believe) and contended that "a successful consultation process ends with a different *representation of the problem* . . . a conceptual shift or *turning*" on the part of the consultee (Hylander, 2004, p. 45). Consultation begins with the consultee's presentation, and the goal of consultation is to bring the consultant's and consultee's presentations and representations into alignment. In engaging in consultation, the consultant engages in three modes of interaction: approach (i.e., trying to see the problem how the consultee sees it), attention (i.e., asking neutral questions and mirroring the consultee's responses back), and autonomy (i.e., challenging the consultee's presentation). The consultant's task is to oscillate between confirming and challenging the teacher's presentation, and consultants must also challenge their own representations. In this process, consultants allow consultees to view their presentations, and it is this process of seeing one's presentation that can eventually result in a conceptual shift on the part of consultees.

Hylander (2004, p. 52) also described pitfalls to consultation that she referred to as "blind alleys in the consultation process" based on the consultee's and the consultant's presentations and representations. The first blind alley is the *bind*. In this case, the consultant's presentation is too close to the consultee's, although their representations differ, and the consultant is either unwilling or unable to challenge the consultee's presentation, resulting in no room for the consultee to view her presentation and experience a turning. The second blind alley is labeled *boredom*. In this case, the consultant and consultee share the same presentation and representation, once again resulting in no space for ideas to develop. A *break* is the third blind alley. In this blind alley, the consultant's presentation and representation are different than the consultee's, and the consultant challenges the consultee's representation but does not challenge her own representation enough, resulting in a growing gulf between consultant and consultee. Hylander concluded by noting that all consultants who are actively engaged in consultation go down blind alleys—they are a part of the process—and the flexibility of the consultant is critical in moving the consultation process forward. With these concepts in mind, we now present the case studies of the trainee consultants.

CASE STUDIES

Case 1: AM Before becoming a consultant-in-training, my prior experience in schools was limited to observing and sometimes assisting in classrooms. As such, it was difficult for me to envision myself doing the work of a consultant; I was concerned that I would not be accepted as a consultant but instead would be seen as an uninformed outsider. These concerns are reflected in my initial conceptual model of consultee-centered consultation (Figure 18.1a). To construct my model, I borrowed heavily from Hylander (2004) in order to supplement my lack of expertise. Hylander (2004) introduced three consultant stances: *approach* (nondirective, where the consultant builds trust by confirming the consultee's presentation); *attention* (directive, where the consultant mirrors the consultee's statements); and *autonomy* (directive or nondirective, where the consultant challenges the consultee with new thoughts or listens to the consultee's proposals). Each of these stances has utility, and it is the consultant's job to move among them as needed, represented in Figure 18.1a by the connecting arrows. However, each of these

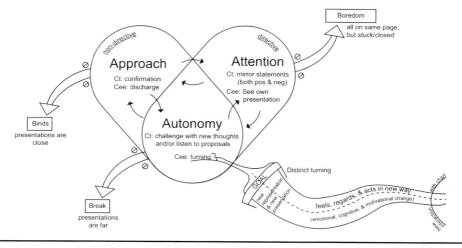

Figure 18.1a AM: Beginning of Semester

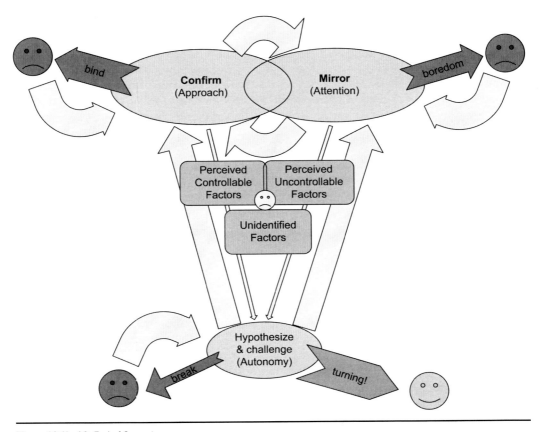

Figure 18.1b AC: End of Semester

stances also comes with the potential hazard of sending the consultation relationship down a blind alley, that is, to a bind, to boredom, or to a break.

My second conceptual model (Figure 18.1b) at the end of the semester retains many aspects from the initial one. I still find it useful to attend to the three stances and associated blind alleys, and I still see the eventual goal as a turning in the consultee. However, I identified the need for at least three changes in my initial model: (a) there should be a representation of the work problem, (b) the size of the elements in the model should reflect frequency of use, and (c) the names of the three stances should reflect how I thought about them during sessions.

I recognized the need for a representation of the work problem while making my initial model, but having no experience with consultation, I was unsure of what it should look like. As I began engaging in consultation, a distinction between *controllable* and *uncontrollable* factors emerged in my discussions. At times, a consultee would present a work problem (e.g., low student motivation) alongside a list of perceived controllable factors (e.g., classroom incentives and competitions) as well as a list of uncontrollable factors that stood in the way (e.g., difficult home lives and poverty).

My challenge was to use our conversations to uncover unidentified factors that might be controllable (e.g., a mismatch between assignment difficulty and student proficiency) and sometimes to reframe uncontrollable factors as potentially manageable ones (e.g., reframing "difficult home lives" as "difficult for parents to access school resources, but maybe teachers/schools can make it easier"). Conversations during supervision and consultation with our professor were invaluable in the process of generating potential reframes of the factors involved in the work problem and in finding ways to introduce these ideas to my consultees. The distinction among controllable, uncontrollable, and unidentified factors most often remained in the background of consultative discussions, but at times it became useful to make the distinction explicit in order ask questions such as what else could we try, what would it look like if we *could* control this factor, and what are we missing?

When making my initial model, I had assumed that the three consultative stances were distinct and would take up roughly equal amounts of time. I was surprised to find that the majority of my time was spent in the approach and attention stances and that these stances felt somewhat overlapping. Thus, in my revised model, these two stances are represented by large overlapping ovals with thick curved arrows leading from one to the other. In contrast, the autonomy stance felt entirely distinct and most useful in relatively infrequent doses. Thus, the autonomy stance is now farther away from the others with only thin arrows providing access and with thick arrows leading away.

The final change I made to my model was to give the consultative stances the names they hold in my head. I changed approach to confirm, attention to mirror, and autonomy to hypothesize and challenge. Most of these name changes happened almost immediately, as I shared my consultation work during supervision and I found it simpler to speak about the actions I was taking as a consultant. However, the word *hypothesize* was added later when I found it to be a useful tool to present my alternate representation of a work problem. After discussing a work problem with a consultee at length, I would turn our attention back to the observable behaviors (e.g., student spends most of math class doodling instead of completing a worksheet), present the consultee's view as one hypothesis (e.g., that the student has low academic motivation), and suggest what another hypothesis could be (e.g., that the student does not understand the mathematical concepts behind the algorithms required on the worksheet and thus cannot remember the steps accurately). This process usually elicited more curiosity about student behavior and allowed us to consider ways to test our hypotheses.

My first year working as a consultant in training gave me invaluable experience that refined my conceptual understanding of consultation. Although the main elements in my initial concept map are retained in my final map, direct experience with consultees as well as conversations with my supervisor and reflecting with my faculty consultant allowed me to refine my thinking about how the three consultant stances are related and gave me useful tactics for defining and addressing work problems. Additionally, I have found this model of consultation to be surprisingly applicable to long-term work with parents when discussing their child's behavior in the home.

Case 2: JN As a beginning consultant, my ideas about consultation were idealistic. I thought that if I could develop a trusting relationship with consultees and follow a prescribed set of steps during consultation, I would be successful at enriching consultees' thinking about challenges that arise in the classroom and possible solutions to those challenges. Similarly, if program faculty and I followed the same set of steps when I brought concerns or problems into consultation as a consultee, I would inevitably develop a clear idea of how to proceed in my work. As a result, my initial concept map was simple and

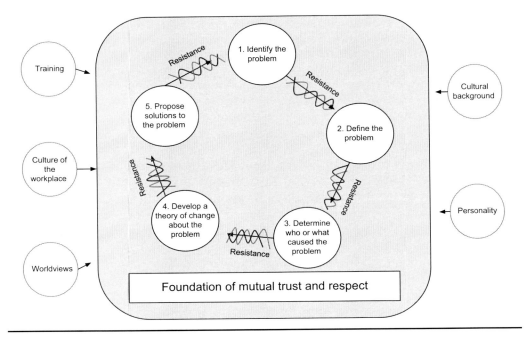

Figure 18.2a JN: Beginning of Semester

prescriptive (Figure 18.2a). I represented the process as a cycle in which the consultant works with the consultee to: (a) identify a problem; (b) define the problem; (c) untangle who or what caused the problem; (d) develop a theory of change about that problem; and (e) propose possible solutions to the problem. I assumed that these steps could be repeated if an appropriate solution was not obtained, but I believed that if a consultant followed these steps carefully, they would rarely need to be repeated.

I acknowledged that the consultant must confirm and challenge the consultee's perceptions during each of these steps. For example, I planned to offer additional information based on observations of the client, ask questions to better understand the consultee's perspective, and hone in on areas of ambiguity or contradiction that could shed light on the consultee's perceptions of the client (a process represented by oscillating lines in Figure 18.2a). During this confirming and challenging process, I also expected that I would encounter resistance—in part because I sometimes felt resistant to the process when I took part in consultation as a *consultee* (e.g., feeling frustrated that solutions were not quickly provided to me by faculty consultants)—and I considered this development a natural and intelligent response to the consultation process that should be addressed directly to move forward with the consultation process. I recognized that the consultation process takes part within a relationship, and thus, in my cognitive map, the process of consultation rests squarely on a foundation of mutual trust and respect without which the process would fall apart. From participating in supervision and in consultation as a consultee, I knew that my comfort asking questions, raising concerns, admitting challenges, and accepting feedback from faculty was affected by my relationships with them; the more trust and respect present in the relationship, the more progress we made.

Finally, I acknowledged that external factors, such as the consultee and the consultant's training, pressure to develop a solution to a challenging problem quickly, and

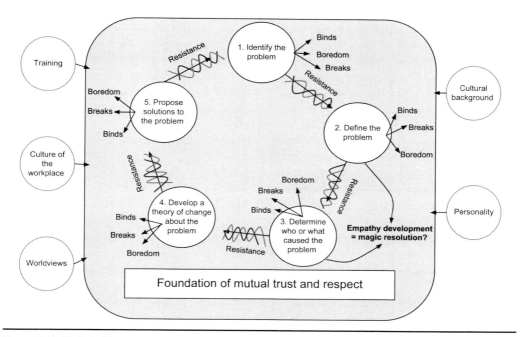

Figure 18.2b JN: End of Semester

worldviews could affect the consultation process. I thought these factors would be particularly important to consider if the consultant and consultee held different beliefs about teaching or had different cultural backgrounds, for example. Additionally, I thought the relative importance of these factors might vary depending on the local and national contexts in which the consultant and consultee are practicing. As a beginning consultant, I assumed that differences in training, worldviews, and perceptions of effective teaching and learning would complicate consultation and that the more similar my beliefs, background, and training were to my consultee, the more easily we could progress through the steps in my concept model.

However, as I began practicing consultation, I quickly discovered that I could follow each aspect of my consultation model but still fail to develop an appropriate solution to the problem. Similarly, when receiving consultation from faculty about my work as a consultant, I could think over the course of many meetings with faculty and my peers without developing a workable solution to a problem—a surprising revelation, as both consultant and consultee in this setting were all familiar with the CCC model. As a result, in my second cognitive map, I indicated that during each step of the problem-solving process, the consultee and the consultant will likely encounter blind alleys (e.g., binds, boredom, or breaks) in which a consultant can and regularly does get stuck (see Hylander, 2004). In my second map, these blind alleys are included as a normative part of consultation, resulting in a more circuitous process.

I also found that consultees and I sometimes viewed classroom problems and their causes very differently. Much of my consultation time, therefore, was spent *thinking* with consultees about the differences in our presentation and representations of the problem. For example, I worked with a preschool teacher who was concerned about a 4-year-old boy who had recently moved to the United States with his family and spoke very limited

English. The consultee often requested that we talk about his aggressive behavior, defiance, and low frustration tolerance (e.g., he sometimes bit other students, often hit other students, sometimes hit teachers) and described him as an "inherently difficult" child with an "irritable temperament." I, on the other hand, viewed him as a child with inadequate language and interpersonal skills to manage the demands of his new school setting. I wondered if he had the vocabulary to ask for things he needed or the social skills to communicate his desires and needs without using aggression.

After weeks of discussion and after obtaining supervision from program faculty, I asked the consultee a new question: "I wonder how it feels to be this child? What's school like for him?" This question, unlike many others about his language skills or his cultural background, allowed the consultee to think about the child's experience at school and, I believe, to begin to develop empathy for the young man (Brodin, 2004). The consultee recognized that it must be difficult to feel frustrated so often, to be reprimanded so frequently, and to not have many friends at school. Thus, although the child continued to struggle with acquiring vocabulary and using prosocial strategies to meet his needs, the consultee's response to him changed dramatically. His behavior was met less often with frustration from his teacher and more often with empathy, which over the course of the next 2 months allowed them to develop a closer, warmer, more positive relationship. In addition, after listening to my consultee's perception of the problem during supervision and consultation, I began to seriously consider to what extent this child's temperament might play into his difficulty with aggressive behavior at school, challenging my representation. With a new appreciation for his teacher's thoughts and observations, I was able to better to work with the child's teacher to create interventions that supported his behavior at school.

I share this story to illustrate three lessons I learned over the course of the semester: (a) modeling empathy can lead to changes in a teacher's behavior that result in an apparently *magic* resolution to the problem (Hylander, 2004) based on the teacher's change in representation, (b) consultation does not need to follow the prescriptive set of steps, and (c) sometimes differences in worldviews and perceptions of problems can be assets to consultation instead of hindrances, meaning that CCC may be a particularly useful tool in settings where consultant and consultee do not share the same culture, nationality, training, or worldviews. As a result, I added empathy development to my cognitive model as a feature that could facilitate reaching a solution in the consultation process.

Practicing consultation, obtaining supervision, and participating in consultation as a *consultee* has allowed my conceptualization of CCC to become more complicated. I initially believed consultation was prescriptive and that good consultants possessed enough interpersonal skills and expertise to avoid blind alleys. As a result of my consultation practicum supported by supervision and consultation, I learned that successful consultation regularly involves working through blind alleys and does not require narrowly following the sequence I laid out for myself in my first map. I am now better able to accept and welcome resistance, roadblocks, and differences in perspective with consultees, which allows me to engage genuinely with them as we co-construct resolutions to classroom problems. I also learned that although external factors such as worldviews, training, and culture do affect the consultation process, sometimes honing in on differences between the consultant and consultee expands the thinking of both the consultee and the consultant, making the CCC process more effective.

Case 3: CK   Initially, I viewed consultation as a relatively straightforward interaction between someone seeking information or help and someone who could provide what was being sought. From this perspective, the consultant school psychologist provided the answers to help the consultee teacher solve her problem. Thus, the teacher's problem is depicted at the center of my first map (Figure 18.3a). I understood the problem to be a concrete issue involving a specific student. I assumed that teachers willingly come to the school psychologist to get answers, and things go awry when teacher fails to listen or correctly implement the consultant's suggestions.

I initially defined and still see consultation as two experts coming together to jointly solve a problem, and I had been trained to view consultation as a nonhierarchical process in my previous graduate program. Thus, both my first and second concept maps place the consultant and consultee at the same level. However, although I was taught that consultation is collaborative and nonhierarchical, my implicit belief was that consultation was an inherently uneven process. Many consultants come to consultation from a position of apparent power and knowledge relative to consultee teachers, and this inequality may be further complicated by differences in gender or ethnic identity. Ethnicity is not reducible to culture (Wimmer, 2013), and the lack of equivalence between ancestry and values or behavioral norms is especially apparent in the diverse San Francisco Bay Area. Nevertheless, when consultants and consultees have backgrounds associated with different degrees of privilege, either the consultant or consultee, or both, may feel vulnerable, may be less able to engage in honest dialogue, or may not feel acknowledged or understood by their counterpart.

My training in consultee-centered consultation helped me better see persistent issues such as those related to hierarchy and appropriately complicated my view of consultation and the problem-solving process. First, I shifted from viewing consultation as *merely* a problem-solving process to a voluntary prevention-oriented dialogue driven by questions (Rosenfield, 2004). Second, I went from seeing it as a consultant-directed process to a consultee-directed one. The consultee's expertise is not recognized simply by *labeling* the process egalitarian. The consultant must acknowledge that the consultee is competent in some domains, has students' best interests in mind, and possesses specific expert knowledge. Third, I moved from viewing the consultation relationship as *triadic,* as described in the literature, to seeing it as mainly *dyadic.* Instead of becoming indirectly

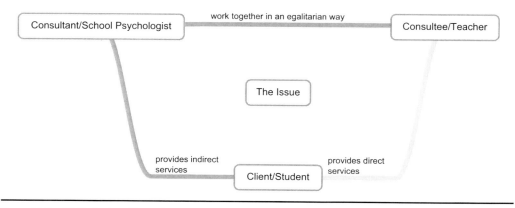

Figure 18.3a CK: Beginning of Semester

involved with a specific student or client, the consultant's main goal is facilitate a more general shift in the consultee's understanding and interaction with current and future students. Correspondingly, the consultant serves not one client, but many *hidden* clients.

In my initial view of consultation, the consultee has a problem and is at a loss to solve it, but the consultant must have *the* answer and the consultee's problem will be solved if she listens to the consultant. The initial map provided no explanation of the underlying processes that bolster this change; it merely highlighted the difference between the consultant's provision of indirect services and the consultee's direct services. In my second map (Figure 18.3b), the central problem is defined as a *mismatch* between expectations and performance. I no longer assume that the consultant has the answer or that the consultee wants the consultant's answer. Additionally, the consultee's presentation of the problem may not accurately reflect the way she has represented it internally. Consultants may experience frustration about teachers' lack of willingness to accept seemingly sensible advice.

In a school setting, the school psychologist may come to view teachers as resistant, unwilling, or incompetent and may experience distress when she senses what she takes for resistance. Likewise, teachers may feel incompetent if they come to a school psychologist for consultation and are immediately told what they are doing right and wrong. Therefore, the idea of mismatching in my second map was shaped by my recognition that the consultant may not always or even often have the answer to the consultee's problem.

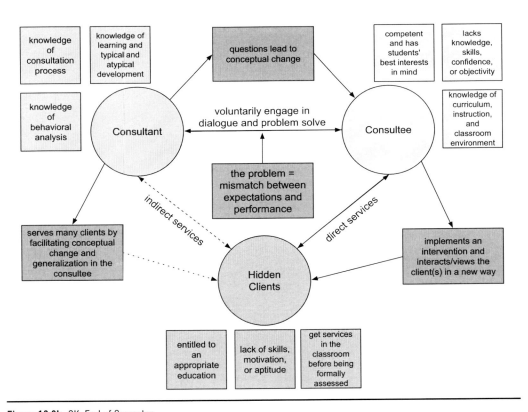

Figure 18.3b CK: End of Semester

However, the consultant's questions are the fuel that drives the problem-solving process, eventually leading the consultee to interact and view the client in a new way.

Beginner consultants may struggle to formulate such questions. Direct instruction of nondirective consultation and questioning techniques may lessen trainee consultants' anxiety and improve their effectiveness (Rosenfield, 2004). Trainee consultants who feel more at ease and who are more skilled are better equipped to engage in productive consultation sessions, thereby improving consultees' perceptions of consultee-centered consultation and clients' outcomes.

Our program incorporates two forms of training. First, trainees discuss their experiences with each other and a faculty consultant. The faculty consultant models consultee-centered consultation. Second, trainees receive more directive supervision. These two forms of training are complementary. The first allows trainees both to learn through observation and to better understand how their consultees may experience the consultation process. The second gives trainees the necessary opportunities to present concerns to their supervisor, receive clear advice, and have questioning techniques expressly modeled (e.g., "You could say, '*I wonder if . . .*'"). As in schools and other consultation settings, the time for consultation in training programs is limited. Resources for trainees in consultee-centered consultation are relatively limited, with some exceptions (e.g., Sandoval, 2014). However, parallels exist between consultee-centered consultation and solution-focused counseling, and solution-focused training materials may be helpful to consultants who wish to have written resources at hand (e.g., Bannink, 2010).

In my more complicated view of consultation, the teacher who seeks out consultation usually does have some problem, which may result from the consultee's lack of knowledge, skills, confidence, or objectivity as in the traditional CCC model. However, the consultant does not make it her mission to unearth the consultee's weaknesses or failures, and although the consultant has some responsibility for the student in most school contexts, she is not emotionally attached to or in charge of the student. Outside of rare instances of misconduct, the consultant sees the student as the consultee's charge. Additionally, the consultant would rather empower the consultee to solve her problem for herself than solve it for her. It is hoped, moreover, that this trust and agency will allow the consultee to generalize what she learns or discovers to future problematic situations. In addition to including brief explanations of this process in my second map, I illustrate this shift in my thinking by weakening the lines linking the consultant and client relative to those between the consultee and client.

Instead of immediately attacking the problem at hand, the consultant should try to get some distance from the problem by first asking the consultee appropriate questions and maybe recalling relevant stories and metaphors which may facilitate conceptual change for the consultee (Mang, 2004). This process works *because* the consultee is seen indeed as an expert in her own right; the consultant truly trusts her colleague's expertise and does not just endorse it hypothetically. At the same time, the consultant has specific knowledge of the consultation process. The consultant realizes that (a) the consultee has put herself in a vulnerable position by admitting she needs help and (b) the consultee may have the answer to her own question. In sum, the consultee-centered, consultee-directed model of consultation allows both teacher and consultant to feel respected.

Case 4: CGr   At the beginning of the school year, when I became a new consultant, I conceptualized consultation as a developmental process that proceeded in a stage-like

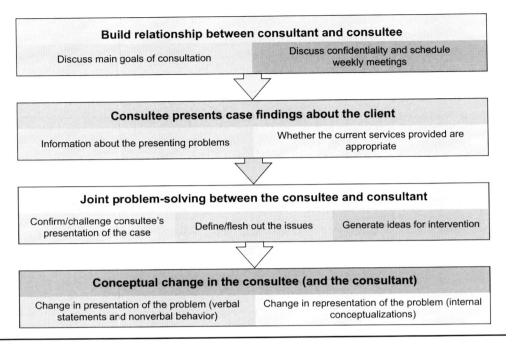

Figure 18.4a CGr: Beginning of Semester

fashion with a predefined order. To help me navigate the process, I created a cognitive map (Figure 18.4a) that I could refer to when I needed guidance as my consultation relationships and work progressed. In this map, I laid out major milestones or stages that I identified in the readings early in the course about the theoretical framework supporting the CCC model. Within each stage, I depicted subgoals that helped me break down the process into smaller steps for myself. In the sections that follow, I briefly discuss my experiences in each of the four stages.

Building the Relationship   As a new consultant, my first goal was to build positive and productive relationships with the two teachers who were my consultees. With this goal in mind, I planned to discuss with each teacher our work together, but I knew that I needed to take the lead and focus on individual students who needed our support. On my first day, the first words one of the teachers uttered, half out of breath (as she pointed to a student), were "Fix him!" I thought, in panic, "She expects me to provide direct services to her students," but I responded, "I am here to work together with you to discuss problems that your students are having. We can pool our resources together and come up with ideas for intervention. I'm not able to be in your class on a daily basis, so, ultimately, you're in a better position to carry out consistent interventions for students on a daily basis." It was a difficult way to start a new relationship (Guvå, 2004), but the teacher *seemed* willing to try. Upon trying to schedule time for consultation, I discovered that one consultee (Ms. A), an overwhelmed kindergarten teacher who also had a 2-month-old baby at home, hardly ever took a break. We were never able to keep to a consistent schedule, though we somehow managed to squeeze in brief meetings between her classes.

Consultee Presents the Problem   I was fortunate to work with two teachers who openly discussed their students' challenges. By the way they talked about their experiences, they made it clear they wanted their students to receive help. However, engaging them about changes they would personally be willing to make was difficult. Ms. A deflected discussions about interventions she could make by moving to other topics and cutting meetings short. She viewed her students' families as engaging in permissive parenting resulting in dependent immature behavior. Ms. B excelled at analyzing contributing factors, and we often discussed a particular third-grade boy focusing on a new problematic behavior every week. Ms. B was convinced that he was not capable of recognizing others' feelings. Our discussions led to insights and new empathy for the student when we analyzed the ways that his mother's mental health problems made her unavailable to him at home.

Joint Problem-Solving   Though we developed complex understandings of the students, by the middle of the year I was left with an undeniable sense of frustration; it was the end of the semester and our conversations yielded insights but no tangible changes ensued in the teacher's practice. I brought up my concern in my weekly supervision meeting at the end of the first semester and received thoughtful reflection from my supervisor that left me with many questions to consider over winter break. However, something shifted during the spring semester because my supervisor finally gave me the explicit "go ahead" to formulate suggestions for interventions during discussions with the teachers. It was relieving to receive advice that I could take action on, and I was especially pleased when the teachers were receptive to some of the ideas I presented. During the last quarter, consultation transformed into a space for constructive feedback about the outcomes and feasibility of the interventions we tried. We experienced some successes and some failures. In one case, we were able to get a very disruptive student to stay on task for increments that increased by 5 minutes per day. The student's success in achieving his goals boosted his confidence and, in turn, he had more positive interactions with peers and teachers. When interventions did not work out, we gained helpful data that informed our working formulation of the problem, and we returned to the drawing board to incorporate our new insights into the next trial.

Conceptual Change   I cannot help but think that the greatest impact made from consultation came from carving out a space in the busy school day each week to step back and discuss the students' problems. Having a container for this discussion to analyze complex contributing factors was a powerful intervention in itself, an intervention that had far-reaching effects that extended beyond any one of the individual ideas we tried to implement. I learned to sit with uncertainty and explore ideas that enabled me to actualize the ultimate goal of this type of consultation: to work with a teacher to foster a conceptual change in his understanding of a student's problem (Sandoval, 1996). Furthermore, our weekly supervision course provided a safe space for me to reflect upon our conversations and gain insight from knowledgeable colleagues about how to proceed.

Rethinking Consultation   At the end of the semester, I revised my original cognitive map to incorporate the understanding I gained in my work throughout the year (see Figure 18.4b). I kept the four stages, but I added a third column (far right) in which I included pertinent considerations from practice. For example, in Stage 1, I found that I had to clarify and reclarify each of our roles during consultation to avoid falling prey to

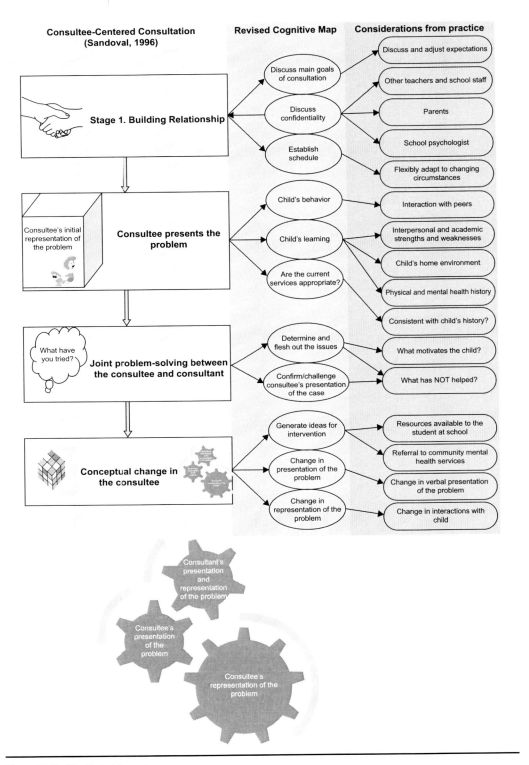

Consultee-Centered Consultation (Sandoval, 1996)

Revised Cognitive Map

Considerations from practice

Stage 1. Building Relationship

- Discuss main goals of consultation
- Discuss confidentiality
- Establish schedule

- Discuss and adjust expectations
- Other teachers and school staff
- Parents
- School psychologist
- Flexibly adapt to changing circumstances

Consultee's initial representation of the problem

Consultee presents the problem

- Child's behavior
- Child's learning
- Are the current services appropriate?

- Interaction with peers
- Interpersonal and academic strengths and weaknesses
- Child's home environment
- Physical and mental health history
- Consistent with child's history?

What have you tried?

Joint problem-solving between the consultee and consultant

- Determine and flesh out the issues
- Confirm/challenge consultee's presentation of the case

- What motivates the child?
- What has NOT helped?

Conceptual change in the consultee

- Generate ideas for intervention
- Change in presentation of the problem
- Change in representation of the problem

- Resources available to the student at school
- Referral to community mental health services
- Change in verbal presentation of the problem
- Change in interactions with child

Consultant's presentation and representation of the problem

Consultee's presentation of the problem

Consultee's representation of the problem

Figure 18.4b CGr: End of Semester

untenable demands on my time and requests to provide direct service to students. When it came to scheduling consultation meetings, I had to remain flexible about the format our consultation sessions would take. In discussing confidentiality, I found that I had to explicitly differentiate my role as a consultant from the regular school psychologist's role as a provider of direct services to students.

In Stage 2, when the teacher presented the students' problems to me, it was sometimes helpful for me steer our focus beyond the student's specific behavior in the classroom to more broad considerations of the student with peers and with family in the home environment. In Stage 3, I found that it was important to consider motivating factors that reinforced the child's problematic behavior or habits and to review the interventions that had been tried before. In Stage 4, it was helpful to list the potential resources available to the child inside the school as well as in the community. The ultimate test of our progress was measured when I took a step back and traced how the consultees' understanding and representations of their students' problems changed throughout the course of our discussions. These turnings (Hylander, 2004) represented the light at the end of the tunnel, and when we reached this point, I knew consultation was working and we had the potential to derive new solutions together.

Case 5: CGe In September 2012, I began a 1-year consultee-centered consultation placement at a San Francisco Bay Area elementary school. Each week, I spent Friday mornings in a first grade classroom and Friday afternoons in a fifth grade classroom. As consultant-trainee, my goal was to build trust with my consultees, to support my consultees, and to carefully facilitate behavioral change in my consultees—all while accepting that my consultees could accept or reject my service and fail to change their behaviors. Broad instead of precise, teacher- instead of student-focused, my work as a consultant-trainee led me to think less about curriculum-based measures, testing, and interventions and more about teachers' knowledge, skills, and confidence.

Over the course of consultation, I tracked my development as a consultant-trainee through two self-designed models, each of which was aimed at pictographically representing consultee-centered consultation. One model was created after 3 weeks as a consultant-trainee, the other after 3 months. Both models were premised on Lambert's (1983) three phases of consultation: the first phase, relationship building and role clarification; the second, problem identification and intervention generation; and the third, mutual understanding of roles and use of interactions to explore, propose, and rule out solutions. Reflecting on my consultant-trainee relationships, I believe that the relationships reached Lambert's Phase 1 and 2 interactions during the first 3 months of consultation and intermittently entered Phase 3 thereafter.

During the first 3 months my relationship with each consultee was characterized by a relentless focus on the consultee, respect for the consultee's insights, and curiosity about the consultee's "stories" of students. Consistent with Lambert's (1983) Phase 1 description, I spent much time observing the consultees, the students, and the broader school milieu. I asked the consultees many questions and always withheld judgment about the consultees' answers. Fundamental to the question-asking process was my use of the empathy, tolerance, and flexibility referenced in Figure 18.5a.

The Phase 1 focused approach yielded similar results for each consultee. Both consultees enjoyed the challenge of being asked questions that tapped into their professional expertise and both were particularly eager for the questions to yield immediate

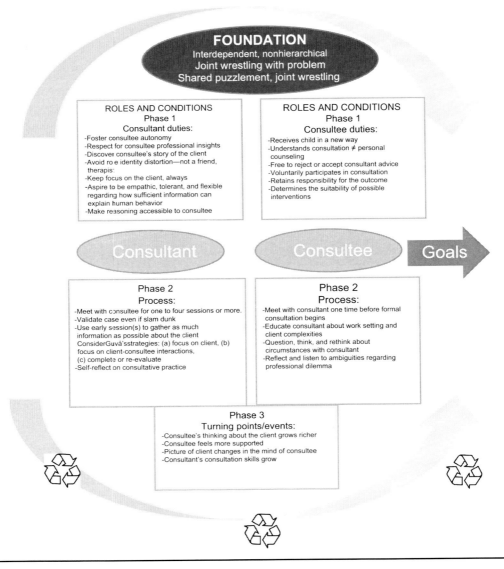

ROLES AND CONDITIONS
Phase 1
Consultant duties:
-Foster consultee autonomy
-Respect for consultee professional insights
-Discover consultee's story of the client
-Avoid role identity distortion—not a friend, therapist
-Keep focus on the client, always
-Aspire to be empathic, tolerant, and flexible regarding how sufficient information can explain human behavior
-Make reasoning accessible to consultee

ROLES AND CONDITIONS
Phase 1
Consultee duties:
-Receives child in a new way
-Understands consultation ≠ personal counseling
-Free to reject or accept consultant advice
-Voluntarily participates in consultation
-Retains responsibility for the outcome
-Determines the suitability of possible interventions

Consultant

Consultee

Goals

Phase 2
Process:
-Meet with consultee for one to four sessions or more.
-Validate case even if slam dunk
-Use early session(s) to gather as much information as possible about the client ConsiderGuvá'sstrategies: (a) focus on client, (b) focus on client-consultee interactions, (c) complete or re-evaluate
-Self-reflect on consultative practice

Phase 2
Process:
-Meet with consultant one time before formal consultation begins
-Educate consultant about work setting and client complexities
-Question, think, and rethink about circumstances with consultant
-Reflect and listen to ambiguities regarding professional dilemma

Phase 3
Turning points/events:
-Consultee's thinking about the client grows richer
-Consultee feels more supported
-Picture of client changes in the mind of consultee
-Consultant's consultation skills grow

FOUNDATION
Interdependent, nonhierarchical
Joint wrestling with problem
Shared puzzlement, joint wrestling

Figure 18.5a CGe: Beginning of Semester

intervention strategies. Consequently, I moved quickly with both consultees into Lambert's (1983) second phase conversations. For example, in the instance of Consultee A, the most pressing concern was her class's boisterous, unwieldy transition times. During our Phase 1 discussion, Consultee A recognized she needed a behavior management system, and during our Phase 2 discussion, Consultee A identified the type of system she wanted. Over the course of eight sessions, Consultee A, with my support and indirect guidance, refined the behavior management system. During the refining process, Consultee A took the lead in amending the behavior management system, a process in which she worked toward the "question, think, and rethink about circumstances" goal referenced in Figure 18.5a.

Although my work with both consultees was successful in the early consultation period, the intensity with which both consultees desired immediate interventions could have undermined the consultee-centered component of the relationship. Thankfully, the consultee-centered component of the relationship was retained through ongoing role definition and clarification in Phase 1. I communicated to my consultees that our consultative relationship would develop as we explored and expanded our perspectives on situations and brainstormed the advantages and disadvantages of different interventions.

In the second half of the year's consultation placement, my consultees and I engaged in dialogues that shifted between Phases 1 and 2, a shift that is represented pictographically as a "recycle" sign in Figure 18.5a. During our dialogues I continued to support consultee autonomy. I listened more carefully than I had as a new consultant-trainee and attempted to look objectively at my consultees' realities while also trying to have some subjective experience of their feelings. I asked many questions and encouraged the consultees to do the same. I asked and wondered so many things that one consultee compared me to Penny from *Inspector Gadget* (Chalopin & Heyward, 1983). Such light-heartedness, particularly in the latter months of the consultation period, was common in my discussions with both consultees.

Information gathering and empathic, reflective listening, week in and week out, eventually led my consultees to arrive at the cognitive restructuring associated with Phase 3 (Lambert, 1983). Consultee A realized she was feeling resentful toward her challenging group of students. This realization helped Consultee A to carve out a more justly designed behavior management system. Consultee B, after a long struggle with a student's attention issues, realized that the behavior of the student's mother was distracting her from thinking about the student's problems in an unbiased way. This realization led Consultee B to name emotions she felt toward the parent; to ponder the source of the emotions—jealousy, insecurity, ineptitude; and to explore how the emotions were interfering with her relationship with the student.

The emergence of my consultees' Phase 3 thinking (Lambert, 1983) was the result of months-long application of the key ingredients of consultee-centered consultation: relationship building and coordinate interdependence; psychoeducation; information gathering; and empathic, reflective listening. Of course, behind this rather simplistic list of ingredients for successful consultation is a more nuanced description of ingredients that I employed once I had become a more experienced consultant. For example, as a more seasoned consultant, I built the relationship through use of metaphors, humor, and storytelling. I learned to be patient because role clarification via psychoeducation ended up being an ongoing process as opposed to short one. When facilitating the coordinate interdependence, I became comfortable with my consultees' discomfort about being the center of the relationship and the originators of the ideas. I also became less afraid to ask difficult questions as part of the information-gathering process.

As I grew to appreciate the subtleties of CCC, I created an updated conceptual model using symbols to reflect the nuances necessary for successful consultation. My updated model, seen in Figure 18.5b, depicts 16 different images. Each of these apparently disparate images helps to convey my more sophisticated understanding of key components of consultation, as I explain below. It is the consultant's job to help consultees *look in the mirror* to facilitate cognitive restructuring, and consultants need to pay attention to the affective and *metaphorical* aspects of the dialogues with the consultee. We ask questions to understand the consultee's view of the *puzzle* that the client poses, and we choose our

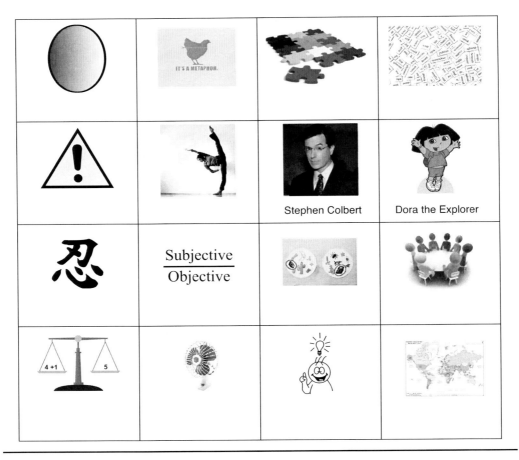

Figure 18.5b CGe: End of Semester

words carefully to facilitate a joint questioning and wondering about the problem that the consultee has. The warning sign is a reminder that skepticism and resistance are normative in this process and related to both consultant and consultee reluctance to change their behavior; thus, consultants need to be incredibly *flexible* both in our approach to the consultee and in terms of the theoretical frameworks that we bring to bear.

In his satiric role as a color-blind reporter on *The Colbert Report*, a news satire that aired for several years on Comedy Central, Stephen Colbert provided an ironic reminder that although consultants should *not* be color- or culture-blind, they should also avoid intervention paralysis manifested in Colbert's inability to respond to cultural issues. In contrast, *Dora the Explorer*, a Latina cartoon character in the U.S., reminds consultants that they *must* explore issues about culture and human differences while remembering that relationship building and role clarification may take a long time; *patience* matters. Consultants need be empathetic, in that they try to have a *subjective* understanding of the consultee's situation while also looking and helping the consultee look *objectively* at the reality of the situation. In discussing interventions, *matching* the consultee's rationale can lead to greater acceptance of interventions, so consultants need to know and be able to uncover the types of interventions their consultees prefer. Many great ideas can emerge in the consultant-consultee dyads as well as in consultation *groups* involving other teachers or parents. CCC is premised on the consultee and consultant as *equals* sharing views, but it is the consultant's task to *oscillate* between confirming and challenging the consultee's presentation of the case leading to a *new understanding* of the problem. Finally, pictures or concept maps are useful tools in helping consultants understand the consultee's issues, and these can also serve as a benchmark against which to gauge changes (Sandoval, 2004).

My updated conceptual model also captures the cross-cultural components of consultation represented by comedian Stephen Colbert and the image of Dora the Explorer. The image of the flexible woman also symbolizes the need for consultants to be flexible with their cultural understanding, which can be defined as consultants' knowledge of their own culture, respect and value for the cultures of others, the awareness of the impact of their own culture on others, and knowledge of interventions appropriate for the cultures of the consultees (Ingraham, 2000).

Looking back on the consultation placement, I enjoyed my growth as a consultant, the growth of my consultees' problem-solving skills, and seeing my consultees take pride in and ownership for successful interventions. When outcomes were less successful, I enjoyed reframing questions and rethinking possibilities based on my consultee's insights and knowledge base. I also enjoyed the weekly supervision and consultation components of my graduate program. During these weekly sessions, I was often able to share issues related to my consultation placement and to digest questions, resulting in insights that led me to experience the cognitive restructuring symbolized in the mirror in Figure 18.5b. The opportunity to become the consultee every month provided an opportunity for me to know how it felt to be on the receiving end of consultation.

I am grateful that I developed in my understanding of the ingredients for successful consultation. My development is illustrated in the movement from the regimented conceptual model I designed as a novice consultant (Figure 18.5a) to the more nuanced model I designed with some experience (Figure 18.5b). Moving forward, I feel confident that I can productively use my consultation skills across organizational, cultural, and geographic contexts. Thus, although my consultation experience began in an educational setting in the San Francisco Bay Area, I may use my skills in noneducational settings across the country or around the world.

CONCLUSION

Trainee consultants, whether in the U.S. or elsewhere, often begin the process of learning consultation with either too much confidence or too little. The former perceive consultation as a rigid, formulaic process that will inevitably result in solving the problem that the consultee has brought, especially if the consultee will do what they say. The latter are stymied by their status as students and their perceived lack of expertise and standing in the eyes of consultees. Both of these viewpoints are represented in this article. Trainees on both sides of this divide often find it much easier to begin with behavioral consultation, as the interview guides associated with that approach (Kratochwill & Bergan, 1990) provide a safety net on which to fall back on. However, trainees in CCC have to live in ambiguity (Thörn, 2004) and use unscripted conversations to build relationships with the client, in a fashion that is similar to but not identical with a psychotherapeutic relationship.

As reflected in the five student voices in this chapter, we have learned several things about CCC and about training consultants in this model. The first is the idea that learning to consult is quasi-developmental, as with learning other skills. As the reflections show, over the course of one semester, consultant trainees moved from unidirectional stage-like views of consultation that were primarily based on the first sets of readings that they encountered to much more fluid conceptualizations. Most important, they abandoned the notion of a consultation formula, even in the conceptualizations that still retained some sense of linear sequencing. Moreover, the comments suggest that the students have learned to incorporate reflections from their practice into ongoing understanding, a process that the program facilitates for five semesters after they have completed the second concept map and which we hope will result in a lifetime of reflection in their consultation practice. Second, the students recognized the importance of not only building a relationship with the consultee but trying to understand the problem from the consultee's point of view (e.g., Knotek, 2012).

This latter aspect is a critical one in CCC, and it is the one that makes it a model that is useful in different cultural and national contexts. Behavioral consultation's generalizability is based on the fact that the basic behavioral principles (e.g., reinforcement) apply to organisms across cultural and national boundaries; thus, while what is *reinforcing* may differ, the effect of reinforcement is the same. Similarly, the generalizability of CCC is based on fact that its principles do not change across contexts, cultures, and nationalities. As mentioned previously, in 2004, Lambert (see pp. 15–17) outlined several principles of CCC that apply across cultures and international settings, and none of these principles was specific to a nation or culture. Thus, even while the specific content discussed in consultation might change and the humor and metaphors that are used may be culture and nation specific, the fundamental processes—for example, the focus on the client, the promotion of conceptual change, the recognition that CCC is to some extent consultee-driven, the importance of language use, among others—remain the same and all speak to the way in which CCC is useful in the U.S. (e.g., Ingraham, 2000; Sandoval, 2014), Europe (e.g., Hylander & Guvå, 2004; Johannessen, 2004) and beyond.

There are individuals who are ardent advocates of one type of consultation over all others. The limited number of meta-analyses (Gibson & Chard, 1994; Medway & Updyke, 1985; Reddy, Barboza-Whitehead, Files, & Rubel, 2000) that we have in this area tells us that both behavioral consultation and CCC are effective in changing consultee behavior. Given the sociohistorical context of UC Berkeley and its commitment to free speech and social justice, CCC is ideally suited to our training model. Although we would be remiss if we did not expose our students to other training models related to learning, programs that do not train their students to engage in mutually respective, nonhierarchical problem-solving relationships are remiss, because at the core of every consultation model, there is a problem that requires a collaborative relationship to begin to get to a solution.

REFERENCES

Anderson, D. L. (2011). *Organizational development: The process of leading organizational change.* Thousand Oaks, CA: Sage.

Bannink, F. (2010). *1001 solution-focused questions.* New York, NY: Norton.

Brodin, M. (2004). What does he look like? From the inner world of the consultee to the inner world of the client (with a little help from a question). In N. M. Lambert, I. Hylander, & J. H. Sandoval (Eds.), *Consultee-centered consultation: Improving the quality of professional services in schools and community organizations* (pp. 265–278). Mahwah, NJ: Lawrence Erlbaum.

Caplan, G., & Caplan, R. B. (1999). *Mental health consultation and collaboration*. Prospect Heights, IL: Waveland Press.

Chalopin, J., & Heyward, A. (Producer). (1983). *Inspector Gadget*. Television series. New York, NY: Nickelodeon.

Garcia, M. (2004). Reflectivity in consultation. In N. M. Lambert, I. Hylander, & J. H. Sandoval (Eds.), *Consultee-centered consultation: Improving the quality of professional services in schools and community organizations* (pp. 359–369). Mahwah, NJ: Lawrence Erlbaum.

Gibson, G., & Chard, K. M. (1994). Quantifying the effects of community mental health consultation interventions. *Consulting Psychology Journal: Practice and Research, 46,* 13–25. doi: 10.1037/1061–4087.46.4.13

Guvå, G. (2004). Meeting a teacher who asks for help but not for consultation. In N. M. Lambert, I. Hylander, & J. H. Sandoval (Eds.), *Consultee-centered consultation: Improving the quality of professional services in schools and community organizations* (pp. 255–264). Mahwah, NJ: Lawrence Erlbaum.

Hatzichristou, C. (2004). Alternative school psychological services: Development of a model linking theory, research, and service delivery. In N. M. Lambert, I. Hylander, & J. H. Sandoval (Eds.), *Consultee-centered consultation: Improving the quality of professional services in schools and community organizations* (pp. 115–132). Mahwah, NJ: Lawrence Erlbaum.

Hylander, I. (2004). Analysis of conceptual change in consultee-centered consultation. In N. M. Lambert, I. Hylander, & J. H. Sandoval (Eds.), *Consultee-centered consultation: Improving the quality of professional services in schools and community organizations* (pp. 45–61). Mahwah, NJ: Lawrence Erlbaum.

Hylander, I. (2012). Conceptual change through consultee-centered consultation. *Consulting Psychology Journal: Practice and Research, 64,* 29–45. doi: 10.1037/a0027986

Hylander, I., & Guvå, G. (2004). A model for consultation with day care and preschools. In N. M. Lambert, I. Hylander, & J. H. Sandoval (Eds.), *Consultee-centered consultation: Improving the quality of professional services in schools and community organizations* (pp. 65–77). Mahwah, NJ: Lawrence Erlbaum.

Ingraham, C. L. (2000). Consultation through a multicultural lens: Multicultural and cross-cultural consultation in schools. *School Psychology Review, 29,* 320–343.

Ingraham, C. L. (2004). Multicultural consultee-centered consultation: Supporting consultees in the development of cultural competence. In N. M. Lambert, I. Hylander, & J. H. Sandoval (Eds.), *Consultee-centered consultation: Improving the quality of professional services in schools and community organizations* (pp. 133–148). Mahwah, NJ: Lawrence Erlbaum.

Johannessen, E. M. (2004). Complicating the thinking of the consultee. In N. M. Lambert, I. Hylander, & J. H. Sandoval (Eds.), *Consultee-centered consultation: Improving the quality of professional services in schools and community organizations* (pp. 247–253). Mahwah, NJ: Lawrence Erlbaum.

Kelman, H. C. (1965). Manipulation of human behavior: An ethical dilemma for the social scientist. *Journal of Social Issues, 27,* 31–46.

Knotek, S. E. (2012). Utilizing culturally responsive consultation to support innovation implementation in a rural school. *Consulting Psychology Journal: Practice and Research, 64,* 40–62. doi: 10.1037/a0027993

Kratochwill, T. R., & Bergan, J. R. (1990). *Behavioral consultation in applied settings*. New York, NY: Plenum Press.

Lambert, N. M. (1983). Perspectives on training school-based consultants. In J. Meyers & J. Alpert (Eds.), *Training in consultation: Perspectives from behavioral, mental health, and organizational consultation* (pp. 3–20). Mahwah, NJ: Lawrence Erlbaum.

Lambert, N. M. (2004). Consultee-centered consultation: An international perspective on goals, process, and theory. In N. M. Lambert, I. Hylander, & J. H. Sandoval (Eds.), *Consultee-centered consultation: Improving the quality of professional services in schools and community organizations* (pp. 3–20). Mahwah, NJ: Lawrence Erlbaum.

Lambert, N. M., Hylander, I., & Sandoval, J. (2004). *Consultee-centered consultation: Improving the quality of professional services in schools and community organizations*. Mahwah, NJ: Lawrence Erlbaum.

Mang, M. (2004). Use of metaphors, parables, and anecdotes in consultee-centered consultation: School-based applications. In N. M. Lambert, I. Hylander, & J. H. Sandoval (Eds.), *Consultee-centered consultation: Improving the quality of professional services in schools and community organizations* (pp. 301–312). Mahwah, NJ: Lawrence Erlbaum.

Medway, F. J., & Updyke, J. F. (1985). Meta-analysis of consultation outcome studies. *American Journal of Community Psychology, 13,* 489–505. doi: 10.1007/BF00923263

Newell, M. L. (2012). Transforming knowledge to skill: Evaluating the consultation competence of novice school-based consultants. *Consulting Psychology Journal: Practice and Research, 64,* 8–28. doi: 10.1037/a0027741

Reddy, L. A., Barboza-Whitehead, S., Files, T., & Rubel, E. (2000). Clinical focus of consultation outcome research with children and adolescents. *Special Services in Schools, 16,* 1–22. doi: 10.1300/J008v16n01_01

Rosenfield, S. (1987). *Instructional consultation*. Mahwah, NJ: Lawrence Erlbaum.

Rosenfield, S. (2004). Consultation as dialogue: The right words at the right time. In N. M. Lambert, I. Hylander, & J. H. Sandoval (Eds.), *Consultee-centered consultation: Improving the quality of professional services in schools and community organizations* (pp. 337–347). Mahwah, NJ: Lawrence Erlbaum.

Rosenfield, S. (Ed.). (2012). *Becoming a school consultant: Lessons learned.* New York, NY: Routledge.

Rosenfield, S., & Gravois, T. A. (1996). *Instructional consultation teams: Collaborating for change.* New York, NY: The Guilford Press.

Sandman, L., & Munthe, C. (2010). Shared decision making, paternalism, and patient choice. *Health Care Analysis, 81*, 60–84. doi: 10.10C7/s10728–008–0108–6

Sandoval, J. (1996). Constructivism, consultee-centered consultation, and conceptual change. *Journal of Educational and Psychological Consultation, 7*, 89–97. doi: 10.1207/s1532768xjepc0701_8

Sandoval, J. (2004). Conceptual change in consultee-centered consultation. In N. M. Lambert, I. Hylander, & J. H. Sandoval (Eds.), *Consultee-centered consultation: Improving the quality of professional services in schools and community organizations* (pp. 37–44). Mahwah, NJ: Lawrence Erlbaum.

Sandoval, J. (2014). *An introduction to consultee-centered consultation in the schools: A step-by-step guide to the process and skills.* New York, NY: Routledge.

Sheridan, S. M. (1997). Conceptual and empirical bases of conjoint behavioral consultation. *School Psychology Quarterly, 12*, 119–133. doi: 10.1037/h0088954

Thörn, S. (2004). Allowing ambiguity and listening to the contradictions. In N. M. Lambert, I. Hylander, & J. H. Sandoval (Eds.), *Consultee-centered consultation: Improving the quality of professional services in schools and community organizations* (pp. 279–289). Mahwah, NJ: Lawrence Erlbaum.

Wimmer, A. (2013). *Ethnic boundary making: Institutions, power, networks.* New York, NY: Oxford University Press.

Part VI

RESEARCHING CONSULTATION

19

CONDUCTING SCHOOL-BASED CONSULTATION AS PUBLISHABLE RESEARCH

*Stephen D. Truscott, Moriah A. Kearney, Yanique T. Matthews,
and Kirnel Daniel*

Every day psychologists, mental health professionals, and educational specialists in schools and communities across the globe work with teachers and colleagues to improve the lives of children. These efforts may focus on improving a specific child's academic achievement, implementing evidence-based classroom management practices in an elementary school, or enhancing the intersection of community and school services, but all such efforts have common features, such as sharing interdisciplinary expertise, collaborating with multiple people who work with children, and working within the prevailing social and political contexts. The professionals who engage in such activities use their professional training, knowledge of the local culture, and experience to guide their work (Coyne & Trombetta, 2007; Leon, Campagnaro, & Matos, 2007; Saklofske, Schwean, Harrison, & Mureika, 2007: Zhou, 2007). That combination of professional knowledge and experience is important to successful consultation and collaboration and is valuable to the program participants. It is also valuable to share this knowledge and experience with the global community of professionals who engage in similar work.

Of course, implementing a school-based project that responds to an identified need may be different from implementing the project with the intent to publish and present the results. Professionals who work in schools often experience tension between having our work be informed by educational science and working within the reality of what is possible to implement in the daily practice of schools (Nastasi et al., 2000). The tension between the science and everyday practice can result in what has been called the science–practice or research–practice gap (e.g., Wandersman, 2003), which occurs when common practices do not align with research-based recommendations.

The science–practice gap sometimes complicates school-based consultation projects, but it can also serve as the impetus to work toward useful adaptations of the science to the local school context. Stoner and Green (1992) recommended thinking about each school-based project as a local experiment that employs scientific evidence as a starting point, adapts the scientific knowledge to the local conditions and contexts, and then employs scientific methods to evaluate the results of the experiment. Similarly, Nastasi and Jayasena (2014) reported on a 20-year international public health intervention for school-aged children using Participatory Culture-Specific System Consultation (PCSC), through which scientific evidence is combined with knowledge from the local context. In PCSC, the researchers (consultants) and local stakeholders co-design, -implement, and -evaluate the project using scientific methods.

PCSC was developed for international collaborations in developing nations, but the basic tenets can be applied in many settings. Following similar methods, Research and Development in Organizations (RADIO; Timmins, Bham, McFadyen, & Ward, 2006) was developed as a collaborative action research framework that features fluid negotiations between positivist scientific research approaches and the needs/resources of local educational organizations. Although these approaches differ in scope, each strives to bridge the gap between science and practice by carefully considering the presenting situation, adapting established research findings to local contexts, and then evaluating the results using evidence. Conceptualizing school-based consultation projects as potentially publishable research follows a similar process.

Typically, publishable projects require considerable thought before the project begins to ensure that the work follows a careful design, adopts a clear theoretical model, intentionally includes critical elements of that model, and collects detailed information about the characteristics of the participants and settings. Outcome data collection and analysis strategies also need to be well defined and implemented consistently in research projects. To be publishable, applied projects and studies must include rationales and descriptions for *why* the project was designed in a particular way, *who* the project involved, *how* the project was actually implemented, and *what* results were obtained from all of that effort. Addressing these requirements may seem overwhelming because most professionals who do consultative work in schools already have more than enough to do, but treating consultative practice as research may improve the efficacy and outcomes of that work precisely because it forces one to think carefully about the *why*, *who*, *how*, and *what* elements of the project.

PURPOSE OF THE CHAPTER

This chapter aims to encourage colleagues who conduct consultative and collaborative school-related projects to present and publish their work and thereby contribute to our collective knowledge of consultation practice, theory, and research. Although consultative services are common in practice, there is a clear need for research and theory development to examine and inform our work. The combined efforts of international researchers could begin to address these needs by building from what is already known about school-based consultation; developing some shared definitions of approaches and methods; clarifying differences in theories, perspectives, and practices that distinguish various approaches; and then systematically investigating elements of the consultative and collaborative processes as they are applied in different sociopolitical, educational, and national contexts.

This chapter is intended to provide information about some of the issues that SBC practitioners and researchers should consider as they implement projects. It was based on the first author's knowledge and experiences as an SBC practitioner, researcher, journal editorial board member, and past editor of the *Journal of Educational and Psychological Consultation (JEPC)*. The chapter was informed by our ongoing examination of reviewers' and editors' comments for all general manuscripts submitted to *JEPC* between 2007 and 2013. The co-authors contributed their knowledge and experiences as doctoral school psychology students who are learning to implement SBC practice and research projects, and each added her significant international perspective. Finally, we searched the literature for relevant international perspectives on school consultation and solicited ideas from five consultants who have substantial international experience (Ingrid Hylander, Bonnie Nastasi, Abigail Harris, Chryse Hatzichristou, and Sylvia Rosenfield).

For readers who are experienced researchers, some of the suggestions in the chapter may seem like obvious elements of any research project. Although that may be the case, these elements were commonly overlooked in manuscripts submitted to *JEPC*. We hope we have provided a useful overview and reference about specific things to consider when conducting SBC research and preparing it for professional dissemination. For less experienced readers who are considering implementing SBC projects and conducting publishable research, we hope this chapter will serve as a guide to critical elements to consider and resources to explore as they move toward sharing their findings with colleagues.

DEFINITION OF SCHOOL-BASED CONSULTATION

In this chapter, we embrace a broad definition of school-based consultation (SBC) to include collaborative efforts through which professionals work to improve services provided to children by others. Such a broad definition includes many forms of indirect service to children, including approaches such as traditional school-based consultation (e.g., Curtis & Meyers, 1988), consultation teams (e.g., Rosenfield & Gravois, 1996), behavioral consultation (e.g., Sheridan, Clarke, & Ransom, 2014), teacher professional development (e.g., Villegas-Reimers, 2003), coaching (e.g., Denton & Hasbrouck, 2009), Consultee-Centered Consultation (e.g., Hylander, 2004), Wagner's adapted consultation model (Wagner, 2000), organizational consultation (e.g., Truscott, Cosgrove, Meyers, & Eidle-Barkman, 2000), Participatory Culture-Specific System Consultation (Nastasi, Varjas, Bernstein, & Jayasena, 2000), and professional collaboration (Cook & Friend, 2010). We also include consultation approaches based on public health or population-based models (e.g., Nastasi, 2004), which may be better suited to some national, social, and cultural contexts or specific issues.

Adopting such a broad definition serves multiple purposes. First, the potential contexts and circumstances faced by international consultants vary so much between, within, and across nations that a broad definition better captures the scope of the work undertaken by our readers. Second, we want to encourage indirect service providers and researchers from multiple perspectives and fields to communicate with each other. Finally, although there are certainly commonalities across existing indirect service delivery models, there are few, if any, clear and widely accepted operational definitions for many of the key elements of these different approaches. The lack of clear operational definitions presents many challenges to researchers, who must describe their efforts in replicable terms. The lack of clear operational definitions also provides opportunities to adopt flexible approaches that bridge various models. In any event, until some universal classification system is devised, we suggest that researchers clearly describe and define the critical components of their specific indirect service procedures for publication and professional communication purposes.

RESOURCES FOR SCHOOL-BASED CONSULTATION RESEARCH

The *Handbook of Research in School Consultation* (Erchul & Sheridan, 2014) is an excellent resource when designing and conducting SBC projects and studies. It is easily the most comprehensive source for detailed information on SBC research in the United States. The detailed sections and chapters cover specific methodological issues, consultation approaches, and research considerations that will be helpful to consultants implementing projects and may be critical as the work moves forward toward dissemination. The chapters and commentaries also suggest topics and research approaches that can address gaps in the literature, which may be of particular interest to doctoral students and emerging scholars. SBC theory development has been progressing for over 40 years in the U.S., and the handbook reflects that maturity. However, the *Handbook of Research in School Consultation* (Erchul & Sheridan, 2014) does not specifically offer an international perspective.

The *Handbook of International School Consultation* (Hatzichristou & Rosenfield, this volume) provides multiple perspectives and approaches that are tailored to international work in a wide variety of contexts and is the first large-scale compilation of school-based consultation knowledge to specifically target an international audience. It is an excellent resource for future consultation projects and research. There is also a body of SBC research and scholarly literature about individual projects, countries, and collaborations that provides important international perspectives on SBC. For example, Hatzichristou (2002; Greece), Kasler and Elias (2012: Israel), Kennedy, Frederickson, and Monsen (2008: Great Britain), Wagner (2000: Great Britain), and Thornberg (2014: Sweden) address sociopolitical, educational, and cultural contexts in their respective nations. *Consultee-Centered Consultation: Improving the Quality of Professional Services in Schools and Community Organizations* (Lambert, Hylander, & Sandoval, 2004) is an excellent resource for researchers interested in consultee-centered consultation, and it includes chapters from prominent international researchers (e.g., Hylander and Hatzichristou).

Professional conferences and special interest groups are remarkable sources for information and collaboration. The International School Psychology Association (ISPA) annual conference convenes each year in a different nation, and ISPA hosts special interest meetings at U.S. conferences. ISPA events present formal and informal information exchange and networking opportunities. The Consultee-Centered Consultation special interest group also often holds meetings associated with major school psychology conferences and as separate special interest conferences (http://communities.nasponline.org/communities/community-home?CommunityKey=3cfd43f6–5593–4c68–8e91–0b1dc9528ee5).

If travel is not possible, then low-cost ways to view conference proceedings and interact with other researchers are available via the web. Increasingly, conferences offer virtual sessions and archived presentations that can be accessed anywhere. We have also used web-based research networks such as ResearchGate (www.researchgate.net) to make contacts and access articles that inform our work. Organizations such as the National Association of School Psychologists often have online communities that can facilitate international collaboration and support for SBC. For example, the Society for the Study of School Psychology (SSSP) Early Career Forum offers essays about succeeding in academic careers (www.ssspresearch.org/earlycareerforum). Such tools have incredible potential and may be particularly important for researchers working with limited resources.

Large organizations such as the American Psychological Association (APA) and American Educational Research Association (AERA) have international divisions (e.g., APA Division 52) and many of the subdivisions have international interest groups. APA Division 16 (school psychology) recently developed important international initiatives (e.g., www.apadivisions.org/division-16/leadership/working-groups/globalization/index.aspx). Some of these organizations offer small research grants targeted toward international work. Notably, ISPA and the SSSP recently initiated small research grants to support international researchers (http://ssspresearch.org/awards?quicktabs_7=3).

Overall, SBC researchers can enhance the quality of their consultation and research by accessing resources that consolidate the relevant SBC scientific literature, reviewing the scholarly work specific to their focal county and local culture, and facilitating meetings with colleagues and potential collaborators at conferences, special interest group meetings, and online.

CONSIDERING THE WHY, WHO, HOW, AND WHAT OF CONSULTATION PROJECTS

In this section we will examine how strategically considering the *Why*, *Who*, *How*, and of consultation projects can guide project and research decisions to be more productive and more likely to be publishable. For the purposes of this chapter, a consultation *project* is a service provider's response to a specific presenting issue or case. A consultation *approach* consists of the consultation strategies and techniques that the service provider chooses to employ in a specific consultation project. A consultation *model* informs and generally guides the service provider's work but may be superseded in a specific case. For example, a consultant brought in to assist with a crisis may choose to respond with a *project* using an expert and directive *approach* to deal with the immediate situation, even though she usually works from a consultee-centered collaborative *model*.

Determining the SBC Approach by Considering Why

Before starting a consultation project, it is important to think strategically about the approach you will take and *why* that specific approach makes sense for your goals in that context under those circumstances. After carefully assessing the presenting issues and contexts and then considering the intervention options, consultants must choose a particular consultation approach. To do that, it is useful to think about the interventions, programs, organizational processes, or technologies that consultants provide as *innovations* (Wandersman, 2003; Wandersman et al., 2008). Consultants who explicitly identify the consultation problem, strategically select an innovation that addresses that problem, and then consider how best to transfer the innovation to the setting can develop a clear rationale for choosing a particular consultation approach. They choose that specific approach because it allows them to address the problem using the preferred innovation. For example, if the presenting problem they have identified is an individual child's behavior and the innovation is a behavioral intervention plan, then the consultant may choose a behavioral consultation approach (Sheridan et al., 2014) that is designed to transfer a specific behavioral intervention plan (the *innovation*) to the child's teacher. If the identified presenting problem is improving how all teachers in a school link assessment data to instructional interventions, then the consultants may choose an instructional consultation team approach (ICT; Rosenfield & Gravois, 1996), because ICT and its attendant instructional technologies are designed to be school-wide innovations.

Consultation, public health, and community psychology researchers and theorists have considered innovation transfer (e.g., Nastasi et al., 2000; Timmins et al., 2006; Wandersman, 2003; Wandersman et al., 2008) and developed useful transfer models. Essentially, consultants who strive to implement innovations can design their consultation activities on a continuum from *research-to-practice* or *source-based* models to *community-centered* or *user-based* models (Wandersman et al., 2008). Research-to-practice models start from the scientific evidence and seek to have consultees and organizations implement the intervention, curriculum, or process as closely as possible to the original design. These models are sometimes referred to as *expert* approaches to consultation in which the consultants have expertise and prescribe an evidence-based response for the presenting problem. Manualized interventions that prescribe specific steps following explicit protocols are one form of expert-driven innovation. At the other end of the continuum, community-centered models seek to work with consultees to understand the problem in context, design acceptable innovations based on both scientific evidence and local knowledge, and then implement and evaluate the site-specific innovation. Action research is an example of a community-based approach. Such models are sometimes categorized as *collaborative* approaches to consultation. Both approaches have advantages and disadvantages, and many consultation models fall somewhere between the ends of the continuum. Various situations may call for more emphasis on expert consultation models or a more collaborative approach, depending on the nature of the problem, goals for the consultation, and organizational/cultural/national context.

The consultants' assumptions about innovation transfer are particularly important to examine before undertaking international collaborations. Consultants may assume that interventions and processes developed in their home country can easily transfer to different national and cultural contexts. However, such assumptions can easily undermine the effort (Williams & Staulters, 2014). Carefully considering the salient aspects of the situation before the project starts and developing a rationale for why you should adopt a specific consultation approach for the situation is always a good idea because you can use that information to match the consultation and research approaches to meet the local conditions.

The Sociopolitical Context

In Gerald Caplan's (1970) account of the beginning of mental health consultation (MHC), he described the situation in the new state of Israel after World War II. As large numbers of children immigrated to Israel, often after having suffered wartime trauma, Caplan and a small staff of mental health workers were overwhelmed by the responsibility of providing mental health services to thousands of children in widespread institutional settings (Caplan, Caplan, & Erchul, 1995). Caplan's answer to the impossibility of serving these children directly was to develop MHC as a process through which mental health professionals worked with adult caregivers to help them understand and address the children's presenting issues. When we think about why Caplan developed MHC, it is clear that the context required an approach focused on working with adults because he practiced in an emerging nation with very few specialists and limited resources. The emphasis was on helping children, but the method was to do so indirectly by providing consultation services to adults, and the strategies associated with MHC target these adult caregivers.

What is relevant and accurate in one context, however, may or may not apply to other situations. Contemporary consultants sometimes work in rich and mature educational contexts with ample services and an array of supporting educational specialists. But, the consultation theories and approaches developed in such settings may not be applicable in others. For example, direct behavioral approaches to consultation (e.g., Watson & Robinson, 1996) that focus on outcomes for individual and small groups of children, including functional behavioral analysis, intensive behavioral interventions, ongoing measurement, and performance monitoring of the teacher's implementation may be possible in some U.S. and other resource-rich schools, but they are clearly not universally applicable, not even in many resource-rich countries. Consultants working in other situations may instead focus on socially and culturally specific issues such as improving instruction for children who live in rural communities with few resources or professional development for educators who have limited training (e.g., Watkins, Hall, & Worrell, 2014; Williams & Staulters, 2014). Such circumstances require broad efforts and measures of school progress. The sociopolitical context should be a critical determinant of the consultation approach adopted, and one should be careful about making assumptions as the sociopolitical context can and often does vary substantially within and across schools and communities.

Societal values and beliefs also inform consultation practices and research. Generally, the U.S. society values, among other things, individualism, merit-based advancement, market-driven economic principles, competition, and technology (Fischer, 2008; Williams, 1970). The U.S. inclination to value individualism and merit-based advancement influences education by focusing attention on society's obligation to provide equal opportunity to individuals, who are then responsible for taking advantage of the opportunities (or not). The society is consequently responsible for providing equal opportunity, but not necessarily for addressing social disparities or social agendas (equity). In this view, individual students advance by taking advantage of the opportunities through their work ethic and natural talents.

These beliefs influence SBC research by establishing parameters under which such research can be accomplished. Most SBC in the U.S. addresses improvement of children's basic skills, such as improving reading skill and appropriate behavior, rather than more esoteric issues such as enhancing happiness or life satisfaction. In part, this basic skills focus is driven by our legal and social contexts. To cite a famous special education court decision, U.S. schools are not required to provide a Cadillac when a Chevrolet will do (*Doe v. Board of Education of Tullahoma City Schools* [1993] as cited in Thomas & Rapport, 1998). Whether such policies or the educational methods linked to them best serve the needs of rapidly diversifying populations, children from minority racial/ethnic groups, impoverished children, or new immigrants is a much debated question, both in the U.S. (e.g., Bon, 2012; De Vito, 2007) and globally (e.g., Gilmour & Soudien, 1994; Organization for Economic Co-operation and Development, 2012). Recent publications in SBC reflect interest in moving research and theory to address broad issues in education and society (e.g., multicultural consultation, [Chapter 7 in this volume or Ingraham, 2004]; social emotional learning [Kasler & Elias, 2012]; and social justice [Shriberg & Fenning, 2009]).

The U.S. societal values outlined previously are different from those experienced in other parts of the world. Many European countries, for example, are social democracies that emphasize collective societal responsibility over individualism and have stronger governmental interest in addressing social disparities (e.g., Sweden: www.everyculture.com/Sa-Th/Sweden.html). We have seen these values reflected in published consultation research that features collaborative efforts between schools and local town or city government services (e.g., Kasler & Elias, 2012; Thornberg, 2014). Consultation research conducted in other countries also often includes planning for multiple factors that are generally not included in U.S. efforts. For example, international projects often include nongovernmental organization partners in additional to government institutions and schools (e.g., Nastasi & Jayasena, 2014) and must include attention to health and public issues that impact school access and attendance (Lockheed & Harris, 2005).

Such sociocultural differences can and do create contexts that influence the approaches, foci, expected outcomes, processes, and research methods that are used in consultation work throughout the world. Research about these different approaches and contexts has the potential to enrich our general knowledge of the consultative and collaborative processes and to add valuable information to consultation practice and research methods internationally. International consultation approaches based on public health and population models, for example, can inform researchers working on large scale problems everywhere, while treatment-focused approaches employed in resource-rich countries can inform efforts for specific populations in other nations.

The Scientific Context

Much foundational research in education and psychology was based on naturalistic observation and philosophical thought leading to theory development that was subsequently applied to the general population and tested through research. For example, Freud, Piaget, and Erikson all developed their theories based on observations of limited samples of people, intensive thought about the meaning of their observations, and explication of their theories as representative of general behavior. This naturalistic approach is derived from fields like biology, philosophy, and anthropology. It is especially useful when the studied phenomena are complex and relatively unknown. A competing approach to educational and psychological research comes from what are sometimes called the "hard sciences" such as physics, chemistry, and mathematics. This experimental model also contributed foundational psychology research from theorists such as Wundt, Hall, Cattell, and Skinner. Experimental psychology relies on accurate measurement and experimental manipulation of the studied phenomena to determine causal relationships between variables.

The naturalistic and experimental approaches have competed throughout the history of psychological and educational research and continue to do so in multiple venues, including SBC research. A central issue in the debate between experimentalists and naturalists centers on competing demands for experimental control derived from reducing external variables versus the need to understand human behavior in the full context of social settings. Experimentalists argue that such reduction is necessary to accurately establish causality, and naturalists argue that reduction changes the context of the studied phenomenon so much that it neither accurately depicts what occurs in actual contexts nor reflects the connections that exist between various stimuli and variables (e.g., Hylander, 2003). School-based consultation and related researchers face these competing demands routinely.

Although the debate about experimental versus naturalistic approaches continues, there is a clear preference in U.S. psychology-related journals for experimental studies and research that features careful definitions of the variables and sophisticated statistical analyses. Even journals that accept qualitative studies may publish many more articles from quantitative paradigms, in part because more research from the behavioral perspective is produced in the U.S. For example, in a recent article commemorating the 25th anniversary of the *Journal of Educational and Psychological Consultation*, Truscott, Lopez, Fish, and Margolis (2015) reported that 44% of the applied research articles focused on behavioral consultation compared to 16% for collaborative models, and only one research study specifically examined consultee-centered consultation.

The familiar scientific method depends on developing constructs that are valid, reliable, measurable, and observable and on being able to isolate problems and solutions enough to be able to accurately attribute causality to the experiment. This scientific method is the essence of both the evidence-based practice and the problem-solving approaches that have been central to SBC research in the U.S. since the 1970s (e.g., Bergan & Tombari, 1976; Frank & Kratochwill, 2014; Stoiber & Waas, 2002). The "gold standard" for such research is the randomized controlled trial (What Works Clearinghouse Procedures and Standards Handbook [Version 3.0] p. 11, U.S. Department of Education, March 2013) which is increasingly employed in large-scale educational research and is now used in the U.S. as the primary criterion to establish an educational intervention as evidence-based. Consequently, research that features objective and reliable measures, clearly defined key constructs that can be isolated to determine causality, replicable procedures, and a means to test the significance of the results is generally favored over more naturalistic research or descriptions of applied work that is often "messy" compared to controlled experiments.

However, the nascent state of SBC research and complexity of consultation-related processes create a problem for researchers seeking to conduct experimental studies of SBC. We do not yet have clearly defined key constructs nor objective and reliable measures for most of the work that we do. Consequently, there is a need for much more research from a variety of paradigms (Hylander, 2003; Truscott et al., 2015).

The following is a brief review of just a few gaps in the school-based consultation literature. Naturalistic approaches, such as ethnographic and qualitative research, are needed to develop grounded theories of the consultative and collaborative processes (e.g., Hylander, 2003). There is a clear and continuing need for analog and simulation studies of the consultation and collaborative processes (e.g., Newell, Newell, & Looser, 2013), because theories and approaches need to be tested before it makes sense to expend all of the time and resources required for an actual consultation project. Small-*n* approaches are needed to investigate specific elements of the consultation process. For example, the impact of consultee choice (Andersen & Daly, 2013) and collaborative versus expert consultation (Kelleher, Riley-Tillman, & Power, 2008) on intervention integrity have both been examined using innovative small-*n* experimental designs. Careful program evaluations are needed to report on outcomes of indirect service efforts and provide ideas about approaches that can be investigated further. Large studies of professional development projects and similar efforts are needed to better understand how elements of SBC can be scaled-up to address systemic issues (e.g., Truscott et al., 2012). Mixed-method (Johnson & Onwuegbuzie, 2004) studies are needed to understand the relationships between consultation processes, participant reactions, and student outcomes. There is also critical need to test existing approaches and processes in different national, social, cultural, and multicultural contexts as we cannot reasonably assume that theories developed in some contexts will translate to all. In summary, there is a tremendous need for SBC research using a variety of research paradigms. Clearly, opportunities exist for practitioners and researchers throughout the world to contribute to our collective understanding of school-based consultation and collaboration.

Identifying Who *Is Involved in SBC Research*

At minimum, there are three sets of participants involved in consultation and collaborative work in schools: the consultants, the consultees, and the clients. Often, there are more than three sets of participants, particularly if the project involves community, school, nongovernmental agency, and international partners. Implementing successful consultative and collaborative projects requires explicit attention to the characteristics, situations, and preparation of all three groups. The consultative and collaborative training, experiences, preferences, and beliefs of the consultants are important because the consultants must implement the consultation. Considering the consultants' need for training in consultation methods, adult learning, and how schools function before the project is implemented can prevent many problems later on. Similarly, considering the existing knowledge, working conditions, inclinations, and collaborative experiences of the consultees before the project begins can identify potential consultee needs and social contexts, possible consultation strategies, and contextually-relevant client-centered interventions beforehand (e.g., Knotek, 2012; Timmins et al., 2006). For example, intensive behavioral consultation models directed at individual students may be evidence-based, but may not be appropriate in a school with few resources, large class sizes, and teachers who have limited preparation (Watkins et al., 2014; Williams & Staulters, 2014). Carefully considering the characteristics of the children can provide critical information about the types of interventions that are needed and the potential sociocultural impact of intervention approaches. The need to carefully consider the circumstances of the people involved in SBC is important in any project, but this is especially pertinent when the consultants, consultees, and clients come from different nations or sociocultural backgrounds.

Research publications and presentations require complete descriptions of each of the three participant groups (APA, 2010). In addition, any special information about school conditions, organizational culture, and previous educational experiences is important to include because such contextual factors may impinge on the current effort. Such descriptions can appear in either the participants' section of the manuscript or as a specific subsection on the setting.

Determining How *the SBC Research Project Will Be Implemented*

Successful SBC projects are implemented strategically and purposefully because different indirect service approaches accomplish different outcomes. Meyers' (1989, 2002) adaptation of Caplan's (1970) classification of consultation targets as client-centered (student-centered), consultee-centered (teacher-centered), or system-centered can be useful to consider as the project is designed. In this framework, client-centered work is focused on changing children's behavior; consultee-centered work is focused on changing teachers' skills, knowledge, or beliefs; and system-centered work is focused on changing some aspect of the organization that will improve functioning and services to children. Each of these targets requires a different consultation approach, and each approach is comprised of specific techniques and activities.

Once the consultation target and approach are determined, consultants must attend to *how* they actually conduct the activities associated with that approach. Too often researchers attend to what they want the consultees to do but pay much less attention to their own activities and consultative strategies. It is important to remember that consultation is an *intentional* process. In other words, just as researchers might think about how well teachers implement a targeted intervention (i.e., intervention fidelity), they must think about the fidelity of their own consultative efforts. Consultation activities, regardless of theoretical model, should follow specific sequences in much the same way that therapists strategically guide the counseling process with an individual. For example, organizational consultation begins with needs assessment, behavioral consultation begins with problem identification, and mental health consultation begins with an assessment of the consultee's needs (i.e., lack of knowledge, skill, confidence, or objectivity). If these steps are not completed, then the possibility for positive outcomes is diminished.

For SBC research, it is important to document how the project was implemented and whether and why any deviations occurred. There are multiple ways to accomplish this documentation, depending on the research approach that was adopted. For experimental research and other approaches, periodic checklists or debriefing measures can assess the integrity with which the consultation plan is being implemented (e.g., Noell & Gansle, 2014). Such methods allow researchers to be confident that the plan was implemented as intended and to attribute causality. For naturalistic research, "thick" descriptions of the implementation provide documentation of the consultation process and often allow rich analysis of the contextual relationship between the consultants' and participants' actions and interactions (Meyers, Truscott, Meyers, Varjas, & Kim, 2014). Documenting how the project was implemented increases confidence that the findings are attributable to the consultation project, allows other researchers to learn from your project, and is critical to moving SBC research forward.

Identifying **What** *the SBC Project Will Accomplish*

Carefully designed SBC projects that consider the sociocultural and educational contexts address the needs and situations of the people involved and that follow an identified approach that is implemented well have a better chance of achieving the project goals. It is important to consider exactly *what* those goals are as you design the project in order to determine how you will assess your progress and outcomes. For example, if your goals are to introduce a reading instructional innovation that: (a) teachers use to (b) improve instruction for struggling students, then you need to assess both (a) that the teachers used the innovation and (b) that instruction improved for the struggling students. There are multiple ways to measure each of those goals, and your choices will be governed by the resources you have and what is possible in the context. Direct measures of the targeted behavior are the most credible, but indirect measures can also be employed. In this example, a direct but resource-intensive measure of "teacher use" could be classroom observations to see if the teacher is implementing the innovation. Less resource-intensive but still direct measures could include examining a sample of the teachers' lesson plans (artifacts) or having the teachers complete daily checklists that identify the steps of the innovation and where those steps were completed in the lessons. These are just examples; there are many possibilities from which to choose. Interviews, focus groups, and surveys are useful ways to collect the teachers' perceptions of the innovation, but for the example goal of "teacher use," such self-reports are less credible than direct measures of behavior.

There are also measurement decisions to be made for "improved instruction." The most credible would be some measure of the targeted students' reading progress that was sensitive to short-term changes and was used to compare baseline (before the innovation) to post-innovation data, such as oral reading fluency (Hosp, Hosp, & Howell, 2007). Such a measure actually exceeds the research goal of "improved instruction" because it would also provide evidence about whether the students benefited from the instruction. Large-scale academic achievement assessments, such as yearly school-wide tests, would not be as useful for the previous example because such tests usually do not measure specific skills in detail, are not as sensitive to short-term growth, and are only administered occasionally (so you must wait a long time between data points). Another way to approach the "improved instruction" goal would be to compare key instructional behaviors at baseline and postinnovation. Targeted behaviors could include items such as the length of time devoted to reading instruction per day or the inclusion of direct instruction of reading vocabulary, depending on the specific project goal. Such an approach would be most defensible if the selected innovation had very strong evidence that it was effective with the types of students targeted in the study. This type of measure is limited, however, as no evidence is collected that the "improved instruction" actually benefited the targeted students.

Collecting goal-related consultation outcome data entails multiple decisions and is subject to many trade-offs between the ideal and what is possible with the available resources in the setting. Yet, identifying exactly *what* the project is designed to accomplish sets the parameters for what data are collected at what points in the process. It may seem obvious, but the data collected should be guided by the research questions, which should guide the design. Unfortunately, we have seen many research manuscripts that suffered from having research questions that were not answerable with the data that were collected.

Attending to the proposed consultee-focused activities requires collecting data on the consultant-consultee interactions and strategies and assessment of changes in the consultees' behavior, beliefs, knowledge, and/or skills. Consultee self-reports can be reasonable sources for some such data and can be collected relatively easily via surveys and focus groups. However, observable data provide greater confidence and pre- and postproject observations of consultee behavior and/or artifacts provide good measures of consultee change. For example, if the SBC project is directed at increasing the teachers' knowledge of classroom management, then observations focused on the classroom management techniques the teachers actually use or artifacts collected from their classrooms (e.g., classroom management plans) will provide good evidence about whether the goal has been met.

Student data (i.e., the clients) can be important to collect because the ultimate goal for indirect service is to improve the students' lives. Outcome goals can be set for individual students, classrooms, or systems depending on the scope of the project. For example, if the project goal is to improve a small group of students' behavior, then classroom observations of the specific and well-defined behaviors (such as initiating positive social contact with peers during recess) are the gold standard. Unstructured teacher and parent reports collected occasionally are less credible for research purposes because they are subject to bias. Naturally occurring data, such as discipline referrals, attendance, or results of scheduled tests, can function as measures of student outcomes for some projects. Overall, the idea is to purposefully match the SBC approach, method, design, and data collected to the project purpose and research questions.

THE CRUCIAL, BUT OFTEN NEGLECTED, CONSULTATION PROCESS DATA

Consultee behavior is only part of the story. Describing how consultation activities were implemented to result in changes in the teachers' behaviors is the sometimes neglected heart of consultation research. There is a critical need for consultation research that examines both whatever innovation is implemented with the students (or other clients) and the consultation "intervention" used with the teachers (or other consultees). It is important, as noted earlier, that consultation researchers attend to the fidelity of their efforts. Without documentation that the consultation process, activities, and interpersonal variables met key conditions of the approach, one cannot attribute the results to the consultation project.

There are several strong lines of school consultation-related behavioral research focused on performance monitoring as a means to increase teachers' fidelity to an intervention plan (e.g., Kaufman, Codding, Markus, Tryon, & Kyse, 2013; Sanetti & Collier-Meek, 2014). In these studies, the consultants provide explicit feedback and corrective action to the teachers as they implement an expert-designed child intervention. Participatory consultation models (Nastasi et al., 2000; Timmins et al., 2006) also typically include descriptions of the consultation intervention. There are fewer such studies using other consultation approaches, but some are available (e.g., Hylander, 2004; Truscott et al., 2000). Teacher use and consultation method evidence are valuable for more than just research purposes. In most cases, such data are actionable if collected as the project progresses because the consultants can adjust their strategies as needed if progress toward the goals is not occurring.

Moving Your Work toward Publication

SBC projects that are carefully designed and implemented should be shared with the international community of practitioners and researchers who do similar work. Following the guidelines above provides the basic elements needed to conduct work that is publishable, but there are additional steps to move your effort towards actual publication. The remainder of this chapter provides information that is important to consider as you prepare your manuscript to share with international colleagues.

Publication requires careful definitions and explanation of exactly what process the researchers studied, careful description of the participants in the process (consultants, teachers, and children), detailed explanation of the procedures used, and clear, explicit outcome measures (teacher change, student outcomes, organizational improvements) (APA, 2010). For international work, careful descriptions of the educational context are also required since the audience may not be familiar with the differences between the studied educational system and what they typically experience (see, e.g., Harris and Ueda, this volume, for examples of what to address). Critical contextual variables such as teacher training, class size, the ebb and flow of a school year, and school organizational structures may vary considerably across the world. If the authors are not familiar with presenting SBC research for publication, then it makes sense to identify similar articles that were previously published to use as examples to guide the manuscript preparation.

Table 19.1 lists key elements of a SBC research study in the general order they would be presented in a research manuscript. It is intended as an outline of the important elements to include in a research manuscript and as a guide to the types of information that should be included. The exact order is not fixed, and it should be modified as needed to present the research as clearly as possible. Readers are referred to Chapter 2 of the *Publication Manual of the American Psychological Association* (6th ed.) (APA, 2010) for a more detailed presentation of the information in Table 19.1. Condensed information from the APA *Publication Manual* is available for free at https://owl.english.purdue.edu/owl/resource/560/01/.

Table 19.1 Key Elements of a School-Based Consultation Research Publication

Introduction

Organization	The introduction should flow from larger issues and general findings to specific issues and the need for research about the exact topic of the study. In other words, the reader should be able to reasonably predict the research problem and questions before they are provided.
Review of previous research	The literature review should be thorough and include the most important previous work that is related to the current study; including international studies. Seminal works should be cited. Relevant work from the last 10 years should be highlighted, if possible.
	Ideas informed by previous research studies should be differentiated from ideas informed by theoretical writing. When citing research studies, include some indication of the type of research (e.g., clinical trial, small-n, experimental, qualitative case study). Be careful not to overstate the generalizability of previous research.
Key constructs	Key constructs should be defined clearly and thoroughly.
Statement of the problem	The introduction should culminate in a clear and specific statement of the problem being examined and the process being employed in the research.
Research questions	Research questions vary between approaches (e.g., qualitative vs. quantitative), but the introduction should conclude with clear research questions (or a research statement) that will be addressed by the study. Be careful to make sure the research questions are answerable by the research that was conducted.

Method

Context	Describe the context of the study including relevant detail about the educational setting such as the school system (e.g., grade levels included, school year, and national educational requirements), demographics of the groups served, and existing support services available. When the context varies substantially from that of other nations, it is useful to make comparisons.
Participants	In SBC research there are three groups of participants: (1) the consultees (e.g., teachers); (2) the clients (children or students); and (3) the consultants. Describe each group and include demographic and other relevant details such as the teachers' training, experience, and familiarity with consultation; the student socio-economic status; and the consultants' training, experience, and theoretical orientation.
Explicate assumptions	Make your assumptions explicit and defend them, for example, that teachers in three different schools are similar enough to group their results together, or that results from several different consultants can be combined because they followed the same core procedures.
Consultation procedures	Describe the theoretical orientation of the consultation approach (e.g., behavioral, consultee-centered, organizational) and the consultation procedures employed (with details) used in the approach (e.g., frequency and descriptions of the consultation meetings, problem-solving sequence).
Fidelity to consultation procedures	Measures of the fidelity to the process are needed to establish that the participants did what the researchers intended them to do. In SBC research there are often two categories of fidelity: (1) consultation procedures (i.e., did the consultants follow the intended consultation procedures?) and (2) client intervention procedures (i.e., did the teachers implement the interventions derived from the consultation).
Measures	Describe the measures used in the research, including psychometric information when available (e.g., reliability and validity of the measures). If the measures are study-specific, describe how they were developed and how they correspond to key research constructs. Include citations that support the use of the measures when possible.

Research design	Describe the research design, a rationale for using that design, and citations to support the procedures. Qualitative studies often require more explanation of the design as reviewers may be less familiar with qualitative approaches.
Research procedures	Describe how the data were collected, when, and under what circumstances.
Analyses	Use accepted analysis procedures. Describe the analyses used and a rationale for those analyses. Make explicit analysis decisions and support the decisions with citations. In qualitative research, describe and support the analysis procedures (e.g., coding and construction of themes) and provide information about the "trustworthiness" of the analyses (e.g., interrater coding agreement, triangulation of findings). Use citations to support your analyses.

Results

Present clear data	Use tables as appropriate, with enough information for reviewers to independently verify the results. With statistical procedures, include measures of statistical significance and effect (e.g., effect size) as appropriate. With qualitative data, include quotes and triangulation data to support the interpreted results. With small-n data, use accepted methods to present and interpret visual data.
Limit interpretations	Describe what the results are, but interpretations about what the results mean are presented in the discussion section, not the results section.
Qualitative exception	In some qualitative research, the results and discussion are presented together. This approach is acceptable if it is made explicit, but keep in mind that not all journal reviewers are familiar with qualitative approaches.

Discussion

Start with most important interpretation	After an introductory paragraph, begin the discussion with the most global findings from the research and support the global findings with more detailed interpretations.
Interpret the results in the context of previous research	Refer to the literature review and interpret the current findings in the context of what was previously known or thought. Explicate how the current results confirm, refute, or extend the information cited in the literature review.
Do not overinterpret results	It is common to want to extend the results beyond what it is possible to "know with certainty" from any given research study. Be careful not to do that, and use tentative language in the discussion unless you are certain of the result. The generalizability of findings is particularly prone to overinterpretation.
Implications	The implications for research should be integrated with previous literature and include some discussion of what still needs to be investigated. Be cautious with the implications for practice unless you are certain the results are generalizable to other situations.
Limitations	All research has limitations. Include a frank discussion of the limitations of the research that demonstrates that you understand what the current research can and cannot contribute to the literature. The limitations need not be exhaustive, but they should include the primary issues.

Special Considerations When Conducting and Publishing SBC Research in Different Contexts

Tremendous opportunities exist for conducting international SBC research that adds important and useful information to our collective efforts to improve the lives of children. There are also challenges that must be addressed for international SBC research to reach its potential. We will address some of these opportunities and challenges in this section of the chapter, which is derived from our own experiences and from ideas shared with us by the highly accomplished colleagues we consulted. We are grateful to Ingrid Hylander, Bonnie Nastasi, Abigail Harris, Chryse Hatzichristou, and Sylvia Rosenfield for sharing their thoughts and observations with us.

OPPORTUNITIES

SBC Researchers, Educators, and Children Need Diverse Perspectives

Researchers from the U.S. produce the majority of SBC publications and often employ well-developed SBC approaches, research designs, and theory. That combined knowledge has value to international SBC practitioners and researchers. However, that does not mean the ideas and approaches presented by researchers in the U.S. are always correct or complete. Researchers from other nations have also investigated SBC and developed knowledge that is important to share with researchers in the U.S. Educating children to become well-rounded world citizens who are fulfilled, contributing, and mentally healthy adults is an incredibly complex process about which there are many opinions and approaches, but few absolutes. SBC researchers across the globe are attempting to find ways to improve the educational process for individual children, groups of children, and schools as organizations in a large, highly complex, and rapidly changing global environment. Publishing multiple perspectives from differing national and societal contexts may give SBC researchers different ways to think about SBC, different approaches to take with teachers and children in their own countries, and refinements on SBC processes and approaches that enhance their efforts. Without information from diverse settings, approaches, and underlying concepts, there is a danger that researchers who share the same values and beliefs can fall into a circular epistemological trap. Exposure to a broad array of perspectives about SBC will add value to our conceptualizations about how to best help children via indirect services.

Publishing and Presenting SBC Research Expands the Audience and Potential Impact of the Work

Researchers who publish their findings and ideas want the broadest possible audience to increase the opportunities for others to be influenced by their ideas, approaches, and findings. SBC work that is published, particularly in premier journals, increases the potential impact of that work. Respected journals are widely indexed in leading research databases, which further enhances the likelihood that SBC research will be seen by other researchers.

The increasing availability of electronic search capabilities, such as Google Scholar, improves access to researchers throughout the world. We are cautious, but intrigued by the possibilities of open access publishing outlets such as the *Electronic Journal of Research in Educational Psychology* and *Health Psychology Report* as vehicles to increase and improve international communication about SBC practice and research. Similarly, electronic networks, websites, and search engines have the potential to link researchers and facilitate collaboration to develop SBC theory and practice.

Publishing International SBC Research Expands Opportunities for International Collaboration

Researchers and universities now actively seek opportunities for international collaboration. Such collaborations are sought across the globe and are valued in academics' tenure and promotion decisions. Accessing the broad base of potential research collaborators expands the expertise and resources available to global researchers beyond what might be available in their immediate settings. Knowledge gained from such collaborations has the potential to benefit children, educators, and schools in all of the collaborators' home countries.

Such collaborations involve complexities and challenges, to be sure, but we believe the potential benefits far outweigh to potential concerns. Many universities have international offices that provide support for such collaborations. Organizations such as SSSP and ISPA offer small grants to support international work. Governmental and nongovernmental organizations also offer potential support for international SBC researchers. For example, the Foundation for Educational Exchange between Canada and the United States of America (Fulbright Canada; www.fulbright.ca/) and the U.S Institute of International Education (Fulbright Program: www.iie.org/fulbright) support international research exchanges and collaborations (see also Harris & Ueda, this volume).

CHALLENGES
Lack of Existing Consultation Services and Training
SBC services are not always available in all countries or to all schools within any given nation, even in nations that are resource-rich. Similarly, professional training in consultation methods and research is not universally required or even available for school professionals. It is difficult to conduct SBC research if the services or training are not available. There may be opportunities to work with community-based organizations or universities to develop programs that provide such training and services on a case-by-case basis, but doing so will take concerted effort, planning, and resource development (see Kassay & Terjesen, this volume, on the development of such a program in Vietnam). Similarly, education and special education are not universally provided to all children. In such cases, there is a need for systems development and policy to address the need for universal access to education before SBC research is possible.

Differing Cultural, Social, Political, and Practice Beliefs and Agendas
International efforts to improve education may enlist consultants from different nations and cultures that have disparate beliefs about fundamental social structures such as basic human rights, the role of religion in society, and girls' rights to education. This can result in clashes between the agendas of the external consultants and the hosts. Such differences are important to consider and resolve before the work begins but will likely continue to be potential sources of concern throughout the project and require ongoing communication between the project participants to reduce the likelihood that conflicts will become intractable. Similarly, international consultants may be accustomed to practices that are quite different from those of the host country (Rosenfield, 2014), such as prescriptive versus collaborative professional services. Again, communication and humility are warranted as the partners work to resolve conflicts. Overall, it is critical that international consultants temper their theoretical and cultural epistemologies with the understanding that context matters and remain open to learning new and important information from all of the participants (see, e.g., Nastasi, this volume; Nastasi & Jayasena, 2014).

Language Differences

Differences between conversational second language skill and formal academic writing present an ongoing impediment to publishing global SBC research. It is one thing to be able to write and speak conversationally in a second language, but it is quite another to write in the formal academic style that is required for publication. Unfortunately, small but consistent mistakes in grammar and word usage can make the difference between manuscripts that are accepted with revisions and those that are rejected. Some, but not all, editors may be willing to work with international authors to revise manuscripts that have strong research or conceptual merit. We suggest that international researchers enlist assistance from researchers who are very familiar with the journal's academic language requirements when preparing manuscripts for publication, either to provide editing assistance or to become a collaborating co-author. As noted, researchers often welcome opportunities to collaborate with international colleagues and resources exist to facilitate such partnerships.

Merino-Soto (2014) raised another concern about language issues in cross-national practice. He posited that consultants should be able to read and speak in the consultee's native language rather than assume the participants will be able to translate from the consultant's preferred language. Merino-Soto (2014) also suggested that focusing the international work on developing local consultation teams and practitioners could address language and cultural issues in cross-national efforts. In some ways the problems of communication across disciplines, perspectives, cultures, and settings may manifest somewhat differently in international work, but they apply to school-based consultation in every setting. Effective consultants everywhere work to understand the local context, establish effective communication with participants, translate innovations into usable knowledge, and develop the local capacity to address challenges and improve performance.

CONCLUSION

We encourage our colleagues to contribute to the global research on SBC by publishing and presenting well-designed and carefully implemented consultative and collaborative work. To support that effort, we provided general guidelines to SBC practitioners and researchers who conduct consultation projects that benefit children. We also described the important elements to include in research manuscripts and provided some guidance about the types of outlets that should be considered for such work. Our intent was to provide information that may help readers access opportunities to increase the audience for their work and inform SBC research on a wider scale. Our hope is that SBC practitioners and researchers see this chapter as an invitation to publish, inform SBC researchers throughout the world, and form collaborative partnerships. We are all working to better understand how SBC can improve the lives of children though improvements in the educational process. That is an ambitious and honorable endeavor, which can be enhanced if we work together.

REFERENCES

Andersen, M., & Daly, E. I. (2013). An experimental examination of the impact of choice of treatment components on treatment integrity. *Journal of Educational & Psychological Consultation, 23*, 231–263. doi: 10.1080/10474412.2013.845493

APA. (2010). *Publication manual of the American Psychological Association* (6th ed.). Washington, DC, US: American Psychological Association.

Bergan, J. R., & Tombari, M. L. (1976). Consultant skill and efficiency and the implementation and outcomes of consultation. *Journal of School Psychology, 14*, 3–14. doi: 10.1016/0022-4405(76)90057-1

Bon, S. C. (2012). Examining the crossroads of law, ethics, and education leadership. *Journal of School Leadership, 22*, 285–308.

Caplan, G. (1970). *The theory and practice of mental health consultation*. New York, NY: Basic Books.

Caplan, G., Caplan, R. B., & Erchul, W. P. (1995). A contemporary view of mental health consultation: Comments on "Types of mental health consultation" by Gerald Caplan (1963). *Journal of Educational and Psychological Consultation, 6*, 23–30. doi: 10.1207/s1532768xjepc0601_2

Cook, L., & Friend, M. (2010). The state of the art of collaboration on behalf of students with disabilities. *Journal of Educational and Psychological Consultation, 20*, 1–8.

Coyne, J., & Trombetta, C. (2007). The service of school psychology in Italy. In S. R. Jimerson, T. D. Oakland, & P. T. Farrell (Eds.), *The handbook of international school psychology* (pp. 199–210). Thousand Oaks, CA: Sage Publications.

Curtis, M. J., & Meyers, J. (1988). Consultation: A foundation for alternative services in the schools. In J. Graden, J. Zins, & M. Curtis (Eds.), *Alternative educational delivery systems: Enhancing instructional options for all students* (pp. 35–48). Washington, DC: National Association of School Psychologists.

Denton, C. A., & Hasbrouck, J. (2009). A description of instructional coaching and its relationship to consultation. *Journal of Educational and Psychological Consultation, 19*, 150–175.

De Vito, D. (2007). The gap between the real and the ideal: The right to education amid fiscal equity legislation in a democratic culture. *Ethics and Education, 2*, 173–180. doi: 10.1080/17449640701610111

Erchul, W. P., & Sheridan, S. M. (Eds.). (2014). *Handbook of research in school consultation: Empirical foundations for the field*. New York, NY: Routledge.

Fischer, C. S. (2008). Paradoxes of American individualism. *Sociological Forum, 23*, 363–732.

Frank, J. L., & Kratochwill, T. R. (2014). School-based problem-solving consultation: Plotting a new course for evidence-based research and practice in consultation. In W. P. Erchul & S. M. Sheridan (Eds.), *Handbook of research in school consultation* (pp. 18–39). New York, NY: Routledge/Taylor & Francis Group.

Gilmour, D., & Soudien, C. (1994). Disadvantage in South African education: The issue of equality and equity in transformative policy and research. In A. Dawes, D. Donald, A. Dawes, & D. Donald (Eds.), *Childhood & adversity: Psychological perspectives from South African research* (pp. 122–135). Claremont, South Africa: David Philip Publishers.

Hatzichristou, C. (2002). A conceptual framework of the evolution of school psychology: Transnational considerations of common phases and future perspectives. *School Psychology International, 23*, 266–282. doi: 10.1177/0143034302023003322

Hatzichristou, C., & Rosenfield, S. A. (This volume). *The handbook of international school consultation*. Abingdon, UK: Routledge.

Hosp, M. K., Hosp, J. L., & Howell, K. W. (2007). *The ABCs of CBM*. New York, NY: Guilford.

Hylander, I. (2003). Toward a grounded theory of the conceptual change process in consultee-centered consultation. *Journal of Educational and Psychological Consultation, 14*, 263–280.

Hylander, I. (2004). Analysis of conceptual change in consultee-centered consultation. In N. L. Lambert, I. Hylander, & J. H. Sandoval (Eds.), *Consultee-centered consultation: Improving the quality of professional services in schools and community organizations* (pp. 45–61). Mahwah, NJ: Lawrence Erlbaum Associates, Inc.

Ingraham, C. (2004). Multicultural consultee-centered consultation: Supporting consultees in the development of cultural competence. In N. M. Lambert, I. Hylander, J. H. Sandoval, N. M. Lambert, I. Hylander, & J. H. Sandoval (Eds.), *Consultee-centered consultation: Improving the quality of professional services in schools and community organizations* (pp. 133–148). Mahwah, NJ, US: Lawrence Erlbaum Associates Publishers.

Johnson, R. B., & Onwuegbuzie, A. J. (2004). Mixed methods research: A research paradigm whose time has come. *Educational Researcher, 33*, 14–26.

Kasler, J., & Elias, M. J. (2012). Holding the line: Sustaining an SEL-driven whole-school approach in a time of transition. *Journal of Educational & Psychological Consultation, 22*, 227–246. doi: 10.1080/10474412.2012.706130

Kaufman, D., Codding, R. S., Markus, K. A., Tryon, G. S., & Kyse, E. N. (2013). Effects of verbal and written performance feedback on treatment adherence: Practical application of two delivery formats. *Journal of Educational and Psychological Consultation, 23*, 264–299. doi: 10.1080/10474412.2013.845494

Kelleher, C., Riley-Tillman, T. C., & Power, T. J. (2008). An initial comparison of collaborative and expert-driven consultation on treatment integrity. *Journal of Educational and Psychological Consultation, 18*, 294–324. doi: 10.1080/10474410802491040

Kennedy, E. K., Frederickson, N., & Monsen, J. (2008). Do educational psychologists "walk the talk" when consulting? *Educational Psychology in Practice, 24*, 169–187. doi: 10.1080/02667360802256733

Knotek, S. E. (2012). Utilizing culturally responsive consultation to support innovation implementation in a rural school. *Consulting Psychology Journal: Practice and Research, 64*, 46–62. doi: 10.1037/a0027993

Lambert, N. M., Hylander, I., & Sandoval, J. H. (2004). *Consultee-centered consultation: Improving the quality of professional services in schools and community organizations.* Mahwah, NJ, US: Lawrence Erlbaum Associates Publishers.

Leon, C., Campagnaro, S., & Matos, M. (2007). School psychology in Venezuela. In S. R. Jimerson, T. D. Oakland, & P. T. Farrell (Eds.), *The handbook of international school psychology* (pp. 427–435). Thousand Oaks, CA: Sage Publications.

Lockheed, M. E., & Harris, A. M. (2005). Beneath education production functions: The case of primary education in Jamaica. *Peabody Journal of Education, 80*, 6–28. doi: 10.1207/S15327930pje8001_2

Merino-Soto, C. (2014). Lessons learned from a consultation process overseas. *Journal of Educational and Psychological Consultation, 24*, 340–344. doi: 10.1080/10474412.2014.929964

Meyers, J. (1989). The practice of psychology in the schools for the primary prevention of learning and adjustment problems in children: A perspective from the field of education. In L. A. Bond & B. E. Compas (Eds.), *Primary prevention and promotion in the schools* (pp. 391–422). Thousand Oaks, CA, US: Sage Publications, Inc.

Meyers, J. (2002). A 30 year perspective on best practices for consultation training. *Journal of Educational and Psychological Consultation, 13*, 35–54. doi: 10.1207/S1532768XJEPC1301&2_05

Meyers, J., Truscott, S. D., Meyers, A. B., Varjas, K., & Kim, S. Y. (2014). Qualitative and mixed methods designs in consultation research. In W. P. Erchul, S. M. Sheridan, W. P. Erchul, & S. M. Sheridan (Eds.), *Handbook of research in school consultation* (pp. 103–137). New York, NY, US: Routledge/Taylor & Francis Group.

Nastasi, B. K. (2004). Meeting the challenges of the future: Integrating public health and public education for mental health promotion. *Journal of Educational and Psychological Consultation, 15*, 295–312.

Nastasi, B. K., & Jayasena, A. S. (2014). An international partnership promoting psychological well-being in Sri Lankan schools. *Journal of Educational and Psychological Consultation, 24*, 265–282. doi: 10.1080/10474412.2014.929965

Nastasi, B. K., Varjas, K., Bernstein, R., & Jayasena, A. (2000). Conducting participatory culture-specific consultation: A global perspective on multicultural consultation. *School Psychology Review, 29*, 401–413.

Nastasi, B. K., Varjas, K., Schensul, S. L., Silva, K. T., Schensul, J. J., & Ratnayake, P. (2000). The participatory intervention model: A framework for conceptualizing and promoting intervention acceptability. *School Psychology Quarterly, 15*, 207–232.

Newell, M. L., Newell, T. S., & Looser, J. A. (2013). Examining how novice consultants address cultural factors during consultation: Illustration of a computer-simulated case-study method. *Consulting Psychology Journal: Practice and Research, 65*, 74–86. doi: 10.1037/a0032598

Noell, G. H., & Gansle, K. A. (2014). Research examining the relationships between consultation procedures, treatment integrity, and outcomes. In W. P. Erchul, S. M. Sheridan, W. P. Erchul, & S. M. Sheridan (Eds.), *Handbook of research in school consultation* (pp. 386–408). New York, NY, US: Routledge/Taylor & Francis Group.

Organization for Economic Co-operation and Development. (2012). *Equity and quality in education: Supporting disadvantaged students and schools.* Paris: OECD. Retrieved from http://asiasociety.org/files/oecd-0512report.pdf

Rosenfield, S. A. (2014). Reflecting on the role of competence and culture in consultation at the international level. *Journal of Educational and Psychological Consultation, 24*, 330–339. doi: 10.1080/10474412.2014.929963

Rosenfield, S. A., & Gravois, T. A. (1996). *Instructional consultation teams: Collaborating for change.* New York, NY: Guilford.

Saklofske, D. H., Schwean, V. L., Harrison, G. L., & Mureika, J. (2007). School psychology in Canada. In S. R. Jimerson, T. D. Oakland, & P. T. Farrell (Eds.), *The handbook of international school psychology* (pp. 39–51). Thousand Oaks, CA: Sage Publications.

Sanetti, L. H., & Collier-Meek, M. A. (2014). Increasing the rigor of procedural fidelity assessment: An empirical comparison of direct observation and permanent product review methods. *Journal of Behavioral Education, 23*, 60–88. doi: 10.1007/s10864–013–9179-z

Sheridan, S. M., Clarke, B. L., & Ransom, K. A. (2014). The past, present, and future of conjoint behavioral consultation research. In W. P. Erchul, S. M. Sheridan, W. P. Erchul, & S. M. Sheridan (Eds.), *Handbook of research in school consultation* (pp. 210–247). New York, NY: Routledge/Taylor & Francis Group.

Shriberg, D., & Fenning, P. A. (2009). School consultants as agents of social justice: Implications for practice: Introduction to the special issue. *Journal of Educational & Psychological Consultation, 19*, 1–7. doi: 10.1080/10474410802462751

Stoiber, K., &Waas, G. A. (2002). A contextual and methodological perspective on the evidence-based movement within school psychology in the United States. *Educational and Child Psychology, 19*, 7–21.

Stoner, G., & Green, S. K. (1992). Reconsidering the scientist-practitioner model for school psychology practice. *School Psychology Review, 21*, 155–166.

Thomas, S. B., & Rapport, M. K. (1998). Least restrictive environment: Understanding the directions of the courts. *The Journal of Special Education, 32,* 66–78. doi: 10.1177/002246699803200201

Thornberg, R. (2014). Consultation barriers between teachers and external consultants: A grounded theory of change resistance in school consultation. *Journal of Educational and Psychological Consultation, 24,* 183–210.

Timmins, P., Bham, M., McFadyen, J., & Ward, J. (2006). Teachers and consultation: Applying research and development in organisations (RADIO). *Educational Psychology in Practice, 22,* 305–319. doi: 10.1080/02667360600999419

Truscott, S. D., Cosgrove, G., Meyers, J., & Eidle-Barkman, K. A. (2000). The acceptability of organizational consultation with prereferral intervention teams. *School Psychology Quarterly, 15,* 172–206.

Truscott, S. D., Kreskey, D., Bolling, M., Psimas, L., Graybill, E., Albritton, K., & Schwartz, A. (2012). Creating consultee change: A theory-based approach to learning and behavioral change processes in school-based consultation. *Consulting Psychology Journal: Practice and Research, 64,* 63–82. doi: 10.1037/a0027997

Truscott, S. D., Lopez, E., Fish, M. C., & Margolis, H. (2015). The Journal of Educational and Psychological Consultation: A quarter century of contribution, a future of challenge and optimism. *Journal of Educational and Psychological Consultation, 25,* 2–15. doi: 10.1080/10474412.2014.994635

U.S. Department of Education, Institute of Education Sciences, What Works Clearinghouse. (2013, March). *What Works Clearinghouse: Procedures and standards handbook (version 3.0).* Retrieved from http://whatworks.ed.gov

Villegas-Reimers, E. (2003). *Teacher professional development: An international review of the literature.* Paris, France: International Institute for Educational Planning.

Wagner, P. (2000). Consultation: Developing a comprehensive approach to service delivery. *Educational Psychology in Practice, 16,* 9–18. doi: 10.1080/026673600115229

Wandersman, A. (2003). Community science: Bridging the gap between science and practice with community-centered models. *American Journal of Community Psychology, 31,* 227–242.

Wandersman, A., Duffy, J., Flaspohler, P., Noonan, R., Lubell, K., Stillman, L., & Saul, J. (2008). Bridging the gap between prevention research and practice: The interactive systems framework for dissemination and implementation. *American Journal of Community Psychology, 41,* 171–181. doi: 10.1007/s10464-008-9174-z

Watkins, M. W., Hall, T. E., & Worrell, F. C. (2014). From central guidance unit to student support services unit: The outcome of a consultation process in Trinidad and Tobago. *Journal of Educational and Psychological Consultation, 24,* 283–306. doi: 10.1080/10474412.2014.929962

Watson, T. S., & Robinson, S. L. (1996). Direct behavioral consultation: An alternative to traditional behavioral consultation. *School Psychology Quarterly, 11,* 267–278. doi: 10.1037/h0088933

Williams, R. M. (1970). *American society.* New York, NY: Knopf.

Williams, S. S., & Staulters, M. L. (2014). Instructional collaboration with rural educators in Jamaica: Lessons learned from an international interdisciplinary consultation project. *Journal of Educational and Psychological Consultation, 24,* 307–329. doi: 10.1080/10474412.2014.929968

Zhou, H. (2007). School psychology in China. In S. R. Jimerson, T. D. Oakland, & P. T. Farrell (Eds.), *The handbook of international school psychology* (pp. 53–59). Thousand Oaks, CA: Sage Publications.

Part VII

A FINAL WORD

20

MAPPING THE GLOBAL FUTURE OF SCHOOL-BASED CONSULTATION

Sylvia Rosenfield and Chryse Hatzichristou

On medieval maps, the notation "here be dragons" indicated the possible perils looming in uncharted areas. Having explored in the previous chapters the known state of school-based consultation in countries around the world, it is time to reflect on the current and future training, practice, and research in this complex domain. Although not a complete worldview, our chapter authors represent multiple countries, specifically Australia, Canada, England, Greece, Hong Kong, Israel, Sweden, and the U.S., with projects done in diverse other countries such as Ghana, India, Jamaica, Japan, and Vietnam. Although the chapters include a stronger representation of authors from the U.S., the degree of congruence among the authors across national boundaries in policies, issues, concerns, and beliefs is compelling. In this concluding chapter, we wish to present our reflection on the state of school consultation that the authors of this volume have provided as well as address some recommendations for the future.

CULTURAL WORLDVIEWS

During the last two decades, there has been growing interest and an emerging body of literature for the study of multicultural/cross-cultural aspects of consultation. Though there has been some progress, there is a continuing need for awareness and study of the cultural influences on consultation processes and outcome, including the study of various interrelated aspects of one's culture beyond the usual researcher categorization of ethnicity (Ingraham, 2003). Ingraham (2008) points out the limitations in various research methodologies and frameworks that presume "culture is a variable or category of variable rather than a paradigm or worldview that permeates one's thoughts and actions" (p. 286).

Ken Robinson (2008), in his classic TED talk "Changing Education Paradigms," noted that one of the goals of education is to pass along the culture of one's country in a world that is undergoing globalization. In his presentation, he noted that every country is trying to figure out how to educate their children so that they have a sense of cultural identity while recognizing that they are also taking part in the process of globalization. In Chapter 8, Ortiz and Melo consider the importance of understanding the development of cultural knowledge and language acquisition in working as a consultant in educational settings as well as the dilemmas of students caught in the process of acculturation.

Even within families, as Hughes (Chapter 7) demonstrates so comprehensively, cultural issues arise. As Lowman (2015) states, "consultants are always crossing cultural boundaries, even within their own cultures, because every organization they work with has a unique culture of its own, as do the groups and individuals within those organization" (p. x). Other chapter authors, such as Nastasi, Harris and Ueda, and Brock and Jimerson, consider how culture impacts systems consultation efforts across national boundaries. In all these chapters, there is a clear message that consultants in the global village need to be clear about their own cultural values and their impact on their work. Glover and Friedman (2015) conclude:

> Perhaps the most important thing we have learned is that professional consultants . . . need to adapt to the social and cultural context wherever they might be working. The global community has many opportunities for consultants . . . who are able to . . . avoid stereotyped cultural prescriptions. . . . The ability to reconcile diverse stakeholders' models is needed for realizing sustainable results in the complex world of real cultural differences. Being wary of hidden biases and cultural traps is essential to being transculturally competent.
>
> (p. 149)

TRAINING

Being a school consultant is an enormous responsibility. Consultants impact individuals directly (e.g., teachers, administrators, parents) and indirectly (e.g., students), and they influence systems (e.g., classrooms, teams, schools, and even school districts). But consultants cannot consult effectively in their professional practice (a) if they do not have sufficient opportunities to practice these skills within the safety net of training, (b) if they do not receive meaningful feedback via supervision, and (c) if they do not know what they do not know. Consultants cannot develop the content knowledge and process skills that are needed to effectively consult given the limited time for consultation training that is provided in most graduate programs, as research has documented (e.g., Anton-Lahart & Rosenfield, 2004; Hazel, Laviolette, & Lineman, 2010).

There is an implicit assumption in consultation courses with a focus on knowledge, the typical course required in many programs, that students can apply that content in their work in schools. Recent work on expertise suggests otherwise. It has been demonstrated consistently that knowledge alone does not lead to expertise in practice. We all know a lot of things that do not impact our behavior, such as the dangers of texting and driving. Charbonneau (2016), in an APA Society of Consulting Psychology listserv discussion of the impact of training on consultants, wrote the following important message about training consultation skills:

> Let me add that I see a potential danger in our community of focusing development on insight at the expense of skills. . . . I am often surprised these days in my consulting work at how little managers and executives seem to have received in actual skills development: communication, negotiation, leading difficult conversations, leading effective meetings, leading performance conversations etc. . . . All of these topics come with actual techniques that can be taught and learned, rather than having our now

very aware and busy clients left to their own devices re-invent the wheel on their own. These techniques really make a huge difference.

These comments could be equally relevant for educationally based consultants.

Moreover, according to experts on expertise, it is not just practice but "the right sort of practice over a sufficient period of time [that] leads to improvement. Nothing else" (Ericsson & Pool, 2016, p. 14). Ericsson and Pool (2016) make the case for extensive practice of crucial skills, and their definition of practice is worth considering. They describe "deliberate practice" in building skills as consisting not of routine practicing that is automatic and easy but following specific guidelines: moving out of your comfort zone, purposeful in the sense of improving one particular aspect of your performance, and obtaining feedback in order to correct performance problems. In a study on teaching science, Ebert-May et al. (2011) evaluated the effects of professional development workshops on science teachers and found that not only did the teachers not utilize what they had learned in the workshops, but they appeared unaware that they were not using the new skills. They concluded that more was needed for the teachers to be able to use their new skills.

Looking across national boundaries, it seems that students share concerns about their consultation training. For example, Hatzichristou et al. (Chapter 5) compared concerns of consultant students at the University of Athens to those in the U.S. (Rosenfield, 2012) and found that graduate school psychology students in Greece identified common areas, such as understanding context, building the consultation relationship, communication, and how to systematically address consultee needs. Hatzichristou et al. concluded that irrespective of country or educational and cultural settings, all school communities share common needs and worries. The needs that were brought up in supervision and consultation sessions were undoubtedly context and school specific, but they had also remarkable similarities for all participants.

This commonality has the potential to form the basis for developing a training model for the development of effective and well-structured training courses across the world, similar to what Brock and Jimerson (Chapter 11) describe in their chapter on crisis intervention. They built a model of training that was viable across countries, from the U.S. to Japan. The different case examples and training models presented in this volume have the potential to be applied in different countries and lead the way to the development of a transnational model of consultation training.

Although many authors touched on the issue of training, three chapters focused on this topic (Chapters 16, 17, and 18) and one other chapter (Chapter 5) demonstrated how a comprehensive training program could be integrated into a larger national practice model. In each of these chapters, there is respect for the complexity of the consultation process and the developmental progression of students. Worrell et al. (Chapter 18) highlighted the complexity and progression from the perspective of the students. But the generation of this complexity relies on a structured and intense training structure based on time and support. Ingraham (Chapter 17) demonstrates how diversity issues can be incorporated into the training process and suggests a number of exercises to enhance the development. Kennedy et al. (Chapter 16) address the critical issue that Ericsson and Pool (2016) raise, specifically supervision and feedback as students practice their new skills. A research program is also needed to document the effectiveness of the training as it is applied in the world of practice. Newell and Newman (2014), in their review of the empirical basis for consultation training, found a limited and dated empirical base and called for the emergence of a reenergized "consultation training agenda focused on identifying the most effective practices for teaching psychologists to consult" (p. 443).

Moreover, the time is also ripe to add an international component to this agenda. Relevant findings evident in most of the chapters of this volume point to the benefit of making a systematic effort to include not only multicultural components in our graduate curricula of school psychology but also international/transnational resources and readings regarding consultation theory, research, and practice. Currently, attention to international issues in school psychology training is very limited. Oakland and Hatzichristou (2014a) examined school psychology programs globally and some of the country-specific processes and factors that influenced the development of school psychologist training and preparation. In addition, Oakland and Hatzichristou (2014b) examined the academic and professional development components of school psychology training programs in seven countries, including their emphasis on multicultural and international issues. They found that while multicultural and transnational components are more commonly infused in graduate courses, attention to international/transnational issues is very limited. An emphasis on the inclusion of an international perspective and framework in training would provide added scope to the process.

PRACTICE

When we began the selection of authors for this volume, there was an expectation that we would find multiple areas where school consultation was the dominant practice of school psychologists and other mental health and educational professionals working in the schools. Several authors described strong and interesting models of consultation services. For example, Hylander (Chapter 2) noted the proactive use of consultation for the promotion of student well-being and learning as well as the prevention of problems.

However, Maital (Chapter 13) states that psychological consultation and systems thinking is still central to the practice of school psychologists in Israel, where Caplan (1970) introduced the concept of Mental Health Consultation. But in practice, many school psychologists focus on individual cases, relying mainly on traditional assessment and psychotherapy techniques.

From England (Farrell & Woods, Chapter 12) to Australia (Bowles, Chapter 4), authors noted the lack of implementation of consultation services in the schools. Further, even when authors noted that their national literature recommended consultation practice, the reality was different. Authors expressed similar concerns about the difference between desired outcomes and actual implementation.

Moreover, there was consistency in authors' beliefs about why this was true. For example, Maital (Chapter 13) suggested that

> psychologists, trained to seek intrapsychic factors in individual difficulties, may assume that reliance on systems-level consultation may not really resolve psychological

difficulties. They may believe that they would "miss" the real source of difficulty and not treat it or resolve the problem.

Similarly, in spite of a long and positive history of consultation services in Swedish schools, Hylander (Chapter 2) still finds that

> a barrier to consultation in both compulsory schools and preschools is teachers not wanting to do anything until they know the result of an assessment. To turn a request for an assessment into a request for consultation is still one of the greatest challenges for school-based psychologists, just as it was 40 years ago.

How to combine direct and indirect roles as school-based practitioners is an issue common across many countries (e.g., Chapter 3, 12, 13). We need to address how changes in our role occur and who needs to be involved in the change process, an issue discussed in Chapters 4, 13, and 14.

Several authors suggested interventions for addressing the role of school psychologists as consultants. If there is one essential takeaway from this concern, it may well be the important role of advocacy that was mentioned by a number of the chapter authors. Both in training and in practice, strong advocacy for consultation is a critical need across the globe. There is also a role for technology to support consultants. Cole and Wiener (Chapter 3) incorporated technology to support caregivers, educators, and psychologists in Canada. The Center for Psychology in the Schools, an American Psychological Association unit, has also developed some websites that would be useful for school consultants, such as a set of modules on teaming (http://www.apa.org/ed/schools/cpse/). Some authors have invested in group training sessions to help practitioners address their role. For example, Lam (Chapter 14) brought together a group of consultants in Hong Kong to help them brainstorm strategies for working with teachers who were resistant to using consultant services to support them in integrating new instructional methods.

At the systems level, consultation has served some unique implementation efforts. For example, Hazel (Chapter 15) demonstrates how consultation can support the implementation of children's rights in educational settings in the U.S. Kassay and Terjesen (Chapter 10) have documented their work at the international level, demonstrating how school psychology faculty in the U.S. used consultation to support the development of school psychology training in Vietnam. Similarly Brock and Jimerson (Chapter 11) have internationalized the crisis intervention curriculum and enabled consultants across the globe to intervene in those exceptional circumstances.

RESEARCH

Within school psychology, there is a general commitment to the scientist-practitioner model. As stated by Truscott et al. (Chapter 19):

> Professionals who work in schools often experience tension between having our work be informed by educational science and working within the reality of what is possible to implement in the daily practice of schools (Nastasi et al., 2000). The tension between the science and everyday practice can result in what has been called

the science–practice or research–practice gap (e.g., Wandersman, 2003), which occurs when common practices do not align with research-based recommendations.

They acknowledge how complicated consultation research is and provide a roadmap for practitioners to contribute to the research enterprise.

The research model that Truscott et al. describe is particularly relevant given the latest findings of a recent collaboration among social science researchers (Open Science Collaboration, 2015). In their work, the collaborating researchers replicated findings of 100 peer-reviewed psychology studies and found that only a little more than a third of the significant findings were replicated, often with a lower effect size. Other areas, such a medicine, suffer similarly from problems with replication. In the complex reality of schools, the importance of gaining additional data on so-called evidence-based interventions is clear. Not only can consultants provide information about processes, strategies, and interventions and monitor their implementation, but they can also add to the database about what works, where, and how effectively.

The importance of consultation in enhancing the implementation integrity of evidence-based practices is an important contribution given the complexity of real-world contexts. Bryk (2016) describes a model of implementation called *adaptive integration* that takes into account the complexity of the intervention and the diversity of contexts into which the intervention will be implemented. Ortiz and Melo (Chapter 8) also note the fragile nature of evidence-based research:

> When an intervention program is described as being empirically or scientifically validated, it merely indicates that within the context of experimental conditions, on average, the group of children who received the intervention improved academically more than another group that did not receive the intervention. However, this does not mean that *all* children benefited or improved or that all children will learn via that technique. In addition, it does not mean that it is even the best technique available.

Truscott et al.'s consultation practitioner as researcher could provide not only support for implementation but also a rich source of evidence for how different programs are implemented in the schools and a richer "what works in what context" set of practices.

The limited history of replication of educational and psychological research also suggests another essential potential contribution of the school consultant role. Those consultants who utilize a problem-solving process, including implementation monitoring and outcome evaluation, can be strong partners to schools at every level, from individual students to systems interventions at the school and district levels. It is time for school consultants to advocate strongly for their roles in this process.

FINAL THOUGHTS

Reconceptualizing school psychologists' roles as consultants at a global level is still a work in progress (e.g., Ehrhardt-Padgett, Hatzichristou, Kitson, & Meyers, 2003; Newell et al., 2010; Oakland, Hatzichristou, Farrell, & Jimerson, 2014), even though a significant advancement in the recognition of the presence of culturally and linguistically diverse children and families in school psychological practice has been noted (see, e.g., Chapters 7 and 8). For example, the ever-increasing immigrant and refugee student populations in the educational systems of multiple countries indicate that most school psychologists are likely to encounter global issues at the local level as they serve immigrant and refugee populations. The need for consultation services in schools and other educational institutions becomes more critical than ever; it reminds us of the context in which Caplan (1970) introduced mental health consultation as a solution to the large influx of immigrants to Israel and the shortage of mental health personnel. *Transnational competence* represents multicultural competence at an international level (Hatzichristou & Lampropoulou, 2004; Hatzichristou, Nastasi, Kaufman, Lopez, & Hess, 2014a, b; Newell et al., 2010); in consultation training and practice, such competence is critical to the effectiveness of school psychology service delivery in the 21st century.

There has been a further shift to internationalizing university psychology curricula, emphasizing the need for changing the curriculum from an ethnocentric model to an international model in order to respond to the existing and emerging global context in which we live (Leong, Leach, Marsella, & Pickren, 2012). Attending to the "pressing concerns of the human spirit for identity, purpose and meaning by advocating justice, equality and peace" becomes central to the need to educate for a global psychology (Marsella, 2010, p. 340). As Gardner (2004) states, "education is fundamentally and primarily a values undertaking" (p. 236) and needs to include new skills and understandings for a global era. He further proposes new skills and understandings that education for a global era needs to encompass, including "knowledge of and ability to interact civilly and productively with individuals from quite different cultural backgrounds—both within one's own society and across the planet" (Gardner, 2004, p. 254). Developing multicultural/ transcultural awareness, knowledge, and skills is a lifelong process of learning aimed at the development of a professional identity closely related to our personal development (Hatzichristou, 2002).

Reflecting on our collaborative process of co-editing this handbook, it becomes so apparent to us that the magical journey of synthesizing diverse but similar perspectives, knowledge, cosmopolitan ideologies, and experiences is deeply rooted in universal human needs and expressions of respect, appreciation, openness, reflection, personal and professional development, care, and support that give a unique *meaning* in our lives. When Lambert (2004) first listened in 1989 to three psychologists from Sweden, visitors to University of California at Berkeley, share their problems and challenges as consultants, she noted that "it was as if they had been in Berkeley working in the same school sites, not thousands of miles away in Sweden" (p. 11). Our authors, over a decade later, suggest that there is still considerable truth in her statement. However, there is also a wealth of knowledge that the authors in this volume have shared not just about problems and challenges but also about strategies and innovation that would improve consultation services. By sharing this work, we hope that the future of consultation will be enhanced and a global network in training, research, and practice can be established.

REFERENCES

Anton-Lahart, J., & Rosenfield, S. (2004). A survey of preservice consultation training in school psychology programs. *Journal of Educational and Psychological Consultation, 15*, 41–62.

Bryk, A. (2016, March 17). *Fidelity of implementation: Is it the right concept?* Carnegie Foundation for the Advancement of Teaching. Retrieved from www.carnegiefoundation.org/blog

Caplan, G. (1970). *The theory and practice of mental health consultation.* New York: Basic Books.

Ebert-May, D., Derting, T. L., Hodder, J., Momsen, J. L., Long, T. M., & Jardeleza, S. E. (2011). What we say is not what we do: Effective evaluation of faculty professional development programs. *BioScience, 61,* 550–558.

Ehrhardt-Padgett, G. N., Hatzichristou, C., Kitson, J., & Meyers, J. (2003). Awakening to a new dawn: Perspectives of the future of school psychology. *School Psychology Quarterly, 18,* 483–496.

Ericsson, A., & Pool, R. (2016). *Peak: Secrets from the new science of expertise.* New York: Houghton Mifflin Harcourt.

Gardner, H. (2004). How education changes: Considerations of history, science and values. In M. M. Suarez-Orozco & D. B. Qin-Hilliard (Eds.), *Globalization: Culture and education in the new millennium* (pp. 235–258). Berkeley, CA: University of California Press.

Glover, J., & Friedman, H. L. (2015). *Transcultural competence: Navigating cultural differences in the global community.* Washington, DC: American Psychological Association.

Hatzichristou, C. (2002). A conceptual framework of the evolution of school psychology: Transnational considerations of common phases and future perspectives. *School Psychology International, 23*(2), 1–17.

Hatzichristou, C., & Lampropoulou, A. (2004). The future of school psychology conference: A cross-national approach to service delivery. *Journal of Educational and Psychological Consultation, 15,* 313–333.

Hatzichristou, C., Nastasi, B., Kaufman, J., Lopez, E. C., & Hess, R. S. (2014a, February). *Transnational-global considerations in school psychology training and practice.* Symposium conducted at the meeting of the National Association of School Psychologists, Washington, DC.

Hatzichristou, C., Nastasi, B., Kaufman, J., Lopez, E. C., & Hess, R. S. (2014b, August). *From multicultural to transnational global philosophy in school psychology training and practice.* Symposium conducted at the APA Annual Convention, Washington, DC.

Hazel, C. E., Laviolette, G. T., & Lineman, J. M. (2010). Training professional psychologists in school based consultation: What the syllabi suggest. *Training and Education in Professional Psychology, 4,* 235–243.

Ingraham, C. L. (2003). Multicultural consultee centered consultation: When novice consultants explore cultural hypotheses with experienced teacher consultees. *Journal of Educational and Psychological Consultation, 14,* 329–362.

Ingraham, C. L. (2008). Studying multicultural aspects of consultation. In W. P. Erchul & S. M. Sheridan (Eds.), *Handbook of research in school consultation* (pp. 269–291). New York, NY: Lawrence Erlbaum Associates.

Lambert, N. (2004). Consultee-centered consultation: An international perspective on goals, process and theory. In N. M. Lambert, I. Hylander, & J. Sandoval (Eds.), *Consultee-centered consultation: Improving the quality of professional services in schools and community organizations* (pp. 3–19). Mahwah, NJ: Lawrence Erlbaum.

Leong, F. T. L., Leach, M. M., Marsella, A. J., & Pickren, W. E. (2012). Internationalizing the psychology curriculum in the USA: Meeting the challenges and opportunities of a global era. In F. T. L. Leong, W. E. Pickren, M. M. Leach, & A. J. Marsella (Eds.), *Internationalizing the psychology curriculum in the United States* (pp. 1–9). New York, NY: Springer.

Lowman, R. L. (2015). Series editor foreword. In J. Glover & H. L. Friedman (Eds.), *Transcultural competence: Navigating cultural differences in the global community* (pp. vii–x). Washington, DC: American Psychological Association.

Marsella, A. J. (2010). Education and training for a global psychology: Foundations, issues and actions. In M. J. Stevens & U. P. Gielen (Eds.), *Toward a global psychology: Theory, research, intervention and pedagogy* (pp. 333–361). New York, NY: Psychology Press.

Newell, M. L., Nastasi, B. K., Hatzichristou, C., Jones, J. M., Schanding, G. T., Jr., & Yetter, G. P. (2010). Evidence on multicultural training in school psychology: Recommendations for future directions. *School Psychology Quarterly, 25,* 249–278.

Newell, M. L., & Newman, D. (2014). Assessing the state of evidence in consultation training: A review and call to the field. In W. P. Erchul & S. M. Sheridan (Eds.), *Handbook of research in school consultation* (2nd ed., pp. 421–449). New York: Routledge.

Oakland, T. D., & Hatzichristou, C. (2014a). International perspectives on academic and professional preparation of school and educational psychologists: Introduction to a special issue of the International Journal of School & Educational Psychology. *International Journal of School & Educational Psychology, 2,* 150–153.

Oakland, T. D., & Hatzichristou, C. (2014b). Professional preparation in school psychology: A summary of information from programs in seven countries. *International Journal of School & Educational Psychology, 2,* 223–230.

Oakland, T. D., Hatzichristou, C., Farrell, P., & Jimerson, S. (2014, July). *Program preparation that addresses multicultural and international issues.* Symposium entitled: "Professional practices and changing role of school psychologists". International School Psychology Association Conference, Kaunas, Lithuania.

Open Science Collaboration. (2015). Estimating the reproducibility of psychological science. *Science, 349,* 943–951.

Robinson, K. (2008). *Changing education paradigms.* Ted Talk. Retrieved from https://www.ted.com/talks/ken_robinson_changing_education_paradigms

Rosenfield, S. (2012). Introduction: Becoming a school consultant. In S. A. Rosenfield (Ed.), *Becoming a school consultant: Lessons learned* (pp. 1–22). New York, NY: Routledge.

CONTRIBUTORS

Terence Bowles is a senior lecturer in educational psychology in the School of Education at the University of Melbourne. He is the author of more than 50 peer-reviewed papers. His research programs focus on clinical and normal functioning, motivation, learning, communication, and relationships. He has published on change management, adaptive functioning, social and emotional learning time orientation, and affect and talent development. He has served as the editor and editorial board member of a number of journals and serves on the university ethics committee. He is committed to advancing the practice of psychologists in particular in areas of consulting and leadership.

Stephen E. Brock is a professor and the school psychology program coordinator at California State University, Sacramento (CSUS). He worked for 18 years as a school psychologist (Lodi Unified School District) before joining the CSUS faculty. As a school psychologist, he helped develop the district's school crisis response protocol. He currently serves as a member of NASP's School Safety and Crisis Response Committee and is the author of the PREP*a*RE curriculum. He was the lead editor of *Best Practices in School Crisis Prevention and Intervention (NASP)* and lead author of *School Crisis Prevention and Intervention.* His work has included school-based crisis intervention; systems-level school crisis response; suicide prevention, intervention, and postvention; violence prevention; and threat assessment.

R.J. Cameron was founder of the professional doctorate in educational psychology at University College London and, following retirement in 2012, is now an honorary research associate at the UCL Department of Clinical, Educational and Health Psychology. He is currently co-director of the Pillars of Parenting Social Enterprise and a private consultant in child and educational psychology. In 2005, he was given the British Psychological Society's national award for distinguished contributions to the teaching of psychology, and in 2010 he received their annual award for his distinguished contribution to educational and child psychology.

Anna Casey (nee McGee) earned her Ph.D. in school psychology at the University of California, Berkeley in 2016. Her research centers on mathematics teaching and learning with a particular focus on teachers' decisions around their use of mathematics curricular materials.

Ester Cole is a psychologist in private practice. She was previously a supervising psychologist for a board of education. Her work focused on the development of multicultural and consultation services. She taught at the University of Toronto (OISE) and York University. Dr. Cole published numerous articles in journals and professional publications and co-edited and contributed to several manuals and books. She was the president of the Canadian Association of School Psychologists, the chair of the Psychology Foundation of Canada, and the president of the Ontario Psychological Association and the Canadian Register of Health Service Psychologists. She is a member of the APA Council of Representatives.

Kirnel Daniel is a doctoral student in the Georgia State University school psychology Ph.D. program. Her research interests include urban student populations, intervention implementation and evaluation, and professional development.

Sandra Dunsmuir is the director of the educational psychology group at University College London. She has had extensive experience working as an educational psychologist in four different local authorities and continues to practice on a regular basis with children, their families, and teachers in school and community settings. Sandra's research interests integrate empirical research and psychological theory with a particular focus on relationships and communication; interventions to support children's learning; cross-professional collaborative working; supervision; and the use of cognitive behaviour therapy (CBT) with children, young people, their families, and school staff. She is past chair of the British Psychological Society Division of Educational and Child Psychology.

Peter Farrell is professor emeritus in educational psychology at the Manchester Institute of Education, a former president of the International School Psychology Association (ISPA), and fellow of the British Psychological Society. He has extensive experience as a trainer of educational psychologists in the United Kingdom and has worked with psychologists in several countries giving advice on the development of psychological services. He is currently the chair of an ISPA committee that manages the international accreditation of school psychology training programmes. He has been a keynote speaker at 17 international conferences on issues related to international school/educational psychology.

Georgios Georgouleas is a school psychologist working at Arsakeia-Tositseia Schools of FilekpaideftikiEtaireia, Athens, Greece. He has obtained his MA in school psychology at National & Kapodistrian University of Athens and is now a Ph.D. candidate in developmental psychology in the Department of Psychology of the same university. He is a member of the scientific team of the Center for Research and Practice in School Psychology at the Department of Psychology, University of Athens, Greece. His research interests and work experience include mental health promotion, intervention programs, counseling/consultation, and adolescent development.

Christine E. Gerchow is a 2015 graduate of the University of California, Berkeley, school psychology program. She is currently a postdoctoral psychologist intern specializing in functional family therapy (FFT) for probation involved youth and their families.

Chloe Green is a doctoral candidate in school psychology at University of California, Berkeley. She studies the neuropsychological underpinnings of mathematical learning. She is particularly interested in early interventions for children at risk for math learning disabilities.

Abigail Harris is an associate professor in school psychology at Fordham University in New York. She has over two decades of experience in the Caribbean, Africa, and Central America using systemic consultation to support national educational reform efforts and improve educational quality.

Chryse Hatzichristou is professor of school psychology and chair of the Department of Psychology at the National and Kapodistrian University, Athens, Greece. She is also director of the Graduate Program in School Psychology and the Center for Research and Practice in School Psychology at the Department of Psychology. Her extensive research publications and books include topics on mental health and resilience promotion in school communities, psychosocial adjstment of migrant students and at-risk groups, crisis intervention, school-based consultation, social and emotional learning and evidence-based interventions in schools, and multicultural and transnational issues in school psychology training and practice. She has served as secretary of the executive committee of ISPA, member and co-chair of the Committee of International Relations in Psychology of APA, and chair of the Globalization WG of School Psychology Division of APA. She has received in 2010 the ISPA Outstanding International Scholar Award.

Cynthia Hazel is the chair of the Teaching and Learning Sciences Department and a professor in the Child, Family, and School Psychology Program at the University of Denver. Dr. Hazel's research interests include consultation, student school engagement, on-time high school graduation, and preventing bullying. She has published two books and numerous articles and presented internationally to promote equity and population-wide wellness for children, families, and school communities.

Candice A. Hughes is a faculty member in the School Psychology Department and serves as an adjunct faculty to the International Psychology Department at the Chicago School of Professional Psychology. She lived abroad as an expatriate for 14 years in three different countries. During that period, she worked over a 10-year period as a mental health professional in three international schools in Europe where she gained extensive experience working with children and their families from multiple countries about cultural transition issues. Her primary professional focus is working with school communities to better address the needs of their culturally diverse family members.

Ingrid Hylander is associate professor and senior researcher and a former research leader at the Division of Family Medicine, Department of Neurobiology, Caring Sciences and Society, KarolinskaInstitutet (Huddinge, Stockholm) and former associate professor at Linkoping University, Department of Behavioral Sciences. She has worked professionally for about 30 years as school psychologist, clinical child psychologist, and consultant to early childhood education and is a licensed psychologist with specialist diplomas in educational psychology and in clinical psychology. Her research interests are group psychology, professional consultation and interprofessional collaboration, and qualitative research methods. She has published articles, chapters, and books on consultation, interprofessional collaboration, self-development, and qualitative research methods.

Colette L. Ingraham's research interests focus on multicultural and cross-cultural school consultation, systemic and MTSS interventions, and multicultural issues. She is especially interested in consultee-centered consultation (individual, group, and organizational), applied and action research, and ways to promote social justice and educational equity in diverse schools and communities. She is involved in research using restorative and trauma-informed practices in schools, services for English language learners, and prevention, early interventions, and tiered systems of support. She is also involved in studying how consultants learn school consultation.

Shane R. Jimerson is a professor at the University of California, Santa Barbara, in the Department of Counseling, Clinical, and School Psychology. Dr. Jimerson is currently editor of the *School Psychology Quarterly* journal, president of the International School Psychology Association, and previous president of Division 16 (school psychology) of the American Psychological Association. With over 320 publications, including over 25 books, his scholarship has provided insights regarding the developmental pathways of school success and failure, the effectiveness of early prevention and intervention programs, and school psychology internationally. He has contributed over 200 presentations to diverse audiences across more than 25 countries.

Kimberly S. Kassay is a school psychologist in Westport, Connecticut. She also works with children and families in private practice in Purchase, New York. She has taught, presented, and published nationally and internationally. During her graduate studies at St. John's University, she became involved in the early stages of the collaborative efforts between her university and Hanoi National University of Education to develop a school psychology training program. She traveled to Vietnam and worked closely with faculty and professionals from the United States and Vietnam to plan and evaluate preparation and implementation of the newly established school psychology training program.

Moriah A. Kearney is a doctoral student in the Georgia State University school psychology Ph.D. program. Her research interests include consultants' epistemologies, the effects of trauma on children, and therapeutic interventions for children and young adults.

Emma Kate Kennedy is the deputy director of the educational psychology training program at the Tavistock and Portman NHS Foundation Trust. She is educational psychologist in the clinic's multidisciplinary lifespan team for children, young people, and adults with autism spectrum disorders and learning disabilities, and she also runs a psychology consultancy service for children, families, and schools. Her research interests include effective integrated working in multiteam systems, consultation in the context of professional action, and developing initial and in-service applied psychology training in the context of the Tavistock's psychoanalytic, systemic, and attachment-focused traditions.

Claire E. Kunesh is a doctoral student in human development at the University of California, Berkeley. Her research interests include the influence of family- and school-level factors on immigrant and ethnic minority adolescents' educational outcomes.

Shui-fong Lam is a professor in the Department of Psychology at the University of Hong Kong. She is also the director of the master's program in educational psychology, a professional training program for educational psychologists. She received the Outstanding Teaching Award from the University of Hong Kong in 2012 and the Outstanding International Scholar Award from the International School Psychology Association in 2015. Her research interests lie in achievement motivation, parenting, instructional strategies, and positive psychology. She is also concerned with the improvement of psychoeducational services in school systems.

Aikaterini Lampropoulou is a school psychologist working in a clinical setting. She obtained her MA in school psychology at National & Kapodistrian University of Athens, and she is a member of the scientific team of the Center for Research and Practice in School Psychology at the Department of Psychology, University of Athens, Greece. In addition, she has been teaching undergraduate and graduate courses in school psychology. Her research interests and work experience include mental health promotion, intervention programs, counseling/consultation, and family–school partnership. Dr. Lampropoulou has many research publications and presentations and has conducted many workshops.

Emilia C. Lopez is a professor in the graduate program in school psychology at Queens College, City University of New York. In addition to teaching courses focused on consultation and multicultural issues, she is the director of the bilingual and multicultural specializations in that program. Her scholarly interests are in the areas of multicultural consultation, multicultural competencies for school psychologists, bilingual school psychology, and working with school interpreters.

Sharone L. Maital is a senior educational psychologist in Israel where she lives and works. She recently retired from her post as deputy head psychologist of the Northern Region of the Israel Educational Psychology Services. She continues to supervise and train school psychologists, focusing on consultation. In addition, Dr. Maital is an adjunct lecturer in the Graduate Program in Educational Psychology at Jezreel Valley Academic College and in the Faculty of Education at Haifa University. She has written articles on an ecosystemic approach to consultation, Internet-based services, and multicultural approaches to consultation, and she recently co-edited a forthcoming Israeli handbook of school psychology in Hebrew.

Yanique T. Matthews is a doctoral student in the Georgia State University school psychology Ph.D. program. Her research interests include services for children with neurodevelopmental disabilities, special education, and effective assessment of autism.

Kristan E. Melo is a certified school psychologist in New York State and a doctoral candidate in St. John's University's bilingual school psychology program. She earned her MS in bilingual school psychology from St. John's University and her BA in psychology and creative writing from the City University of New York: Hunter College. She serves as a senior member of the St. John's University Bilingual Research Team and has served as a consultant to APA's Coalition for Psychology in Schools and Education. Melo publishes and conducts research on evaluation of English learners as well as on early childhood education.

Spiridoula Mihou received her Ph.D. in school psychology in the Department of Psychology at National and Kapodistrian University of Athens, Greece. She is also a member of the scientific team of the Center for Research and Practice in School Psychology at the University of Athens. Her primary research interests include children and adolescents' psychosocial adjustment and resilience. She has also been involved in a European-funded program Education of Roma Children as coordinator and in an international project "An Examination of Individual and Contextual Factors Contributing to Resilient Classrooms and Schools." She has been working with diverse student populations and families.

Jessica Ernandes Naecker completed her Ph.D. in school psychology at University of California, Berkeley in 2016. Her research focuses on how elementary school children reason about social inequality and how reasoning about social inequality is associated with children's social behavior.

Bonnie Kaul Nastasi is professor of psychology at Tulane University and co-directs the trauma specialization in the school psychology doctoral program. She received her Ph.D. from Kent State University in 1986. Her research focuses on using mixed methods to develop and evaluate culturally constructed assessment and intervention approaches for promoting mental health and reducing health risks domestically and internationally. She is active in professional development of school psychologists as child rights advocates. She is past president of APA's Division 16, past co-chair of APA's Committee on International Relations in Psychology, current president-elect of International School Psychology Association, and Division 16 representative to the APA Council.

Samuel O. Ortiz is professor of psychology at St. John's University, New York. He earned his Ph.D. in clinical psychology from University of Southern California with postdoctoral training in bilingual school psychology at San Diego State University. He has served as VP for professional affairs (APA Division 16), chair of APA's Committee on Psychological Tests and Assessment, and member of APA's Coalition for Psychology in Schools and Education and the Presidential Task Force on Educational Disparities. Dr. Ortiz publishes and conducts research on evaluation of English learners, cross-battery assessment, and learning disabilities. His books include *Assessment of Culturally and Linguistically Diverse Students: A Practical Guide* and *Essentials of Cross-Battery Assessment* (3rd edition).

Sylvia Rosenfield is professor emerita at the University of Maryland (UMD); she was co-director of the Lab for IC Teams at UMD. Her primary research interests focus on consultation training, practice, and research; she has published four books and multiple other publications on these topics and has presented related workshops and papers. She received the National Association of School Psychologists Lifetime Achievement Award (2013) and the American Psychological Association Distinguished Career Contributions to Education and Training Award (2000). She is an APA fellow of Divisions 13 (consulting), 15 (educational psychology), and 16 (school psychology) and past president of Division 16.

Mark D. Terjesen is associate professor at St. John's University and program director of the school psychology (PsyD and MS) programs. Dr. Terjesen has studied, published, and presented at a number of national and international conferences and trained many professionals internationally in school psychology and the use of cognitive behavioral practices with children and families. He has served as president of the School Division of the New York State Psychological Association, the president of the Trainers of School Psychologists, as past president of Division 52 (international psychology) of the American Psychological Association, of which he is also a fellow.

Stephen D. Truscott is an associate professor and the coordinator of the Georgia State University school psychology Ph.D. program. He was the editor of the *Journal of Educational and Psychological Consultation* from 2008 to 2013. His research interests include school-based consultation, professional development for teachers, and interprofessional education.

Mio Ueda is a doctoral candidate in school psychology at Fordham University. She has experience working as an early childhood special educator, providing one-on-one support to preschool age children with autism and other developmental disabilities within home and school settings. Her dissertation research focuses on the experience in Japan of mothers of children with autism.

Judith Wiener is a professor in the Department of Applied Psychology and Human Development at the University of Toronto (OISE). She has worked as a school psychologist and in clinical settings. Her primary clinical expertise is assessment and psychosocial interventions with children and adolescents with learning disabilities and ADHD, including immigrants and refugees. Her current research is on the self-perceptions and family and social relationships of these children and adolescents. She has over 80 book chapters and refereed journal publications, and she co-authored the book *Psychological Assessment of Culturally and Linguistically Diverse Children and Adolescents: A Practitioner's Guide.*

Kevin Woods is a professor of educational and child psychology at the University of Manchester, where he is director of the professional training program for practitioner school psychologists. He has worked in a variety of roles as a registered practitioner school psychologist for 25 years. His research and publication interests include the role and work of practitioner psychologists, student assessment needs, test anxiety, dyslexia, and children's rights. He has also worked as an expert witness child psychologist and trainer within the family law courts.

Frank C. Worrell is a professor and director of the school psychology program at the University of California, Berkeley. His research interests include psychosocial development, cultural identities, and the translation of research findings into school-based practice.

INDEX